Lecture Notes in Computer Science

Lecture Notes in Artificial Intelligence 15570

Founding Editor

Jörg Siekmann

The series Lecture Notes in Artificial Intelligence (LNAI) was established in 1988 as a topical subseries of LNCS devoted to artificial intelligence.

The series publishes state-of-the-art research results at a high level. As with the LNCS mother series, the mission of the series is to serve the international R & D community by providing an invaluable service, mainly focused on the publication of conference and workshop proceedings and postproceedings.

Edna Barros · Josiah P. Hanna · Hiroyuki Okada ·
Elena Torta
Editors

RoboCup 2024: Robot World Cup XXVII

Springer

Editors
Edna Barros
Federal University of Pernambuco
Recife, Brazil

Josiah P. Hanna
University of Wisconsin–Madison
Madison, WI, USA

Hiroyuki Okada
Tokyo Information Design Professional University
Tokyo, Japan

Elena Torta
Eindhoven University of Technology
Eindhoven, The Netherlands

ISSN 0302-9743 ISSN 1611-3349 (electronic)
Lecture Notes in Artificial Intelligence
ISBN 978-3-031-85858-1 ISBN 978-3-031-85859-8 (eBook)
https://doi.org/10.1007/978-3-031-85859-8

LNCS Sublibrary: SL7 – Artificial Intelligence

This Springer imprint is published by the registered company Springer Nature Switzerland AG
The registered company address is: Gewerbestrasse 11, 6330 Cham, Switzerland

Preface

The RoboCup initiative seeks to advance robotics and artificial intelligence (AI) through competitions that challenge the forefront of these technologies. The 2024 edition of RoboCup took place in Eindhoven, The Netherlands at Genneper Parken from July 17th to July 22nd. The Eindhoven University of Technology organized the event in collaboration with the non-profit foundation Promotech2050, which represents the Eindhoven RoboCup teams.

This book presents the proceedings of the 27th annual RoboCup International Symposium that was held at the Evoluon in Eindhoven on July 22nd, 2024. The technical challenges brought on by the RoboCup initiative motivate novel scientific and engineering strategies for developing complete, advanced robotic systems. The RoboCup Symposium fosters the sharing of these approaches and advances the science of robotics by enabling scientists and practitioners to build upon the progress of others. This book also presents contributed technical papers from the champions of the 2024 competition's constituent leagues. These papers describe the key approaches necessary for winning the respective competition.

In 2024, the RoboCup Symposium received a total of 58 submissions, which were then reviewed by the 54 members of the Program Committee. Each paper was read and evaluated by at least two and usually three reviewers per submission in a single-blind review. After receiving scores from the Program Committee, the Program Chairs decided to accept 24 regular scientific papers and 10 papers for a development track. Overall, the acceptance rate was 58%. Eight accepted papers were given oral presentations at the symposium, and the rest were presented as posters. Champion papers from RoboCup winners were reviewed by members of the respective league executive committees and the Program Chairs.

Among the 34 accepted research papers, five papers were nominated as best paper award finalists. The awards committee evaluated the finalists based on the paper as well as their associated reviews and presentations and selected one best paper:

Direction and Distance Estimation of Whistle Events on a NAO Robot by Diana Kleingarn, Dominik Brämer, and Rainer Martin.

In addition to the accepted papers, the RoboCup 2024 Symposium hosted two wonderful invited keynote talks:

- **Chieko Asakawa**, T. J. Watson Research Center and Carnegie Mellon University, USA & Japanese National Museum of Emerging Science and Innovation, Japan. Title: *AI suitcase: A navigation robot for the visually impaired.*
- **Javier Alonso-Mora**, Delft University of Technology, the Netherlands. Title: *Motion Planning and Task Assignment among Decision-Making Agents.*

We are indebted to a great number of people without whom the Symposium could not have taken place. First, we thank all of the Program Committee for their time and expertise to ensure that accepted papers met a high bar. Second, we thank the awards committee for their time reading and evaluating the five candidates for the best paper. Finally, we are grateful to the local organizers who handled the event setup and actively helped create the program. In particular, we thank Arnoud Visser, Femke van Beek, Ömür Arslan, and Lotte de Koning for ensuring the Symposium ran smoothly.

December 2024

Edna Barros
Josiah P. Hanna
Hiroyuki Okada
Elena Torta

Organization

Program Committee Chairs

Hanna, Josiah P.	University of Wisconsin–Madison, USA
Barros, Edna	Federal University of Pernambuco, Brazil
Torta, Elena	Eindhoven University of Technology, Netherlands
Okada, Hiroyuki	Tokyo Information Design Professional University, Japan

Program Committee

Akiyama, Hidehisa	Okayama University of Science, Japan
Araújo, Victor	Federal University of Pernambuco, Brazil
Arslan, Omur	Eindhoven University of Technology, Netherlands
Barros, Edna	Federal University of Pernambuco, Brazil
Behnke, Sven	University of Bonn, Germany
Bianchi, Reinaldo	Centro Universitário FEI, Brazil
Brienza, Michele	Sapienza University of Rome, Italy
Cavalcanti, Lucas	Federal University of Pernambuco, Brazil
Chen, Xieyuanli	National University of Defense Technology, China
Contreras-Toledo, Luis	TID Professional University, Japan
De Bortoli, Marco	Graz University of Technology, Austria
Dorer, Klaus	Hochschule Offenburg, Germany
Duarte, Christopher	University of Miami, USA
Estivill, Vladimir	Universitat Pompeu Fabra, Spain
Ferrein, Alexander	FH Aachen University of Applied Sciences, Germany
Gabel, Thomas	Frankfurt University of Applied Sciences, Germany
Genter, Katie	University of Texas at Austin, USA
Gies, Valentin	Toulon University, France
Hanna, Josiah P.	University of Wisconsin–Madison, USA
Hart, Justin	University of Texas at Austin, USA
Hori, Sansei	Kyushu Institute of Technology, Japan
Ito, Masahide	Aichi Prefectural University, Japan
Labiosa, Adam	University of Wisconsin–Madison, USA

MacAlpine, Patrick	University of Texas at Austin, USA
Machado, Mateus	Federal University of Pernambuco, Brazil
Magalhães Braga, Pedro	Federal University of Pernambuco, Brazil
Melo, João	Federal University of Pernambuco, Brazil
Mitrevski, Alex	Hochschule Bonn-Rhein-Sieg, Germany
Mizuchi, Yoshiaki	Tamagawa University, Japan
Moos, Arne	Technical University of Dortmund, Germany
Musumeci, Emanuele	Sapienza University of Rome, Italy
Nakashima, Tomoharu	Osaka Prefecture University, Japan
Nardi, Daniele	Sapienza University of Rome, Italy
Nardin, Luis Gustavo	École des Mines de Saint-Étienne, France
Noda, Itsuki	Hokkaido University, Japan
Norouzi, Asad	LeddarTech, Canada
Obst, Oliver	Western Sydney University, Australia
Ojalvo, Julio	University of Miami, USA
Okada, Hiroyuki	Tokyo Information Design Professional University, Japan
Okada, Aiko	Tokyo Info. Design Professional University, Japan
Oomes, Stijn	University of Amsterdam, Netherlands
Orozco González, Marina	University of Amsterdam, Netherlands
Pasternak, Katarzyna	University of Miami, USA
Pavlichenko, Dmytro	University of Bonn, Germany
Pazelli, Tatiana	Federal University of São Carlos, Brazil
Pimentel, Fagner	FEI University Center, Brazil
Polani, Daniel	University of Hertfordshire, UK
Reis, Luis	University of Porto, Portugal
Rossi, Alessandra	University of Naples Federico II, Italy
Sugiura, Toko	National Institute of Technology, Japan
Schwertfeger, Sören	ShanghaiTech University, China
Shayesteh, Mohammad	Islamic Azad University, Iran
Simões, Marco	University of Coimbra, Portugal
Stelter, Sebastian	Cranfield University, UK
Steup, Christoph	Otto-von-Guericke University Magdeburg, Germany
Stolzenburg, Frieder	Harz University of Applied Sciences, Germany
Suppa, Marek	Comenius University in Bratislava, Slovakia
Suthakorn, Jackrit	Mahidol University, Thailand
Tonidandel, Flavio	FEI University Center, Brazil
Torta, Elena	Eindhoven University of Technology, Netherlands
van Beek, Femke	Eindhoven University of Technology, Netherlands
Villar-Corrales, Angel	University of Bonn, Germany
Villing, Rudi	Maynooth University, Ireland

Visser, Ubbo	University of Miami, USA
Visser, Arnoud	University of Amsterdam, Netherlands
Wiley, Timothy	RMIT University, Australia
Wong, Aaron	Newcastle University, UK
Zare, Nader	Linnaeus University, Sweden

Contents

Best Paper Award

Scientific Track

Best Paper Award

Direction and Distance Estimation of Whistle Events on a NAO Robot

Diana Kleingarn[1(✉)], Dominik Brämer[1], and Rainer Martin[2]

[1] Robotics Research Institute, Section Information Technology, TU Dortmund University, 44227 Dortmund, Germany
diana.kleingarn@tu-dortmund.de

[2] Institute of Communication Acoustics Ruhr-Universität Bochum, 44801 Bochum, Germany

Abstract. In order to achieve a more human-like soccer game, the robots should not only recognise a whistle but, more importantly, decide which whistle event is relevant and which is 'noise' from visitors or games from adjacent fields. Furthermore, each robot should be able to determine the sound source independently, without wireless messages between the robots, as this will allow a fair comparison with human teams in the future.

For this task, we propose a neural network approach to evaluate the time-of-arrival difference and a second approach to estimate the distance of the sound source using the direct-to-reverberation ratio (DRR) and spectral analysis. We were able to achieve accuracies of a few degrees for direction estimation, in particular, with distance estimation also delivering reasonable results. Furthermore, we were able to implement the entire system efficiently on the NAO robot's integrated hardware.

Keywords: Sound source localisation · Whistle recognition · Convolutional neural network

1 Introduction

Robots are designed to serve a specific purpose, such as playing soccer in our case. However, in addition to their main task, they have to react to specific events, such as a whistle. With our whistle recognition [3], we demonstrated a robust method for detecting whistles reliably. This resulted in the necessity of discarding whistles from neighbouring fields since reacting to referee commands from other fields is not beneficial for the game. Whistle recognition was first introduced in the Standard Platform League (SPL) in 2015 to indicate the start of a game. By now, a whistle indicates the beginning of a kickoff, a goal, and the end of the game [2]. In addition, official RoboCup events provide multiple soccer fields close to each other for one league, with different leagues possibly nearby. With the implemented time delay of the game controller signal sent to the robots, recognising and reacting to the whistle is necessary. However, falsely

E. Barros et al. (Eds.): RoboCup 2024, LNAI 15570, pp. 3–15, 2025.
https://doi.org/10.1007/978-3-031-85859-8_1

detecting a whistle from another field can currently only be noticed when the expected game controller signal is missing after the set delay. So, the problem addressed here is not the recognition of whistle events but distinguishing between relevant whistles and whistles from other fields that can be labelled as noise.

The described task contains two parts: estimating the sound source's direction and distance, described in Sects. 3 and 4. This information, combined with knowledge about the soccer field and the robot's location, can be used to decide whether the detected whistle is relevant. In Sect. 1.1, we give an overview of existing solutions for sound source localisation. One of the most common difficulties in distance estimation is overfitting to a specific room. This is unfortunate for soccer robots which are supposed to play everywhere, just like humans. Therefore, the goal is to make the localisation of the whistle as independent from the room as possible. The issue is also described in detail in Sect. 1.1, which leads to the dataset described in Sect. 2.

Another main criterion for RoboCup teams is the runtime. To maintain a fluent game, added tasks should not block or slow down the motion, vision or behaviour. Additionally, according to the rules of the SPL league, all robots have to be autonomous and are not supposed to be altered, so they must use the integrated hardware of the NAO robot. So, in the evaluation, Sect. 5, not only the performance in terms of correct detections is analysed, but also if the execution time still fits in the set timeframe of 30 ms for one cognition frame. The final Section summarises the results and provides an overview of future projects.

1.1 Related Work

Although the problem of Sound Source Localization (SSL) has been addressed many times, it is still an area that has not been fully explored. Usually, this topic involves finding a speaker's location so that most methods concentrate on the frequency range of human speech [1,6,14,15]. Currently, the SPL league does not use speech as a form of communication, so audio perception focuses exclusively on whistle recognition. Whistles usually have a fundamental frequency between 2 kHz and 3.5 kHz and between one and three overtones. In comparison, the fundamental frequency of voiced speech ranges between 50 and 450 Hz and its spectrum features a larger number of overtones typically up to 4 kHz [11]. Since this league is still in the early stages of audio processing, and the design of the NAO robot bears some challenges compared to the classic microphone array approach, not many solutions are suitable for a direct comparison.

In Li et al. [6], the authors show an SSL approach using a NAO V5 head. However, they also describe challenges such as the integrated fans near the microphones, insufficient processing power, which improved with the newer robot version but is still a major restriction, and the sound quality of the integrated microphones. The newer robot version now uses omnidirectional microphones. To overcome some of the challenges, the authors in [6] decided to outsource the computations, which the SPL rules [2] prohibit, and to use vision as an additional source of information. Adding vision, something humans do automatically, can provide helpful information. However, the robot in Li et al. [6] was placed on a table, compensating the difference in height between humans and the NAO robot (58 cm). Other points of interest next to the one speaker, like a second one or, in our case, a ball as the highest priority, were not examined. They use a direct-path estimator to calculate the location of a speaker. Therefore, they use phase and level differences between two diagonal microphone pairs of the NAO robot in the short-time Fourier transform (STFT) domain. In Fig. 1, the top view of a NAO V6 head is shown to highlight the position of the four microphones. The changes between the robot versions, besides the colour, are not visually noticeable since they are related to the integrated hardware, like processors or sensors, not to the overall design of the robot.

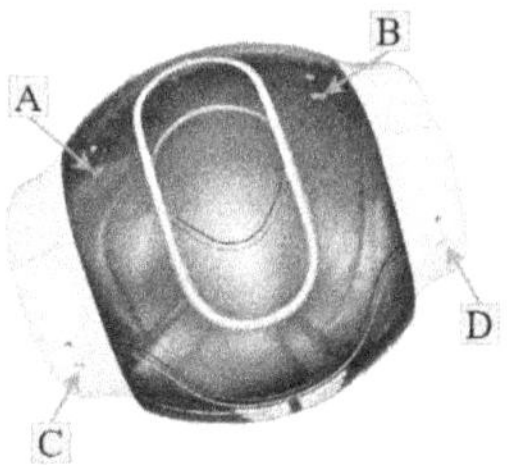

Fig. 1. Top view on NAO head with four microphones A, B, C, and D.

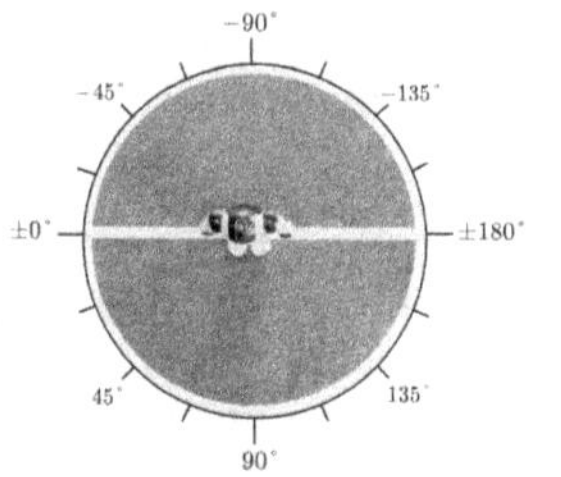

Fig. 2. NAO robot with azimuth labels.

Fig. 3. The robot is in a penalised position (left) and walking (right).

Kushwaha et al. [4] propose a machine-learning approach using a convolutional recurrent neural network (CRNN). One of the primary difficulties they faced was overfitting to specific datasets. Two of the five datasets used were generated, while the other three were recorded. Additionally, two of the recorded datasets and one of the generated datasets featured only one room or church, whereas the remaining three utilised nine or sixteen unique rooms without any indication of their distinguishing characteristics. Naturally, different rooms have unique acoustics due to differences in their structure, size and design. So, this effect can also be described as overfitting to specific rooms or categories of rooms.

The most common field of application for SSL is an at-home setting, e.g. service robots. This kind of application, described in [1,10], is limited to relatively fixed settings in living areas. In Cho et al. [1], the authors evaluate their proposed search space clustering method to speed up the steered-response power-phase transform (SRP-PHAT) based SSL method in a classroom. Sewtz et al. [10] chose a conversation setting between two speakers in the robot's field of view to combine hearing and vision. The setting was shown in a picture displaying a living room or an office with an L-shaped bookshelf. Both works produced good results, but only in a limited range of use cases. However, this work aims to use SSL for any soccer game or showcase scenario with as little calibration as possible.

Considering information about the room acoustic as presented in [15], the direct-to-reverberant energy ratio (DRR) has shown to be beneficial in multiple cases. Furthermore, Zohourian et al. [16] demonstrated the importance of using an accurate inter-microphone distance and head-related transfer functions (HRTFs). However, instead of measuring both, we chose a machine learning approach to learn the relation between the microphones instead of measuring it.

2 Dataset

Preparing the dataset is one of the most critical steps in training a neural network. With the goal of estimating the distance and the direction of the whistle, we needed this information as labels. In addition, the information about the room where the whistle was recorded was kept as a label. This is important because, as explained in Sect. 1.1, overfitting to a particular room or category of rooms can be an issue. This information is also helpful for debugging as it helps keeping track of the variety of rooms.

We recorded the complete dataset on several of our robots to take the HRTF of the NAO head into account. For easier handling of the robots, they were brought into the penalised position, shown in Fig. 3 (left), which does not allow any movement and, therefore, avoids inaccuracies due to head movements. During the recording process, we checked that the used robots had at least three functioning microphones and discarded recordings with more than one broken one. However, the goal was to use mainly fully functioning robots. So, of the 142 recordings we made, only four are of robots with one broken microphone. We did not discard those four recordings to increase the diversity of the data. For each recording, we pressed the whistle, shown in Fig. 5, five times at different heights before either turning the robot or moving to the next position. Although the rules [2] briefly describe how to use the whistle, it is common that every referee has a unique style of holding the whistle, or in some cases, they use a regular one in contrast to the one we showed. To be prepared for any height difference, we decided to split the five different heights at which we pressed the whistle between an outstretched arm over the head and an outstretched arm downwards next to the body, leading to the three additional positions: at eye level, chest level, and hip level.

As the mentioned picture of the whistle in Fig. 5 shows, the airflow can only leave the whistle through a specific opening, leading to a directed signal. Therefore, we rotated and tilted the whistle differently for all five whistle placements per position. Depending on the room where the recording took place, the desired distance between the robot and the sound source, and the robot's position in this room, we either turned the robot or let the person with the whistle walk around the robot in discrete intervals. So, the sound source had a fixed distance to the robot for each recording. These recordings cover 360° around the robot in discrete steps of 45° in most cases. Some files have smaller intervals of 22.5° or bigger ones of 90°. In Fig. 2, the direction labels are displayed. Table 1 shows the complete list of distance and room labels.

When locating a specific sound source, the data is supposed to contain this sound, with background noise, but not noise without this sound. We used the neural network described in [3] with a low threshold to automatically extract the

Table 1. List of Labels for test and training.

Training rooms	Training distances in meter	
Arena	0.7	1.0
Audimax Hamburg	1.6	1.9
Basement	2.0	2.5
Hallway upstairs	3.0	3.1
MMI Lab (reverberant)	3.5	4.5
MMI Lab with Curtains	5.4	6.0
Meeting Room	7.0	7.7
Staircase	8.5	9.0
	10.0	15.3

Test rooms	Test distances in meter	
Arena	0.7	1.9
Hallway downstairs	3.1	4.5
MMI Lab (reverberant)	5.0	7.7
MMI Lab with Curtains	9.0	12.4
Outdoor Field in Rome		

whistle events from each recording. The first few frames mainly contain direct sound without reverberations, which is important for estimating the direction and distance. This is why a low threshold is used to capture the first frames. The goal is to have whistle events exclusively in the dataset, but each whistle event separately. However, we started by grouping 1024 samples into one frame with half-overlapping windows to use the whistle detection referenced above. This windowed time domain data is one part of the dataset we provide. Afterwards, we apply the Hamming window as a window function, transform the windowed data into the frequency domain using an FFT, and calculate the phases from these complex spectrograms. These complex spectrograms and the phases are the second part of the dataset. Due to its versatility, every form of scaling or post-processing is possible from this point. To now extract the whistle events, first, each recording is analysed to find the longest whistle sequence per file, the reference sequence X_{ref}. Multiplied with our attention multiplier, which is set to $a_{\text{mul}} = 1.25$, we obtain the attention length $a_{\text{len}} = |X_{\text{ref}}| \cdot a_{\text{mul}}$. All frames are grouped into one big whistle frame X_{w}, as long as the number of frames in which no whistle is detected is lower than a_{len}.

In the next step, we slide X_{w} gradually two frames forward, generating three whistles in the dataset per recorded whistle. Additionally, this approach ensures robustness if the robot detects a whistle later than desirable. The process mentioned above is only utilised to calculate the distance.

We divide the dataset generated in this way into a training dataset, a test dataset and an evaluation dataset. By including 125 of the recording sessions, with 15312 whistle events in the training dataset, 12 sessions with 1272 whistle events in the test dataset and seven sessions with 1050 whistle events in the evaluation dataset.

3 Direction Detection

Estimating the direction of the sound source, here a whistle, is one part of determining whether the whistle sound is likely to belong to the soccer field the robot is standing on. In contrast to most at-home scenarios described in Sect. 1.1, we focus on the azimuthal angle while paying no attention to the elevation. The azimuth in relation to the robot is shown in Fig. 2.

When working with sound, it is beneficial to also consider room acoustics [5]. As shown in Fig. 4, the direction of sound is determined by its direct path. However, in any scenario except the free field, reverberation should be considered. To avoid any confusion caused by reflections, we have decided to skip frames that contain reverberation. Based on measurements taken in our lab, we found that only the first two frames contain mostly direct sound. However, due to inaccuracies in detection, we have found that using the first three frames (93 ms) leads to a better performance.

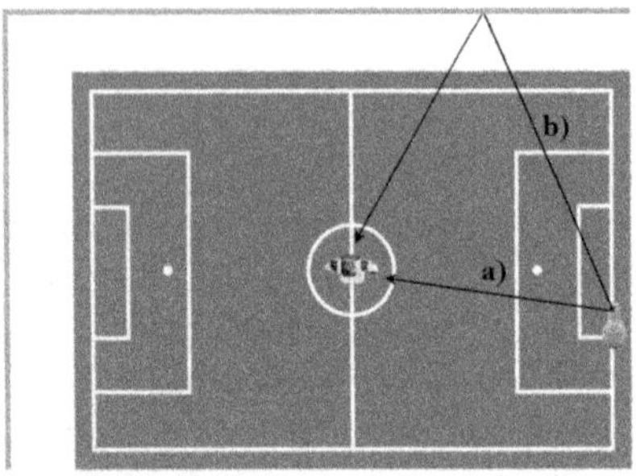

Fig. 4. Example of the path of direct sound a) and reflected sound b).

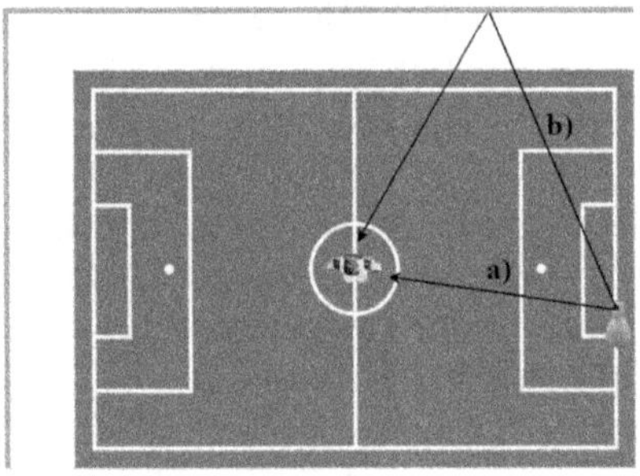

Fig. 5. Illustration of the direction of sound radiation for the hand whistle utilized by us and by the SPL.

Since we are using a neural network for the direction estimation, we first want to introduce our training loss. Due to a slight imbalance in our direction training data, we decided to adopt the shrinkage loss proposed by Lu et al. [8], as it penalises easy-to-learn samples and can, therefore, focus more on difficult samples. We have also decided to represent the direction as an angle between 0 and 360° instead of −180 to 180°, which we use as an angle in our datasets, as it is easier to process with our framework. To combine this with the loss, we do not compare the pure angles with each other but convert them into direction vectors on a unit circle and use the resulting distance on the unit circle between the vectors as the error part of the shrinkage loss. This also prevents the problem of mishandling values close to 0° so that, for example, 5° and 355° produce the same error and not an absolute error of 5 in one case and 355 in the other.

As previously demonstrated by Li et al. [6] and Cho et al. [1], phases carry a significant amount of directional information. Therefore, we use the phases and time domain data as input for our direction estimation. Both data are processed in parallel by one backbone each to create a feature vector. Since Li et al. [6] have already shown that an inter-microphone level difference is helpful in recognising a direction, we use the feature vector derived from the time domain to refine the phases further. We use an attention system [12] that adjusts the phase feature vector for this. The resulting vector is combined with the time-domain feature vector and is then processed by a fully connected network to provide a value for our direction estimation. The entire structure of our neural network can be seen in Fig. 6. Note that, apart from the output layer, which uses a sigmoid function as activation, each dense layer uses Mish [9] as an activation function. We opted for Mish over ReLU (Rectified Linear Unit) activation function because Mish is non-monotonic and self-regularising, which leads to improved neural network robustness and performance [9].

Although we use three frames for the subsequent direction estimation, the neural network only works with a single frame at a time. Since a single whistle consists of several frames, we separate the whistle sequence, described in Sect. 2, and shuffle them. As described in Sect. 2, we use multiple datasets: a training dataset, a validation dataset and an evaluation dataset. In this process, we utilise solely the training and validation datasets to gather 256 randomised whistle frames to create our batches. Then, we receive the training and validation batches and proceed to train our neural network for 2500 epochs, using early stopping to prevent overfitting.

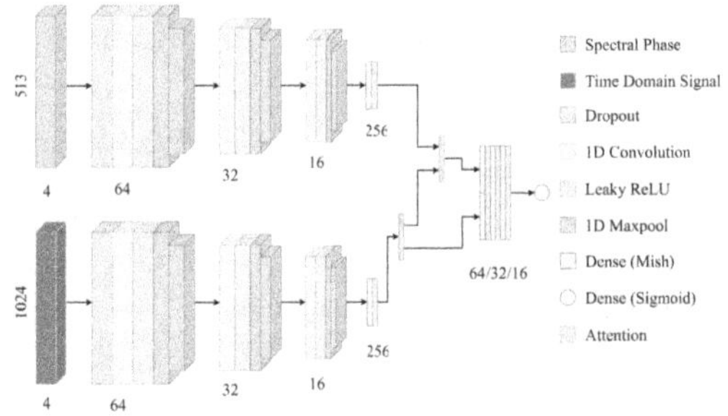

Fig. 6. Overview of our proposed whistle direction estimation neural network architecture. The numbers indicate the filter count of the convolution or the number of dense units, and a step indicates that the input is reduced by half.

4 Distance Estimation

The second part of SSL, in our case, is the distance. Despite being more challenging, this part is also more important for deciding whether the sound is relevant to the robot. The aim is to achieve a human-like perception. However, human distance estimation is not highly accurate [13], people also rely on their vision for accurate estimates. This can be challenging for the Nao robots due to the difference in height and their small field of view (60.9° horizontally and 47.6° vertically). As noticed during the visual referee challenge, the robots can either see where they go or watch what the referee does above hip level. Accordingly, we focus on information that the robot can easily acquire and does not interfere with its movements or the ongoing game (see Sect. 1.1).

In addition, we grouped distances into five bins/classes [17] with the boundaries 2 m, 4.5 m, 6.75 m and 9 m to have a finer grid than just the distinction between near and far while still not expecting an absolutely precise result. Unlike the direction detection, where we focused on the beginning of the sound, the later frames are also helpful for distance estimation. By analysing the test and training dataset, we discovered that 18 frames are, on average, a good window size to capture most of one whistle event.

Therefore, our neural network uses an 18-frame-wide spectrogram and a DRR value for each frequency feature of the spectrogram as input for distance estimation. Both inputs are processed in parallel by one backbone each. The spectrogram backbone starts with a Gaussian noise layer. It continues with four convolution blocks, each consisting of a 2D convolution and a leaky ReLU activation function layer followed by 2D max-pooling. After this, the spectrogram backbone ends with a 3-layer wide, fully connected network, which forms a feature vector. The DRR backbone is similar to the spectrogram backbone, except it utilises 1D convolutions instead of 2D ones. Both backbones create a feature vector, which is then multiplied and fed into another four-layer wide, fully connected network that starts with a leaky ReLU activation layer. This last network produces a probabilistic estimation of the likelihood that the current input belongs to each of our five distance groups.

During training, only whole whistle sequences are processed, and the DRR is calculated using the first three frames as the direct part and the following 15 frames as the reverberation. As already described in Sect. 3, only the training and validation dataset is used here. The loss function we use to train the distance estimation is an adapted version of the focal loss [7].

5 Evaluation

For the evaluation, we recorded five new sessions in three rooms. Two of these recordings were made in rooms not included in the test or training dataset described in Sect. 2. The other three were recorded on our soccer field in our lab. The recordings in the other rooms, a seminar room and an office, followed the procedure described in Sect. 2. The robot had a fixed position in the room with a 4.05 m distance to the whistle in the seminar room and a 1.25 m distance in the office. In this setting, turning the robot in 45° steps was more reasonable than having the person move. However, to capture as many different rotations and tilts of the whistle as possible, we decided to whistle ten times per height and position around the robot. Other than that, the procedure per position for all five recordings remained the same.

In our lab, we changed the positions of the robots and the whistle to create a more realistic setting. The whole setup is shown in Fig. 7 with dots indicating positions with a whistle while circles mark the positions of the robots. Additionally, the colour red indicates that these locations were used in both lab recordings, while the blue ones were only used in the first bigger test. Although the marks on the field are clear, the actual position differed, whether the person holding the whistle was standing on this spot or positioned the whistle exactly on the marked spot. This led to an offset of up to 45 cm.

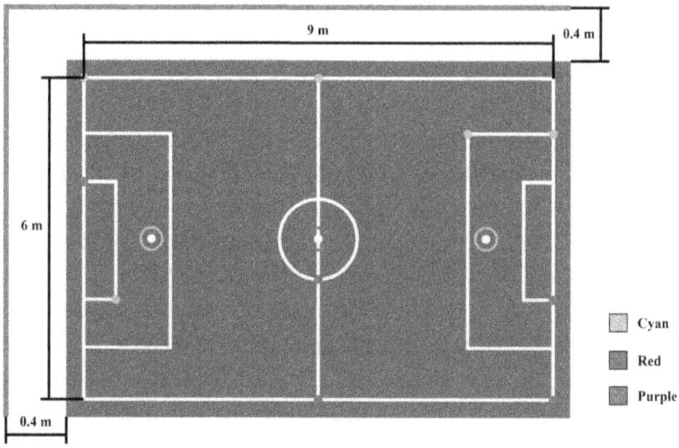

Fig. 7. Soccer field according to the rules [2] with walls coloured in purple. The circles mark the position of the robots K, B, and V, while the dots mark the place of sound sources. The red colour indicates that these points were used for both recordings, and the cyan-coloured positions were added for the lab evaluation.

During the first lab recording, three robots were placed on the described marks simultaneously to ensure equal conditions. Again, all robots were in the penalised position, as shown in Fig. 3. This posture is different from the shown posture during walking. In addition, movement creates noise, and the additional head movement needs to be tracked to compute a direction in relation to the robot's body instead of the head. During walking, it can also not be guaranteed that the robot's body is always perfectly aligned in a 90 ° angle to the centre line. Another difficulty is the so-called backlash, meaning the sensor measuring the head angle can have an offset or the sensor update is delayed. Because of these difficulties, we decided to add a more realistic test. Therefore, we had one robot walk on the spot in the centre circle while moving the head. This second recording covered the same area of the field but with fewer positions on the field. It was more of a brief test to see if the results could be actually used in a game.

The results are displayed in Tables 2 and 3. As a metric for the evaluation, we chose the median error, mean error and the standard deviation over one recording. In terms of the direction, the error is given in degree. However, it is more challenging with respect to distance estimation because the output label is calculated by choosing the distance bin with the highest probability. As described in Sect. 4, the hard decisions can cause larger errors than expected. So, one distance bin next to the actual label is still acceptable, while two or more bins apart are not desirable. To acknowledge that, the distance error ranges between 0 and 1, with 1 meaning the ground truth and the prediction is as far apart as possible with five bins.

Table 2 shows the results of the recordings with standing robots. Since the datasets to train and validate the neural networks were recorded with standing robots, the expectation was that they would perform better than the ones with a walking robot. Additionally, a majority of the mentioned datasets were recorded on our field, while the other two rooms we chose for the evaluation were not included in the test or training dataset. Surprisingly, the tests on the soccer field, a known area, have a median direction error of 12°, while the median direction error for the unknown rooms amounts to 2° and 5°. The median distance error for some tests was 0.25, meaning one bin next to the ground truth. But the robots B and V had a better perception with a median distance error of 0. While there is no explanation for the differences in the robots, except for robot K, which had one broken microphone, the unexpected result regarding the direction can mostly be explained with the person holding the whistle. During the evaluation on the field, the person paid attention to standing on the designated spot, leading to an offset of the whistle of up to half an arm's length, as described above. However, in the other two rooms, the whistle-holder paid special attention to holding the whistle at the desired azimuth angle towards the robot. It is important to know that robot K, with one broken microphone, performed slightly less well than the other robots, but not to a point at which it would show in the median error.

Table 2. Direction and distance errors in an evaluation with standing robots, the letters in brackets describe which robot was used for the evaluation. $\tilde{x}$, $\bar{x}$, and σ denote the median, mean error, and standard deviation. The distance error is normalized on the maximum deviation represented by four distance bins. Therefore, a normalized distance error of 0.25 corresponds to a deviation by one bin.

	Direction Error			Normalized Distance Error		
	$\tilde{x}$	$\bar{x}$	σ	$\tilde{x}$	$\bar{x}$	σ
Penalty mark (right) [B]	12°	14°	13°	0.0	0.16	0.22
Kick-off point [K]	12°	16°	19°	0.25	0.21	0.17
Penalty mark (left) [V]	12°	14°	15°	0.0	0.17	0.21
Conference Room [B]	2°	4°	5°	0.0	0.16	0.23
Office [E]	5°	14°	24°	0.25	0.23	0.18

The second part of the evaluation, shown in Table 3, was mainly to verify if the proposed solution can be used for a RoboCup game. Walking, in combination with head movement, significantly increased the complexity of the problem. This effect is mostly visible when one microphone is not working. While the difference in performance during the first part of the evaluation was barely noticeable, during walking, the one missing microphone caused the percepts to be mirrored on either the x or y-axis regularly. This led to a median direction error of 58°. The median distance error was not affected. However, considering all the other error sources mentioned above, the result is still acceptable, although a robot with functioning microphones is preferable.

The walking evaluation with robot B, which had four functioning microphones, is on par with the field evaluation with the standing robots in regard to direction detection. Overall, the distance estimation is similar to the first part of the evaluation. However, as discussed before, we would interpret varying accuracies as mostly related to how precisely the whistle-holder positioned the whistle.

Table 3. Direction and distance errors in an evaluation with walking robots, the letters in brackets describe which robot was used for the evaluation. $\tilde{x}$, $\bar{x}$, and σ denote the median, mean error, and standard deviation. The distance error is normalized on the maximum deviation represented by four distance bins. Therefore, a normalized distance error of 0.25 corresponds to a deviation by one bin.

	Direction Error			Normalized Distance Error		
	$\tilde{x}$	$\bar{x}$	σ	$\tilde{x}$	$\bar{x}$	σ
Goal (left) [B]	15°	40.2°	69.6°	0.25	0.25	0.0
Center circle [B]	11.5°	11.8°	6.4°	0.25	0.14	0.15
T-junction [B]	8.5°	9.3°	6.6°	0.0	0.14	0.22
Goal (right) [B]	10.5°	14.3°	10.3°	0.25	0.25	0.0
Corner (right) [B]	13.5°	17.8°	17.3°	0.25	0.47	0.25
Overall (3 mics) [K]	58°	72.5°	51.2°	0.25	0.34	0.22

Lastly, it was important that besides the results, the runtime is realistic for the robot. As mentioned in Sect. 1, the upper limit is 30 ms. The entire processing pipeline needs around 25 ms to recognise the whistle and estimate the direction and distance. Only outliers break the 30 ms mark, but this is not a problem as the estimation of the direction and distance is only active if a whistle has also been detected. When no whistle is detected, sufficient time for computing other tasks is available.

6 Conclusion and Future Work

In this paper, we showed an SSL approach that is, in general, fast enough to be used on a NAO robot while also being accurate enough to help decide whether or not the whistle is relevant to the ongoing game. Taking the partially inaccurate placement of the whistle during our data collection effort into account, the direction detection has a median deviation of a few degrees. The distance estimation seems quite robust due to the rough classification in five distance groups. However, it can be investigated whether a change to a regression or curriculum learning can further decrease the error. While the performance of the direction and distance estimation is promising, the main task for the future is optimising the computational process to avoid the sporadic computational peaks that are not within the set limits.

References

1. Cho, Y., Yook, D., Chang, S., Kim, H.: Sound source localization for robot auditory systems. IEEE Trans. Consum. Electron. **55**, 1663–1668 (2009). https://doi.org/10.1109/TCE.2009.5278040
2. RoboCup Technical Committee: Robocup standard platform league (NAO) rule book (2024). https://spl.robocup.org/wp-content/uploads/SPL-Rules-2024.pdf
3. Kleingarn, D., Brämer, D.: Neural network and prior knowledge ensemble for whistle recognition. In: Buche, C., Rossi, A., Simões, M., Visser, U. (eds.) RoboCup 2023: Robot World Cup XXVI, pp. 17–28. Springer, Cham (2024)
4. Kushwaha, S.S., Roman, I.R., Fuentes, M., Bello, J.P.: Sound source distance estimation in diverse and dynamic acoustic conditions (2023)
5. Kuttruff, H.: Room Acoustics. CRC Press (2016)
6. Li, X., Girin, L., Badeig, F., Horaud, R.: Reverberant sound localization with a robot head based on direct-path relative transfer function. In: 2016 IEEE/RSJ International Conference on Intelligent Robots and Systems (IROS). IEEE (2016). http://dx.doi.org/10.1109/IROS.2016.7759437
7. Lin, T.Y., Goyal, P., Girshick, R., He, K., Dollár, P.: Focal loss for dense object detection. In: Proceedings of the IEEE International Conference on Computer Vision, pp. 2980–2988 (2017)
8. Lu, X., Ma, C., Ni, B., Yang, X., Reid, I., Yang, M.H.: Deep regression tracking with shrinkage loss. In: Proceedings of the European Conference on Computer Vision (ECCV), pp. 353–369 (2018)
9. Misra, D.: Mish: a self regularized non-monotonic activation function. arXiv preprint arXiv:1908.08681 (2019)
10. Sewtz, M., Bodenmüller, T., Triebel, R.: Sound source localization for robotic applications (2020). https://api.semanticscholar.org/CorpusID:231829935
11. Vary, P., Martin, R.: Digital Speech Transmission and Enhancement, 2nd edn. Wiley/IEEE Press (2023)
12. Vaswani, A., et al.: Attention is all you need. In: Advances in Neural Information Processing Systems, vol. 30 (2017)
13. Zahorik, P., Brungart, D.S., Bronkhorst, A.W.: Auditory distance perception in humans: a summary of past and present research. Acta Acust. Acust. **91**(3), 409–420 (2005)
14. Zohourian, M., Enzner, G., Martin, R.: Binaural speaker localization integrated into an adaptive beamformer for hearing aids. IEEE/ACM Trans. Audio Speech Lang. Process. **26**(3), 515–528 (2018). https://doi.org/10.1109/TASLP.2017.2782491
15. Zohourian, M., Martin, R.: Binaural direct-to-reverberant energy ratio and speaker distance estimation. IEEE/ACM Trans. Audio Speech Lang. Process. **28**, 92–104 (2020). https://doi.org/10.1109/TASLP.2019.2948730

16. Zohourian, M., Martin, R., Madhu, N.: New insights into the role of the head radius in model-based binaural speaker localization. In: 2017 25th European Signal Processing Conference (EUSIPCO), pp. 221–225 (2017). https://doi.org/10.23919/EUSIPCO.2017.8081201
17. Zohourian, M., Stinner, J., Martin, R.: Speaker distance estimation using binaural hearing aids and deep neural networks. Universitätsbibliothek der RWTH Aachen (2019)

Scientific Track

A ROS 2-Based Navigation and Simulation Stack for the Robotino

Saurabh Borse[1(✉)], Tarik Viehmann[2], Alexander Ferrein[1], and Gerhard Lakemeyer[2]

[1] The Mobile Autonomous Systems and Cognitive Robotics Institute, FH Aachen University of Applied Science, 52066 Aachen, Germany
borse@fh-aachen.de

[2] Knowledge-Based Systems Group, RWTH Aachen University, 52074 Aachen, Germany

Abstract. The Robotino, developed by Festo Didactic, serves as a versatile platform in education and research for mobile robotics tasks. However, there currently is no ROS 2 integration for the Robotino available. In this paper we describe our work on a Webots simulation environment for a Robotino platform extended by LIDAR sensors. A ROS 2 integration and a pre-configured setup for localization and navigation using existing ROS packages from the Nav2 suite is provided. We validate our setup by comparing simulations with real-world experiments conducted by three Robotinos in a logistics environment in our lab. Additionally, we tested the setup using a ROS 2 hardware driver for the Robotino developed by team GRIPS of the RoboCup Logistics League. The results demonstrate the feasibility of using ROS 2 and Nav2 for navigation tasks on the Robotino platform showing great consistency between simulation and real-world performance.

Keywords: Robotics · ROS 2 · Nav2 · Webots · Robotino

1 Introduction

The Robotino is a mobile robot platform for science and education developed and distributed by Festo Didactic, featuring a holonomic drive, close-range infrared sensors and an *Inertial Measurement Unit* (IMU). It can be used for developing navigation and mapping methods [4,7], it is being used in applications such as office mail delivery [20], or in production logistics scenarios such as the *RoboCup Logistics League*(RCLL) [16].

The latest Robotino platform is using Ubuntu 18.04 and 20.04 as base OS. C++ and REST APIs are provided as well as graphical programming support and *Robot Operating System*(ROS) 1 nodes. However, ROS 1 [19] is nearing its end of life in 2025 and its successor, ROS 2 [13], offers more advanced features, including an extensive framework for navigation named as *Nav2* [14]. In order to make use of this framework, several components need to be configured according

E. Barros et al. (Eds.): RoboCup 2024, LNAI 15570, pp. 19–31, 2025.
https://doi.org/10.1007/978-3-031-85859-8_2

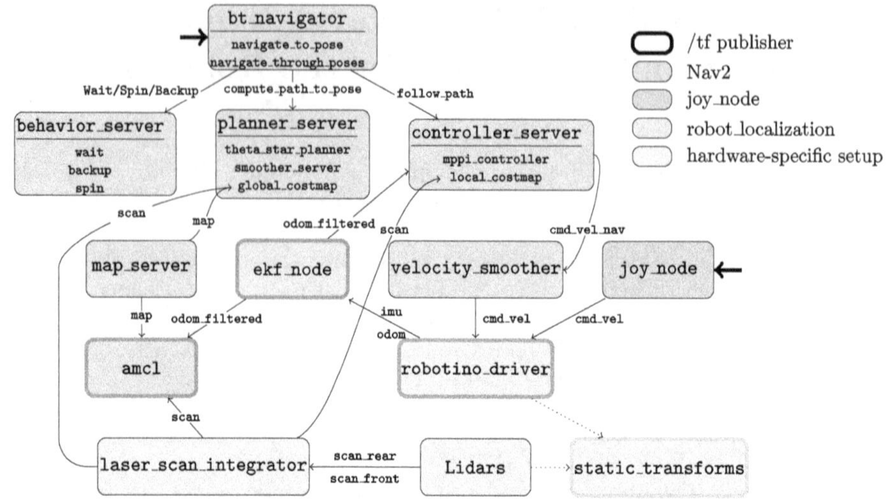

Fig. 1. ROS components overview

to the characteristics of the robot at hand, including components for planning, path following, localization and sensing.

In this paper, we present a ROS 2 integration for Robotino navigation, seamlessly bridging simulation and real-world deployment for rapid prototyping and testing of navigation algorithms, by leveraging the Webots simulation framework [15,22]. This approach accelerates development, reduces costs, and enables reliable performance comparisons in common environments.

Figure 1 depicts an overview of the presented Robotino ROS 2 integration. In order to obtain native support for the latest ROS 2 LTS version "Humble", we deployed Ubuntu 22.04 and installed the core drivers from older debian packages. The installed packages are: *rec-rpc* and *robotino-dev* for interprocess communication; *robotino-api2* that offers a C++ interface to the hardware; and *robotino-daemons* that provides the services (*rpcd*, *controld3* and *gyrod*) to start and stop the driver. We further extend the Robotino 4 with two SICK TiM571 *LIght Detection And Ranging*(LIDAR) sensors using 3D printed mounts[1]as shown in Fig. 2.

The core component of the system is the robotino driver that models the drive kinematics and odometry of the Robotino (see Sect. 3.1). It translates linear and angular velocity commands, which are published over a *cmd_vel* topic given either by an input device like a joystick or by the Nav2 stack, into corresponding motor velocities. The Robotino driver not only controls drive kinematics and odometry but also interfaces with built-in sensors like the gyroscope, infrared sensors and bumpers. It publishes sensor data over corresponding topics and provides the static transforms for each sensor relative to the *base_link*.

[1] 3D models can be found at https://github.com/carologistics/hardware/tree/master/cad/robotino/stl.

Furthermore, it provides *joint_state* data vital for odometry calculations and localization. Similarly, the external LIDARs need to provide their data in ROS, which we also account for in our simulation setup. For the real LIDARs official packages provided by SICK are used to interface the data to ROS.

The rest of the paper is as follows. We present our implementation of a driver for the Webots simulation framework [15,22] in Sect. 3. While the Robotino platform has no official ROS 2 driver yet, a ROS 2 driver (using the RobotinoApi2[2] and developed by team GRIPS from the RCLL [6]) is used to interface with the hardware for our real world experiments. The rest of the system is set up to seamlessly process data from both, simulated environments and real-world trials without a distinction of the data source. The data from both individual LIDARs is accumulated to a common *scan* topic while an Extended Kalman Filter [8,10] is used to fuse the odometry and IMU data for robust localization of the robot. These steps provide the input for the Nav2 stack, which is used for localization and navigation as described in Sect. 4. To demonstrate our results, we compare the runs of three Robotinos on a field of the RCLL in simulation with the same runs conducted in the real world in Sect. 5. Then we conclude.

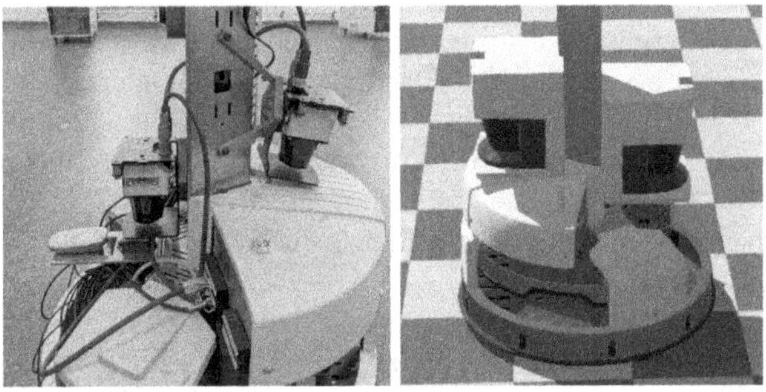

Fig. 2. LIDAR setup in simulation and on the real robot

2 Related Work

Pitonakova et al. [18] compare Gazebo, V-REP, and ARGoS for simulating mobile robot with differential and omnidirectional drive. They performed a number of benchmarks and evaluated the performance in terms of the Real Time Factor (RTF) and the CPU and memory utilization. Their research concludes that Gazebo is faster for large environments, while ARGoS is able to handle more robots in small environments.

Shamshiri et al. [21] compared in their research Webots, Gazebo, ARGoS, and V-REP simulations on platforms for agricultural robotics. In their work,

[2] https://wiki.openrobotino.org/index.php?title=API2.

they compared these simulators based on performance, availability of a ROS 2 interface, a multi-physics engine, robot and sensor libraries. They come to the conclusion that V-REP fits best for their requirements and domain.

Symeonidis et al. [1] presented a comprehensive comparison between different simulators. They highlight Gazebo and Webots for their broad community support and interoperability with ROS 2, but see drawbacks in Gazebo regarding visual realism and computational overhead. Meanwhile, according to their study, Webots offers fast GPU-bound rendering and a vast library support for robotic models, but has poor domain randomization tools and customization options for environments. AirSim and CARLA provide high visual realism and extensive 3D assets, but tend to be computationally intensive. Finally, CoppeliaSim offers multiple physics engines and versatile programming approaches.

As our main concern in this work is the interoperability with ROS 2, we opted to use the Webots simulator to develop the navigation stack for the Robotino in this environment. In the following, we outline other contributions for the navigation tasks of the Robotino platform.

Zwilling et al. [24] introduce an environment created with Gazebo simulator, establishing a direct connection with the semi-autonomous game controller called referee box ensuring that it accurately mimics real-world dynamics. However, the limitations lie in its reliance on the Fawkes framework rather than ROS 2.

The work of Abdo et al. [2] focused on visual odometry and localization using the Robotino. Experiments were conducted in simulation with Robotino Sim Professional and Matlab for acquiring and processing ground truth data, as well as on actual hardware. The study evaluated visual odometry performance in challenging environments and concluded on the efficacy of visual odometry for localization.

Nizamettin et al. [11] focused on visual odometry and implemented a navigation framework using *NI-LabVIEW* and the Festo navigation software stack. They evaluated the system in both simulation and real-world settings. The study identified two key limitations of visual odometry: inefficiency in extreme ambient light and difficulty detecting dynamic obstacles of similar color to the surroundings.

Bischoff et al. [3] propose an hierarchical reinforcement learning (RL) architecture for mastering complex robot movements, focusing on navigation tasks with the Robotino. By decomposing movements into primitives, the approach enhances planning and execution efficiency. Results on a mobile robot platform demonstrate the efficacy of the hierarchical RL framework, with potential applications in real-time navigation and dynamic obstacle avoidance.

3 Webots Robotino Driver

In order to provide a proper integration of the Robotino in Webots with ROS 2 interfaces, several existing resources can be used, including a pre-built model of the Robotino and its sensors as well as the ROS 2 bridge *webots_ros2* to establish seamless communication between ROS 2 and the Webots sensor and control interfaces.

The main task is to provide a control driver that translates incoming velocity commands to motor control actions using a kinematic model of the robot as well as providing feedback about the executed actions in form of calculated odometry information and sensor readings, while exhibiting similar properties as the control interfaces of the real hardware. In the following sections, we present the different models used in our simulation environment.

3.1 Drive Kinematics

The drive kinematics of the Robotino is characterized by its three side wheels enabling omnidirectional control, as depicted in Fig. 3. The position and orientation of each wheel with respect to the robot's frame of reference play a crucial role in determining its motion and maneuverability [12,17].

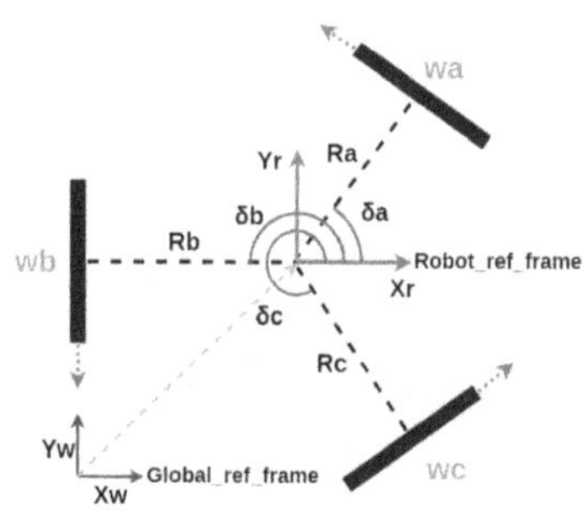

Fig. 3. Representation of the pose of the robot relative to the world reference frame (X_W, Y_W). The frame (X_R, Y_R) is the robot frame of reference, with X_R depicting its front. (R_a, R_b, R_c) represents the radial distances and $(\delta_a, \delta_b, \delta_c)$ represent the angular orientation of wheels relative to the robot frame of reference

Kinematic Model. The kinematic model of the omnidirectional motion system facilitates the calculation of the rotational speeds $(\omega_{M1}, \omega_{M2}, \omega_{M3})$ of the three omnidirectional wheel motors needed (in rpm) to execute a given motion command $C = (v_x, v_y, \omega)$, where, v_x and v_y are the translational velocity in x and y direction in m/s, respectively. ω is the angular velocity about z-axis (in rad/s). Palacín et al. [17] describe the kinematic model that we use as defined in Eq. 1.

$$\begin{bmatrix} \omega_{M1} \\ \omega_{M2} \\ \omega_{M3} \end{bmatrix} = \underbrace{\begin{bmatrix} -\sin(\delta_a) & \cos(\delta_a) & R_a \\ -\sin(\delta_b) & \cos(\delta_b) & R_b \\ -\sin(\delta_c) & \cos(\delta_c) & R_c \end{bmatrix}}_{:=K} \cdot \begin{bmatrix} v_x \\ v_y \\ \omega \end{bmatrix} \cdot \frac{1}{r} \cdot \frac{60}{2\pi} \cdot \frac{16}{1} \cdot S_c \tag{1}$$

r represents the wheel radius (in [m]), K the kinematic matrix and $\frac{16}{r}\frac{60}{2\pi}$ converts the resulting velocity to rpm. The robotino is equipped with motors GR 42x40,20W coupled with a planetary gearbox PLG 42S with a reduction ratio of 16. Additionally, to compensate for the absence of a motor model and gearbox in the simulation environment, we adjusted the linear and angular velocities by an empirically determined scaling factor, $S_c = 0.009375$. This adjustment aimed to mimic the behavior of the real robot accurately. We determined the scaling factor by issuing identical velocity commands via the *cmd_vel* topic to both the physical robot and the simulated one in an open field, covering identical distances, and then comparing the travel times required in each case.

Inverse-Kinematic Model. The inverse kinematic model of the omnidirectional motion system enables the determination of the motion parameters $C = (v_x, v_y, \omega)$ based on the measured actual rotational speed of the motors $(\omega_{M1}, \omega_{M2}, \omega_{M3})$. The robotino is equipped with incremental encoders, which facilitate measuring the rotational speed of the motors $(\omega_{M1}, \omega_{M2}, \omega_{M3})$. These rotational speeds can be converted to the angular velocities of the wheels $(\omega_a, \omega_b, \omega_c)$. Finally, the translational velocity of the robot referred to its reference frame v_x, v_y and its angular rotational velocity ω can be computed by inverting the kinematic matrix from Eq. 1, as shown in Eq. 2.

$$\begin{bmatrix} v_x \\ v_y \\ \omega \end{bmatrix} = K^{-1} \cdot \begin{bmatrix} \omega_{MA} \\ \omega_{MB} \\ \omega_{MC} \end{bmatrix} \cdot r \cdot \frac{2\pi}{60} \cdot \frac{1}{16} \cdot \frac{1}{S_c} \tag{2}$$

In the used Robotino model, the wheels are placed with uniform radii ($R = R_a = R_b = R_c$) and angular positions ($\delta_a = 60°, \delta_b = 180°, \delta_c = 300°$) as depicted in Fig. 3.

3.2 Odometry

The odometry we deploy for the simulated Robotino relies on the inverse kinematic analysis shown in Sect. 3.1 to estimate the robot's motion parameters (v_x, v_y, ω) relative to the its frame of reference given the motor feedback. Following a time interval ΔT, the robot's incremental position $(\Delta x, \Delta y, \Delta z)$ is determined by integrating the motion parameters (v_x, v_y, ω). This incremental position is then added to the previously known position (x_i, y_i, z_i) of the robot with respect to the world coordinate frame to update its current position (x_f, y_f, z_f). Here, T_m represents the transformation matrix, transforming the pose from the robot frame of reference to the global frame of reference. With a sufficiently small ΔT and subject to the accuracy of the encoder data, the odometry can thus be calculated according to Eq. 3 [17].

$$\begin{bmatrix} x_f \\ y_f \\ \theta_f \end{bmatrix} = \begin{bmatrix} x_i \\ y_i \\ \theta_i \end{bmatrix} + \underbrace{\begin{bmatrix} \cos(\theta_i) & -\sin(\theta_i) & 0 \\ \sin(\theta_i) & \cos(\theta_i) & 0 \\ 0 & 0 & 1 \end{bmatrix}}_{:=T_m} \cdot \begin{bmatrix} v_x \\ v_y \\ \omega \end{bmatrix} \cdot \Delta\,\mathrm{T} \tag{3}$$

While comparing the calculated odometry in simulations with the one obtained from a real Robotino, we observed notable inaccuracies occurring in the simulation, caused by unusual wheel slippage and inaccuracies due to time discretization in the simulation engine. We therefore also implemented an alternative method to obtain the odometry in simulations, by adding a GPS sensor to the model that directly retrieves the current pose. This alternative odometry source is used in our experiments in Sect. 5.

3.3 Sensing

In addition to Robotino's built-in sensors such as the infrared and IMU sensors, we extend the simulated Robotino model by SICK LMS 291 sensors, which are already defined in Webots and provide a similar coverage. By default, Webots provides a sensor plugin that facilitates the use of sensors within the simulation environment. Through the standard *webots_ros2_driver*, data is published over ROS topic in every time step of the webots simulation. Additionally, we provide static transforms of the sensors with respect to the *base_link* reference frame.

3.4 Control

The driver controls the movement of the Robotino in a separate act thread, which has a configurable frequency. Whenever it receives velocity data from the *cmd_vel* topic, it stores the incoming message. The data is used in the control loop of the act thread which converts it through the kinematics calculations of Sect. 3.1 to motor velocities and applies those velocities in simulations. After applying the velocity, the data of the incoming message is deleted, hence the Robotino stops, if no new velocity commands arrive. This also means that the frequency of the act loop in the driver should match the frequency of the controllers sending velocity commands.

4 Localization and Navigation

With the presented setup for acting and sensing, we utilize the ROS 2 ecosystem to provide a basic setup for mobile robotics application by configuring a localization and navigation.

The Nav2 stack offers a node for *Adaptive Monte Carlo Localization*(AMCL) (see, e.g. [5]), which is performing decently without further tuning. However, the motion model needed adaptations to fit the kinematics of the Robotino. Additionally, as odometry information from the wheels tends to be rather inaccurate, sensor fusion is used to additionally incorporate the data from the (IMU) sensor to improve the accuracy of the estimated pose. The *robot_localization* suite in ROS offers implementations for common sensor fusion algorithms such as the *Extended Kalman Filter*(EKF) [8,10] and *Unscented Kalman Filter*(UKF) [9] algorithms. We deploy the *ekf_node* that publishes odometry over *odom_filtered* and also publishes the transform between *odom* and *base_link*. Meanwhile, AMCL publishes the transform from *map* to *odom*.

The *nav2_bringup* package offers sensible base configurations for planning, path following and recovery behaviors, which we took as baseline for further tuning. We mainly focus on the planning and path following, as recovery behaviors are more likely to be tweaked to domain-specific needs.

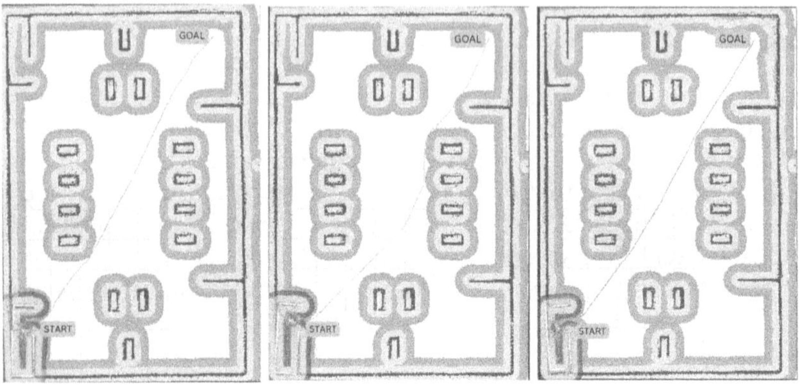

(a) NavFn Planner (b) SmacPlanner 2D (c) Theta Star Planner

Fig. 4. A comparison of the global plans generated by different planner plugins for the same goal.

The *planner server* within Nav2 implements the server responsible for managing planner requests and accepts inputs such as the goal location and the name of the desired planner plugin. We compare the three planner plugins that Nav2 offers for omnidirectional robots, namely *NavFn*, *Smac* and *Theta Star*. In Fig. 4 shows one of the instances. The *Theta Star* planner uses A* search with line of sight (LOS) checks to create any-angle paths, avoiding typical zig-zag patterns. Thus, it generates more direct trajectories compared to other planners and is the most suitable choice for this application.

The Controller Server in the Nav2 Stack takes care of the low-level motion control to move the robot to a desired goal pose. The default configuration suggests to use a basic progress and goal checker as well as a *Dynamic Window Approach Based*(DWB) [14] controller as a path follower. While the DWB controller is reactive and uses a constant action model, the *Model Predictive Path Integral*(MPPI) controller [23] is an alternative, which uses model predictive control to adjust trajectories on-the-fly, instead of splitting the task into a planning and execution stage.

Due to our objective of being able to navigate in environments with frequent dynamic obstacles (such as other robots), we opted for the MPPI controller, which is more flexible compared to the DWB controller due to it's optimization-based trajectory planning. The MPPI controller is particularly advantageous for its ability to predict future states of the robot using a dynamic model and optimize control actions over a finite time horizon. This predictive capability allows the controller to anticipate obstacles and dynamically adjust trajectories, making it well-suited for navigating through complex and dynamic environments.

Table 1. Main MPPI controller parameters

Parameters and values					
`time_steps`	`model_dt`	`frequency`	`motion_model`	`batch_size`	`vx_min`
80	0.05	20	Omni	2000	-0.7
`vx_max`	`wz_max`	`vy_max`	`vx_std`	`vy_std`	`wz_std`
0.7	0.8	0.7	0.4	0.4	0.4

The main considerations for configuring the MPPI controller evolve around the kinematics constraints to create a sampling distribution and the prediction horizon which depends on controller frequency, cost map size and sampling points. The core parameters of the MPPI controller are listed in Table 1.

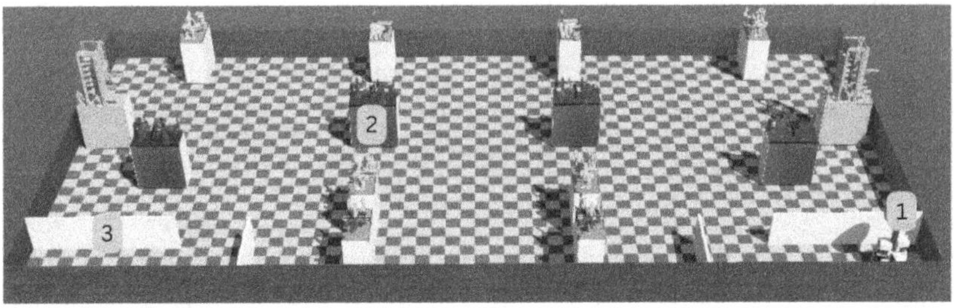

Fig. 5. Simulation map with 1 mobile robot(s), 2. static machines 3. Border walls.

5 Evaluation

As a test environment, we utilize a 6 m × 12 m field, resembling a setup from the RCLL, with cuboid machines serving as static obstacles (see Fig. 5). In each experiment, robots are assigned the task of traversing five randomly generated paths. Each path consists of four waypoints, with the robots starting at the first point and then traveling to the other three points in sequential order. The waypoints are randomly selected from points of interest in close proximity to and facing the machine sides. Each experiment is repeated five times to gauge the consistency and ROS 2 bags were recorded for all experiments.[3]

In experiment (E1), a single robot was used in both simulation and the real world. In experiment (E2), all three robots were deployed for navigation trials.

[3] https://zenodo.org/records/10938688.

Table 2 depicts the execution times for the paths. We note that the ratio of total execution time in real world trials relative to simulation trials is ≈ 1.01, hence the real world trials are about 1% slower than simulation trials in this setting.

Table 2. Five distinct run per path (P) with either using one robot (E1) or using 3 robots (R1, R2 and R3) simultaneously (E2)

P	E1		E1 Sim		E2 R1		E2 Sim R1		E2 R2		E2 Sim R2		E2 R3		E2 Sim R3	
	Avg	Δ	Avg	Δ	Avg	Δ	Avg	Δ	Avg	Δ	Avg	Δ	Avg	Δ	Avg	Δ
1	45.45	3.94	51.36	17.11	49.99	16.33	49.19	9.59	46.15	49.38	24.53	2.47	53.97	8.52	56.86	17.08
2	47.77	33.26	46.41	16.67	61.11	31.01	53.23	20.64	52.65	63.39	25.69	8.19	68.83	66.88	59.29	31.11
3	38.24	16.03	33.58	5.75	54.56	43.79	41.12	6.29	68.91	50.75	50.81	11.96	60.66	25.58	60.98	20.17
4	35.45	9.81	37.85	12.16	47.00	14.58	46.90	17.48	52.03	36.64	50.08	40.39	67.91	23.31	69.29	16.62
5	47.06	11.60	43.13	5.14	65.17	21.94	59.43	51.42	49.67	27.19	41.02	10.27	42.28	34.84	34.94	18.53

Additionally, paths driven on the first and second experiment are plotted in Fig. 6a and 6b. We observe that in simulations, the robot sometimes executes sharp curves, whereas trajectories in real-world trials tend to be smoother, which we attribute to the wheel slippage also observed when using inverse kinematics for pose estimation. Also, the turning behavior in both environments could be improved (especially for real world trials), as it can involve translational movement instead of rotating on the spot or rotating while heading forward as expected.

Next, we conducted tests using three robots to gather data in dynamic environments. Each robot operates independently and perceives the others as dynamic obstacles. The execution times are recorded in Table 2. One can observe that the real-world trials are about 16% slower than simulation trials in this setting, when accumulating the execution times of all robots. The major performance delay can be largely attributed to the increased situations, where recovery behaviors were triggered. We conclude that this is a result of less precise position estimates (resulting from normal odometry data compared to perfect gps-based odometry, approximative static obstacle positions from being placed by humans as well as semi-transparent obstacles causing worse sensor readings).

Visualizations of the driven paths of the test instances 3, 4 and 5 are plotted in Fig. 6c, 6d and 6e. In Fig. 6f, the run of path 2 is depicted, which was among the worst performances due to collisions and recovery behaviors causing slow trajectories.

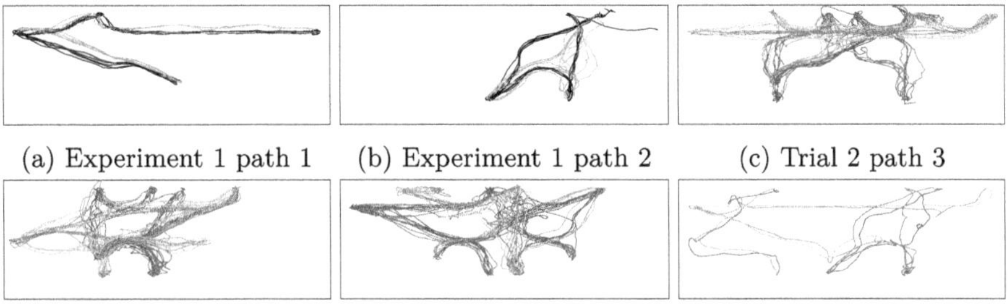

(a) Experiment 1 path 1 (b) Experiment 1 path 2 (c) Trial 2 path 3

(d) Trial 2 - path 4 (e) Trial 2 path 5 (f) Trial 2 path 2, run 2

Fig. 6. Plots of the driven paths of each robot. Black indicates solo runs, blue, red, and green indicate paths of robots 1,2 and 3, respectively. Lighter colors are used to depict paths driven in simulation. (Color figure online)

6 Conclusion

We proposed a ROS 2 setup for a Festo Robotino extended by two LIDAR sensors. It provides localization and navigation on known maps using the Nav2 framework. A Webots environment is presented that mirrors the physical setup and is used to test the framework described in this paper. By comparing simulation trials to experiments carried out on a fleet of three Robotinos we showed that the behavior in simulation matches the behavior in the real world, especially in environments without dynamic obstacles. However, some unexpected wheel slippage was observed in simulation trials that is not occurring in real trials.

To build on the presented results, future work will consider the creation of custom recovery behavior, which considers costmap data to prefer driving collision-free, a possible utilization of the robots' infrared sensors for collision monitoring and leveraging bumper sensor to reduce the collision impact and aid in recovery. Additionally, Multi Agent Path Finding (MAPF) should be explored for planning optimal collision free paths for the group of robots.

Acknowledgments. This work was partially funded by the Deutsche Forschungsgemeinschaft (DFG, German Research Foundation) under Germany's Excellence Strategy – EXC-2023 Internet of Production – 390621612, the EU ICT-48 2020 project TAILOR (No. 952215) and Research Training Group 2236 (UnRAVeL) and the Faculty of Electrical Engineering and Computer Science of FH Aachen University of Applied Sciences.

References

1. Chapter 18 - simulation environments. In: Iosifidis, A., Tefas, A. (eds.) Deep Learning for Robot Perception and Cognition, pp. 461–490. Academic Press (2022)
2. Abdo, A., Ibrahim, R., Rawashdeh, N.: Mobile robot localization evaluations with visual odometry in varying environments using festo-robotino (2020)
3. Bischoff, B., Nguyen-Tuong, D., Lee, I.H., Streichert, F., Knoll, A.: Hierarchical reinforcement learning for robot navigation. In: The European Symposium on Artificial Neural Networks (2013)
4. Derbas, A.M., Tutunji, T.A.: Slam algorithm for omni-directional robots based on ANN and EKF. In: 2023 IEEE Jordan International Joint Conference on Electrical Engineering and Information Technology (JEEIT), pp. 80–86 (2023)
5. Fox, D., Burgard, W., Dellaert, F., Thrun, S.: Monte Carlo localization: efficient position estimation for mobile robots. In: Proceedings of the Sixteenth National Conference on Artificial Intelligence and the Eleventh Innovative Applications of Artificial Intelligence Conference Innovative Applications of Artificial Intelligence, AAAI 1999/IAAI 1999, pp. 343–349. American Association for Artificial Intelligence, USA (1999)
6. Fürbaß, L., et al.: RoboCup logistics league graz robust and intelligent production system GRIPS. Graz University of Technology, Technical report (2023)
7. Hassanien, M.: Exploring and mapping indoor environment for mobile robots using different ways of scanning. Int. J. Eng. Res. Technol. **V8** (2019)
8. Jazwinski, A.: Stochastic processes and filtering theory. Mathematics in Science and Engineering, no. 64. Academic Press, New York (1970)
9. Julier, S.J., Uhlmann, J.K.: A new extension of the kalman filter to nonlinear systems. In: The 11th International Symposium of Aerospace/Defense Sensing, Simulation and Controls, Multi Sensor Fusion, Tracking and Resource Management II, Orlando, pp. 182–193 (1997)
10. Kalman, R.E.: A new approach to linear filtering and prediction problems. J. Basic Eng. **82**(1), 35–45 (1960)
11. Kulaç, N., Engin, M.: Developing a machine learning algorithm for service robots in industrial applications. Machines **11**(4) (2023)
12. Li, Y., et al.: Kinematic modeling of a combined system of multiple mecanum-wheeled robots with velocity compensation. Sensors **20**(1) (2020)
13. Macenski, S., Foote, T., Gerkey, B., Lalancette, C., Woodall, W.: Robot operating system 2: design, architecture, and uses in the wild. Sci. Robot. **7**(66), eabm6074 (2022)
14. Macenski, S., Martin, F., White, R., Ginés Clavero, J.: The marathon 2: a navigation system. In: 2020 IEEE/RSJ International Conference on Intelligent Robots and Systems (IROS) (2020)
15. Michel, O.: Webots: professional mobile robot simulation. J. Adv. Robot. Syst. **1**(1), 39–42 (2004)
16. Niemueller, T., Lakemeyer, G., Ferrein, A.: The RoboCup logistics league as a benchmark for planning in robotics. In: 2nd ICAPS Workshop on Planning in Robotics (PlanRob) (2015)
17. Palacín, J., Rubies, E., Clotet, E., Martínez, D.: Evaluation of the path-tracking accuracy of a three-wheeled omnidirectional mobile robot designed as a personal assistant. Sensors **21**(21) (2021)

18. Pitonakova, L., Giuliani, M., Pipe, A., Winfield, A.: Feature and performance comparison of the v-rep, gazebo and argos robot simulators. In: Giuliani, M., Assaf, T., Giannaccini, M.E. (eds.) Towards Autonomous Robotic Systems, pp. 357–368. Springer, Cham (2018)
19. Quigley, M., et al.: Ros: an open-source robot operating system, vol. 3 (2009)
20. Rawashdeh, N., Alwanni, H., Sheikh, N., Afghani, B.: Control design of an office mail delivery robot based on the festo robotino platform (2019)
21. Shamshiri, R., et al.: Simulation software and virtual environments for acceleration of agricultural robotics: features highlights and performance comparison. Int. J. Agric. Biol. Eng. **11**, 12–20 (2018)
22. Webots. Open-source Mobile Robot Simulation Software. http://www.cyberbotics.com
23. Williams, G., Drews, P., Goldfain, B., Rehg, J.M., Theodorou, E.A.: Aggressive driving with model predictive path integral control. In: 2016 IEEE International Conference on Robotics and Automation (ICRA), pp. 1433–1440 (2016)
24. Zwilling, F., Niemueller, T., Lakemeyer, G.: Simulation for the robocup logistics league with real-world environment agency and multi-level abstraction. In: RoboCup 2014: Robot World Cup XVIII 18, pp. 220–232. Springer (2015)

Using Off-the-Shelf Deep Neural Networks for Position-Based Visual Servoing

Matteo Tschesche[1(✉)], Till Hofmann[2], Alexander Ferrein[1], and Gerhard Lakemeyer[2]

[1] Mobile Autonomous Systems and Cognitive Robotics Institute, FH Aachen University of Applied Sciences, Aachen, Germany
{tschesche,ferrein}@fh-aachen.de

[2] Knowledge-Based Systems Group, RWTH Aachen University, Aachen, Germany
{hofmann,lakemeyer}@kbsg.rwth-aachen.de

Abstract. Visual servoing is a well-established technique for object grasping and controls the robot in a closed-loop fashion. It typically uses hand-crafted features or a neural network that directly learns the control output. We propose an alternative approach that uses an off-the-shelf neural network object classifier and can therefore compute target poses without manually selected features while also not requiring training from scratch. Instead, the object classifier only needs to be fine-tuned on a domain-specific dataset, significantly reducing the amount of required training data. We describe a task sequencing approach that can control a robot with a mobile base and an additional gripper, which is a typical setup in many robotics applications. We evaluate the approach in the RoboCup Logistics League and demonstrate the reliability and speed of the proposed approach.

Keywords: sensory-motor control · visual servoing · 3D perception

1 Introduction

Grasping objects is an essential part of almost every robotics application. While motion planning allows for computing trajectories to reach a goal pose, a motion planner typically operates in an open-loop fashion, i.e., it senses the target and computes the path once and then executes it until completion. In contrast, in *visual servoing* [7], a closed-loop controller updates its target and adapts its movements in every iteration and can therefore react to moving targets and sensor errors, but typically does not plan long trajectories. Usually, visual servoing uses manually selected features, which are often based on simple shapes such as lines, or circles [9]. While this has been used successfully in many applications, it requires careful fine-tuning of the selected features and does not allow for complex objects or shapes. Alternatively, some approaches directly learn a closed-loop controller, i.e., a neural network determines the next control output given an input image from a camera [25]. However, this typically requires

E. Barros et al. (Eds.): RoboCup 2024, LNAI 15570, pp. 32–43, 2025.
https://doi.org/10.1007/978-3-031-85859-8_3

training a neural network from scratch and therefore requires large amounts of training data.

In this paper, we propose a visual servoing architecture that uses a neural network as object detector in order to determine the pose of the target object but then uses a classical control law to determine the control outputs. This allows us to use an off-the-shelf object detector such as YOLOv4 [5] for object detection and therefore alleviates the need for expensive training. Instead, a pre-trained network can be used that only requires fine-tuning on a domain-specific dataset.

The proposed framework supports kinematically redundant robots that have a wide-range but inaccurate mobile base and an additional close-range but accurate gripper. The two components are combined with *task sequencing*, which first searches the target object using the robot's navigation stack and switches to a closed-loop controller once the target object has been detected. It then moves the mobile base to a target region near the target object, before it adjusts its pose by moving the gripper until the target pose has been reached with high accuracy. This allows wide-range and precise movements while also being fast.

We evaluate the approach in several tasks from the RoboCup Logistics League (RCLL) [30]. In the RCLL, a team of robots needs to transport workpieces between machines in order to execute a sequence of manufacturing steps. Hence, each robot needs to pick workpieces from and put workpieces on the machine's conveyor belt, grab workpieces from a shelf, and feed workpieces onto a slide. As each assembly process involves numerous grasping tasks, speed and reliability of grasping is a crucial factor in the design of the robots. As we will see, the proposed approach is able to execute grasping tasks more reliably but also faster than a baseline approach using the iterative closest point(ICP) algorithm, which has been successfully used in previous iterations of the competition.

The remainder of the paper is structured as follows. In Sect. 2, we discuss related work, before we describe our approach in greater detail in Sect. 3. We evaluate the proposed visual servoing approach and compare it against the baseline in Sect. 4 and finally conclude in Sect. 5.

2 Related Work

Visual servoing [6,7,14] is the task of moving a camera or robot to match the current configuration of visual features with a target configuration. In contrast to motion planning [18], visual servoing uses a closed control loop and typically does not involve collision avoidance, but uses real-time visual information to compute the next control inputs until the goal is reached. The controller may directly determine joint inputs or provide set-point inputs to a joint-level controller, which is sometimes referred as a *dynamic look-and-move* controller [14]. Typically, the camera is moving with the robot (*eye-in-hand*), but other configurations such as a static camera observing the robot workspace are also possible [7].

Visual servoing can be formulated as an optimization problem of minimizing the error $\mathbf{e}(t) = \mathbf{f}(t) - \mathbf{f}^*$ between the target features $\mathbf{f}^*$ and the current features $\mathbf{f}(t)$ at timestep t. Depending on the choice of features $\mathbf{f}$, we can distinguish *image-based visual servoing* and *position-based visual servoing* [7,15], where the former directly uses the image feature measurements in the image plane to compute the error, while the latter estimates the camera pose and compares the estimated camera pose to the target pose. Position-based visual servoing requires a geometric model and a calibrated camera system, while mapping the image space to the workspace in image-based visual servoing sometimes results in control problems and non-convergent behavior [7]. Hybrid approaches try to avoid these drawbacks [9], e.g., 2-$\frac{1}{2}$-D visual servoing [26] combines image features with 3D data by determining a partial estimate for the camera pose without requiring a camera model, and partitioned visual servoing [10] decouples the z-axis motions from the other degrees of freedom.

Typically, visual servoing requires carefully designed visual features which are usually based on detecting simple shapes such as circles as lines or identifying predefined tags [9]. More recently, visual servoing has been combined with various learning approaches to allow for more complex features [25]. Several approaches learn the relative pose of a pair of images, e.g., based on optical flow estimation [32], convolutional neural network (CNNs) [4,17], or siamese neural networks [38]. Alternatively, a policy that directly determines the control inputs can be learned, e.g. with CNN-based regression [34], unsupervised reinforcement learning [16,20,21,31], or one-shot imitation learning [1]. While these approaches can be used without fine-tuning visual features, they typically require large amounts of training data and sometimes suffer from the reality gap, that is, while they work well in simulation, reproducing similar precision in real-world domains is challenging. As an alternative and similar to the approach proposed in this paper, pre-trained neural networks can be used to detect objects, which then serves as input for visual servoing. This has been used successfully with stereo cameras for navigating drones towards wind turbines [12] and only using a RGB data for aligning bolster springs in railway maintenance application [23]. In contrast to the former approach, our approach does not require a stereo camera. The latter approach requires the image plane to be parallel to the object plane, while our approach allows arbitrary initial yaw rotations.

A robot is said to be *kinematically redundant* if it has more degrees of freedom than required for the given task [8]. This can be exploited, for, say, enlarging the stable area of the task [29], avoiding joint limits [11], or for achieving secondary goals [28]. *Task sequencing* [27] combines several subtasks by executing each task in a pre-defined order, e.g., by first constraining only a few degrees of freedom while the robot is far away from the goal and then adding constraints as the robot gets closer to the goal [27]. A *task priority strategy* [8,11] assigns a priority to each task and only enables a lower priority task while the higher priority task has reached its goal. A similar approach can also be used to combine a mobile base with a robotic arm [24], where the mobile base is prioritized while the robot far away from the goal, while the arm is prioritized for grasping tasks.

For the RCLL, several approaches have been described to solve manipulation tasks. The team GRIPS uses a closed-loop approach using a LiDAR as sensor [35]. As the shape of the machines used in the RCLL is known, a clustering algorithm can be used to compute the pose of the machine. From this pose, the goal pose for grasping can be derived. A closed-loop sliding mode controller is used to reach the computed goal pose. Before adopting the approach proposed in this paper, the team Carologistics used an open loop approach with multiple stages [13]. In a first stage, similar to [35], the machine's pose is estimated from the LiDAR. Next, a plane fitting algorithm based on RANSAC is used to detect the front of the conveyor belt, using point cloud data from an RGB-D camera. Finally, the exact pose of the conveyor belt is computed with an ICP algorithm. In every stage, the robot moves to the computed pose without additional sensor feedback. This approach serves as baseline for the evaluation in Sect. 4.

3 Visual Servoing with an Off-the-Shelf Object Detector

In the following, we describe our position-based visual servoing approach consisting of 3D object localization, triangulation, and a control approach based on task sequencing. In order to determine the goal pose, we use the pre-trained and fine-tuned object detector YOLOv4 [5]. This allows us to use learned features rather than manually defined hard-coded features while avoiding the need of large amounts of training data, as we only need to fine-tune the object detector to the domain at hand. Furthermore, assuming geometrical constraints given by the domain, determining the 3D position of the target location is sufficient, as roll, pitch, and yaw can be inferred, for instance, because the target object is known to be placed on a flat surface. Given the location of the target object in the 2D image and the known shape of the target object, the 3D goal position is computed by means of triangulation. Finally, as the robot is kinematically redundant, we use task sequencing to first move the mobile base to the vicinity of the goal and then use the robot's gripper to reach the goal region.

3.1 3D Object Localization

The controller needs a 6D pose as target input. However, it is often sufficient to determine the 3D position of the target and then infer the rotation from the environment. This is the case in the RCLL: the conveyor belt and slide are known to be placed level on the machines, i.e., there is no rotation relative to the machine, and the machine itself stands flat on the ground. Similarly, workpieces are always placed flat on the conveyor belt and are rotationally symmetric about the yaw axis, hence we can assume that its yaw is zero. This allows us to use an off-the-shelf object detector that only uses RGB input, which computes a bounding box of the target object in the image. As the shape of the object is known, triangulation can be used to determine the 3D position. In this paper, we use YOLOv4 [5] and YOLOv4-tiny [37] to compute bounding boxes of the target objects. YOLOv4 uses a CNN architecture and is fast enough to be used in a closed-loop approach while also being precise enough to determine the goal pose with sufficient accuracy. It is pre-trained on the COCO dataset [22] and we fine-tuned the detection layers on a domain-specific training set.

Triangulation. Assuming the shape of the target object is known, we can raycast through bounding box corners and apply triangulation to project the detected 2D bounding boxes from image space to 3D Euclidean space, as shown in Fig. 1. We use the lower bounding box corners for the projection $\mathbf{i_1} = (u_1\ v_1)^T$ and $\mathbf{i_2} = (u_2\ v_2)^T$ where $v_1 = v_2 = v$, shown as blue dots in image and Euclidean space. They are used to determine the raycast direction for p_1 given by (Δ_{x_1}, Δ_y) and for p_2 by (Δ_{x_2}, Δ_y) normalized for $z = 1$. Using the known object width, w_o, and a calibrated camera with focal lengths f_x in pixel-width and f_y in pixel-height, the object positions $\mathbf{p_m} = (x_m\ y_m\ z_m)^T$ in the middle between $\mathbf{p_1} = (x_1\ y_1\ z_1)^T$ and $\mathbf{p_2} = (x_2\ y_2\ z_2)^T$ of the projection of bounding box corners to the 3D Euclidean space can be computed using the angle between the raycast of p_m and the z axis defined by α as follows:

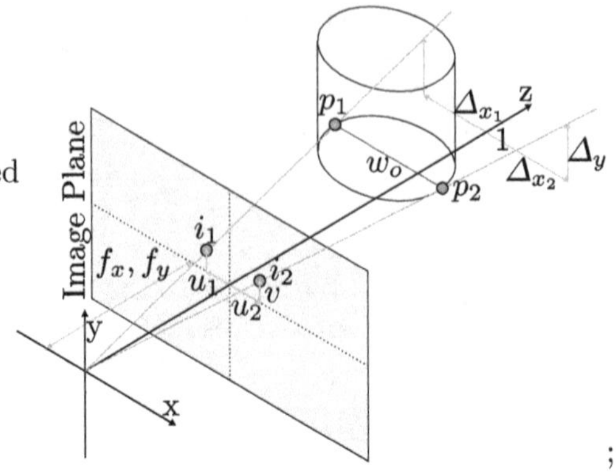

Fig. 1. 3D projection of a workpiece.

$$p_m = \begin{pmatrix} \Delta_{x_1} \left(\frac{\cos\alpha\, w_o - \sin\alpha\, w_o\, \Delta_{x_2}}{\Delta_{x_2} - \Delta_{x_1}} + \frac{\sin\alpha\, w_o}{2} \right) + \frac{\cos\alpha\, w_o}{2} \\ \Delta_y \left(\frac{\cos\alpha\, w_o - \sin\alpha\, w_o\, \Delta_{x_2}}{\Delta_{x_2} - \Delta_{x_1}} + \frac{\sin\alpha\, w_o}{2} \right) \\ \frac{\cos\alpha\, w_o - \sin\alpha\, w_o\, \Delta_{x_2}}{\Delta_{x_2} - \Delta_{x_1}} + \frac{\sin\alpha\, w_o}{2} \end{pmatrix};$$

Target Poses. Using p_m and the known height h of the object, we can compute the center and upper edge of the target object. Since kinematically redundant robots typically have a mobile base that is less accurate than the gripper, it is often useful to define two different goal poses, one for the mobile base and one for the gripper. The target pose for the gripper is set to be just above the target object such that the robot can move down the gripper to reach the target. The target pose for the mobile base is set further away from the actual goal to avoid collisions.

3.2 Controllers

Once we have determined the target pose for the mobile base $(x_b^*\ y_b^*\ \psi_b^*)^T$ and the gripper $(x_g^*\ y_{g^*}^*\ z_g^*)^T$, we can use simple linear controllers to reach each from its current pose $(x_b\ y_b\ \psi_b)^T$ and $(x_g\ y_g\ z_g)^T$ for base and gripper respectively. As the mobile base is omni-directional, we can compute control outputs for translational speeds $v_{b,x}$, $v_{b,y}$, and the rotational speed $v_{b,\psi}$ separately. We use a P controller [3] to determine the desired speed $\mathbf{v}_b = \left(v_{b,x}\ v_{b,y}\ v_{b,\psi}\right)^T$ at timestep t:

$$\begin{pmatrix} v_{b,x} \\ v_{b,y} \\ v_{b,\psi} \end{pmatrix} = \begin{pmatrix} \max\left(v_{b,x}^{\min}, \min\left(v_{b,x}^{\max}, a_{b,x} \cdot t, |x_b^* - x_b| \cdot \frac{v_{b,x}^{\max}}{a_{b,x}^{\text{dec}}\, s_{b,x}}\right)\right) \\ \max\left(v_{b,y}^{\min}, \min\left(v_{b,y}^{\max}, a_{b,y} \cdot t, |y_b^* - y_b| \cdot \frac{v_{b,y}^{\max}}{a_{b,y}^{\text{dec}}\, s_{b,y}}\right)\right) \\ \max\left(v_{b,\psi}^{\min}, \min\left(v_{b,\psi}^{\max}, a_{b,\psi} \cdot t, |\psi_b^* - \psi_b| \cdot \frac{v_{b,\psi}^{\max}}{a_{b,\psi}^{\text{dec}}\, s_{b,\psi}}\right)\right) \end{pmatrix}$$

Here, $\mathbf{v}_b^{\min} = \left(v_{b,x}^{\min}\ v_{b,y}^{\min}\ v_{b,\psi}^{\min}\right)^T$ and $\mathbf{v}_b^{\max} = \left(v_{b,x}^{\max}\ v_{b,y}^{\max}\ v_{b,\psi}^{\max}\right)^T$ are the minimal and maximal possible velocities respectively. The acceleration is constant and defined by the factors $\mathbf{a}_b = \left(a_{b,x}\ a_{b,y}\ a_{b,\psi}\right)^T$. The velocity required while decelerating is computed based on the required distance $\mathbf{s}_b = \left(s_{b,x}\ s_{b,y}\ s_{b,\psi}\right)^T$ to stop at the target, the difference between target and current pose, the current velocity, and the constant deceleration $\mathbf{a}_b^{\text{dec}} = \left(a_{b,x}^{\text{dec}}\ a_{b,y}^{\text{dec}}\ a_{b,\psi}^{\text{dec}}\right)^T$.

The gripper uses three separate stepper motors for the x, y, and z axis, each being controlled independently using a P controller. We define control output for the x axis, the other axes are controlled analogously. First, the maximal possible speed $v_{g,x}^p(i)$, that can be decelerated before reaching the target, at timestep i is computed by:

$$v_{g,x}^p(i) = \sqrt{2\, a_{g,x}\, \left|x_g^* - x_g(i)\right|}$$

Here, the constant acceleration $a_{g,x}$ and error in x direction between the x position $x_g(i)$ at timestep i and target x position x_g^* are used.

The velocity $v_{g,x}(i)$ in x direction at timestep i is computed using the maximum speed of the gripper's x axis $v_{g,x}^{\max}$ as follows:

$$v_{g,x}(i) = \begin{cases} \min(v_{g,x}^{\max}, v_{g,x}(i-1) + \frac{a_{g,x}}{v_{g,x}(i-1)} & \text{if } v_{g,x}^p(i) > v_{g,x}(i-1) \\ v_{g,x}(i-1) - \frac{a_{g,x}}{v_{g,x}(i-1)} & \text{else} \end{cases}$$

The velocities are applied by computing the time between each motor step using the ramp algorithm [2].

3.3 Task Sequencing

As the robot's three degrees of freedom (DOF) mobile base and three DOF gripper are kinematically redundant, we use task sequencing as shown in Fig. 2 to coordinate the subtasks.

Search. In the first subtask, the robot is far away from the goal and may possibly not sense the target. Instead, it uses the expected pose (e.g., based on the known machine position) to instruct the robot's navigation stack in order to

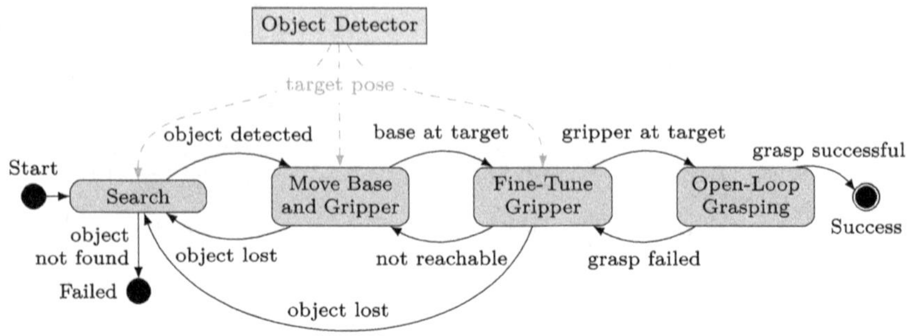

Fig. 2. Task sequencing.

reach a position from which the target object is visible. As the robot gets closer to the machine and the machine is detected, the expected position is computed relative to the observed position of the machine, which improves the accuracy and increases the robustness. Once the object is detected reliably and the robot is within a threshold to the target pose, the next subtask is activated. If the navigation fails to reach the target region the complete task fails.

Move Base and Gripper. Once the target object is reliably detected and the robot is close to the target, the first visual servoing task is activated, which moves the mobile base and gripper simultaneously. The base velocity is reduced as the distance towards the machine decreases. If vision of the object is lost, the controller switches back to *Search*. The goal of this subtask is to move the mobile base to its target pose within a threshold, using the target pose and control law as described above. At the same time, the gripper is moved to its expected target pose assuming the robot's mobile base precisely reaches its target pose.

Fine-Tune Gripper. Once the mobile base has reached its target, the gripper needs to be moved to reach its target pose. As the mobile base can only move imprecisely, the gripper pose typically needs to be readjusted even if the gripper already reached its target pose in the previous subtask. This subtask succeeds if the gripper reaches its target pose within a small threshold. In case the object moved and is no longer in range of the gripper, the previous subtask is reactivated to re-adjust its base. If the object is no longer visible, the procedure switches back to *Search*.

Open-Loop Grasping. After the gripper has reached its target pose, the object is grasped in an open loop fashion, assuming that the workpiece will not move. This subtask consists of three poses which need to be reached consecutively. It starts from the visual servoing target pose, moves down the gripper, and either picks the workpiece up or puts it down. Afterwards, the gripper is moved back in its default pose.

Table 1. Performance and speed of YOLOv4 and YOLOv4-tiny with a minimum IoU of 50% and 75%, showing the F1 score, average precision for workpieces (AP_{wp}), conveyor belts (AP_c), and slides (AP_s), mean average precision (mAP), and inferences per second (IPS).

Object Classifier	min. IoU	F1	AP_{wp}	AP_c	AP_s	mAP	IPS (s^{-1})
YOLOv4	50	**0.97**	**0.9966**	**0.9888**	**0.9804**	**0.9886**	0.904
	75	0.92	0.9741	0.9147	0.8217	0.9035	0.904
YOLOv4-tiny	50	0.91	0.9720	0.9526	0.8688	0.9311	**18.904**
	75	0.74	0.7976	0.7553	0.4263	0.6597	**18.904**

4 Evaluation

We evaluate our visual servoing framework[1] and its components in several scenarios of the RCLL. First, we analyze whether YOLOv4 and YOLOv4-tiny are performant enough to be used for real-time object detection on a robot. As a robot typically has no dedicated GPU, all inferences needs to be done on a CPU. Hence, inference time on a CPU is crucial. Next, we compare the novel visual servoing approach against our previous approach, which was based on ICP (Fig. 3).

4.1 Object Detection

We compare the `darknet`[2] implementations of YOLOv4 and YOLOv4-tiny with 3 detection layers, which were fine-tuned on object classes from the RCLL.

Training. We used 4000 labeled images for training and used several augmentation techniques to improve robustness. Each image was rotated by 0°, 90°, 180°, or 270°. Additionally, the dataset was augmented by applying cropping and padding, hide and seek [33], and CutMix [39], using random images from the COCO dataset [22] as replacement.

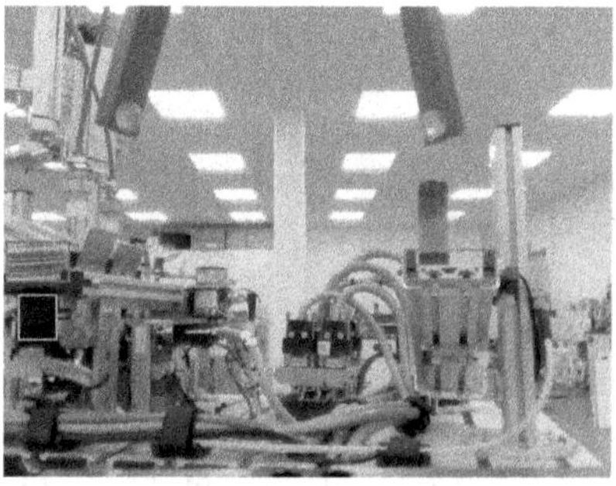

Fig. 3. Object detection with bounding boxes for a workpiece (blue), conveyor belt (green), and slide (red). (Color figure online)

Results. Table 1 shows a comparison of YOLOv4 and YOLOv4-tiny with a minimum Intersection over Union (IoU) of 50% and 75% on 300 test images

[1] The code including weights of the neural network is available at https://zenodo.org/records/11032321.

[2] https://github.com/kiyoshiiriemon/yolov4_darknet.

using an AMD Ryzen 5 1600 CPU. We can see that YOLOv4 performs better than YOLOv4-tiny, but accomplishes less than one inference per second, which is too slow for closed-loop visual servoing, typically requiring 5 to 10 inferences per second to work reliably. On the other hand, for YOLOv4-tiny, we can see that a minimum IoU of 75% does not perform well with a mean average precision (mAP) of 0.6597. However, with a minimum IoU of 50%, performance is significantly better while also faster with approximately 19 inferences per second, thus being both performant enough and fast enough to be used for visual servoing.

4.2 Comparison of VS and ICP

We compare our visual servoing approach with the ICP approach previously used by Carologistics [13]. We do so by benchmarking several grasping tasks with varying machine (BS, CS, RS) and initial robot poses (A, B, C, D, and E with different orientations), as shown in Fig. 4. We evaluate picking tasks of a randomly chosen workpiece for each machine's output side of the conveyor belt as well as each cap station's shelf, as well as putting tasks for each machine's input side of the conveyor belt. This results in seven pick and three put tasks for each starting pose and hence 100 different tasks overall. The workpiece configuration was chosen randomly. This setup covers every possible manipulation task in the RCLL from multiple starting poses.

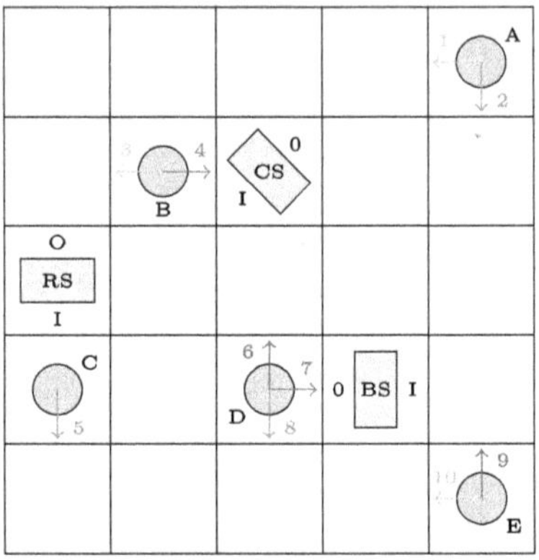

Fig. 4. Field configuration for the evaluation tasks with a base station (BS), ring station (RS), and cap station (CS) with input (I) and output (O), and 10 different initial robot poses (A-E).

The results are shown in Fig. 5. We can see that for almost all tasks, the VS approach was faster than the ICP approach. On average, the ICP approach required 26.1 s, while the VS approach required 21.1 s. Furthermore, the VS approach was also more reliable, as it succeeded in 99 out of 100 tasks, while the ICP approach was only successful in 92 out of 100 tasks. On the robot's Intel Core i5-8400H CPU, the VS approach updates the target pose with approximately 19 Hz and thus is sufficiently fast to run on the robot.

Grasping Challenge As an additional benchmark, we evaluated the VS approach in the RCLL Grasping Challenge, where the task of a team of three robots is to move a workpiece from a machine's output to its input, three times for each of the three machines [19]. The team Carologistics won this challenge in 2022 using the ICP approach described above, requiring 225 s to complete the task. In comparison, the VS approach only required 123 s, decreasing the total execution time by 45%.

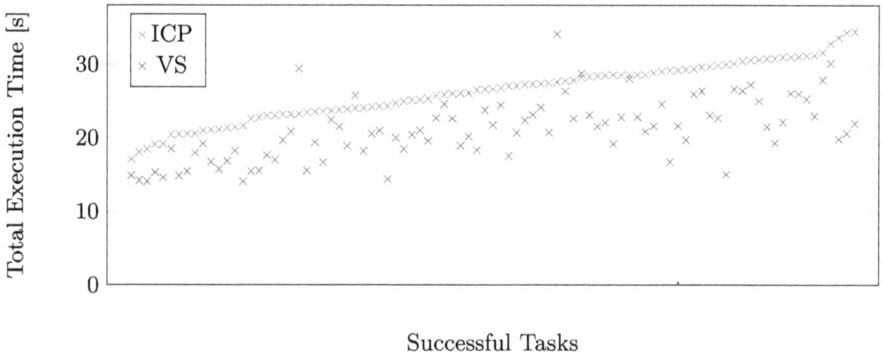

Fig. 5. Total execution time of each attempt, showing only tasks where both the ICP approach and the VS approach were successful. The tasks are ordered by the execution time needed by the ICP approach.

In conclusion, the proposed approach is more reliable and faster than the previous approach based on ICP, which was the best approach in the 2022 grasping challenge.

5 Conclusion

In this paper, we have described a visual servoing framework for kinematically redundant robots with a mobile base with a wide range of motion but low accuracy and a limited-range but highly accurate gripper. Using an off-the-shelf neural network object classifier such as YOLO, the framework is capable of precise grasping without fine-tuning manually selected features but also with only little requirement for training. As we can use a pre-trained neural network, we only need to apply domain-specific fine-tuning to obtain a suitable object detector. The detected object position in image space is then used to compute the target pose of the robot by means of triangulation. A task sequencing approach exploits the kinematic redundancy by first aligning the mobile base to the target with a high tolerance and then moving the gripper closely to the target pose.

We demonstrated the effectiveness of the proposed visual servoing approach by comparing it to a previous approach based on ICP in several scenarios of the RCLL. The visual servoing approach was not only more reliable but also executed the tasks significantly faster. The proposed visual servoing approach contributed to the success of the team Carologistics at RoboCup 2022 [36].

Acknowledgements. This work was supported by the Federal Ministry of Education and Research (BMBF) under grant No. 02L19C602 and the EU ICT-48 2020 project TAILOR (No. 952215).

We thank the reviewers for their feedback and suggestions, in particular for a suggestion that may improve and simplify the pose computation.

References

1. Argus, M., Hermann, L., Long, J., Brox, T.: FlowControl: optical flow based visual servoing. In: IROS, pp. 7534–7541 (2020)
2. Austin, D.: Generate stepper-motor speed profiles in real time. EMSP **1** (2005)
3. Bajpai, P.: Chapter 24 - process control. In: Biermann's Handbook of Pulp and Paper, 3rd edn, pp. 483–492. Elsevier (2018)
4. Bateux, Q., Marchand, E., Leitner, J., Chaumette, F., Corke, P.: Training deep neural networks for visual servoing. In: ICRA, pp. 3307–3314 (2018)
5. Bochkovskiy, A., Wang, C.Y., Liao, H.Y.M.: Yolov4: optimal speed and accuracy of object detection (2020)
6. Chaumette, F., Hutchinson, S.: Visual servo control. I. Basic approaches. IEEE Robot. Autom. Mag. **13**(4), 82–90 (2006)
7. Chaumette, F., Hutchinson, S., Corke, P.: Visual servoing. In: Siciliano, B., Khatib, O. (eds.) Springer Handbook of Robotics, pp. 841–866. Springer, Cham (2016). https://doi.org/10.1007/978-3-319-32552-1_34
8. Chiacchio, P., Chiaverini, S., Sciavicco, L., Siciliano, B.: Closed-loop inverse kinematics schemes for constrained redundant manipulators with task space augmentation and task priority strategy. IJRR **10**(4), 410–425 (1991)
9. Cong, V.D., Hanh, L.D.: A review and performance comparison of visual servoing controls. IJIRA **7**(1), 65–90 (2023)
10. Corke, P., Hutchinson, S.: A new partitioned approach to image-based visual servo control. IEEE Trans. Robot. Autom. **17**(4), 507–515 (2001)
11. De Luca, A., Ferri, M., Oriolo, G., Giordano, P.R.: Visual servoing with exploitation of redundancy: an experimental study. In: 2008 IEEE International Conference on Robotics and Automation, pp. 3231–3237 (2008)
12. Durdevic, P., Ortiz-Arroyo, D.: A deep neural network sensor for visual servoing in 3D spaces. Sensors **20**(5), 1437 (2020)
13. Hofmann, T., Limpert, N., Mataré, V., Ferrein, A., Lakemeyer, G.: Winning the RoboCup logistics league with fast navigation, precise manipulation, and robust goal reasoning. In: Chalup, S., Niemueller, T., Suthakorn, J., Williams, M.-A. (eds.) RoboCup 2019. LNCS (LNAI), vol. 11531, pp. 504–516. Springer, Cham (2019). https://doi.org/10.1007/978-3-030-35699-6_41
14. Hutchinson, S., Hager, G., Corke, P.: A tutorial on visual servo control. IEEE Trans. Robot. Autom. **12**(5), 651–670 (1996)
15. Janabi-Sharifi, F., Deng, L., Wilson, W.J.: Comparison of basic visual servoing methods. IEEE/ASME Trans. Mechatron. **16**(5), 967–983 (2011)
16. Jin, Z., Wu, J., Liu, A., Zhang, W.A., Yu, L.: Policy-based deep reinforcement learning for visual servoing control of mobile robots with visibility constraints. IEEE Trans. Industr. Electron. **69**(2), 1898–1908 (2022)
17. Jokić, A., Petrović, M., Miljković, Z.: Semantic segmentation based stereo visual servoing of nonholonomic mobile robot in intelligent manufacturing environment. Expert Syst. Appl. **190**, 116203 (2022)
18. Kavraki, L.E., LaValle, S.M.: Motion planning. In: Springer Handbook of Robotics, pp. 139–162. Springer (2016)
19. Knoflach, L., Kohout, P., Imhof, S., Rohr, A., Swoboda, D., Viehmann, T.: RoboCup Logistics League: Rules and Regulations 2022 (2022)
20. Lampe, T., Riedmiller, M.: Acquiring visual servoing reaching and grasping skills using neural reinforcement learning. In: IJCNN, pp. 1–8 (2013)

21. Lee, A.X., Levine, S., Abbeel, P.: Learning visual servoing with deep features and fitted Q-iteration. In: ICLR (2022)
22. Lin, T.Y., et al.: Microsoft COCO: common objects in context. In: ECCV (2014)
23. Liu, H., Li, D., Jiang, B., Zhou, J., Wei, T., Yao, X.: MGBM-YOLO: a faster light-weight object detection model for robotic grasping of bolster spring based on image-based visual servoing. JINT **104**(4), 77 (2022)
24. Liu, J., et al.: Garbage collection and sorting with a mobile manipulator using deep learning and whole-body control. In: Humanoids, pp. 408–414 (2021)
25. Machkour, Z., Ortiz-Arroyo, D., Durdevic, P.: Classical and deep learning based visual servoing systems: a survey on state of the art. J. Intell. Robot. Syst. **104**(1), 1–27 (2021). https://doi.org/10.1007/s10846-021-01540-w
26. Malis, E., Chaumette, F., Boudet, S.: 2 1/2 D visual servoing. IEEE Trans. Robot. Autom. **15**(2), 238–250 (1999)
27. Mansard, N., Chaumette, F.: Tasks sequencing for visual servoing. In: IROS (2004)
28. Mansard, N., Chaumette, F.: Directional redundancy: a new approach of the redundancy formalism. In: IEEE CDC, Seville, Spain, pp. 5366–5371 (2005)
29. Mansard, N., Chaumette, F.: Task sequencing for high-level sensor-based control. IEEE Trans. Rob. **23**(1), 60–72 (2007)
30. Niemueller, T., Ewert, D., Reuter, S., Ferrein, A., Jeschke, S., Lakemeyer, G.: RoboCup logistics league sponsored by festo: a competitive factory automation testbed. In: Automation, Communication and Cybernetics in Science and Engineering 2015/2016, pp. 605–618. Springer (2016)
31. Sadeghzadeh, M., Calvert, D., Abdullah, H.A.: Self-learning visual servoing of robot manipulator using explanation-based fuzzy neural networks and Q-learning. J. Intell. Robot. Syst. **78**(1), 83–104 (2015)
32. Saxena, A., Pandya, H., Kumar, G., Gaud, A., Krishna, K.M.: Exploring convolutional networks for end-to-end visual servoing. In: ICRA, pp. 3817–3823 (2017)
33. Singh, K.K., Lee, Y.J.: Hide-and-seek: forcing a network to be meticulous for weakly-supervised object and action localization. In: 2017 IEEE International Conference on Computer Vision (ICCV), pp. 3544–3553 (2017)
34. Tokuda, F., Arai, S., Kosuge, K.: Convolutional neural network-based visual servoing for eye-to-hand manipulator. IEEE Access **9**, 91820–91835 (2021)
35. Ulz, T., Ludwiger, J., Steinbauer, G.: A robust and flexible system architecture for facing the robocup logistics league challenge. In: RoboCup 2018, pp. 488–499. Springer (2018)
36. Viehmann, T., Limpert, N., Hofmann, T., Henning, M., Ferrein, A., Lakemeyer, G.: Winning the RoboCup logistics league with visual servoing and centralized goal reasoning. In: RoboCup 2022, pp. 300–312. Springer (2023)
37. Wang, C.Y., Bochkovskiy, A., Liao, H.Y.M.: Scaled-yolov4: scaling cross stage partial network (2021)
38. Yu, C., Cai, Z., Pham, H., Pham, Q.C.: Siamese convolutional neural network for sub-millimeter-accurate camera pose estimation and visual servoing. In: IROS, pp. 935–941 (2019)
39. Yun, S., Han, D., Oh, S.J., Chun, S., Choe, J., Yoo, Y.: CutMix: regularization strategy to train strong classifiers with localizable features. In: ICCV, pp. 6023–6032 (2019)

Deep Learning Based Measurement Model for Monte Carlo Localization in the RoboCup Humanoid League

Jasper Güldenstein(✉), Niklas Fiedler, and Jianwei Zhang

Informatics Department, Universität Hamburg, 22527 Hamburg, Germany
{jasper.gueldenstein,niklas.fiedler}@uni-hamburg.de

Abstract. We propose a deep learning based measurement model for Monte Carlo self-localization to improve the robustness to robot calibration errors in the RoboCup Humanoid League context. A deep neural network estimates the distance between a line mask computed by the vision pipeline from a camera image and given pose candidates. This distance is then used to derive weights for the particles of the Monte Carlo localization. The network is trained using images generated by applying a perspective transformation on the map of the field. We use a style transfer model to preprocess the input data for finetuning the model to build robustness towards noise and detection errors in real-world data. Our model is more robust to erroneous head pose measurements than the baseline. Further, we show significant improvements in global localization.

Keywords: Robot Self Localization · Particle Filter · Deep Learning · State Estimation

1 Introduction

For most mobile robots, knowing and tracking their position in the environment is essential to achieving their goals [16]. This is especially true in the RoboCup Humanoid Soccer League [2]. Accurate localization allows for precise navigation. This enables the robot to position itself purposefully and strategically to achieve its goals. Furthermore, it enhances multi-agent system capabilities as information about the environment can be shared in global instead of local coordinates. In the RoboCup soccer context, this allows, for example, sharing the position of the ball or opponents, which may not be visible from all robots' positions.

This paper presents a novel approach to localization. A neural network is proposed as the measurement model required in particle filter (Monte Carlo [6]) localization. In particle filter localization, a set of particles represents the belief of the robot's pose. Particles are firstly updated based on odometry information with the motion model. In the following step, the measurement model estimates the likelihood of each particle being the robot's true pose, given its observations.

E. Barros et al. (Eds.): RoboCup 2024, LNAI 15570, pp. 44–55, 2025.
https://doi.org/10.1007/978-3-031-85859-8_4

Afterwards, particles are resampled based on their likelihood. We describe several related approaches that use this form of localization in Sect. 2.

Our work builds upon the RoboCup Humanoid League KidSize team Hamburg Bit-Bots' codebase. A previous iteration of the localization has been developed and described by Hartfill [7]. The current version of the Hamburg Bit-Bots' localization uses a mask of the detected field lines in the camera image (line mask) generated by the vision neural network YOEO [18]. They use inverse perspective mapping to project the line mask onto the ground plane in Cartesian coordinates. The particle filter estimates the likelihood by calculating the overlap of these lines with a known map for each particle. This localization was successfully used in previous competitions: In the Virtual RoboCup 2021, the team came in third; in the Virtual Season 2022, second; in the Virtual Season 2023, first; and in the RoboCup German Open 2024, first. We use this approach as our baseline against which we compare. While the approach works well in an idealized scenario, it suffers greatly from errors in the robot's head pose measurement. The inverse perspective mapping is sensitive to this and produces results that significantly degrade the localization's performance. The Wolfgang OP [4] used by the Hamburg Bit-Bots and in this research features a series elastic element in the neck joint to prevent the head from breaking when falling. This element introduces significant uncertainty.

To overcome this, we propose using a deep neural network as the measurement model to estimate the particles' likelihood. Instead of operating on the inverse perspective mapped line detections, it processes the vision's output, i.e. the line mask, directly and the robot's head joint angles to estimate the particles' likelihood.

2 Related Work

Particle filters are an established self-localization method for mobile robots [16]. In the RoboCup Humanoid League, many teams rely on this method. The winners of the past three competitions used a variation of this approach. Davydenko et al. used the lines detected by Hough Transforms for their measurement [5]. Hayashibara et al. used lines and goalposts detected by a neural network [8]. Finally, Allali et al. used field features and the goalposts detected by a neural network in their localization [1]. All three approaches share that the features are inverse perspective mapped from image space to Cartesian coordinates using the robot's estimate of its camera pose.

Dasilva et al. describe the necessity of accurate calibration for this type of approach to be viable [15]. Inverse perspective mapping is sensitive to head pose estimate errors and may require significant calibration effort to be viable for localization in the RoboCup Humanoid domain.

Outside of RoboCup, various advancements to conventional particle filters are proposed. Differentiable particle filters are end-to-end trained recurrent neural networks that use the particle filtering algorithm as a prior and implicitly learn both the motion and measurement model. The latent state of the recurrent network consists of the particles in the filter. The concept was first introduced by Jonschkowski et al. [10]. In the same year, Karkus et al. proposed a very similar approach [12], including several advancements. For example, their model features a differentiable approximation of resampling and fuses information from multiple sources. In contrast to a fully differentiable particle filter, approaches like that presented by Lu et al. [13] extract features from the input data using deep neural networks to create rated pose candidates. Afterward, these candidates are further processed in recurrent neural networks, which can utilize a temporal context.

However, these are not optimally suited to our use case. The motion model of the robot may significantly differ between robots of the same type due to wear and ground surface (i.e., the robot may slip more or less on different materials). Adapting an end-to-end model to such conditions would require time-consuming retraining, which may not be feasible in the RoboCup competition setting, as new labeled training data must be collected. Our model only requires fine-tuning on unlabeled data to adapt to a new environment and manual tuning of the odometry model, which, in our experience, requires little effort.

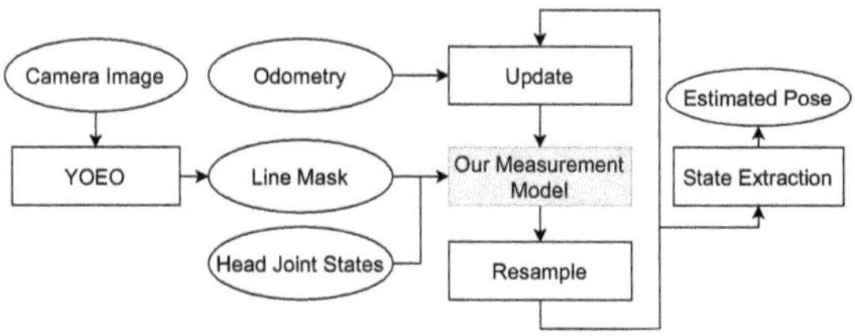

Fig. 1. Schematic representation of the overall algorithm. A camera image is fed through the YOEO [18] vision pipeline to produce a mask of the detected field lines. Our trained measurement model uses this line mask and head joint states to estimate the likelihood of a set of particles to be the robot's true pose. The typical steps of the particle filter are performed. The pose estimate is extracted from a subset of the most likely particles.

3 Approach

We propose a novel measurement model using a deep neural network to rate pose candidates given an input line mask as depicted in Fig. 1. A particle filter is used for robot self-localization. It is a Bayes filter implementation that allows for non-linear state transitions and measurement models. The current belief is represented as a set of particles, each representing a possible system state. In the update step, the particles are moved in the state space accordingly to the motion model using the robot odometry. All particles are then weighted based on how well their individual state fits the measurement taken by the robot through the measurement model. Afterwards, the particles are resampled based on their weights. Instead of using the conventional measurement model, which requires the input line mask projected into Cartesian space, our model directly uses the raw line mask in image space and the head joint states. Based on this information, the linear distance in x and y and the angular distance of potential pose candidates (the particles in the filter) are estimated for the observed situation. The distances are then used to derive a weight for each particle. We do not change the motion model in our system.

Formally, the problem can be described as follows: We need to assign a weight ω_p to each particle $p = (x_p, y_p, yaw_p)$ given the head joint states encoded as follows $j = (\cos(\text{pan}), \sin(\text{pan}), \cos(\text{tilt}), \sin(\text{tilt}))$ where pan and tilt are the joint encoder readings of the robot's head joints and the binary line mask $m \in [0,1]^{256\times192}$. This assignment is done by training a model to approximate the function $F_\theta(m, j, p) = (\Delta x, \Delta y, \Delta yaw)$ with $(\Delta x, \Delta y, \Delta yaw)$ being the estimated distances between the particle's pose and the pose at which the observation m was taken. The particle weight is defined as $\omega_p = 1/(|\Delta x|+|\Delta y|+|\Delta yaw|)$. We tried different weightings of angular and linear error and found no significant improvement compared to this simple formula.

3.1 Input Processing

Our vision pipeline utilizes the YOEO architecture [18], which produces bounding box detections of objects relevant in the RoboCup domain besides a segmented image of lines in the image with little additional computational effort. This is achieved by utilizing the YOLO encoder for both the bounding box and segmentation mask, followed by separate decoders for bounding boxes and masks. The network is trained and evaluated on a large dataset [3], which allows it to robustly detect the lines on diverse images. The conventional measurement model requires the lines to be inverse perspective mapped into Cartesian space, while our proposed deep learning based approach does not.

3.2 Training Data Generation

To generate sufficient training data, we randomly sample robot poses in the field of play. Further, we sample head joint angles and calculate the resulting camera pose using forward kinematics. We apply a perspective transformation on a binary image of the field lines to generate a binary 256×192 pixel image from the camera's perspective.

CAST, an arbitrary image style transfer network proposed by Zhang et al. [19], is used with the provided weights to increase the robustness of the network to imperfect input data. In the following, we refer to it as style-net.

The style-net takes two images as input: one to define the content of the output image and another to describe the style. It then generates a new image that portrays the content of the first image in the style of the second image. This process introduces noise and loss of detail, similar to real-world recordings. Figure 2 illustrates an example of a style image, a line mask created by a perspective transform, and the resulting image produced by the style-net, which depicts the same scene as the line mask with realistic noise. Due to the high computational effort, this is not efficient enough for the whole training process. Thus, after training the model on perspective transforms only, we finetuned it using the samples produced by the style-net based on the generated images.

In addition to the generated image, we sample 128 poses from a normal distribution around the pose used to generate the corresponding image and calculate the distances Δx, Δy, and Δyaw as the label. We chose the standard deviation of these distributions as $1m$ and $1rad$, respectively. Angles are encoded as $\sin(\theta)$ and $\cos(\theta)$ for the network to avoid problems with discontinuity.

Fig. 2. Exemplary images produced by the data generator and the style-net. On the left, a line mask, as produced by the vision pipeline, is shown. It is used as a style definition for the style-net to process the perspective-transformed image.

3.3 Neural Network

Figure 3 shows an overview of the proposed network architecture. We used a pre-trained resnet18 [9] with weights provided by torchvision[1]. Using pretrained weights showed to speed up the training process in early experiments. We only use a single input channel (binary mask) compared to the three used in their training (RGB), so the weights of the first layer of the network are discarded. Further, we discard the fully connected layers after the convolutional ones. Instead, we utilize seven 1D convolutional layers. We repeat the image encoding produced by the resnet18 and the robot head joint encoding for each pose candidate and concatenate the pose candidate encoding. This allows for processing each pose-, head-joint- and image-encoding combination with the same weights. Further, this enables a variable number of pose candidates to be processed. The network outputs the signed estimated distances Δx, Δy, and Δyaw. During training, the loss is calculated using the mean squared error.

We trained the model using PyTorch[2] in Python. Firstly, the model is trained on images that have not been modified with the style-net algorithm (see Sect. 3.2). Secondly, we continue training the model but apply the style

[1] https://pytorch.org/hub/pytorch_vision_resnet/ (last accessed 19 Apr 2024).
[2] https://pytorch.org/ (last accessed 21 Apr 2024).

transfer to the input images. The training was performed on an Nvidia GeForce RTX 4090. The first training phase required around 8 h of training time, while the finetuning training phase was run for 12 h.

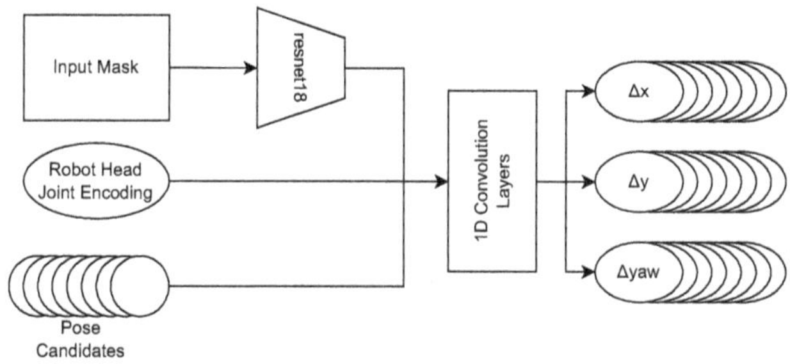

Fig. 3. Overview of the proposed network architecture. An input line mask is fed into a resnet with 18 convolutional layers. The image encoding and robot head joint encoding are combined with a variable number of pose candidates and fed through several 1D convolutional layers.

3.4 Integration

We integrated the measurement model into the existing localization pipeline of the Hamburg Bit-Bots by defining a new measurement model that utilized the neural network to weigh the particles. We serialize the model trained in Python using TorchScript. It is then loaded and executed in the measurement model from the modified Bit-Bots localization written in C++[3].

4 Evaluation

To evaluate the performance of the measurement model, we conduct several experiments. In each experiment, we keep the particle filter parameters fixed between the trained measurement model and the classical approach of line matching. The experiments were performed in the RoboCup Humanoid League Webots simulation environment [14], which was used for the Virtual Competition in 2021[4]. Camera images were rendered in Webots and passed through the Bit-Bots vision pipeline with the YOEO neural network to extract the line mask. We chose to perform the experiments in simulation as the robot's precise pose and camera pose are required for accurate evaluation.

[3] https://github.com/bit-bots/bitbots_main/tree/feature/deep_localization/bitbots_navigation/bitbots_localization (last accessed 17 Jun 2024).

[4] https://humanoid.robocup.org/hl-2021/v-hsc/ (last accessed 22 Apr 2024).

We tried using the reflective marker-based tracking system OptiTrack[5] to capture the real robot's camera pose for real-world experiments. However, accurate calibration between the marker's position and the pose of the robot's camera, in combination with the tracking system's inaccuracies, proved infeasible. Specifically, the orientation of a rigid body is inferred from the positions of several markers. This is prone to more error if the markers are closer to each other. The possible physical marker configuration was limited as they were mounted to the robot's head, which has a significant range of motion. To compare the approach to the baseline, an accurate estimate of the orientation of the robot's head would be required.

We conducted the following experiments, which we describe in the ensuing subsections. Firstly, we quantify the model's performance in a global localization (kidnapped robot) scenario. Secondly, we show the model's ability to track the robot's pose when it is following a trajectory. Then, we present the effects of introducing an angular error in the head joint state measurement. We compare the results of our proposed method to the currently used measurement model as a baseline. Further, in the first two evaluations, we evaluate our network with and without finetuning using the style-net to investigate whether the goal of improving the domain transfer was reached.

Additionally, we measured the computation time required to execute each filter step. The calculation time required for the baseline approach depends heavily on the number of pixels detected as lines and the inverse perspective mapped. We calculated its average filter iteration to take around 15ms. The performance of our approach was measured at 10ms. This is, however, subject to the availability of computing hardware, as we used GPU acceleration to run our network.

4.1 Global Localization

In this experiment the robot is placed at a random position and orientation on one half of the soccer field. The particle filter is initialized on this field half as depicted in Fig. 4a and allowed 10 s to converge. The robot is only initialized on one half of the field as it is symmetric. This problem is usually overcome in the RoboCup context by the knowledge that the robot is initialized on the teams own half and through pose tracking.

This experiment is performed for 64 poses each for the approach, the approach before finetuning, and the baseline. The results are presented in Fig. 5 and Table 1. Both the histograms and quantitative metrics indicate a superior performance of the proposed approach compared to the baseline. Further, the finetuning significantly increased the probability of good convergence. We observed that the line-matching baseline often converges to local maxima as some of the sampled poses have a significant overlap of the measured lines and the map. Figure 4b shows an example.

[5] https://optitrack.com/ (last accessed 19 Apr 2024).

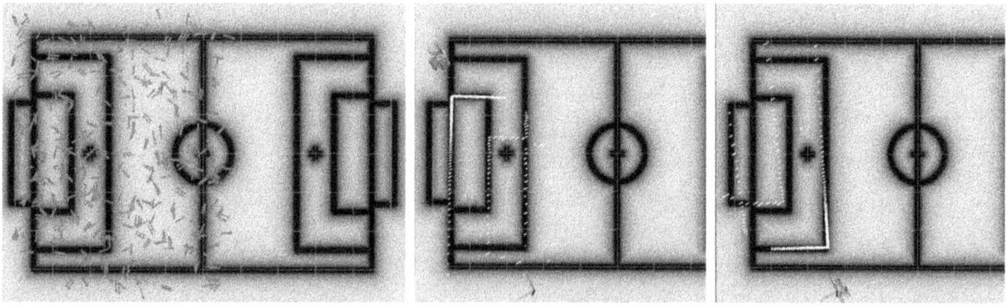

(a) Particle filter initialized on one field half. The 300 pose candidates are spread uniformly.

(b) Particle filter with conventional measurement model converging in a local optimum.

(c) Particle filter converging on the actual robot pose.

Fig. 4. Visualizations of the particle filter state in RViz2 [11].

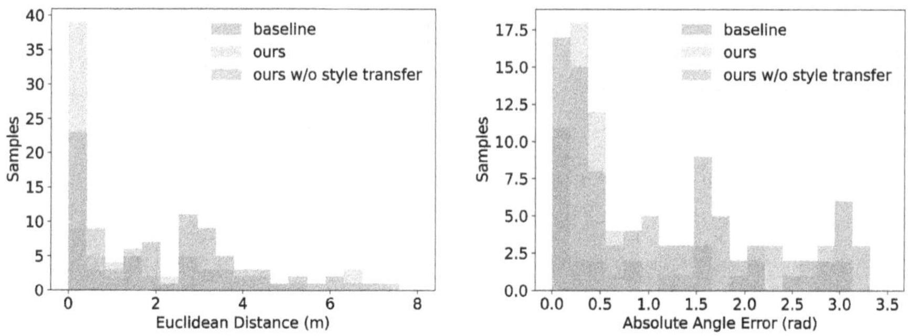

Fig. 5. Histograms of the Euclidean distance error (**left**) and the angle error (**right**) of the global localization experiment for both our approach (with and without finetuning with style transfer) and the baseline.

4.2 Pose Tracking

After a successful global localization or when starting the robot at a known pose, the localization task is to accurately track the robot's pose during movements. We evaluate the pose tracking performance by generating a set of 10 trajectories using colored noise as described by Timmer and Koenig [17] and implemented by Patzelt et al.[6]. We chose the smoothing parameters and scale to stay within the velocity and acceleration limits of the robot platform. No falls occurred during the execution of the experiments. The trajectories have a length of 30 s with 10 poses per second. An exemplary trajectory is depicted together with pose tracking results of both our approach and the baseline in Fig. 6. The robot's pose is initialized randomly in the central region of the field where the x coordinate is uniformly sampled in $(-3, 3)$, the y coordinate in $(-2, 2)$, and its orientation in $(-\pi, \pi)$. This avoids collision with the goalposts while allowing for variance

[6] https://github.com/felixpatzelt/colorednoise (last accessed 19 Apr 2024).

Table 1. Performance of the global localization experiment for Euclidean distance error d and absolute angle error α with respective standard deviations σ.

Approach	median d	mean d	σ d	median α	mean α	σ d
Baseline	2.711	2.605	**1.672**	1.475	1.347	1.078
Ours w/o style transfer	0.793	1.660	1.723	0.467	0.961	0.948
Ours	**0.263**	**1.332**	1.982	**0.383**	**0.669**	**0.737**

in the starting pose. The trajectories and starting poses are identical for the experiments using the baseline and the proposed approach.

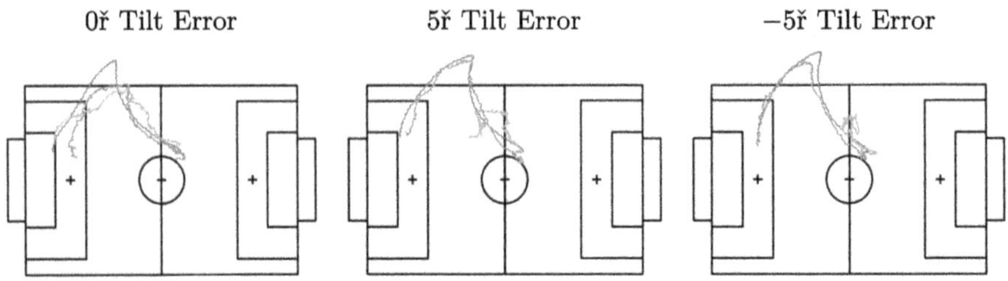

Fig. 6. Exemplary test trajectories and pose tracking results from our approach and the baseline with a calibration error of 0^{circ}, 5^{circ}, and -5^{circ} applied to the head tilt measurement. The ground truth is drawn in **blue**, the baseline in **orange**, and our approach in **green**. (Color figure online)

For each trajectory, we initialize the robot to the sampled starting position and orientation. The particle filter is initialized at this pose and allowed to settle for 5 s. We command the velocities calculated from the generated trajectory to the walking engine. We track the robot's pose, estimated by the localization and the ground truth from the simulator. The tracked pose is the `base_link` of the robot located at the bottom of the robot's torso.

We present a histogram of the deviation of both approaches to the ground truth in Euclidean distance and angular error in Fig. 7. Further, Table 2 quantifies the mean and median error. The baseline outperforms our approach by a small margin. While the difference between mean distance error and mean angular error is very small, at 0.015 m and 0.01 rad, the difference in the median is more pronounced. This can be explained by the histograms shown in Fig. 7: The baseline produces very small errors with occasional outliers, while our method consistently causes small errors.

Again, similar to the previous experiment, the results show that finetuning using the style transfer training data yields consistent performance improvements. Thus, we consider it a successful approach to improving the network's robustness and assisting with the transfer to different styles of lines on fields.

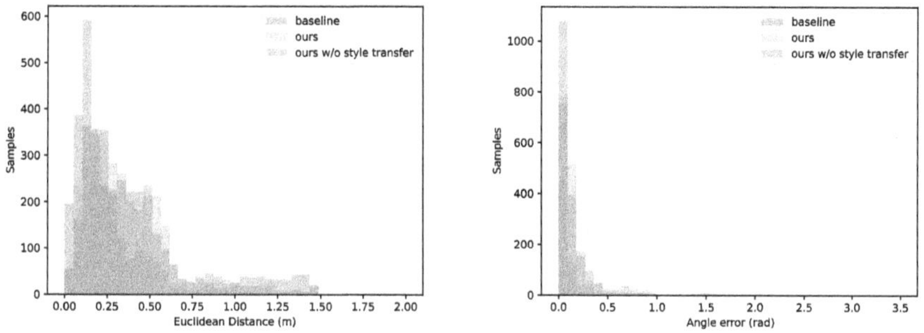

Fig. 7. Histograms of the linear Euclidean distance and the absolute angular difference between tracked robot pose and ground truth for both approaches

Table 2. Performance of the pose tracking experiment for Euclidean distance d and absolute angle error α with respective standard deviations σ.

Approach	median d	mean d	σ d	median α	mean α	σ d
Baseline	**0.201**	**0.331**	0.353	**0.043**	**0.100**	0.228
Ours w/o style transfer	0.329	0.393	0.286	0.088	0.140	0.209
Ours	0.307	0.346	**0.211**	0.077	0.110	**0.167**

4.3 Angular Error

The orientation of the robot's head in relation to the ground plane is usually tracked using an Inertial Measurement Unit (IMU) and forward kinematics. This estimation has several error sources. Firstly, the IMU may be mounted with an offset, or the axes of the accelerometer may be calibrated with an offset. Secondly, the joint encoders used to calculate the forward kinematics may have an offset. Thirdly, the robot model may have inaccuracies compared to the physical robot due to tolerances and deformation. Furthermore, the robot may have an elastic element such as the Wolfgang OP [4], which introduces uncertainty in the head joint measurement.

We re-performed the experiments presented in Sect. 4.2 and introduced an artificial angular error on the cameras' tilt angle. This is the most severe error in the Wolfgang OP robot platform due to the elastic element.

Table 3 shows the performance of the proposed approach compared to the measurement model with different errors applied to the camera tilt angle for the tracking experiment. As mentioned in Sect. 4.2, the baseline outperforms our approach in the task with a 0^{circ} error. However, with a camera tilt angle error of 3^{circ} and -3^{circ}, the performance of the baseline method significantly deteriorates, while ours is relatively stable. In case of a larger error, such as 5^{circ} and -5^{circ}, our approach outperforms the baseline. This is also evident in the exemplary visualization of pose tracking trajectories in Fig. 6.

This shows that the proposed measurement model handles the angular error significantly better than the conventional line matching approach. This is caused by the lines not aligning well to the map of the field after the inverse perspective mapping was performed with the angle error.

The results present a trade-off between robustness to angle measurement deviation and performance under ideal conditions. A more robust approach may prove favorable as many sources of error accumulate on the real robot platform. If suitable computational acceleration is available, our approach has comparable performance to the baseline and can be used on a mobile platform.

Table 3. Results of the pose tracking experiments with an error induced to the robot's head tilt angle for Euclidean distance d and absolute angle error α with respective standard deviations σ.

HeadTilt Error	Approach	median d	mean d	σ d	median α	mean α	σ d
0^{circ}	Baseline	**0.201**	**0.331**	0.353	**0.043**	**0.100**	0.228
	Ours	0.307	0.346	**0.211**	0.077	0.110	**0.167**
3^{circ}	Baseline	**0.229**	0.402	0.416	**0.047**	0.166	0.505
	Ours	0.334	**0.393**	**0.254**	0.075	**0.122**	**0.208**
-3^{circ}	Baseline	**0.245**	**0.393**	**0.461**	**0.045**	**0.116**	0.240
	Ours	0.316	0.440	0.920	0.080	**0.115**	**0.164**
5^{circ}	Baseline	0.530	0.826	0.756	0.179	0.404	0.706
	Ours	**0.364**	**0.436**	**0.334**	**0.085**	**0.148**	**0.227**
-5^{circ}	Baseline	0.384	0.702	0.738	0.105	0.186	0.266
	Ours	**0.369**	**0.413**	**0.270**	**0.092**	**0.135**	**0.189**

5 Conclusion

We introduced a neural network based measurement model integrated into a particle filter for humanoid robot localization. We show significantly better global localization performance and better robustness to calibration errors compared to the previously used approach by the Hamburg Bit-Bots. Further, with the style transfer net, we introduce a way of efficiently adapting the trained network to noisy and sparse input data by finetuning on stylized generated data.

Further enhancements may be achieved by introducing multiple modalities, such as the robot's IMU measurements or more detection of the vision pipeline. More elaborate networks, such as attention mechanisms, may be required to take full advantage of these. Additionally, the performance under degraded conditions such as occluded lines or bad segmentation results (e.g. due to natural lighting conditions) should be investigated.

Acknowledgments. This research was partially funded by the German Research Foundation (DFG) and the National Science Foundation of China in project Crossmodal Learning, TRR-169. We would also like to thank Florian Vahl for insightful discussions and his work on the localization, Timon Engelke for initial work on the perspective transformation, and the whole team of the Hamburg Bit-Bots.

References

1. Allali, J., et al.: Rhoban football club: robocup humanoid kid-size 2023 champion team paper. In: RoboCup 2023: Robot World Cup XXVI. Springer (2024)
2. Asada, M., von Stryk, O.: Scientific and technological challenges in robocup. Ann. Rev. Control Robot. Auton. Syst. **3**, 441–471 (2020)
3. Bestmann, M., et al.: TORSO-21 dataset: typical objects in RoboCup soccer 2021. In: RoboCup 2021: Robot World Cup XXIV (2021)
4. Bestmann, M., Güldenstein, J., Vahl, F., Zhang, J.: Wolfgang-op: a robust humanoid robot platform for research and competitions. In: IEEE Humanoids 2021 (2021)
5. Davydenko, E., Khokhlov, I., Litvinenko, V., Ryakin, I., Osokin, I., Babaev, A.: Starkit: robocup humanoid kidsize 2021 worldwide champion team paper. In: RoboCup 2021: Robot World Cup XXIV. Springer (2022)
6. Dellaert, F., Fox, D., Burgard, W., Thrun, S.: Monte Carlo localization for mobile robots. In: Proceedings 1999 IEEE International Conference on Robotics and Automation, vol. 2, pp. 1322–1328. IEEE (1999)
7. Hartfill, J.: Feature-based Monte Carlo localization in the RoboCup humanoid soccer league. Master's thesis, Universität Hamburg (2019)
8. Hayashibara, Y., et al.: Robocup2022 kidsize league winner CIT brains: open platform hardware sustaina-op and software. In: RoboCup 2022: Robot World Cup XXV. Springer (2023)
9. He, K., Zhang, X., Ren, S., Sun, J.: Deep residual learning for image recognition. In: Proceedings of the IEEE Conference on Computer Vision and Pattern Recognition (CVPR) (2016)
10. Jonschkowski, R., Rastogi, D., Brock, O.: Differentiable particle filters: end-to-end learning with algorithmic priors. In: Robotics: Science and Systems (2018)
11. Kam, H.R., Lee, S.H., Park, T., Kim, C.H.: Rviz: a toolkit for real domain data visualization. Telecommun. Syst. **60**, 337–345 (2015)
12. Karkus, P., Hsu, D., Lee, W.S.: Particle filter networks with application to visual localization. In: Conference on Robot Learning, pp. 169–178 (2018)
13. Lu, W., Zhou, Y., Wan, G., Hou, S., Song, S.: L3-net: towards learning based lidar localization for autonomous driving. In: Proceedings of the IEEE/CVF Conference on Computer Vision and Pattern Recognition, pp. 6389–6398 (2019)
14. Michel, O.: Cyberbotics ltd. webots^{TM}: professional mobile robot simulation. Int. J. Adv. Robot. Syst. **1**(1), 5 (2004)
15. da Silva, F.B.D.R., de Albuquerque Máximo, M.R.O., Yoneyama, T., Barroso, D.H.V., Aki, R.T.: Calibration of inverse perspective mapping for a humanoid robot. In: RoboCup 2023: Robot World Cup XXVI. Springer (2024)
16. Thrun, S., Burgard, W., Fox, D.: Probabilistic Robotics. MIT Press (2005)
17. Timmer, J., Koenig, M.: On generating power law noise. Astron. Astrophys. **300**, p707 (1995)
18. Vahl, F., Gutsche, J., Bestmann, M., Zhang, J.: Yoeo–you only encode once: a CNN for embedded object detection and semantic segmentation. In: IEEE International Conference on Robotics and Biomimetics (ROBIO) (2021)
19. Zhang, Y., et al.: A unified arbitrary style transfer framework via adaptive contrastive learning. ACM Trans. Graph. (2023)

Semantic Path Planning for Heterogeneous Robots from Building Digital Twin Data

Karameldeen Omer[1,3](✉), Koen de Vos[2], Pieter Pauwels[2], Elena Torta[2], and Andrea Monteriù[1]

[1] Università Politecnica delle Marche, Ancona, Italy
k.i.m.omer@pm.univpm.it
[2] Eindhoven University of Technology, Eindhoven, Netherlands
[3] University of Khartoum, Khartoum, Sudan

Abstract. This paper presents an innovative approach to semantic path planning for mobile robots by integrating semantic data from building digital twins. Semantic and metric information extracted from the digital twin is used to assign weights to a connectivity graph, allowing for path computation using the A* algorithm. Our method excels at generating robot-specific maps that combine both geometric and semantic data, diverging from traditional static maps. This semantic integration equips robots with diverse navigation skills, enabling them to navigate complex environments within large smart facilities.

A key innovation of this work is our path planner, which utilizes semantic data from Building Information Modeling (BIM) databases. This marks a significant advancement in mobile robotic navigation, accommodating robots with varying navigation abilities. The significance of this work lies in the seamless integration of semantic data, enhancing the adaptability and efficiency of mobile robots, regardless of their navigation skills. This coordinated navigation system not only improves safety but also optimizes shared space management for both humans and robots.

Keywords: Robot Digital Twin · Robot-Specific Maps · Semantic Mapping for Mobile Robot Navigation · Human-Centered Design · Semantic Path Planning · Building Information Modeling (BIM)

1 Introduction

The integration of mobile robots into various environments has been on a consistent upward trend. These environments are diverse, ranging from smart homes to settings where robots provide support in Ambient Assisted Living [6,20] to more dynamic settings like restaurants, warehouses, and hospitals. In these settings, autonomous robotic solutions are employed for diverse purposes. For instance, in residential settings, there is often a mix of different robots such as those designed for mobility assistance, cleaning, and various service tasks [2,4]. Similarly, in

E. Barros et al. (Eds.): RoboCup 2024, LNAI 15570, pp. 56–67, 2025.
https://doi.org/10.1007/978-3-031-85859-8_5

commercial and industrial spaces like warehouses, factories, and hospitals, specialized robots are utilized for specific tasks such as medicine delivery, cleaning, healthcare support in contaminated areas, and order picking [3]. Each of these scenarios highlights the coexistence and cooperation of different robotic systems (human-to-robot, robot-to-robot) within the same space they share with a human while having to adapt to the unique needs and challenges of their respective environments.

Despite significant progress in robotics, modern localization and navigation techniques continue to face challenges, particularly in maintaining safety for both humans and robots. Traditional methods such as SLAM (Simultaneous Localization and Mapping) often falter in dynamic environments where changes occur frequently, causing inaccuracies in mapping [14]. Additionally, the process of creating maps for expansive, multi-level buildings demands considerable time and resources. Another notable issue is the reliance on manual intervention for navigation, which hampers the robots' ability to operate autonomously.

In this paper, we introduce a novel approach designed to tackle a key issue in the field of robotic navigation. We focus on a method of semantic mapping that captures the static characteristics of various elements commonly present in indoor settings. This includes their geometry, and the properties, which are vital for efficiently running a robot through large indoor spaces.

A key innovation of our approach is the creation of robot-specific maps. These maps are not one-size-fits-all, furthermore, we have developed a new path planning based on the A* algorithm. This algorithm is designed to chart optimal routes for each robot, adhering to stringent safety standards and specific navigation requirements. The result is a navigation solution that not only enhances safety and efficiency for the robots but also empowers them to access and navigate areas that are most suitable for their unique capabilities.

This paper is systematically organized to provide a comprehensive exploration of the topic. Started by introducing the subject followed by a concise overview of the preliminary research conducted by our team, laying the groundwork for the current study. The paper then progresses into a detailed examination of semantic map generation, elaborating on the integration of semantic information into this process. Subsequently, the focus transitions to the development of our innovative path-planning algorithm. This algorithm is uniquely designed to utilize semantic data, enabling it to customize navigation paths under the specific capabilities and safety requirements of individual robots. In the results section, we present the results from the simulated case and the strengths and limitations of our approach. The conclusion section goes further, analyzing the outcomes of our research. Here, we identify potential areas for refinement and address the challenges encountered.

2 Stat of the Art

This project builds on the foundational work of Hendrikx *et al.* [8], and extends it by developing a more advanced, robot-specific approach to localization and navigation using Building Information Modeling (BIM) [22] data. Hendrikx *et al.*'s work demonstrated how semantic data extracted from a BIM model could be utilized in creating a world model representation tailored for individual robots. This representation enables robots to query semantic objects in their vicinity and use a graph-based method for localization, incorporating explicit map features. The innovative aspect of this approach is its ability to assist robots in navigating to new locations using data from the BIM model.

Our project further explores and enhances the application of BIM models in robot localization. Previous studies have shown diverse methods of integrating BIM data for this purpose. For instance, Acharya, Khoshelham, and Winter [1] utilized a Convolutional Neural Network (CNN) to identify features from synthetic images derived from a BIM model, aiding robots in pinpointing their location. Laska [13] proposed a similar CNN-based method, but instead of identifying specific locations, it broadly determines the zone or area where the robot is situated. This approach offers the advantages of faster training and reduced computational requirements.

Another significant contribution in this field is from Schaub *et al.* [19], who used synthetic point clouds obtained from BIM models for comparison with the robot's local point cloud data to determine the robot's location. This method is particularly noteworthy as it does not necessitate retraining for each new building, making it more scalable and adaptable.

Kim and Peavy [10, 18] took a different approach by converting the entire BIM model into a dynamic URDF (Unified Robot Description Format) model, where dynamic elements, like doors and windows, are interactive, allowing for more realistic simulation and interaction for robots. This URDF model is beneficial not only for localization but also for navigation purposes.

Our research in robot navigation substantially builds upon and extends the foundational work of de Koning *et al.* [11]. Their research demonstrated the effective use of maps generated from Building Information Modeling (BIM [22]) for robot navigation, a concept closely aligned with the work of Karimi et al. [9]. Utilizing this as a baseline, our project seeks to enhance these methods by developing more complex, robot-specific maps and navigation paths. We leverage the comprehensive semantic data available from BIM models to achieve this. Our goal is to establish a more efficient, safe, and adaptive system for robotic navigation, particularly suited to environments that are both diverse and subject to frequent changes.

3 Project Overview

The core of this work extends the research conducted by the same team at TU/e which was fully reported by Pieter Pauwels [17], focusing on the development of localization and navigation maps for robots using a graph database. The process is divided into several key phases as could be summarized as described in Fig. 1.

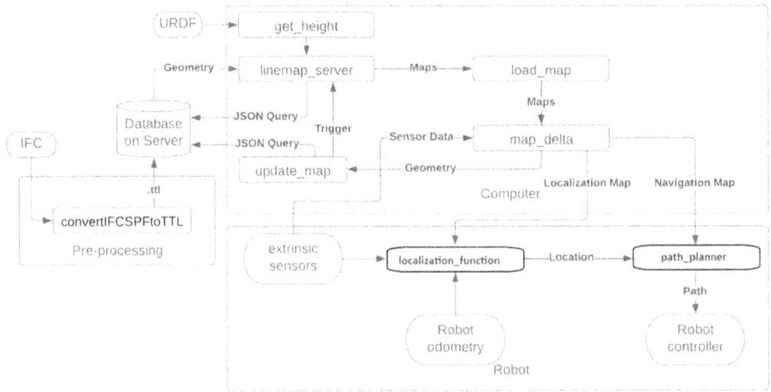

Fig. 1. Process diagram from BIM data to robot navigation as the digital twin.

3.1 Digital Twin

BIM models include not just structural details like walls, doors, and windows, but also other relevant information such as the materials used, the layout of rooms, and the location of furniture or other obstacles. By integrating BIM data, the digital twin of the robot can interact with a detailed 3D model of the building or environment. The data exchange could be summarized in these points:

- Conversion of an Industry Foundation Classes (IFC) file into a Terse RDF Triple Language (TTL) file, representing a graph database [16].
- Storage of the TTL file, containing semantic and geometric data of the building, on a server as graph data. The server's role is limited to data storage.

3.2 Database and Server Processing

- The server, written in Go programming language [5], acts as an intermediary between the robot and the database.
- It manages data retrieval (SELECT queries) and database updates (UPDATE queries) via POST requests.
- The server's API facilitates data exchange but is not designed for complex computations.

3.3 Detailed Map Generation Steps

Robots initiate map loading by requesting LiDAR sensor data and robot height from the URDF, and then two types of maps will be generated; a localization map at the sensor's height and a navigation map covering the space between the robot's height and the floor.

1. **Querying elements:** Retrieving elements from the IFC or the server [7].

2. **Generating meshes:** Creating meshes for each element using faces and vertices data.
3. **Slicing meshes:** Generating sliced meshes for localization or navigation maps.
4. **Generating polygons:** Converting sliced meshes into polygons for mapping.
5. **Obtaining coordinates:** Extracting x and y coordinates from polygons.
6. **Plotting the map:** Using coordinates to plot line, point, and grid maps as required.

3.4 Research Motivation: Integration of Semantic Data

The team has implemented all the above-mentioned pipelines except two parts which we try to cover during this work:

- encoding of semantic data about space, equipment, and structural elements during map generation;
- detailed explanation of how this semantic data is encoded and decoded during the robot's path planning phase.

Each section contributes to creating a system for efficient robot navigation, combining database management, geometric processing, and semantic data integration. The following sections provide a detailed explanation of each component.

4 Proposed Solution

This section outlines our innovative approach to enhancing robot navigation using Building Information Modeling data. The solution comprises two primary components: the generation of semantic maps, and the development of a novel path planner utilizing these maps.

4.1 Semantic Map Generation

Our approach utilizes a Python script to convert complex 3D BIM data into functional 2D maps for robot navigation. These maps are rendered in grayscale, with distinct shades representing various architectural elements such as walls and glass. This color-coding facilitates the embedding of semantic information within the maps, allowing robots to recognize and interact with different environmental features.

The map generation process involves several steps. Firstly, we select relevant building elements from the BIM database, gathering their geometric data—faces, edges, and vertices—to construct accurate meshes at specific elevations. These elevations correspond to the robot sensors' positioning, crucial for precise localization. Next, we process these elements into two types of maps: localization maps, created as planes, and navigation maps, generated as volumes. Each type of map employs a unique method to represent the building's layout.

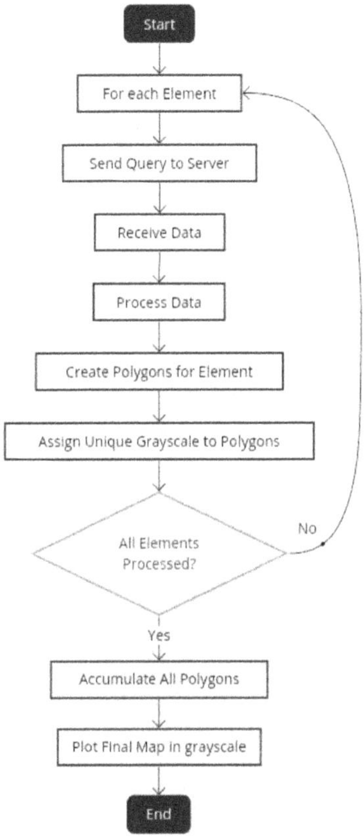

Fig. 2. Flowchart for the proposed method.

To encode semantic information in the navigation maps, each occupied cell is linked to a specific building element. During the map plotting phase, distinct grayscale values are assigned to each element class, representing different types of environmental features. This encoding allows for the inclusion of additional classes if necessary, simply by modifying the map generation scripts.

The process involves extracting elements from the database, retrieving their geometry, and organizing them into discrete vectors. Unlike previous methods that combined vertices and faces sequentially from all queried elements [11], this approach treats each element individually precisely. We iterate over these elements, then generate all the polygons and assign them specific grayscale values belonging to the element.

Finally, we plot the processed polygons with their corresponding grayscale values, producing the final map. The flowchart shown in Fig. 2 summarizes the process for the proposed approach.

4.2 Path Planner Development

Our path planner is an enhanced version of the A* algorithm [23], specifically adapted to integrate semantic data extracted from the BIM model. This data, which includes various static obstacles in different standard gray (ranging from black to white, or 0–255 in grayscale values) [12], is embedded into the navigation map. The primary goal of our path planner is to navigate efficiently while giving different considerations for each obstacle in the map.

The innovative aspect of our approach lies in the handling of these obstacles separately. Each type of obstacle is first identified and then assigned specific penalties based on user-defined requirements for the robot's path. This penalty is a crucial part of our path-planning process. It involves calculating the distance of each cell from key static obstacles (for example walls, glass partition, or sofa), and then applying penalties accordingly, based on a set of predefined rules. The modified A* algorithm works as follows:

- Initialize the planner with the navigation map dimensions.
- Process the map to detect obstacles (walls, glass, etc.) and calculate distance transforms for each cell.
- Begin the A* algorithm by adding the starting point to the open list.
- For each successor node evaluated, check if it's not in the open list and add it, factoring in the calculated scores based on penalties and distances.
- If a successor node is already in the open list but can be reached via a more optimal path in the new evaluation, update its scores and parent node accordingly.
- Continue this process until the goal is reached. Then, trace back the path from the goal to the starting point by following the parent nodes.

The penalty for each cell in the grid is determined by measuring the distance from the nearest wall or glass obstacle. This distance is then used to apply a penalty value according to predefined thresholds. The penalty parameters are symbolically represented as follows in Fig. 3.

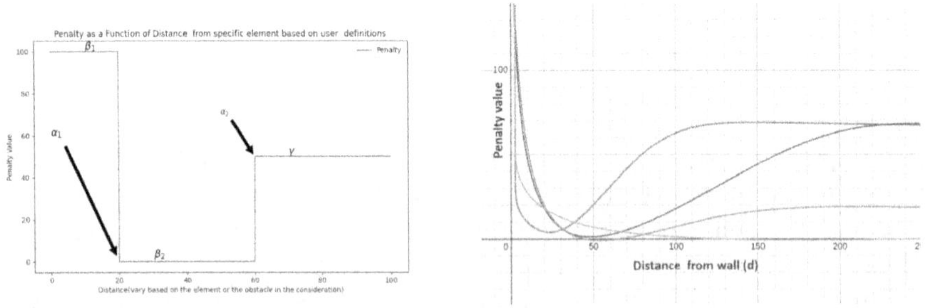

Fig. 3. Penalty as a distance function, on the left as a piecewise function, on the right as a continuous function.

The penalty is calculated using a piecewise function based on the distance from any object presented on the map as

where $\alpha_1, \alpha_2, \beta_1, \beta_2, \gamma \geq 0$ and

- slopes α_1 and α_2 represent the values at which the penalty decreases as the distance from the obstacle increases;
- the threshold β_1 indicates a distance beyond which the penalty sharply drops;
- the threshold β_2 represents the distance beyond which no penalty is applied;
- the line γ represents the minimum penalty value that is applied once the distance is beyond β_2.

The penalty function also could be calculated as a continuous function as below

$$\text{Penalty}(d) = A \times e^{-k_1(d-\mu_1)^2} + C \times \log((d - \mu_2 + k_2)) \quad (1)$$

where

- d: distance from the wall or obstacle;
- A, C: scaling constants for the two components of the function;
- k_1: determines the rate of decrease of the penalty near the wall;
- μ_1: typically set to 0, denotes distance offset for the first component;
- μ_2: represents the distance at which the logarithmic penalty begins to have a notable effect;
- k_2: offset to ensure the value inside the logarithm is always positive.

5 Implementation

The implementation of the proposed method has been done in the simulation of a simple scenario. Our current simulation focuses on two primary static obstacles from the BIM data: walls and glass partitions. The flexibility of our script allows for the inclusion of additional classes as needed. All implementation has been executed within the Robot Operating System (ROS) environment, as detailed in [21]. Specifically, the path planner was adeptly integrated as a plugin into the ROS navigation stack, aligning with the standards outlined in [24]. We utilize BIM files to create a simple building environment that comprises two rooms connected by a hallway, with one room adjoining the hallway through a glass partition. In this setup, the robot's navigation algorithm is designed to find the most efficient path from one room to another. When a feasible route involves passing through the glass partition, the robot is expected to maintain a safe distance from the glass while staying closer to the walls. Figure 4 shows the map for walls and glass; the color is only for visualization because the original map is gray, so it could be hard for the naked eye to differentiate the scale.

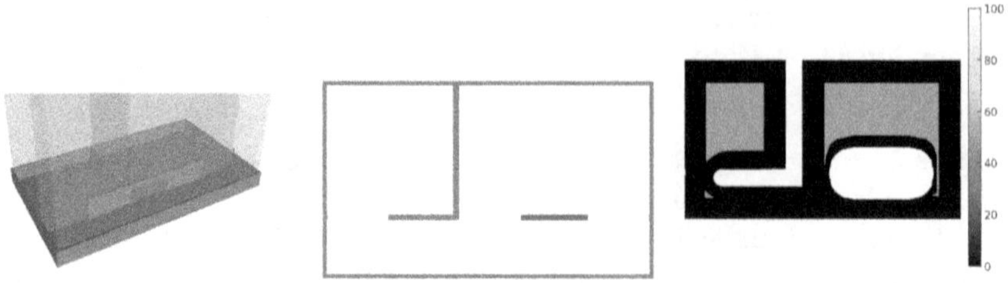

Fig. 4. From left, 3D model for the simulated environment and its projected map for wall and glass, with glass in blue, lastly on the right visualization of Wall and Glass Penalty as heatmap, warmer colors indicate higher penalties, while cooler colors represent lower penalties. The penalties are calculated based on the specified thresholds for proximity to walls and glass. (Color figure online)

5.1 Penalty Calculation

The penalty calculation through a function that assigns two distinct values to each cell: one representing the proximity to glass and the other to walls. The penalty values are configured to be high when a cell is close to a wall or glass, decrease to zero with increasing distance, and then rise again as the distance becomes excessively large. This gradation is clearly illustrated in the visualizations provided in Fig. 4.

Furthermore, the final penalty for each cell is computed based on user-defined criteria, allowing customization of the robot's behavior. Users can specify how the penalties for walls and glass are combined, thus tailoring the overall penalty landscape through which the robot navigates. This flexible approach ensures that the robot's navigation is not only efficient but also aligns with specific safety requirements and desired behaviors in different environments. This method underlines the practical implementation of our path planning algorithm, demonstrating its adaptability and effectiveness in controlled scenarios.

6 Results and Discussions

The simulation results for our path planning method, designed to demonstrate the integration of semantic map data from graph databases in a simplified environment, have positively affirmed the concept's viability. In this test scenario, the system adeptly managed 'wall' and 'glass' obstacles, highlighting its applicability for real-time robotic navigation. The simulation was set up to assess whether the robot could maintain a safe distance from walls while avoiding glass partitions, as dictated by the penalty parameters. The results showed that, in most instances, the robot navigated effectively, closely following the walls and steering clear of glass areas as shown in Fig. 5, which illustrate two different robot path-planners, one path planned with conventional A* on the right the generated path from our semantic path planner.

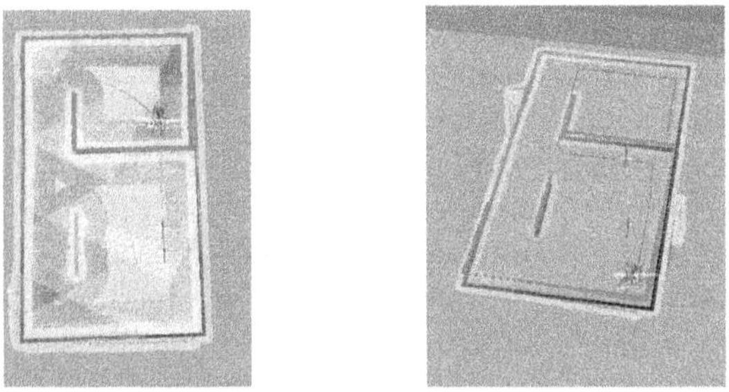

Fig. 5. Difference between conventional and semantic A* path planning: on the left with normal A*, on the right using semantic A*.

This successful outcome in a basic setup underscores the potential of this approach to meet specific user-defined navigation requirements and to adapt path planning based on a robot's unique navigation capabilities.

The preliminary results from our path planning system, while requiring further refinement, show great promise and mark a notable advancement in sophisticated, context-aware robotic navigation. One key observation from the simulations is the critical role of accurately setting penalty values. Incorrect or imprecise penalty configurations can lead to suboptimal navigation outcomes, as evidenced in the provided figures. These illustrations depict how the same navigation goal can yield dramatically different paths for the robot, depending on the penalty values assigned. In cases where these values are not properly defined, the robot may choose significantly longer or less efficient routes, highlighting the importance of fine-tuning these parameters to achieve optimal navigation performance (Fig. 6).

Fig. 6. Effect different heuristic scale factors and penalty costs on the path planning

7 Conclusion

The concept of integrating semantic map data into our path planning system is pivotal not only for advancing robotic navigation but also in the context of digital twin technology and human-centered design. This approach significantly contributes to safer navigation for robots with diverse skills, aligning with the principles of a digital twin and human-centric design.

From a human-centered design perspective, the system prioritizes safe interaction between robots and humans in shared spaces. By understanding and interpreting the environment semantically [15], robots can navigate more intuitively and respond appropriately to human presence and activities. This aspect is crucial in environments like healthcare facilities, warehouses, and public spaces, where seamless and safe interaction between robots and humans is essential.

Furthermore, the ability to customize navigation paths based on the specific skills of different robots ensures that each robot can operate optimally within its capabilities while maintaining safety standards. This adaptability is particularly important in complex environments where robots with varying functionalities coexist.

In summary, the integration of semantic map data into path planning is not just an advancement in robotic navigation technology; it's a step towards creating more responsive and safe navigation robotic systems, aligning with the evolving concepts of digital twins and human-centered design.

References

1. Acharya, D., Khoshelham, K., Winter, S.: BIM-posenet: indoor camera localisation using a 3D indoor model and deep learning from synthetic images. ISPRS J. Photogramm. Remote. Sens. **150**, 245–258 (2019)
2. Benavidez, P., Kumar, M., Agaian, S., Jamshidi, M.: Design of a home multi-robot system for the elderly and disabled. In: 2015 10th System of Systems Engineering Conference (SoSE), pp. 392–397 (2015). https://doi.org/10.1109/SYSOSE.2015.7151907
3. Boysen, N., Briskorn, D., Emde, S.: Parts-to-picker based order processing in a rack-moving mobile robots environment. Eur. J. Oper. Res. **262**(2), 550–562 (2017)
4. Ciabattoni, L., Ferracuti, F., Foresi, G., Freddi, A., Monteriù, A., Pagnotta, D.P.: Real-time fall detection system by using mobile robots in smart homes. In: 2017 IEEE 7th International Conference on Consumer Electronics - Berlin (ICCE-Berlin), pp. 15–16 (2017)
5. Donovan, A.A., Kernighan, B.W.: The Go Programming Language. Addison-Wesley Professional (2015)
6. Ferracuti, F., Freddi, A., Iarlori, S., Monteriù, A., Omer, K.I.M., Porcaro, C.: A human-in-the-loop approach for enhancing mobile robot navigation in presence of obstacles not detected by the sensory set. Front. Robot. AI **9** (2022)
7. Gui, N., Wang, C., Qiu, Z., Gui, W., Deconinck, G.: IFC-based partial data model retrieval for distributed collaborative design. J. Comput. Civ. Eng. **33**(3), 04019016 (2019)
8. Hendrikx, R., Pauwels, P., Torta, E., Bruyninckx, H.P., van de Molengraft, M.: Connecting semantic building information models and robotics: an application to 2D lidar-based localization. In: 2021 IEEE International Conference on Robotics and Automation (ICRA), pp. 11654–11660. IEEE (2021)

9. Karimi, S., Iordanova, I., St-Onge, D.: An ontology-based approach to data exchanges for robot navigation on construction sites. arXiv preprint arXiv:2104.10239 (2021)
10. Kim, K., Peavy, M.: BIM-based semantic building world modeling for robot task planning and execution in built environments. Autom. Constr. **138**, 104247 (2022)
11. de Koning, R., Torta, E., Pauwels, P., Hendrikx, R., van de Molengraft, M.: Queries on semantic building digital twins for robot navigation. In: 9th Linked Data in Architecture and Construction Workshop, LDAC 2021, pp. 32–42. CEUR-WS.org (2021)
12. Kumar, T., Verma, K.: A theory based on conversion of RGB image to gray image. Int. J. Comput. Appl. **7**(2), 7–10 (2010)
13. Laska, M., Blankenbach, J.: Deeplocbim: learning indoor area localization guided by digital building models. IEEE Internet Things J. **9**(16), 15323–15335 (2022)
14. Li, Y.: Researches advanced in the slam for dynamic environment. In: Journal of Physics: Conference Series, vol. 2634, p. 012054. IOP Publishing (2023)
15. Naik, L., Blumenthal, S., Huebel, N., Bruyninckx, H., Prassler, E.: Semantic mapping extension for openstreetmap applied to indoor robot navigation. In: 2019 International Conference on Robotics and Automation (ICRA), pp. 3839–3845. IEEE (2019)
16. Pauwel, P.: Ifctolbd. https://github.com/ISBE-TUe/IFCtoLBD. Accessed 2023
17. Pauwels, P., de Koning, R., Hendrikx, B., Torta, E.: Live semantic data from building digital twins for robot navigation: overview of data transfer methods. Adv. Eng. Inform. **56**, 101959 (2023). https://doi.org/10.1016/j.aei.2023.101959. https://www.sciencedirect.com/science/article/pii/S1474034623000873
18. Peavy, M., Kim, P., Oyediran, H., Kim, K.: Integration of real-time semantic building map updating with adaptive Monte Carlo localization (AMCL) for robust indoor mobile robot localization. Appl. Sci. **13**(2), 909 (2023)
19. Schaub, L., Podkosova, I., Schönauer, C., Kaufmann, H.: Point cloud to BIM registration for robot localization and augmented reality. In: 2022 IEEE International Symposium on Mixed and Augmented Reality Adjunct (ISMAR-Adjunct), pp. 77–84. IEEE (2022)
20. Silva, V.D., Roche, J., Shi, X., Kondoz, A.: IoT driven ambient intelligence architecture for indoor intelligent mobility. In: 2018 IEEE 16th International Conference on Dependable, Autonomic and Secure Computing, 16th International Conference on Pervasive Intelligence and Computing, 4th International Conference on Big Data Intelligence and Computing and Cyber Science and Technology Congress (DASC/PiCom/DataCom/CyberSciTech), pp. 451–456. IEEE Computer Society, Los Alamitos (2018)
21. Stanford Artificial Intelligence Laboratory et al.: Robotic operating system. https://www.ros.org
22. Volk, R., Stengel, J., Schultmann, F.: Building information modeling (BIM) for existing buildings–literature review and future needs. Autom. Constr. **38**, 109–127 (2014)
23. Wang, H., Qi, X., Lou, S., Jing, J., He, H., Liu, W.: An efficient and robust improved a* algorithm for path planning. Symmetry **13**(11), 2213 (2021)
24. Wiki, R.: Writing a global path planner as plugin in ros (2015)

Planning the Path with Reinforcement Learning: Optimal Robot Motion Planning in RoboCup Small Size League Environments

Mateus G. Machado(✉), João G. Melo, Cleber Zanchettin, Pedro H. Braga, Pedro V. Cunha, Edna N. S. Barros, and Hansenclever F. Bassani

Centro de Informática, Universidade Federal de Pernambuco, Av. Prof. Moraes Rego, 1235 - Cidade Universitária, Recife, Pernambuco, Brazil
{mgm4,jgocm,cz,phmb4,pvc3,ensb,hfb}@cin.ufpe.br

Abstract. This work investigates the potential of Reinforcement Learning (RL) to tackle robot motion planning challenges in the dynamic RoboCup Small Size League (SSL). Using a heuristic control approach, we evaluate RL's effectiveness in obstacle-free and single-obstacle path-planning environments. Ablation studies reveal significant performance improvements. Our method achieved a **60% time gain** in obstacle-free environments compared to baseline algorithms. Additionally, our findings demonstrated **dynamic obstacle avoidance capabilities**, adeptly navigating around moving blocks. These findings highlight the potential of RL to enhance robot motion planning in the challenging and unpredictable SSL environment.

Keywords: Reinforcement Learning · Motion Planning · Robot Control

1 Introduction

The RoboCup Small Size League (SSL) is a robot soccer competition that focuses on the problem of multi-robot cooperation and control in a highly dynamic environment [28]. This challenging game requires controlling a team of up to 11 robots to work together to perform passes, dribbles, and shots on goal in a coordinated and effective way. The effectiveness of these actions hinges on precise path-planning tailored to the distinct motion models of each robot [9].

Figure 1 represents the general workflow for planning a robot's motion within the SSL environment. Given a target position and orientation in the environment (depicted in orange), the process unfolds in three key steps. Initially, global planning calculates a geometric path, represented by a set of coordinates in the configuration space, guiding the robot toward the desired target. Subsequently, the local planner generates a sequence of desired states, comprising positions and velocities, forming a trajectory aligning with the previously computed path.

E. Barros et al. (Eds.): RoboCup 2024, LNAI 15570, pp. 68–79, 2025.
https://doi.org/10.1007/978-3-031-85859-8_6

Finally, the motion control module determines the requisite control inputs for the robot to transition from its current state to the next desired state.

Reinforcement Learning (RL) has emerged as a promising approach for robotic control tasks [15,18]. RL offers a paradigm where agents learn optimal strategies through interaction with their environment. This learning paradigm finds a natural application in the SSL, as it allows agents to adapt and improve their decision-making processes in response to the dynamic and unpredictable nature of the game [29].

We discern a hierarchical structure by adapting the motion planning workflow to RL learning environments. While the motion control module directly governs the robot's actions, the global and local planning modules serve as intermediary sub-goals to be achieved. We refer to the motion control task as **goToPoint**, with global and local planning denoted as **path-planning**.

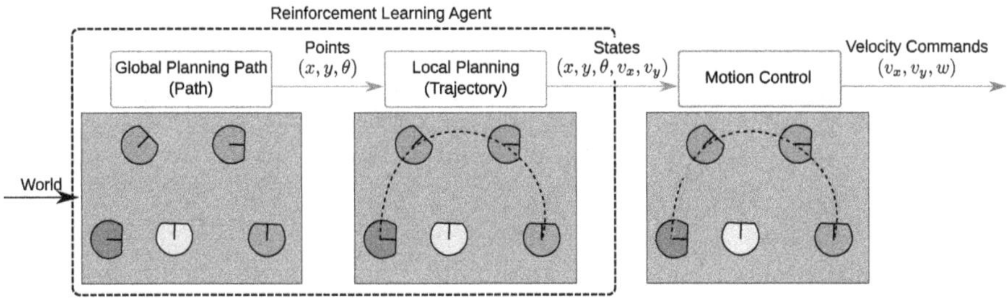

Fig. 1. General workflow for robot motion planning and control, divided into Global planning, local planning, and motion control. The first two stages plan the points and velocities the agent should follow, while the last controls the robot. This Work focuses on the first two modules of this workflow.

Building upon this foundation, we propose a model-free path-planning methodology, leveraging goal-conditioned policies that take the goal state as input [13,25], and yield sub-goals to be executed by an omnidirectional motion control [27]. Sim2Real is a subfield of Machine Learning focused on mitigate the gap between simulated and real-world environments [8,12]. While RL environments traditionally model the entire motion planning system, integrating a Sim2Real module becomes imperative to transfer learned models to real-world settings. Our methodology circumvents this challenge, as the path-planning model remains agnostic to the training environment, whether simulated or real.

Our primary contribution lies in a methodology for employing Reinforcement Learning in the path-planning task, creating a model that seamlessly transitions from simulation to reality [9,10]. We evaluate the efficacy of the Soft Actor-Critic (SAC) [11] algorithm across both baseline and proposed learning environments, shedding light on discrepancies inherent in the baseline's reliance on goToPoint to address the path-planning task. Additionally, we introduce two state-of-the-art methods to mitigate action instability and craft intuitive trajectories. Finally, through empirical validation, we demonstrate the readiness of our model for real-world deployment.

2 Related Work

Traditionally, motion planning systems are conceptualized as single complex agents aimed at solving the entire system [6,7,21]. However, a hierarchical understanding of the system [22,30] delineates a manager-worker structure, with the path-planning task delegated to a manager agent and goToPoint executed by a worker agent. In our approach, we base the environment development on the managerial treatment of the environment in existing works.

In Reinfocement Learning, the reward function quantifies the impact of an action on the environment and serves as a crucial component to guide the agent through the learning process [29]. Our baseline work [4] endeavors to solve the path-planning task for robots in the Small Size League (SSL) of RoboCup [28]. As elucidated in subsequent sections, [4] adopts a reward system emphasizing direct impact actions, culminating in an inherently unstable goToPoint agent.

The challenge of ensuring the robustness of RL algorithms in handling continuous actions has been extensively studied in the realm of robot learning [17,24,26]. A hallmark of a proficient path-planning algorithm lies in its ability to generate a minimal set of stable output points. Contrarily, algorithms such as the one proposed in [4] exhibit instability, rendering them impractical for real-world deployment. To address this, we employ two learning methods for the agent [14,20], to produce a model characterized by desired features such as action stability and simplicity.

Our methodology establishes a conducive learning environment for the path-planning task, anchored on three core pillars: a reward system centered on agent actions, action stability, and simplicity in action selection. Our results yield path-planning agents capable of generating intuitive trajectories for human comprehension. While the motion control aspect for SSL robots has been extensively explored in prior works [1–3], our deliberate abstraction of this module enables our agents to seamlessly integrate into real-world setups, facilitating a plug-and-play deployment paradigm.

3 Motion Planning Learning Environments

We adopted a similar environment structure guided by the fundamental principles of [4]. However, we explore RL-based path-planning to abstract the motion control module, following the pipeline presented in Fig. 1[1].

[1] Agents, both trainable and trained, are available at https://github.com/goncamateus/Planning-the-path-with-rl.

3.1 Baseline Environment

Cruz *et al.* [4] explore two RL-based motion planning approaches: RL-based path-planning to a given control system and a single-component approach, where the RL agent learns both motion planning and control. As a starting point for this work, we have successfully replicated their environments within the rSoccer framework [18], employing the first approach as a Baseline environment for this research. The state space within these environments is characterized by a 13-dimensional vector: (x^t, y^t, $cos(\theta^t)$, $sin(\theta^t)$, v_x^t, v_y^t, x^r, y^r, $cos(\theta^r)$, $sin(\theta^r)$, v_x^r, v_y^r, ω^r), where t and r labels account for target and robot respectively. Also, in applying RL-based path-planning to a given motion control, the action space consists of a 6-tuple $(x, y, v_x, v_y, \sin\theta, \cos\theta)$, generating a sub-goal at each environment step. Notably, these vectors are subject to normalization concerning the maximum values in each dimension, except for the angular components, represented as sine and cosine values.

The reward system in [4] is defined by $R_T(s,a) = R_d(s,a) + R_\theta(s,a) + R_t(s,a)$, where:

$$R_d(s,a) = \begin{cases} -\mathrm{d}(s,a), & \text{if } \mathrm{dist}(s,a) > D_{th} \\ 10, & \text{otherwise} \end{cases}$$

$$R_\theta(s,a) = \begin{cases} \frac{-\delta(s,a)}{\pi}, & \text{if } \delta(s,a) > \theta_{th} \\ 1, & \text{otherwise} \end{cases}$$

$$R_t(s,a) = \begin{cases} 1000, & \text{if } \mathrm{dist}(s,a) > D_{th} \text{ and } \delta(s,a) > \theta_{th} \\ 0, & \text{otherwise} \end{cases}$$

Here, s and a are state and action, $\mathrm{d}(s,a)$ and $\delta(s,a)$ are the distance and angle difference to the target, with thresholds D_{th} and θ_{th}, respectively. As elucidated in Sect. 2, these rewards do not depend directly on the actions taken but on the robot's actuators. See in Fig. 2a a graphical representation of the angle difference and the distance to the target.

3.2 Proposed Environment

Firstly, we simplified the learning problem by imposing two main constraints: the agent's actions velocity components magnitude is constrained to zero; the goal also has the target velocity magnitude constrained to zero. Therefore, the Local Planning, as seen in Fig. 1, is in form of $x, y, \theta, 0, 0$. The state and action spaces remain the same as in the Baseline.

The reward system proposed by [4] accounts only for the robot's properties, underscoring the agent's responsibility to optimize its actions and achieve the desired objectives. We introduced an action-centric reward structure by adding action features to our reward system, emphasizing states where the robot is on the cusp of achieving favorable outcomes within each reward component.

Therefore, the whole reward system, R_d, R_θ, and R_t, outlined in Sect. 3.1 remains the same but changes the reference from the robot to the sub-goal action of our path-planning agent. Note in Fig. 2b a visual difference between our Proposed environment and the Baseline.

In our proposed reward system, the agent is penalized if the generated path is incompatible with the target. This strategic shift ensures that the agent's learned actions align more closely with the desired trajectory, fostering a genuine path-planning capability and reinforcing the agent's focus on optimal and effective target-reaching strategies.

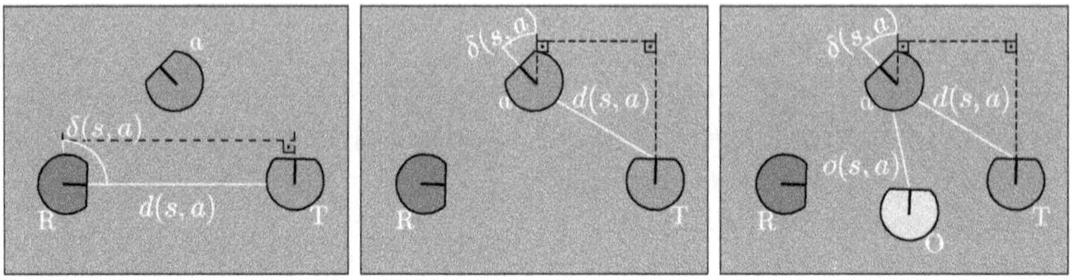

(a) Baseline (b) Proposed (c) Obstacle

Fig. 2. Visualization of the "Baseline", "Proposed", and "Obstacle" learning environments with example rewards. The circles blue (R), magenta (a), yellow (O), and orange (T) represent the robot's position, the action taken, the obstacle, and the target goal, respectively. The white arc and lines illustrate the angular difference, $\delta(s, a)$, and distances, $d(s, a)$, $o(s, a)$, to target and obstacle, respectively. (Color figure online)

3.3 Proposed Obstacle Environment

The obstacle setup inherits the Proposed environment and adds an enemy robot as the obstacle. Therefore, the state space for this environment is incremented by a 5-dimensional vector referent from the obstacle: $x^o, y^o, v_x^o, v_y^o, \omega^o$. The obstacle moves randomly, varying its speed in a range of $[0, 1]m/s$ each step. In this environment, we also add penalties for hitting the obstacle and the actions being close to it. When the agent hits an obstacle, the episode fails, and the penalty is the inverse of reaching the target.

At each step, we penalize the agent's proximity from the obstacle with a parametric Gaussian in function of the distance between the action and the obstacle $o(s, a)$, expected value $\mu = 0$, and variation $\sigma = 1$. Therefore, we can describe the reward system as $R_T(s, a) = R_d(s, a) + R_\theta(s, a) + R_t(s, a) + R_{obst}(s, a) + R_{hit}(s, a)$, where $R_{hit}(s, a) = -1000$ if the robot hits the obstacle; otherwise, 0. See the addition of the obstacle distance reward in Fig. 2c.

4 Mitigating Action Instability

The prominent issue of erratic and non-smooth actions learned by RL policies is well-recognized, posing potential concerns such as overheating and energy wastage problems in practical applications [5,16]. In our context, this problem manifests as the agent controlling the robot not through angular or linear velocities but via poses. We introduce two techniques known to be effective in addressing this challenge in our training process.

The *Frame skip* wrapper simplifies action sequences by repeating a given action for a specified number of steps. As it demonstrated to enhance agent performance in Atari games using Deep Q-Networks [14,19], we apply this wrapper with a skip rate of 16 in the rSoccer framework [18]. This adjustment significantly reduces the number of actions per episode from 1200 to a maximum of 75.

Mysore *et al.* [20] introduce an intuitive regularization technique, achieving an impressive 80% reduction in power consumption during robot experiments. This technique, termed *Conditioning for Action Policy Smoothness* (**CAPS**), introduces an additional loss term for the Actor in an Actor-Critic setup. CAPS aims to penalize actions that exhibit significant differences for similar states, promoting smoother and more controlled behavior.

5 Results

We evaluate the agent's performance in the presented environments, namely Baseline, Proposed, and Obstacle, comparing their episodic lengths and the Cumulative Pairwise Action Distance (**CPAD**), a novel proposed measure designed to assess the stability of executed actions. This metric quantifies the overall displacement solely in the (x, y) position and is mathematically defined as: $D(A) = \sum_{i=0}^{K-1} \text{Dist}(A_i, A_{i+1})$, where A represents the actions undertaken throughout the episode, and K denotes the episode length.

CPAD offers valuable insights into the agent's behavioral stability. Specifically, a consistently directed focus on a particular (x, y) position results in a cumulative distance of 0. Conversely, rapid and erratic movements yield higher cumulative distances. As such, a lower CPAD is a crucial indicator of more stable and consistent actions, a pivotal attribute in motion planning.

Next topics unveils the results obtained from trained agents using the Soft Actor-Critic (**SAC**) [11] method in the setups described in Sect. 3. It is important to note that, given our use of the SAC algorithm for training agents, adjustments were made to accommodate the CAPS algorithm. SAC's policy entropy factor α is a parameter of the policy learning method to induce exploration during training. This parameter is originally set as trainable to, for example, explore at the beginning of training and then having stable actions. When applying CAPS at SAC, the α parameter hinds the stability loss, and the learning in general. Therefore, we set α as a constant throughout the SAC-CAPS algorithm execution.

5.1 Comparing Baseline and Proposed Environments

This evaluation assesses SAC agents in both Baseline and Proposed environments using four different setups: **1)** Vanilla, **2)** with Frame Skip, **3)** with CAPS, and

4) with both Frame Skip and CAPS (FSCAPS). These setups provide insights into the model's adaptability within a real-world environment.

Table 1 shows the proposed metrics results for obstacle-free environments. Notably, both metrics gradually decrease with the addition of action-stabilizing methods. The Proposed environment consistently outperforms the Baseline, showcasing improved agent motion.

Table 1. Test results distributions are presented for obstacle-free environments over 1000 episodes. Pairwise comparisons are conducted for each setup using the methods outlined in Sect. 4. The Vanilla experiments involve running agents in the environments described in Sect. 3 without any action stabilizing method. The Frame Skip and CAPS experiments are similar but include either the frame skip or CAPS method. The FSCAPS experiments encompass both stabilization methods.

		Episode Length(steps)			CPAD(m)		
	Env	IQR	Max	Min	IQR	Max	Min
Vanilla	Baseline	1200(1200-1200)	1200	52	20.84(14.42-26.75)	47.66	1.39
	Proposed	**128(102-152)**	**1200**	**35**	**6.03(3.93-8.07)**	**16.43**	**0.20**
Frame Skip	Baseline	198(150-265)	1200	49	13.53(11.03-16.55)	38.40	3.46
	Proposed	**119(95-141)**	**223**	**33**	**1.31(0.60-2.12)**	**6.80**	**0.01**
CAPS	Baseline	1200(731-1200)	1200	37	13.97(9.61-16.31)	22.86	1.91
	Proposed	**113(91-134)**	**1200**	**33**	**1.29(0.81-1.87)**	**3.81**	**0.14**
FSCAPS	Baseline	**109(87-130)**	**196**	**34**	0.58(0.36-0.87)	2.22	0.02
	Proposed	114(92-137)	193	31	**0.06(0.05-0.08)**	**0.16**	**0.00**

When evaluating individual experiments through a "Baseline *vs* Proposed" lens, our proposed environment consistently demonstrates superior performance in both episode length and CPAD metrics. The Vanilla experiment, notable improvements of **90% for episode length** and **71% for CPAD** were observed. Incorporating the Frame Skip wrapper yielded a significant performance enhancement, reducing task completion time by approximately **80 steps** (equivalent to 6% of the total episode) and achieving a **90%** improvement in the CPAD metric. In the CAPS experiment, inspired by [20], we achieved a **78%** CPAD reduction compared to Vanilla-Proposed. This outcome underscores the limitations of baseline-trained agents in attaining the precision of our proposed approach.

Combining action-stabilizing methods in the FSCAPS experiments showcases enhanced performance. The Baseline-trained agent exhibits marginally improved episode length, while the Proposed-trained agent demonstrates a remarkable **tenfold improvement** in action precision. Therefore, the gain in episode length is deemed negligible compared to the Proposed agent's superior transfer capability to a real-world environment.

In comparing experiments within our proposed environment, the final temporal gain between Vanilla and FSCAPS experiments is modest, with only 14 simulated steps (1% of the total episode) faster. However, examining the CPAD metric reveals a substantial increase in action stability with each addition, resulting in a final gain **100 times better** than the environment alone. See in Fig. 3 trained agents for our proposed environment in each experiment. These compelling results encourage further research, particularly in environments with obstacle setups.

(a) Vanilla (b) Frame Skip (c) CAPS (d) FSCAPS

Fig. 3. Trained Soft Actor-Critic agents operating within the Proposed environment across various experiments. The orange circle denotes the target goal, while the red dots trace the actions executed by the agent throughout the episode. The red line visually maps the trajectory followed by the robot. As depicted in Fig. 3d, the agent demonstrates precision by consistently reaching the target without deviation. (Color figure online)

5.2 Evaluating Obstacle Avoidance

The proposed Obstacle environment is evaluated using SAC agents following the scheme outlined in Sect. 5.1. This environment features a simple scenario with a single mobile robot acting as the obstacle. Uniquely in this setup, the percentage of hitting the obstacle is introduced as an additional metric, providing insights into the adaptability of our previous research in obstacle-laden environments.

Table 2 presents results from experiments in the Obstacle environment. Preliminary results indicate that the baseline method struggled to solve the task consistently within the imposed training time. In contrast, our final method, FSCAPS, introduces a robust and adaptable approach for environments with obstacle. Understandably, variations in actions are observed as the agent needs to navigate around the moving obstacle. The low rate of collisions suggests that the agent effectively learned the purpose of the environment, even at maximum speed, with the episode length nearly identical to the setup without obstacles.

Table 2. Test results distributions are presented for the environment with obstacle over 1000 episodes.

	Episode Length(steps)			CPAD(m)			Collision
	IQR	Max	Min	IQR	Max	Min	
Vanilla	1200(1200-1200)	1200	132	12.38(10.70-14.21)	35.03	4.10	12.38%
Frame Skip	1200(1200-1200)	1200	148	6.03(5.24-6.90)	11.35	2.23	5.61%
CAPS	1200(1200-1200)	1200	670	11.35(10.55-12.17)	20.60	4.10	1.32%
FSCAPS	**115(113-158)**	**1200**	**79**	**1.27(1.06-1.53)**	**5.87**	**0.55**	**0.61%**

5.3 Real Environment Results

After obtaining stable and accurate results in a simulated environment, the trained agents were subsequently deployed in a real-world setting. We integrated our model into the RobôCIn SSL-Unification software [3] using the TorchScript module [23] for compilation and adaptation purposes. It is important to note that the RobôCIn SSL-Unification software employs its own motion control system, whereas our agents were trained using a general omnidirectional motion control approach [27].

The agents utilized in these experiments included the Vanilla agent, trained in an obstacle-free environment, and the FSCAPS agent, trained in our proposed "Obstacle" environment. For experiments involving obstacles, we employed a fixed obstacle to ensure safety.

Table 3 presents the episode length and CPAD for the experiments on the real-world. The Vanilla agent failed to complete the task in any of the ten trials. The CPAD metric suggests unstable paths extending to a length of 25 fields, turning it unpractical to real-world.

In contrast, the FSCAPS agent exhibited consistent results across both environment setups. These findings align with our approach of developing a methodology that is agnostic to the motion control system, thereby facilitating deployment in real-world scenarios.

Table 3. Test results distributions are presented for real-world setup over 10 episodes.

	Episode Length(steps)			CPAD(m)		
	IQR	Max	Min	IQR	Max	Min
Vanilla	1200(1200-1200)	1200	1200	227.93(227.06-230.79)	235.06	225.45
FSCAPS	159(155-160)	162	135	0.10(0.10-0.10)	0.99	0.09
Obstacle	140(131-151)	171	109	2.10(2.04-2.15)	2.32	2.01

6 Discussion

In analyzing agent adaptability, FSCAPS demonstrates significant superiority in acquiring efficient strategies in challenging environments. The combination of Frame Skip with CAPS accelerates adaptation to obstacle dynamics, evidenced by reduced episode durations and collision rates. This suggests more effective learning and better generalization compared to isolated methods. Environmental parameters significantly impact path planning efficacy, with FSCAPS exhibiting greater robustness against environmental variations. This emphasizes the need for strategies resilient to fluctuations.

Compared to state-of-the-art approaches, FSCAPS not only outperforms in efficiency and safety but also strikes a balanced solution, especially in complex obstacle environments where real-time adaptation is crucial. Navigation failures revealed that Pure and Frame Skip methods struggled with unpredictable obstacles. The integration of CAPS enhances predictability and action smoothness, reducing collision rates.

While longer episodes offer more experience, they can induce fatigue. FSCAPS reduces episode duration without compromising safety, offering a sustainable training approach. However, generalizing FSCAPS to untested scenarios requires further exploration to validate its real-world robotic applications.

7 Conclusion

In this study, we comprehensively evaluated Reinforcement Learning (RL) applied to the intricate challenges of robot motion planning within the RoboCup Small Size League (SSL). Leveraging a heuristic control approach, we explored various learning environments, comparing the performance of SAC agents in both Baseline and Proposed setups.

Our exploration in obstacle-free environments showcased the Proposed environment's effectiveness in reducing action instability, and enhancing agent performance. The Frame Skip wrapper further improved efficiency, and the combined use of Frame Skip and CAPS in the "FSCAPS" experiments demonstrated significant performance gains.

Transitioning to obstacle-laden environments, the initial experiments faced challenges in consistently solving tasks, emphasizing the complexity introduced by mobile obstacles. However, our final method, "FSCAPS", exhibited evident adaptability, effectively navigating around obstacles with a minimal rate of collision.

Furthermore, we validated the adaptability of our model in a real-world setting without compromising performance in terms of trajectory length or precision. This corroborates the efficacy of our approach, emphasizing the importance of initially addressing high-level tasks for seamless model adaptation between simulation and real-world deployment.

These results underscore the significance of our research in advancing RL techniques for robot motion planning, particularly in dynamic and challenging

SSL environments. The strategic integration of heuristic control and innovative stabilizing techniques demonstrates the potential for improved decision-making and adaptability in dynamic robotic scenarios, paving the way for advancements in the field of autonomous robotics.

References

1. Abiyev, R.H., Akkaya, N., Gunsel, I.: Control of omnidirectional robot using z-number-based fuzzy system. IEEE Trans. Syst. Man Cybern. Syst. **49**(1), 238–252 (2018)
2. Abiyev, R.H., Günsel, I.S., Akkaya, N., Aytac, E., Çağman, A., Abizada, S.: Fuzzy control of omnidirectional robot. Procedia Comput. Sci. **120**, 608–616 (2017)
3. Araújo, V., et al.: Robôcin ssl-unification: a modular software architecture for dynamic multi-robot systems. In: Robot World Cup, pp. 313–324. Springer (2023)
4. Cruz, J.V.S.: Exploring reinforcement learning in path planning for omnidirectional robotsoccer (2023). https://repositorio.ufpe.br/handle/123456789/51592
5. Duan, Y., Chen, X., Houthooft, R., Schulman, J., Abbeel, P.: Benchmarking deep reinforcement learning for continuous control. CoRR abs/1604.06778 (2016). http://arxiv.org/abs/1604.06778
6. Eysenbach, B., Salakhutdinov, R., Levine, S.: Search on the replay buffer: bridging planning and reinforcement learning (2019)
7. Fang, M., Zhou, C., Shi, B., Gong, B., Xu, J., Zhang, T.: Dher: hindsight experience replay for dynamic goals. In: International Conference on Learning Representations (2018)
8. Gao, R., et al.: Objectfolder 2.0: a multisensory object dataset for sim2real transfer. In: Proceedings of the IEEE/CVF Conference on Computer Vision and Pattern Recognition (CVPR), pp. 10598–10608 (2022)
9. Gasparetto, A., Boscariol, P., Lanzutti, A., Vidoni, R.: Path planning and trajectory planning algorithms: a general overview, pp. 3–27. Springer, Cham (2015)
10. González, D., Pérez, J., Milanés, V., Nashashibi, F.: A review of motion planning techniques for automated vehicles. IEEE Trans. Intell. Transp. Syst. **17**(4), 1135–1145 (2016). https://doi.org/10.1109/TITS.2015.2498841
11. Haarnoja, T., et al.: Soft actor-critic algorithms and applications. CoRR abs/1812.05905 (2018). http://arxiv.org/abs/1812.05905
12. Hu, X., Li, S., Huang, T., Tang, B., Huai, R., Chen, L.: How simulation helps autonomous driving: a survey of sim2real, digital twins, and parallel intelligence. IEEE Trans. Intell. Veh. **9**(1), 593–612 (2024). https://doi.org/10.1109/TIV.2023.3312777
13. Kaelbling, L.P.: Learning to achieve goals. In: IJCAI, vol. 2, pp. 1094–1098. Citeseer (1993)
14. Kalyanakrishnan, S., et al.: An analysis of frame-skipping in reinforcement learning. CoRR abs/2102.03718 (2021). https://arxiv.org/abs/2102.03718
15. Lillicrap, T.P., et al.: Continuous control with deep reinforcement learning. In: Bengio, Y., LeCun, Y. (eds.) 4th International Conference on Learning Representations, ICLR 2016, San Juan, Puerto Rico, 2–4 May 2016, Conference Track Proceedings (2016). http://arxiv.org/abs/1509.02971
16. Mahmood, A.R., Korenkevych, D., Vasan, G., Ma, W., Bergstra, J.: Benchmarking reinforcement learning algorithms on real-world robots. CoRR abs/1809.07731 (2018). http://arxiv.org/abs/1809.07731

17. Mankowitz, D.J., et al.: Robust reinforcement learning for continuous control with model misspecification. arXiv preprint arXiv:1906.07516 (2019)
18. Martins, F.B., Machado, M.G., Bassani, H.F., Braga, P., Barros, E.S.: rSoccer: a framework for studying reinforcement learning in small and very small size robot soccer. In: Alami, R., Biswas, J., Cakmak, M., Obst, O. (eds.) RoboCup 2021. LNCS (LNAI), vol. 13132, pp. 165–176. Springer, Cham (2022). https://doi.org/10.1007/978-3-030-98682-7_14
19. Mnih, V., et al.: Playing atari with deep reinforcement learning. CoRR abs/1312.5602 (2013). http://arxiv.org/abs/1312.5602
20. Mysore, S., Mabsout, B., Mancuso, R., Saenko, K.: Regularizing action policies for smooth control with reinforcement learning. CoRR abs/2012.06644 (2020). https://arxiv.org/abs/2012.06644
21. Nair, A.V., Pong, V., Dalal, M., Bahl, S., Lin, S., Levine, S.: Visual reinforcement learning with imagined goals. In: Advances in Neural Information Processing Systems, vol. 31 (2018)
22. Narasimhan, K., et al.: Feudal reinforcement learning. arXiv preprint arXiv:1811.03244 (2018)
23. Paszke, A., et al.: Pytorch: an imperative style, high-performance deep learning library (2019)
24. Perrusquía, A., Yu, W.: Continuous-time reinforcement learning for robust control under worst-case uncertainty. Int. J. Syst. Sci. **52**(4), 770–784 (2021)
25. Pong, V., Gu, S., Dalal, M., Levine, S.: Temporal difference models: model-free deep RL for model-based control. arXiv preprint arXiv:1802.09081 (2018)
26. Rahul, M., Chiddarwar, S.S.: Deep reinforcement learning with inverse jacobian based model-free path planning for deburring in complex industrial environment. J. Intell. Robot. Syst. **110**(1), 4 (2024)
27. Siegwart, R., Nourbakhsh, I.R., Scaramuzza, D.: Introduction to Autonomous Mobile Robots. MIT Press (2011)
28. Small Size League Technical Committee: Rules of the RoboCup Small Size League 2023. https://robocup-ssl.github.io/ssl-rules/sslrules.pdf
29. Sutton, R.S., Barto, A.G.: Reinforcement Learning: An Introduction. The MIT Press (2018)
30. Sutton, R.S., Precup, D.: Learning multi-level hierarchies with hindsight. In: International Conference on Machine Learning, pp. 861–868 (1998)

Holes and Clashes in Simulated Soccer: When a Real-Time Simulation System Meets Compute-Hungry Agents

Thomas Gabel(✉) and Eicke Godehardt

Faculty of Computer Science and Engineering, Frankfurt University of Applied Sciences, 60318 Frankfurt am Main, Germany
{tgabel,godehardt}@fb2.fra-uas.de

Abstract. The paper addresses the challenges and implications of (lacking) synchronization between agents in real-time multi-agent simulation systems. Based on two specific manifestations of mis-synchronization in 2D Soccer Simulation, termed holes and clashes, the paper makes two contributions: First, it provides a thorough historical review of the problem's existence and urgency of occurrence, covering the time from the very early beginnings of the RoboCup initiative in the late 1990s till today. Second, it presents the results of an exhaustive empirical study that reveals quantitatively what impact synchronization problems may have on the playing performance of a simulated soccer team.

1 Introduction

Our story begins with a match of our soccer simulation team FRA-UNIted against the team Tehran during RoboCup 2022. Using flip book-style, Fig. 1 visualizes one peculiar scene in which our team's agent #2 (blue) performed a failing tackle at $t = 4792$ in a situation where the tackle success probability was zero, whereas it would have been quite promising to perform that tackle a time step earlier, i.e. at $t = 4791$ where its chance of success would have been 84.6%.

Knowing that our team's calculation for the tackle decision is efficient and fail-safe, the observed behavior seemed miraculous. Inspecting the game's logfile revealed that #2 intended to perform its tackling at $t = 4791$, but that the corresponding command *arrived late*, i.e. not until the succeeding time step, followed by a turn command which was intended for $t = 4792$. That situation is called a *hole* (no command at $t = 4791$) with a subsequent *clash* of two commands, where the soccer simulator executes only the first of the commands arrived and disregards the latter.

Given that the situation took place near our team's penalty area and having agent #2 forced to ten cycles of inactivity after its failed tackle, the opponent team scored a goal. Challenged by this instance, we decided to research on the topic of holes and clashes in soccer simulation 2D in more depth. This paper presents our findings: In Sect. 2, we start by introducing some necessary

E. Barros et al. (Eds.): RoboCup 2024, LNAI 15570, pp. 80–92, 2025.
https://doi.org/10.1007/978-3-031-85859-8_7

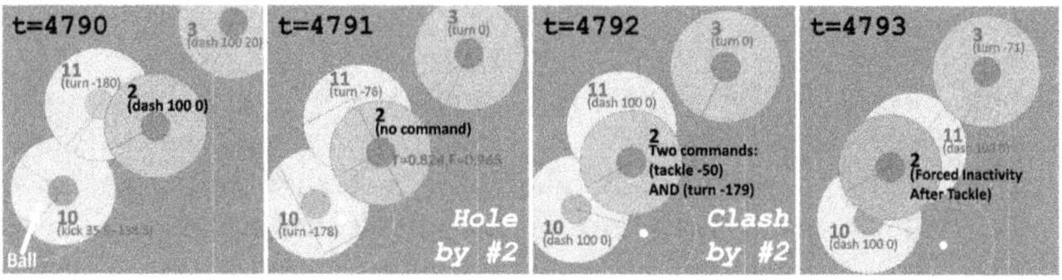

Fig. 1. Tracking the Sequence of Actions of Player #2: After a dash with 100% power into direction 0°, the rectangle inside player #2 at $t = 4791$ indicates a tackle success probability of $T = 0.824$. Instead of doing the tackle, however, #2 issues no command at all – a hole arises. In the subsequent cycle $t = 4792$, two commands from #2 arrive at the server – a clash. While the latter command is ignored by the server, the former one, a tackle into direction –50°, is executed. Though this would have been a good action at $t = 4791$, it is doomed to fail at $t = 4792$ since now the ball is already so distant that the tackle success probability is zero. After the tackle has failed, #2 is, according to the rules of the simulation, forced to 10 steps of inactivity starting at $t = 4793$ which allow the opponent players #10 and #11 to dribble ahead.

notation and discuss related work. Section 3 provides a historical review on the occurrence of holes and clashes covering the entire history of the RoboCup initiative. Finally, in Sect. 4 we analyze and show empirically how significant the impact of clashes is on a team's soccer-playing performance.

2 Foundations

In RoboCup's 2D Simulation League, two teams of simulated soccer-playing agents compete against one another using the Soccer Server [12] as real-time soccer simulation system which facilitates playing soccer in a client/server-based style. It simulates the playing field, communication, the environment and its dynamics, while the player clients connect to the server and send their intended actions once per simulation cycle to the server. The server takes all agents' actions into account, computes the subsequent world state and provides all agents with information about their environment via appropriate messages over UDP.

Decision making must be performed in real-time or, more precisely, in discrete time steps: Every 100ms the agents can execute a basic action and the world-state will change based on the individual actions of all players. The set of available actions include dash, turn, kick, tackle, and some other types of action each of which can be parameterized by some action or direction argument. Most importantly, only one action can be executed per time step which is why these basic actions must be combined cleverly in consecutive time steps in order to create "higher-level actions" like intercepting balls or doing dribblings, and that missing one of them in a sequence may hamper an agent's overall intentions.

2.1 Notation

In the early days of RoboCup's soccer simulation it was a challenge to assure synchronization between clients and server. On the one hand, the UDP protocol used for exchanging messages did not guarantee the arrival of some packet at the target implying that the agents' states were eventually not synchronized with the server cycle. On the other hand, games are run under real-time constraints and, depending on the particular hardware employed at a RoboCup tournament's venue, the agents' computational thirst at times exceeded the available resources often resulting in messages to arrive too late at the server's side.

Definition of Holes and Clashes
In its nowadays used setup, each agent is allowed to send a single body-related command to the Soccer Server in each time step. We define a *Hole* as a situation where no such body-related command has arrived at the Soccer Server from an agent. Thus, there can be up to eleven holes per team per step. And given that the default duration of a match is ten minutes (i.e. 6000 simulation cycles), there might be up to 66.000 holes per team per match.

Generally, the occurrence of a hole *may* indicate a potential problem, but it does not necessarily have to. While a hole certainly represents an agent's missed opportunity to act, there might also be times where it intentionally sends no command, if, for example, it sees no need to act.

A *Clash* denotes the situation where the Soccer Server receives more than only one body-related command within one simulation cycle from one specific agent. Variations in the speed with which a network packet containing a command is transmitted used to be an erstwhile cause for clashes. Today's main cause for clashes are compute-hungry agents or, stated differently, underpowered simulation machines. If an agent's calculations for determining its next action takes longer than 100ms and, thus, then the command cannot arrive at the Soccer Server within the current simulation cycle, but will so when the next one has already started. If, moreover, the agent's subsequent action arrives in time, two commands will have arrived within the time step's 100ms time window in which case the Soccer Server executes the former and discards the latter.

While a hole *may* indicate some problem, a *clash* certainly does so as one of the commands issued by the agent will be dropped. An overview of a selection of situations in which holes and clashes occur, is provide in Fig. 2. The flipbook example from RoboCup 2022 visualized in Fig. 1 represents a classic clash.

2.2 Related Work

Time synchronization in distributed systems is a prominent research topic, notably in the areas of (wireless) sensor networks, internet of things and distributed computing [10], but of course also in the domain of robotics and robotic soccer [8,13]. In Soccer Simulation 2D the task of synchronizing the soccer-playing clients with the server was a major challenge in its first decade and was discussed frequently in the literature. In [7], a comparative study is presented on

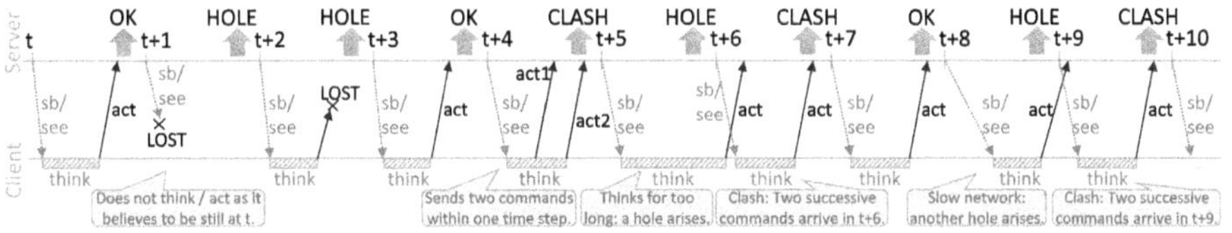

Fig. 2. The Soccer Server maintains the beat by sending "sense body" (sb) and "see" messages to clients at the beginning of a cycle. These messages are received sooner or later by an agent, depending on the network, or, in extreme cases, may get lost ($t+1$). When received, the agent takes this as the start of the next time step, incorporates the transmitted data into its world model, starts calculating its next action and, finally, sends it to the server. The required calculation (think) should be finished fast (i.e. in less than 100ms) to ensure that the act message arrives at the server within the current cycle. Holes occur when messages got lost ($t+2$) or when an agent's command arrives too late at the server, either because of a slow network ($t+8$) or due to too demanding computations by the agents, finished too late for the message to arrive at the server within the current cycle ($t+5$). Clashes may occur if it (erroneously) sends multiple commands within a single cycle ($t+4$, seldomly observed in practice). If, however, a clash occurs immediately after a hole (sometimes also called a "black hole"), then most certainly something "is wrong" with the network, the timing, the computational demands, or generally with the synchronization of server and clients ($t+6$ and $t+9$).

different synchronization mechanisms between players and the environment, differences among which are attributed to the occurrence of holes and clashes which are detected in a match's log file in a similar manner as we do. Different authors attempted to find counter strategies to get along with synchronization offsets [11] or took a formal approach to overcome the linear stochastic asynchronous control problem in simulated soccer [14].

In later years, the focus shifted away from holes and clashes mainly because synchronization became less of an issue due to matured network technology and faster machines. Besides, version 12 of the Soccer Server (2008) introduced a so-called synchronized viewing mode which, effectively, abolished the concept of asynchronously sending visual information and sense-body perception [7] since all teams switched to the new, simpler mode. A brief, yet general review of the development of the league and its changing foci can be found in [15].

Many discussions in the simulation community's veteran `robocup-sim` mailing list referred to holes and clashes, as well. Yet, the second-to-last thread in that list with reference to the topic at hand originates from 2007: ATHumboldt's former team leader R. Berger reports on an "abnormal number of holes and clashes in [...] qualification games", "found a correlation between the size of the team logfile that is recorded by the [league manager] script and the mentioned synchronization problems", and linked "these effects [to] logging to a non-local NFS-imported directory". Ever since, extensive logging by teams has been forbidden in general during tournaments. The last thread on that topic in the mentioned mailing list is from 2023 by the first author of this paper [9] about a noticeable reoccurrence of holes and clashes in 2022's RoboCup tournament which we summarize below. Finally, in preparation of the RoboCup 2023 tournament, a thorough analysis of the situation during recent tournaments has been conducted by O. Amini (Cyrus) and A. Rad and published online [3].

3 Historical Review

In the first years after the start of the RoboCup initiative in 1996, soccer simulation teams primarily fought with unreliable network connections between server and host machines and with delayed or dropped packets that resulted in both, holes and clashes. As network technology became more reliable, around 2001/02 the focus started to shift towards computational issues and the task of guaranteeing to cease an agent's inferencing and calculations within 100ms of time.

Methodology. We performed an extensive techno-archaeological study to investigate the question how many holes and clashes occurred during historic RoboCup events. For this, we retrieved all historical RoboCup world championships log files which are available online on `chaosscripting.net` (covering the very beginnings in 1996 and ceasing in 2017) as well as on `robocup.info` (covering competitions from 2004 till the very recent tournament in 2023) [1]. In total, we focused on the almost 3400 official world championships matches that took place on-site in the previous 28 years. We had to skip a few of the very early years where the log file format was subject to heavy changes and was preserved only in binary format where it would have meant enormous effort to analyze and interpret the artifacts of that time with today's tools.

In the first years our study covers, holes were prevalent (e.g. the 1996 tournament saw more than 1.6 million holes in total), but their frequency of occurrence diminished over the years (e.g. from 6.600 holes per team per match on average during RoboCup 2001 in Seattle to 32 during the RoboCup 2023 in Bordeaux, cf. Fig. 3, top). Yet, these numbers are a volatile basis for further analyses, since holes are counted, too, if some player erroneously disconnects or gets trapped in an endless loop due to a programming bug and, henceforth, sends no more commands at all. Therefore, all our further analyses focus exclusively on clashes occurring immediately after holes (aka black holes) as this combination hints most likely to problems in timing and synchronization of agents and the server.

Even when focusing on clashes solely, it is hard to draw general conclusions because team-internal problems and bugs might distort any statistic on clashes. We therefore conducted an analysis to identify outliers, i.e. teams whose binaries performed extraordinarily conspicuously in terms of producing holes and clashes, using the local outlier factor (LOF) algorithm [6]. Although it is not guaranteed that all teams with severe internal problems are identified this way, we empirically found that several "beknown" outliers were successfully filtered out using this approach, including Damavand'23 (heavy problems on the last tournament day), FRA-UNIted'18 (mistakenly left logging enabled in first rounds), or problems of Java-based teams like KickOffTUG'09 to name just a few.

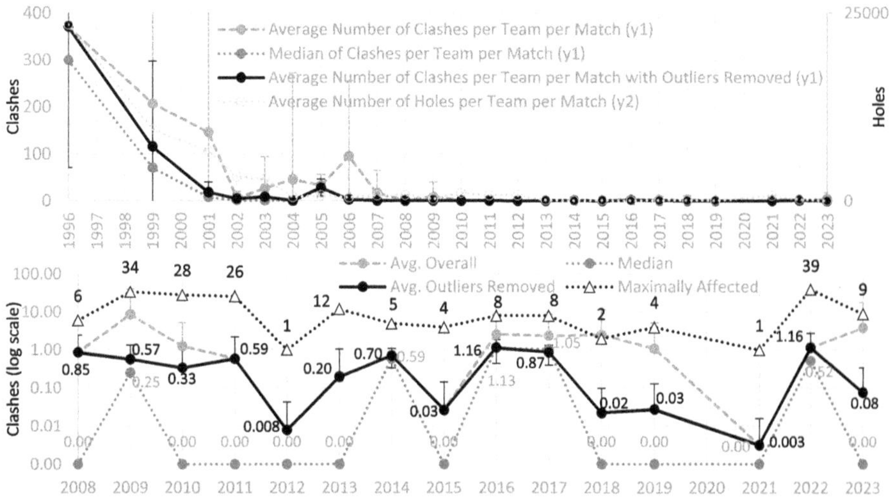

Fig. 3. Historical Review on the Occurrence of Holes and Clashes: The top chart witnesses that the average number of holes per team per match (secondary ordinate) has diminished substantially over the years. More relevantly, both charts highlight the development of clashes (black holes): The median and average number of clashes per team per match has seen a strong decline in RoboCup's first decade. However, the problem of their occurrence has never fully disappeared. Using a log scale ordinate, the bottom chart puts an emphasis on the more recent 15 years and also includes data on games that were maximally biased by clashes (after having removed outliers).

Discussion. Essentially, when observing multiple teams with a moderate number of clashes within one season's tournament, this is a strong indication that there is or, better, was a general issue with the competition set-up. Figure 3 (bottom) visualizes our findings: We report both, the number of clashes per team per match averaged over all teams (with and without outliers) as well as this value for the median team. Additionally, we have plotted the maximum number of clashes of the non-outlying teams over all matches – a value that can be used to confirm or reject the conclusion that competition results were, at least in part, biased by clashes. So, for example teams YuShan'22 and FRA-UNIted'22 had to face 4.6 and 4.2 clashes per match on average, but there were matches with as many as 39 or 32 clashes.

The 2022 RoboCup tournament stands out insofar as two of the considered measures, the average number of clashes per team per match, as well as the maximum amount of clashes in a game (outliers removed in either case), obtain an all time high in that year for the period of the past 15 years. Since also the median stands out within the previous six years, we will return to this point in a later section.

4 Interdependency of Clashes and Team Performance

While our discussion has so far concentrated only on the pure existence of holes and clashes, their impact on an ongoing match has been disregarded. Our example from the Introduction, however, illustrates the fact that there is some – in all likelihood negative – influence on the playing performance of a team. In what follows, we aim at quantifying that effect.

4.1 Relation Between Clashes and Agent CPU Utilization

Assuming a stable network connection and a constant access to compute power, the occurrence of clashes is essentially subject to the amount of computations made by an agent when determining its next action ("think" in Fig. 2). Each soccer simulation team applies very different algorithms and, henceforth, consumes a different amount of CPU power in each time step. If for some agent it holds $\delta = o + t + a > 100\,\mathrm{ms}$, where o is the time a see message sent by the Soccer Server needs to arrive at the agent, a is the time an act message sent by an agent needs to arrive at the server, and t the agent's "thinking" time, then a hole arises and a clash in the subsequent cycle becomes likely.

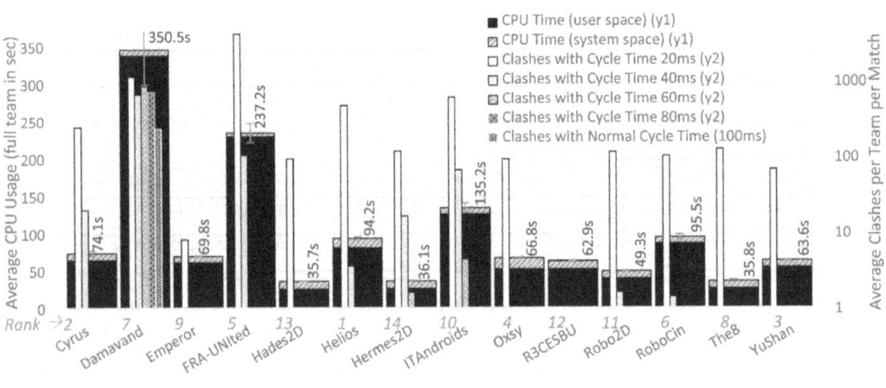

Fig. 4. CPU Utilization vs. Forced Clashes: The average summed CPU usage of an entire team during one match varies strongly across the 2023 SS2D teams (wide bars). We can easily provoke the emergence of clashes by artificially speeding up the timing of the Soccer Server, i.e. reducing the length of a single time step to $t_{step} < t_{default}$; the average number of clashes per team per match for $t_{step} \in \{20, \ldots, 100\}$ are plotted using narrow bars on the log-scale secondary y-axis.

Focusing on all teams participating in last year's world championships (2023), we determined the average required CPU utilization by the agents. Figure 4 shows the average summed CPU time that the ensemble of the processes of a team spent during a single match in total (default duration of a match is 600 s), executing code in user space (time spent by the processes executing their own code) plus the seconds executing code in system space, particularly the time spent by the Linux kernel on behalf of the process, such as handling system calls or executing kernel-level tasks[1]. The reported CPU times depend, of course, on the hardware and were produced by the teams playing on an x86_64 Intel Core i7-1165G7 CPU with 8 cores at 2.8 GHz with the Soccer Server's default timing of $t_{default} = 100\,\text{ms}$.

4.2 Modifications to the Soccer Server's Timing

Speeding up the simulation (tested up to a factor of five), we can easily provoke clashes since agents will frequently fail to ensure $\delta \leq t_{step}$. As expected, there is a strong correlation between the agent's general demand for compute power and the number of clashes they produce when faced with a sped-up simulation. The narrow bars in Fig. 4 show that 12 out of the 14 teams considered generate more than 100 clashes per team per match for $t_{step} = 20\,\text{ms}$, with this number dropping when t_{step} is increased, until for $t_{step} \geq 80$ no more clashes are observed (except for the already discussed outlier Damavand) on the hardware mentioned. Note that in this setting the machine's eight cores are shared across both teams, granting (with the mentioned exception) sufficient computational resources to any of the 25 processes involved in a match (2×11 players, 2 coaches, 1 server).

4.3 Limitations of Computational Resources

Another way to provoke the appearance of holes and clashes, is to artificially restrain the computational resources granted to the agents while sticking with the default timing. This can be achieved when running the mentioned 25 processes within Docker [5] containers each, as it is regularly done during RoboCup world championships since 2022 [4]. So, while we considered "bare metal" matches in the preceding sections, we now focus on Docker-based settings. In addition to that, we abandon the inspection of a full age group of teams, but focus on a single pair made up of our team FRA-UNIted and 2023's champion Helios [2].

4.3.1 Limiting the Number of Cores per Teams Using Docker, it is straightforward to specify on start-up which CPU cores can be utilized by which team. In preliminary experiments we verified, that zero holes and clashes occur for the considered match-up when both can utilize four or more cores. Using three cores, Helios never produces a clash, while FRA-UNIted starts doing so due to its higher computational demand (cf. Fig. 4).

Figure 5 summarizes what happens, if Helios remains to be allowed to exploit three cores, while FRA-UNIted's ensemble of 12 agents must share three, two, or only one core(s). As to be expected, the sheer amount of clashes increases with the restriction of computational resources. Using three cores we observe,

[1] As an interesting side note, we found that more compute does not necessarily imply a better ranking in the tournament, with both variables being only slightly negatively correlated (Pearson correlation of –0.228).

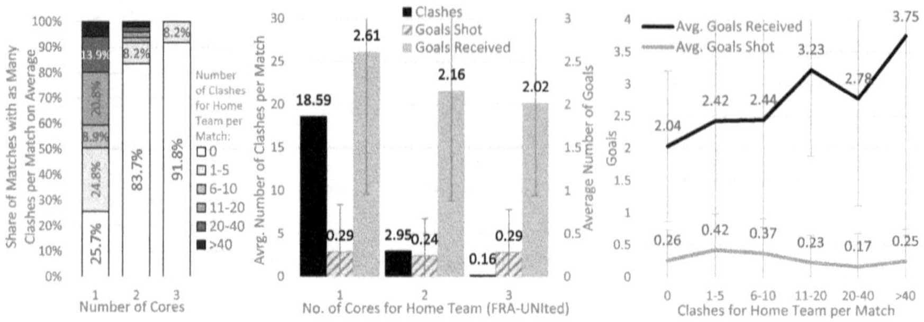

Fig. 5. Focusing on the fixture of the 2023 binary of FRA-UNIted (rank 5, dubbed home team) and champion Helios, the impact of reducing the available CPU cores for one team only (home team) is shown: Less than 3 cores imply more matches with a larger share of clashes (left) and an increased number of goals received (middle). Right: The average score of a match depends on the amount of clashes the home team had.

that there is no clash at all in 92% of the matches, while in the remaining 8% of the matches only 1–5 clashes occur. By contrast, sharing a single core only, merely a quarter of the matches remains clash-free, while in 40% of the matches more than 10 clashes occur. The middle part of the figure visualizes, how limiting the number of cores for one competitor (here: FRA-UNIted) affects its overall performance: When the number of cores is decreased, the amount of clashes occurring increases and simultaneously that team receives more goals against. This relation is made more transparent in the right part of the figure where matches with a certain number of clashes are grouped and average match results for those groups are plotted. Starting from ten clashes per match, a clear deterioration of the overall team performance must be acknowledged.

4.3.2 Constraining Core Usage of an Agent We performed a more fine-grained analysis of the impact of clashes on a team's playing strength by instructing the Docker containers that run a player process to consume only a *fraction* of a CPU core's computing power. Initial tests have shown that a CPU core share of 0.3 per agent yields zero holes/clashes for neither FRA-UNIted nor Helios on the mentioned hardware, which is fully in line with our previous observations since 11 players plus the coach would make up for up to 3.6 utilized cores per team.

In a series of test games, we varied the CPU power granted to either team's agents within $I = [0.01, 0.3]$ cores per agent and measured the number of holes and clashes as well as average scores. Figure 6's abscissa (left) lists all CPU share settings examined in the format as $x : y$ where $x \in I$ is the CPU share granted to any agent of the home team (FRA-UNIted) and $y \in I$ the share granted to any away team agent (Helios). The undistorted clash-free default setting is highlighted (gray background), left of which we have scenarios that thwarted the home team and right of which scenarios that impede the away team.

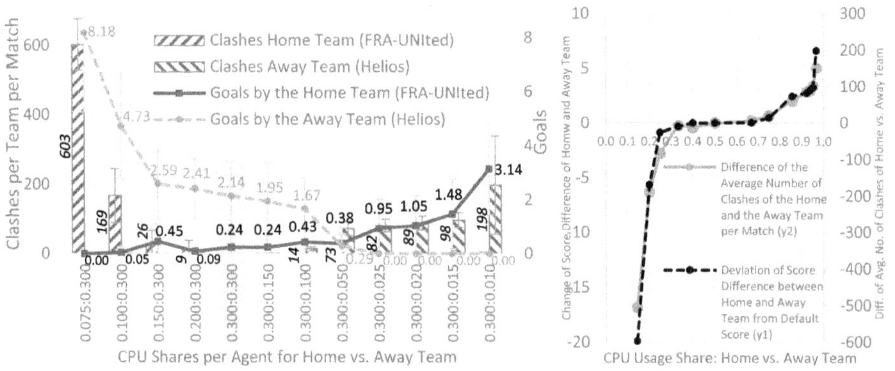

Fig. 6. The left chart shows how the balance of powers between the two considered teams changes w.r.t. clashes which we provoke by constraining the CPU core usage of a team's agents. The right chart takes an equal usage of compute power ($0.5 = \frac{0.3}{0.3+0.3}$) as baseline and opposes the difference of clashes (y_2) for both teams with changes in the score difference (y_1), highlighting the strong correlation between both.

Besides the expectable insight that holes and clashes do apparently compromise a team's performance in terms of goals scored/received, it is striking to realize that as little as about ten clashes per team per match yield a significant change of the average score and, moreover, that as little as approximately 70 clashes (0.30 : 0.05 setting) depose last year's the champion team making it play inferior to that year's rank 5 team. We emphasize that all the clash values we report refer to the overall number of clashes for the *entire team* per match (not per agent per match).

The right part of Fig. 6 stresses the relation between clashes and performance by visualizing the same data differently. The x-axis denotes the share of home and away team CPU usage shares – a value of 0.5 indicates a fair sharing of resources whereas a value of 0.2 means that the home team was granted only 20% of the overall computing power and the away team took 80%. The gray/black curves show the variations relative to the default setting ($0.3 : 0.3 \mathrel{\widehat{=}} 0.5$) in terms of for which team clashes occur as well as how, thus, the average score difference between home and away team changes. We observe a strong correlation between clashes and score difference shift (Pearson correlation of 0.74).

4.4 Competition-Like Set-Ups

Given that small amounts of clashes can distort soccer simulation games substantially, care must be taken with competition set-ups. To this end, the local organizers of the RoboCup 2023 soccer simulation 2D tournament did an excellent job by performing exhaustive analyses and tests in advance which are precisely documented [3] and which made the tournament a clash-free one.

This section addresses one factor that we judge to be a catalyst for the frequent re-occurrence of clashes in the preceding year's competition (2022, cf. Fig. 3), where we observed 10 matches with ≥ 10 clashes per team per match (maximum: 39). As a matter of fact, since the number of cores per team was 12 in that tournament and considering our findings from Sect. 4.1, it is obvious that, actually, no clashes should have occurred at all.

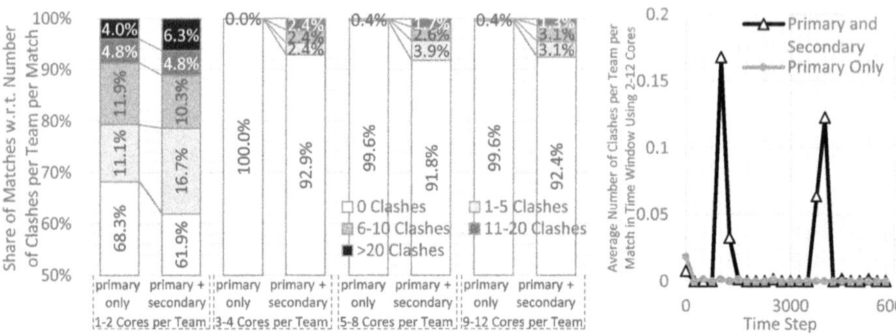

Fig. 7. Left: Running a single (primary) or two matches (primary and secondary) simultaneously on the same CPU cluster: We plot the share of clashes during primary matches (0, 1–5, 6–10, 11–20, or more than 20 clashes per team per match) and compare what happens, if that match runs solitarily vs. when some secondary match is started and run in separated Docker containers on the same CPU cluster. Apparently, more and more games become affected by clashes to varying degrees. Right: Throughout our experiments, two secondary matches of 500 time steps length were started. A first one within the first half of the primary match, the second one in the second half. The histogram shows the average number of clashes per team per match using a window size of 250 and reveals a clear link between clashes and the start-up phase of the secondary match. Note that this histogram covers only matches with three or more cores per team such that the lack of compute power as a cause for clashes is filtered out.

For an accurate replication of a competition site, we used a CPU cluster of 8× Dell PowerEdge R7525 with 32 cores at 3.0 GHz and executed randomly selected Docker-based matches using the officially released 2023 binaries using 25 full cores per match in Ubuntu 22.04. Alongside, however, we started and stopped random Docker-based matches whose containers were run on the remaining cores. We were not interested in the results or clashes of those secondary matches, but in the question whether the existence of a parallel match exerts some interference with the run of the primary one. Unfortunately, we had to corroborate that conjecture as Fig. 7 shows. While expectable when the primary match was distributed on a few cores only, we observe the emergence of a critical amount of clashes per team per match even when the computational load of the primary match is spread across a large number of cores (e.g. 9–12), as soon as a secondary match takes place. The right part of Fig. 7 reveals the cause. The start-up of a Docker-based match takes about 45 s and includes the launch of 25 Docker containers. We timed our experiments such that the primary match was superimposed with two such secondary matches (each one lasting 500 time steps) of which the first was launched in the first half and the second one in the second half time of the primary match. The corresponding peaks around $t = 1000$ and $t = 4000$ confirm the interference resulting from the fact that the operating system is in many instances occupied largely by the simultaneous start-up of the secondary match.

Inspecting the exact game starting times and time required for a Docker-based match start-up we could confirm that the clash that resulted in a missed tackling (cf. Fig. 1) took place exactly when on the same machine, despite using 25 separate CPU cores, the game between RoboCIn and HfutEngine was started simultaneously and, therefore, was very likely the result of the problems delineated in this section. Therefore, we conclude that running two or even more Docker-based soccer simulation 2D matches on a single machine, even when equipped with an abundance of cores, might distort games and ought to be disregarded or at least safeguarded by extensive tests in advance.

5 Conclusion

Establishing a reliable synchronization in real-time multi-agent systems is a delicate task. The Soccer Simulation 2D community as a whole met this challenge already in the late 1990s and thought it to be solved, with holes and clashes as main manifestations of mis-synchronization remaining as a side issue nowadays. The results of the analyses we presented in this paper show which significance the topic has had historically in the preceding 25 years of soccer simulation. In particular, our experiments revealed that, over the past few years, the topic has witnessed a clear resurgence in relevance.

Acknowledgements. This research has been supported by the German Federal Ministry of Education and Research under grant number 13FH027Kl1.

References

1. The RoboCup Online Archives of Soccer Simulation 2D Binaries and Logfiles. http://archive.robocup.info/Soccer/Simulation/2D/. https://chaosscripting.net/files/competitions/RoboCup/. Accessed June 2024
2. Akiyama, H., Nakashima, T., Hatakeyama, K., Fujikawa, T., Hishiki, A.: HELIOS2023: RoboCup 2023 soccer simulation 2D competition champion. In: RoboCup 2023: Robot World Cup XXVI. Springer, Heidelberg (2024). https://doi.org/10.1007/978-3-031-55015-7_32
3. Amini, O., Rad, A.: Unraveling the Mysteries of the Hole and Clash (Black Hole) Problem. https://www.rcss.dev/holesclashes. Accessed June 2024
4. Amini, O., Rad, A., Zare, N.: SS2D Docker Tournament Runner. https://github.com/RCSS-IR/SS2D-Docker-Tournament-Runner. Accessed June 2024
5. Boettiger, C.: An introduction to docker for reproducible research. ACM SIGOPS Oper. Syst. Rev. **49**(1), 71–79 (2015)
6. Breunig, M., Kriegel, H., Ng, R., Sander, J.: LOF: identifying density-based local outliers. In: Proceedings of the 2000 ACM SIGMOD International Conference on Management of Data, pp. 93–104. ACM, Dallas (2000)

7. Butler, M., Prokopenko, M., Howard, T.: Flexible synchronisation in robocup environment: a comparative analysis. In: RoboCup 2000, pp. 119–128 (2001)
8. Cavalcanti, L., Joaquim, R., Barros, E.: Optimized wireless control and telemetry network for mobile soccer robots. In: Alami, R., Biswas, J., Cakmak, M., Obst, O. (eds.) RoboCup 2021. LNCS (LNAI), vol. 13132, pp. 177–188. Springer, Cham (2022). https://doi.org/10.1007/978-3-030-98682-7_15
9. Gabel, T.: The RoboCup-sim Mailing List Archive. https://lists.robocup.org/archives/list/robocup-sim@lists.robocup.org/2023/5/. Accessed June 2024
10. Levesque, M., Tipper, D.: A survey of clock synchronization over packet-switched networks. IEEE Commun. Surv. Tutor. **18**(4), 2926–2947 (2016)
11. Montgomery, J.D., Mackworth, A.K.: Adaptive synchronisation for a robocup agent. In: Kaminka, G.A., Lima, P.U., Rojas, R. (eds.) RoboCup 2002. LNCS (LNAI), vol. 2752, pp. 135–149. Springer, Heidelberg (2003). https://doi.org/10.1007/978-3-540-45135-8_11
12. Noda, I., Matsubara, H., Hiraki, K., Frank, I.: Soccer server: a tool for research on multi-agent systems. Appl. Artif. Intell. **12**(2–3), 233–250 (1998)
13. Oliveira, L., Almeida, L., Santos, F.: A loose synchronisation protocol for managing RF ranging in mobile ad-hoc networks. In: Röfer, T., Mayer, N.M., Savage, J., Saranlı, U. (eds.) RoboCup 2011. LNCS (LNAI), vol. 7416, pp. 574–585. Springer, Heidelberg (2012). https://doi.org/10.1007/978-3-642-32060-6_49
14. Polani, D.: Towards a probabilistic asynchronous linear control theory. In: Polani, D., Browning, B., Bonarini, A., Yoshida, K. (eds.) RoboCup 2003. LNCS (LNAI), vol. 3020, pp. 720–728. Springer, Heidelberg (2004). https://doi.org/10.1007/978-3-540-25940-4_71
15. Prokopenko, M., Wang, P.: Disruptive innovations in robocup 2D soccer simulation league: from cyberoos'98 to gliders2016. In: Behnke, S., Sheh, R., Sarıel, S., Lee, D.D. (eds.) RoboCup 2016. LNCS (LNAI), vol. 9776, pp. 529–541. Springer, Cham (2017). https://doi.org/10.1007/978-3-319-68792-6_44

Lightweight Real-Time Gesture Recognition for Dynamic Soccer Referee Signals

Murray Owens(✉) and Timothy Wiley

School of Computing Technologies, RMIT University, Melbourne, Australia
s3783779@student.rmit.edu.au, timothy.wiley@rmit.edu.au
https://rmit.edu.au/ailab

Abstract. We present a lightweight keypoint-based Recurrent Neural Network (RNN) approach to the 2023 RoboCup Standard Platform League Visual Referee Challenge. The goal of the challenge is to classify 13 different static and dynamic referee gestures during a robotic soccer match. The developed solution must be lightweight and perform well from anywhere on the field. Multiple referees may be present on the field, with the distinguishing trait of the visual challenge referee being their red gloves. We use the lightweight Convolutional Neural Network pose detector BlazePose to extract the pose key-points. To isolate the referee in the frame, HSV colour segmentation is used to find red glove regions and mask unneeded sections of the image. A lightweight RNN is used to classify the sequence of keypoints. We compare the results of our work to previous solutions developed for the 2022 Visual Referee Challenge. Analysis on real-time testing shows our method achieves strong performance for all gestures on many different locations on the soccer field.

Keywords: Human Gesture Recognition · Recurrent Neural Networks

1 Introduction

With the increasing commonplace of robotic systems, human-robot interaction (HRI) has been an area of significant interest. These robotic systems need to be easily interactable for people to feel safe, comfortable and trusting. One important part of HRI is human gesture recognition. Body language is an integral part of human-to-human communication. For robots to better interact with humans they must be able to quickly and accurately recognize body language.

One application of this technology is in RoboCup. The goal of RoboCup is 'By the middle of the 21st century, a team of fully autonomous humanoid robot soccer players shall win a soccer game, complying with the official rules of FIFA, against the winner of the most recent World Cup'. In the official FIFA rules, referees use hand and arm signals to convey important match information to the

E. Barros et al. (Eds.): RoboCup 2024, LNAI 15570, pp. 93–103, 2025.
https://doi.org/10.1007/978-3-031-85859-8_8

players. To achieve the 2050 goal, robots must be able to quickly and accurately recognize and interpret these referee signals.

RoboCup Soccer Standard Platform League (SPL) is an international robotic soccer league. To facilitate achieving the 2050 goal, RoboCup Soccer SPL holds technical challenges to further research in specific areas of autonomous robotics. One challenge is the 'In-Game Visual Referee Challenge' [13], which tasks players to autonomously identify referee hand signals. There are three types of signals included: static single hand signals, static multi-hand signals and dynamic signals. In the 2022 and 2023 challenges, the referee wears red gloves to distinguish them from other assistants. The challenge takes place when the head referee whistles (kick-off, goal or end-of-play), after which they perform the selected gesture for 10 s. We define real-time as staying within the 10 s the referee performs the gesture. The full description of the 2023 Visual Referee Challenge is included in the RoboCup SPL 2023 Technical Challenge rule book [13]. The RoboCup Soccer SPL currently uses the SoftBank NAO V6 robot, which has limited processing power (Atom E3845 Quad core 1.91 GHz 4 GB DDR3). This limitation necessitates the development of lightweight solutions. Previous works made for the 2022 challenge [10,11,15] must be adapted to work with the new constraints introduced in the 2023 challenge: recognizing the gestures during a game scenario and distinguishing the dynamic multi-stage gestures.

We propose to use a quick color segmentation approach to locate the referee based on the position their red gloves. Unneeded regions of the image are masked to isolate the referee and reduce background noise. The lightweight person tracker BlazePose [3] is utilized to extract the keypoints of the referee's body and arms. A lightweight Recurrent Neural Network (RNN) is used to classify the referee gestures based on these keypoints quickly and accurately.

Our novel contribution for this work is the development of a lightweight solution to the 2023 RoboCup SPL Visual Referee Challenge that improves upon existing methods by allowing for accurate recognition of dynamic referee gestures from many different locations on the field.

2 Related Work

The RoboCup SPL Visual Referee Challenge is a problem that is within the field of human gesture and action recognition. In recent years Convolutional Neural Networks (CNN) have been the main approach for many computer vision tasks. Though CNNs are computationally heavy, lightweight CNNs have been used for object detection on the NAO [2,6]. OpenPose [4] is a CNN-based skeleton feature extractor used for human pose estimation. It calculates the pose of multiple people within an image using simultaneous confidence maps and part affinity fields. OpenPose has previously been utilized on NAO hardware for gesture recognition [7,14], which shows the possibility of using DNN skeletal feature extractors on the NAO's hardware. BlazePose [3] is a lightweight single-person tracker, which reduces its complexity compared to OpenPose. While less accurate than the previous architectures, it runs significantly faster making it ideal for real-time use on low-powered systems. We propose to use BlazePose to extract reasonably accurate skeleton features, while remaining efficient enough to run at real-time on the limited NAO hardware.

Recurrent neural networks (RNN) are a type of neural network that retain a memory of previous states. This memory makes RNNs useful for problems that involve sequential data. A major issue with RNNs is the exploding/vanishing gradient problem, which reduces their effectiveness for long sequences. Long short-term memory (LSTM) [8] is a type of RNN that uses memory cells with three gates: 'input', 'forget' and 'output'. These gates control how previous states affect the current state by limiting or forgetting them, diminishing the effect of the gradient problems. LSTM-based action recognition can be achieved on low power edge devices using a lightweight network [1]. However, a more efficient approach may be to use an RNN while decreasing the length of the image sequence. Gated Recurrent Units (GRUs) [5] are another type of RNN that use memory gates to avoid the vanishing gradient problem. GRUs use less gates and parameters than LSTMs, which reduce their computational complexity. This makes GRUs useful for real-time sequence classification on low-powered systems.

Several approaches were developed for 2022 RoboCup SPL Visual Referee Challenge. Lohani [10] found the position of the face using a quick cascade classifier and the red gloves using HSV color segmentation. These positions and their angles are used to classify the signal based on a set of heuristic rules. While this approach is faster than heavier CNNs [4,12], it cannot differentiate between gestures that have similar hand locations. This could be improved by using additional arm joints. Vermaas [15] utilized Blazepose [3] and a small multilayer perception consisting of one hidden layer with 256 neurons for classification. Like Lohani's approach, Vermaas used single image classification over multiple frames, making it unsuitable for classifying the dynamic gestures. Molnar [11] used a 2DCNN GRU which achieved a validation accuracy of 94.6%. These approaches were designed with the referee standing directly in front of the robot and must be adapted to recognize the gestures from anywhere on the field.

3 Methodology

Besides positioning, the only information that differentiates the challenge referee from assistants is their red gloves. By segmenting the red color in the image, we can obtain the location of the two red gloves and thus the referee.

3.1 Feature Extraction

Similar to Lohani's [10] approach, we first convert the image to HSV and extract red color regions. We then find the convex hull bounding box for the red regions. This bounding box is applied to the original image, masking all areas in the x-coordinate not covered by the bounding box. The y-coordinates are not used to segment the image as it could cut off the head or waist. This approach results in large unneeded sections of the background being removed.

Blazepose provides 33 keypoints, covering different positions on face, arms, torso and legs. The x and y values of each keypoint are divided by the width and height of the image respectively to normalize them between 0–1. Because the referee gestures are made using arm movements, we use the keypoints of the shoulders (11,12) elbows (13,14) wrists (15,16) and left hip (23). Vermaas [15] noted that additional keypoints from the face and legs helped to improve the accuracy of their approach. However, Lohani [10] was able to achieve a reasonable accuracy using a less complex rule classifier with only 4 features. To ensure that our approach is translation invariant, the distance to the right hip (keypoint 24) is used rather than image coordinate values. The hip was chosen as it is a static position and does not move while the referee is performing the signal.

Certain gestures, such as pushing free kick and goal, are distinguishable only by their elbow keypoint. The lightweight RNNs does not have the complexity to accurately distinguish between these gestures with just this keypoint. To help further improve the accuracy of these less complex networks two signals we include the angle between the shoulder, elbow and hand. The degrees are divided by 360 to normalize them between 0–1 to ensure that the values of the angles are within the same range as the Blazepose keypoints.

3.2 RNN Architecture

We use a 30 unit 2 layer RNN to classify the referee gestures. While lightweight and computationally/memory efficient, this smaller network has difficulty distinguishing the minute details between similar gestures. Because of this, an RNN with one 128 unit layer and one 64 unit layer is also developed. This larger network has more parameters and is slower, but is able to better distinguish the finer details between gestures. For both of these network sizes RNN, LSTM and GRU units are applied to develop a classifier that achieves a good accuracy while minimizing the number of parameters and inference time.

An important aspect of the recurrent network is the number of frames in the sequence. Having more can reduce the effect of individual incorrect skeletal estimates. However this introduces other issues, such as the vanishing/exploding gradient problem. Because of this we use a small sequence length. This allows us to limit the vanishing gradient problem. Additionally, processing less frames with the pose estimator decreases the amount of computational power needed. An issue with shorter sequence lengths is enough data to accurately classify the dynamic gestures may not be obtained. A minimum time of 3–5 s is needed to obtain the full signal information for the dynamic gestures. We propose to sample a smaller number of frames over a period of 5 s. A limitation with this approach is it requires minimum time of 5 s to classify even the static non-moving gestures. However, it ensures that enough information is obtained no matter whether the gesture is static or dynamic. The NAO V6 camera captures at 30fps, giving 150 total frames in 5 s. We experiment with different subsampling rates over this period of 15, 20, 25, 30 and 50 timesteps to determine the ideal number that balances accuracy and computation time.

Adam [9] is used to optimize weights during training. To allow the optimizer to settle at the optimal minimum, the learning rate is lowered to 0.0005. The batch size is set to 32 to increase training speed. To reduce overfitting we use dropout, regularization and early stopping. RNN layers have two types of dropout: input and recurrent. For the RNNs, both of these values are set to 0.1. For the GRUs and LSTMs the value is set to 0.2 to account for the increased complexity. We used L2 regularization with a value of 0.001. Early stopping with a patience of 50 is used to save the epoch with the best accuracy on the validation set.

4 Results

Our code is written in Python 3. OpenCV is used for the color segmentation and masking. The networks are developed using the TensorFlow Keras API. The models are converted to OnnxRuntime for inference on the NAO V6 CPU (Atom E3845 Quad core 1.91 GHz 4 GB DDR3).

We created our own data set for the purpose of training and evaluating the model. The training set consists of 449 videos consisting of 2 different people performing the gestures, taken from different positions on the RoboCup field such as the midfield, corners and penalty marks. These videos include different lighting conditions. By horizontally mirroring these sequences, the amount of data is doubled to 898 sequences. Additionally, we collected 65 videos for validation. This validation set is comprised of 3 different people who are not present in the training set, to ensure the model is accurate with different body types. These are mirrored to get a total of 130 validation videos. To train and evaluate the classifier we need the true value of the body keypoints. For each sequence the keypoints for 150–160 frames are collected. Manually labelling the keypoints for each frame in all 1028 sequences is difficult and time consuming. The key-point labelling process is automated with Blazepose Heavy [3].

The color segmentation and masking approach is able to quickly remove unwanted sections of the image. Shown in Fig. 1 the color segmentation locates the two referee gloves and masks the rest of the image, isolating the referee. The method runs quickly on the NAO hardware with an average processing time of 9.1ms. One limitation of this approach is that red color sections in the background expand the visible section of the image, increasing the amount of background noise. However, this is a reasonable trade-off given the speed of the approach. Another limitation is that the masking can cut sections of the referee during the goal gestures when viewing the referee at an angle. This also occurs in extreme lighting conditions, where the color segmentation is unable to locate one or both of the gloves. To ensure that the referee is not cutoff, a 100 pixel buffer is added to the visible zone. Though this increases the noise in the background, it ensures that the referee is always present in the frame. Despite the limitations, this approach is still a quick and sufficient method of isolating the referee.

We evaluate the addition of the arm angles to the 30-unit and 128-64 unit architectures. With a smaller number of parameters the 30-unit RNN network

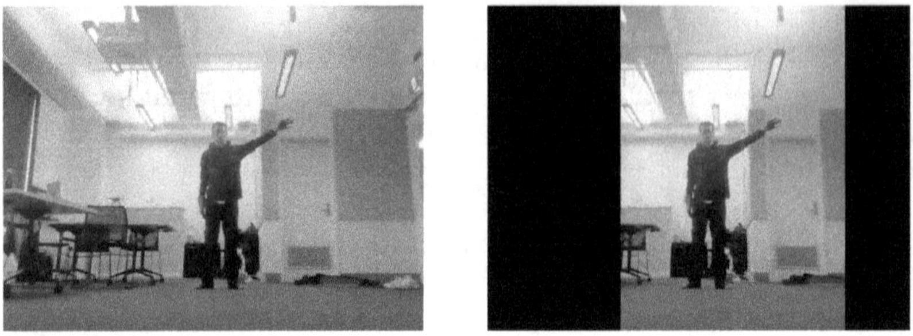

(a) Before color segmentation and masking

(b) After color segmentation and masking

Fig. 1. Example to demonstrate red colour segmentation and masking. 100-pixel margin is applied to prevent the referee being cut off in certain gestures. (Color figure online)

is unable to distinguish the minute difference between the goal and pushing free kick gestures, achieving an accuracy of only 30% on both the goal signals. The addition of the arm angles increases the accuracy of both the goal poses increases to 70%. The 128-64 unit RNN without the arm angle features achieved an accuracy of 97%. The increased complexity allows it to accurately distinguish the goal and pushing free kick gesture without the extra arm angle features. Because of this, we use the arm angles only into the 30-unit networks.

Tables 1a and 1b show the accuracy each sequence length with the different architectures. The highest scoring architecture for the 30 unit network is the 20 length LSTM with an F1 score of 0.95. The highest scoring architecture for the 128/64 unit network is the 20 length RNN with an F1 score of 0.96. These results show that a sequence length of 20 is the ideal length, since it has the highest accuracy while also requiring less frames to be processed.

Table 1. F1 score of different sequence lengths for RNN, LSTM and GRU

(a) 30 unit

Architecture	15	20	25	30	50
RNN	0.86	0.88	0.88	0.91	0.81
LSTM	0.92	0.95	0.89	0.90	0.91
GRU	0.87	0.92	0.89	0.89	0.92

(b) 128-64 unit

Architecture	15	20	25	30	50
RNN	0.93	0.96	0.92	0.91	0.77
LSTM	0.89	0.90	0.94	0.92	0.95
GRU	0.95	0.95	0.92	0.95	0.95

Tables 2a and 2b show the inference run-time of the different architectures. Our LSTM and GRU architectures are significantly slower than the RNN architectures, taking 3×–4× times longer to predict. From the highest scoring architectures mentioned previously, the 30 unit 20 length LSTM has an inference speed of 10.3 ms while the 128/64 unit 20 length RNN has a speed of only 4.5 ms

Table 2. Inference time of sequence lengths for architectures on NAO (ms)

(a) 30 unit

Architecture	15	20	25	30	50
RNN	2.5	3.3	4.0	5.0	8.4
LSTM	7.6	10.3	12.4	15.0	25.0
GRU	8.1	10.9	13.3	16.2	26.8

(b) 128-64 unit

Architecture	15	20	25	30	50
RNN	3.4	4.5	5.5	6.6	10.7
LSTM	13.0	17.5	21.4	25.8	42.0
GRU	11.8	16.7	20.4	23.9	40.0

To evaluate our approach, we simulate real game conditions with our two best architectures. The first architecture is the 128/64 unit RNN model. It achieved an accuracy of 95.7% on the training set, and achieved the highest accuracy of all the architectures on the validation set with an accuracy of 96.9%. The second architecture is the smaller 30 unit LSTM. This model achieved an accuracy of 98.6% on the training set and 94.6% on the validation set. These two architectures are tested to determine which best balances speed and accuracy.

4.1 Simulated Game Testing

Evaluation is done on the NAO V6 robot. OpenCV is used to capture video from the NAO. The initial image size is 640×480, and is downsampled to 256×256. We follow a similar procedure to the RoboCup SPL challenge [13]. First, the visual referee code is run on the NAO robot. After 5 s the referee performs the chosen gesture, which is then held for 10 s. This procedure is repeated on different locations on the field, shown in Fig. 2. These positions give a good variety of distances and angles from the referee. A test directly in front of the referee is not performed, as the NAO V6 camera is unable to capture the entire referee. We also test our solution on the four corners of the field positions (shown in Fig. 2 as black dots), to evaluate difficult positions. The results for these extreme positions are separated from the other field positions. Each gesture is performed twice for each position to ensure a comprehensive evaluation.

Figure 3 shows the results for simulated game testing on both architectures. The 128/64 unit RNN achieves an overall accuracy of 93%. One issue with the architecture is its lower accuracy when classifying the goal red gesture, having an accuracy of 55%. These incorrect predictions were made from the 3 midfield positions. This is due to the removal of the arm angle features, which makes it difficult to distinguish the goal red and pushing free kick gestures. The results from other gestures and positions show good accuracy. The 30 unit LSTM achieves an accuracy of 92.66%. The LSTM model with arm angles can accurately distinguish the goal and pushing free kick gestures. However, the red goal kick gesture has an accuracy of 68% due to difficulty recognizing it when positioned on the right half of the field. In terms of speed, the RNN is slightly faster than the LSTM with average runtimes of 5.35 and 5.61 s respectively.

We compare our approach to other methods for the 2022 Visual Referee Challenge. For the previous approaches, the runtime is measured as the time needed

Fig. 2. Positions for simulated game testing. The blue dot represents the location of the referee. The red and black dots represent the locations of the robot. The black dots represent the extreme corner positions. (Color figure online)

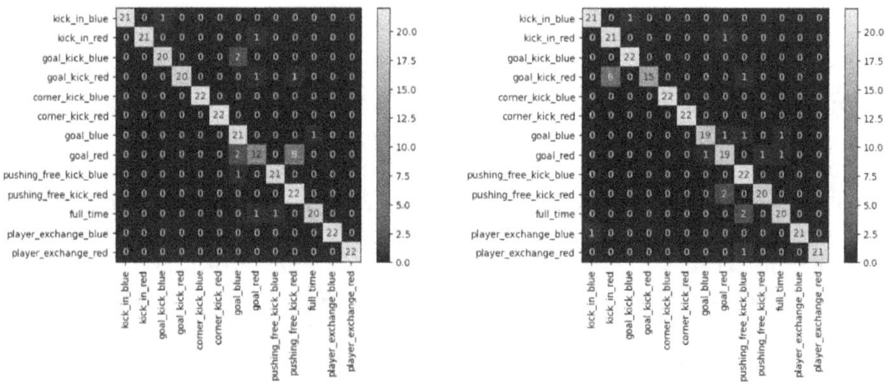

(a) 128/64 unit RNN

(b) 30 unit LSTM

Fig. 3. Comparison of our proposed 128/64 RNN and 30 unit LSTM architecture.

to process and predict a single image. Lohani's hybrid approach took 0.38 s on average to classify a single image. While useful for quickly recognizing the static gestures, it is less useful for the dynamic gestures which require additional time to gain enough information to classify them. We achieved an accuracy of 93% for both RNN models, significantly greater than the hybrid's 77% accuracy. Lohani's highest accuracy approach, utilizing Stacked Hourglass [12], achieved an accuracy of 93%. The Stacked HG takes 5.27 s to process a single image while ours take 5.35 s to process a sequence of 20 images. While we achieved slightly less accuracy than Vermaas [15] and Molnar [11], who reportedly achieved 100% and 95% accuracy in the 2022 challenge, these methods were designed for the 2022 Visual Challenge, which is an easier task because it took place on one specific position on the field and did not include the dynamic gestures. Thus, our approach achieves similar results in a more challenging environment (Table 3).

Table 3. Comparison to Lohani's [10] Visual Referee approaches.

Model	Runtime (seconds)	Accuracy
Hybrid [10]	0.38[a]	0.77
OpenPose [10]	7.30[a]	0.90
Stacked HG [10]	5.27[a]	0.93
Our BP RNN	**5.35**[b]	**0.93**
Our BP LSTM	**5.61**[b]	**0.93**

[a]Processing time on a single image
[b]Processing time on a sequence of 20 images

Table 4 shows the F1 scores for the extreme corner positions. Our approach achieves fairly good results for the bottom corners, apart from our larger RNN which achieves an F1 score of 0.62 on the bottom left corner. The performance on the top corners is poor for both models. The main difficulty from this position is accurately detecting the referee's pose from the referee's side where parts of the body are obscured. However, this a fair trade-off to achieve real-time classification that is accurate in many other positions on the field.

Table 4. F1-score for the difficult corner positions.

Architecture	Bottom-Left	Bottom-Right	Top-Left	Top-Right
128/64 RNN	0.62	1.00	0.35	0.15
30/30 LSTM	0.92	0.96	0.52	0.16

5 Conclusion

In this paper, we proposed a lightweight RNN solution the 2023 RoboCup SPL Visual Referee Challenge. A combined color segmentation and lightweight CNN pose detector is used to quickly locate the challenge referee and extract their skeletal features, then using an a lightweight RNN to classify a sequence of images sampled over a period of 4–5 s. Experiments under game conditions show that our proposed solution is accurate and is quick enough to run in real-time on the NAO hardware. It has a strong performance on most locations on the field. Our solution is easily able to distinguish the static kick-in gestures from the dynamic player-exchange gestures. Though slower than the previous hybrid method [10], the additional time is needed to gain enough information to classify the dynamic signals. Future work can be done improve our approach. Firstly, both the proposed models have difficultly distinguishing similar gestures at certain angles. Secondly, the red gloves may not be used in future competitions, requiring the development of a new method of segmenting the referee.

References

1. Agarwal, P., Alam, M.: A lightweight deep learning model for human activity recognition on edge devices. In: International Conference on Computational Intelligence and Data Science (2019). https://doi.org/10.1016/j.procs.2020.03.289
2. Albani, D., Youssef, A., Suriani, V., Nardi, D., Bloisi, D.D.: A deep learning approach for object recognition with NAO soccer robots. In: Behnke, S., Sheh, R., Sarıel, S., Lee, D.D. (eds.) RoboCup 2016. LNCS (LNAI), vol. 9776, pp. 392–403. Springer, Cham (2017). https://doi.org/10.1007/978-3-319-68792-6_33
3. Bazarevsky, V., Grishchenko, I., Raveendran, K., Zhu, T., Zhang, F., Grundmann, M.: Blazepose: on-device real-time body pose tracking (2020). https://arxiv.org/abs/2006.10204
4. Cao, Z., Hidalgo, G., Simon, T., Wei, S.E., Sheikh, Y.: Openpose: realtime multi-person 2d pose estimation using part affinity fields. IEEE Trans. Pattern Anal. Mach. Intell. (2019). https://doi.org/10.1109/TPAMI.2019.2929257
5. Cho, K., Merrienboer, B., Bahdanau, D., Benigo, Y.: On the properties of neural machine translation: encoder-decoder approaches. In: Proceedings of SSST-8, Eighth Workshop on Syntax, Semantics and Structure in Statistical Translation (2014). https://doi.org/10.3115/v1/W14-4012
6. Cruz, N., Lobos-Tsunekawa, K., Ruiz-del-Solar, J.: Using convolutional neural networks in robots with limited computational resources: detecting NAO robots while playing soccer. In: Akiyama, H., Obst, O., Sammut, C., Tonidandel, F. (eds.) RoboCup 2017. LNCS (LNAI), vol. 11175, pp. 19–30. Springer, Cham (2018). https://doi.org/10.1007/978-3-030-00308-1_2
7. Di Giambattista, V., Fawakherji, M., Suriani, V., Bloisi, D.D., Nardi, D.: On field gesture-based robot-to-robot communication with NAO soccer players. In: Chalup, S., Niemueller, T., Suthakorn, J., Williams, M.-A. (eds.) RoboCup 2019. LNCS (LNAI), vol. 11531, pp. 367–375. Springer, Cham (2019). https://doi.org/10.1007/978-3-030-35699-6_28
8. Hochreiter, S., Schmidhuber, J.: Long short-term memory. Neural Comput. **9**(8), 1735–1780 (1997). https://doi.org/10.1162/neco.1997.9.8.1735
9. Kingma, D., Ba, J.: Adam: a method for stochastic optimization (2014). https://arxiv.org/abs/1412.6980
10. Lohani, P., Wiley, T.: Hybrid methods for real-time video sequence identification of human soccer referee signals. In: RoboCup 2023: Robot World Cup XXVI (2023). https://doi.org/10.1007/978-3-031-55015-7_12
11. Molnar, L.: Visual Referee Detection on Nao Robots for RoboCup SPL 2022. Bachelor's thesis, Swiss Federal Institute of Technology Zurich, Zurich (2022)
12. Newell, A., Yang, K., Deng, J.: Stacked hourglass networks for human pose estimation. In: Leibe, B., Matas, J., Sebe, N., Welling, M. (eds.) ECCV 2016. LNCS, vol. 9912, pp. 483–499. Springer, Cham (2016). https://doi.org/10.1007/978-3-319-46484-8_29
13. RoboCup: Robocup standard platform league (nao) technical challenges (2023). https://spl.robocup.org/wp-content/uploads/SPL-Challenges-2023.pdf. Accessed 7 Mar 2023

14. Schneider, P., Memmesheimer, R., Kramer, I., Paulus, D.: Gesture recognition in RGB videos using human body keypoints and dynamic time warping. In: Chalup, S., Niemueller, T., Suthakorn, J., Williams, M.-A. (eds.) RoboCup 2019. LNCS (LNAI), vol. 11531, pp. 281–293. Springer, Cham (2019). https://doi.org/10.1007/978-3-030-35699-6_22
15. Vermaas, D.: RoboCup The Visual Referee Challenge. Bachelor's thesis, University of Amsterdam, Amsterdam (2022)

Quantized Neural Networks for Ball Detection on the NAO Robot: An Optimized Implementation

Felix Thielke[1,2](✉)

[1] University of Bremen, Bremen, Germany
fthielke@uni-bremen.de
[2] Fraunhofer MEVIS, Bremen, Germany

Abstract. Improving the latency of neural networks on low-end hardware such as the NAO robot used in the RoboCup Standard Platform league has been a relevant research topic since deep learning models can be effectively used for real-time computer vision. This paper focuses on optimizing the implementation of quantized neural networks (QNNs) for ball detection on the NAO V6 robot. The goal is to improve inference speed and reduce memory usage.

A direct quantization scheme is employed, where weights and activations are represented as 8-bit integers. SIMD instructions available on the NAO's processor architecture are utilized for efficient calculations. Quantization-aware training is used to train the models, and their inference is realized via automatically generated assembly code.

The quantized models achieve a speedup of approximately 2× compared to float models. However, there is a slight decrease in model performance, as indicated by lower AUROC scores and mean ball IoU values for the quantized models. Paired t-tests confirm the statistical significance of the differences between float and quantized models.

The optimized implementation of QNNs for ball detection on the NAO robot provides a practical speedup while maintaining reasonable model performance, however choosing simpler architectures leads to a better trade-off between latency and performance than quantization. Future work could involve comparing the results with the XNOR-Net for ball detection on the NAO and exploring the proposed approach in other RoboCup applications. All code used in the experiments is publicly available at https://github.com/fthielke/NaoQNN.

Keywords: neural network quantization · ball detection · open source

1 Introduction

Since the breakthrough of artificial neural networks as tools for solving many computer vision tasks, they have been applied to many real-world applications, including mobile robotics. In the RoboCup competitions, many real-time vision

E. Barros et al. (Eds.): RoboCup 2024, LNAI 15570, pp. 104–115, 2025.
https://doi.org/10.1007/978-3-031-85859-8_9

tasks are now solved using neural networks, but most solutions face the problem of limited computational resources.

To improve the inference speed and reduce the memory usage, it has been proposed to quantize the weights and activations of neural networks to integers with low bit widths. Different methods for the quantization of operations in neural networks have been proposed. A direct approach is to map all network weights to the range of an integer with a specified bit width by defining an affine mapping of integer values to floating point values using scale and zero-point parameters [4]. As an advantage of this method, existing models trained with floating point numbers can be converted to this quantized format after training, however it is also possible to train the model in a quantization-aware fashion [5]. In the latter case, it is possible to improve the model performance by making the model aware of the step-wise mapping to integers by applying a cascade of sigmoid functions to all activations in the architecture [18].

An end to end method for training neural networks with low bit widths was proposed in the form of the XNOR-Net [9]. This approach replaces all matrix multiplications in a neural network architecture with two operations, XNOR and bitcount (also called popcount). Using the XNOR-Net, it is possible to achieve speedups even when quantizing models to bit widths smaller than the register size of vector registers—weights typically use between 1 and 4 bits—while only suffering small performance decreases compared to models using 32-bit floating point (float32) operations [8].

The aim of this work is to apply quantization to improve the performance of neural networks running on the NAO robot used in the RoboCup Standard Platform league. While quantization has been successfully applied in multiple domains, to the best of the author's knowledge none of the available implementations are written with the hardware of the NAO V6 in mind: a 64-bit Intel Atom CPU of the Silvermont generation. As shown by Yao et al. for an object detection model, using a generic implementation of QNNs (as implemented in TensorFlow Lite[1]) can even lead to worse performance than the corresponding models using floating-point numbers [19]. Instead, the target platforms of existing works are FPGAs [16], ARM processors using the NEON instruction set [4,8], NVIDIA GPUs [15] and Intel Xeon processors using the AVX-512 VNNI instruction set extensions [10]. Common to all mentioned specialized implementations is the use of SIMD instructions, which allow to perform calculations with vectors instead of scalar operands. On the NAO's processor, SIMD instructions from the SSE instruction sets up to SSE4.2 are available [3].

Using quantized neural networks (QNNs) on NAO robots has already been explored by previous works, however none of them could empirically show a large speedup resulting from quantizing small neural networks feasible for real-time execution compared to an optimized floating-point implementation. Using a neural network for detecting whether image patches contain balls, O'Keeffe and Villing systematically evaluated the model performance of different convolutional neural network (CNN) architectures when converted to XNOR-Nets [6,7]. While

[1] https://www.tensorflow.org/lite/.

they calculated a theoretical speedup of up to 40×, they did not provide an actual implementation of the inference optimized for the NAO and thus could not perform any empirical evaluation.

Cruz et al. evaluated the use of XNOR-Nets for a robot detection model based on an implementation that does not use SIMD instructions and found that they could achieve large speedup factors (up to 11×) for large models [1]. However, for the only architecture fast enough to be used in a real-time application (< 1 ms), the implementation using 32-bit floating point numbers turned out to be slightly faster than the XNOR-Net version.

Yan et al. achieved an inference speedup of 2.46× compared to a basic floating-point implementation by replacing the weights of convolutional layers in their model architecture with only -1 and 1 and using an optimized implementation using SSE instructions [17].

As this work's main contribution, an implementation of QNN training and inference optimized for the NAO V6 robot is presented and compared with respect to its performance and latency to the CompiledNN library [14], which currently provides the fastest inference time for many small floating point models on NAO robots [19]. Ball detection is chosen as the application used in this work: since the problem of detecting balls in image patches within acceptable time is already solved, the focus can be placed on improving inference speed while maintaining model performance.

2 Materials and Methods

2.1 Model Architectures

As a baseline model for ball detection, the one currently employed by the team B-Human is used, which was published as part of their 2019 code release [11]. This model consists of three parts: an encoder, a classification head to decide whether the input patch contains a ball and a regression head which predicts the relative position of the ball in the input patch [12].

Figure 1 shows the four different variants of the encoder architecture that are used for experiments: the original architecture (a) as well as three variants which aim to improve the inference time. The first variant is an encoder where the convolutional layers do not use zero-padding (b), then in the second additionally all convolutional blocks are replaced with separable convolutions [13] (c) and the third variant the spatial resolution is reduced as early as possible via a 4×4 strided convolution in the first layer (d).

For the decoder part containing the classification and regression heads, the original architecture as shown in Fig. 2 is used, with the minor difference that the classification output uses two neurons and a Softmax activation instead of one neuron with a Sigmoid activation.

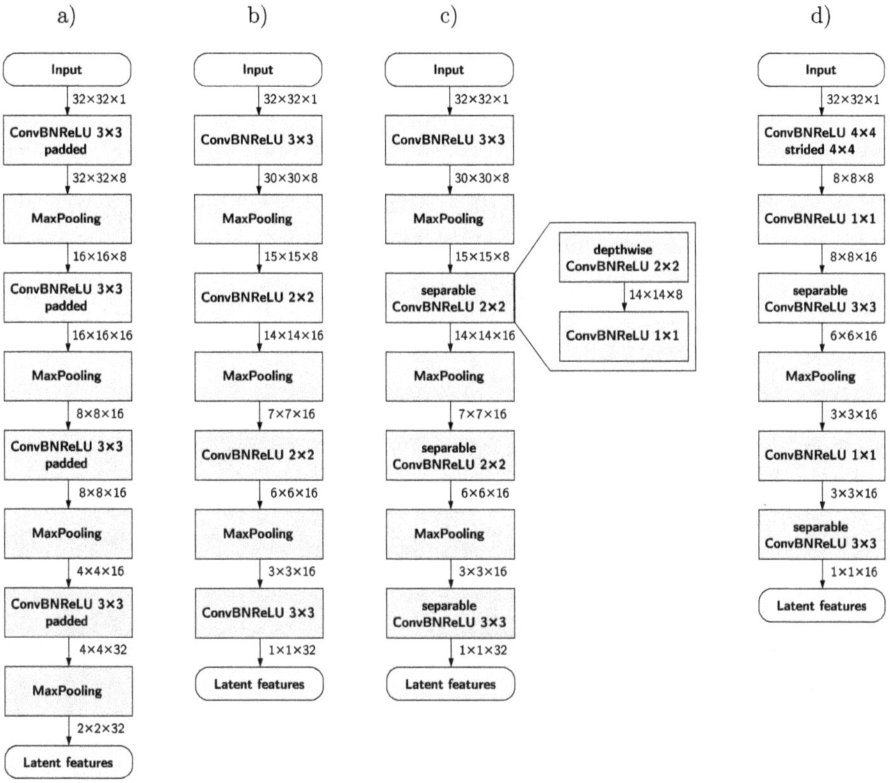

Fig. 1. Encoder architectures used in the experiments.

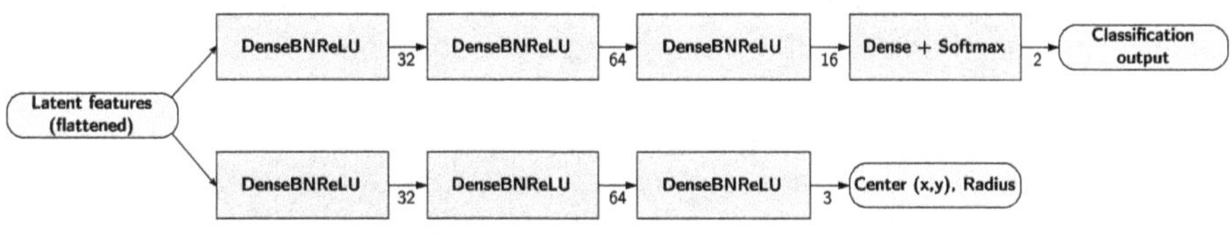

Fig. 2. Decoder architecture used in the experiments.

2.2 Data

For training models, the same public dataset with which the original model was trained is used.[2] This dataset consists of 139 509 gray-scale patches of size 32×32 px which were extracted from NAO camera images recorded during both real and simulated soccer games. 26 265 (18.8 %) of these patches contain a ball, which is annotated with its center and radius within the patch.

Since the data split of the original training is not documented, a new random dataset split was created such that half of the validation and test sets consist

[2] https://b-human.informatik.uni-bremen.de/public/datasets/b-alls-2019/.

of positive samples, resulting in the subsets shown in Table 1. As there is also no documentation regarding which patches stem from which robots and games, samples from the different subsets will most likely be correlated and not fully independent. Therefore all evaluation performed on the test set can only measure how well models generalize to data not seen during training, but not how well the models generalize to unseen data in general. This circumstance is acceptable for comparing different model architectures in the context of this work, but has to be kept in mind for productive use of the resulting models.

Table 1. Split of the data into training, validation and test sets. Here, positive examples are patches that contain a ball.

	Training set	Validation set	Test set
Positive examples	22 326	1 313	2 626
Negative examples	109 305	1 313	2 626
Total	131 631	2 626	5 252

2.3 Quantization Method

A direct quantization scheme is chosen for the experiments, where all representations of weights and activations fit into 8-bit integer registers. Most other works using direct quantization use 32-bit integer registers for accumulating the results of the point-wise multiplications [4,10,20]. In case of the Silvermont's 128-bit SIMD registers, this means that the multiplication steps can operate on 16 values at once, but the following accumulation steps only operate on 4 values at once. Since the number of accumulation steps scale logarithmically with the filters, this is not a problem for large models. However, for small numbers of filters as employed in the neural network architectures in this work, using 32-bit accumulators effectively adds a bottleneck to the inference. Therefore, in this work 16-bit (`int16`) registers are used for accumulation instead.

While it is common to use either signed (`int8`) or unsigned (`uint8`) integers for both weights and activations [5], there is no SIMD instruction in the Silvermont architecture for `uint8`/`uint8` or `int8`/`int8` multiplication. Instead, the SSSE3 instruction PMADDUBSW is particularly suited for the task, as it performs 16 multiplications and 8 additions at once with low latency [2], but requires either weights or activations to be `int8` while the other is `uint8`.

By choosing to use signed integers for weights and defining their zero-point to be zero, some calculations can be saved at runtime. To avoid overflows from only having 16-bit accumulators, all weights are clamped such that they only use the lower 6 bits of their registers. Since weights are signed, `uint8` has to be used for activations. This circumstance also provides an advantage for the resulting latency: by packing the accumulated 16-bit results into uint8 registers with saturation (using the PACKUSWB instruction), the ReLU activation function is effectively applied at the same time at no additional cost.

Using the presented quantization scheme, the inference step for all combinations of convolutional or fully-connected layers with optional batch normalization and a ReLU activation function can then be realized as shown in Fig. 3. All of these steps can be efficiently implemented using SIMD instructions available on the NAO's processor architecture. The remaining layers in the chosen architecture are MaxPooling layers, which can be directly implemented for the uint8 activations, and the final Softmax/Sigmoid layers, which are not necessarily needed for inference: since these functions are strictly monotonic, a threshold for binary classification can also directly be applied to their input. For the regression outputs of the ball model, which shall predict the ball size and offset within the patch, a fixed linear mapping from the uint8 outputs in the range [0, 255] to the expected output ranges from the training data is defined.

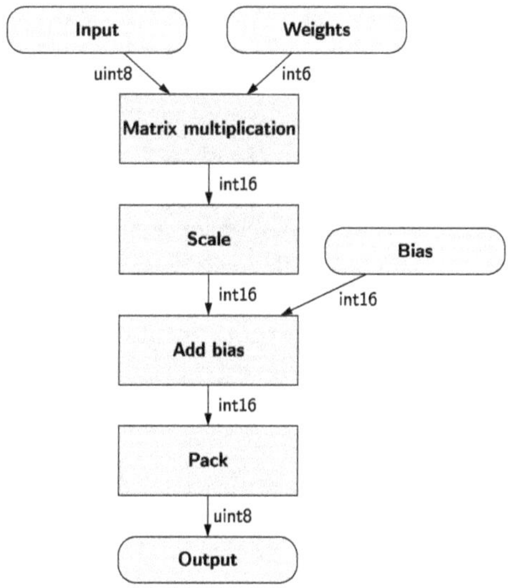

Fig. 3. The inference steps under the proposed quantization scheme for a neural network building block consisting of a convolutional or fully-connected layer, an optional batch normalization layer and a ReLU activation function.

Quantized models in this work are trained using a quantization-aware training setup in which at training time, model parameters are stored as float32 but the quantization step is already performed during the forward pass and taken into account when calculating gradients during backpropagation.

2.4 Training Configuration

For each of the four architectures, both standard floating-point trainings and quantization-aware trainings under the proposed quantization scheme are performed, resulting in a total of eight different model configurations.

Initial experiments have shown that many quantization-aware training runs with the proposed quantization scheme do not converge. Given the amount of constraints set on the trainable parameters, it could be that finding a minimum during gradient descent is strongly dependent on the initial random initialization of the parameters. However, since each training step for the given models is very fast and the models do not require much GPU memory to train, it can be afforded to train the same configuration many times and even train multiple models at the same time on the same machine.

For each of the model configurations, 10 training runs are performed. During a training run, a model with randomly initialized parameters is trained for 100 000 training steps with a batch size of 128 patches. To sort out non-converging models early, the F_1 score of the classifier head is calculated for the validation data after 5 000 iterations. If this score is below 0.85, the training run is aborted and restarted with a new random initialization of the model parameters.

For all training runs, a combined loss function is employed which aims to help the optimizer optimize equally for both the classification and the regression tasks of the model. This loss function equally weights a classification loss composed of the categorical cross-entropy and the soft Dice loss with a regression loss, which is composed of the mean absolute and mean squared errors for both circle and radius.

All training runs use the Adam optimizer and a polynomial learning rate schedule with an exponent of 0.9 which starts at the learning rate 10^{-2} and ends at 10^{-6}.

2.5 Evaluation

Since a trade-off between inference latency and model performance is to be expected, metrics are employed to measure both these factors for the trained models.

Given that models shall solve both a classification task and a regression task, the model performance is measured for both these tasks. For the classification task, in practice robot soccer code uses different configurable or automatically adjusted thresholds for the model outputs. To estimate the overall separation between positive and negative classes regardless of a specific threshold, the area under the receiver-operating characteristic curve (AUROC) is employed as a measure for the classification performance.

Since the goal of the regression task is predicting the position and size of the ball within the given image patch, the performance of this regression is estimated by calculating the intersection over union (IoU) of predicted balls compared to the reference data. As the models always return values at the regression outputs regardless if a ball is present and the classification performance should not impact the regression metrics, the IoU is only calculated for patches that do in fact contain a ball according to the reference annotations.

Inference latency in the context of this work is measured as the mean duration it takes for a NAO V6 robot to calculate the model output for a single patch under optimal conditions. To properly assess the latency, each experiment is structured as follows: first 100 warmup runs are performed, then the inference for either a single sample or a batch of samples is performed 100 times while time is measured using the C++ class `std::chrono::steady_clock`. The mean time per sample can then be calculated by dividing the total time by both the number of runs and the batch size. To avoid artifacts from unrelated CPU load, each experiment is repeated 100 times, and the minimum result is reported.

3 Results

As Table 2 shows, all models generally achieve large AUROC scores and differ only within about 1.3 percent points. However, the score for quantized models is always below the one of the corresponding float version. For the mean ball IoU, the difference is more pronounced, hinting at the possibility that the regression task is harder for the quantized models due to the reduced value ranges. As can be seen in Fig. 4, the center and radius predictions of the quantized models are accurate in unambiguous cases.

Paired t-tests were used to show that all differences in metrics between float and corresponding quantized models are statistically significant ($p < 0.05$), i. e. for all model architectures examined in this work, the quantization process using quantization-aware training always leads to a reduction in model performance with respect to the given metrics.

Figure 5 shows the relative inference time differences and absolute performance differences of the models compared to their quantized equivalents. Except for the original model a), differences both in inference time and performance seem to be larger for smaller architectures. The overall gain in inference latency can be summarized as being a factor of about 2 with a maximum observed speedup of 2.419. The original architecture is an exception, with a speedup of only 1.219. However, this outlier can be explained with unused potential for optimization: unlike all other inference implementations, the algorithm for execution of padded convolutions with quantized parameters used in this work was not specifically optimized for the NAO's processor architecture due to time constraints.

An overview of the results for all models trained in this work can be seen in Fig. 6. It shows that overall, quantized models offer the best inference latency while float models achieve the best model performance. Looking at differences between the models, choosing a simpler architecture leads to a better trade-off between latency and performance than training a quantized version of the same architecture.

Table 2. Resulting metrics of the trained models on the test set.

Architecture		AUROC	Mean ball IoU	Latency (μs)
a)	float	0.9994 ± 0.0001	0.8549 ± 0.0008	197.892
	quantized	0.9908 ± 0.0135	0.7968 ± 0.0201	162.288
b)	float	0.9991 ± 0.0002	0.8472 ± 0.0013	80.179
	quantized	0.9966 ± 0.0009	0.7941 ± 0.0044	40.669
c)	float	0.9981 ± 0.0004	0.8175 ± 0.0033	58.033
	quantized	0.9899 ± 0.0019	0.7586 ± 0.0090	28.379
d)	float	0.9978 ± 0.0003	0.8119 ± 0.0025	17.651
	quantized	0.9860 ± 0.0057	0.7453 ± 0.0133	7.296

Fig. 4. Visualization of the center and radius predictions of the float (top row) and quantized (bottom row) model d.

4 Conclusion

In this work, a specialized implementation of directly quantized neural networks for the NAO robot was presented. It could be shown that in practice, quantizing small neural networks for the given processor architecture achieves a speedup of about 2×. However, quantization of models seems to only be worthwhile after having exhausted the possibilities given by tweaking the architecture: for the models examined in this paper, reducing the amounts of layers and filters resulted in larger speedups at less performance cost compared to quantization.

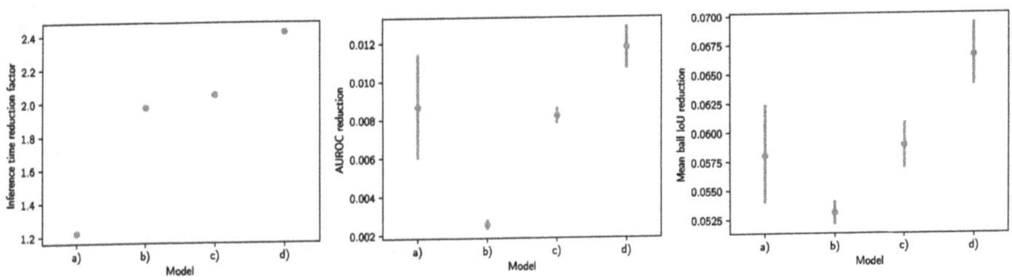

Fig. 5. Differences of inference times and performance metrics between float models and the corresponding quantized variants.

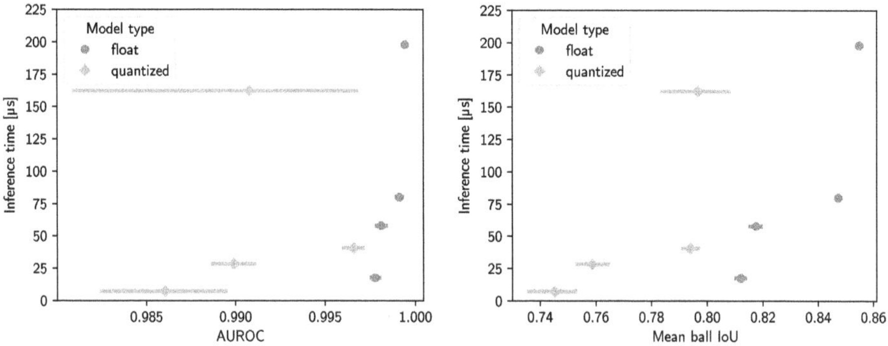

Fig. 6. Mean and 95% confidence interval of performance metrics of trained models for the test set compared to the corresponding minimum mean inference time on a NAO V6.

All code used for training the models and generating the X86 assembly code for inference is publicly available on GitHub.[3] Using this code, anyone using NAO V6 robots or comparable setups with Silvermont CPUs can retrain their models with quantization and benefit from the speedup, as long as they use a similar set of configurations as used in this work—only the layers used in the experiments are currently supported by the framework.

In the future, it would be interesting to directly compare the results achieved in this work with using the XNOR-Net for a similar ball model on the NAO. Such a comparison is particularly desirable because the XNOR-Net was already employed for other applications in the RoboCup SPL [1,6,7].

Further future works may evaluate the proposed approach on more RoboCup applications such as robot detection or field line tracking to examine how the results observed for the already small ball detection architecture scale for larger neural networks.

The currently implemented method of assembly code generation in Python could also be rewritten in C++ and thus integrated into the CompiledNN library. Such an integration would allow for simpler usage in a running system without requiring to use the specific software environment of the current ahead-of-time compilation.

Acknowledgments. The author thanks the RoboCup SPL team B-Human for providing the NAO V6 robot used for the experiments in this study, and in particular Arne Hasselbring for the many valuable discussions.

Disclosure of Interests. The author has no competing interests.

References

1. Cruz, N., Lobos-Tsunekawa, K., Ruiz-del-Solar, J.: Using convolutional neural networks in robots with limited computational resources: detecting NAO robots while

[3] https://github.com/fthielke/NaoQNN.

playing soccer. In: Akiyama, H., Obst, O., Sammut, C., Tonidandel, F. (eds.) RoboCup 2017. LNCS (LNAI), vol. 11175, pp. 19–30. Springer, Cham (2018). https://doi.org/10.1007/978-3-030-00308-1_2
2. Fog, A.: Instruction Tables (1996–2022). https://www.agner.org/optimize/instruction_tables.pdf
3. Fog, A.: The microarchitecture of Intel, AMD, and VIA CPUs (1996–2023). https://www.agner.org/optimize/microarchitecture.pdf
4. Jacob, B., et al.: Quantization and training of neural networks for efficient integer-arithmetic-only inference. In: 2018 IEEE/CVF Conference on Computer Vision and Pattern Recognition, pp. 2704–2713 (2018). https://doi.org/10.1109/CVPR.2018.00286
5. Liang, T., Glossner, J., Wang, L., Shi, S., Zhang, X.: Pruning and quantization for deep neural network acceleration: a survey. Neurocomputing **461**, 370–403 (2021). https://doi.org/10.1016/j.neucom.2021.07.045
6. O'Keeffe, S., Villing, R.: Evaluating quantized convolutional neural networks for embedded systems. In: McDonald, J., Markham, C., Winstanley, A.C. (eds.) Irish Machine Vision and Image Processing Conference Proceedings 2017, pp. 261–264. Irish Pattern Recognition & Classification Society (2017)
7. O'Keeffe, S., Villing, R.: A benchmark data set and evaluation of deep learning architectures for ball detection in the RoboCup SPL. In: Akiyama, H., Obst, O., Sammut, C., Tonidandel, F. (eds.) RoboCup 2017. LNCS (LNAI), vol. 11175, pp. 398–409. Springer, Cham (2018). https://doi.org/10.1007/978-3-030-00308-1_33
8. Peng, P., You, M., Xu, W., Li, J.: Fully integer-based quantization for mobile convolutional neural network inference. Neurocomputing **432**, 194–205 (2021). https://doi.org/10.1016/j.neucom.2020.12.035
9. Rastegari, M., Ordonez, V., Redmon, J., Farhadi, A.: XNOR-Net: imagenet classification using binary convolutional neural networks. In: Leibe, B., Matas, J., Sebe, N., Welling, M. (eds.) ECCV 2016. LNCS, vol. 9908, pp. 525–542. Springer, Cham (2016). https://doi.org/10.1007/978-3-319-46493-0_32
10. Rodriguez, A., et al.: Lower numerical precision deep learning inference and training. Intel White Paper (2018). https://www.intel.com/content/dam/develop/external/us/en/documents/lower-numerical-precision-deep-learning-jan2018-754765.pdf
11. Röfer, T., et al.: B-Human team report and code release 2019 (2019). http://www.b-human.de/downloads/publications/2019/CodeRelease2019.pdf
12. Röfer, T., et al.: B-Human 2019 – complex team play under natural lighting conditions. In: Chalup, S., Niemueller, T., Suthakorn, J., Williams, M.-A. (eds.) RoboCup 2019. LNCS (LNAI), vol. 11531, pp. 646–657. Springer, Cham (2019). https://doi.org/10.1007/978-3-030-35699-6_52
13. Sandler, M., Howard, A., Zhu, M., Zhmoginov, A., Chen, L.C.: MobileNetV2: inverted residuals and linear bottlenecks. In: 2018 IEEE/CVF Conference on Computer Vision and Pattern Recognition, pp. 4510–4520 (2018). https://doi.org/10.1109/CVPR.2018.00474
14. Thielke, F., Hasselbring, A.: A JIT compiler for neural network inference. In: Chalup, S., Niemueller, T., Suthakorn, J., Williams, M.-A. (eds.) RoboCup 2019. LNCS (LNAI), vol. 11531, pp. 448–456. Springer, Cham (2019). https://doi.org/10.1007/978-3-030-35699-6_36
15. Wu, H., Judd, P., Zhang, X., Isaev, M., Micikevicius, P.: Integer Quantization for Deep Learning Inference: Principles and Empirical Evaluation (2020). https://doi.org/10.48550/arXiv.2004.09602

16. Xu, J., Huan, Y., Zheng, L.R., Zou, Z.: A low-power arithmetic element for multi-base logarithmic computation on deep neural networks. In: 2018 31st IEEE International System-on-Chip Conference (SOCC), pp. 43–48 (2018). https://doi.org/10.1109/SOCC.2018.8618560
17. Yan, Q., Li, S., Liu, C., Chen, Q.: Real-time lightweight CNN in robots with very limited computational resources: detecting ball in NAO. In: Tzovaras, D., Giakoumis, D., Vincze, M., Argyros, A. (eds.) ICVS 2019. LNCS, vol. 11754, pp. 24–34. Springer, Cham (2019). https://doi.org/10.1007/978-3-030-34995-0_3
18. Yang, J., et al.: Quantization networks. In: 2019 IEEE/CVF Conference on Computer Vision and Pattern Recognition (CVPR), pp. 7300–7308 (2019). https://doi.org/10.1109/CVPR.2019.00748
19. Yao, Z.B., Douglas, W., O'Keeffe, S., Villing, R.: Faster YOLO-LITE: faster object detection on robot and edge devices. In: Alami, R., Biswas, J., Cakmak, M., Obst, O. (eds.) RoboCup 2021. LNCS (LNAI), vol. 13132, pp. 226–237. Springer, Cham (2022). https://doi.org/10.1007/978-3-030-98682-7_19
20. Yao, Z., et al.: HAWQ-V3: dyadic neural network quantization. In: Proceedings of the 38th International Conference on Machine Learning, pp. 11875–11886. PMLR (2021)

Decision Tree-Like Dynamic Conditional Stand-Up Routines for NAO Robots

Diana Kleingarn(✉) and Dominik Brämer

Robotics Research Institute, Section Information Technology, TU Dortmund University, 44227 Dortmund, Germany
diana.kleingarn@tu-dortmund.de

Abstract. A reliable stand-up movement is particularly important for humanoid robots. This becomes even more important in competitions such as the Standard Platform League (SPL), as a lying robot is an obstacle for other robots on the field and can neither effectively defend nor score a goal. Therefore, we have developed a system enabling the NAO robots to stand up reliably even with worn-out joints and on challenging floors. Here, we combine conditions influenced by the environment with an online-learned score for different parts of the stand-up movement. This enables us to stand up more reliably on a wide range of floor conditions.

Keywords: Stand-up movements · Online learning

1 Introduction

This paper explores the application of a decision tree-like approach to facilitate the selection of optimal stand-up motions, aiming to enhance the efficiency and effectiveness of humanoid robots in diverse real-world scenarios. For soccer robots, standing up is a key ability they need for a game. Otherwise, there would be a problem in case a robot falls. However, this task is often overlooked due to the fact that standing up is totally natural for humans.

Motion, in general, depends heavily on the robot's state, such as the temperature of the joints, battery charge or wear, which causes joint play. In our case, joint play is defined as the additional movement in the joint caused by the play in the gearing of the motors or the plastic skeleton of the robot, which gets looser over time. Additionally, the environment, mainly the floor, can help a motion or add more difficulties. For SPL games, it is common to have a different field at each event. Although field dimensions are fixed, the organizer decides whether to tape or spray the lines, making the artificial grass harder by spray paint. To prevent the robots from breaking when they fall, a cushion layer is added in most cases. These setups may affect the motion.

However, the goal of this league is to have autonomous robots, which ideally need as little supervision as possible while still being able to play everywhere.

E. Barros et al. (Eds.): RoboCup 2024, LNAI 15570, pp. 116–126, 2025.
https://doi.org/10.1007/978-3-031-85859-8_10

Therefore, it is not an option to manually test which motion performs best on each robot on the field. For our stand-up approach, we took inspiration from humans; see Sect. 3. We split the movements into smaller parts and allow a decision tree-like [6] choice depending on the robot's position in the room, the upper body angle, and the learned experience of which parts were successful in the past. In Sect. 3.2, we discuss possible motion aborts [2] as a backup plan to prevent robot damage and speed up the process if a motion can not be executed successfully. However, it would clearly be better to avoid the necessity of an interrupt. Therefore, some parts of the stand-up motion have a joint error compensation, described in Sect. 3.3, which is inspired by the proposed error compensation the SPL team from Bremen (B-Human) presented in their code release [1]. In Sect. 4, we evaluate the proposed approach by comparing it on different surfaces with an older version before the changes.

2 Related Work

As Stückler et al. stated back in 2006 [10], it is not a straightforward task for humanoid robots to survive falling to the ground and then getting up again. Here they propose their first general standing-up methods for kid-size humanoid robots. They were developed with a simulation and tested under real-world conditions at the RoboCup in 2005.

A decade later, Jeong et al. proposed a reinforcement learning approach [4] to generate more robust stand-up movements from a set of currently used motion sequences. This method involves a Gaussian Mixture Model and Q-learning to improve stand-up movement sequences (keyframes) for adult-size robots.

In 2021, Stelter et al. demonstrated an approach to generate fast and reliable stand-up motions for humanoid robots [9]. In developing this system, they have moved away from the keyframe-based methods previously used in the industry and created a new approach based on splines. This method is built and optimized with a simulation for kid-size humanoid robots.

All the presented approaches were designed and optimized for robots developed by the team itself, making it more difficult for teams from other leagues, such as the SPL, to adopt them. Another possible approach to learn stand-up motions is by using a motion tracking system, as Mistry et al. demonstrate with their sit-to-stand transition movement [5]. This is not applicable to the NAO robots of the SPL league as they are too different in anatomy and strength to a human body. One example is the NAO robot's hip-yaw pitch, that makes it impossible for the robot to move both legs completely independent. Another detail that almost all approaches have in common is that they were all trained in a simulation and then tested on a real robot to overcome the reality gap. This is easier for the mentioned researcher as they work with self-developed robots and can simulate them much more accurately, which is not yet possible with the NAO robot. This is why we decided to continue using the handmade keyframes but to link them in a significantly different way.

3 Stand-Up Routine Architecture

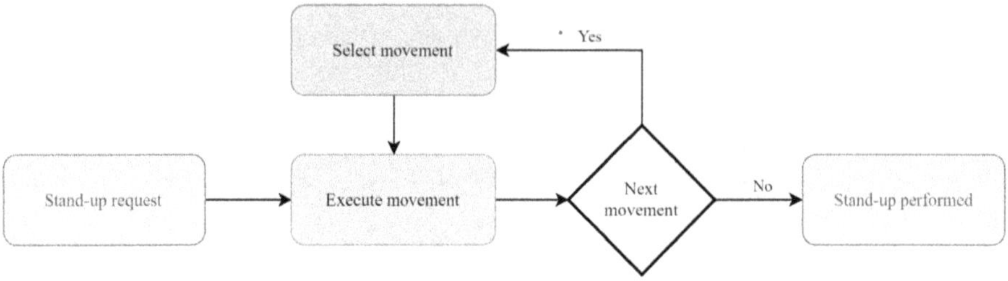

Fig. 1. Rough overview of our proposed stand-up routine architecture. The red box is explained in more detail in Sect. 3.1 and the blue box in Sect. 3.2 and Sect. 3.3. (Color figure online)

Our stand-up approach is divided into three main components:

1. a decision tree-like conditional movement selection,
2. interception movements,
3. a compensation for joint play.

The decision tree-like linking between different stand-up movements builds our stand-up routines out of the possible keyframes. Additionally, interception movements are supposed to reduce damage to the robots while they enable our robots to recover from an incorrectly performed stand-up more quickly at the same time. However, a motion without interceptions will always be faster, so we use the joint play compensation to counteract the wear of the robots. Our recent robust stand-up architecture comprises these three components working together. Figure 1 provides an overview of where the individual components are located in our architecture.

3.1 Conditional Movement Selection

Our movement selection procedure includes three types of conditions:

1. forced transitions,
2. transitions based on external influences, like the robot's position in the room or its upper body angle or rotation,
3. online learned transitions based on the probability of failure of certain parts of the motion.

We use all three decision types as conditions for changing from one partial stand-up movement to the next and forming a decision tree of movements based on a start movement. Figure 2 shows a part of the possible decision paths we use in our approach. To avoid overloading the figure, we decided not to show the transitions for possible interception movements, including a return from all yellow

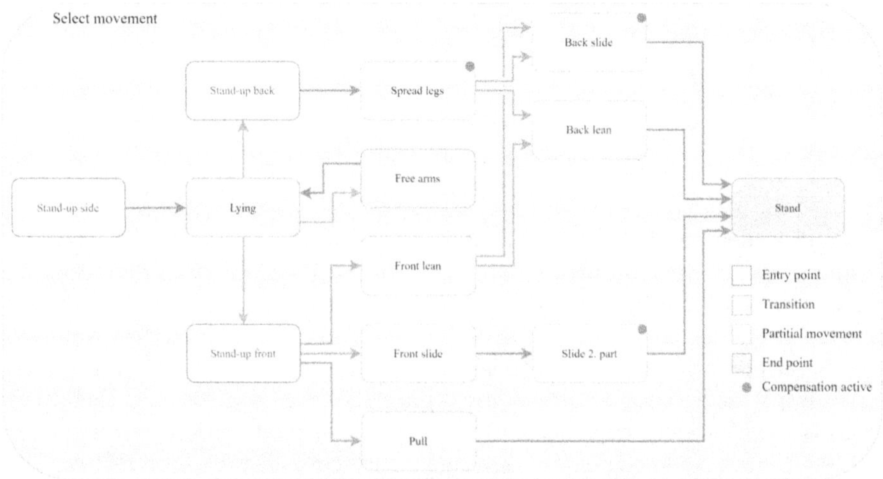

Fig. 2. Overview of our movement selection process, it involves forced transitions (red arrows), environmentally influenced transitions (green arrows), and learned transitions (blue arrows). (Color figure online)

and purple boxes to the transition in orange, shown in Fig. 4. The green paths are determined based on a ranking system and the relevant environment. Given a sequence of conditions, each one is examined for possible applicability, and the first applicable condition is selected. The position of the robot in space plays a crucial role here.

From here on, we will focus more on the decisions learned online. In the beginning, all blue (online learned) paths still have the same probability of being selected, as the robot has not yet required a stand-up attempt. Therefore, we assume that every possible stand-up movement path could possibly be successful. We did not collect any data points to build a statistic at this stage, so the final decision on which path we use is updated only after three stand-up attempts.

According to a fall statistic [8], our 7 robots on the field combined fell on average 57.7 times per game during RoboCup 2023. This value does not consider the actual time of the games or the number of robots on the field. For this reason the statistic also gives a normalised average, 68.7 falls per game for the Nao Devils, considering the described factors. A more recent not yet published fall statistic [7] shows a better result, which confirms that our robots fall down relatively often. On average 47 times (not normalised) in every match of the RoboCup German Open 2024, so most robots exceeded the threshold value used to decide which path to use for successfully getting up.

We use the following updating rules for each possible selection:

$$\tau^{t+1} = \tau^t + 1 \mid \text{if stand-up motion is aborted} \tag{1}$$

$$\rho^{t+1} = \rho^t + 1 \mid \text{if stand-up motion is started} \tag{2}$$

$$\sigma = \frac{\tau}{\rho}. \tag{3}$$

τ, ρ and σ denote the number of aborted stand-up movements, the number of started stand-up movements, and the current failure rate of the stand-up movement, respectively. After collecting enough data points, we use the path with the lowest failure rate. We assume this point is reached after three stand-up tries. Some potential errors need to be considered when calculating our statistics. For example, if a robot is picked up during the stand-up routine, the stand-up motion potentially triggers one of the possible interception movements or registers that it is already upright and goes directly into the *stand* motion, and we are unable to know whether the robot might have managed to get up after all or not.

Therefore, we have a correction mechanism that corrects τ and ρ by simply restoring the state before the stand-up attempt. As more and more data is collected in the course of an SPL game, each robot can put together the combination that suits it best. We also deliberately decided against storing this information in a long-term memory, as the condition of the robot can change too quickly due to heating, wear and tear, battery charge and more. As wear and tear plays a significant role in whether a partial stand-up movement is usable, we have also built the option of making minor changes to the movements during execution, see Sect. 3.3. However, this allows the robot to determine its ideal stand-up combination in the initial phase of a game and thus use a version optimized for this game.

3.2 Interception Movement

In this section, we examine the role and efficiency of various interception movement strategies to prevent falls and ensure overall stability of the stand-up movement. The first strategy originates from the idea that the robot is supposed to be able to move its arms and legs even when lying on the floor. In case a robot falls on its arm, while the next movement requires a movement of the arms, it is clear that this movement is impossible as long as the arm is stuck. B-Human was the first team to show how to resolve this issue [1]. With a similar idea, we designed a motion in which the robot lifts its hip to free the arm. During the motion *lying* in Fig. 2, the robot verifies if the motion *free arms* is necessary using the joint error of the arms.

Another critical point during the stand-up motion is the beginning of the *stand-up front* motion. This motion uses the arms to push the robot towards a more upright position. Since the motion will likely fail if the arms cannot reach the desired position, forming a T shape, the robot aborts the movement under this condition and starts over again.

Fig. 3. Robot in *sit* position.

In the later stages of the movement, the body angle mostly determines whether an interception or abort is necessary. When the aimed body angle is not reached, even taking a tolerance into account, it is highly likely that the robot is not in balance and can not finish the motion successfully. Various interception movements are differently reasonable depending on the following conditions:

1. the stage of the stand-up,
2. how upright the upper body is,
3. whether the feet are supporting the robot.

As long as the robot's centre of gravity is close to the ground, the default intercept movement is called *play dead*. This movement switches all joints to an unstiff mode. Only when the stand-up motion has progressed enough so that a regular movement to intercept a fall can be executed, the decision is changed from *play dead* to the in-game fall-down protection.

In both described cases, the robot would start the stand-up process from *lying* again, Fig. 2. This takes time and is not, in all cases, necessary. Humans would also rather make a smaller adjustment to their stand-up motion when they lose balance instead of lying down again. When transferring the idea to robots, the robot's limitations need to be considered. In the case of the NAO robot, the arms are weak compared to the legs, so they can prevent a nearly upright sitting robot, like in Fig. 3, from losing balance; however, supporting most of the robot's weight is unrealistic. The general idea of trying to intercept the robot's stumble during a stand-up routine with some form of sitting motion was first introduced by B-Human [2], who currently don't use this method. This motion is typically used when the robot is upright enough to perform the motion while not having progressed in the *stand* part. During a *stand* motion, the robot's centre of gravity is high enough to cause damage to the robot in case of a direct transition to the *sit* motion.

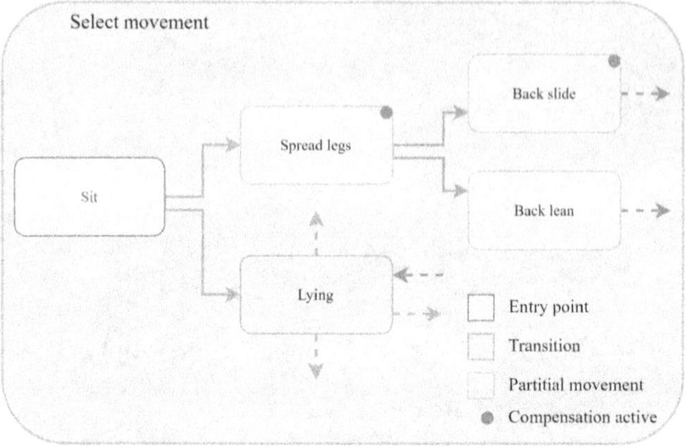

Fig. 4. Overview of our interception movement process, it involves forced transitions (red arrows), environmentally influenced transitions (green arrows), and learned transitions (blue arrows). The dashed lines indicate the transitions returning to Fig. 2. (Color figure online)

Figure 4 shows how the robot can continue after this *sit* motion. When the interception was successful, the robot can directly continue with the stand-up routine. This is mainly determined using the upper body angle to check whether the robot is actually sitting. As long as the robot has an upper body angle of less than 45° consisting of the maximum upright angle of 25° plus a tolerance of 20° for the stand-up motion, the robot is considered **not lying**, and the motion was successful. For reference, a robot standing upright has a body angle of 0°. In this desired case, the speedup of the process, compared to starting the stand-up all over again, is noticeable. It takes the robot about 5 s to stand up out of the sitting position, while it takes 8 s from a lying position. Additionally, the distance the robot falls is shorter for the *sit* motion than for a complete abortion of the stand-up motion.

When the motion was not successful, the robot would start from the *lying* position. Although the *sit* movement is not executed correctly every time, it is still enough to see an improvement. The success rate is highly dependent on the robot, its wear, and the joint play. A robot which is able to perform this motion has a success rate of 50%. However, the main challenge of integrating this movement is triggering it at the correct time. The robot needs enough time to execute the movement, but it is also supposed only to trigger an interception if no other option is available.

In the first step, we decide for which parts of each keyframe the possibility of aborting this motion is reasonable. Afterwards, we measured the desired target body angle using a debugging mode. To consider joint play, we allow a tolerance determined by a comparison of the course of the body angle between a successful and a failed attempt. For example, for the last frame of the motion *front lean*, the target body angle is 14°, while we allow a tolerance of 20° backwards.

Additionally, the direction in which the robot is falling is necessary since this sit movement is designed for backward stumbling and would cause more harm if used in another direction. So, when the robot is no longer *on ground*, but in a stand-up motion, the body angle is leaving the allowed range, and the robot falls backwards, the *sit* motion is triggered.

3.3 Compensation of Wear

The wear and tear of the robot is a major problem, which was also determined by Fiedler et al. [3] in their research. For this reason, we have decided to implement a compensation for the joint error induced by wear and tear in our stand-up routine for essential partial movements. These movements are marked by a red dot in both Fig. 2 and Fig. 4. The method of compensation is inspired by an implementation used for a similar purpose by the SPL team B-Human [1]. In contrast to the implementation of B-Human, the joint at which this compensation is to be carried out is not specified, but the joint with the most significant error is automatically compensated. It is possible to specify which joints should absorb a particular joint's error and to which degree. The robot decides which joint to compensate based on the joint with the largest error, limited to the joints from the hip downwards. The compensation itself is then carried out during the partial movement's execution as soon as a threshold value of 8° for the error of one of the joints is exceeded. Where possible, each leg of the NAO robot is considered separately. We have also set the maximum compensation to a value of 10°, with the option to adjust this value for each partial movement.

4 Evaluation

To evaluate the benefits of the proposed changes, we compare the recent version to the version published for the code release 2022 on different surfaces. We start with the artificial grass in our lab, then add a carpet of artificial grass as a second layer, and finally add two layers of pool mats (4 mm each) between the artificial grass in our lab and the carpet on top. In this setup, the floor has varying degrees of resilience to ensure the motion does not overfit to our lab. Figure 4 shows the results of these stand-up tests with two different robots. The robots had eight attempts to stand up from both sides, front and back. It is important to note that the stand-up statistic requires three tries, as described in Sect. 3.1, to determine which motion works better, while the old version has two stand-up front versions and one stand-up back version. The old stand-up version switches between the two fixed motions when one is not executed correctly, leading the robot to fall during the stand-up routine.

Additionally, we acknowledged the wear of the robots by choosing older, worn-out robots. As mentioned in [3], worn-out robots have larger joint angle errors than new robots. These errors need to be compensated for the worn-out robot to still manage the required movements. The internal value **hardware quality** gives feedback about the status of the leg joints and is defined between zero and one, with one referring to new robots. The robots we chose, B and C, have quality scores of 0.0 and 0.35, respectively. During the tests with the new version, we noticed that we needed to reset the statistics between the stand-up front and the stand-up back evaluation. The statistic is supposed to find a stable motion, which at that time required the robot to stand stable for a defined amount of time. So when the human supervising the test is laying the robot on the ground too soon after the stand-up motion, this motion is counted as not successful for the statistic, although it was successful in regard to the test.

We started the evaluation with the easiest surface and continually increased the level of difficulty. For attempts which needed the *sit* motion, we decided to count the attempt as successful as long as the motion was not aborted, meaning the robot was not lying on the floor during this motion. As demonstrated in Fig. 5, with one exception on the field, the new version performs equally well or better than the old version. Also, the results with the new stand-up on the more resilient floor are similar to the ones on the regular field in our lab. However, we needed to cancel the test with the old stand-up on robot C midways due to robot

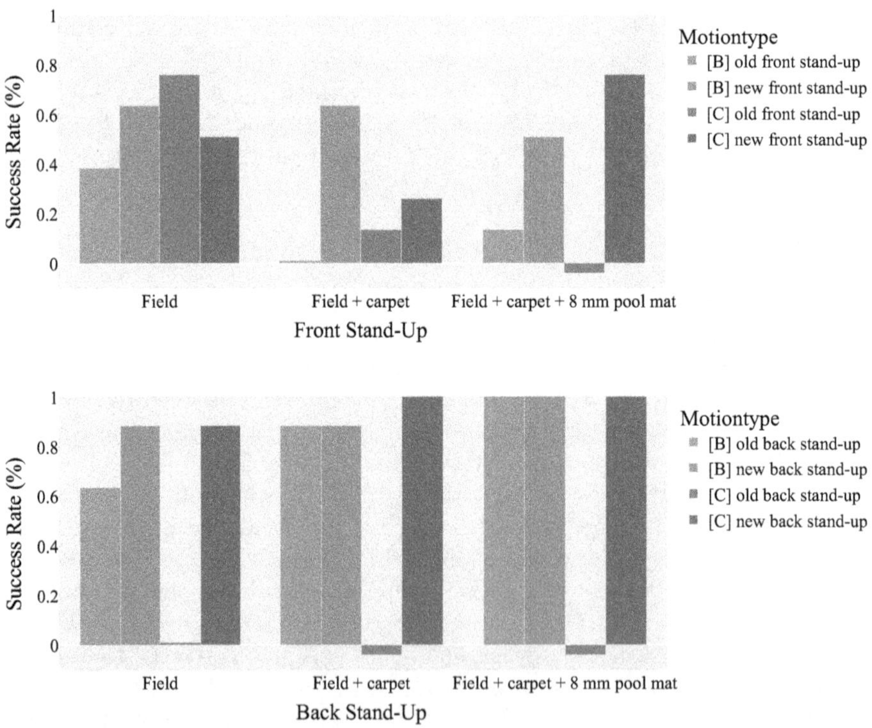

Fig. 5. These are the results of our tests with the new and old stand-up movement framework on two different Robots. The negative value indicates that we had to stop the test because the robot broke down during it.

safety reasons. The missing tests are indicated with a success rate below zero. Because of these safety concerns, we chose not to do the comparison with new robots. However, standing up was not an issue for intact robots during recent test games. Overall, the stand-up back motions are more reliable and stable than the stand-up front. A possible explanation for this observation is the use of arms in this sequence of motions. While the arms are more passively used when the robot is lying on its back, they actually need to push the robot up and support it when it is lying on its front. A similar observation has already been made by Stückler et al. [10], who found that standing up from the front is significantly more complex than from behind due to joint angle limitations.

5 Conclusion and Future Work

This paper shows a stand-up routine approach for humanoid robots that use a mixture of environmentally influenced conditional branches and learned branches that connect partial movement keyframes. As part of these new stand-up routines, we have also introduced various novel interception movements that we have integrated into our approach. In addition, we have built a mechanism that can adapt our keyframe movements to the robots' current wear and tear during execution.

As discussed in the evaluation, Sect. 4, the stand-up front movements are, in general, more difficult than the stand-up motions when the robot is lying on its back. Nevertheless, it is the goal to have reliable motions independent of the direction in which the robot fell. A possible solution would be to consider the robot's quality status, legs and arms, for the transitions between the motions. Additionally, the SPL team from Bremen, B-Human, introduced a joint error prediction [3], which allowed them to compensate the errors earlier, leading to smaller errors and a more stable stand-up routine. Therefore, we want to adopt this type of prediction in our implementation of joint angle error compensation and improve our automatic selection process for when and which joint angle error should be compensated.

References

1. B-Human Team: B-Human Code Release (2022). https://github.com/bhuman/BHumanCodeRelease/releases/tag/coderelease2022
2. B-Human Team: Keyframe Motions - B-Human (2023). https://docs.b-human.de/coderelease2023/motion/motion-keyframemotionengine/#keyframe-parameters
3. Fiedler, J., Laue, T.: Neural network-based joint angle prediction for the nao robot. In: Robot World Cup, pp. 66–77. Springer, Heidelberg (2023). https://doi.org/10.1007/978-3-031-55015-7_6
4. Jeong, H., Lee, D.: Learning complex stand-up motion for humanoid robots. In: Proceedings of the AAAI Conference on Artificial Intelligence, vol. 30 (2016)
5. Mistry, M., Murai, A., Yamane, K., Hodgins, J.: Sit-to-stand task on a humanoid robot from human demonstration. In: 2010 10th IEEE-RAS International Conference on Humanoid Robots, pp. 218–223. IEEE (2010)

6. Quinlan, J.R.: Induction of decision trees. Mach. Learn. **1**, 81–106 (1986)
7. Reichenberg, P.: RoboCup German Open 2024 Fall Statistic (2024)
8. Reichenberg, P.: RoboCup Fall Statistic 2023 (2024). https://b-human.informatik.uni-bremen.de/public/Statistics/2023/
9. Stelter, S., Bestmann, M., Hendrich, N., Zhang, J.: Fast and reliable stand-up motions for humanoid robots using spline interpolation and parameter optimization. In: 2021 20th International Conference on Advanced Robotics (ICAR), pp. 253–260. IEEE (2021)
10. Stückler, J., Schwenk, J., Behnke, S.: Getting back on two feet: reliable standing-up routines for a humanoid robot. In: IAS, pp. 676–685. Citeseer (2006)

A Mental Simulation Based Decision-Making Algorithm for the RoboCupSoccer Goalkeeper

Antoine Dizet[2,4(✉)], Ubbo Visser[3], and Cédric Buche[1,4]

[1] CROSSING, CNRS IRL 2010, Adelaide, Australia
[2] Lab-STICC, CNRS UMR 6285, Brest, France
[3] University of Miami, Coral Gables, USA
[4] ENIB, Plouzané, France
dizet@enib.fr

Abstract. The RoboCup, an international robotics competition, serves as a platform to improve robot capabilities. In the RoboCup Soccer leagues, continuous enhancements target critical aspects like robot perception, locomotion, shooting, and decision-making. This paper introduces a novel decision-making strategy based on a mental simulations architecture integrating prediction algorithms to anticipate diverse potential outcomes of ongoing actions. Implemented within the context of a goalkeeper scenario in the RoboCup Soccer 3D simulation league, this strategy allows the robot to recognize potential future threats, thus preventing the opposing team from scoring opportunities. A comparative analysis demonstrates the efficacy of employing complex algorithms over traditional decision-making approaches such as state machines. Notably, as the complexity of the robot's operating environment increases.

Keywords: RoboCup · Soccer · Goalkeeper · Robotic · Simulation · Decision-making

1 Introduction

Effective decision-making in competitive environments, such as the RoboCup Soccer, confers a considerable advantage. Optimal player positioning and timely choices, such as passing or shooting, significantly enhance the chance of victory. In pursuit of enhancing decision-making abilities, this paper proposes a solution inspired by the work of Polceanu et al. (2015) [16], which demonstrated notable performance [15]. Both proposed approaches in the previously cited paper bring significant improvements for the goalkeeper's stop rates (200%) and validate the applicability of the novel mental model based decision-making process. The results were obtained from a free kick scenario, where the initial position of the ball varied, resulting in changes to both its distance from the goal and its shooting angle. In order to explore and evaluate the capabilities as well as the limits of decision-making based on mental simulations, our proposal is an extension of

E. Barros et al. (Eds.): RoboCup 2024, LNAI 15570, pp. 127–139, 2025.
https://doi.org/10.1007/978-3-031-85859-8_11

previously conducted work. Continuing to use the goalkeeper as the agent within the 3D simulation environment, we assess its performance in both constrained scenarios such as free kicks, as well as during a more generalized scenario, which is the full match. Mental simulations are made more complex by incorporating all agents present on the field, applying a decision-making algorithm coupled with a prediction algorithm to define the various future actions and positions that the different player can take. This paper will begin by presenting the state of previous research concerning goalkeepers (cf. Sect. 2). It will be structured into two main sections: the first focusing on non-humanoid leagues, including SSL (Small Size League), MSL (Middle Size League), and 2D simulation (cf. Sect. 2.1). The second addressing humanoid leagues, including SPL (Standard Platform League), Humanoid league, and 3D simulation (cf. Sect. 2.2). The third section of the paper (cf. Sect. 3) will explain various aspects of our contribution, such as the algorithm's architecture and the correlation between prediction algorithms and mental simulations, aiming to enhance the goalkeeper's behavior. Following the description of different test scenarios in our developments (cf. Sect. 3.2), we will proceed to present and analyze the obtained results (cf. Sect. 4). Lastly, potential enhancements and future work will be deliberated (cf. Sect. 5).

2 State of the Art

2.1 Non-humanoid Leagues (SSL, MSL, Sim 2D)

In terms of decision making, the literature contains a variety of complex algorithms (e.g. Q-learning) and non-complex algorithms (e.g. state machine) (cf. Table 1). There are state machines with [11] allowing to stop 64.6% of the goals [12]. Reinforcement learning is also used [4]. [21] propose a comparison between a reinforcement learning algorithm and a hard-coded algorithm in SSL, the results are in favour of artificial intelligence with an average stopping rate of 18.9% for the hard-coded algorithm, 32.1% and 53.24% for the reinforcement learning algorithms, respectively NR and EBR. Other interesting approaches are in the literature such as a Danger Theory Based strategy in 2D simulation with an efficiency of around 80% [17] and a requirements derivation method applied to a SSL goalkeeper [6]. The two following articles follow the implementation of a goalkeeper in 1999 for the MSL league [2,3], the first one presents a Genetic programming approach with encouraging results on a simulator while the second one presents a landmark-based self-localisation method of the robot. In order to intercept the ball before the goal, it is possible to compute the intersection point between the trajectory of the ball and the future trajectory of the robot [19]. So we find mainly the AI/Hard-coded algorithm duality, such as state machines, with a slight advantage for reinforcement learning although the stop rates of state machines are correct.

2.2 Humanoid Leagues (SPL, Humanoid, Sim 3D)

Here again the choice of a state machine is a possibility (cf. Table 2). [8,9] raise interesting questions about the installation of an NAO goalkeeper. [9] explain a

Table 1. Non-Humanoid Leagues goalkeeper developments

Goal	Paper	Solution	Result	Robot
Goalkeeper for MSL	[11]	State machine	A goalkeeper misses the ball, basically in two situations: Not seeing the ball and seeing the ball but not being able to move fast enough to catch it	MSL
Design a MSL Goalkeeper	[12]	State machine	64.6% of goals saved	MSL
Evolving goalkeeper behaviour	[4]	Hand-coded & Q-learning	Performance ratio between 4 and 10 (ratio 3 = 75% stop rate)	
Penalty kick goalkeeping for SSL	[21]	Hard coded vs Q-learning	Average stop rate (simulation): Hard coded (18.9%), NR(32.1%), EBR(53.24%)	SSL
Build a goalie behaviour	[17]	Danger Theory Based strategy	Effectiveness above 80%	2Dsim
Motion-control strategy for a goalkeeper MSL	[2]	Genetic programming (GP)	The preliminary results obtained on a simulator are encouraging	MSL
Design Goalkeeper	[3]	Landmark-based robot self-localisation	The robot is able to perform its tasks in real time	MSL
MSL Goalkeeper, Detect positions of the ball to predict the interception point	[19]	Image processing & Hand-coded algorithm	The experimental results show the accuracy and effectiveness of this strategy	MSL

conflict encountered between the software performances and the hardware limits of the robot, which not reach the intersection point with the ball trajectory in time. One year later, [8] shows good results, the ball is correctly traced, 100% of the time, the robot is correctly positioned 84% of the time and thus stops 62% of the shots. Contrary to what has been shown in the previous section, a comparison between a Q-learning algorithm and a hard-coded algorithm in 3D simulation shows that complex algorithm is less efficient, but could be improved [7]. The use of Q-learning coupled with a Petri Net nevertheless obtains good results [10]. A diving strategy, published in 2018, consists in voluntarily dropping the robot so that it can stop the ball [14]. This strategy has been implemented in 3D simulation and is not applicable to the SPL league without taking the risk of breaking the robot. Two promising approaches were published in 2015 in a single article [15]. Both methods were carried out in 3D simulation. The first one proposes a deterministic behaviour using a Kalman filter and a linear regression. The second, based on mental simulations, predicts the future state of the environment according to its current state. The results obtained are: an average stop rate of 27.23% according to the shooting distance and 32.3% according to the shooting angle for the deterministic algorithm and 46.8% according to the shooting distance and 59% according to the shooting angle for the other one. The use of a state machine for goalkeeper decision making is a possible solution. The results obtained by non-hard-coded algorithms within a simulation are also good and can be an alternative to the state machine.

Table 2. Humanoid Leagues goalkeeper developments

Goal	Paper	Solution	Result	Robot
Goalkeeper behaviour	[9]	State machine	Conflict between software performance and hardware capacity, the goalkeeper can't reach the point in time	NAO
Goalkeeper behaviour	[8]	State machine	The architecture allowed the robot to track the ball nearly 100% of the time, position itself properly 84% of the time, and save goals from 62% of the trajectories tested	NAO
Goalkeeper strategy	[7]	Q-learning vs Hard coded	The Q-learning algorithm is less efficient but can be enhance	NAOsim
New learning- based behaviour model for a soccer goalkeeper	[10]	Petri nets & Q-learning	Results of theoretical analysis of some case studies show impressive performance improvement in goalkeeper task execution	
Goalkeeper strategy	[14]	Diving behaviour	stop rate 46.6%	NAOsim
Goalkeeper strategy sim 3D	[15]	Deterministic behaviour (Linear Regression/Kalman filter) & Mental model approach	stop rate: Deterministic behaviour: distance 27,23%, angle 32,3%, mental model approach: distance 46,8%, angle 59%.	NAOsim

2.3 Mental Simulations and ORPHEUS

In light of the literature, it is noticeable that the algorithm used by [15] is the one that achieves the best results. Two algorithms are presented in this paper. In this article, we will focus on the one that uses mental simulations based on the ORPHEUS algorithm [16]. ORPHEUS is an agent architecture that provides a generic approach as support for decision-making developed in 2015. An agent has an imaginary space constructed from perceiving reality, which autonomously predicts possible outcomes in diverse real-world situations. The mental simulations algorithm allows modeling an environment and digitally evolving it to generate several possible futures. The first step is to model the real environment in which the agent operates (cf. $r(t)$ in Fig. 1) in the form of an initial mental image (cf. $s(t)$ in Fig. 1). From the initial mental image (cf. $s(t)$ in Fig. 1), we generate an initial set of potential future scenarios (cf. $s(t+1)$ and $s'(t+1)$ in Fig. 1). These potential future scenarios also take the form of mental images, enabling us to iterate the process of generating future scenarios. Several applications of this algorithm have demonstrated the relevance of this architecture and the interest of this decision-making strategy for an agent [16]. This algorithm was used on a goalkeeper in the RoboCup 3D Simulation environment in 2015 [15].

3 Proposal

The results were obtained in 2015 in the context of a free kick scenario, changing the initial position of the ball. We propose in this paper a potential improvement

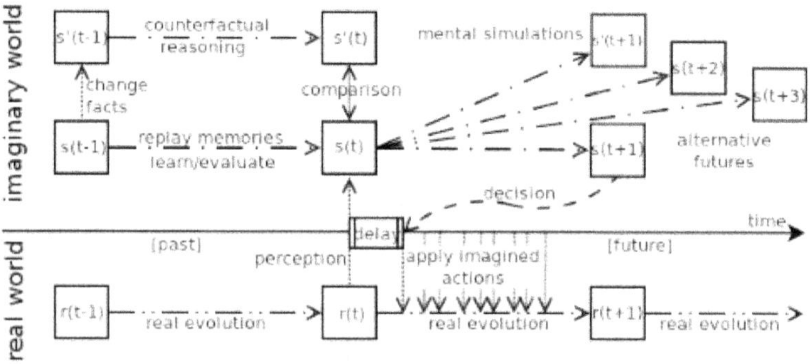

Fig. 1. ORPHEUS algorithm architecture

of what was proposed in 2015. We have now extended this work to a more complex and dynamic environment, the full match. Unlike previous proposals [15], mental simulations are modified and made more complex. Instead of generating a range of possible futures by evolving our agent in various mental simulations, we evolve the environment (ball and other players) in mental simulations to extract the most risky possible future situations to assist our agent in making a decision in advance. To enhance the goalkeeper's decision-making skills, we propose an algorithm centered on predicting the evolution of the environment. From the current state of the goalkeeper's surroundings, we generate multiple potential future scenarios (cf. Figure 1). Subsequently, we identify and prioritize those scenarios posing a high risk (i.e., a high probability of conceding a goal). The goalkeeper then takes action to mitigate the risk, ideally intercepting the ball before the opposing team scores a goal. We have chosen a time step of half a second between $s(t)$ and $s(t+1)$ (cf. Figure 1) for our use case and we generate about twenty mental images per generation, depending on our computer calculation capacity.

3.1 Prediction Model

The primary objective is to characterize the robot's environment. We use the robot's sensors to construct a representation of its surroundings. This enables us to position various dynamic entities, such as the ball and other robots, on the soccer field. These distinct mental entities are characterized by their physical attributes, including weight, height, shape, as well as their x and y coordinates on the soccer field. Each mental entity is linked to a prediction model designed to forecast potential movements. To generate these prediction models for future x and y coordinates, we employed a neural network implemented with TensorFlow [1], the training results using this neural network show good performance in coordinate (x and y) prediction (cf. Table 3). The prediction model for the ball is trained on a dataset comprising numerous instances of moving ball positions generated by the PyBullet simulator [5]. The ball shares the same characteristics (weight, size, shape) as the standard office ball used in the RoboCupSoccer Standard Platform League. Similarly, the player prediction model is trained on a dataset containing multiple instances of moving player positions, generated from the official RoboCupSoccer Simulation 3D league simulator [18,20], and the behavioral software of the UT Austin Villa team [13]. We have chosen to associate a prediction model with each agent, one for the ball and one for the players, instead of a full unified prediction for all the elements together in order to be able to remove or add one or more agents in the various test scenarios.

Table 3. TensorFlow Neural Network Training Score

	ball position	player's position
X Root mean square error (m^2)	0.0008	0.0085
Y Root mean square error (m^2)	0.0021	0.0098

3.2 Test Environment

To assess and validate the decision-making algorithm, we've established a testing environment where the goalkeeper operates. Using the RoboCupSoccer 3D Simulation software, we use the code from the UT Austin Villa team behavior software [13] as a foundation to integrate our advancements. Within this testing environment, the goalkeeper continuously logs the necessary information in real-time to construct the mental images, including player and ball positions. We've designed three test scenarios: the first involves a shot with only one opposing player and the goalkeeper, with numerous shots taken from various positions on the soccer field. The second scenario involves two opposing players, with one passing the ball to the second player attempting to score. And the third scenario is a full match. To evaluate our algorithm's performance, we compare the stop rates across different goalkeeper types: absence of a goalkeeper, a basic goalkeeper behavior using a simple state machine, and a goalkeeper employing behavior based on prediction and evolution of mental images. Assessing the stop rate when no goalkeeper is present allows us to evaluate the shooter's performance, facilitating a more comprehensive analysis of the stop rates of the other goalkeeper types. Failure to score a goal is possibly due to various factors, including the player's fall preventing a shot before the time limit expires, shots off target, or shots lacking sufficient strength to reach the goal.

4 Results

4.1 First Scenario: A Shooter Versus the Goalkeeper

In this scenario, the shooter is sequentially positioned at 12 different locations on the field. These positions are determined by the distance between the shooter and the goalkeeper (3 m, 5 m, and 7 m) and the shooting angle range ([0°, –30°], [–30°, –50°], [–50°, –70°], and [–70°, –90°]). Each combination of distance and angle is assigned a position number from 1 to 12 (cf. Fig. 2). For instance, position number 5 indicates that the shooter is positioned 5 m away from the goalkeeper and at a shooting angle ranging between –50° and –70°.

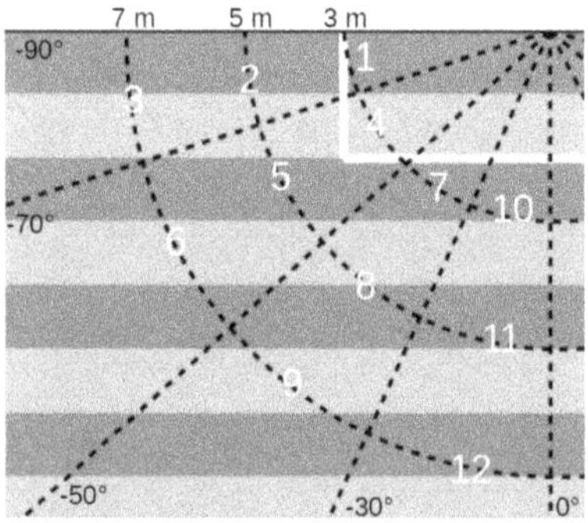

Fig. 2. Kicker positions

After the kicker is positioned in one of the 12 designated spots, they proceed to shoot multiple times. To ascertain the reliability of each goalkeeper's stop rate, we examined the progression of the stop rate at each position. At each position, the stop rate reached a stable level after approximately 150 shots (cf. Fig. 3).

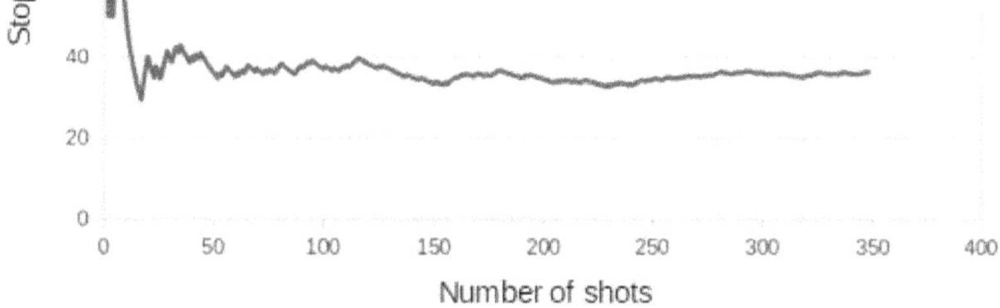

Fig. 3. Basic Goalie stop rate evolution at the 11th position

While 150 shots may appear sufficient to yield relevant outcomes, we conducted 350 shots per position for each goalkeeper type (No goalkeeper, basic goalkeeper, mental simulation-based goalkeeper) to ensure the most reliability of the results. The outcomes from this scenario reveal that the stop rates between the basic goalkeeper and the goalkeeper using mental images are closely aligned (cf. Table 4). We attribute this to the brevity of each simulation, lasting approximately 15 s per shot, and the relatively uncomplicated nature of the scenario. The primary advantage of mental simulations with prediction algorithms lies in their capacity to foresee potential future events, enabling the goalkeeper to proactively make decisions. Hence, a scenario lacking complexity and brevity does not accurately reflect the algorithm's potential performance. Consequently, we devised a second, more intricate scenario.

Table 4. First scenario results

Position number	No Goalie stop rate	Basic Goalie stop rate	Mental simulation goalie stop rate
1	40.75%	62.18%	61.84%
2	51.15%	85.34%	82.08%
3	81.43%	91.11%	96.53%
4	9.83%	54.57%	53.29%
5	22.41%	59.89%	59.25%
6	65.61%	84.53%	88.83%
7	11.17%	34.48%	26.65%
8	16.47%	38.51%	33.52%
9	75.93%	74.43%	84.86%
10	8.67%	24.71%	21.84%
11	13.54%	30.17%	28.08%
12	77.87%	83.62%	88.54%

4.2 Second Scenario: A Shooter and a Teammate Versus the Goalkeeper

The aim of this scenario is to introduce complexity and prolong the simulation to underscore the benefits of decision-making using mental simulation and prediction algorithms. In this second scenario, two opposing players are involved. Initially, one player possesses the ball and passes it to the other player, who then attempts to score a goal. To introduce variability, the shooter is positioned at location 10 while the other player's position ranges from 1 to 9 (cf. Figure 2). We conducted 150 shots per position (cf. Table 5). Notably, in this second scenario, the stop rate of the goalkeeper employing mental simulation with prediction algorithms is slightly higher than that of the basic goalkeeper (cf. Table 5). This underscores that the use of complex algorithms for decision-making confers an advantage in more complex situations. Additionally, we observed that the stop rate in the absence of a goalkeeper is higher than in the first scenario. As this stop rate serves to assess the player's goal-scoring performance, it becomes evident that the presence of more agents leads to increased errors.

Table 5. Second scenario results

Position number	No Goalie stop rate	Basic Goalie stop rate	Mental simulation goalie
1	38.76%	52.24%	57.46%
2	54.29%	60.99%	61.22%
3	80.66%	81.33%	82%
4	39.04%	72.72%	75.18%
5	41.55%	48.2%	48.28%
6	40.56%	56.34%	59.31%
7	60.56%	81.69%	79.33%
8	61.97%	63.43%	67.11%
9	32.57%	49.26%	52.03%

4.3 Third Scenario: Full Match

Previously, we observed that as the environment becomes more complex, decision-making using mental simulations appears to perform well. With the aim of creating the most complex environment possible, we conducted full matches by swapping the goalkeeper of one of the two teams. Initially, we conducted mirror matches to assess the relevance of the scenario regarding the goalkeeper's impact (cf. Fig. 4).

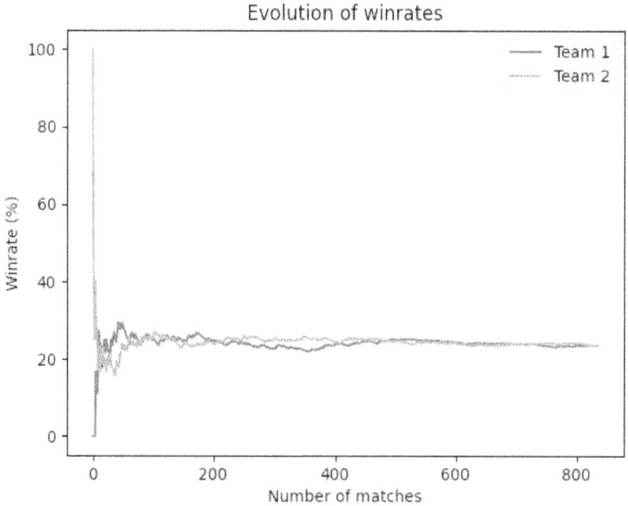

Fig. 4. Winrate evolution match mirror

We notice that after a certain number of matches, the win rate stabilizes at 23.5% for both teams, a perfect equality with a total of 53% of the matches being draws (cf. Table 6). Subsequently, we removed the goalkeeper from one team to visualize the impact of the goalkeeper in a team (cf. Fig. 5). We observe that the team without a goalkeeper has only 16.2% compared to 28.4% for the team with a goalkeeper, highlighting the importance of a goalkeeper in a team (cf. Table 7).

Table 6. Match mirror results

	Team 1 (State machine)	Team 2 (State machine)	Draw match
Win-rates	23.5%	23.5%	53%

Table 7. No goalkeeper results

	With goalkeeper (State machine)	Without goalkeeper	Draw matchs
Win-rates	28.4%	16.2%	55.4%

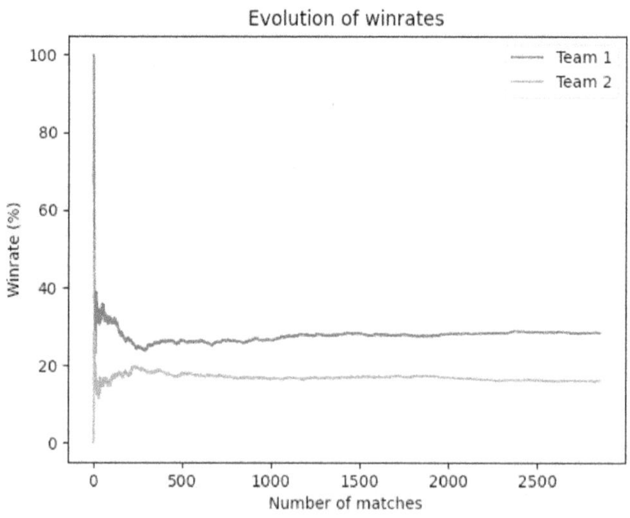

Fig. 5. Winrate evolution with no goalkeeper (in Team N°2)

To assess the performance of our decision-making algorithm using mental simulations, we replaced the behavior of one goalkeeper by the mental model algorithm previously described. We notice that the win rate of the team using mental simulations is slightly higher, although not significantly dominant (cf. Table 8).

Table 8. Mental simulation results

	State machine	Mental simulation	Draw matchs
Win-rates	22.7%	25.3%	52%

5 Conclusion and Future Work

Making effective decisions in competitive settings provides a significant advantage. We propose an improvement on work carried out in 2015 [15]. Based on the ORPHEUS [16] agent architecture, we have extended the test scenario to a full match and modified the architecture of the mental simulations to include all the entities present on the field. To evaluate the performance of our approach, we compared the results of our goalkeeper against a goalkeeper using a simple state machine as decision-making algorithm. The results obtained show a slightly better performance than goalkeepers using a simple state machine, although the win-rate difference between the two behaviors remains close. These results are encouraging and we will continue to improve the test environment in order to refine the results. In fact, in this article, we compared our approach based on mental simulations with an outdated simple state machine. In order to validate the performance of such an approach today, we would need to compare the performance of our behavioral algorithm with the goalkeeper algorithms used by RoboCup teams today. We are now working on porting this algorithm to a real robot, to check whether the computing capacity of a NAO V6 is sufficient to use this approach. The performance of such an algorithm a real robot will be harder to achieve than in simulation (it's easier to make 150 shots in simulation than with real robots). We are therefore considering a possible validation approach. Although successful porting to a physical robot will at least be a proof of concept.

Acknowledgment. This work benefits from the support of CERVVAL, Brittany region.

References

1. Abadi, M., et al.: Tensorflow: a system for large-scale machine learning. In: OSDI, Savannah, GA, USA, vol. 16, pp. 265–283 (2016)
2. Adorni, G., Cagnoni, S., Mordonini, M.: Genetic programming of a goal-keeper control strategy for the RoboCup middle size competition. In: Poli, R., Nordin, P., Langdon, W.B., Fogarty, T.C. (eds.) EuroGP 1999. LNCS, vol. 1598, pp. 109–119. Springer, Heidelberg (1999). https://doi.org/10.1007/3-540-48885-5_9
3. Adorni, G., Cagnoni, S., Mordonini, M.: Landmark-based robot self-localization: a case study for the robocup goal-keeper. In: Proceedings 1999 International Conference on Information Intelligence and Systems (Cat. No. PR00446), pp. 164–171. IEEE (1999)

4. Bozinovski, S., Jaeger, H., Schoel, P.: Engineering goalkeeper behavior using an emotion learning method. In: Proceedings of RoboCup Workshop, KI99: Deutsche Jahrestagung fuer Kuenstliche Intelligenz, pp. 48–56. Citeseer (1999)
5. Coumans, E., Bai, Y.: Pybullet, a python module for physics simulation for games, robotics and machine learning (2016)
6. Farias, G.B., Maximo, M.R., Afonso, R.J.: Requirements derivation for the goalkeeper of the robocup small size league. J. Control Autom. Electr. Syst. **33**(4), 1329–1341 (2022)
7. Fossel, J.D.: Using q-learning to control robot goal keeper behaviour (2010)
8. Garcıa, J.F., Rodrıguez, F.J., Fernández, C., Matellán, V.: Design an evaluation of robocup humanoid goalie. J. Phys. Agents **4**(2), 19–26 (2010)
9. García, J.F., Rodríguez, F.J., Fernández Llamas, C., Matellán Olivera, V., et al.: Designing a minimal reactive goalie for the robocup spl (2009)
10. Gholami, A., Bigham, B.S.: A learned soccer goalkeeper petri net model. In: 2017 Artificial Intelligence and Robotics (IRANOPEN), pp. 102–108. IEEE (2017)
11. Jamzad, M., et al.: A goal keeper for middle size robocup. In: Stone, P., Balch, T., Kraetzschmar, G. (eds.) RoboCup 2000. LNCS (LNAI), vol. 2019, pp. 583–586. Springer, Heidelberg (2001). https://doi.org/10.1007/3-540-45324-5_92
12. Lausen, H., Nielsen, J., Nielsen, M., Lima, P.: Model and behavior-based robotic goalkeeper. In: Polani, D., Browning, B., Bonarini, A., Yoshida, K. (eds.) RoboCup 2003. LNCS (LNAI), vol. 3020, pp. 169–180. Springer, Heidelberg (2004). https://doi.org/10.1007/978-3-540-25940-4_15
13. MacAlpine, P., Stone, P.: UT Austin Villa RoboCup 3D simulation base code release. In: Behnke, S., Sheh, R., Sarıel, S., Lee, D.D. (eds.) RoboCup 2016. LNCS (LNAI), vol. 9776, pp. 135–143. Springer, Cham (2017). https://doi.org/10.1007/978-3-319-68792-6_11
14. MacAlpine, P., Torabi, F., Pavse, B., Sigmon, J., Stone, P.: UT Austin Villa: RoboCup 2018 3D simulation league champions. In: Holz, D., Genter, K., Saad, M., von Stryk, O. (eds.) RoboCup 2018. LNCS (LNAI), vol. 11374, pp. 462–475. Springer, Cham (2019). https://doi.org/10.1007/978-3-030-27544-0_38
15. Masterjohn, J.G., Polceanu, M., Jarrett, J., Seekircher, A., Buche, C., Visser, U.: Regression and mental models for decision making on robotic biped goalkeepers. In: Almeida, L., Ji, J., Steinbauer, G., Luke, S. (eds.) RoboCup 2015. LNCS (LNAI), vol. 9513, pp. 177–189. Springer, Cham (2015). https://doi.org/10.1007/978-3-319-29339-4_15
16. Polceanu, M.: ORPHEUS: Reasoning and Prediction with Heterogeneous rEpresentations Using Simulation. Ph.D. thesis, Université de Bretagne Occidentale (UBO) (2015)
17. Prieto, C.E., Nino, F., Quintana, G.: A goalkeeper strategy in robot soccer based on danger theory. In: 2008 IEEE Congress on Evolutionary Computation (IEEE World Congress on Computational Intelligence), pp. 3443–3447. IEEE (2008)
18. Stoecker, J., Visser, U.: RoboViz: programmable visualization for simulated soccer. In: Röfer, T., Mayer, N.M., Savage, J., Saranlı, U. (eds.) RoboCup 2011. LNCS (LNAI), vol. 7416, pp. 282–293. Springer, Heidelberg (2012). https://doi.org/10.1007/978-3-642-32060-6_24
19. Wang, X., et al.: The goalkeeper strategy of RoboCup MSL based on dual image source. In: Almeida, L., Ji, J., Steinbauer, G., Luke, S. (eds.) RoboCup 2015. LNCS (LNAI), vol. 9513, pp. 165–174. Springer, Cham (2015). https://doi.org/10.1007/978-3-319-29339-4_14

20. Xu, Y., Vatankhah, H.: SimSpark: an open source robot simulator developed by the robocup community. In: Behnke, S., Veloso, M., Visser, A., Xiong, R. (eds.) RoboCup 2013. LNCS (LNAI), vol. 8371, pp. 632–639. Springer, Heidelberg (2014). https://doi.org/10.1007/978-3-662-44468-9_59
21. Zolanvari, A., Shirazi, M., Menhaj, M.: A q-learning approach for controlling a robotic goalkeeper during penalty procedure (2019)

Analysis of the Introduction Trajectory Planning in Control Applied in Small Size League Robots

Riei Rodrigues(✉), Lucas Cavalcanti, João Melo, Edna Barros, and Hansenclever F. Bassani

Centro de Informática, Universidade Federal de Pernambuco., Av. Prof. Moraes Rego, 1235 - Cidade Universitária, Recife, Pernambuco, Brazil
{rjmr,lhcs,jgocm,ensb,hfb}@cin.ufpe.br
https://robocin.com.br/

Abstract. Navigating mobile robots is a widely studied problem for Autonomous Mobile Robots. Together with path planning and robot navigation, trajectory planning comes to fill gaps related to the dynamics of the robot's movement. Trajectory planning brings the challenge of evaluating the performance gains obtained from strategies without this module. This work starts with a test methodology inserted in a robot soccer game, a dynamic environment with moving obstacles and objectives. The methodology explores various capabilities of the strategies along with the introduction of Bang-Bang trajectories with the Smith predictor and its evaluation. This work determines each approach's advantages and verifies the optimization advantages for the proposed state synchronization. The results show a 12% increase in the average speed during movement and a reduction of 26% of the time needed to navigate between two points compared with the visibility graph approach.

Keywords: Mobile Robotics · Path Planning · Trajectory Planning · Bang-Bang Trajectories

1 Introdution

Autonomous Mobile Robots are increasingly present in our daily lives, helping to carry out tasks such as vacuum cleaners, deliveries made by drones, and even autonomous cars [1]. These applications share the fundamental need to navigate the environment autonomously, dynamically responding to changes efficiently to fulfill their navigation task of getting from one point to another in space.

To move autonomously, as defined by Siegwart et al. [2], a robot needs four capabilities: Perception, Localization, Cognition, and Motion Control. If a robot does not have a robust perception system, it may not be able to react to changes in the external world, hindering obstacle avoidance. Acquiring this ability is currently a significant challenge for more critical areas such as autonomous cars,

Supported by Centro de Informática (CIn - UFPE) and RobôCIn Robotics Team.

E. Barros et al. (Eds.): RoboCup 2024, LNAI 15570, pp. 140–151, 2025.
https://doi.org/10.1007/978-3-031-85859-8_12

which seek to share space with human drivers and pedestrians on city streets, as discussed by Hussain et al. [3]. Moreover, perception is critical to the robot's localization in the environment, which defines the obstacles' positions.

There are two types of perception systems: local and global. In local perception, information is perceived by the robot itself. On the other hand, global perception has a global view of the context. For example, RoboCup Small Size League (SSL) [4] category, as they are based on image detection with SSL-Vision [5], processing of colors and patterns for tracking objects in the scene, information from the world has noise and a natural delay between capturing the image and sending the information, generating instability and uncertainty.

To minimize perception uncertainty, SSL teams improve information reliability by processing world-view information with filters, such as Kalman filters [6], which considers the current sequence of images and not just the latter. Although it improves data consistency, Kalman filter affects the perception delay of the world. Furthermore, we still have a limitation on the update frequency with RGB cameras, which are around 60 Hz in SSL context, generating an interval of approximately 0.016 s to obtain an update of the world.

SSL matches offer various scenarios in which other robots move around the field, representing dynamic obstacles, and the goalkeeper areas represent static obstacles. Under SSL rules, the ball cannot be pushed more than one meter and must be kicked, reaching a speed of up to 6.5 m/s, which generates sudden changes in-game objectives and contexts. Furthermore, the fact that the robots are omnidirectional forces the exploration of their maneuverability.

The trajectory planning goal is to improve compliance between the planning and execution of a movement for a better performance of the navigation system, in contrast with approaches that directly couple path planning with control. However, evaluating trajectory planning systematically and understanding its advantages and disadvantages are not widely discussed for mobile robots, as this depends heavily on the context of the application.

In this work, a methodology for creating systematic tests and collecting data from real use cases will be proposed to analyze the adoption of trajectory planning in the soccer matches of SSL, comparing the Bang-Bang Trajectory (BBT) trajectories in comparison with the navigation strategy of the Visibility Graph (VG), which does not consider trajectory. Furthermore, this work proposed a new method, called Synchronized State Bang-Bang Trajectories (SSBBT), that aims to meet the real-time control with a predictor minimizing the system perception delay, which limits the performance of BBT, presents performance gains compared to the other versions analyzed.

2 Background

Conceptually, trajectories and paths are objects of different natures. While path only considers the geometric perspective and the points in space, a trajectory is directly associated with the robot that will execute that movement, considering the dynamics of the robot's kinematics moving over time. According to the definition of Lynch et al. [7], a trajectory is the combination of a path with its geometric positions, with a temporal dimension that respects the robot's movement capabilities, and the time resolution between points to enable smooth and fluid navigation.

As defined by Gasparetto et al. [8], ideally, a navigation task is implemented in three steps, each the specific responsibility, sequentially from the abstract definition:

1. Path planning: Finding a possible path from the robot's current position to the goal, considering the current state of the world. This phase starts with a geometric objective, its position, and the obstacles. The output is a list of points for the robot to reach its destination, the geometric path.
2. Trajectory planning: Computing interactions between the robot's dynamics with obstacles considering its performance in the world over time. The interactions consider the geometric path, the robot's current state (position, speed, and acceleration), and its motion capabilities (acceleration and speed limits). The output is a list of robot movement states over time that connects the current state to the desired final state, respecting the robot's limits.
3. Control: Process planning to obtain effective robot actions based on the current state of the robot and the planned state. With this information, the difference between the planned and current state is calculated and used to control the robot, seeking to synchronize these two states at each cycle.

2.1 Bang-Bang Trajectory

Lynch et al. [7] demonstrates that, from a path function that relates the position space (s), $\theta(s)$, and a trapezoidal profile, we can find the optimal time and a speed profile that respects the movement possible to be performed by the actuators.

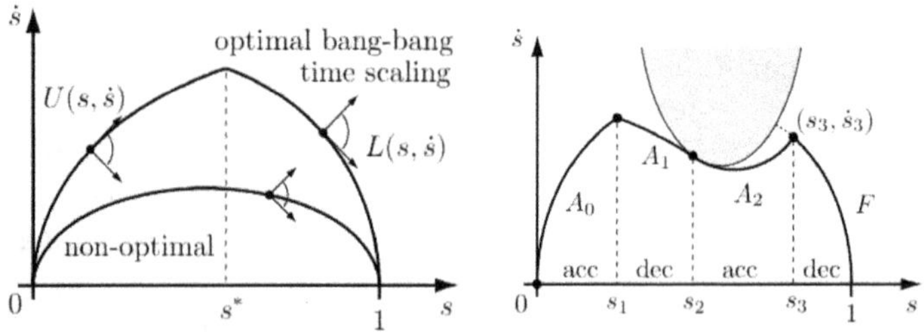

(a) Non-optimal time scale and the profiled scale Bang-Bang.

(b) Depending on the state of the robot and the world, it will be necessary to divide it into more than one trajectory segment.

Fig. 1. Graphs in $\theta(s, \dot{s})$ plane with speed profiles for a navigation task. Lynch et al. [7].

Timescale optimizations can be developed as a function of the Cartesian plane $\theta(s, \dot{s})$. We can derive functions from these optimizations that limit the maximum and minimum acceleration for each robot's state in time $L(s, \dot{s}) \leq \ddot{s} \leq U(s, \dot{s})$. Integrating these functions on time, we obtain the limiting speed curve, the acceleration cone, shown in Fig. 1(a).

After defining the robot's operation limits, maximizing the area in the $\theta(s, \dot{s})$ plane is possible and creates a time scale that operates within limits, switching between extremes. This is the principle of the Bang-Bang Trajectory Technique (BBT). This profile accelerates maximally on the curve $U(s, \dot{s})$ up to a certain $S*$ and then decelerates maximally on the curve $L(s, \dot{s})$.

A bottleneck for using trajectories is the complexity of modeling a robot's capabilities as a function of its state. For example, omnidirectional robots allow movement in any direction. Optimizations are possible, and Purwin et al. [9] showed that equations can be simplified and grouped into five cases, considering the current velocity with the planned trajectory.

Whenever the current status is determined, it is possible to keep the robot moving at high performance by calculating its trajectory in real-time. The robotics teams Tigers [10] and Er-Force [11] also adopted in their Bang-Bang implementation the velocity profiles from trapezoidal trajectories, the version implemented in this work was described in [12]. Their approaches differ in how the trajectory from the origin to the destination is divided into sub-problems. Tigers' approach creates a constellation of fixed points around the robot's current position and tests the possible combinations, forming a tree from the robot's position to its destination. On the other hand, ER-Force's approach randomly searches for a pivot state between the current state and the destination that prioritizes speed and avoids collision with the closest obstacle as a priority.

2.2 Related Work

Costa et al. [13] analyzed navigation in non-ideal environmental conditions with noise and uncertainty. In addition, they explored complex environments, which require the coordination of multiple robots. In Costa et al. work, the capacity of three algorithms is analyzed: Multi Robot A* (MRA*), Dynamic Visibility Graph A* (DVG+A*), and Probabilistic Safety Barrier Certificates (PrSBC). Analyzing the task of coordinating the navigation of multiple robots in an SSL match, presenting the context of their implementations and how the tests were performed.

To validate each algorithm, Costa et al. propose a testing methodology with antipodal tests and tests with other robots that actively try to block their path, collecting the computational time, navigation time, minimum distance between robots, and number of collisions.

3 Methodology

In robotics soccer games, like SSL, the development of navigation tasks in a match varies greatly depending on how teams interact and the environment.

As a result, analyzing navigation leads to many uncertainties and variations between executions, making a robust comparative analysis between strategies complex. To minimize these problems, this work proposes to analyze the team's execution during games and use fixed test cases that follow the same distribution and navigation characteristics during games.

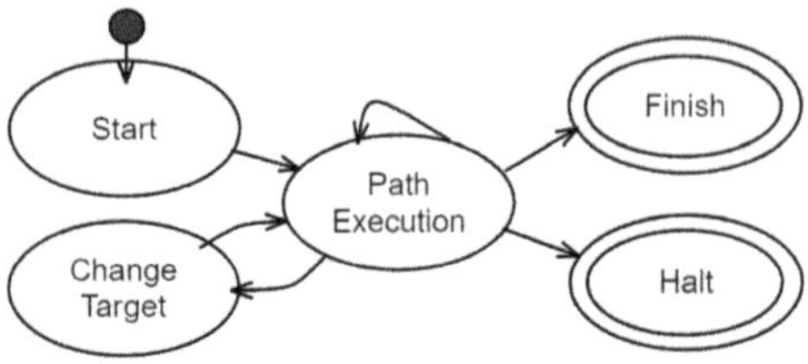

Fig. 2. Navigation states in an SSL match, each cycle, a transition is performed, the initial state is indicated with an entry arrow, and the terminal state is indicated with a double circle.

During the direct execution, without interruptions or changes, as shown in Fig. 2, the robot at rest receives a new navigation activity with a new objective. At the subsequent cycle of the *Start* state, the robot goes to the Path-Execution state and stays there until reaching the objective, when it transitions to the *Finish* state, completing the task. However, since this is a dynamic environment, the navigation task objective can change at each cycle in the Path-Execution, transitioning to the *Change-Target* state and then returning to the *Path-Execution* state with a new task defined. Lastly, at any time in the game, the referee may require an emergency stop, and the robot will go to the *Halt* state, where all robots must stop moving.

From the RoboCup SSL match logs, it is possible to reproduce any game situation at the team's software from a past game. With this, it is possible to generate statistics on browsing behavior within the game. Using this data makes it possible to replicate the distribution of behaviors in isolated scenarios, making them consistent with real scenarios.

With the execution of the replay of the RoboCup 2023 match logs, 3105 samples of machine executions were obtained. The movements interrupted by a halt command from the referee, which represented 8.5% of the samples, were ignored. By analyzing the remaining 91.5% machine executions, the distribution shown in Table 1 was obtained. Data show that the standard deviation is greater than the average time due to the considerable variation in the targets' objectives. During the game, the robots may want to move a few millimeters or a few meters, and, in addition, during the journey, objectives may change, taking the robot to travel further distances. The generated data presents the same average and standard deviation observed in real scenarios, approximated by a Gaussian distribution.

Table 1. Statistical distribution of execution flows of the navigation state machine in Fig. 2.

Parameter	AVG	STD
Execution Time to Finish (s)	3.95	4.05
Time from Last Change Target State to Finish (s)	0.35	0.43
Completion Rate to Target in Change Target State (%)	0.89	0.13
Distance to Goal in Start State (m)	0.75	1.25
Distance to Target when leaving Change Target State (m)	1.47	1.43
Number of Passes in the Change Target State	24	28

3.1 Visibility Graph Strategy

In the strategy based on the Visibility Graph (VG), we have two main modules in which movement planning appears implicitly only in navigation. As defined by Lynch et al. [7], the path planning step creates a representation of the world in a graph with the obstacles being simplified polygons connected by visible edges, having as output a list of intermediate positions to reach the destination. From the path, the discrete navigator creates a velocity vector in the direction of the next destination, according to the minimum and maximum speeds allowed to be sent to the robot. When the objective is reached, it is exchanged for the next one until the final destination is reached.

The navigation, together with intermediate destinations, causes a strategy bottleneck because the movement inertia requires reduced speed to avoid collisions and stick to the planned path. The robot distorts the path due to an uncompensated force, generating collisions and invasions.

3.2 Bang-Bang Trajectory Strategies

The Bang-Bang Trajectories (BBT) strategy start with a path planning based on an exploratory algorithm for sampling the valid space, a list of intermediate states (position, speed, acceleration) is created from the current position to the destination. The planning trajectory with intermediate states and the robot's current state combined with the robot's dynamic limits builds a plan from the current position until the final objective. By making enough iterations in this planning loop, we have a trajectory that approximately represents the minimum time to that destination and in the context of the world.

Movement planning lists the robot's movement states over time, including position, velocity vector, and time to that point. From the list of states over time planned for the robot based on the current estimated state and the current perceived state of the robot, the state browser calculates the necessary action to follow the planned, taking as output the speed of action that the robot must apply at that time to its motors.

In a context where the control system sends a command for execution remotely on the robot, the actuation delay impacts the system's responsiveness. The communication delays cause commands to be executed late by the robot, and the perception of the effects of these commands also takes time to be noticed.

To minimize delay effects, work like that developed by Velasco-Villa et al. [14], uses a Smith predictor to reduce errors associated with delay in tracking the trajectory of omnidirectional mobile robots. Based on this, the Synchronized State Bang-Bang Trajectories (SSBBT) navigation system was developed, as shown in Fig. 3, in which a predictor was added based on the current state perceived by the global view external to the robot, with a delay to the real one, and a buffer with the commands sent within the time window of actuation delay, it is capable of predicting the current state by applying these N commands, considering the robot kinematic constants, to the state seen from the vision and estimating their effects.

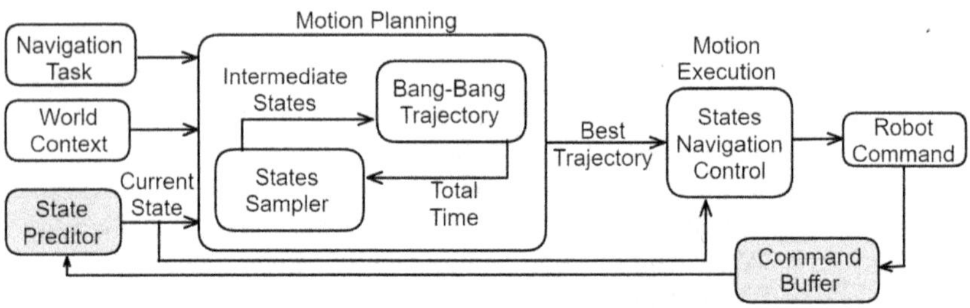

Fig. 3. Flow of execution of the Bang-Bang Trajectory (BBT), in gray, modules adding to Synchronized State Bang-Bang Trajectories (SSBBT).

The following commands were sent to measure the actuation delay window, the first half of the cycle with a linear velocity of 1 m/s and the remaining with zero; between the commands sent and the perception of the robot's speed in the global view, it is possible to obtain a temporal displacement representing the actuation delay.

3.3 Test Cases

For systematically evaluating each navigation strategy, analyzing the possible flows of states in Fig. 2 and recurring characteristics of the games, test cases were created to standardize the navigation tasks during a game. They were grouped into three sets:

- Simple movements, the robot starts from rest and reaches its destination, avoiding obstacles, going through the following sequence of states in the navigation state machine: Start → Path Execution → Finish.
- Redirected movement, when the robot starts moving towards a destination, but during the journey, it is redirected to another destination because something changed in the context of the game. The robot goes through the following states: Start → (Path Execution ↔ Change Target) → Finish.

- Marking movement avoids the prohibited area, a stressful environment, and reduced space for navigation where enemy robots move to random points within the risk region, and the defending team needs to move while avoiding collisions and invasions.

To define the distance of the objective at the Start and Change-Target state, the number of objective changes, when they occur, and their frequency, the distribution parameters presented in Table 1 were used at the random generation of navigation tasks and their possible modifications.

Three contexts are considered for simple and redirected movements: In the first experiment, only the robot was controlled on the field, with the goalkeeper areas as static obstacles (scenario 1). In the second experiment, the 11 stationary robots were randomly scattered across the field (scenario 2). In the last experiment, 11 robots can randomly change places with another robot, moving across the field and creating an interaction scenario with dynamic obstacles (scenario 3).

The Simulator-CLI [15] was adopted to evaluate all the proposed test cases and create a more realistic environment with noises and delay; for each type of test and each scenario, 100 navigation tasks were designed and executed. In addition to the simulator, the RobôCIn robots were used to compare the performance of the strategies and the robustness of the analyses in a more complex real-world environment for control and perception. Scenario 1 was tested for simple movement and movement with redirection.

3.4 Metrics and Data Analyzed

During the execution of each test, logs were recorded to analyze the execution of the navigation tasks. For each state in Fig. 2, the current timestamp, the collisions, and invasion fouls following the SSL rules [16] and SSL referee [17] implementation were recorded in the log, together with the following data:

- Start: Distance from the robot to the objective and estimated time.
- Path Execution: The trajectory calculated to the destination, position, and speed from vision, reference position and speed considered at the trajectory, position considering the execution time, position error, time error, error for the execution time position, and the state calculated by the predictor.
- Change Target: Distance from the robot to the old objective and from the robot to the new objective, estimated time to the new objective, and the current execution time.
- Finish: The current time and the total execution time.

The following metrics are analyzed to define the performance of navigation strategies:

- Average speed and execution time to measure how fast the robot moved during the execution of the task.

- Consistency of the path generated throughout the execution, using the scattering algorithm, as the path is recalculated, to analyze the accuracy of the execution and how much the navigation performance distorts the planned path when applying it to the robot.
- Root Mean Square Error (RMSE) of the position in time between the current and expected state, in strategies with trajectory planning, used to analyze synchrony between the estimated state and the real state of the robot.

We propose to compute the path dispersion score to analyze the consistency metric throughout the generated path. The path dispersion algorithm fills a matrix with the dimensions of the field and all paths calculated along the task to the destination, assigning a weight to the robot's planned position in time. At each cycle, a loop iterates over the planned path to the final destination, writing a weight in the position corresponding to the planning in the matrix. Each cycle starts with the weight one and goes with decay with a factor of 0.95 for each 50-millimeters distance traveled. After normalizing by real traveled distance, if no distortion or path uncertainty occurs, the resulting score tends to the value of one.

4 Results

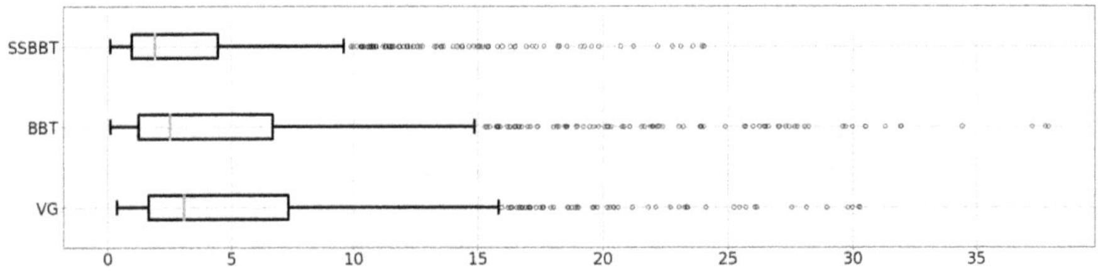

Fig. 4. Distribution of total time (in seconds) taken by each strategy to perform navigation tasks in tests with the simulator.

When analyzing Fig. 4, we see that the SSBBT strategy completes navigation in less time, compared to the VG technique, achieving an average reduction of 26%. Furthermore, as shown in Fig. 5(a), while the base version of BBT has speeds around 10% below the VG strategy, the improved version, SSBBT, presented on average an improvement of 12% in average speed.

Analyzing the results presented in Fig. 5(b), the VG presented a low dispersion as a direct consequence of the robot's lower speed, reflected in the lower average speed and longer time to perform the navigation presented. These speed reductions create a bottleneck to keep the control system stable for high-performance applications like SSL.

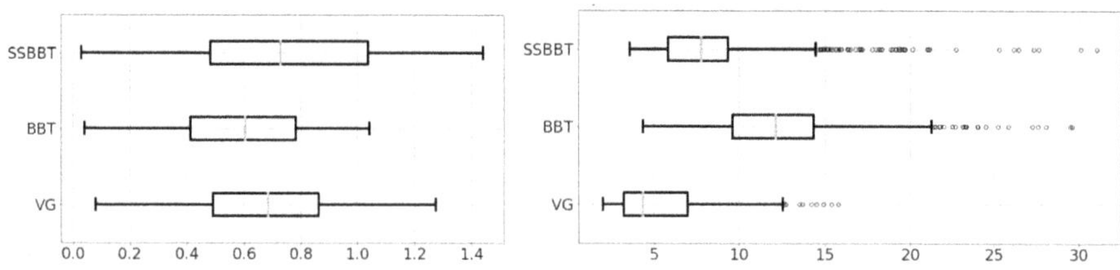

(a) Average speed (m/s). (b) Dispersion (1).

Fig. 5. Box plot of result of tests with the simulator for the strategies: Bang-Bang Trajectory (BBT), Visibility Graph (VG), Synchronized State Bang-Bang Trajectories (SSBBT).

The perception delay impacts the responsiveness of the control system in perceiving the robot's response to the applied action, a characteristic that generates an apparent inertia to execute changes according to the planned trajectory; thus, the dispersion shown in Fig. 5(b) between the base Bang-Bang trajectories BBT is, on average, 60% higher, compared to the improved version, SSBBT.

Furthermore, the uncertainty of paths for scenarios with more complex dynamic obstacles contributed to the dispersion observed in strategies that use Bang-Bang trajectories. In these scenarios, due to limitations in the implementation and modeling of obstacles, Bang-Bang trajectories proved to be sensitive to world state changes, increasing dispersion.

Table 2. Average of the execution results with the real robot, applying the simple and redirected movement tests in scenario 1.

Strategy	Total Time (s)	Average Speed (m/s)	Dispersion (1)
VG	7.713 ± 4.554	0.513 ± 0.156	15.484 ± 3.540
BBT	8.417 ± 8.422	0.612 ± 0.174	13.751 ± 2.286
SSBBT	6.223 ± 4.983	0.708 ± 0.206	11.969 ± 2.220

With the tests in the real environment shown in Table 2, it is possible to observe results that reinforce those previously analyzed in the simulated environment. SSBBT demonstrated a 20% time reduction and a 38% increase in average speed compared to the VG. BBT, even with a higher average speed, due to the delay in correcting the robot when redirecting objectives, results show an increase in distance traveled and execution time. Finally, for dispersion, we realize that the greater complexity of guaranteeing the execution of the movement in the real robot, with a discrete point-to-point control, together with the analysis of only scenario 1, without obstacles that lead the Bang-Bang to uncertain paths, we obtain a reduction in dispersion in strategies that use Bang-Bang trajectories. SSBBT reaches 23% less dispersion than VG.

Analyzing the RMSE errors between strategies that use Bang-Bang trajectories, it is possible to conclude that the global view provides accurate data with a position error in time of 0.0522 $\pm$ 0.013 m, while the SSBBT presented an error of 0.071 $\pm$ 0.019 m, 36% higher due to estimation noise and oscillations in the actuation delay.

In addition to data directly associated with navigation performance, during the tests, invasions of prohibited areas and collisions with other robots were analyzed to evaluate each strategy's navigation safety.

Table 3. Collision and invasion events throughout the tests, divided by strategy.

Strategy	Amount of Collisions	Average speed of Collisions (m/s)	Amount of Invasion	Size Average of Invasion (m)
VG	3	1.696	67	0.01363
BBT	3	1.867	28	0.00373
SSBBT	0	N/A	70	0.00686

As for collisions in Table 3, obtaining conclusive data was impossible due to each strategy's low occurrence of collisions. It would be necessary to carry out more specific tests, such as those presented by Costa et al. [13], to test the limits of the techniques.

Regarding invasions shown in Table 3, in the VG strategy, they occur because the robot navigates the boundaries of obstacle polygons. In this way, errors in matching planned and executed navigation lead to invasions, an idea reinforced by the fact that the BBT strategy has reduced invasions by around 140%. However, even with trajectory planning, the SSBBT strategy presented several invasions similar to VG, the noise in the current state estimate, leading the predictor to have an exaggerated anticipatory bias in navigation, hindering the completion of the obstacle avoidance maneuver.

5 Conclusion and Further Work

In this work, the gains involved in introducing a trajectory planning system are notable, along with the need to use a state predictor to gain advantages, even with the increase in dispersion tolerated by the increase in speed obtained. Thus, this work made it possible to systematically measure the gains of the SSBBT technique in speed and time reduction.

For future work, it is important to define the coverage rate obtained with proposed tests to expand them. Minimizing uncertainty when defining the path to improve strategies involving Bang-Bang trajectories is essential.

References

1. Misaros, M., Stan, O.P., Donca, I.C., Miclea, L.C.: Autonomous robots for services—state of the art, challenges, and research areas. Sensors **23**(10), 4962 (2023)

2. Siegwart, R., Nourbakhsh, I.R., Scaramuzza, D.: Autonomous mobile robots, A Bradford Book (2011)
3. Hussain, R., Zeadally, S.: Autonomous cars: research results, issues, and future challenges. IEEE Commun. Surv. Tutor. **21**(2), 1275–1313 (2018)
4. Kitano, H., Asada, M., Kuniyoshi, Y., Noda, I., Osawa, E.: Robocup: the robot world cup initiative. In: Proceedings of the First International Conference on Autonomous Agents, AGENTS '97, p. 340347. Association for Computing Machinery, New York (1997)
5. Zickler, S., Laue, T., Birbach, O., Wongphati, M., Veloso, M.: SSL-vision: the shared vision system for the robocup small size league. In: Baltes, J., Lagoudakis, M.G., Naruse, T., Ghidary, S.S. (eds.) RoboCup 2009. LNCS (LNAI), vol. 5949, pp. 425–436. Springer, Heidelberg (2010). https://doi.org/10.1007/978-3-642-11876-0_37
6. Yang, S., Baum, M.: Extended kalman filter for extended object tracking. In: 2017 IEEE International Conference on Acoustics, Speech and Signal Processing (ICASSP), pp. 4386–4390 (2017)
7. Lynch, K.M., Park, F.C.: Modern Robotics: Mechanics, Planning, and Control, 1st edn. Cambridge University Press, Cambridge (2017)
8. Gasparetto, A., Boscariol, P., Lanzutti, A., Vidoni, R.: Path planning and trajectory planning algorithms: a general overview. In: Carbone, G., Gomez-Bravo, F. (eds.) Motion and Operation Planning of Robotic Systems. MMS, vol. 29, pp. 3–27. Springer, Cham (2015). https://doi.org/10.1007/978-3-319-14705-5_1
9. Purwin, O., D'Andrea, R.: Trajectory generation for four wheeled omnidirectional vehicles. In: Proceedings of the 2005, American Control Conference, 2005, vol. 7, pp. 4979–4984 (2005)
10. Ommer, N., Ryll, A., Geiger, M.: Tigers mannheim (team interacting and game evolving robots) extended team description for robocup. In: RoboCup Small Size League, Mannheim, Germany (2019)
11. Wendler, A., Heineken, T., Er-force 2020 extended team description paper. In: RoboCup Small Size League, Erlangen, Germany (2020)
12. Araújo, V., et al.: Robôcin ssl-unification: Aămodular software architecture forădynamic multi-robot systems. In: Buche, C., Rossi, A., Simões, M., Visser, U. (eds.) RoboCup 2023: Robot World Cup XXVI, pp. 313–324. Springer, Cham (2024). https://doi.org/10.1007/978-3-031-55015-7_26
13. da Silva Costa, L., Tonidandel, F.: Multi-robot path planning with safety based control applied to the small size league robots. In:Buche, C., Rossi, A., Simões, M., Visser, U. (eds.) RoboCup 2023: Robot World Cup XXVI, pp. 78–89. Springer, Cham (2024). https://doi.org/10.1007/978-3-031-55015-7_7
14. Velasco-Villa, M., del Muro-Cuellar, B., Alvarez-Aguirre, A.: Smith-predictor compensator for a delayed omnidirectional mobile robot. In: 2007 Mediterranean Conference on Control & Automation, pp. 1–6 (2007)
15. Bergmann, P., et al.: Er-force 2022 extended team description paper. In: RoboCup Small Size League, Erlangen, Germany (2022)
16. RoboCup. Laws of the RoboCup Small Size League 2023. Small Size League Technical Committee (2024)
17. Magel, L.: Development of an autonomous referee software for the small size league. In: Robocup Small Size League, Mannheim, Germany (2016)

Cross Language Soccer Framework: An Open Source Framework for the RoboCup 2D Soccer Simulation

Nader Zare[1(✉)], Aref Sayareh[1,2], Alireza Sadraii[1], Arad Firouzkouhi[1,4], and Amilcar Soares[3]

[1] CYRUS Robotic Team, Halifax, Canada
nader@cyrus2d.com, asayareh@mun.ca, amilcar.soares@lnu.se, arad.firouzkouhi@aut.ac.ir
[2] Memorial University of Newfoundland, St. John's, Canada
[3] Department of Computer Science and Media Technology, Linnaeus University, Växjö, Sweden
[4] Amirkabir University of Technology, Tehran, Iran
https://www.cyrus2d.com , https://github.com/CLSFramework

Abstract. RoboCup Soccer Simulation 2D (SS2D) research is hampered by the complexity of existing C++-based codes like Helios, Cyrus, and Gliders, which also suffer from limited integration with modern machine learning frameworks. This development paper introduces a transformative solution: a gRPC-based, language-agnostic framework that seamlessly integrates with the high-performance Helios base code. This approach not only facilitates the use of diverse programming languages including C#, JavaScript, and Python—but also maintains the computational efficiency critical for real-time decision-making in SS2D. By breaking down language barriers, our framework significantly enhances collaborative potential and flexibility, empowering researchers to innovate without the overhead of mastering or developing extensive base codes. We invite the global research community to leverage and contribute to the Cross Language Soccer (CLS) framework, which is openly available under the MIT License, to drive forward the capabilities of multi-agent systems in soccer simulations (https://github.com/CLSFramework,https://github.com/CLSFramework/cross-language-soccer-framework/wiki).

Keywords: RoboCup · Soccer Simulation 2D · Python · Proxy

1 Introduction

Soccer, a sport universally celebrated for its dynamic nature and strategic gameplay [1–3], serves as a captivating domain for artificial intelligence research. The RoboCup organization was established to advance the abilities of autonomous agents to understand and play soccer. The ultimate objective of this organization

E. Barros et al. (Eds.): RoboCup 2024, LNAI 15570, pp. 152–163, 2025.
https://doi.org/10.1007/978-3-031-85859-8_13

is to create a fully autonomous team that can defeat the FIFA World Cup champion by the year 2050 [4–7]. Soccer Simulation 2D League (SS2D) is a platform that promotes the development of artificial intelligence in multi-agent environments [8–13]. Figure 1 provides a detailed visualization of the Soccer Simulation 2D game environment.

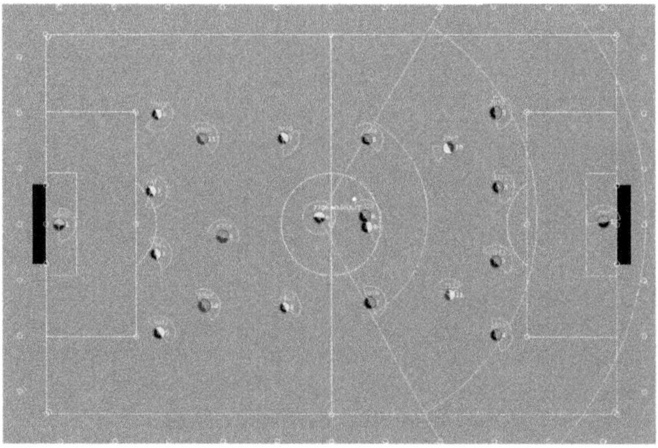

Fig. 1. An overview of Soccer Simulation 2D Environment

Existing widely-used C++-based codes like Helios, Cyrus2D, and Gliders offer tools that allow researchers to focus on the decision challenges within the environment [14,15,20]. Nevertheless, due to the inherent complexity of C++ and its limited integration with machine-learning frameworks, incorporating machine-learning methods into these frameworks poses significant challenges. Addressing these challenges involves the development of new frameworks in alternative languages. However, creating frameworks in different languages is a time-consuming process, and the performance of these languages may not be sufficiently high for making timely decisions. For example, Python, a widely used and straightforward programming language, lacks the necessary performance capabilities in the context of SS2D [26].

Recognizing the advantages of a high-performance base code, such as Helios, which completely supports SS2D server features, we propose a novel solution. This development paper introduces an innovative approach to overcome language barriers and enhance flexibility. By connecting the robust Helios base code to other languages using gRPC, we aim to provide researchers with the freedom to work in their preferred languages without compromising the performance benefits offered by C++. This approach empowers researchers to focus on the intelligence aspects of their agents, leveraging the high-quality and high-performance foundation laid by Helios.

As illustrated in Fig. 2, the Cross Language Soccer framework architecture seamlessly integrates the Helios base code with a language-agnostic gRPC server.

This connection facilitates efficient communication and collaboration between the high-performance Helios base code and multiple programming languages, empowering researchers in the RoboCup 2D Soccer Simulation domain.

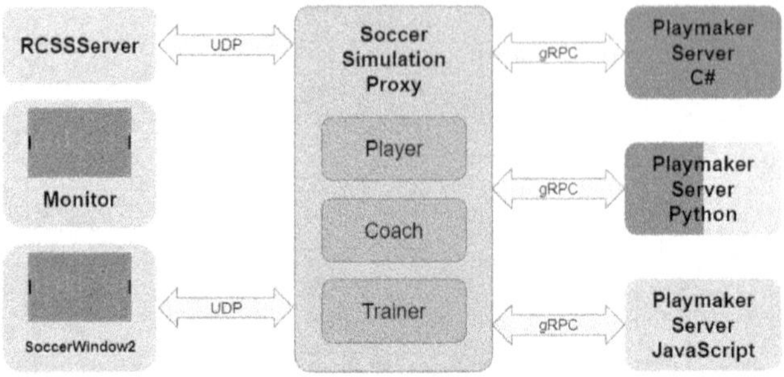

Fig. 2. CLS Framework Architecture: The diagram depicts the interconnected components of the CLS framework approach. The modified version of the Helios base code called Soccer Simulation Proxy communicates with a language-agnostic gRPC Playmaker Server, providing a flexible environment for researchers working with various programming languages in RoboCup 2D Soccer Simulation.

In the following sections, we provide a detailed explanation of our approach, including the framework's architecture, implementation details, and its implications for research in the SS2D environment.

2 Background

The RoboCup Soccer Simulation 2D server (server) has two main jobs: it runs soccer games and interacts with coaches, players, trainers, and monitors. It communicates by sending observations to agents, receiving low-level actions from them, and applying them to the game. Various teams have contributed base codes to the RoboCup soccer simulation, for instance, the "CMUnited" team from Carnegie Mellon University (USA) [16,17], the "UvA Trilearn" team from the University of Amsterdam (The Netherlands) [18], the "MarliK" team from the University of Guilan (Iran) [22], the "HELIOS" team from AIST Information Technology Research Institute (Japan), the "Wrighteagle" team from the University of Science and Technology of China [19], the "Gliders2d" team from the University of Sydney (Australia) [20,21], and the "Cyrus2d" and "Pyrus" teams from Dalhousie University (Canada) [13,15,26].

The Helios base code provides in processing observations by denoising them and constructing a detailed world model that contains all of the information required for decision-making, such as an intercept table. Also, its richness in functionality, encompasses high-level actions (e.g., BodyGoToPoint, BodySmartKick), offensive planners (e.g. ChainActions), and extensive logging functionality, offering graphical logs through the SoccerWindow2 application.

In navigating the complexities of existing base codes like Cyrus and Gliders, which are built upon the powerful Helios base code, researchers often face challenges due to their intricacy. While these codes provide robust capabilities, applying new algorithms or working with them requires a deep understanding of both soccer simulation 2D and the base codes. Moreover, their reliance on C++ poses hurdles, as the language lacks abundant machine-learning frameworks and is relatively challenging for researchers less familiar with SS2D or C++. On the other hand, the Pyrus base code, developed in Python, offers a more accessible option but sacrifices performance.

Half Field Offense (HFO) is an environment tailored for reinforcement learning in soccer simulations, focusing exclusively on half-field scenarios [24]. This framework modifies the standard Soccer Simulation 2D server, limiting it to half-field play, which restricts its applicability to full-match scenarios and broader training objectives. Furthermore, HFO only supports C++ and Python, excluding other programming languages. Its specialized nature and lack of support for recent server updates or features also restrict its utility for researchers looking to utilize the latest developments in soccer simulation.

To address these challenges, we propose a novel solution by using Remote Procedure Call (RPC) technology, specifically gRPC (Google Remote Procedure Call). We implemented the gRPC client on the Helios base, so it facilitates efficient communication between the base and other languages. Therefore, we streamline the development process and enhance the flexibility of researchers. This approach allows developers to benefit from the high performance of C++ for computationally intensive tasks, such as denoising and world modeling, while enabling them to implement or improve Helios base decision-making logic in languages like C#, JavaScript, Python, or others.

The use of gRPC offers several advantages, including low latency, language-agnostic communication, and efficient serialization of data. This integration helps researchers work in their preferred languages without sacrificing the performance advantages of the Helios base code. In summary, our solution facilitates a bridge between the efficiency of C++ and the flexibility of other languages, empowering researchers in the SS2D domain.

3 Cross Language Soccer Framework

We have introduced a new approach called Cross Language Soccer Framework to enhance the flexibility and interoperability of RoboCup Soccer Simulation 2D (SS2D). The Cross Language Soccer approach consists of two components: Soccer Simulation Proxy and Playmaker Server. The Soccer Simulation Proxy is an extended version of the Helios base that can send decision-making information to the Playmaker Server. It can receive high-level actions from the Playmaker Server and send them to RoboCup Soccer Simulation Server and/or SoccerWindow2. On the other hand, the Playmaker Server receives information from the client and selects the appropriate actions to be sent back to the client. We have implemented some sample servers in C#, Python, and JavaScript, but it can also be implemented in other languages to make use of their features.

3.1 Soccer Simulation Proxy

We have modified the Helios base code to enhance its interaction capabilities with the gRPC server[1]. Specifically, the base code now transmits detailed information about each game cycle to the server, which in response, sends back a series of potential actions. This bidirectional communication enables the Playmaker Server to effectively process and make strategic decisions based on the incoming data.

To facilitate this enhanced functionality, the client is designed to serialize various data types—such as the WorldModel, FullState WorldModel, Server Parameters, Player Parameters, and Player Types—into gRPC messages during each game cycle. Conversely, it also deserializes incoming gRPC action messages back into Helios base actions.

These improvements ensure that the Helios base maintains its inherent efficiency and performance, while now being able to seamlessly interact with a diverse array of programming languages through gRPC. This modification not only preserves the robustness of the original system but also expands its utility and applicability in multi-language research environments.

3.2 Playmaker Server

The Playmaker Server acts as the decision-making hub within our framework, receiving and processing messages from the Soccer Simulation Proxy. Based on the detailed information conveyed in these messages, it evaluates the current game state and strategically generates corresponding actions to be executed in the simulation.

To demonstrate the versatility and language-agnostic design of our framework, we have developed initial implementations of the Playmaker Server in three different programming languages: C#[2], Python[3], and JavaScript[4]. These examples serve to showcase the server's capability to operate effectively across diverse programming environments. Looking ahead, we aim to extend this functionality by developing additional server implementations in other languages, further broadening the framework's accessibility and appeal to a global research community.

3.3 Benefits of Using gRPC

To facilitate robust communication between the Playmaker Server and the Soccer Simulation Proxy, we employ gRPC, a high-performance, open-source universal RPC framework. The core of this communication setup is a Protocol Buffer, which defines the structure of messages and services. This Protocol Buffer is

[1] https://github.com/CLSFramework/soccer-simulation-proxy.
[2] https://github.com/CLSFramework/playmaker-server-csharp.
[3] https://github.com/CLSFramework/playmaker-server-python.
[4] https://github.com/CLSFramework/playmaker-server-nodejs.

instrumental in generating an abstract server and client-side objects for each message, utilizing libraries that support multiple programming languages.

The adoption of gRPC streamlines the integration process for researchers working in different programming environments. It eliminates the cumbersome need for manual serialization and deserialization of messages. Researchers can directly utilize the automatically created objects for decision-making and action generation, which are then seamlessly communicated to the SS2D-Proxy-Client. This efficient data handling mechanism not only accelerates development but also enhances the flexibility and scalability of server implementations across diverse research contexts.

3.4 Protocol Buffer Definitions

The communication protocol between the modified version of the Helios base and the Playmaker Server is defined using Protocol Buffers (ProtoBuf). The gRPC service 'Game' comprises several Remote Procedure Call (RPC) functions for obtaining player, coach, and trainer actions, as well as sending initialization messages and server parameters. The 'State' message encapsulates crucial information about the game state, including agent type and a detailed world model. Figure 3 provides an overview of the 'Game' service and highlights key messages utilized in the Protocol Buffer. Detailed explanations of the RPC functions and messages are presented in the subsequent sections.

```
message PlayerAction {
  oneof action {
    Dash dash = 1;
    Turn turn = 2;
    Kick kick = 3;
    ...
    Body_GoToPoint body_go_to_point = 16;
    Body_SmartKick body_smart_kick = 17;
    ...
    HeliosShoot helios_shoot = 58;
    HeliosChainAction helios_chain_action = 59;
    ...
  }
}
message PlayerActions {
  repeated PlayerAction actions = 1;
}
message Player {
  Vector2D position = 1;
  Vector2D seen_position = 2;
  Vector2D heard_position = 3;
  ...
}
```

```
message WorldModel {
  InterceptTable intercept_table = 1;
  string our_team_name = 2;
  string their_team_name = 3;
  ...
  repeated Player teammates = 8;
  repeated Player opponents = 9;
  repeated Player unknowns = 10;
  map<int32, Player> our_players_dict = 11;
  map<int32, Player> their_players_dict = 12;
  ...
}
message State {
  AgentType agent_type = 1;
  WorldModel world_model = 2;
  WorldModel full_world_model = 3;
}
service Game {
  rpc GetPlayerActions(State) returns (PlayerActions) {}
  rpc GetCoachActions(State) returns (CoachActions) {}
  rpc GetTrainerActions(State) returns (TrainerActions) {}
  rpc SendInitMessage(InitMessage) returns (Empty) {}
  rpc SendServerParams(ServerParam) returns (Empty) {}
  rpc SendPlayerParams(PlayerParam) returns (Empty) {}
  rpc SendPlayerType(PlayerType) returns (Empty) {}
}
```

Fig. 3. Definition of Protocol Buffer Messages and RPC Functions for the 'Game' Service in SS2D-Proxy. The illustration outlines essential structures and functions used for communication between the Helios base and the SS2D-Proxy-Server.

3.5 Key RPC Functions

In our framework, several key Remote Procedure Call (RPC) functions facilitate communication between the Soccer Simulation Proxy and Playmaker Server components. A Soccer Simulation Proxy agent calls 'SendInitMessage', 'SendServerParams', 'SendPlayerParams', and 'SendPlayerType' once to send parameters to Playmaker server, and calls 'GetPlayerActions', 'GetCoachActions', or 'GetTrainerActions' to receive Action message in each cycle. Below is an overview of these essential RPC functions and their roles:

- **GetPlayerActions(State)**: Returns a list of player actions based on the provided game state.
- **GetCoachActions(State)**: Retrieves coach actions corresponding to the given game state.
- **GetTrainerActions(State)**: Fetches trainer actions based on the provided game state.
- **SendInitMessage(InitMessage)**: Sends an initialization message and receives an acknowledgment.
- **SendServerParams(ServerParam)**: Transmits server parameters and acknowledges receipt.
- **SendPlayerParams(PlayerParam)**: Sends player parameters and receives an acknowledgment.
- **SendPlayerType(PlayerType)**: Sends player type information and acknowledges receipt.

3.6 Message Definitions

This section presents some of the important gRPC messages used in our framework[5]. The Soccer Simulation Proxy sends the 'ServerParam', 'PlayerParam', and 'PlayerType' messages once, while the 'State' message is sent in each cycle. The Playmaker Server receives the 'State' message and responds with 'PlayerAction', 'CoachAction', or 'TrainerCction' messages.

- **State**: The 'State' message encapsulates the agent type and a detailed 'WorldModel,' containing essential game state information such as team names, player details, ball position, game mode, and scores.
- **PlayerAction**: The 'PlayerActions' message consists of a list of 'PlayerAction' messages, each representing an action that a player can perform during a game cycle. These actions cover a wide range of behaviours, including movement, ball interaction, communication, and specific strategies like those implemented in the Helios base code.
- **TrainerAction**: Represents actions initiated by a trainer during the game.
- **CoachAction**: Represents actions initiated by a coach during the game.
- **ServerParam**: Contains parameters related to the game server, contributing to the game's configuration.
- **PlayerParam**: Encompasses parameters specific to individual players, influencing their behaviour in the game.

[5] https://github.com/CLSFramework/cross-language-soccer-framework/wiki/Environment-Messages.

- **PlayerType**: Provides insight into a player's style, helping to differentiate and classify players on the field.

As depicted in Fig. 4, the message flow illustrates the seamless communication between the SS2D Proxy Base, SS2D Proxy Server, Soccer Window 2 Monitor, and the SS2D Server. This visual representation offers insights into the data exchange dynamics within the proposed SS2D-Proxy framework.

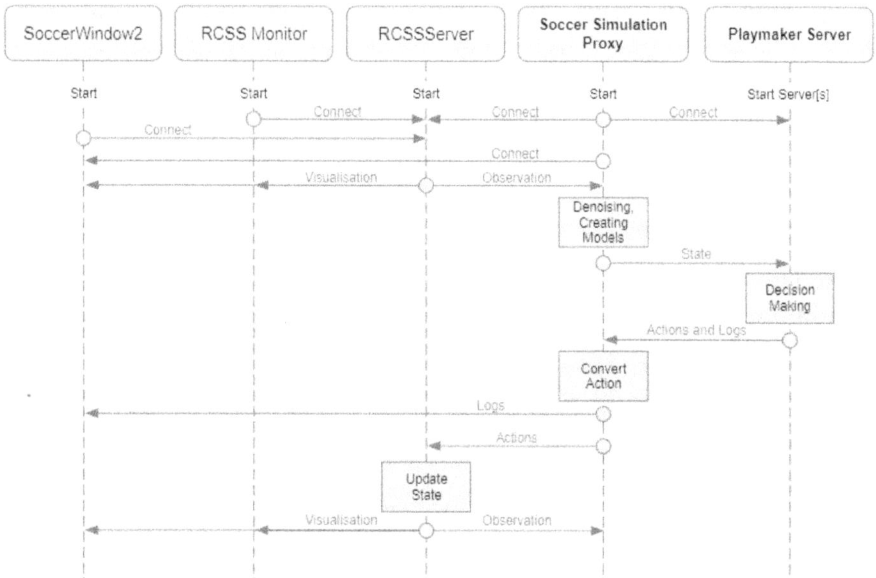

Fig. 4. SS2D-Proxy Message Flow: The diagram illustrates the message flow between key components, showcasing the interconnected communication pathways among the SS2D Proxy Base, SS2D Proxy Server, Soccer Window 2 Monitor, and the SS2D Server in the development of the SS2D-Proxy framework.

In summary, the SS2D-Proxy approach fosters collaboration and flexibility in RoboCup SS2D research, enabling seamless communication between the high-performance Helios base code and diverse programming languages through the gRPC protocol. This integration lays the groundwork for advancing intelligent multi-agent systems in the dynamic domain of RoboCup Soccer Simulation 2D.

4 Development Features

This section highlights key development challenges encountered while building the framework and the innovative solutions implemented to address these challenges. These solutions are designed to simplify the setup and use of our framework, enhancing its accessibility for researchers and participants in the RoboCup competition.

4.1 Cross-Platform Compatibility Challenges

Challenge: Setting up the Soccer Simulation Server, Soccer Simulation Proxy, and Soccer Simulation Monitor on Ubuntu was initially complex due to multiple dependencies and configuration requirements.

Solution: We provide Linux AppImages for the Soccer Simulation Server, Soccer Simulation Proxy, and Monitor. These AppImages are self-contained and include all necessary components and dependencies, allowing users to download and execute them with ease. To customize or extend the functionality of the Playmaker Server, researchers simply need to install language-specific dependencies using NPM for JavaScript, PIP for Python, or .NET for C#. This approach significantly simplifies the initial setup process, enabling researchers to quickly start developing and testing their strategies.

4.2 Windows Compatibility

Challenge: Building and running the Soccer Simulation Server, Soccer Simulation Proxy, and Monitor on Windows platforms is not directly supported due to compatibility issues.

Solution: We recommend using Windows Subsystem for Linux (WSL) to run the server components, while the Playmaker Server can run natively on Windows. Alternatively, we provide a Dockerized version of the framework, allowing users to deploy the Soccer Simulation components in Docker containers and connect them seamlessly to the Playmaker Server running on Windows.

4.3 RoboCup Competition Preparation

Challenge: Participants in the RoboCup competition need a reliable and easy-to-setup environment to compete without technical issues.

Solution: We offer an AppImage of the Soccer Simulation Proxy that integrates smoothly into the Playmaker project. This setup ensures that teams can participate in the RoboCup competition with minimal setup and without compatibility concerns.

4.4 Support for Reinforcement Learning Research

Challenge: Researchers aiming to implement reinforcement learning algorithms require a flexible and robust environment compatible with modern RL frameworks.

Solution: Our framework includes sample Python code that researchers can use as a foundation for training agents. Additionally, we provide mechanisms for controlling the Soccer Simulation Server via a trainer agent, facilitating the implementation and testing of advanced RL algorithms.

4.5 Integration with Gym Environments

Challenge: Researchers familiar with developing RL algorithms in gym environments need a comparable setup to apply their expertise in the soccer simulation context [25].

Solution: We have developed sample projects that mimic the design of gym environments, allowing researchers to leverage existing RL libraries and techniques. This approach provides a familiar and efficient starting point for developing new RL strategies in our soccer simulation framework.

4.6 Geometric Computations

Challenge: Developing efficient geometric computations for decision-making processes can be time-consuming and complex.

Solution: To expedite and simplify the development of geometric computations, we have integrated the Python Pyrus Geom library (pyrusgeom), specifically designed for the PYRUS soccer simulation base code. This library, readily available via PIP, provides robust and optimized geometric computation functions, enabling researchers to implement sophisticated decision-making algorithms more efficiently.

5 Conclusion

In conclusion, the SS2D-Proxy approach presented in this paper addresses the challenges associated with existing C++-based codes in RoboCup Soccer Simulation 2D (SS2D) research. The complexities and learning difficulties posed by these codes, coupled with the time-consuming process of developing new base codes for each language, motivated the need for a versatile solution.

Our innovation involves connecting the widely adopted Helios base code to a language-agnostic framework using gRPC. This approach facilitates seamless communication between Helios and different languages, such as C#, Python, and JavaScript. By doing so, we empower researchers to work in their language of choice without compromising the high-quality, high-performance features offered by the C++ Helios base code.

The integration of gRPC not only streamlines communication but also introduces efficiency through low-latency data exchange and language-agnostic capabilities. Researchers can now focus on developing intelligent multi-agent systems in SS2D without the burdensome task of creating an entire base code.

Our solution enhances collaboration, allowing researchers to leverage the strengths of C++ for computationally intensive tasks, while developing decision-making logic in languages that better suit their preferences and expertise. The protocol buffer definitions and RPC functions provide a standardized and efficient means of communication between Helios and the gRPC server, ensuring a seamless exchange of game state information and actions.

In summary, the SS2D-Proxy approach opens new avenues for collaborative research in the RoboCup SS2D domain. It bridges the gap between the efficiency of C++ and the flexibility of multiple languages, paving the way for advancements in intelligent multi-agent systems within the dynamic context of RoboCup Soccer Simulation 2D.

Acknowledgments. We extend our heartfelt appreciation to Professor Stan Matwin and Professor Amilcar Soares for their exceptional support and guidance over the past three years. Their mentorship has been instrumental in shaping the trajectory of our research in the CYRUS team.

Special thanks are extended to Professor Hidehisa Akyama for his pivotal work on the Helios base and Soccer Simulation 2D server. His pioneering efforts have laid a solid foundation for researchers in the field, including ourselves.

These acknowledgments stand as a tribute to the collaborative spirit and mentorship that have played a crucial role in the development and realization of this project.

References

1. Bangsbo, J., Peitersen, B.: Soccer Systems and Strategies. Human Kinetics, Champaign (2000)
2. Pollard, R., Reep, C.: Measuring the effectiveness of playing strategies at soccer. J. R. Stat. Soc. Ser. D (The Statistician) **46**(4), 541–50 (1997)
3. Rein, R., Memmert, D.: Big data and tactical analysis in elite soccer: future challenges and opportunities for sports science. Springerplus **5**(1), 1–3 (2016)
4. Burkhard, H.D., Duhaut, D., Fujita, M., Lima, P., Murphy, R., Rojas, R.: The road to RoboCup 2050. IEEE Robot. Autom. Mag. **9**(2), 31–38 (2002)
5. Noda, I., Matsubara, H.: Soccer server and researches on multi-agent systems. In: Proceedings of the IROS-96 Workshop on RoboCup, pp. 1–7, November1996
6. Kitano, H., Asada, M., Kuniyoshi, Y., Noda, I., Osawa, E.: Robocup: the robot world cup initiative. In: Proceedings of the First international Conference on Autonomous Agents, pp. 340–347, February 1997
7. Kitano, H., Asada, M., Kuniyoshi, Y., Noda, I., Osawa, E., Matsubara, H.: RoboCup: a challenge problem for AI. AI Mag. **18**(1), 73–73 (1997)
8. Noda, I., Stone, P.: The RoboCup soccer server and cmunited clients: implemented infrastructure for MAS research. Auton. Agents Multi-Agent Syst. **7**(1–2), 101–120 (2003)
9. Stone, P., Riley, P., Veloso, M.: Defining and using ideal teammate and opponent models. In: Proceedings of the 12th Annual Conference on Innovative Applications of Artificial Intelligence (2000)
10. Butler, M., Prokopenko, M., Howard, T.: Flexible synchronisation within RoboCup environment: a comparative analysis. In: RoboCup 2000: Robot Soccer World Cup IV, pp. 119–128. Springer, London, UK (2001)
11. Prokopenko, M., Wang, P.: Disruptive innovations in RoboCup 2D soccer simulation league: from cyberoos'98 to gliders2016. In: Behnke, S., Sheh, R., Sariel, S., Lee, D.D. (eds.) RoboCup 2016: Robot World Cup XX [Leipzig, Germany, June 30 - July 4, 2016]. LNCS, vol. 9776, pp. 529–541. Springer (2017)
12. Prokopenko, M., Wang, P., Marian, S., Bai, A., Li, X., Chen, X.: Robocup 2d soccer simulation league: Evaluation challenges. In: Akiyama, H., Obst, O., Sammut, C., Tonidandel, F. (eds.) RoboCup 2017: Robot World Cup XXI [Nagoya, Japan, July 27-31, 2017]. LNCS, vol. 11175, pp. 325–337. Springer (2018)

13. Zare, N., Sayareh, A., Sarvmaili, M., Amini, O., Matwin, S., Soares, A.: Engineering features to improve pass prediction in 2D soccer simulation games. In: RoboCup 2021: Robot World Cup XXIV. Springer (2021)
14. Akiyama, H., Nakashima, T.: Helios base: an open source package for the robocup soccer 2d simulation. In: Robot Soccer World Cup 2013 Jun 24, pp. 528–535. Springer, Berlin, Heidelberg
15. Zare, N., et al.: Cyrus2D base: source code base for RoboCup 2D soccer simulation league. In: RoboCup 2022: Robot World Cup XXV, pp. 140–151. Springer International Publishing, Cham (2023)
16. Stone, P., et al.: Overview of robocup-2000. In: Stone, P., Balch, T.R., Kraetzschmar, G.K. (eds.) RoboCup 2000: Robot Soccer World Cup IV. LNCS, vol. 2019, pp. 1–28. Springer (2000)
17. Stone, P., Riley, P., Veloso, M.: The CMUnited-99 champion simulator team. In: Veloso, M., Pagello, E., Kitano, H. (eds.) RoboCup-99: Robot Soccer World Cup III. LNAI, vol. 1856, pp. 35–48. Springer Verlag, Berlin (2000)
18. Kok, J.R., Vlassis, N., Groen, F.: UvA Trilearn 2003 team description. In: Polani, D., Browning, B., Bonarini, A., Yoshida, K. (eds.) Proceedings CD RoboCup 2003. Springer, Padua (2003)
19. Bai, A., Chen, X., MacAlpine, P., Urieli, D., Barrett, S., Wrighteagle, S.P.: UT Austin villa: RoboCup 2011 simulation league champions. In: RoboCup,: Robot Soccer World Cup XV 15 2012, pp. 1–12. Springer, Berlin, Heidelberg (2011)
20. Prokopenko, M., Wang, P.: Gliders2d: Source Code Base for RoboCup 2D Soccer Simulation League. CoRR abs/1812.10202 (2018)
21. Prokopenko, M., Wang, P.: Fractals2019: combinatorial optimisation with dynamic constraint annealing. In: Robot World Cup, pp. 616–630. Springer, Cham, July 2019
22. Tavafi, A., Nozari, N., Vatani, R., Yousefi, M.R., Rahmatinia, S., Pirdir, P.: MarliK 2012 Soccer 2D simulation team description paper. In: RoboCup 2012 Symposium and Competitions: Team Description Papers, Mexico City, Mexico, June 2012
23. Kurach, K., et al.: Google research football: a novel reinforcement learning environment. In: Proceedings of the AAAI Conference on Artificial Intelligence, vol. 34, No. 04, pp. 4501–4510, April 2020
24. Hausknecht, M., Mupparaju, P., Subramanian, S., Kalyanakrishnan, S., Stone, P.: Half field offense: an environment for multiagent learning and ad hoc teamwork. In: AAMAS Adaptive Learning Agents (ALA) Workshop, vol. 3, May 2016. sn
25. Brockman, G., et al.: Openai gym, 2016. arXiv preprint arXiv:1606.01540
26. Zare, N., et al.: Pyrus Base: An Open Source Python Framework for the RoboCup 2D Soccer Simulation, 2023. arXiv preprint arXiv:2307.16875

Position and Altitude of the Nao Camera Head from Two Points on the Soccer Field Plus the Gravitational Direction

Stijn Oomes[1] and Arnoud Visser[2(✉)]

[1] Oomes Vision Systems, Amsterdam, The Netherlands
[2] Intelligent Robotics Lab, Universiteit van Amsterdam, Amsterdam, The Netherlands
a.visser@uva.nl
https://www.intelligentroboticslab.nl/

Abstract. To be able to play soccer, a robot needs a good estimate of its current position on the field. Ideally, multiple features are visible that have known locations. By applying trigonometry we can estimate the viewpoint from where this observation was actually made. Given that the Nao robots of the Standard Platform League have quite a limited field of view, a given camera frame typically only allows for one or two points to be recognized.

In this paper we propose a method for determining the (x, y) coordinates on the field and the height h of the camera from the geometry of a simplified tetrahedron. This configuration is formed by two observed points on the ground plane plus the gravitational direction. When the distance between the two points is known, and the directions to the points plus the gravitational direction are measured, all dimensions of the tetrahedron can be determined.

By performing these calculations with rational trigonometry instead of classical trigonometry, the computations turn out to be 28.7% faster, with equal numerical accuracy.

The position of the head of the Nao can also be externally measured with the OptiTrack system. The difference between externally measured and internally predicted position from sensor data gives us mean absolute errors in the 3–6 cm range, when we estimated the gravitational direction from the vanishing point of the outer edges of the goal posts.

1 Introduction

RoboCup is an event where robot capabilities are tested by playing a game of soccer between one team against another [12]. Already from the beginning of the competitions, the importance of visual localization was recognized [3,11]. Since that start methods like Visual Odometry have been developed, but those methods rely on enough dense and distinctive textures [1]. In the RoboCup often not much more than the green turf is visible, with an occasional white line (if not obstructed by other robots nearby). When a L-, T- or X-intersection on a

E. Barros et al. (Eds.): RoboCup 2024, LNAI 15570, pp. 164–175, 2025.
https://doi.org/10.1007/978-3-031-85859-8_14

white line-crossing can be observed [16], a distinctive point on the field has been recognized (although due to the symmetry of the field unfortunately not unique). Two of those distinctive points are enough to estimate the location where this observation is made, as demonstrated in this paper.

2 Rational Trigonometry

To understand the relations between observable variables (measurements with one or more cameras) and not directly observable variables (3D properties of objects and their configurations) transformations have to be defined. Rational Trigonometry [23] uses quadrances and spreads instead of distances and angles. The quadrance is defined as the quadratic sum of differences in the coordinate values of two points. The spread is defined as a proportion of quadrances; for a right triangle it is the opposite quadrance divided by the hypotenuse quadrance. Both quantities can be easily converted back and forth to the well-known concepts of distance and angle, although they are defined *independently*. A **quadrance** Q is the square of the distance d. This makes it in essence a measure of area in Euclidean space. Quadrances have dimension m^2.

$$Q = d^2 \tag{1}$$

A spread measures the divergence between two lines. A **spread** s is the square of the sine of an angle α.

$$s = \sin^2 \alpha \tag{2}$$

Spreads have a range between $[0 - 1]$ and are dimensionless, but is actually the ratio of quadrances (so dimension $\frac{m^2}{m^2}$). This characteristic has important consequences, because this range is better balanced than the ranges of ^{circ}s ($[0 - 360^{circ}]$) and radians ($[0 - 2\pi]$) once translations and rotations have to be combined. It also means that the spread has no sign, and is actually the same value for adjacent angles. This prevents many ambiguity checks in the calculations.

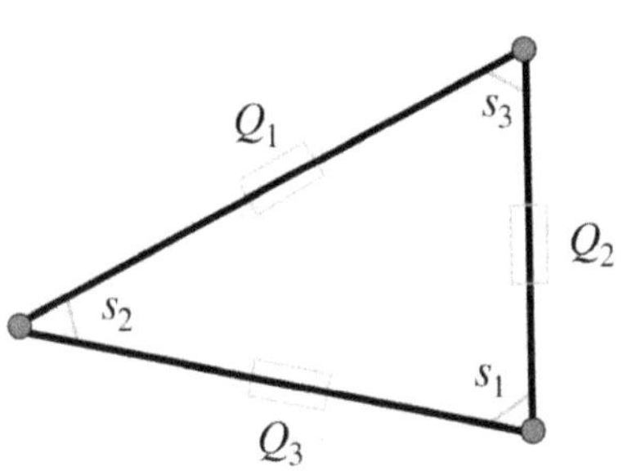

Fig. 1. The quadrances Q_i and spreads s_i of a triangle.

The relation between quadrances and spreads of triangle, as illustrated in Fig. 1 is given by the **Spread law** of rational trigonometry:

$$\frac{s_1}{Q_1} = \frac{s_2}{Q_2} = \frac{s_2}{Q_2} \tag{3}$$

Yet, for the method applied in this paper mostly the **Cross law** of rational trigonometry is used:

$$(Q_1 + Q_2 - Q_3)^2 = 4Q_1Q_2(1 - s_3) \tag{4}$$

The Cross law (Eq. 4) can be used to calculate an unknown quadrance Q_3 from two known quadrances Q_1 and Q_2 and the spread s_3 between those two quadrances (and opposite the unknown quadrance Q_3). Once s_3 and all three quadrances $Q_{1...3}$ of a triangle are known, the other two spreads s_1 and s_2 can be calculated from the Spread law (Eq. 3).

3 Method

The first phase is the detection of the relevant objects in the world, that is, on the soccer field. Those are the white lines on the green field, especially the X-, T-and L-intersections. Of course there are also objects like the goals, the ball and the other robots; team-members and opponents are distinguishable by their different colored jerseys [18]. The distance between two of those points detected on the field can be used to estimate the position where those points are observed from the camera position. The position of the X-, T-and L-intersections are specified in the Standard Platform League rule book [21], so their distances are known.

For efficiency reasons in RoboCup typical scan-line techniques are used to detect lines, searching for regions of white pixels surrounded with green pixels [16]. Yet, many other white objects are present on the field (such as goal-posts, the ball and other robots), so additional filters are needed to reduce the number of false positives [4]. Instead of hand-crafting such filters for the lines and their crossings, we used a state-of-the-art detector.

The X-, T-and L-intersections in this paper are detected with the detector based on YOLO v8, a detector which is slightly easier to fine-tune on new types of objects than YOLO v9 [22]. The detector is based on the YOLO v8 XL model pretrained on the COCO dataset, further finetuned on 1309 L-intersections, 1229 T-intersections and 806 X-intersections. This intersections were already annotated in the TORSO-21 dataset [2], but further extended with annotated mages recorded by the Dutch Nao Team [10]. This dataset, including the YOLO v8 XL model trained on this data, is publicly available[1]. This model achieved a precision of 86.1% and a recall of 84.2%. An example of such detection of two X-intersections can be seen in Fig. 2. The intersections further away are also detected, but with a too low confidence to be displayed (a confidence below 50%). From the rule book it is known that the distance between the two X-intersections is 1.5 m.

[1] https://universe.roboflow.com/fieldmarks/splfieldmark, courtesy Gijs de Jong.

Fig. 2. The X-intersection detected on the Standard Platform League field.

3.1 Position from 3 Known Points

When three points are known in the world, one can formulate a third ^{circ} polynomial which once solved gives 4 solutions. This is known as the **P3P** problem, which was first solved by Grunert [8] and further refined by Finsterwalder & Scheufele [5]. Grunert solution is nicely described by [9], which starts with the following three equations generated by the law of cosines:

$$\begin{aligned} x^2 + y^2 - 2xy\cos(\alpha) &= a^2 \\ x^2 + z^2 - 2xz\cos(\beta) &= b^2 \\ y^2 + z^2 - 2yz\cos(\gamma) &= c^2 \end{aligned} \tag{5}$$

Finsterwalder has shown that this is equivalent with solving λ in this third ^{circ} polynomial for the P3P problem:

$$\begin{aligned} &\lambda^3\, c^2(c^2\sin^2\alpha - a^2\sin^2\gamma) + \\ &\lambda^2\left[a^2(b^2 - a^2)\sin^2\gamma - c^2(2b^2 + c^2)\sin^2\alpha + 2a^2c^2(1 - \cos\alpha\cos\beta\cos\gamma)\right] + \\ &\lambda\left[a^2(a^2 - c^2)\sin^2\beta + b^2(b^2 + 2c^2)\sin^2\alpha - 2a^2b^2(1 - \cos\alpha\cos\beta\cos\gamma)\right] + \\ &b^2[a^2\sin^2\beta - b^2\sin^2\alpha] = 0 \end{aligned} \tag{6}$$

After the overview of Haralick [9] several other researchers came with solutions for the P3P problems, such as [7] and [15].

When a fourth point is known one can disambiguate between the four solutions, which makes P3P a special case of the PnP problem with n the number of known points. Yet, in our case only two points are known: $n = 2$.

3.2 Position from 2 Points on the Field and Gravity

The two point problem can be solved if we have a robot and a measure of the direction of gravity. Actually, there are two ways to get a measure on the direction of gravity. Initially we used the measurement of the an Inertial Measurement Unit (IMU) on-board of the robot. By also using the measurement values of the pitch and yaw angles of the head relative to the torso, this direction is transformed to the coordinate frame of the camera. Yet, together with timing errors small directional deviations resulted in positional errors in the range of 8–25 cm range. As a check, we also derived the gravitational direction from the perspective in the image, from the vanishing point of the outer edges of the goal posts. Here we found that the mean absolute errors are much better in the 3–6 cm range. So, for the rest of this paper we use the gravitational direction from the perspective, although this means that this direction can only be estimated when parallel verticals structures are visible. With better calibration of the gravitational direction from the IMU and the kinetic chain, we could skip this intermediate step.

For two points on the soccer field we know the distance, so also the quadrance L. We can determine their directions in camera coordinates from the projection in the image. With the direction of gravity g, we can convert those two directions to the spreads p_1 and p_2 between the visual directions and the gravitational direction g. The three vectors form a tetrahedron with the camera on top, as illustrated in Fig. 3. The spread between the two visual directions is q_{12}. The quadrance H is along the gravitational direction g and that is the parameter to be determined.

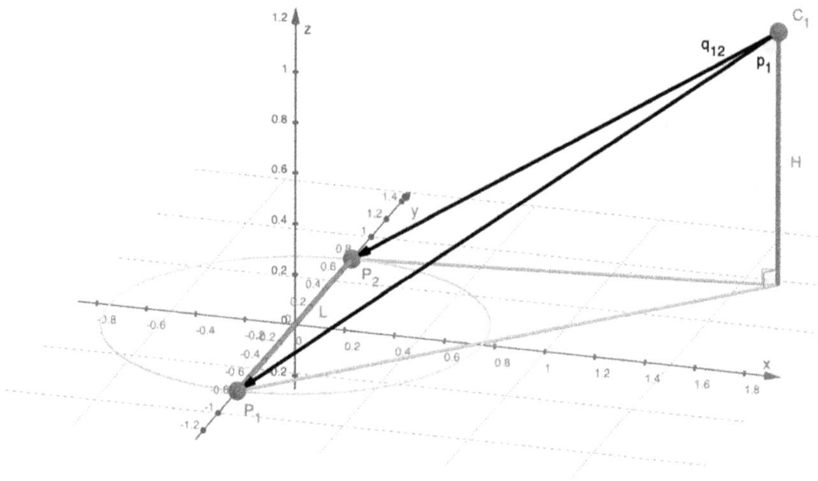

Fig. 3. A line L between two known points seen from a camera. The red points on the ground plane are the intersections of middle line and circle of which the quadrance L is known. The red point on the top right is the camera point. Together with the foot of the altitude these points form a tetrahedron with two right angles. The altitude quadrance H can be determined from quadrance L and the spreads p_1, p_2, and q_{12} (Color figure online).

The tetrahedron has 4 vertices, 6 edges, and 4 faces. So, in the tetrahedron 6 distances/quadrances can be distinguished (see the three colored pairs in Fig. 3) and 12 angles/spreads. One quadrance L and five spreads are known: (p_1, p_2, q_{12}) and the two right angles formed by H and the ground plane. The other spreads and quadrances can be derived from those measurements.

From the three measured spreads p_1, p_2, and q_{12} and the known quadrance L we can determine the vertical height, denoted as the quadrance H:

$$H = \frac{(1-p_1)(1-p_2)}{(1-p_1)+(1-p_2)-2\sqrt{(1-p_1)(1-p_2)(1-q_{12})}} L \tag{7}$$

If we define P1 in Fig. 3 as the origin, and the Y-axis is the vector along line L in the direction of P2, the (X, Y) coordinate where quadrance H touches the ground plane can be calculated:

$$X = \frac{(1-p_1)(1-p_2)[q_{12}-(1-p_1)-(1-p_2)+2\sqrt{(1-p_1)(1-p_2)(1-q_{12})}]}{[(1-p_1)+(1-p_2)-2\sqrt{(1-p_1)(1-p_2)(1-q_{12})}]^2} L \tag{8}$$

$$Y = \frac{[(1-p_2)-\sqrt{(1-p_1)(1-p_2)(1-q_{12})}]^2}{[(1-p_1)+(1-p_2)-2\sqrt{(1-p_1)(1-p_2)(1-q_{12})}]^2} L \tag{9}$$

Note that in both equations no transcendental trigonometric functions like $\sin(\phi)$, $\arccos(\phi)$ and $tan(\phi)$ are used.

3.3 Classical Trigonometry

The same method can also be formulated with distances and angles, which gives the following equations:

$$x = \frac{\cos(\alpha_1)\cos(\alpha_2)\sqrt{\sin^2(\beta_{12})-\cos^2(\alpha_1)-\cos^2(\alpha_2)+2\cos(\alpha_1)\cos(\alpha_2)\cos(\beta_{12})}}{\cos^2(\alpha_1)+\cos^2(\alpha_2)-2\cos(\alpha_1)\cos(\alpha_2)\cos(\beta_{12})} l \tag{10}$$

$$y = \frac{\cos^2(\alpha_2)-\cos(\alpha_1)\cos(\alpha_2)\cos(\beta_{12})]}{\cos^2(\alpha_1)+\cos^2(\alpha_2)-2\cos(\alpha_1)\cos(\alpha_2)\cos(\beta_{12})} l \tag{11}$$

$$h = \frac{\cos(\alpha_1)\cos(\alpha_2)}{\sqrt{\cos^2(\alpha_1)+\cos^2(\alpha_1)-2\cos(\alpha_1)\cos(\alpha_2)\cos(\beta_{12})}} l \tag{12}$$

When optimized (removing redundant calculations), this algorithm requires 17x a transcendental function-call to calculate $\cos(\phi)$ and $\sin(\phi)$.

4 Computational Experiments

Wildberger claims that rational trigonometry increases both the computational accuracy and the computational speed when compared to classical trigonometry [23]. Let us check whether we have found any evidence for this claim.

If we look at the accuracy of both computations we do not find any significant differences. The deviations start showing up around the 12th decimal. That is way beyond the measurement accuracy and precision for our position measurements.

The code to calculate the camera positions from two points on the field with *quadrances* and *spreads* was executed multiple times on a Nao v6 robot, which indicates that one calculation takes on average $2.47 \cdot 10^{-05}$ s. The implementation was in Python 2.7, the language supported by the standard Aldebaran NaoQi image, so could be further optimized in C++ or RUST. Yet, the Python implementation can already be used for a comparison with the same calculation with traditional method based on *angle* and *distance*, which needed for one calculation on average was $3.18 \cdot 10^{-05}$ s (Table 1). This indicates that the rational algorithm on the Nao v6 robot is ≈28.7% faster, because it performs the calculations with only divisions and square-roots as computational heavy operations, in contrast with the trigonometric functions like $\cos(\phi)$ and $\sin(\phi)$ used in the classical method.

Table 1. Execution time of algorithm in seconds

# runs	50x	500x	5000x	50.000x	500.000x
classical algorithm	$1.58 \cdot 10^{-3}$	$1.59 \cdot 10^{-2}$	$1.61 \cdot 10^{-1}$	$1.59 \cdot 10^{0}$	$1.59 \cdot 10^{+1}$
rational algorithm	$1.24 \cdot 10^{-3}$	$1.24 \cdot 10^{-2}$	$1.23 \cdot 10^{-1}$	$1.23 \cdot 10^{0}$	$1.23 \cdot 10^{+1}$

5 Metrical Experiments

To see the relative location (x, y, h) of the camera in the head of the Nao v6 robot relative to two points on the soccer field, we recreated two Simultaneous Localization and Mapping experiments, which were used as Technical Challenge in 2004 and 2005 [19,20].

The 2004 SLAM challenge specified five points: $[(160, 100), (180, -30), (50, -100), (-210, 0), (-100, 50)]$ - all cm from the origin at the center of the field. Those points were marked with red tape on the field. The 2005 SLAM challenge specified another five points: $[(130, 120), (220, -150), (-160, -120), (-210, 90), (270, 0)]$, they were marked with black tape on the field.

The soccer fields of 2004 and 2005 were smaller than the current field, so all points are sampled near the center (see Fig. 5a) The collected data is publicly available[2]. As can be seen from Fig. 4.(f-j), the black points from the 2005 SLAM challenge are slightly further from the center, so here the center circle is always fully visible. Also the weather conditions changed; the sun was casting shadows when the 2005 SLAM locations were recorded.

[2] https://github.com/physar/landmark_based_slam_dataset.

(a) (b) (c) (d) (e)

(f) (g) (h) (i) (j)

Fig. 4. Viewpoints from the 2004 and 2005 SLAM challenge locations

To provide ground truth, the Nao robot was equipped with a rigid body marker of the OptiTrack system (see Fig. 5b), consisting of eight Flex 13 cameras, which can record movements with a 3D accuracy of ±0.20 mm in a tracking area of ±8 m $\times$ 4 m [6].

The estimates of location of the observations made on the 10 marked positions from the 2004 and 2005 SLAM challenge are summarized in Table 2 and 4. As can be seen from Table 2, no predictions were made for red point 3 and point 5, because the center circle was not in full view. Also can be seen from the two tables combined that in half of the cases (4 of the 8 marked positions) a reasonable good estimate is given, while for the other half the estimate is clearly off (indicated with a red italic font). Yet, this clearly wrong location-estimates can be filtered out by setting a threshold on the predicted height, for instance by the constraint that the height as to be in the range (+0.440, +0.550).

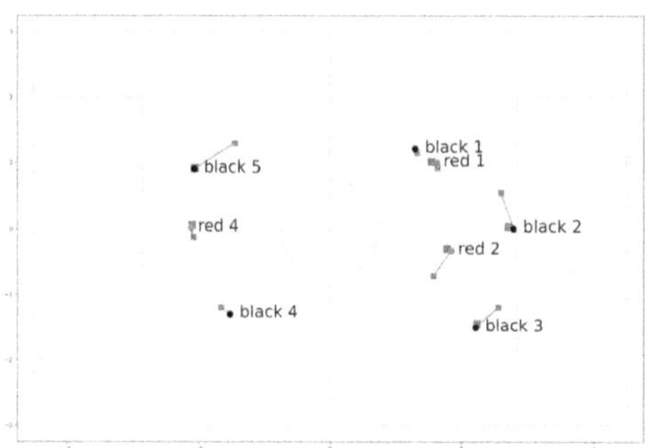

(a) (b)

Fig. 5. Top view of the 2004 and 2005 SLAM challenge locations and a Nao robot with an OptiTrack rigid body marker

Table 2. Predictions of the observations at the 2004 SLAM challenge locations

	x	y	h	
2004 SLAM challenge				
red point 1	+1.600	+1.000		m
OptiTrack reference	+1.626	+1.004	+0.449	m
prediction with g-vector from IMU	+1.637	+0.939	+0.483	m
prediction with visual g-vector	+1.545	+1.023	*+0.369*	m
red point 2	+1.800	−0.300		m
OptiTrack reference	+1.849	−0.330	+0.452	m
prediction with g-vector from IMU	*+1.576*	*−0.721*	*+0.364*	m
prediction with visual g-vector	+1.784	−0.306	+0.468	m
red point 3	+0.500	−1.000		m
red point 4	−2.100	0.000		m
OptiTrack reference	−2.115	+0.014	+0.452	m
prediction with g-vector from IMU	−2.083	−0.125	+0.448	m
prediction with visual g-vector	−2.100	+0.056	*+0.390*	m
red point 5	−1.000	+0.500		m

Yet, a reliable observation prediction in only half of the cases is not good enough to be useful as input for a localization algorithm. To test whether the origin of this failure comes from the IMU measurement of the g-vector, we also estimated the g-vector from the goal-posts, when they were visible in the field of view. This improved the prediction of the observation locations considerably. With a visual g-vector we found the following errors between the prediction and the reference measurement from the OptiTrack system as indicated in Table 3.

Table 3. Difference between predictions with visual g-vector and the OptiTrack reference system

	x	y	h	
mean absolute error	0.044	0.030	0.076	m
standard deviation	0.037	0.017	0.069	m

Note that for black point 1 and point 3 of the 2005 SLAM challenge (Table 4) no goal-posts were in the field-of-view, so visual g-vector could be estimated. Also note for red point 1 and point 4 of the 2004 SLAM challenge (Table 2 the (x, y) prediction with the visual g-vector is quite good, but that the constraint on the height-estimate would indicate that this observation could better be skipped.

In general, a small error in the viewing direction can give large errors in position estimates. The underlying origin of this small error in estimating the g-vector by the IMU can be drift of the accelerometer itself, or a buildup of an error the kinematic chain of several joints between orientation of the head relative to the torso (where the IMU is located).

Table 4. Predictions of the observations at the 2005 SLAM challenge locations

	x	y	h	
2005 SLAM challenge				
black point 1	+1.300	+1.200		m
OptiTrack reference	+1.296	+1.217	+0.460	m
prediction with g-vector from IMU	+1.296	+1.157	+0.538	m
black point 2	+2.700	0.000		m
OptiTrack reference	+2.791	+0.003	+0.472	m
prediction with g-vector from IMU	*+2.596*	*+0.549*	*+0.606*	m
prediction with visual g-vector	+2.706	+0.027	+0.597	m
black point 3	+2.200	−1.500		m
OptiTrack reference	+2.207	−1.505	+0.474	m
prediction with g-vector from IMU	*+2.560*	*−1.199*	*+0.577*	m
prediction with visual g-vector	+2.230	−1.449	+0.502	m
black point 4	−1.600	−1.200		m
OptiTrack reference	−1.513	−1.298	+0.454	m
prediction with g-vector from IMU	−1.654	−1.298	+0.499	m
black point 5	−2.100	+0.900		m
OptiTrack reference	−2.070	+0.907	+0.425	m
prediction with g-vector from IMU	*−1.439*	*+1.302*	*+0.301*	m
prediction with visual g-vector	−2.058	+0.919	+0.449	m

6 Discussion

Finding the viewpoint from a limited number of 'known' points depends strongly on the accuracy of the 'known' part. The Inertial Measurement Unit (IMU) should in principal give an accurate estimate of the g-vector. Yet, this g-vector is measured inside the torso of the robot, which requires a coordinate transformation from the torso to the camera in the head. Kneip [13] assumes that this transformation is fixed and accurately established with a calibration procedure [17], which is unfortunately not possible on a moving robot. When the g-vector was estimated from the perspective lines in the image, instead of the IMU measurement, the results actually improved. This indicates that our measurement strongly depends on a good estimate of the g-vector.

A better estimate could also be accomplished by combining the constraints from multiple known points, as demonstrated by several solutions available in the OpenGV library [14]. In this paper only the X-intersections of middle line and circle were used. Yet, the Standard Platform field has many other useful points, such as the L-corners of the penalty area or the T-intersections at the edge of the field. All these type of intersections can be recognized with the YOLO v8 detector. Yet, the field of the view of the Nao robot is limited, so even in most cases not more than two known points are visible. Including the goal-posts as 'known' points would increase the number of candidates, but it remains a challenge to have at least three or four of those points visible. When playing a soccer match with the occlusion of the opponents nearby, the situation will be even worse. Having an algorithm that can give a reasonable estimate on just two 'known' points remains valuable.

7 Conclusion

In this paper the claim that the use of rational trigonometry can reduce the time to calculate a triangulation is reproduced in a robotics application. This is beneficial for a robotics platform like the Nao robot, where computation time is scarce.

In addition, this paper demonstrates that for a known orientation relative to the g-vector, observing two 'known' points in the environment is enough to get an estimate on the pose of the camera. The accuracy depends on an accurate measurement of the g-vector by either an Inertial Measurement Unit or the vanishing point from two vertical lines. Estimates that are completely off can be filtered out by setting a boundary of the height estimate; the height of the robot is known, measurements above that height are only possible when the robot is lifted from the ground.

The estimates of the relative position to two 'known' points can be the input of a full-scale localization or a landmark based simultaneous localization and mapping algorithm, which keeps track of those observations over time, combined a model of the movement of the robot.

Acknowledgement. We like to thank Madelon Bernardy for her support in collecting a dataset, including the reference measurements with the OptiTrack system. We like to thank Gijs de Jong for extending the YOLO v8 XL detector with annotated training data for the X- T- and L-intersections.

References

1. Alkendi, Y., Seneviratne, L., Zweiri, Y.: State of the art in vision-based localization techniques for autonomous navigation systems. IEEE Access **9**, 76847–76874 (2021)
2. Bestmann, M., et al.: Torso-21 dataset: typical objects in RoboCup soccer 2021. bit-bots' github repository (April 2021)
3. Enderle, S., Ritter, M., Fox, D., Sablatnög, S., Kraetzschmar, G., Palm, G.: Vision-based localization in RoboCup environments. In: RoboCup 2000: Robot Soccer World Cup IV, pp. 291–296. Springer, Berlin, Heidelberg (January 2001)
4. Farazi, H., Allgeuer, P., Behnke, S.: A monocular vision system for playing soccer in low color information environments. In: Proceedings of the 10th Workshop on Humanoid Soccer Robots, International Conference on Humanoid Robots (November 2015)
5. Finsterwalder, S., Scheufele, W.: Das rückwärtseinschneiden im raum. Sitzungsberichte der Mathematisch-Physikalischen Klasse der K.B. Akademie der Wissenschaften zu München, pp. 591–614 (November 1903). band XXXIII

6. Furtado, J.S., Liu, H.H.T., Lai, G., Lacheray, H., Desouza-Coelho, J.: Comparative analysis of optitrack motion capture systems. In: Advances in Motion Sensing and Control for Robotic Applications, pp. 15–31. Springer (June 2019)
7. Gao, X.S., Hou, X.R., Tang, J., Cheng, H.F.: Complete solution classification for the perspective-three-point problem. IEEE Trans. Pattern Anal. Mach. Intell. **25**(8), 930–943 (2003)
8. Grunert, J.A.: Das pothenot'sche problem, in erweiterter gestalt; nebst bemerkungen über seine anwendungen in der geodäsie. Grunerts Archiv fur Mathematik und Physik, pp. 238–248 (1841)
9. Haralick, R.M., Lee, C.N., Ottenburg, K., Nölle, M.: Analysis and solutions of the three point perspective pose estimation problem. In: CVPR, vol. 91, pp. 592–598 (June 1991)
10. Hidde, G.J., Lekanne gezegd Deprez, H., Visser, A.: The Dutch Nao Team synthetic dataset. Universiteit van Amsterdam (June 2020). https://doi.org/10.21942/uva.12570902.v1
11. Iocchi, L., Nardi, D.: Self-localization in the RoboCup environment. In: RoboCup-99: Robot Soccer World Cup III, pp. 318–330. Springer (June 2000)
12. Kitano, H., Asada, M., Kuniyoshi, Y., Noda, I., Osawa, E.: RoboCup: the robot world cup initiative. In: Proceedings of the First International Conference on Autonomous Agents, pp. 340–347 (February 1997)
13. Kneip, L., Chli, M., Siegwart, R.: Robust real-time visual odometry with a single camera and an IMU. In: Proceedings of the British Machine Vision Conference 2011. British Machine Vision Association (September 2011)
14. Kneip, L., Furgale, P.: Opengv: a unified and generalized approach to real-time calibrated geometric vision. In: 2014 IEEE International Conference on Robotics and Automation (ICRA), pp. 1–8 (September 2014)
15. Kneip, L., Scaramuzza, D., Siegwart, R.: A novel parametrization of the perspective-three-point problem for a direct computation of absolute camera position and orientation. In: CVPR 2011, pp. 2969–2976 (August 2011)
16. Laue, T., de Haas, T.J., Burchardt, A., Graf, C., Röfer, T., Härtl, A., Rieskamp, A.: Efficient and reliable sensor models for humanoid soccer robot self-localization. In: Proceedings of the 4th Workshop on Humanoid Soccer Robots, pp. 22–29 (December 2009)
17. Lobo, J., Dias, J.: Relative pose calibration between visual and inertial sensors. Int. J. Robot. Res. **26**(6), 561–575 (2007)
18. Owusu, P.P.D.: Recognizing all opponents: a real-time object detection approach for robotic soccer jerseys. Bachelor thesis, Universiteit van Amsterdam (February 2024)
19. RoboCup Technical Committee: Technical challenges for the RoboCup 2004 legged league competition (June 2004)
20. RoboCup Technical Committee: Technical challenges for the RoboCup 2005 legged league competition (June 2005)
21. RoboCup Technical Committee: RoboCup Standard Platform league (NAO) rule book (March 2024)
22. Wang, C.Y., Yeh, I.H., Liao, H.Y.M.: Yolov9: learning what you want to learn using programmable gradient information. preprint arXiv 2402.13616 (February 2024)
23. Wildberger, N.J.: Divine Proportions: Rational Trigonometry to Universal Geometry. Wild Egg Pty Ltd., Sydney, Australia (August 2005)

LLCoach: Generating Robot Soccer Plans Using Multi-role Large Language Models

M. Brienza[1(✉)], E. Musumeci[1], V. Suriani[2], D. Affinita[1], A. Pennisi[3], D. Nardi[1], and D. D. Bloisi[3]

[1] Department of Computer, Control, and Management Engineering Sapienza University of Rome, Rome, Italy
{brienza,musumeci,affinita,nardi}@diag.uniroma1.it

[2] School of Engineering, University of Basilicata, Potenza, Italy
vincenzo.suriani@unibas.it

[3] Department of International Humanities and Social Sciences, International University of Rome, Rome, Italy
domenico.bloisi@unint.eu

Abstract. The deployment of robots into human scenarios necessitates advanced planning strategies, particularly when we ask robots to operate in dynamic, unstructured environments. RoboCup offers the chance to deploy robots in one of those scenarios, a human-shaped game represented by a soccer match. In such scenarios, robots must operate using predefined behaviors that can fail in unpredictable conditions. This paper introduces a novel application of Large Language Models (LLMs) to address the challenge of generating actionable plans in such settings, specifically within the context of the RoboCup Standard Platform League (SPL) competitions where robots are required to autonomously execute soccer strategies that emerge from the interactions of individual agents. In particular, we propose a multi-role approach leveraging the capabilities of LLMs to generate and refine plans for a robotic soccer team. The potential of the proposed method is demonstrated through an experimental evaluation, carried out simulating multiple matches where robots with AI-generated plans play against robots running human-built code.

Keywords: Humanoid Robotics · Planning and Reasoning · Team Coordination Methods

1 Introduction

Recent advancements in Language Modeling, particularly the proliferation of technologies associated with Large Language Models (LLMs), have unlocked numerous ways to enhance embodied AI systems with common sense knowledge [16]. The expansive scope of LLMs serves as a vast repository of information, facilitating multi-modal interactions with textual and visual data.

E. Barros et al. (Eds.): RoboCup 2024, LNAI 15570, pp. 176–188, 2025.
https://doi.org/10.1007/978-3-031-85859-8_15

When appropriately queried, LLMs provide access to semantic cues that are crucial for bridging the conceptual gap between abstract planning domains and intricate and unpredictable real-world environments [12]. Consequently, they are increasingly integrated into embodied AI systems [3].

In this work, we present a first attempt to use generative AI in the context of robot soccer for creating successful game plans using an approach to leverage the LLMs' chain of thought and generate game tactics by impersonating a coach. In particular, we present a multi-role pipeline, featuring four stages in which the capabilities of a foundation model are exploited to generate and refine a plan for a soccer robot (see Fig. 1). Robot soccer offers an ideal environment for planning within a multi-robot, highly dynamic environment [14]. Here, we focus on the RoboCup Standard Platform League (SPL), which involves teams of Aldebaran NAO V6 humanoid robots competing autonomously in soccer matches. Participating teams are tasked with executing multi-agent strategies aimed at securing victory in the matches. It is worth noting that, in SPL matches, the applicability of commonsense knowledge is constrained, given that a detailed understanding of game rules and the capabilities of robots during soccer matches is often specialized knowledge. Access to such information, including the actions available to each agent, is typically facilitated through a Retrieval-Augmented Generation (RAG) system [1]. The contribution of this work is two-fold:

1. A methodology for extracting high-level strategies from videos of RoboCup soccer matches.
2. A pipeline for creating detailed, multi-agent plans that can be directly executed by a NAO robot using its available set of basic actions.

Experimental results are obtained in a simulated environment by performing multiple matches where the robots with the AI-generated plans play against the robots running the code[1] used by SPQR Team in RoboCup 2023. The code and the additional material mentioned in this paper are publicly available at https://sites.google.com/diag.uniroma1.it/llcoach/.

The rest of the paper is organized as follows. Section 2 presents a brief overview of related work, while Sect. 3 showcases the methodology and the proposed architecture. Experimental results are shown in Sect. 4. Finally, Sect. 5 draws the conclusions and future directions.

2 Related Work

Before the advent of the LLMs, few approaches have been proposed for coaching teams of robots. The first attempt is represented by a language to coach a RoboCup team [10], where COACH UNILANG is presented for Simulated 3D League. More recently, in SPL, [8] presented an approach to conditioning the robot's behavior before or during the time of the match.

More recently, LLMs have been used as planners for both structured [11] and unstructured environments [5]. However, when using LLMs as planners,

[1] https://github.com/SPQRTeam/spqr2023.

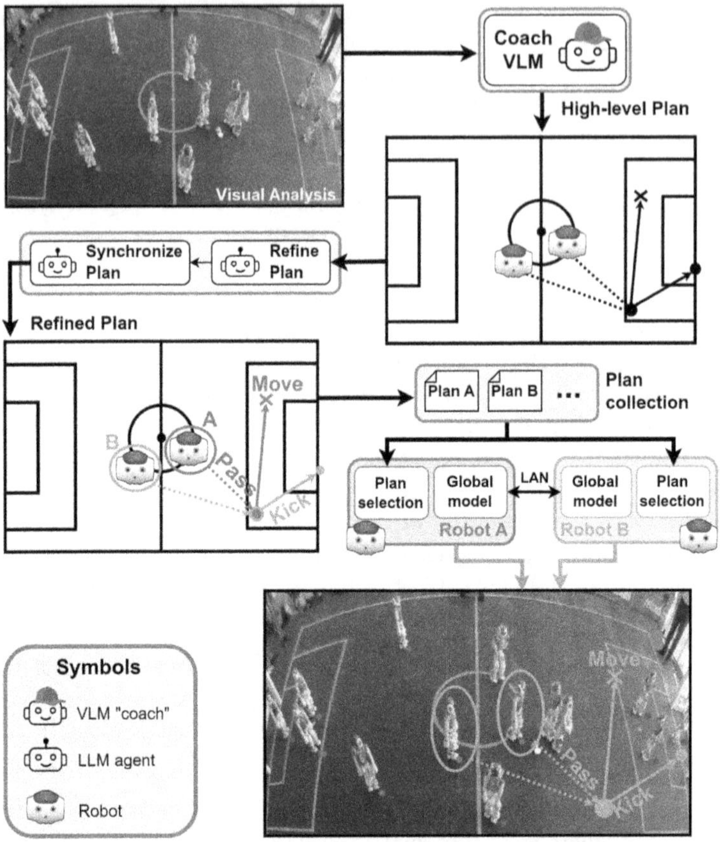

Fig. 1. The LLCoach architecture includes high-level plan generation by the VLM coach, which is then refined to a low-level plan, executable in robot matches.

especially for embodied AI (where visual cues must be conveyed through text), there is the possibility of incurring hallucinations, causing skewed or imprecise results. Hallucination is a phenomenon typically observed when the provided textual inputs are too structured and long. For such a reason, it proves beneficial to provide examples of desired output and to define roles for the LLM in a request, by instructing the model on its role and providing constraints on how to perform its task. Demanding to each role a very specific task in a pipeline composed of multiple steps allows to obtain a better final result that would be too complex for the model with a single, lengthy, and complex query. Thanks to the introduction of VLMs [9], LLMs can get both textual and visual inputs reducing the length of the context that must be provided textually in scenarios where visual cues are essential to understand the requested task. Such an approach alleviates the issue of hallucination in applications of embodied AI. However, due to their considerable size in terms of parameters and the consequent computational demands for a single training or inference step, LLMs are less likely to be employed in embedded systems. Moreover, fine-tuning them is an exceedingly resource-intensive endeavor, seldom justifiable for enhancing the accuracy of tasks reliant on specialized commonsense knowledge.

To better fit unknown domains, Retrieval-Augmented Generation (RAG) is implemented within intricate pipelines. Here, segments of potentially lengthy documents are indexed based on their semantics in an embedding space and stored within a Vector Index. This approach facilitates enhanced and expedited customization of LLM query results compared to traditional fine-tuning methods. Moreover, additional pieces of information can be seamlessly integrated into the supplementary knowledge base by appending them to the Semantic Database. This capability enables, for instance, the generation of documents from semantically akin templates [7].

RAG-based systems offer interesting applications to robotics. In [15], RAG-Driver is presented as a novel multimodal RAG LLM for high-performance, explainable, and generalizable autonomous driving. RAGs in robotics offer the possibility to enrich the available commonsense knowledge with more specialized knowledge about the environment or the robotic agent's capabilities.

3 Proposed Approach

Figure 2 shows our multi-role LLM-based planning sequential pipeline, featuring four steps, namely *Action Retrieval*, *Coach VLM*, *Plan Refinement*, and *Plan Synchronizer*.

Input. Although commonsense knowledge is usually enough for most generic tasks, in the case of robot soccer, specific knowledge must be provided. Thus, the prompts for the LLM-based generation steps along the pipeline are constructed from case-specific information. In particular, case-specific knowledge includes:

- The *domain*, containing a natural language description of the application (a soccer match between autonomous robots), the definition of tokens representing the locations of waypoints, described in natural language as a discrete distribution of several relevant locations. This allows managing the complexity of planning in a continuous coordinate space by delegating the grounding of waypoint locations (into actual spatial coordinates) to the robot control framework, where a world model will be available.
- A *planning goal*: "*The own team should score a goal in the opponent's goal.*"
- A description of robot team formations and agent capabilities in natural language, containing tokens associated with the actions they can perform.

Actions are described using natural language, following a structure similar to STRIPS actions (similar to Planning Domain Definition Language [4]) where tokens used from the domain and agent descriptions are used to give the LLM a better understanding of their pre-conditions and effects.

To prevent hallucination, the generation process is subdivided into several subsequent generation steps, centered on the interaction with an LLM or a VLM,

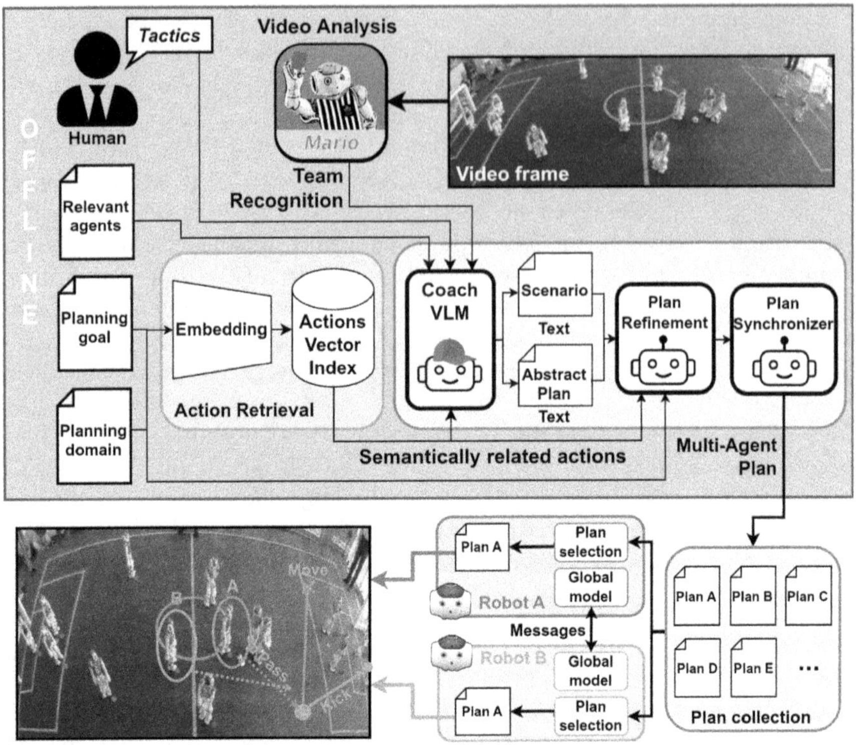

Fig. 2. The pipeline is subdivided into an offline component and an online one, executed in real-time. The offline component collects plans by passing video frames to the coach VLM, and refines them using a multi-role LLM pipeline, using only actions obtained by RAG. The online component retrieves and executes the most fitting plan according to the world model, shared between robots.

each with a properly engineered prompt to minimize its size and increase the quality of the information provided to the model.

3.1 Action Retrieval

To minimize the size of the prompts sent to the LLM or VLM modules requiring an understanding of agent actions, in an attempt to prevent hallucination, actions are stored in a Semantic Database, where each data node corresponds to the vector embedding of their natural language description. The semantic database leverages a Vector Index for efficient storage and retrieval of action definitions.

The Action Retrieval module retrieves actions from the database based on their semantic similarity with the input plan. A *Sentence Transformer*, specifically the MPNet model [13], is employed to compute this semantic similarity. This embedding space is crucial for both populating the database and perform-

(a) (b)

Fig. 3. MARIO visual tool, transforming robot pose (original (a), simulation (b)).

ing retrieval operations. Actions stored in the database follow a STRIPS-like template:

```
ACTION_ID: the name of the action
DESCRIPTION: a high-level description that explains what
the action does.
ARGS: ARG_NAME : ARG_VALUE specifies action arguments.
PRECONDITIONS: conditions that must be satisfied to execute the action.
EFFECTS: the expected result
```

During retrieval, the planning domain and goal are also embedded within this same space, so that only relevant actions may be extracted using a k-nearest neighbor search based on cosine similarity, measuring the alignment between the required task and the actions stored in the database. This enables the extraction of pertinent actions only, minimizing the prompt length for subsequent pipeline steps and improving its quality.

3.2 Coach VLM

Visual Analysis. To acquire the necessary frame information for the coach's utilization of the VLM to generate the desired output, we leverage MARIO [2], a tool specialized in soccer match video analysis.

MARIO extracts a representation of the soccer game using its tracking capabilities and converts it into a 2D plan view applying a homography geometrical transformation. This representation is useful to characterize video frames in a way that a VLM can easily understand. In particular, each robot is marked with a dot representing the color of the robot's jersey, which indicates the team color (see the bottom-left of Fig. 2).

VLM Module. The *coach* module exploits the capabilities of GPT4-Vision [9], a recent Visual Language Model (VLM). A video frame resulting from the visual analysis of a relevant action, like the one in Fig. 3, is provided to the Visual Language Model, along with a textual prompt. While the video frame provides a detailed view of the current configuration of agents and obstacles on the field, the textual prompt is used to instruct the VLM on its task and constraints. In particular, the coach is instructed to perform two tasks:

1. Generating a schematic description of the video frame.
2. Generating a high-level plan in natural language.

The prompt for the first task is based on the following template.

```
As a coach assisting the red team, provide a precise summary using the
formatting below. Each player's position should be related to designated
waypoints on the field.
SCENARIO:
[ROLE_OWN_TEAM] is at [WAYPOINT]
[ROLE_OPPONENT_TEAM] is at [WAYPOINT]
...
BALL is at [WAYPOINT]
```

Given the proven capabilities of LLMs as few-shot learners [12], the prompt is enriched by an example of an ideal output structure. Then, a description of the robot roles in the multi-agent team is added, followed by a list of the available movement waypoints, with a semantic description for each one. Upper-case words are used in an attempt to increase attention over specific tokens.

The second task consists of generating a high-level plan in natural language, describing the optimal strategy to achieve the planning goal, given the same inputs as the first task. The prompt follows the template:

```
After describing the SCENARIO, provide coaching advice.
Your suggestions should utilize the following actions: [ACTIONS]
Recommend player movements to achieve the objective [PLANNING_GOAL]
Your attitude is to perform the following tactics [TACTICS]
```

Here:

- *[ACTIONS]* is replaced with actions extracted at the retrieval step.
- *[PLANNING_GOAL]* is the original planning goal for the current task, which consists simply in "*The own team should score a goal in the opponent's goal.*"
- *[TACTICS]* allow additional customization of the planning goal (which is instead fixed).

In addition to the task, several constraints over the desired output are added:

```
Respect the sequential execution of actions,considering that the previous
action changes the game situation. Constraints on passing: a robot
cannot pass or kick the ball if it has passed it before, receive
the ball only if you are at the target location otherwise, consider
robot movement actions.
```

Then an example of ideal output is provided, to enforce a specific structure:

```
COACH ADVICE:
[give the actions to be performed avoiding conditionals
but describing the precise steps to be performed in sequence.]
```

The output of the VLM is the concatenation of the responses to the two tasks:

1. A structured description of the scenario represented in the input video frame.
2. A multi-agent high-level plan, featuring all the relevant agents detected in the provided snapshots, that represents the suggested strategy for the task, for the given domain, extracted actions, described agents, and planning goal.

Therefore, the VLM returns the initial configuration of the agents and obstacles in the video frame, and an ideal strategy to pursue the planning goal.

Role Retrieval. A description of the relevant roles in the multi-agent team is provided to the Coach VLM in the input prompt. In this way, the Coach module implicitly identifies the roles of the robots in the multi-agent strategy, by mapping the robot in the video frame to the role assigned in the high-level plan, based on its relevance in the strategy. To enable the coach to do so, relevant roles, such as the goalie (the goalkeeper), the jolly (tasked with moving around to receive passes), or the striker (tasked with managing the ball) are defined in natural language in the input prompt. For example, the striker role is described as follows:

```
- STRIKER: The striker robot is responsible for scoring goals, and is
allowed to perform the following actions: pass_the_ball and kick_to_goal
...
```

Similarly, it is possible to describe waypoints (locations reachable by robots on the field) in natural language:

```
OUR_GOAL: Our team's goal area.
...
```

Having discretized the field in a distribution of waypoints, it is possible to identify robot roles by comparing their position on the field with the assignment to waypoints that the VLM returns in its first task.

3.3 Plan Refinement

The plan obtained up until now is a high-level abstract plan, containing tokens representing real-world entities, such as agents, the ball, waypoint locations on the field, and actions. Still, to be executed, two problems have to be solved:

- The plan must be translated into a more structured version, so that a parser may be used to build a Finite-State Machine that is readily executable by the robotic agents.
- Given that several agents concur with the execution of this plan, a hint on the synchronization between the actions of different agents must be provided.

Plan Grounding. The first issue can be solved by transforming the original high-level abstract plan, into a more structured version of the plan. To this aim, the LLM is instructed to satisfy the following task:

```
Generate a high-level plan for the team using the coach's recommendations
in the shortest number of steps using the planning domain, the planning
goal, and the scenario. Don't write actions for the opponent team players.
```

This simple task prompt is then followed by:

- The same planning domain provided to the VLM.
- The actions retrieved by the action database.
- Constraints about the structure of the plan, to make sure that actions are written as `ACTION_ID AGENT_ID ARGUMENTS` (where `AGENT_ID` is the agent acting), followed by a list of possible values for the `ACTION_ID` token (the retrieved actions).
- A list of possible values for the `AGENT_ID` field, containing all the relevant roles for the plan, and descriptions of the agents, in natural language.
- Several more fine-grained constraints to ensure that the result is desirable.
- The "scenario", is the configuration of elements on the field extracted from the output of the VLM.
- Finally, the high-level plan to be refined, presented as "COACH RECOMMENDATIONS"

The result is a more structured version of the high-level plan returned by the "coach" VLM, with action names and arguments correctly grounded in the domain tokens.

Plan Synchronizer. At this stage, actions in the generated plan feature multiple agents but still follow a sequential order. To obtain a multi-agent plan, there should be some indication of how actions performed by different agents at the same time should be synchronized. For this reason, the component of *Plan Parallelization* instructs the LLM to return a plan where actions that are executed by different agents at the same time are put together in a "`JOIN{...}`" block. The prompt provided to the LLM is then further enriched with a positive example of a valid result and several negative examples of results to avoid, with a brief explanation of the reason that makes them invalid. The resulting plan will then look like:

```
pass_the_ball STRIKER {'SENDER': STRIKER, 'RECEIVER': JOLLY}
JOIN {pass_the_ball JOLLY {'SENDER': STRIKER, 'RECEIVER': JOLLY},
      kick_to_goal JOLLY {}}
```

3.4 Plan Execution

The offline portion of the pipeline is used to generate a collection of plans from a given set of video frames, as in Fig. 2. Collected plans are then selected based on their similarity to the real-world scenario. The similarity between the two scenarios can be performed using a clustering technique where the current game scenario is obtained by the global model perceived by the robot. An accurate generation of plans based on various game situations allows for the handling of almost all game situations during matches and allows the robots to apply when needed a suitable behavior that maximizes the likelihood of scoring a goal.

4 Experimental Results

This section illustrates the experimental results obtained from the evaluation in a simulated environment of the results of the current work, with the primary objective of assessing its effectiveness in generating high-quality plans collected by processing video frames from real RoboCup SPL matches.

Prompt Engineering. To obtain the desired results, an initial phase of prompt refinement was required. The prompt of the VLM "coach" module could be more information-rich with a smaller risk of hallucination, given the multi-modal input. Providing both a video frame and textual input allows the coach to give better insight into the subsequent stages along the pipeline. The accuracy of the output at this stage is key, as any error at this stage could mislead the entire generation pipeline. The application domain constitutes a critical component of the prompt for this module, particularly in a use case where the objective is to describe the location of the players based on both an image and a text description. The main obstacle is the representation of 2D coordinates within the provided frame, which cannot be easily achieved using a VLM due to its difficulty in working on cartesian coordinates. Instead of coordinates, tokens representing waypoints are used as a way of discretizing the field, by marking significant field locations. The description of these tokens should not mislead the VLM and the significance of waypoints must be explained in natural language. For example, an earlier iteration of the prompt contained the waypoint "KICKING_POSITION": initially described as a "vantage point", whose semantics are far from having a geometric value. The final version of the prompt avoids such bias-inducing mistakes by describing it as a "favorable position". This improved dramatically the results of the scenario description task.

The second task assigned to the coach consisted of generating a plan given the situation depicted in the provided input frame. Ideally, the plan should be structured according to an easily parsable template. A first attempt at generating a structured plan directly using the VLM resulted in heavy hallucination. To overcome this problem, the VLM was instead tasked with generating a high-level plan, as if it were a soccer coach. To exert more control on the overall strategy, the possibility to customize the overall "tactics" was added, for example by specifying whether passes were desirable or if the strategy should be offensive or defensive. A subsequent plan refinement module was added, to refine the high-level plan into a parsable plan. This module used only a textual input, therefore it was key to minimize the input token count, to avoid hallucination.

Setup. The VLM Coach module relies on the OpenAI *GPT 4 Turbo* model with vision while the text-only modules feature the latest OpenAI *GPT 3.5 Turbo* model *gpt-3.5-turbo-0125*. Tests were conducted in a simulated environment based on SimRobot [6]. Pertinent frames were extracted from historical SPL matches, publicly accessible on the web. For every frame, the robot configuration was replicated within the simulation, reflecting each robot's pose $p_i = (x, y, \theta)$ as extracted from the MARIO, ensuring a faithful recreation of real-world scenarios within the simulated environment. Starting from the same initial configuration, the evolution of plans was considered, comparing the pre-existing behaviors and the plans generated by the presented pipeline. For simplicity, only offensive scenarios were taken into account due to their complexity and larger action space compared to defensive scenarios.

Evaluation. The proposed approach is evaluated using the success rate metric, measuring the team's ability to score goals in offensive situations during gameplay. To assess the effectiveness of our method, we compared two approaches: the baseline approach, relying on the predefined behaviors of the SPQR Team 2023 code release, and the dynamic plans generated by the Large Language Model (LLCoach). In addition to the success rate, we considered the average number of passes and average scoring time in seconds as supplementary metrics to illustrate the evolution of gameplay dynamics over different settings. Considering two different situations from the final match BHuman - HTWK we recreated the robot configurations running eight simulations in total. It is worth noting that, since several API calls are required to obtain and refine the plan throughout the multi-role pipeline, the overall execution time is affected mainly by the inference times of LLM/VLM agents (Table 1).

Table 1. Comparison of success rate, average passes, and seconds played obtained by comparing eight simulations with LLCoach and the human-written code.

Metrics	SPQR Human-written Code	LLCoach
Success Rate	30%	**90%**
Avg. no. of passes	0.60	**1.33**
Avg. scoring time	66 sec.	**29.7 sec.**

5 Conclusions and Future Directions

In this paper, we presented a novel approach to plan generation, exploiting the common knowledge in Large Language Models. The proposed approach represents a first attempt at using generative AI in the context of robot soccer. In particular, we described a complete pipeline, in four stages, where a high-level plan, is progressively refined into a multi-agent plan. The first stage, a Visual Language Model acting as a coach, generates plans from video frames, extracted from videos RoboCup SPL matches. Collected plans can then be run by real NAO robots, as shown by the promising results conducted in the context of RoboCup SPL matches. As future work, we intend to use videos from human soccer matches to create policies for soccer robot players. Our aim is to reduce the gap between robot behaviors and human moves in order to achieve the 2050 RoboCup goal.

Acknowledgement. This work has been carried out while Michele Brienza was enrolled in the Italian National Doctorate on Artificial Intelligence run by Sapienza University of Rome. This work has been supported by PNRR MUR project PE0000013-FAIR.

References

1. Balaguer, A., et al.: Rag vs fine-tuning: pipelines, tradeoffs, and a case study on agriculture (2024)
2. Bloisi, D.D., et al.: Mario: modular and extensible architecture for computing visual statistics in robocup spl (2022)
3. Dorbala, V.S., Mullen, J.F., Manocha, D.: Can an embodied agent find your "cat-shaped mug"? LLM-based zero-shot object navigation. IEEE Robot. Autom. Lett. **9**(5), 4083–4090 (2024)
4. Ghallab, M., et al.: Pddl - the planning domain definition language (August 1998)
5. Huang, W., Abbeel, P., Pathak, D., Mordatch, I.: Language models as zero-shot planners: extracting actionable knowledge for embodied agents. In: International Conference on Machine Learning, pp. 9118–9147. PMLR (2022)
6. Laue, T., Spiess, K., Röfer, T.: Simrobot - a general physical robot simulator and its application in robocup. In: Bredenfeld, A., Jacoff, A., Noda, I., Takahashi, Y. (eds.) RoboCup 2005: Robot Soccer World Cup IX, pp. 173–183. Springer, Berlin, Heidelberg (2006)
7. Musumeci, E., Brienza, M., Suriani, V., Nardi, D., Bloisi, D.D.: LLM based multi-agent generation of semi-structured documents from semantic templates in the public administration domain (2024)
8. Musumeci, E., Suriani, V., Antonioni, E., Nardi, D., Bloisi, D.D.: Adaptive team behavior planning using human coach commands. In: Eguchi, A., Lau, N., Paetzel-Prüsmann, M., Wanichanon, T. (eds.) RoboCup 2022: Robot World Cup XXV, pp. 112–123. Springer International Publishing, Cham (2023)
9. OpenAI: Gpt-4v(ision) system card (2023)
10. Reis, L.P., Lau, N.: Coach unilang-a standard language for coaching a (robo) soccer team. Springer (2002)
11. Silver, T., Dan, S., Srinivas, K., Tenenbaum, J.B., Kaelbling, L.P., Katz, M.: Generalized planning in pddl domains with pretrained large language models (2023)
12. Song, C.H., Wu, J., Washington, C., Sadler, B.M., Chao, W.L., Su, Y.: Llm-planner: few-shot grounded planning for embodied agents with large language models (2023)
13. Song, K., Tan, X., Qin, T., Lu, J., Liu, T.: Mpnet: masked and permuted pre-training for language understanding. In: Advances in Neural Information Processing Systems (2020)
14. Suriani, V., Musumeci, E., Nardi, D., Bloisi, D.D.: Play everywhere: a temporal logic based game environment independent approach for playing soccer with robots. In: RoboCup 2023: Robot World Cup XXVI, pp. 3–14. Springer (2024)

15. Yuan, J., et al.: Rag-driver: generalisable driving explanations with retrieval-augmented in-context learning in multi-modal large language model. arXiv preprint arXiv:2402.10828 (2024)
16. Zhao, Z., Lee, W.S., Hsu, D.: Large language models as commonsense knowledge for large-scale task planning. In: Advances in Neural Information Processing Systems, vol. 36, pp. 31967–31987. Curran Associates, Inc. (2023)

Introduction of Automated Testing and Continuous Metrics & KPI Monitoring in Student-Driven Projects: a Use Case

Thomas Klute(✉)

Robotics Research Institute, Section Information Technology, TU Dortmund University, 44227 Dortmund, Germany
thomas.klute@tu-dortmund.de
https://www.irf.tu-dortmund.de/

Abstract. Managing a RoboCup team requires maintaining and improving playing strength over time to achieve success. This paper demonstrates our approach to applying software engineering methodologies to our RoboCup Standard Platform League (SPL) team. We propose a test strategy that matches the requirements of RoboCup and student-driven projects and give examples of appropriate automated software tests and resulting metrics. Finally, we design and evaluate a Continuous Integration pipeline that automatically handles such tests in a non-disturbing, accompanying manner and computes the resulting performance and quality metrics. Moreover, the pipeline adds visibility via charting and dashboarding and provides feedback to the students. The proposed strategy and Continuous Integration pipeline provide a novel and versatile toolchain for teams to better monitor, maintain, and improve their playing strength over time. These results hold practical significance for RoboCup teams trying to establish quality assurance and performance measurement practices.

Keywords: Test automation · Performance measurement · Continuous Integration · CI pipeline · RoboCup · Quality assurance · SE education

1 Introduction

1.1 Motivation

On the one hand, RoboCup has been designed to be a challenging playground for student education and research activities in robotics, keeping entry hurdles low and providing well-defined sandbox-like environments without much need for safety constraints. On the other hand, the ultimate goal of the RoboCup initiative is to win against the human world soccer champions by the mid-21st century. It is already half-time, as this visionary goal was formulated shortly after RoboCup was founded in 1996 [1]. Achieving this goal requires fostering

E. Barros et al. (Eds.): RoboCup 2024, LNAI 15570, pp. 189–199, 2025.
https://doi.org/10.1007/978-3-031-85859-8_16

aspects not currently emphasized within the RoboCup community [2]: quality assurance (QA) and safety requirements when operating in environments shared with humans. Robotic platforms playing soccer against humans must undergo extensive testing before being approved. Otherwise, playing against such robots could hurt - and that would not be the worst-case scenario.

Additionally, we observe that students entering the industry typically have programming skills but lack experience in software engineering (SE), particularly in software testing. Additional training is needed to develop a proper mindset required for industrial software development, where QA is a must for delivering maintainable, robust, fault-tolerant, and secure software products. This omission becomes even more critical for upcoming challenges in developing the next generation of robots, autonomous cars, and other security-related systems.

We decided to introduce reasonable QA measures to our SPL RoboCup team: to validate certain behaviors and benchmark key performance indicators (KPIs) on how good the robot skills and the team behaviors are. Monitoring and improving our team's playing strength should become a daily task. We want to educate a certain mindset: that continuously measuring software quality and performance is not a burden but a necessity for today's software developers.

1.2 Our Contributions

We define RoboCup-adapted test strategy goals, considering that traditional red/green tests are not suitable if performance should be measured and visualized. We present a novel Continuous Integration (CI) pipeline design based on these goals and provide examples of appropriate automated software tests and resulting metrics. We interview experts on the potential benefits of such a solution for RoboCup teams and the league, and finally, we discuss the results.

This work is divided into the following parts: In Sect. 2, we present an overview of related work. In Sect. 3, we formulate goals to introduce software testing and performance measurement to student-driven projects and derive an appropriate strategy. Section 4 presents a Continuous Integration pipeline architecture that supports our strategy and goals. Section 5 describes the required framework and provides an example of a software test, including KPI measurements. Section 6 presents visualizations and analyses of the data. Finally, in Sects. 7 and 8, we evaluate the solution and discuss the results.

2 Related Work

The National Institute of Standards and Technology (NIST) has defined metrics and KPIs for robotics as part of [4]. We follow the approach and terminology of metrics (something we measure) and KPIs (something we calculate or derive from metrics). M. Russo published a recent review of relevant works on measuring performance metrics in robotics in 2023 [5]. He notes that a "fragmented research field" can be observed, where "no standards exist" and a "limited research scope" is caused by a "lack of research focus on the topic". We interviewed several teams participating in the RoboCup SPL to understand how they approach QA, measure their performance, and improve their playing strength [2]. The findings reveal that while manual measures are already utilized, there is great potential to implement automated methods for monitoring quality. However, such measures are often neglected due to limited time and resources.

For RoboCup, standardizing metrics and KPIs should be possible because of the standardization of the leagues. Furthermore, it should be a suitable playground for research: The humanoid leagues' roadmap mentions continuous performance metrics as crucial for measuring progress and proposes adding the measurement of such metrics to the league and triggering rule changes based on improvements in such metrics [3]: "Gathering the metrics presented in this section will strongly improve the possibilities to assess improvements in the league, allow teams to publish quantitative results to support their claims and provide large amount of data to run learning algorithms." The roadmap proposes a set of metrics that should be tracked from now on, but also states "However, those benefits will come at a cost: significant software development will be required".

The RoboCup SPL league does not currently make such a recommendation. However, we take the humanoid league's recommendation as confirmation that metrics measurement and KPI monitoring are appropriate ways to keep up and foster improvement in a team's playing strength and robot skill quality. The SPL league should develop and publish a similar roadmap.

Dierl, Howar, et al. proposed designing a new kind of SE education program [11], including stand-alone SE projects. Our approach is to apply SE methodologies during the existing graduate projects in the computer science program. Graduate projects should still focus on their primary topics, but SE methodologies should become an accompanying part of software development education.

3 Test Strategy Design

3.1 Software Testing Goals

In this section, we propose reasonable goals for introducing automated software testing for existing research software: Establishing software engineering (SE) methodologies is critical to producing high-quality products [6]. Therefore, testing should accompany student education during any software development project phase. Software testing should not be as time-consuming as the industry requires, where it may account for more than 50% of software development costs [7]. Instead, we propose bringing these topics to the forefront and making them visible to create awareness about the relevance of software testing, metrics measurement, and monitoring of relevant KPIs. Thus, we consider the following goals to be a proper approach:

- G1: Tests should be easy to understand, results should be easy to analyze,
- G2: Tests should be easy to execute locally and in a CI pipeline. They should be repeatable and able to run fully automated,

- G3: Tests should allow the variation of input parameters to generate different test cases from a defined input parameter space,
- G4: Tests should create results that include all relevant metrics and calculate the defined KPIs, e.g., by aggregating the pass/fail rate,
- G5: Each code submission should trigger test runs to detect correlations between performance decrease or improvement and source code submissions,
- G6: If KPIs differ significantly negatively or positively from previous test results, the results should be visible to the submitting developers,
- G7: Ability to continuously monitor the KPIs, including trends and history,
- G8: Finally, the software components used to build such a solution should be open source or at least available for free if used for scientific purposes.

3.2 Test Strategy

The NaoDevils team uses GitHub for source code management (SCM) and has implemented a basic automated smoke test. A GitHub action triggers the smoke test after every commit, checking for compilation errors and simulating a 5-minute match between simulated robots and an immobile dummy team, where a goal is typically scored within seconds. Developers are notified to review their contributions if the test fails. Despite the simplicity of the smoke test, its impact is enormous compared to having no QA at all: it offers near-real-time feedback, helping identify bugs that affect relevant functionality. It serves as virtualized end-to-end test, covering a large amount of source code and ensuring that almost all modules work adequately for the test to pass. Conversely, less obvious issues have a chance to remain undetected, and performance changes are only detected if they result in a goal not being scored. Finally, we would like to note that this test does not address any gap between the simulator and reality.

Based on these initial observations, we wanted to improve the test coverage and gain more insights into specific KPIs of robot skills and team behavior. Choosing such virtualized end-to-end tests as described above over unit tests and integration tests has several advantages:

- Low effort to create test cases after initial infrastructure setup.
- Coverage of large code areas, useful for existing legacy code.
- No need for deep technical knowledge to define tests and assess results.
- High-level tests are largely independent of implementation changes.
- Fully automatable using a CI pipeline and the simulator.

Given our situation and goals, we conclude that such virtualized end-to-end tests are a versatile, valuable, and promising step toward introducing automated software testing and performance measurement. The effort required to set up such tests is acceptable. The results provide valuable feedback to students, developers, and the team. The disadvantage of not covering the gap between the simulator and reality can be mitigated by trying to close such a gap using *sim-to-real* measures. Running tests in a simulator has near zero costs, whereas manually running test games on real robots is time-consuming and comes at high costs due to robots' wear-off. We propose a four-part strategy: 1) Introduce a QA control loop process that guides and improves existing tests and increases test coverage. In case of performance decrease or bugs not detected by the existing tests, new test cases should be added, 2) continuously test team behavior for rule conformance, 3) continuously measure and monitor relevant metrics and KPIs covering relevant robot skills and team behaviors, and 4) periodically conduct real-world tests to compare simulated to real-world results. Identify potential gaps to be addressed through *sim-to-real* measures.

4 CI Pipeline Architecture

Figure 1 shows the proposed CI pipeline architecture. Each developer should have the option to execute relevant test scenes locally (contributes to goal G2) before submitting their contributions to the SCM. Running tests locally allows for experimentation during development to improve the resulting KPIs. The test scene writes detailed test results to a folder.

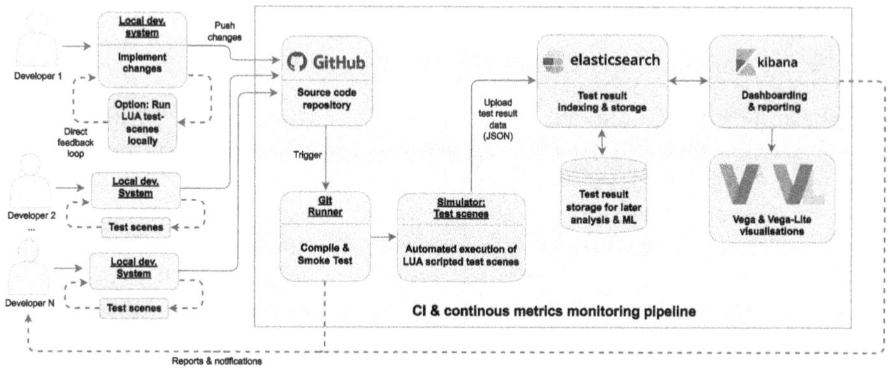

Fig. 1. New CI pipeline design running scripted test scenes automatically, feeding the test results into Elastic Stack for dashboarding, visualization, and reporting.

Additionally, it provides an easy-to-understand indication of the resulting KPIs to the developer (contributes to G1, G4). After a source code contribution is submitted to the SCM, automated software tests are triggered (contributes to G2, G5) consisting of two stages. Stage one contains the compile and smoke test. Stage two adds the more sophisticated scripted software test scenes that orchestrate the test runs, vary input parameters, measure metrics and compute relevant KPIs (contributes to G3, G4). This stage executes the scripted test scenes and automatically uploads the detailed results to an Elasticsearch node [8] for later analysis (contributes to G6, G7). The stored results can then be searched and retrieved by a Kibana node, which is a part of the typical Elastic Stack setup [8]. Kibana enables the processing of test results and offers features for extensive ad-hoc and ex-post analysis, for visualizing and monitoring metrics and KPIs using suitable diagrams, and summarizing test results on a dashboard (contributes to G6). The visualization grammars Vega and Vega-lite [14] allow the assembly of various chart types and interactive graphics. Last but not least, Kibana allows the definition of notifications based on metrics and KPIs (contributes to G7). In addition to running the pipeline on contributions, teams should set up a nightly build and create charts tracking the development of KPIs over time. These charts should be available to all team members. Team leaders and students should be notified of the latest KPI development and trends (contributes to G6, G7). Elasticsearch and Kibana are part of the free and open-source Elastic Stack [8] (contributes to G8).

5 Framework for Simulated End-to-End Tests

To benchmark robot skills and team behaviors, we need a simulation environment capable of (a) simulating scenes as defined by the specific test case and (b) collecting result data and measuring metrics. While the detailed requirements depend on the specific test, a common base functionality is required.

5.1 Enhanced Remote Control of the Simulator

We have been using the popular simulation environment SimRobot [12], as many other SPL teams do. SimRobot was already capable of loading predefined scenes, including a game controller and a partially automatic referee. The "robot console" provides some basic simulation and environment control capabilities. A predefined set of commands can be executed when loading a scene or typing them into the console. The set of commands provided consists of global commands, e.g., for addressing the game controller module to start/stop the gameplay and for handling game situations like corner kicks and penalties. It also provides commands to communicate with each robot and access its internal representations and parameters. However, to achieve our goals, SimRobot still requires some features that we need to add: automated tests require internal control logic to be executed in parallel with the running scene to control the execution and measure relevant metrics. Since the console cannot provide such logic, we need to add something suitable: Now we can load and execute scripts written in the popular scripting language Lua [13] during the simulation. Scripting language support adds much power to the console: all Lua language elements, such as variables, conditional expressions, branching, and loops, can be used, and libraries providing additional functionality may be loaded. The new console includes a "lua" command that loads and executes a Lua script that can add control logic to a scene, govern the automated test, and compose and provide test result data. Due to the simulator's architecture, the Lua script initially registers listener functions for specific events. Such event listeners can be used, for example, to initialize everything the script needs to prepare the test case (SCRIPT_LOADED event), track the ball position (BALL_MOVED event), be notified when a goal is scored (GOAL_SCORED event), and more. The script can orchestrate the test using the ON_UPDATE event listener by tracking the elapsed time and issuing commands at specific times during the test.

5.2 Example Test Case: Benchmarking the Goalkeeper

In this section, we present an example test case, metrics to measure, and KPIs to be calculated and monitored. The example is derived from the basic requirements we defined for our goalkeeper role: balls that are shot at the goal should be defended. With this first example of an automated test, we aim to define metrics and calculate KPIs on how well the goalkeeper implementation can handle balls kicked from different positions at different speeds toward different target positions in the goal. We define the following metrics and KPIs:

Name	Type	Description
distance	metric	the distance between kick position and goal
goal_detected	metric	indicates if the ball is located inside the goal
dive_detected	metric	indicates a dive motion to defend the ball
recovery_time	metric	time in seconds to stand up after dive
prevented_goal_rate	KPI	average of the *not*(*goal_detected*) metric
avg._recovery_time	KPI	average of the *recovery_time* metric

Test Case Definition. We define a single goalkeeper test input as tuple $t_i = (x_s, y_s, v_s, x_t, y_t)$, where x_s, y_s is the start position of the ball, v_s is the starting velocity of the ball motion, and x_t, y_t is the target position of the ball motion. We do not use a robot to kick the ball toward the goal, as this would add an extra dimension of uncertainty regarding the accuracy of the ball motion, including velocity and target coordinates. Instead, we added a command to the simulator that initiates a ball motion using the given velocity and target position. We define the test output tuple as $t_o = (r_{time}, r_{fail}, r_{dist}, r_{dive}, r_{trecover})$, where r_{time} is a timestamp of the test execution, and r_{fail} is a boolean failure flag (*true*: the ball is not defended). We add some additional data for later analysis: r_{dist} is the distance of the kick, r_{dive} is a boolean flag indicating whether the goalkeeper made a dive motion while trying to defend the ball, and $r_{trecover}$ is the time it took the robot to recover after a dive motion, i.e., to get up after the dive. If the robot did not dive, the recovery time is recorded as 0. The test result $t_r = t_i + t_o$ is defined as the concatenation of both tuples and contains all the data required for subsequent analysis. We selected the input data straightforwardly. The output values align with the definition of metrics and KPIs, as seen above. To calculate the KPIs, we must perform many individual tests using different ball positions and velocities targeting different positions in the goal. The number of individual tests performed and the selection of proper input parameters from the search space will influence the KPI value compared to using a

Monte Carlo method with an appropriately high number of test cycles. There is a trade-off between executing a high number of test cycles to approximate the KPI's expected value and running such tests locally without wasting time during software development. Selecting a reasonable set of test cycles is essential for generating realistic KPI values. For simplicity, in this example, we choose uniformly distributed values on a grid as the starting position, using a set of realistic ball velocities between 1.8 and 2.4 m/s.

6 Visualization of Results

Figure 2 shows an example of a dashboard created in Kibana to visualize the "Prevented goal rate (%)" KPI based on the results of multiple test runs: A timeline chart shows the KPI development over a selected time range. The two-dimensional heatmap shows the KPI values per 500 mm · 500 mm intervals of the initial ball position (with the right edge of the diagram showing where the goal and goalkeeper are located) and a breakdown of the KPI per 100 mm target Y position (limited by the left and the right goal post positions at –800 mm and 800 mm), as well as a breakdown pie chart of the KPI by the initial velocity of the ball movement. This test case should be considered only as an example of how to use the basic charting capabilities. The integrated Vega and Vega-Lite visualization grammars can create visualizations beyond the simple examples demonstrated here. In summary, Kibana's visualization and dashboarding options are versatile tools for exploring test result data and visualizing it using a multitude of charting options.

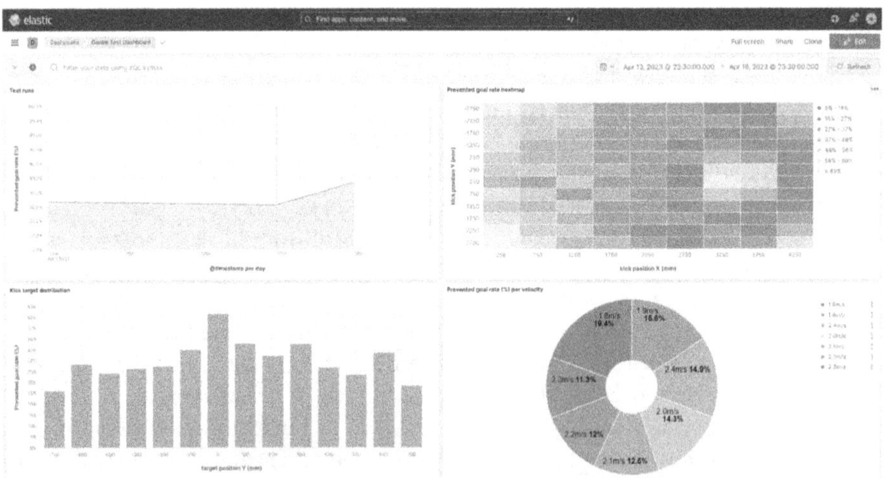

Fig. 2. Example dashboard showing a time range and additional charts focusing on kick position shown as a heatmap, target position, and velocity.

7 Evaluation

We evaluated our approach and the resulting CI pipeline by interviewing seven experts (team leads, technical directors, or equivalents) from six other SPL RoboCup teams (Bembelbots, B-Human, Dutch Nao Team, HTWK Robots, HULKs, Naova) during the competitions in 2023 in Hamburg and Bordeaux. First, we surveyed whether there is a structured approach to QA, software testing, and performance measurement, and if so, what characterizes the approach in detail. Then, we presented our approach and asked for their comments. While the more general results have been published separately [2], we summarize here the comments relevant for the testing and CI pipeline approach. The two main findings are: (a) Currently, no such solution is in use by the SPL teams we interviewed, and (b) in general, all experts found the approach to be suitable (e.g., "definitive suitable", "interesting, impressive", "for sure"). Two experts expressed concern about how the results would relate to reality ("How close is the simulation to reality?", "Useful, but questionable whether this is meaningful in reality. However, generally, a quite good criterion for detecting changes by code submissions."). Three experts expressed interest in adapting the solution (e.g., "Yes, it has the potential to catch lots of issues.", "interesting for own team, but would need to change how time is invested in the team"). One expert noted that he would "partly adapt" the concept and measure and monitor code quality indicators, like test coverage.

8 Discussion

We conclude that a CI pipeline meeting our goals can be built. The components used are available as open-source and free of any license fees. Other tools similar to Elastic Stack, like OpenSearch [9], which is a fork of Elastic Stack, and Prometheus [10] are also available. These tools are typically used for monitoring metrics of large IT infrastructures and alerting in case of reading abnormal metrics values. With some adaptions and integration, they can be versatile tools for continuously monitoring metrics and KPIs as part of a CI pipeline. Building the proposed CI pipeline and aligning functionality to the goals required some experimental work: The simulation environment had to be enhanced with features needed to orchestrate test scenes, collect relevant metrics data, and provide them in a format that can be fed into Elasticsearch. The resulting CI pipeline seems promising and is able to fulfill the goals according to our experiences with the setup. We provide more detailed information containing the setup instructions separatley[1]. Setting up such a solution should be possible by either re-building the pipeline described from scratch or adding missing elements to an existing CI pipeline. Adapting the whole chain to a different RoboCup league or an existing CI pipeline should be an acceptable one-time effort, provided that a proper simulation environment exists that can be automated and remote-controlled. Running the software tests and continuously tracking the resulting metrics can then be achieved at almost no additional cost and effort.

[1] Please visit https://klute.com/research/2024-ContinuousMonitoring.

8.1 Limitations

The most relevant and obvious limitation is using a simulation environment to retrieve test results that need to be considered valid in reality. From our experience, one of the first arguments against the automation of software testing using simulation is that a specific simulation environment X is not quite accurate and behaves differently compared to the reality. Conversely, the *sim-to-real* problem cannot, in our view, be used as an argument against the use of simulation for automated software testing in general. It should be seen as a strong recommendation that improvements to the simulation environment, such as simulator-grounding [15], should be addressed instead. Accurate simulation environments are typically used for prototyping and testing almost every aspect of robotic behavior. Having a suitable simulation environment at hand greatly reduces robot wear-off because testing can be done in the simulation environment rather than on the real robot. Thus, we strongly recommend including software testing as part of every student educational project where students learn to develop software in a team setup over a certain period.

8.2 Future Work and Conclusion

Defining, measuring, and monitoring metrics and KPIs will become key to success in RoboCup, at least in those leagues that measure league progress by monitoring KPI improvements. Performing better in league-defined KPIs will directly correlate with improved skills, playing strength, and team play. Thus, we expect teams to spend more time and effort on these topics in the future. Therefore, guides and solutions that are valuable and adaptable by other teams will be of interest.

References

1. The RoboCup Federation: RoboCup website (1998). https://web.archive.org/web/19981201174356/www.robocup.org/overview/22.html. Accessed 18 Jan 2024
2. Klute, T.: Performance Measurement and Software QA in the RoboCup SPL: a qualitative interview study (2024). https://klute.com/research/2024-SPL-Study/
3. RoboCup Soccer: Humanoid League DRAFT Roadmap (2022). http://humanoid.robocup.org/wp-content/uploads/roadmap_2022.pdf. Accessed 18 Jan 2024
4. Zimmerman, T.A.: Metrics and key performance indicators for robotic cybersecurity performance analysis. NIST (2017). https://doi.org/10.6028/nist.ir.8177
5. Russo, M.: Measuring performance: metrics for manipulator design, control, and optimization. Robotics **12**(1), 4 (2023). https://doi.org/10.3390/robotics12010004
6. Myers, G., Badgett, T., Sandler, C.: The Art of Software Testing (3rd ed.). John Wiley Sons, Hoboken, N.J (2012)
7. Xu, D., Xu, W., Kent, M., Thomas, L., Wang, L.: An automated test generation technique for software quality assurance. IEEE Trans. Reliab. **64**(1), 247–268 (2015). https://doi.org/10.1109/TR.2014.2354172
8. Elastic Stack website. https://www.elastic.co/elastic-stack/. Accessed 18 Jan 2024
9. OpenSearch website. https://opensearch.org/. Accessed 18 Jan 2024

10. Prometheus website. https://prometheus.io/. Accessed 18 Jan 2024
11. Dierl, S., Howar, F., Mues, M., Naujokat, S., Schallau, T.: Do away with the Frankensteinian programs! A proposal for a genuine SE education. In: International Workshop on Software Engineering Education for the Next Generation (SEENG), pp. 26–30. Madrid, Spain (2021). https://doi.org/10.1109/seeng53126.2021.00012
12. Laue, T., Spiess, K., Röfer, T.: SimRobot - a general physical robot simulator and its application in RoboCup. In: Bredenfeld, A., Jacoff, A., Noda, I., Takahashi, Y. (eds.), RoboCup 2005: Robot Soccer World Cup IX, volume 4020 of LNAI, pp. 173–183. Springer (2006)
13. Lua website. https://www.lua.org/about.html. Accessed 18 Jan 2024
14. Vega - Visualization Grammars. https://vega.github.io/. Accessed 18 Jan 2024
15. Desai, S., Karnan, H., Hanna, J.P., Warnell, G., Strong, P.: Stochastic grounded action transformation for robot learning in simulation. In: IEEE/RSJ International Conference on Intelligent Robots and Systems (IROS), pp. 6106–6111. Las Vegas, NV, USA (2020). https://doi.org/10.1109/IROS45743.2020.9340780

Proposal of a Method for Acquiring Characteristics of Large-Diameter Solenoids

Moeko Tominaga[1(✉)], Ayumu Tominaga[2], Yasunori Takemura[1], and Kazuo Ishii[3]

[1] Nishinippon Institute of Technology, 1-11, Aratsu, Kanda-machi, Miyako-gun, Fukuoka 800-0394, Japan
tominaga@nishitech.ac.jp

[2] National Institute of Technology Kitakyushu College, 5-20-1 Shii, Kokuraminamiku, Kitakyushu, Fukuoka 802-0985, Japan
tominaga@kct.ac.jp

[3] Kyushu Institute of Technology, 2-4 Hibikino, Wakamatsu-ku, Kitakyushu-shi, Fukuoka 808-0196, Japan
ishii@brain.kyutech.ac.jp

Abstract. The solenoids used in the RoboCup soccer middle-sized league are large-diameter push solenoids, which are not widely available in the market as a product. Therefore, the relationship between input and output can only be obtained through experiments by researchers who have manufactured the solenoids. Until now, simulations have been performed using FEM and other methods, but it was not possible to analyze the actual plunger motion. In this study, the motion of a plunger is observed using an actual solenoid, and the input-output relationship is clarified. This will allow us to clarify the equation relating ball flight distance and self-inductance as an actual ball ejection device. This research can be utilized not only for Robocup but also for the injection mechanism of Elide Fire Ball and inexpensive and compact ball ejector.

Keywords: Middle Size League · Solenoid · Analysis

1 Introduction

The mechanism for kicking a ball is very important in RoboCup, and its accuracy greatly affects the outcome of the match. In this study, analysis and experiments were conducted to improve the kicking mechanism of "Musashi150," a robot competing in the RoboCup Soccer Middle Size League(MSL). In the middle-size league, the size of the field is getting larger every year, and more precise control of the solenoid is required to pass and shoot the ball accurately. Dynamic response analysis using FEM has been used to analyze solenoids [3,4,8]. However, in fact, it is necessary to measure the flight distance of the ball ejected from the manufactured solenoid and the movement of the plunger, so it is important

E. Barros et al. (Eds.): RoboCup 2024, LNAI 15570, pp. 200–211, 2025.
https://doi.org/10.1007/978-3-031-85859-8_17

to analyze and compare the results. In this study, a prototype solenoid and experiments were conducted to derive a more accurate input-output relationship for a large-diameter solenoid.

2 Solenoid as a Kick Device

2.1 Kick Device in RoboCup

RoboCup Soccer has the goal of achieving soccer with humans by 2050. In order to achieve this goal, robots must have the same or better physical capabilities than humans in terms of soccer. Especially in soccer, if the accuracy of the kicking motion is not improved, even basic behaviors such as passing and shooting become difficult. In RoboCup MSL, a spring-loaded kick device was initially developed. However, the need to change the power of the kick in different situations led to the development of a solenoid kick device [2]. Solenoids are also used in injection mechanisms in small size leagues(SSL) as well as MSL, and geometry parameters are being optimized through FEM analysis [6].

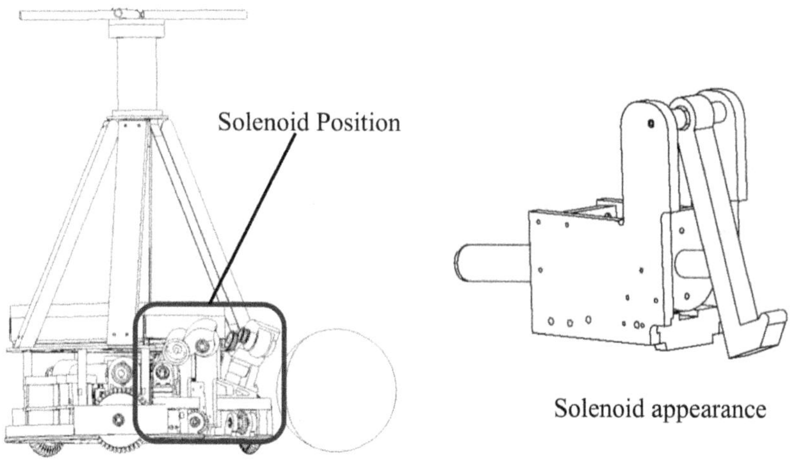

Fig. 1. Outline of A large-diameter, push-type solenoid by Hibikino-Musashi

The solenoid is used as a kicking mechanism to pass the ball to a teammate or shoot at the goalpost, so speed control of the plunger is important. Since the target of injection is the same as a human soccer ball, the plunger must output a maximum force of approximately 7,000 to 8,000N. A large diameter, push-type solenoid is required. A large-diameter, push-type solenoid for kicks currently developed at Hibikino-Musashi is shown in Fig. 1. In addition, details of the components that make up solenoid are shown in Fig. 2. The kick mechanism is

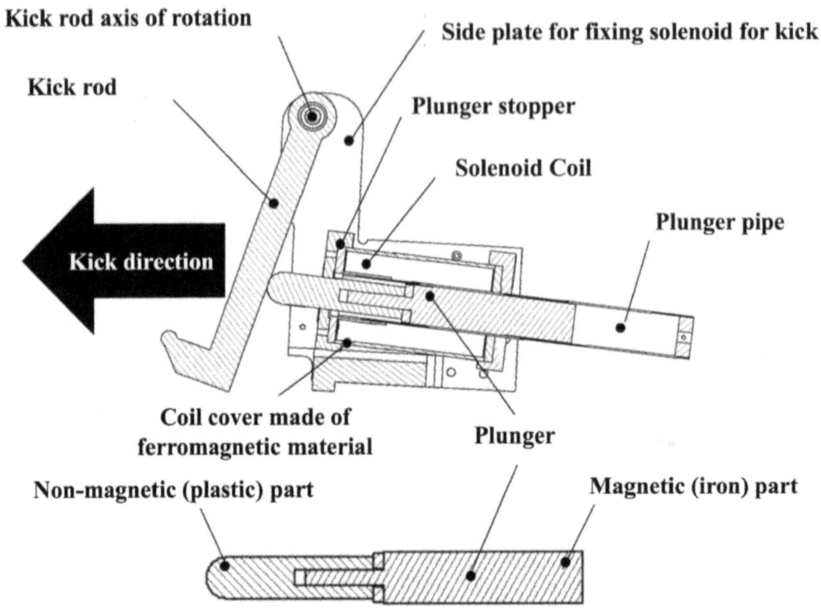

Fig. 2. Detailed solenoid diagram of Hibikino-Musashi

located in front of the robot and can eject the ball when the kick rod hits the ball.

The plunger part is half non-magnetic (plastic) and half magnetic (iron SCM435), and the kick rod is moved by the plastic part protruding from the coil. The following is the procedure for activating the solenoid kick device.

1. When a current flows through the coil, a magnetic field is generated in the coil. The plunger is magnetized and attracted to the coil.
2. Only the resin part of the plunger pops out of the coil.
3. The plunger hits the kick rod and the kick rod rotates around the kick rod rotation axis. The ball is then ejected.
4. When the current stops, the magnetic force disappears and the plunger returns to its initial position by its own weight and the force of a rubber.

Most of the solenoids used in MSL are self-made solenoids due to the lack of sufficient solenoid power and proper size available on the market. These self-made solenoids are analyzed by FEM and the relatively optimal shape is selected from multiple shape patterns, but there are no studies that numerically test the solenoid output in addition to the ball flight distance by actual equipment experiments. As a numerical experiment, a contact-type electromagnetic force measurement method using a mechanical sensor (load cell) can be used to achieve highly accurate measurements [5]. On the other hand, it is necessary to mount the solenoid on a highly rigid solenoid fixture for measurement, which requires a large amount of labor for a single measurement.

2.2 Theory of Electromagnetic Performane of Solenoids

The force output by a plunger in a solenoid is the derivative of its energy with respect to its position. To find it, we need an expression for the change in inductance $L(x)$ with position. Shown in Eq. 1 [7].

$$L(x) = L_0 e^{-\frac{\alpha}{l} x} \tag{1}$$

$$L(0) = L_0 = \frac{\mu_r \mu_0 N^2 A}{l} \tag{2}$$

Set $x = 0$ at the beginning of the armature and l as the length of the entire coil. L_0 is the maximum of the coil inductance as Eq. 2. Here α is given by Eq. 3. r is radius of the coil and μ_r is permeability of the core at r. Also μ_0 is permeability of the core at 0. N is the number of turns and A is the cross-sectional area of the coil.

$$\alpha = \ln(\mu_r) \tag{3}$$

The final force $F(x)$ is shown in Eq. 4. R is the resistance of the conductor wrapped around the coil and V is the voltage.

$$F(x) = -\frac{V^2}{2R^2} \frac{\alpha}{l} L(x) \tag{4}$$

2.3 Requirement Specification and Parameterization

From the equation, Fig. 3 shows the theoretical values relationship between the force and the current value of the solenoid kicker of the RoboCup Soccer middle-size league as a function of the winding diameter. The maximum allowable current is a characteristic of the electronic board manufactured, and if a higher current is allowed, the cost of manufacturing the electronic board will increase significantly. Figure 3 shows that a wire gauge of around 1.8 is optimal. This is because this is the maximum amperage that we can use, while maximizing force.

3 Ball Distance Measurement Experiment Using the Manufactured Solenoid

Based on Sect. 2.3, three solenoids with different wire gauges were fabricated. The fabricated solenoids are shown in Fig. 4 and their parameters are shown in Table 1.

The three solenoids were mounted on a robot as a kicking device (kicker) to measure the distance of the ball. Figure 5 shows the experimental method.

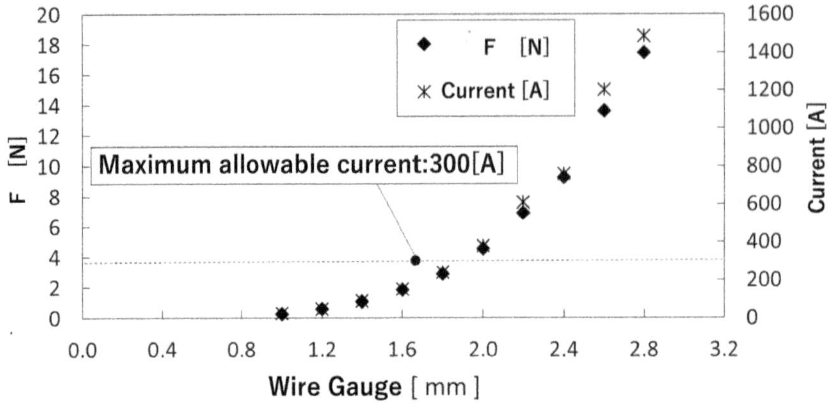

Fig. 3. Relationship between force and current value depending on wire gauge

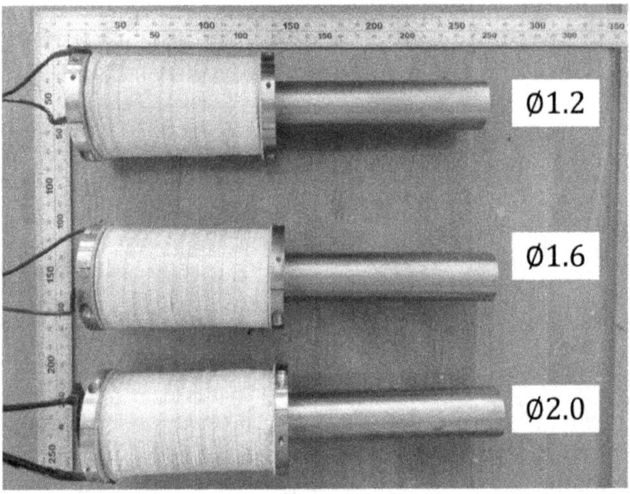

Fig. 4. Manifacutured solenoid kickers fabricated (wire gauge: top $\phi 1.2$, middle $\phi 1.6$, bottom $\phi 2.0$)

Figure 5 shows the experimental procedure. In the experiment, a ball is placed in the same position each time on the device against the robot, and the kick mechanism ejects the ball, which is photographed by a camera from the side direction. The obtained video is used to follow the trajectory of the ball. In this experiment, the distance of the ball is used as the evaluation.

The results are shown in Fig. 6. However, in the experiment with a solenoid with a wire gauge of ϕ 2.0, the rod that directly ejects the ball broke, so data could not be obtained. Rod breakage is shown in Fig. 7.

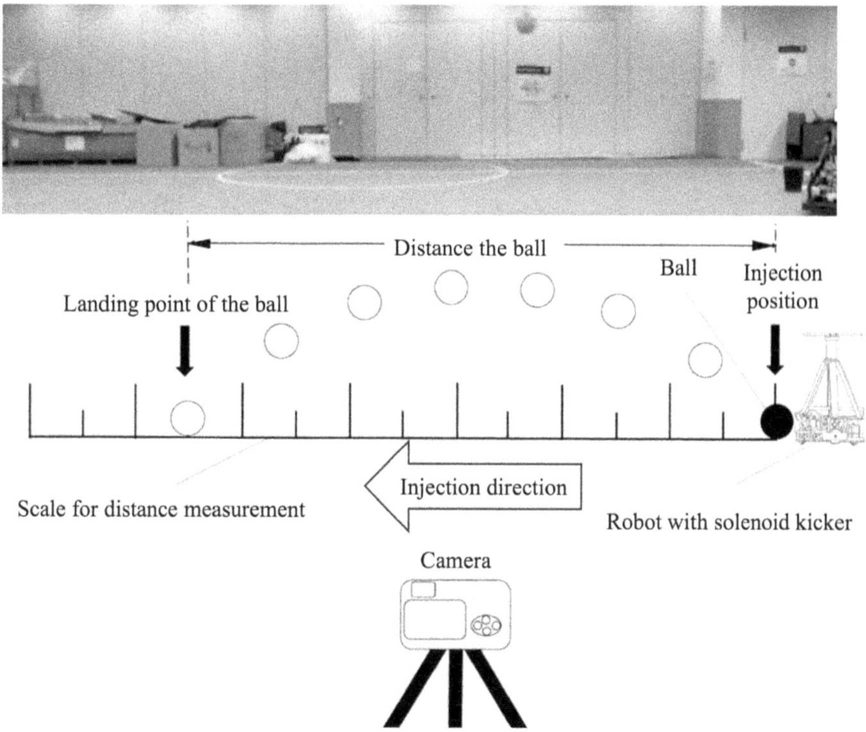

Fig. 5. Schematic diagram of ball distance experiment with solenoid

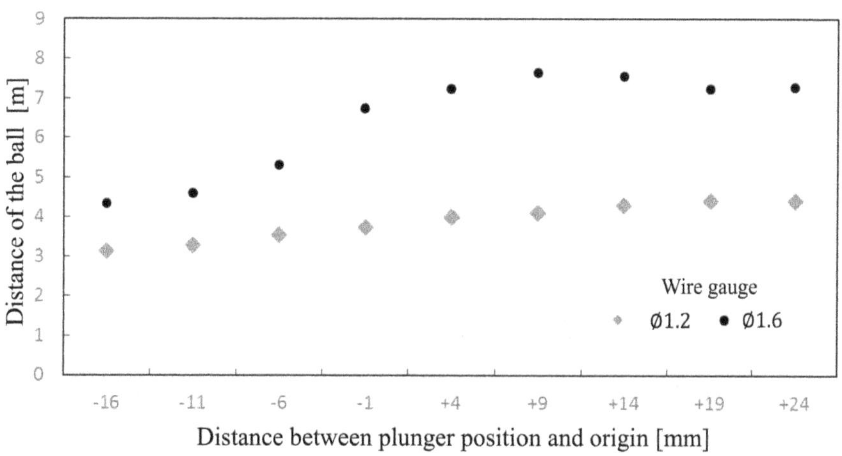

Fig. 6. Measurement result of ball distance in ϕ 1.2 and ϕ 1.6 wire gauge solenoid

Table 1. Detail of the fabricated solenoid kicker

Wire gauge[mm]	Number of turns	Resistance[Ω]
1.2	670	1.282
1.6	400	0.461
2.0	234	0.193

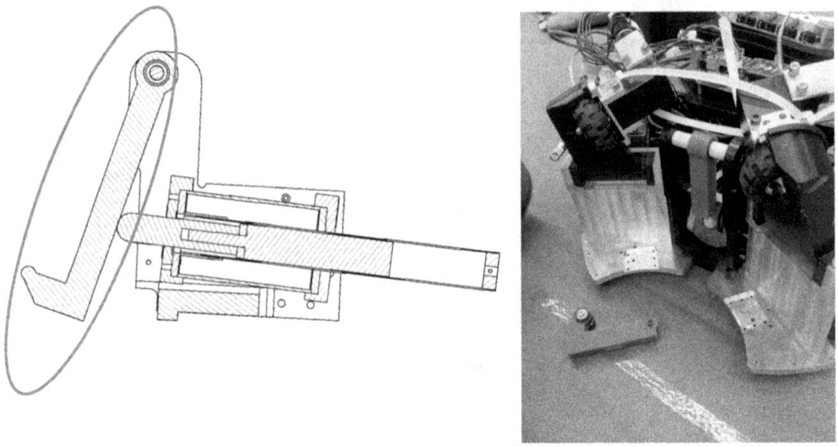

Fig. 7. Rod bloken in ϕ 2.0 wire gauge

The positional relationship between the plunger and the solenoid coil was also investigated. This is because, as many researchers have elucidated, the initial position of the plunger causes a change in the distance of the ball, i.e., the velocity at which the plunger ejects the ball [1]. The plunger initial position coordinates were investigated as shown in Fig. 8.

Figure 6 shows that the distance between the magnetic part and the origin is +24 mm at the initial position for the 1.2 mm winding, and the distance between the magnetic part and the origin is +9 mm at the initial position for the 1.6 mm winding, which gives the longest distance when the ball is kicked. The force on the iron core is determined by its position in relation to the solenoid coil, and it can be considered that the position where the longest distance can be shot is within the length of the currently designed solenoid coil.

4 Experiments in Momentum Derivation

To predict motion energy imparted from the large diameter solenoid to a ball, a displacement measurement system for a plunger has been developed utilizing a one-dimensional Time of Flight (ToF) sensor. The ToF sensor gauges the direct distance to an object illuminated by an infrared laser.

Figure 9 represents the scheme of the proposed method. Initially, the ToF sensor is positioned in the plunger's line of sight, enabling the laser to be directed

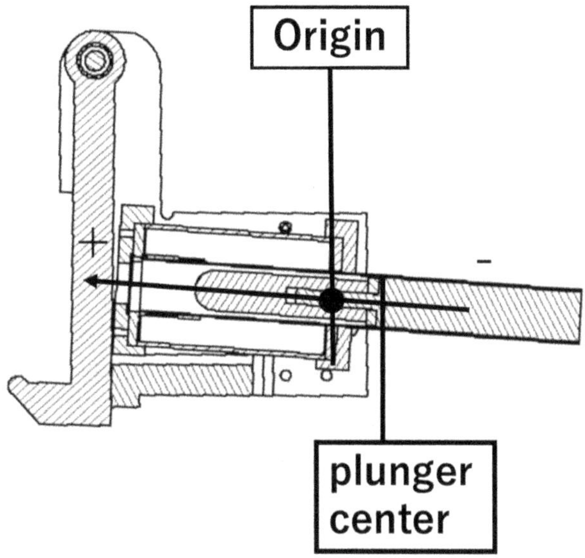

Fig. 8. Origin of solenoid coil and plunger

at the plunger's tip, thereby facilitating distance measurement by the ToF sensor. Subsequently, current is applied to the solenoid coil to actuate the plunger. In this context, the distance value is denoted as d_s when the plunger is at its initial position, while d_e represents the distance when the plunger reaches its terminal position after completing its motion. Thus, the transition of the ToF output value associated with the plunger's motion can be predicted as shown in Fig. 9. Actuating the plunger causes the distance value acquired from the ToF sensor to decrease from d_s to d_e. Leveraging the obtained measurement results, it is feasible to estimate the velocity and kinetic energy of the plunger at each of its positions. Typically, in the kicking mechanism of a soccer robot in the MSL, a leg component used to control the ball's ejection direction is installed in front of the plunger. However, in this study, the motion of the leg component is excluded from observation and analysis. Instead, the focus is solely on observing the motion of the plunger, which directly interacts with the magnetic force generated by the solenoid coil. This approach enables an assessment of its interaction with a magnetic field simulator.

Figure 10 represents the system structure. VL53L0X from STMicroelectronics Co., Ltd. was employed as the ToF sensor in the system. Measurement data is acquired via I2C communication from the sensor, Arduino was used for the data logger interfaced with the sensor. A power supply module was connected to the solenoid coil through an external switch, which is capable of supplying a voltage of 20 V and a maximum current of 2 A to the solenoid coil. While a 90 V voltage is typically used in actual robots in soccer games, concerns over potential damage

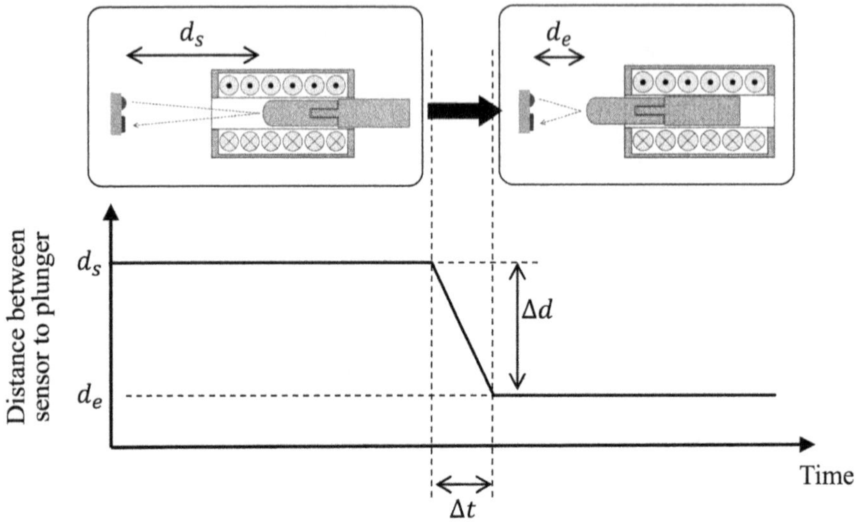

Fig. 9. Plunger displacement measurement method with ToF sensor

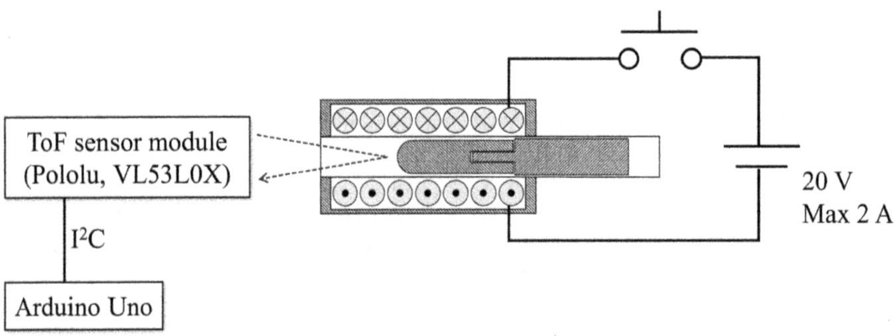

Fig. 10. System structure

to housing and frame constructs prompted a reduction in the input voltage for this study. Figure 11 shows the actual manufactured equipment. Carbon pipes, with a diameter of 22 mm and a thickness of 1 mm, were used for the frames of housing. Both the solenoid coil and the sensor are installed, as shown in Fig. 11. The details of a plunger displacement measurement experiment are desevibed below. The physical parameters of the solenoid coil utilized in the experiment are presented in Table 2.

Figure 12 shows the experimental results of plotting the ToF sensor values at each sample time, with time on the horizontal axis and the measured distance between the ToF sensor and the plunger tip on the vertical axis. In Fig. 12, the horizontal axis represents time and the vertical axis represents the distance between the ToF sensor and the plunger tip. The overall trend of plunger dis-

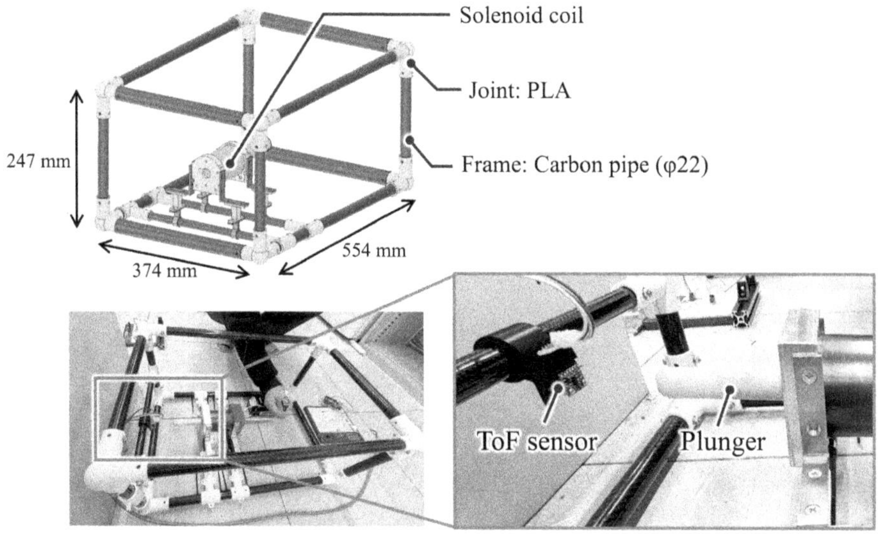

Fig. 11. Housing of the solenoid actuator

Table 2. Solenoid coil specification

Parameters	Value
Wire gauge (mm)	2.0
Number of turns	234
Plunger mass (kg)	0.397
Supply voltage (V)	20
Plunger stroke length (mm)	100

placement shows the same trajectory as predicted depicted in Fig. 9. However, the theoretical ideal value of the flanger displacement distance for the CAD design was 100 mm, whereas the measured distance was about 60 mm.

The instance when the voltage is applied and the plunger initiates motion occurs around 0.4 s, with motion concluding around 0.5 s. During this 0.1 s interval, a plunger displacement of 50 mm was observed. Consider why there was such a difference in Δd. The voltage is applied and the plunger begins to move at around 0.4 s, and the movement ends at around 0.5 s. During this 0.1 s period, 50 mm of plunger displacement was observed. The plunger stroke length, initially designed as 100 mm, was found to deviate significantly from the measurement results obtained with the experimental system. One possible cause of this discrepancy is the shock that occurs when the plunger reaches the end position. In this experiment, a lower voltage was applied than should have been utilized. However, because the plunger travel speed did not decrease sufficiently, the laser

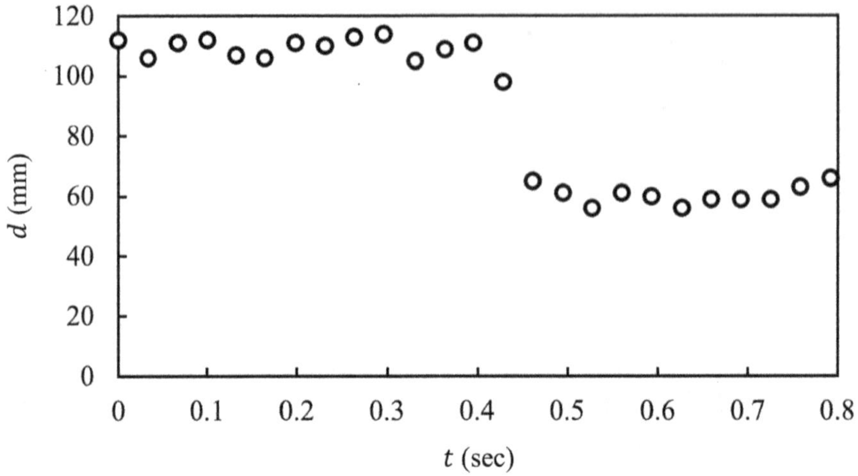

Fig. 12. Measurement result (t-d)

irradiation position of the ToF sensor shifted from the plunger tip, resulting in measurements that were different from those expected.

Conversely, the sample immediately after 0.4 s is anticipated to reflect the outcome of correct laser irradiation of the plunger tip and subsequent measurement. The sample data at and immediately after the 0.4 s mark predicted a plunger motion velocity of 393 mm/s immediately following the application of voltage. Consequently, the kinetic energy was estimated to be 30.6×10^3 J based on the plunger mass.

5 Conclusion

Focusing on the kicking mechanism of a soccer robot in the RoboCup MSL, this study proposed a method to clarify the magnetic and mechanical properties of a large-diameter solenoid, which is the de facto standard for the ball ejection mechanism. First, theoretical values were obtained for the electrical characteristics by calculation. Next, for the mechanical characteristics, we proposed the following two observation methods.

1) A method to observe the distance of the ball using a camera.
2) A method to observe the displacement of the plunger during its motion using a ToF sensor.

As a future issue, it is necessary to evaluate the consistency between the observation and analysis methods using actual equipment and the results of analysis by simulation such as FEM.

References

1. Houtman, W., et al.: Tech United Eindhoven Middle-Size League Winner 2019, pp. 517–528. Chem (2019)
2. Kasaei, S.H.M., Kasaei, S.M.M., Kasaei, S.A.M.: Design and implementation solenoid based kicking mechanism for soccer robot applied in robocup-msl. Int. J. Adv. Robot. Syst. **7**(4) (2010). https://doi.org/10.5772/10490
3. Kawase, Y., Ohdachi, Y.: Dynamic analysis of automotive solenoid valve using finite element method. IEEE Trans. Magn. **27**(5), 3939–3942 (1991). https://doi.org/10.1109/20.104965
4. Mitsutake, Y., Hirata, K., Ishihara, Y.: Dynamic response analysis of a linear electromagnetic solenoid. J. Magn. Soc. Jpn. **20**(2), 517–520 (1996). https://doi.org/10.3379/jmsjmag.20.517
5. Plavec, E., Filipović-Grčić, B., Vidović, M.: The impact of plunger angle and radius on the force and time response of dc solenoid electromagnetic actuator used in high-voltage circuit breaker. Int. J. Electr. Power Energy Syst. **118**, 105767 (2020)
6. Santos, D.D.N., et al.: Geometry analysis and force simulation of a kicker system's flat solenoid to robots for the RoboCup small size league category. In: 2021 Latin American Robotics Symposium, 2021 Brazilian Symposium on Robotics, and 2021 Workshop on Robotics in Education, pp. 300–305 (2021)
7. Schimpf, P.: A detailed explanation of solenoid force. Int. J. Recent Trends Eng. Technol. (IJRTET) **8**(2), 7–14 (2013)
8. Zheng, S.Q., Chen, D.: Analysis of transient magnetic fields coupled to mechanical motion in solenoidal electromagnet excited by voltage source. IEEE Trans. Magn. **28**(2), 1315–1317 (1992). https://doi.org/10.1109/20.123932

On Graph Reduction in Consensus Control of Multi-agent Systems: A Preliminary Study

Amirali Setayeshi[1], Zeynab Ezzati Babi[2], Ali Saadati[1], and Soroush Sadeghnejad[3](✉)

[1] Department of Electrical Engineering, Amirkabir University of Technology (Tehran Polytechnic), Tehran, Iran
{setayeshi,alisaadati}@aut.ac.ir

[2] Human and Robot Interaction Laboratory, School of Electrical and Computer Engineering, University of Tehran, Tehran, Iran
ezzati.z@ut.ac.ir

[3] Bio-Inspired System Design Lab, Department of Biomedical Engineering, Amirkabir University of Technology (Tehran Polytechnic), Tehran, Iran
s.sadeghnejad@aut.ac.ir

Abstract. Since the use of multi-agent systems has significantly increased over the past few decades, it is crucial to study the methods used in this area and take implementation-related practical issues into consideration. For instance, in the formulation of the consensus problem, the communication between the agents is depicted using a graph, where each edge represents a communication link between the agents. In practical terms, there will be significant operational challenges and costs associated with implementing each of these communication channels in various forms. Therefore, in this study, the graph reduction problem has been presented as an optimization problem, accompanied by six distinct cost functions. The objective is to reduce the size of a graph without compromising its fundamental characteristics. Hence, the cost functions provided are formulated to minimize the number of edges in the resulting graph while ensuring that the consensus error remains bounded. Ultimately, simulations were performed to demonstrate the effectiveness of the proposed approach. The outcomes derived from the specified set of cost functions were then compared to several conventional topologies in multi-agent systems.

Keywords: Multi-agent systems · Consensus problem · Graph reduction · Optimization problem · Communication link · Practical issues

1 Introduction

Multiagent systems (MAS) consist of a group of autonomous agents interacting within a shared environment, working collectively to perform tasks that are

E. Barros et al. (Eds.): RoboCup 2024, LNAI 15570, pp. 212–223, 2025.
https://doi.org/10.1007/978-3-031-85859-8_18

beyond the capabilities of individual agents. In robotics, MAS are pivotal in advancing the functionality and adaptability of robots, enabling them to perform complex, dynamic tasks more efficiently [14]. From autonomous vehicle fleets to robotic swarms, MAS has revolutionized the landscape of robotics by introducing enhanced coordination and distributed intelligence.

Robotic soccer teams participate in competitions such as RoboCup, which serves as an opportunity for academics to develop and evaluate robotic systems, with an emphasis on MAS, which demands efficient team strategy and collaborative decision-making processes [1,2,6–8].

One of the most significant challenges in MAS is the consensus problem, where multiple agents must agree on a state or decision through local interactions. This problem is often modelled using graph theory, where agents are nodes and their interactions are edges. The system's consensus-finding efficiency depends on these graphs' structure and behavior.

For formation control, synchronization, and cooperative surveillance, graph architectures can affect consensus speed and reliability [10,13,17,18]. To achieve this goal, it is important to optimize the communication graph, which can be performed in two ways. The first method optimizes a constant graph to reduce control effort and improve the performance index [15]. Second, optimize the system through modifying and minimizing graph connections. The second strategy is the topic of this study, which is frequently followed by lowering the size and number of edges.

Optimizing communication graph size and structure improves operational efficiency, scalability, and reliability, especially in complex robotics areas. Simplifying MAS communication graphs offers many benefits. Smaller communication graphs require fewer messages to be passed among agents. This reduction in communication overhead can speed up decision-making and system responsiveness, especially in time-critical applications. Graph communication links may demand computational resources to manage and maintain.

Reducing edges decreases each agent's computational burden, freeing up resources for processing and performing tasks. Scalability improves with a smaller communication graph, allowing more agents to operate without increasing communication costs. Communication reduction will reduce energy conservation in many robotic applications, such as mobile robots. In a smaller graph, by carefully choosing which nodes communicate directly, the system can be made more robust against failures at specific nodes or links [16,20].

Various approaches have been explored to manage graph optimization. These methods aim to minimize redundant information exchange and enhance system efficiency without sacrificing the speed or quality of consensus achievement.

In [19], the authors optimize the interaction graph of a multi-robot system by maximizing security probability with minimal edges using a weighted matroid intersection algorithm. Moreover, [12] introduces a novel graph-theoretic approach for solving the multi-robot collaborative localization problem through distributed graph optimization, aiming to minimize errors in estimating relative location estimates and optimizing relative poses using g2o graph optimization over dynamic networks, although the computational complexity and implementation in uncontrolled environments pose practical challenges.

On the other hand, [3,11] explore graph coarsening, a widely used technique in scientific computing, and its potential in machine learning. It examines its applications in algebraic multigrid methods and multilevel incomplete LU factorizations. To further comprehend the paper's contribution, consider a set of six agents attempting to solve the consensus problem. These six-agent communications can be represented using several types of graphs. For instance, [4] provides a list of 112 different connected graphs with 6 nodes. In addition, Fig. 1 shows several conventional topologies in multi-agent systems. This research should address two particular questions:

- Is limiting the agents communication required from an operational perspective?
- What is the maximum number of edges that may be eliminated from a complete graph in which each agent is connected to every other agent without compromising the performance of the consensus problem?

In the preceding section, the first problem was addressed from numerous perspectives. Afterwards, we offer a comprehensive answer to the second question in the rest of this research.

The subsequent sections of this article will be structured as follows: a review of the fundamental definitions and theorems pertaining to cooperative control in multi-agent systems and algebraic graph theory will precede the formulation of the problem. A comparison and discussion will conclude the article.

2 Background and Notation

This section begins by presenting the notions and theorems of algebraic graph theory from [5,9]. It then proceeds by providing the preliminary materials necessary for addressing the consensus problem in multi-agent systems from [13,17].

2.1 Algebraic Graph Theory

Consider an undirected graph $G = (V, E)$, where $V = \{v_1, v_2, \ldots, v_n\}$ represents a collection of n nodes and $E \subseteq V \times V$ represents a set of undirected edges.

Definition 1. *The complement of graph G, which is represented by $\overline{G}$, is defined as follows:*

$$V(\overline{G}) = V(G), \quad E(\overline{G}) = \{uv \mid uv \notin E(G)\} \tag{1}$$

Definition 2. *Consider a graph G with a set of vertices $\{v_1, v_2, \ldots, v_n\}$. We can define $\mathbf{A} = (a_{ij})$ as the adjacency matrix of G, where $a_{ij} = 1$ if there is an edge from the vertex v_i to v_j and $a_{ij} = 0$ otherwise.*

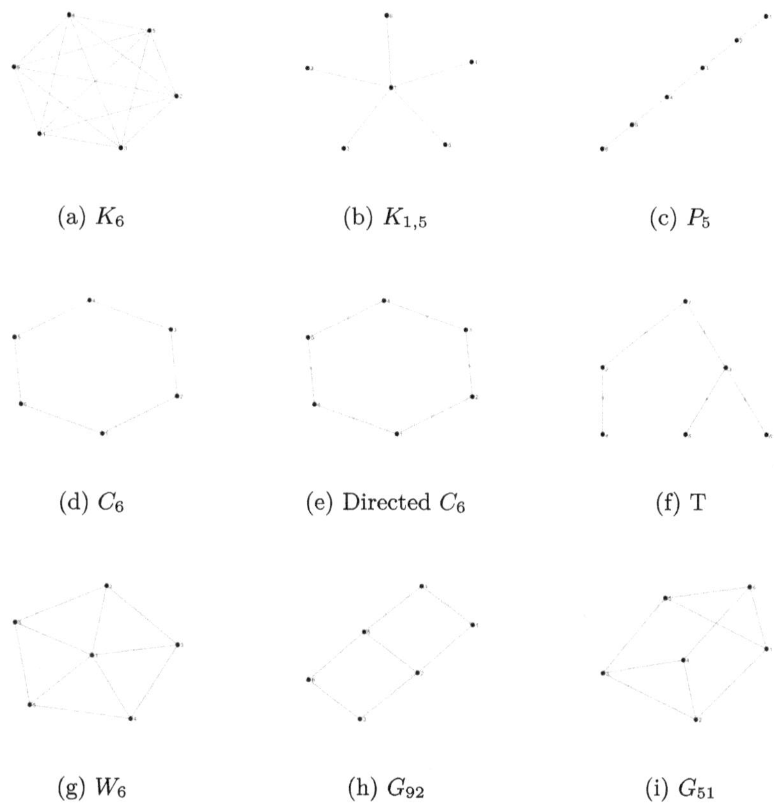

Fig. 1. Conventional topologies used to evaluate cost functions

Definition 3. *Let G be a graph with n vertices and m edges. Let $\mathbf{X}$ denote the incidence matrix of G, with dimensions $m \times n$. This matrix indexes rows corresponding to vertices $v_1, v_2, \ldots, v_n$ and columns corresponding to edges $e_1, e_2, \ldots, e_n$, where each entry ij indicates whether vertex v_i is connected to edge e_i, with a value of 1 and 0 otherwise.*

Definition 4. *Suppose G is a directed graph of order n with a directed incidence matrix $\mathbf{D}$. In this case, the matrix $\mathbf{D}\mathbf{D}^\top$ is the Laplacian matrix of G and denoted by $\mathbf{Q}$.*

Clearly, $\mathbf{Q}$ is a real symmetric $n \times n$ matrix, and if d_i is the degree of vertex v_i and $\mathbf{A}$ is the adjacency matrix of the undirected graph G, then:

$$\mathbf{Q} = \mathbf{D}\mathbf{D}^\top = \mathbf{\Delta} - \mathbf{A} \tag{2}$$

where $\mathbf{\Delta} = \text{diag}(d_1, d_2, \ldots, d_n)$. Therefore, the Laplacian matrix is a symmetric matrix that does not contain any information on the directional characteristics or orientation types present in the graph. Consequently, it is possible to consider any arbitrary pattern for undirected graphs and construct the Laplacian matrix accordingly.

Definition 5. *A directed graph is considered strongly connected if and only if there exists a directed path between any two different nodes in the graph.*

Note that if G is strongly connected, $\text{rank}(\mathbf{Q}) = n - 1$.

Definition 6. *Given a directed graph G, the following are the definitions of the in-degree and out-degree of a node v_i, respectively:*

$$d_{in}(v_i) = \sum_{j=1}^{n} a_{ji}, \quad d_{out}(v_i) = \sum_{j=1}^{n} a_{ij} \tag{3}$$

Definition 7. *Let G be a directed graph. Node v_i is considered balanced if and only if $d_{in}(v_i) = d_{out}(v_i)$. A balanced graph is a directed graph in which all of its vertices are balanced.*

Proposition 1. *Consider a graph G containing n vertices and m edges, wherein $\lambda_1 \geq \lambda_2 \geq \cdots \geq \lambda_n$ represents the eigenvalues of G. The kth spectral momentum of G is:*

$$s_k = Tr\left(\mathbf{A}^k\right) = \sum_{i=1}^{n} \lambda_i^k, \quad k = 0, 1, \ldots \tag{4}$$

Let l and t represent the number loops and triangles in graph G respectively. We have $s_0 = n$, $s_1 = l$, $s_2 = 2m$, and $s_3 = 6t$.

Proposition 2. *Consider a graph G containing n vertices and m edges, wherein $\mu_1 \leq \mu_2 \leq \cdots \leq \mu_n$ represents the eigenvalues of the Laplacian matrix of the graph G. Lets define the τ_k as the kth spectral momentum of $\mathbf{Q}$:*

$$\tau_k = Tr\left(\mathbf{Q}^k\right) = \sum_{i=1}^{n} \mu_i^k, \quad k = 1, 2, \ldots \tag{5}$$

we have:

$$\begin{aligned} \tau_1 &= \sum_{i=1}^{n} d_i = 2\,m \\ \tau_2 &= \sum_{i=1}^{n} d_i^2 + 2\,m \\ \tau_3 &= \sum_{i=1}^{n} d_i^3 + 3\sum_{i=1}^{n} d_i^2 - 6t \end{aligned} \tag{6}$$

Definition 8. *The sum norm of a matrix $\mathbf{A}$ is defined as follows:*

$$\|\mathbf{A}\|_{sum} = \sum_{i,j} |a_{ij}| \tag{7}$$

Put simply, the sum norm is essentially the sum of the absolute values of the matrix elements. This norm will be advantageous in defining one of the cost functions in the subsequent parts.

2.2 Cooperative Control Consensus Problem

The previous sections have demonstrated that the communication between agents in the consensus problem is represented as a graph. Assume that each node in the graph has a similar dynamic. Thus, for the ith agent, we have:

$$\dot{\mathbf{x}}_i = \mathbf{f}_i(\mathbf{x}_i, \mathbf{u}_i) \tag{8}$$

The $\mathbf{x}_i$ denotes the state vector, whereas $\mathbf{u}_i$ represents the control vector for each agent. It is important to note that all vectors have appropriate dimensions. Based on the aforementioned preliminary materials, the subsequent definition and proposition can be posited.

Definition 9. *Determining a distributed control protocol that achieves consistent steady-state values for all states (i.e., $x_i = x_j, \forall i, j,\ i \neq j$) constitutes the consensus problem. The term for this quantity is the consensus value. Furthermore, this problem is commonly known as average consensus when we have $c = \frac{1}{n}\sum_{i=1}^{n} x_i(0)$ for consensus value.*

Proposition 3. *Consider a multi-agent system with associated strongly connected digraph G and single-integrator dynamics for the agents ($\dot{x}_i = u_i$).*

- *The consensus problem is resolved asymptotically by the control variable (9).*
- *The average-consensus problem is resolved globally asymptotically by the control variable (9) iff G is balanced.*

$$u_i = \sum_{v_j \in N_i} a_{ij}(x_j - x_i) \tag{9}$$

where N_i is the collection of neighboring nodes of node v_i.

3 Problem Formulation

The main objective of this study is to formulate graph reduction problems in the form of an optimization problem. The underlying graph should minimize both the number of edges that represent the information flow between agents and the consensus error. In this section, we will begin by outlining the elements of the optimization problem.

The optimization variable for this problem is the components of the adjacency matrix that generate the reduced graph. Given the characteristics of this variable, the numbers assigned to the elements of the adjacency matrix must be restricted to $\{0, 1\}$. Consequently, the optimization problem can be formulated as a zero-one or integer programming problem as follows:

$$\min_{a_{ij} \in \{0,1\}} \quad J_p \tag{10a}$$

$$\text{subject to} \quad \dot{\mathbf{x}}_i = \mathbf{f}_i(\mathbf{x}_i, \mathbf{u}_i), \tag{10b}$$

$$0 \leq a_{ij} \leq 1. \tag{10c}$$

Equation (10b) is considered as the dynamics of each agent. Here, without any loss of generality, we assume that each agent possesses the dynamics of a single integrator. Due to the method's generalizability, it can be implemented in various forms pertaining to agent dynamics. In order to address the optimization problem, six seemingly distinct cost functions are taken into account. Except for one, each of these cost functions consists of two parts. The first term reduces the number of graph edges, while the second element minimizes the consensus error vector's second norm in order to decrease the consensus-mean error:

$$
\begin{aligned}
J_1 &= r\|\mathbf{A}\|_{\text{sum}} + q\ \|\mathbf{e}\|_2 \\
J_2 &= r s_2 + q\ \|\mathbf{e}\|_2 \\
J_3 &= r\tau_1 + q\ \|\mathbf{e}\|_2 \\
J_4 &= \ \|\mathbf{e}\|_2 \\
J_5 &= r s_3 + q\ \|\mathbf{e}\|_2 \\
J_6 &= r\tau_2 + q\ \|\mathbf{e}\|_2
\end{aligned}
\tag{11}
$$

where $e_i = c - x_i$. By minimizing the sum norm of the adjacency matrix in J_1, we effectively insert a zero into this matrix. This results in a reduction in the number of edges. In contrast, using the graph spectrum, J_2, J_3, J_5, and J_6 will involve optimizing the eigenvalues of the adjacency and Laplacian matrix. The sum of the squares of the eigenvalues of the adjacency matrix is equivalent to twice the number of edges, as stated in Proposition 1. Minimizing this sum will result in a reduction of the number of edges in J_2. Proposition 2 was utilized to replicate this issue in a corresponding manner for the Laplacian matrix in J_3. The rationale behind the selection of other cost functions is readily apparent from Propositions 1 and 2. To determine the optimal adjacency matrix, it is necessary to utilize an appropriate optimization algorithm. This study makes use of a genetic algorithm.

Remark 1. *Without compromising the problem's generalizability, the elements and optimization method presented in this study—including the cost function, constraints, and optimization algorithm—can be applied to further multi-agent systems in which the agents have arbitrary dynamics. As an illustrative instance, the investigation and evaluation of first-order systems have been performed in this article.*

4 Simulation Study

This section begins by introducing our proposed optimized graph structure. Then we investigate several conventional topologies frequently used in multi-agent systems. By comparing our approach to these existing graphs, we can evaluate its performance and highlight its advantages in optimizing connections within a multi-agent system. Finally, we will discuss the results of this comparison. For all simulations in this section, we consider the six agents, and the vector of the agent's initial condition is as $x_0 = \left[0.1\ 0.2\ 0.3\ 0.4\ 0.5\ 0.6\right]^\top$. In addition for all scenarios $r = 0.01$ and $q = 1$.

(a) G_1 (b) $\overline{G_1}$

Fig. 2. The graph generated from the optimization problem for J_1 and its complement

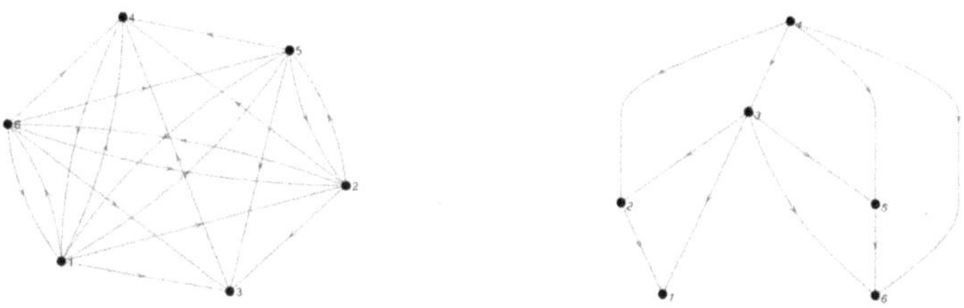

(a) G_2 (b) $\overline{G_2}$

Fig. 3. The graph generated from the optimization problem for J_2 and its complement

Remark 2. *Arrows denoted the direction of communication flow on directed graphs (Fig. 1e), whereas they were absent on undirected graphs (Fig. 1d). Because of the doubled communication cost in undirected graphs due to bidirectional communication, each edge is counted twice in undirected graphs.*

Remark 3. *The settling time of a graph refers to the maximum settling time of any individual agent within the system. This value can be calculated using the following formula:*

$$T_s = \max\left(T_{s_1}, T_{s_2}, T_{s_3}, ..., T_{s_n}\right) \tag{12}$$

Noted that the time it takes for the system output to remain within 2% of the ultimate value is referred to as the 2% settling time.

Figure 2 depicts the optimized graph resulting from the J_1 cost function, which minimizes the sum norm of the adjacency matrix. Besides having only 19 edges (significantly fewer than a complete graph), with T_s it has a settling time close to a complete graph and lower than other conventional topologies, according to Table 1. This suggests that the J_1 and the optimization algorithm have successfully reduced the number of edges, leading to a more compact graph,

(a) G_3 (b) $\overline{G_3}$

Fig. 4. The graph generated from the optimization problem for J_3 and its complement

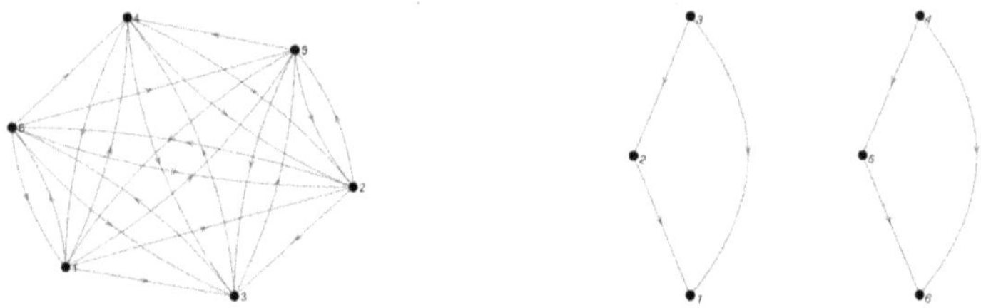

(a) G_4 (b) $\overline{G_4}$

Fig. 5. The graph generated from the optimization problem for J_4 and its complement

without significantly compromising the system's performance as measured by settling time. Several of the cost functions (e.g., J_1) include a term that minimizes the second norm of the error vector, potentially prioritizing performance. Other cost functions (e.g., J_4) may not explicitly target edge reduction but achieve it through the inclusion of different terms in the overall cost function. However, this cost function has demonstrated comparable performance to a complete graph while utilizing fewer edges.

Figure 3 presents the optimized graph resulting from the J_2, which minimizes the sum of the squares of the eigenvalues of the adjacency matrix. This graph has 20 edges, slightly more than the graph associated with J_1. Additionally, Fig. 4 illustrates the optimized graph resulting from the J_3, which minimizes the sum of the Laplacian matrix eigenvalues. Interestingly, similar to the J_1, this graph also has 19 edges. This suggests that for this specific scenario, both J_1 and J_3 might lead to similar graph structures.

Figure 5 depicts the optimized graph resulting from the J_4. This graph exhibits the best settling time among the analyzed graphs and bears a close resemblance to a complete graph with 24 edges, which is more than other graphs and has the best settling time between them. Interestingly, unlike other func-

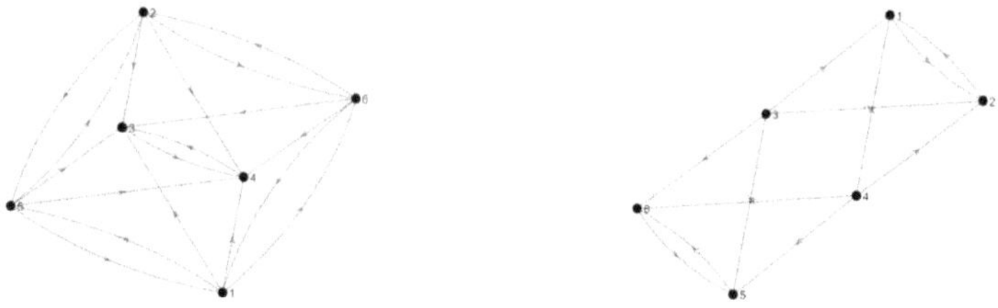

(a) G_5 (b) $\overline{G_5}$

Fig. 6. The graph generated from the optimization problem for J_5 and its complement

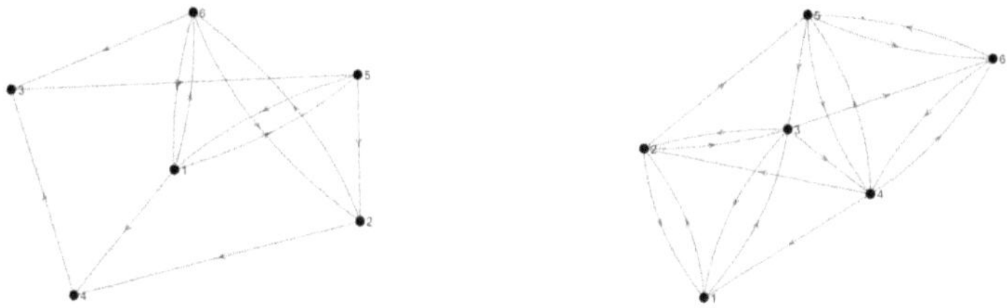

(a) G_6 (b) $\overline{G_6}$

Fig. 7. The graph generated from the optimization problem for J_6 and its complement

Table 1. Results Summary

Graph	# of Edges	T_s [sec]
K_6	30	0.6
$K_{1,5}$	10	3.36
P_5	10	13.07
C_6	12	3.36
Directed C_6	6	6.53
T	5	∞
W_6	20	1.32
G_{92}	14	2.76
G_{51}	18	1.34
G_1	19	0.65
G_2	20	∞
G_3	19	0.65
G_4	24	0.62
G_5	18	0.99
G_6	12	1.32

tions, J_4 does not explicitly aim to minimize the number of edges. Instead, it focuses solely on minimizing the error, potentially explaining the higher number of edges while achieving the fastest settling time. Moreover, Fig. 6 presents the optimized graph resulting from J_5, which minimizes the sum of the cubes of the eigenvalues of the adjacency matrix (or number of the graph triangles). This graph has a compact structure with only 18 edges and achieves a settling time of 0.99 s.

Figure 7 shows the optimized graph resulting from the J_6, which minimizes the skew of the Laplacian matrix eigenvalues. This graph achieves the lowest number of edges (12) among all the optimized graphs (see Table 1). In addition, it has the same edges with undirected graph C_6 and yet more than the star and path graph. G_6 has the highest settling time between G_i, and despite G_6, G_{51}, and W_6 having the same settling time, G_6 has fewer edges than the other two. While the settling time of 1.32 s is slightly higher than some others, it remains acceptable considering the significant reduction in edges.

5 Conclusions

This study aimed to investigate the problem of graph reduction in the context of multi-agent system consensus. First, this problem has been transformed into an integer programming problem through the incorporation of six distinct cost functions. The cost functions are formulated to optimize the number of graph edges and the consensus error simultaneously, using various approaches. The simulation results demonstrate that the graphs have a lower number of edges compared to the complete graph, which achieves the highest performance in the consensus problem. However, the settling time of these graphs is nearly identical. Another intriguing finding is that the ultimate outcome of optimizing the sum of eigenvalues of the Laplacian matrix and the sum norm of the adjacency matrix is entirely indistinguishable from each other. Furthermore, in comparison to other well-known graphs with settling time, the graph derived from the specific cost function demonstrates a lower number of edges. To conclude, the findings derived from this study have a significant impact on the practical implementation of multi-agent systems.

References

1. Affinita, D., Volpi, F., Spagnoli, V., Suriani, V., Nardi, D., Bloisi, D.D.: Multi-agent coordination for a partially observable and dynamic robot soccer environment with limited communication. arXiv preprint (2024).arXiv:2401.15026
2. Antonioni, E., Suriani, V., Riccio, F., Nardi, D.: Game strategies for physical robot soccer players: a survey. IEEE Trans. Games **13**(4), 342–357 (2021)
3. Chen, J., Saad, Y., Zhang, Z.: Graph coarsening: from scientific computing to machine learning (2021)
4. Cvetković, D., Petrić, M.: A table of connected graphs on six vertices. Discret. Math. **50**, 37–49 (1984)

5. Diestel, R.: Graph Theory, second ed. Springer, Berlin (February 2000). electronic edn
6. Gao, Z., et al.: A survey of research on several problems in the robocup3d simulation environment. Auton. Agent. Multi-Agent Syst. **38**(1), 1–61 (2024)
7. Genter, K., Laue, T., Stone, P.: Benchmarking robot cooperation without pre-coordination in the RoboCup standard platform league drop-in player competition. In: 2015 IEEE/RSJ International Conference on Intelligent Robots and Systems (IROS), pp. 3415–3420. IEEE (2015)
8. Gerndt, R., Seifert, D., Baltes, J.H., Sadeghnejad, S., Behnke, S.: Humanoid robots in soccer: Robots versus humans in RoboCup 2050. IEEE Robot. Autom. Mag. **22**(3), 147–154 (2015)
9. Godsil, C., Royle, G.F.: Algebraic graph theory, vol. 207. Springer Science Business Media (2001)
10. Guan, Z.H., Wu, Y., Feng, G.: Consensus analysis based on impulsive systems in multiagent networks. IEEE Trans. Circuits Syst. I Regul. Pap. **59**(1), 170–178 (2011)
11. Jin, Y., Loukas, A., JaJa, J.F.: Graph coarsening with preserved spectral properties (2019)
12. Latif, E., Parasuraman, R.: Dgorl: distributed graph optimization based relative localization of multi-robot systems. In: International Symposium on Distributed Autonomous Robotic Systems, pp. 243–256. Springer (2022)
13. Lewis, F.L., Zhang, H., Hengster-Movric, K., Das, A.: Cooperative control of multi-agent systems: optimal and adaptive design approaches. Springer Science Business Media (2013)
14. Liu, J., Wu, J.: Multiagent Robotic Systems. CRC Press, Boca Raton (2018)
15. Mondal, S., Tsourdos, A.: Optimal topology for consensus using genetic algorithm. Neurocomputing **404**, 41–49 (2020)
16. Monshizadeh, N., Trentelman, H.L., Camlibel, M.K.: Projection-based model reduction of multi-agent systems using graph partitions. IEEE Trans. Control Netw. Syst. **1**, 145–154 (2014)
17. Olfati-Saber, R., Fax, J.A., Murray, R.M.: Consensus and cooperation in networked multi-agent systems. Proc. IEEE **95**(1), 215–233 (2007)
18. Olfati-Saber, R., Murray, R.M.: Consensus problems in networks of agents with switching topology and time-delays. IEEE Trans. Autom. Control **49**(9), 1520–1533 (2004)
19. Wehbe, R., Williams, R.K.: Optimizing topologies for probabilistically secure multi-robot systems. In: 2020 IEEE International Conference on Robotics and Automation (ICRA), pp. 6640–6646. IEEE (2020)
20. Yan, D., Cheng, J., Lu, Y., Ng, W.: Effective techniques for message reduction and load balancing in distributed graph computation (2015)

Enhancing Autonomous Vehicle Control Through Sensor Fusion, NARX-Based Reinforcement Learning with Soft Actor-Critic (SAC) in CARLA Simulator

Seyed Ali Abdollahian[1], Sina Fazel[1], Mohadeseh Rezaei Hadadi[1], Amin Jalal Aghdasian[1], and Soroush Sadeghnejad[2(✉)]

[1] Department of Electrical Engineering, Amirkabir University of Technology (Tehran Polytechnic), Tehran, Iran
{aliabdollahian,sina.fazel,mohadeserezaei,amin.aghdasian}@aut.ac.ir

[2] Bio-Inspired System Design Lab, Department of Biomedical Engineering, Amirkabir University of Technology (Tehran Polytechnic), 15914 Tehran, Iran
s.sadeghnejad@aut.ac.ir

Abstract. This study presents an approach to formulating the optimal control policy for self-driving cars. Our method integrates sensor fusion with deep reinforcement learning, specifically utilizing the Soft Actor-Critic (SAC) algorithm. By leveraging identity mapping and residual structures, we improve agent training through a two-branch fusion technique for vehicle image and tracking sensor data. We introduce a Nonlinear Auto-Regressive model with Exogenous inputs (NARX) within the sensor fusion architecture. This model incorporates actions from previous time steps to capture temporal dependencies in the sensor data, providing a deeper understanding of the environment for the Reinforcement Learning (RL) agent and enhancing decision-making. Our research demonstrates this information fusion approach's effectiveness and highlights our method's advantages through comprehensive comparisons. It illustrates the practical application of reinforcement learning in improving intelligent vehicle decision-making and contributes to the evolving field of autonomous driving. This advancement can positively affect how self-driving cars operate, potentially fostering more trust in the progress of autonomous driving technology.

Keywords: Autonomous Driving · Sensor Fusion · Deep Reinforcement Learning · Soft Actor-Critic · NARX · CARLA

1 Introduction

The field of Autonomous Driving (AD) has changed significantly, highlighting the importance of maintaining safety and dependability in this method of trans-

S. Fazel and M.R. Hadadi—Equal contribution.

E. Barros et al. (Eds.): RoboCup 2024, LNAI 15570, pp. 224–235, 2025.
https://doi.org/10.1007/978-3-031-85859-8_19

portation [30]. AD systems, equipped with collision avoidance and sensor technology, prevent accidents by monitoring vehicle surroundings and responding quickly to unexpected events [30].

AD control tactics range from traditional methods like PID, MPC, and LQR to modern AI-based methods like imitation learning and RL-based control. PID control is simple but requires careful tuning [12], MPC handles complex situations, and LQR optimization efficiently addresses cost functions but requires system dynamics knowledge and potential redesigning for significant changes [4]. Model-free techniques like reinforcement learning offer distinct advantages in contexts where exact modelling is difficult, [20]. Reinforcement learning excels in adaptation and continual learning across domains [27]. Applying RL algorithms to shape driving policies in AD is remarkable [21]. Innovations like Deep Q Learning (DQN) and Deep Deterministic Policy Gradient (DDPG) algorithms have successfully achieved control objectives despite learning optimization challenges from many states [26]. DQN and LSTM architectures and creative observation inputs enable autonomous agents to handle complex situations [19]. Implementing DQN and DDPG algorithms has successfully trained autonomous vehicle control models in realistic simulators [1]. Sensor fusion improves AD systems' environmental perception and comprehension [25]. Sensor fusion improves performance by combining data from several sensors, reducing restrictions and enhancing robustness [3,9,29].

Our study introduces a NARX model to sensor fusion architecture. This NARX model improves sensor data temporal dependencies by using exogenous inputs from prior steps. Capturing these dynamics helps the RL agent grasp the environment's evolution, improving decision-making and control. Our study also introduces sensor data fusion and reinforcement learning-based vehicular control. Combining vehicle photos and tracking sensors improves feature extraction and representation learning. Soft Actor-Critic (SAC) integrates sensor outputs with vehicle speed and position to optimize control command generation and accelerate convergence. Our algorithm is proven effective in real-world driving circumstances through a rigorous examination using the CARLA simulation platform [16]. The paper offers two novel methods: pre-training Soft Actor-Critic (SAC) with Learning from Demonstrations (LfD) and an online combination of SAC, LfD, and LfI [25]. Deep Reinforcement Learning (DRL) algorithms for self-driving cars have improved; therefore, network topologies need more complex data usage strategies. Sensor fusion helps AD systems accurately detect and comprehend their surroundings [3,9,29]. Integrating data from diverse sensors improves perception system robustness and reliability in various driving scenarios, overcomes sensor limitations, and improves autonomous vehicle performance [10,13]. RL makes sensor fusion even more important. As RL-based control systems interact with their environment, the quality of their decisions depends on the perceived information quality [5,21]. Sensor fusion provides integrated and comprehensive environmental models for RL algorithms, improving predictions and decision-making. Adding multi-modal fusion to DRL frameworks can improve decision-making and reliability in complicated contexts [7,15,17].

This study uses sensor data fusion and reinforcement learning to develop a new vehicular control approach.

A dual-branch sensor fusion module merges vehicle pictures and tracking sensors in our method. Residual blocks improve feature extraction and representation learning in this module. SAC combined with sensor fusion integrates image sensor outputs with vehicle speed and position, creating an ideal framework for control commands and speedier convergence. The CARLA simulation platform trained and validated our algorithm in a realistic setting to imitate real-world driving scenarios. A detailed comparative analysis shows how our methodology may outperform state-of-the-art methods. The paper has an introduction, CARLA, SAC, AlexNet, NARX, Methodology, Results, and conclusion. Each offers vital insights into autonomous driving approaches and encourages further research. However, subsequent paragraphs are indented.

2 CARLA

CARLA (Car Learning to Act) stands out as an open-source simulator, meticulously crafted for the development and training of driving systems. Its most compelling feature is the ability to generate simulation results that mirror real-world scenarios with remarkable accuracy. This is made possible by the inclusion of diverse urban environments, complete with varying weather conditions and dynamic traffic scenarios. CARLA also introduces challenges like other vehicles, pedestrians, cyclists, and even animals, elevating the complexity of training environments.

Another standout feature of CARLA is its support for adaptable sensor arrays. These sensors are designed to simulate the data that self-driving cars typically receive, making them a crucial component of the learning process. The array is comprehensive, including a variety of sensors such as cameras, radar, GPS, and Inertial Measurement Units (IMUs). CARLA also offers the flexibility to customize sensor settings and noise levels, enabling a more precise replication of real-world conditions.

Within the CARLA environment, self-driving algorithms can be trained to identify and track objects, predict their behaviour, and make decisions accordingly. But what sets CARLA apart is its ability to enable the evaluation of self-driving performance across various scenarios.

Despite its high level of realism, CARLA has limitations. While it closely mimics reality, it cannot fully replicate real-world conditions and still demands significant computing resources to implement complex scenarios and achieve high sensor accuracy [8,18,23].

3 SAC

SAC is an off-policy algorithm that inherits many features from TD3. However, unlike TD3, SAC utilizes a probabilistic policy represented by π. The core principle of SAC revolves around entropy, which quantifies the randomness of a variable and is denoted by H. To illustrate, if a variable consistently exhibits the same value, its entropy is low; conversely, if it demonstrates a new value each time, its entropy is high [22].

SAC operates within the framework of maximum entropy reinforcement learning (RL). Here, the actor seeks to maximize expected efficiency and entropy simultaneously. This entails achieving task success while allowing the system to behave as randomly as possible [11].

Entropy H is defined as follows:

$$H(P) = E_{x \sim P}[-\log P(x)] \tag{1}$$

Let x be a random variable with density function P in the entropy-regulated RL algorithm. In this algorithm, if the agent adheres to the policy at each step, they receive an additional reward. Consequently, the objective of the RL algorithm becomes the maximization of the reward, formulated as follows:

$$\pi^* = argmax_\pi([E_{\tau \sim \pi}[\sum_{t=0}^{\infty} \gamma^t (R(s_t, a_t, s_{t+1}) + \alpha H(\pi(.|s_t)))]]) \tag{2}$$

In the above equation, the transfer function includes state, action, and reward, respectively. Here, γ represents the discount coefficient, α stands for the trade-off coefficient, π signifies the policy, and s denotes the system's state at that moment. Subsequently, we consider an infinite-horizon discounted setting. In light of this, modified value functions are introduced, wherein the action-state value is adjusted to incorporate and integrate the entropy rewards at each time step.

$$Q^\pi(s_t, a_t) = E[R(s_t, a_t, s_{t+1}) + \gamma(Q^\pi(s_{t+1}, a_{t+1}) + \alpha H(\pi(.|s_{t+1})))] \tag{3}$$

$$= E[R(s_t, a_t, s_{t+1}) + \gamma(Q^\pi(s_{t+1} a_{t+1}) - \alpha \log(\pi(a_{t+1}|s_{t+1})))] \tag{4}$$

This approach comprises a soft parameterized function and a policy represented in a particular form. Each component depends on a distinct set of parameters denoted by ϕ_1, ϕ_2 and θ, respectively. Now, the soft function Q parameters can be trained to minimize the soft Bellman residual. ϕ_1 and ϕ_2 are the parameters of the two Q-networks (Q_1 and Q_2), which estimate the state-action value function $Q(s_t, a_t)$. θ represents the parameters of the policy network, which defines the stochastic policy $\pi(a_t|s_t)$.

$$J_{Q_i} = E_{(s_t, a_t) \sim D}[\frac{1}{2}(Q_\phi(s_t, a_t) - \hat{Q}(s_t, a_t))^2] \tag{5}$$

While the target Q is considered as follows:

$$\hat{Q}(s_t, \overline{\mathrm{a_t}}) = r_t + \gamma(Q(s_{t+1}, \overline{\mathrm{a_{t+1}}}) - \alpha \log(\overline{\mathrm{a_{t+1}}}|s_{t+1})) \tag{6}$$

Here, using the gradient descent method, relation (5) can be improved:

$$\hat{\nabla}_\phi J_Q(\phi) = \nabla_\phi Q_\phi(s_t, a_t)[Q_\phi(s_t, a_t) - \hat{Q}(s_t, a_t)] \quad (7)$$

The policy parameters can be obtained by minimizing the Kullback-Leibler divergence [11]. Through reparameterizing the expectation, we can define the policy objective as:

$$J_\pi(\theta) = E_{st} \sim D[\log \pi_\theta(\overline{a_\theta}(s_t)|s_t) - Q_\phi(s_t, \overline{a_\theta}(s_t))] \quad (8)$$

The approximate of the gradient is provided below:

$$\hat{\nabla}_\theta J_\pi(\theta) = \nabla_\theta \log(\pi_\theta(\overline{a}_t|s_t)) + (\nabla_{\overline{a}_t} \log(\pi_\theta(\overline{a}_t|s_t)) - \nabla_{\overline{a}_t} Q_\theta(s_t, \overline{a}_t)) \nabla_\theta \overline{a}_\theta(s_t) \quad (9)$$

4 NARX

NARX neural network is a deep learning architecture designed for dynamic system analysis, particularly in time series analysis and prediction. It is extensively utilized in system identification and dynamic system control.

Unlike static neural network structures, NARX networks retain information from previous time steps, using this history to predict the system's future behaviour. This approach provides the network with a comprehensive understanding of the system dynamics, facilitating deeper learning.

NARX models are simpler and exhibit lower computational cost and training time compared to RNNs, including LSTM and GRU variants. They are particularly well-suited for problems with known temporal dependencies, offering advantages in interpretability and efficiency. The effectiveness of NARX networks in modeling complex systems can be attributed to their use of nonlinear activation functions. These functions allow the network to account for the influence of external factors, enhancing its ability to minimize prediction errors and approximate the desired system behavior more accurately.

The architecture of NARX, as depicted in Fig. 2, incorporates delayed inputs and outputs into the network. This temporal modelling allows the network to capture temporal dependencies within the data, enhancing its predictive capabilities and overall performance in time series analysis [6,24] (Fig. 1).

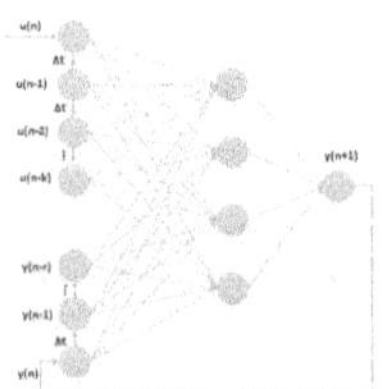

Fig. 1. NARX neural network architecture

5 Methodology

5.1 Reward

Autonomous driving presents a complex optimization problem involving multiple simultaneous parameters. These parameters encompass reaching the destination safely while avoiding obstacles and maintaining proper lane adherence. Optimizing these parameters requires minimizing error through a structured approach.

At the heart of our work, data from the vehicle is harnessed through the front camera and tracking sensor. The integration of this data into a cohesive framework that generates appropriate control commands is a pivotal and challenging task. Vehicle navigation, encompassing longitudinal (acceleration) and lateral (steering) control, with a steering angle typically ranging from -1 to 1 and acceleration from 0 to 1, is a crucial aspect of our autonomous driving system [14].

To address these requirements, a reward function R_t is defined as follows:

$$R_t = \sum_t |v_t \cos(\phi_t)| - |v_t \sin(\phi_t)| - |v_t||d_t| \tag{10}$$

Here, ϕ_t represents the car's angle relative to the route. The term $\cos(\phi_t)$ is incorporated to incentivize reducing the angle ϕ_t towards zero degrees (minimizing lateral deviation from the route). As ϕ_t decreases, $\cos(\phi_t)$ increases, leading to a reduction in error and d_t indicates lateral error.

A higher vehicle speed is also desirable for faster training times and improved overall efficiency. Therefore, the 'speed factor' in the reward function rewards higher speeds. This factor is carefully calibrated to balance the need for speed with the importance of safety and adherence to the route. It encourages the vehicle to maintain a brisk pace without compromising on its ability to navigate safely and accurately.

The reward function is structured to optimize performance, where reaching the destination without incident yields a reward of $+100$ points. Conversely, crossing route boundaries or colliding with obstacles results in a penalty of -200 points. This penalty triggers a 'simulation reset', a process that returns the vehicle to its initial state, allowing it to learn from its mistake and attempt a safer route. This mechanism is crucial in training the autonomous vehicle to avoid such incidents in the future [14,21].

5.2 Sensor Data Fusion

Integrating sensor data, known as Sensor Fusion, empowers Autonomous Driving systems to understand their surroundings comprehensively [3,29]. This technology amalgamates data streams from diverse sensors, aligning them to construct various representations of the vehicle's environment. This process effectively mitigates the limitations and deficiencies inherent in individual sensors, thereby significantly enhancing the system's overall performance [16,28].

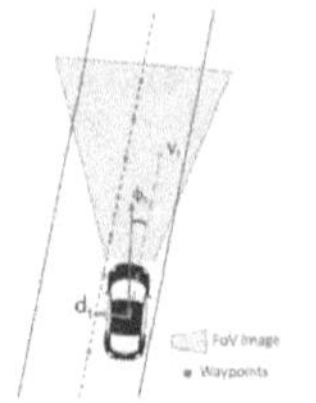

Fig. 2. Reward function parameters based on vehicle orientation [14]

In RL algorithms, the system's performance is shaped by its interactions with the environment, making the quality of the system's understanding of its surroundings and the data it receives from sensors crucial [5,21]. By providing integrated environmental models through Sensor Fusion, the RL algorithm can operate more efficiently and effectively. This enhanced understanding of the environment equips the algorithm to make more accurate decisions [7].

The car is controlled using a combination of Sensor Data Fusion and the SAC algorithm, as depicted in Fig. 4. Information from two branches, the image sensor and the tracking sensor, is integrated by the fusion module. For the image branch, an $F_{W_i}(image)$ convolution layer and a $W_s(image)$ layer are employed (Fig. 3).

$$features = F_{W_i}(image) + W_s(image) \tag{11}$$

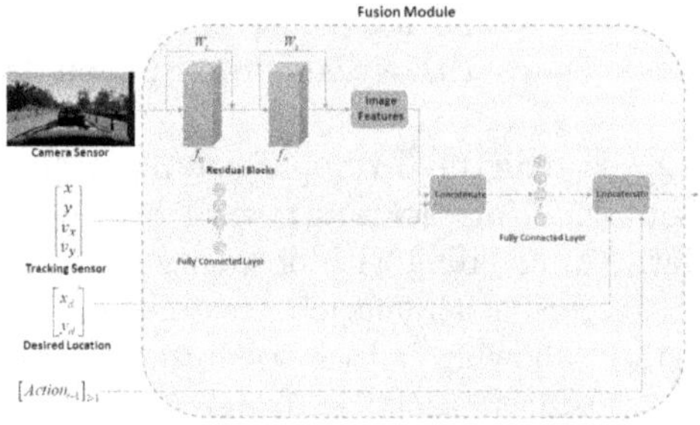

Fig. 3. Sensor fusion model

5.3 Proposed Method Architecture

The approach adopted in this study for self-driving car control involves integrating sensor data with the SAC architecture, leveraging its key features of stability, exploration, and robustness. The fusion structure, depicted in Fig. 5, is applied initially to the Q-network 1, Q-network 2, and Actor components. These

Q-networks are employed to estimate the state-action value function, $Q(s, a)$, which represents the expected cumulative reward of taking action a in state s and following the policy thereafter. The Actor network in the SAC algorithm generates the policy by selecting actions based on the current state to maximize expected returns and policy entropy, facilitating balanced exploration and exploitation during learning. This fusion process involves connecting features extracted from camera and tracking sensor images, which are then processed through FC layers to generate final sensor-derived features. These combined features, along with information on the desired position and previous action, are fed as inputs into the Q-networks and Actor network.

Training the Actor model based on the approximated action-value function allows us to achieve the desired level of performance. To manage the increasing complexity of feature dimensions resulting from more extensive environmental data, optimal information fusion techniques are employed to streamline network operations and minimize complexity.

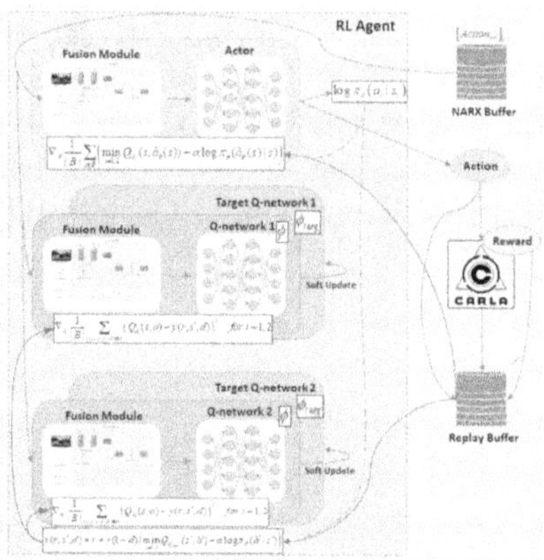

Fig. 4. Proposed DRL control scheme

6 Results

The CARLA simulator was employed in the simulation and results review section. It offers the flexibility to utilize Python libraries and modify environmental dynamics by adding or removing obstacles and vehicles. This capability allows for testing under varied conditions to assess algorithm performance.

To validate the effectiveness of the SAC algorithm, extensive testing was conducted across diverse scenarios within CARLA. These scenarios included the integration of sensor fusion blocks incorporating camera images and tracking sensor data, ensuring consistency in evaluation conditions.

Furthermore, to benchmark the proposed approach, the DDPG algorithm was employed under identical experimental conditions as previous studies. This comparative analysis enables the assessment of the SAC algorithm's superiority over established methodologies like DDPG.

6.1 Training

The proposed approach involves several key steps. The camera image is initially processed through AlexNet [2] and a residual structure to extract 50 features. Subsequently, a fully connected layer incorporates ten features from the tracking sensor to complement the image features. In the Q networks, our agent's input comprises 60 features. Then, these features are passed into a fully connected layer. In this configuration, the fully connected layer shall consist of 60 input features and ten output features upon incorporating four additional actions (gas valve and steering angle from the previous step and desired X and Y); the total input features amount to fourteen.

As shown Fig. 5, we conducted training for the agent over 5000 episodes utilising the Adam optimiser with a learning rate set to 0.0001. Furthermore, a buffer size of 1e6 was employed to facilitate comprehensive exploration. As previously mentioned, the average reward was computed after each episode.

Our approach underwent training and testing on hardware equipped with a 5.2 GHz Ryzen 9 7940HS CPU, an Nvidia Geforce RTX 4090 Ti GPU, and 32 GB of RAM.

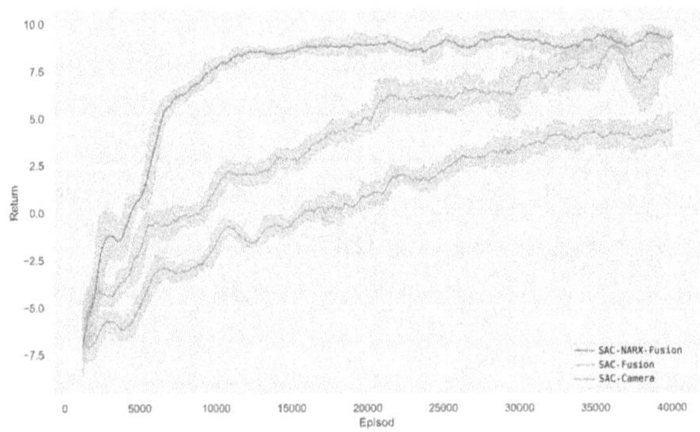

Fig. 5. plot of average reward per episode for three training configurations

6.2 Evaluation

The proposed approaches undergo validation and accuracy assessment using the Root Mean Square Error (RMSE) method. This method is tailored to gauge the disparity between algorithm outputs and ground truth data provided by the CARLA simulator, ensuring a standardized criterion for performance evaluation.

To facilitate comparison among trained agents, 25 distinct routes are delineated and plotted on the CARLA simulator map. These routes serve as guides for the agents and enable the computation of RMSE between the actual and ideal routes, obtained through point interpolation along the roads.

Table presents the RMSE values for each path traversed by the agent over 25 iterations. Additionally, the table includes the maximum and minimum errors encountered along the route, along with the standard deviation (std) of the agent's errors from the starting point to the destination (Table 1).

Table 1. Calculated RMSE in Evaluation phase

Method	Mean	Min	Max	Std
SAC NARX Fusion-based	**0.031**	**0.005**	**0.064**	**0.008**
SAC Fusion-based	0.039	0.006	0.079	0.011
SAC Image-based	0.591	0.189	1.073	0.141
SAC Sensor-based	0.526	0.175	0.919	0.12
DDPG Fusion-based	0.119	0.08	0.158	0.012
DDPG Image-based	0.752	0.24	1.379	0.173
DDPG Sensor-based	0.678	0.318	1.055	0.135

A notable improvement was demonstrated through SAC NARX Fusion in our evaluation results. A significant reduction in overall error was observed when SAC NARX Fusion was employed, indicating that more informed and effective decisions were made by the agent. Conversely, superior performance compared to relying solely on tracking sensors was exhibited by utilizing only images as input for the agent. This distinction arises from the agent's capability to identify road segments and anticipate future actions, particularly during vehicle turning maneuvers, whereas information from tracking sensors solely reflects the current vehicle state.

Furthermore, a relatively lower error rate for the SAC agent was revealed by comparing the SAC and DDPG algorithms. This advantage can be attributed to the effective utilization of a stochastic policy, careful consideration of the entropy function, and an improved exploration process, all aimed at attaining an optimal policy.

The critical role of Sensor NARX Fusion in enhancing the overall performance and robustness of the RL algorithm is underscored by these findings, rendering it a valuable approach for a variety of applications where image and tracking sensor data are available.

7 Conclusion

Our study presents a novel approach to self-driving car navigation, a fusion of sensor data with DRL using SAC algorithm. This innovative method enhances agent training and decision-making capabilities by incorporating identity mapping, residual structures, and a two-branch fusion method for vehicle image and tracking sensor data. The inclusion of a NARX model within the fusion architecture effectively captures temporal dependencies in sensor data, adding a new dimension to our methodology.

Our research has demonstrated the effectiveness and superiority of this fusion strategy through comprehensive comparisons. This work not only carries significant practical implications for advancing intelligent vehicle decision-making but also holds the potential to revolutionize autonomous driving technology.

References

1. Ahmed, M., Lim, C.P., Nahavandi, S.: A deep Q-network reinforcement learning-based model for autonomous driving. In: 2021 IEEE International Conference on Systems, Man, and Cybernetics (SMC), pp. 739–744. IEEE (2021)
2. Alom, M.Z., et al.: The history began from alexnet: a comprehensive survey on deep learning approaches. arXiv preprint arXiv:1803.01164 (2018)
3. Candan, A.T., Kalkan, H.: U-net-based RGB and lidar image fusion for road segmentation. SIViP **17**(6), 2837–2843 (2023)
4. Chen, J., Zhan, W., Tomizuka, M.: Autonomous driving motion planning with constrained iterative LQR. IEEE Trans. Intell. Veh. **4**(2), 244–254 (2019)
5. Chukamphaeng, N., Pasupa, K., Antenreiter, M., Auer, P.: Learning to drive with deep reinforcement learning. In: 2021 13th International Conference on Knowledge and Smart Technology (KST), pp. 147–152. IEEE (2021)
6. Diaconescu, E.: The use of NARX neural networks to predict chaotic time series. Wseas Trans. Comput. Res. **3**(3), 182–191 (2008)
7. Dong, J., Chen, S., Li, Y., Du, R., Steinfeld, A., Labi, S.: Space-weighted information fusion using deep reinforcement learning: the context of tactical control of lane-changing autonomous vehicles and connectivity range assessment. Transp. Res. Part C: Emerg. Technol. **128**, 103192 (2021)
8. Dosovitskiy, A., Ros, G., Codevilla, F., Lopez, A., Koltun, V.: CARLA: an open urban driving simulator. In: Conference on Robot Learning, pp. 1–16. PMLR (2017)
9. Du, J., Huang, X., Xing, M., Zhang, T.: Improved 3D semantic segmentation model based on RGB image and lidar point cloud fusion for automantic driving. Int. J. Automot. Technol. **24**(3), 787–797 (2023)
10. Gite, S., Kotecha, K., Ghinea, G.: Context-aware assistive driving: an overview of techniques for mitigating the risks of driver in real-time driving environment. Int. J. Perv. Comput. Commun. **19**(3), 325–342 (2023)
11. Haarnoja, T., Zhou, A., Abbeel, P., Levine, S.: Soft actor-critic: off-policy maximum entropy deep reinforcement learning with a stochastic actor. In: International Conference on Machine Learning, pp. 1861–1870. PMLR (2018)
12. Honda, K., Okuda, H., Suzuki, T., Ito, A.: MPC builder for autonomous drive: automatic generation of MPCs for motion planning and control. In: 2023 IEEE Intelligent Vehicles Symposium (IV), pp. 1–8. IEEE (2023)

13. Hou, W., Li, W., Li, P.: Fault diagnosis of the autonomous driving perception system based on information fusion. Sensors **23**(11), 5110 (2023)
14. Jalal Aghdasian, A., Heydarian Ardakani, A., Aqabakee, K., Abdollahi, F.: Autonomous driving using residual sensor fusion and deep reinforcement learning. arXiv e-prints, pp. arXiv–2312 (2023)
15. Khalil, Y.H., Mouftah, H.T.: Exploiting multi-modal fusion for urban autonomous driving using latent deep reinforcement learning. IEEE Trans. Veh. Technol. **72**(3), 2921–2935 (2022)
16. Liu, H., Wu, C., Wang, H.: Real time object detection using lidar and camera fusion for autonomous driving. Sci. Rep. **13**(1), 8056 (2023)
17. Liu, W., Xiang, Z., Fang, H., Huo, K., Wang, Z.: A multi-task fusion strategy-based decision-making and planning method for autonomous driving vehicles. Sensors **23**(16), 7021 (2023)
18. May, J., Poudel, S., Hamdan, S., Poudel, K., Vargas, J.: Using the CARLA simulator to train a deep Q self-driving car to control a real-world counterpart on a college campus. In: 2023 IEEE International Conference on Big Data (BigData), pp. 2206–2210. IEEE (2023)
19. Naveed, K.B., Qiao, Z., Dolan, J.M.: Trajectory planning for autonomous vehicles using hierarchical reinforcement learning. In: 2021 IEEE International Intelligent Transportation Systems Conference (ITSC), pp. 601–606. IEEE (2021)
20. Palatucci, E.B.M., et al.: Hierarchical model-based imitation learning for planning in autonomous driving (2022)
21. Pérez-Gil, Ó., et al.: Deep reinforcement learning based control for autonomous vehicles in CARLA. Multimedia Tools Appl. **81**(3), 3553–3576 (2022)
22. Ravichandiran, S.: Deep Reinforcement Learning with Python: Master Classic RL, Deep RL, Distributional RL, Inverse RL, and more with OpenAI Gym and TensorFlow. Packt Publishing Ltd. (2020)
23. Riyanto, R., Azis, A., Tarwoto, T., Deng, W.L.: Training autonomous vehicles in CARLA model using augmented random search algorithm. J. Appl. Data Sci. **2**(2) (2021)
24. Sansa, I., Bellaaj, N.M.: Solar radiation prediction using NARX model. In: Advanced Applications for Artificial Neural Networks. IntechOpen (2018)
25. Savari, M., Choe, Y.: Online virtual training in soft actor-critic for autonomous driving. In: 2021 International Joint Conference on Neural Networks (IJCNN), pp. 1–8. IEEE (2021)
26. Shakya, A.K., Pillai, G., Chakrabarty, S.: Reinforcement learning algorithms: a brief survey. Expert Syst. Appl. 120495 (2023)
27. Yang, J.H., Choi, W.Y., Lee, S.H., Chung, C.C.: Autonomous lane keeping control system based on road lane model using deep convolutional neural networks. In: 2019 IEEE Intelligent Transportation Systems Conference (ITSC), pp. 3393–3398. IEEE (2019)
28. Zhang, Q., Liu, J., Jiang, X.: Lane detection algorithm in curves based on multi-sensor fusion. Sensors **23**(12), 5751 (2023)
29. Zhang, X., et al.: Multi-modal fusion technology based on vehicle information: a survey. IEEE Trans. Intell. Veh. (2023)
30. Zheng, O., Abdel-Aty, M., Wang, Z., Ding, S., Wang, D., Huang, Y.: AVOID: autonomous vehicle operation incident dataset across the globe. arXiv preprint arXiv:2303.12889 (2023)

Digital Environment Description and Reconstruction Using Panoptic Segmentation

João Francisco de Souza Santos Lemos, Gabriel Amaral Dorneles(✉), Igor Pardo Maurell, Stephanie Loi Brião, Rodrigo da Silva Guerra, and Paulo Lilles Jorge Drews Junior

Center for Computational Science - C3, Universidade Federal Do Rio Grande - FURG, Rio Grande, Brazil
gdorneles@furg.br
http://www.c3.furg.br

Abstract. Simulation in the field of robotics is a less costly, safer, more scalable, and more versatile alternative to real-world scenarios. In this work, we present a pipeline for the digital reconstruction of environments using the panoptic segmentation technique . The overall aim is to automate the transcription of real geometries into the digital environment, creating a virtual scene where objects are meticulously segmented, making it possible to manipulate, replicate, remove, and practically move these objects. The methodology is based on Neural Radiance Field for segmentation and reconstruction of scenes, classical methods for manipulating structures, SDFormat as a scene description file, and Gazebo as a 3D robotic simulation platform . The results show that the method is capable of transcribing the scene into a virtual environment and using it as a space for testing, validating, and training robots.

Keywords: panoptic segmentation · simulated environment · surface reconstruction

1 Introduction

Simulation in robotics accelerates the design process, enables detailed testing, and is more cost-effective than real-world experimentation [2]. It provides exhaustive repetition of scenarios, exploring different conditions, and precisely adjusting parameters, something often unfeasible or costly in the physical world. It also facilitates controlled testing without posing risks to the physical safety of agents or causing damage to real-world environments. However, one of its main challenges is the difficulty of constructing scenes that accurately mimic the real world, especially considering time-critical environments such as those presented in the Robocup@Home competition.

The method described in this paper allows for the acquisition of a digital representation of the Robocup competition arena, allowing teams to simulate

E. Barros et al. (Eds.): RoboCup 2024, LNAI 15570, pp. 236–246, 2025.
https://doi.org/10.1007/978-3-031-85859-8_20

different tasks without manually creating the digital environment, a process that can be very challenging and time consuming [14].

This paper presents a novel digitalization pipeline using panoptic segmentation to achieve faithful digital representations of real-world environments, with posed images as input. Panoptic segmentation has been increasingly utilized in the literature to generate a meaningful representations environments [5, 18]. Building upon these results, this research aims to create a tool that can reconstruct a real environment into a virtual scene. In this virtual setting, objects are meticulously segmented, enabling straightforward manipulation, replication, removal, and relocation of these objects.

Our pipeline employs posed images from a given scene and a method based on DM-NeRF [15] for segmentation and reconstruction of the environment with no prior object detection or segmentation. The resulting three-dimensional meshes are then converted into XML files, categorized according to their panoptic classification, to produce an SDF file compatible with simulation software. A depiction of the proposed method can be seen in Fig. 1. The method is evaluated on the DM-SR [15] dataset and we integrate the obtained results into the Gazebo simulation environment through ROS.

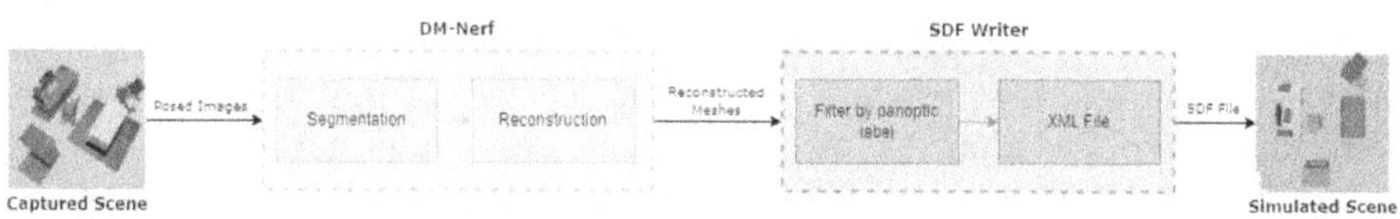

Fig. 1. The proposed pipeline: All individual objects are segmented and reconstructed with the appropriate labels, then transformed into the required format for simulation.

2 Related Work

This section provides an overview of existing research and developments relevant to this work, to contextualize the diversity of methodologies and the progression of ideas in the subject area. The topics explored include panoptic segmentation and reconstruction techniques and 3D scene reconstruction methods.

Image Segmentation: Image segmentation is a fundamental task in computer vision, aiming to partition an image into multiple segments or regions of interest, allowing various downstream tasks such as object detection, recognition, and scene understanding.

Semantic segmentation [3] is a classification where each pixel in an image is assigned a class label representing the category it belongs. Semantic segmentation provides a granular understanding of the image by labeling each pixel. However, instance segmentation [9] takes semantic segmentation a step further by not only assigning class labels to each pixel but also distinguishing between individual object instances. This result is achieved by only categorizing the pixels that are given as relevant in the image, not guaranteeing that all pixels will be classified.

Panoptic Image Segmentation: Panoptic segmentation [6] goal is to unify semantic and instance segmentation into a single task that can segment all pixels in an image, regardless of whether they belong to objects or stuff (e.g., sky, grass, road). In panoptic segmentation, each pixel is labeled with a class label if it belongs to a thing (object) or stuff (background). This holistic approach is crucial for tasks requiring a complete understanding of the visual environment, such as scene understanding and content-aware robotic tasks.

3D Scene Reconstruction: Several methodologies for 3D scene reconstruction from RGB images have been explored in prior research. Dahnert et al. [5] produces results from a single view, so it encounters limitations in reproducing a full scene without employing a mesh registration method. Uni-3d [18] utilizes a multi-view approach but, similarly to Dahnert et al., it relies on traditional reconstruction techniques, which leads to a compromise in the fidelity of the real-world geometry represented. Atlas [12] attempts to address these issues; however, its efficiency is tied to a segmentation method that is purely semantic, resulting in objects lacking specific instance-based information. Contrasting these approaches, this paper employs the DM-NeRF [15] method, which is among the first to include implicit representations of all 3D objects in complex scenes, relying solely on color images and 2D object labels for supervision.

3 Method

In this section, we detail the development of the pipeline designed to digitally recreate a real scene. Figure 1 illustrates the system's architecture, depicting a sequence of four main components along with their respective internal elements.

3.1 Panoptic Segmentation and Reconstruction

Panoptic segmentation [10] unifies semantic and instance segmentation into a single result, assigning semantic labels and indices to all pixels in an image. In contrast to traditional instance segmentation, which employs the concept of relevant classes to decide if a pixel should be classified, panoptic segmentation assigns semantic labels to all pixels, but does not provide specific indices for those that belong to irrelevant classes.

As discussed in Sect. 2, segmentation and reconstruction are well-researched fields with a variety of developed methods, but they are not easily integrated. To connect the two, the segmentation results must be handled by transcribing the data format, filtering the segmentation masks, supplementing the data, and taking other steps to ensure reconstruction can occur.

To address this issue, the DM-NeRF method constructs a triangular mesh by retrieving structures from continuous 3D scenes, segments all objects individually in three-dimensional space, and allows for flexible manipulation of objects. Consequently, the segmentation and reconstruction processes occur simultaneously, since the vector predicted for each of the pixels by segmentation also corresponds to a specific color that is assigned to the vertices in the scene reconstruction.

3.2 Reconstruction Post-processing

Once the scene has been reconstructed, it is important to isolate the objects so that the vertices of each item are separated. This segregation is achieved through a filtering process that utilizes the panoptic label, divided into semantic type labels and instance index labels. These labels enable the distinction between objects of the same category (such as different chairs or tables in the scene, in a domestic environment), and through the semantic tag it is possible to write each object's type within the description file.

Due to the inherent inaccuracies in the reconstruction process, it fails to ensure uniformly smooth surfaces, resulting in uneven terrain. This impairs the navigation and stability of a robotic base. To circumvent this issue, a plane is estimated through primitive segmentation using RANSAC fitting [8]. To find the plane that represents the ground, the sub-mesh of vertices classified with the corresponding label is selected and used as input for the segment plane method of the consolidated Open3D library [13].

The method accepts three arguments: distance threshold θ_t defines the maximum distance a point can have to an estimated plane to be considered a point belonging to it; ransac n defines the number of points that are randomly sampled at each iteration to estimate a plane; and number of iterations λ defines how many times a random plane is sampled and checked. Subsequently, the function outputs a list of indices for points deemed to belong to the plane, alongside a description of the plane through its general equation.

Each vertex of the reconstructed mesh must be interpreted as a point, enabling the plane segmentation method to fine-tune parameters that most accurately describe the ground plane. As a result, each of the vertices has its three-dimensional coordinates projected onto the plane, maintaining the details of the mesh, but with a perfectly smooth floor, a process that is illustrated in Fig. 2.

Once the reconstruction is completed, the representation is in a different coordinate system than the simulator, which leads to mismatches in spatial orientation and positioning when integrating the reconstructed scene into the simulated environment. To address this issue, a coordinate system transformation process is necessary.

Fortunately, estimating a plane provides the information that makes up the normal vector, which is the exact information needed to adjust the orientation. Nonetheless, it is necessary to find the rotation matrix between the scene and

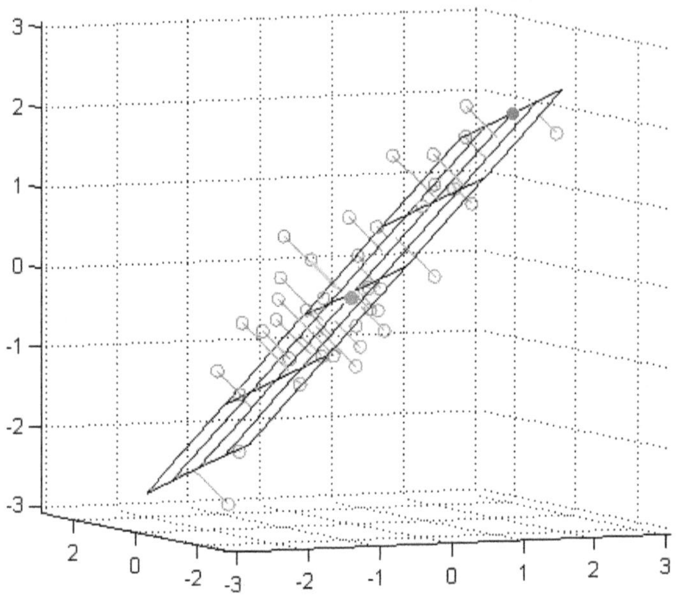

Fig. 2. Points being projected onto a predicted plane [1].

a line parallel to the z-axis. To find the rotation matrix θ between the normal vector $\mathbf{n} = [n_x, n_y, n_z]$ and the positive axis z^+, the scalar product is used:

$$\cos(\theta) = \hat{\mathbf{n}} \cdot [0, 0, 1] = \frac{n_z}{|\mathbf{n}|} \tag{1}$$

In which $|\mathbf{n}|$ is the magnitude of the normal vector and $\hat{\mathbf{n}}$ is the normalized vector. The angle can be calculated using the inverse cosine function.

Applying this angle to the orientation of the overall scene guarantees objects parallel to the z-axis, despite the normal vector not specifying whether the mesh is oriented upwards or downwards. To solve this problem, we determine the height of the mesh on both sides of the floor and orient the side with greater height to face upwards.

3.3 Setting up the Gazebo Scene

To rebuild a scene for robotics simulation, it is important to use a simulator that allows for robot control, sensor integration and provides a user-friendly interface. To ensure this operates smoothly, effective communication among the various components of the robotic system is crucial. The Gazebo simulator was chosen for its integration with ROS, which offers specific interfaces, known as plugins, that enable communication between Gazebo and robotic systems. These plugins, shown in Fig. 3, facilitate the exchange of information between the simulated environment and the various software components operating within the robot.

The Gazebo simulator receives an SDF (Simulation Description Format) file as an input. This file contains the complete description of the simulated environment. To write the file, the ElementTree python library[1] is used, which implements a simple and efficient interface for creating and editing XML data. The real world can be abstractly defined as a collection of objects and backgrounds that relate hierarchically in terms of belonging. This approach makes it possible to use SDF files to describe the scene, since it is essentially composed of labels and attributes in a tree-like structure.

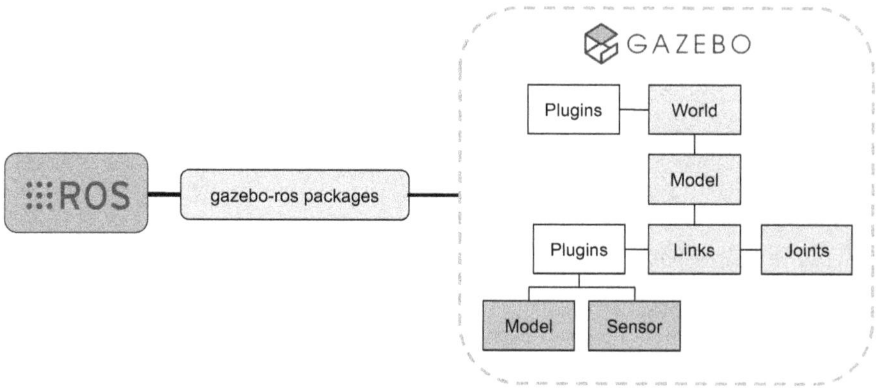

Fig. 3. Communication flow between ROS and Gazebo.

4 Evaluation

This chapter breaks down the results into separate sections, each focusing on the different analyses—quantitative, empirical, or patterns observed. We explain the impact of each process in detail to clarify how they contribute to the overall results. The experiments were designed to assess the effectiveness of the chosen methods and to better understand their performance in a simulated environment.

4.1 Validation Conditions

As validation data for the pipeline, the DM-SR [15] was chosen, a *dataset* made up of residential environments designed precisely for quantitative evaluation of scene reconstruction and panoptic segmentation tasks. It already provides a multi-view capture of the scene with 95 "posed images". Additionally, it includes

[1] ElementTree documentation: https://docs.python.org/3/library/xml.etree.elementtree.html.

semantic and instance annotations for all objects in each image, simplifying the quantification of training and testing metrics.

The dataset is made up of complex domestic scenes with dimensions close to $24\,\mathrm{m}^2$ in area and 3 m in height, containing around 8 objects. The primary focus of our evaluations was the study room model, shown in Fig. 4a, selected due to its large number of elements, a variation of sizes and shapes, sparse positioning, and overlapping objects. With these characteristics, the model effectively addresses most of the main potential challenges presented by an indoor setting in domestic environments, though further investigation is required to address more specific conditions.

4.2 Panoptic Reconstruction

The overall quality of the panoptic reconstruction varies based on the results of two key internal processes of the method, view synthesis and decomposition. In computer graphics, view synthesis involves generating novel images of a specific scene when the only available information is photos taken from different viewpoints. Decomposition is the separation of the elements that make up a scene.

Using the model in the DM-NeRF network and evaluating it with the metrics proposed by Mildenhall et al. [11], the method described in this paper is capable of achieving significant results shown in Table 1.

Table 1. Results obtained from the respective metrics.

Scene	View synthesis			Decomposition (%)
	PSNR ↑	SSIM ↑	LPIPS ↓	
Bathroom	45.22	0.991	0.022	99.20
Bedroom	47.59	0.994	0.018	100.00
Dining Room	38.76	0.987	0.015	99.49
Kitchen	48.90	0.989	0.028	100.00
Reception	41.92	0.996	0.011	99.60
Living Room	43.74	0.981	0.024	100.00
Study Room	39.67	0.995	0.008	100.00
Office	47.01	0.992	0.012	99.12
Mean	44.66	0.991	0.017	**99.58**

PSNR (Peak Signal-to-Noise Ratio) [7] is a metric that, in the case of RGB images, ranges from the worst case at 0 to the best possible result at 58.06. The average PSNR of 44.66 indicates a small difference or error between the original image and its reconstructed version, as PSNR quantifies the ratio between the maximum possible signal energy (original image) and the noise energy (error) affecting its fidelity.

The SSIM (Structural Similarity Index) [16], a metric that ranges from −1 to 1, shows an average SSIM of 0.991. This indicates that the final and reconstructed images are very close to being identical in terms of structure, luminance, and contrast.

The LPIPS (Learned Perceptual Image Patch Similarity) [17] coefficient is inversely proportional to similarity, so the value near 0.015 endorses the significant outcome of the previous metrics in terms of vision synthesis.

(a) "Study Room" environment from the DM-SR dataset [15].

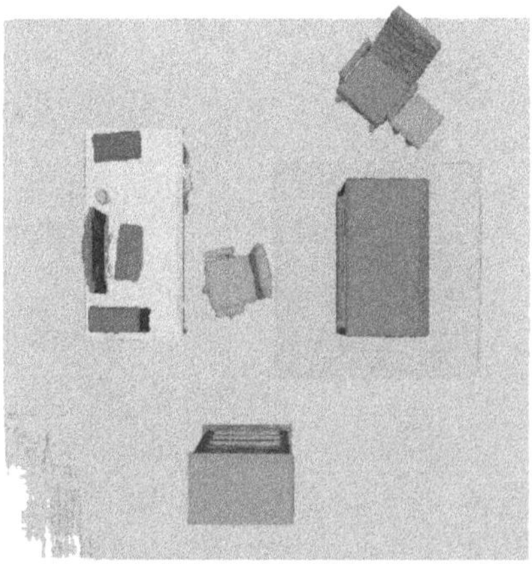

(b) Results from the panoptic reconstruction of "Study Room".

Fig. 4. Comparison between the original and reconstructed scene.

Finally, the average decomposition accuracy percentage being so close to 100 shows that the object vertices are correctly segmented with only minimal noise present. The high quality of the results is apparent when comparing the original scene, shown in Fig. 5a, with the reconstructed scene in Fig. 5b.

(a) Uneven ground plane.

(b) Ground plane after post-processing.

Fig. 5. Comparison between the ground plane before and after post-processing.

The segment plane method described in Sect. 3.2 successfully transformed an uneven ground plane into a continuous plane that retained the mesh details, making it ideal for robot traversal.

In the reconstructed scene, the decomposition of the mesh allows the scene to be mutable, since the objects are not attached. The quality of the separation directly reflects the quality of the segmentation, with colors assigned according to the panoptic class attributed to each vertex, as depicted in Fig. 6.

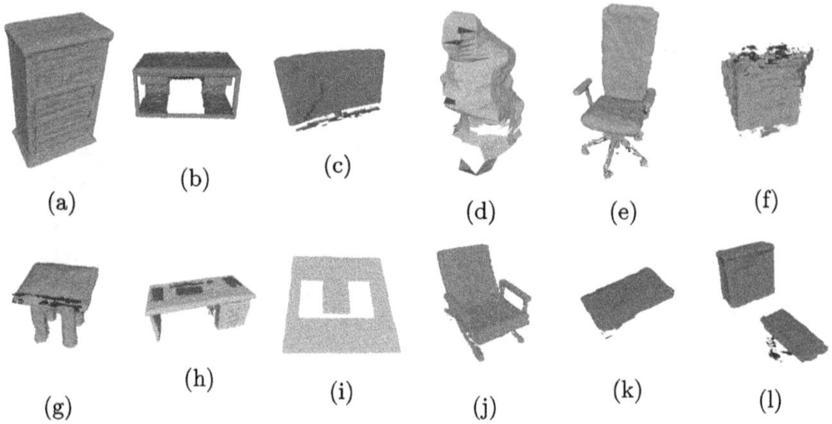

Fig. 6. Objects of the DM-SR dataset segmented and separated by their classes and instances.

4.3 Simulated Environment

As described in Sect. 3.3, the algorithm developed to write the SDF file is simple. It creates a tree structure for the simulated world, assigning the visual characteristics and collision properties to each of the objects. If necessary, the scenario is rotated to align with the orientation of the simulator.

The world allows objects to be replicated, moved, rotated, or removed. The scenario is capable of incorporating other external elements that were not initially present and, as the main feature, serves as a platform that interacts with robots. All these features are displayed in Fig. 7, where new objects, such as cans, are added on top and beside the blue table. In this example, the cabinet is removed, the blue table is replicated, and two robotic bases are positioned in the scene, where they can navigate freely.

One of the applications for these features is the aforementioned Robocup@Home competition, where the limited time allotted for each team in the arena makes creating a simulated environment both challenging and valuable, while the controlled nature of the environment serves as an ideal setting. Using the described method, posed images of the arena can be captured to quickly generate a simulated version of all objects in the scene, allowing different tasks to be tested under conditions similar to the real-world environment, while easily modifying the layout for any specific requirements from different tests.

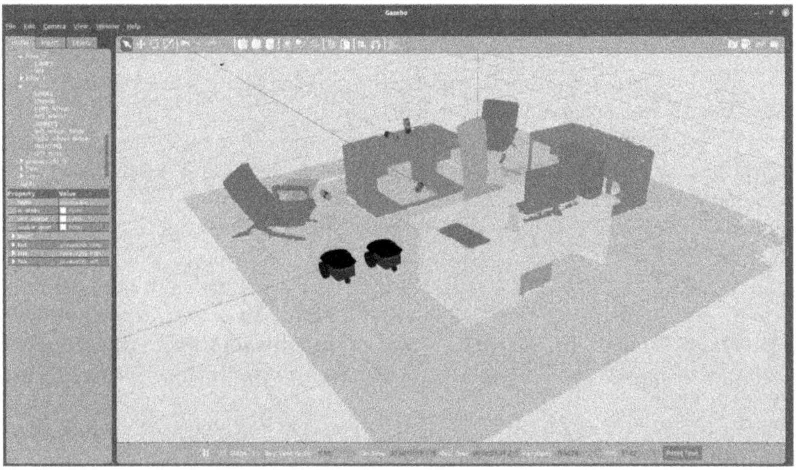

Fig. 7. Simulated environment with newly added, removed, and replicated objects, alongside two robots positioned in the scene. (Color figure online)

5 Conclusions

In this work, we presented a pipeline for the digital reconstruction of environments based on NERFs and using panoptic segmentation. The proposed method aims to create a virtual environment by transcribing real-world geometries, allowing for manipulation, replication, and removal of objects within the scene. Utilizing Gazebo as a simulation environment, the results demonstrate that the method is capable of generating virtual environments for robotic testing and training.

Quantitative evaluations of the scene reconstruction and segmentation processes yielded results with high fidelity and minimal noise. The pipeline was validated on the DM-SR dataset, which features eight typical household rooms. Our method produces accurate digital renditions of real-world environments and integrates them into the Gazebo simulation platform. This enables robots to navigate and interact within the virtual scene, allowing system validation without the risks and costs associated with real-world experiments.

Future work includes assessing the method across various datasets, including custom datasets based on real-world environments. This will help to investigate the method's efficiency in more specific scenarios, particularly those involving cluttered environments. Furthermore, state-of-the-art techniques based on retrieve and deform templates, such as those proposed by Dahnert et al. [4], should be explored to ensure more realistic structures despite incomplete scanning.

Disclosure of Interests. The authors have no competing interests to declare that are relevant to the content of this article.

References

1. Azevedo, R.: Fitting a plane to points using SVD. Mathematics Stack Exchange. https://math.stackexchange.com/q/3501135
2. Choi, H., et al.: On the use of simulation in robotics: opportunities, challenges, and suggestions for moving forward. Proc. Nat. Acad. Sci. U.S.A. **118** (2020). https://api.semanticscholar.org/CorpusID:229281163
3. Csurka, G., Volpi, R., Chidlovskii, B.: Semantic image segmentation: two decades of research (2023)
4. Dahnert, M., Dai, A., Guibas, L.J., Nießner, M.: Joint embedding of 3D scan and CAD objects. CoRR abs/1908.06989 (2019). http://arxiv.org/abs/1908.06989
5. Dahnert, M., Hou, J., Nießner, M., Dai, A.: Panoptic 3D scene reconstruction from a single RGB image. In: Thirty-Fifth Conference on Neural Information Processing Systems (2021)
6. Elharrouss, O., Al-Maadeed, S., Subramanian, N., Ottakath, N., Almaadeed, N., Himeur, Y.: Panoptic segmentation: a review (2021)
7. Fardo, F.A., Conforto, V.H., de Oliveira, F.C., Rodrigues, P.S.S.: A formal evaluation of PSNR as quality measurement parameter for image segmentation algorithms. CoRR abs/1605.07116 (2016). http://arxiv.org/abs/1605.07116
8. Fischler, M.A., Bolles, R.C.: Random sample consensus: a paradigm for model fitting with applications to image analysis and automated cartography. Commun. ACM **24**(6), 381–395 (1981)
9. Hafiz, A.M., Bhat, G.M.: A survey on instance segmentation: state of the art. Int. J. Multimedia Inf. Retrieval **9**(3), 171–189 (2020). https://doi.org/10.1007/s13735-020-00195-x
10. Kirillov, A., He, K., Girshick, R., Rother, C., Dollár, P.: Panoptic segmentation. In: Proceedings of the IEEE Conference on Computer Vision and Pattern Recognition (CVPR), pp. 9404–9413 (2019)
11. Mildenhall, B., Srinivasan, P.P., Tancik, M., Barron, J.T., Ramamoorthi, R., Ng, R.: NeRF: representing scenes as neural radiance fields for view synthesis. CoRR abs/2003.08934 (2020). https://arxiv.org/abs/2003.08934
12. Murez, Z., van As, T., Bartolozzi, J., Sinha, A., Badrinarayanan, V., Rabinovich, A.: Atlas: end-to-end 3D scene reconstruction from posed images (2020)
13. Open3D contributors: open3D: a modern library for 3D data processing (2024). http://www.open3d.org
14. Seppelt, R., Müller, F., Schröder, B., Volk, M.: Challenges of simulating complex environmental systems at the landscape scale: a controversial dialogue between two cups of espresso. Ecol. Model. **24**, 3481–3489 (2009). https://doi.org/10.1016/j.ecolmodel.2009.09.009
15. Wang, B., Chen, L., Yang, B.: DM-NeRF: 3D scene geometry decomposition and manipulation from 2D images (2023)
16. Wang, Z., Bovik, A., Sheikh, H., Simoncelli, E.: Image quality assessment: from error visibility to structural similarity. IEEE Trans. Image Process. **13**(4), 600–612 (2004). https://doi.org/10.1109/TIP.2003.819861
17. Zhang, R., Isola, P., Efros, A.A., Shechtman, E., Wang, O.: The unreasonable effectiveness of deep features as a perceptual metric. CoRR abs/1801.03924 (2018). http://arxiv.org/abs/1801.03924
18. Zhang, X., Chen, Z., Wei, F., Tu, Z.: Uni-3D: a universal model for panoptic 3D scene reconstruction. In: Proceedings of the IEEE/CVF International Conference on Computer Vision (ICCV), pp. 9256–9266 (2023)

Efficient Sequence Model for Early Fall Detection of Humanoid Robots

Khaled Saleh(✉), Thomas O'Brien, Ysobel Sims, Alexandre Mendes, and Stephan Chalup

The University of Newcastle, Newcastle, Australia
khaled.saleh@newcastle.edu.au

Abstract. Ensuring the stability and safety of humanoid robots during dynamic tasks remains a crucial challenge. The ability to predict and prevent falls is pivotal in such contexts, as falls can hinder performance and waste resources. Existing fall detection and prediction methods for humanoid robots vary in their approaches, and data-driven approaches based on neural networks have shown promising results. Nevertheless, these approaches still lack the efficiency required to provide fall predictions within an acceptable timeframe without compromising accuracy. In this paper, we propose a data-driven approach leveraging a lightweight neural network architecture, enabling accurate fall predictions in near real-time. Our framework, relying on raw IMU sensor data, undergoes comprehensive evaluation across diverse fall scenarios and evaluation metrics. Comparative analyses against baseline architectures from the literature affirm its superior performance in humanoid fall detection and prediction.

Keywords: Humanoid · Robotics · Fall · Neural Networks · MLP

1 Introduction

Humanoid robots have long been a focal point in robotics research, representing a synthesis of advanced mechanical engineering, artificial intelligence, and human-inspired design principles. Among the myriad challenges facing developers and researchers in this field, ensuring the stability and safety of humanoid robots during dynamic tasks remains a paramount concern. In contexts such as RoboCup Soccer competitions, where humanoid robots engage in complex interactions and tasks, the ability to predict and prevent falls is of critical importance. As these robots navigate dynamic environments and interact with objects, the risk of falls poses a significant obstacle to their performance and effectiveness. Addressing this challenge requires the development of robust fall prediction algorithms capable of anticipating and mitigating potential instability in real time. Existing fall detection and prediction techniques for humanoid robots can be categorised into three main classes, namely threshold-based methods [10–12], model-based methods [4,6,7], and data-driven methods [2,5,8,14].

E. Barros et al. (Eds.): RoboCup 2024, LNAI 15570, pp. 247–256, 2025.
https://doi.org/10.1007/978-3-031-85859-8_21

Threshold-based methods involve setting specific thresholds for certain sensor observations or measurements to identify potential falls. These sensor observations range from linear acceleration/angular velocities to force sensors. In [10], they combined accelerometer and gyroscope sensor data from a NAO humanoid robot in a simulated environment via Kalman filter, to obtain a single virtual sensor observation. Then, empirically, they defined two different threshold values to determine robot falls while standing or walking. Similarly, Tay et al. [12] utilised a sequence of motion primitives that represents keyframes of the robot's joint angles positions during normal walking. Then, based on a threshold value of the robot's torso angle, they can determine whether the generated sequence of motion primitives by the robot will be feasible (stable) or not. This is based on the assumption that the higher the body angle, the higher the possibility that the robot is going to fall. In [11], by fusing several sensor observations (inertial measurement unit (IMU), force sensor, and depth sensor) using a Kalman filter, and based on several dynamic threshold values (for each sensor type) collected via a set of fall sequences in a simulated environment, they can identify if the robot is in a falling state or not.

Model-based methods involve creating mathematical models representing the robot's dynamics during motion, and they also rely on sensor observations to identify whether the sensor data could lead to a potential fall in the near future. In [6], they relied on a physical model of an NAO robot based on the Linear Inverted Pendulum to model the robot's motion. Then, using the initial measured angle and angular velocity of the robot and the torque generated by all the robot's joint angles, they iteratively simulate whether the robot's movement will result in a stabilised motion or fall motion. In [4], they introduce the concept of Energy Fall Prediction (EFP) as a method for predicting balance states and potential falls for humanoid robots only while they are standing. When a force is applied to the robot while it's standing, they measure the kinetic energy of the robot via IMU sensors as a proxy for measuring the momentum applied to the robot to determine the balance status of the robot. Mummolo et al. [7] introduced a numerical technique to determine balanced and falling states of legged humanoid robots by combining joint-space and Cartesian-space dynamics. They cast it as an optimisation problem that involves system characteristics, physical limitations, and boundary situations, to identify critical velocities signifying maximal disturbances preserving equilibrium. Then, using an iterative process, a stability boundary is calculated, separating balanced and falling states. Balanced states are included within this boundary, whereas excluded states imply falling.

Data-driven methods have recently provided some promising results in tackling the fall detection/prediction problem. They approach the fall detection/prediction problem as a sensor observation classification problem. In [2], they relied on a large number of simulations to obtain sensor observations (derived mainly from an IMU sensor), to train four different machine learning (ML) classifiers to identify fall incidents. In their experiments, the support vector machine (SVM) classifier was shown to be the best-performing model out of the four ML classifiers compared. Similarly, Wu et al. [14], proposed another SVM classifier to classify fall and non-fall incidents of humanoid robots inside simulated environments based on IMU sensor observations. In their experiments, they considered both scenarios of fall - while the robot is standing and while it is walking. In [5], another ML classifier was proposed. However, it was based on the recurrent neural networks architecture, Bidirectional LSTM, rather than the SVM classifier. In their proposed model, it was trained on IMU sensor observations from simulated fall sequences based only on a set of simulated external forces. More recently, Mungai et al. [8], presented another data-driven method based on 1D convolution neural networks to predict potential falls and fall lead time.

While data-driven methods have been improving the false positive rate, which was one of the main issues with previous fall detection and prediction algorithms from the literature, they are not efficient enough during the inference stage for near real-time predictions - or for providing ample lead time for fall prevention and/or recovery. Thus, in this paper, we are proposing a data-driven approach based on an efficient neural network architecture [15] that is lightweight enough to provide accurate fall/non-fall predictions in near real-time.

The remaining sections of the paper are structured as follows. Section 2 outlines the fall data simulation process and the proposed methodology. Section 3 presents the experimental results and performance evaluation of the proposed methodology. Finally, Sect. 4 concludes the paper.

2 Methodology

In this section, we will start by introducing our formulation for the early fall detection problem. Then, we will describe the simulated environment utilised for generating and recording the different scenarios for fall and non-fall sequences. Finally, we introduce our efficient neural network model for early fall detection of humanoid robots.

2.1 Problem Formulation

We cast the early fall detection problem as a time-series classification problem. Given a short sequence $Z_{1:T}$ of sensor observations of length T, we try to predict for the next $T+\delta$ whether the humanoid robot will be falling or not. We chose δ to be 0.5 s empirically. Unlike other approaches in the literature, this unique formulation of the problem, in conjunction with an efficient neural network model, enables us to have a more proactive fall detection/prediction technique. This approach could provide effective indicators about potential falls that humanoid robots may encounter during normal operation, as early as possible.

2.2 Fall Data Simulation

Similar to the common practice in the literature when it comes to collecting fall data [2,5,8,14], we relied on simulation environments to generate such data.

Fig. 1. Force disturbance fall data collection setup.

Fig. 2. Uneven terrain fall data collection setup.

More specifically, we used the robotics simulation software Webots [13] to simulate fall and non-fall sequences of the NUgus humanoid robot. The NUgus platform has 20 degrees of freedom, a mass of 7.65 kg and a height of 90 cm, and is based on the igus Humanoid Open Platform [1].

Fall and non-fall data sequences were generated by having the robot walk forward at a fixed desired velocity of 0.3 m/s using an open-loop walk engine for a maximum duration of 20 s. The simulation environment is then reset after the maximum time has elapsed, or whenever a fall occurs. A fall is determined if the rotation between the z-axis of the world and the torso exceeds a threshold of 55°. We simulated and generated two datasets with varying methods for inducing a fall. The first method involves applying a force ("push") to the robot for a duration of 0.2 s with the magnitude drawn uniformly from the range [30, 60 N]. The force is applied in the "x" (forward) direction at the midpoint between the hips of the robot at a random time point drawn uniformly from the range [3, 20 s], illustrated in Fig. 1. The second method involves having the robot walk over uneven terrain, as shown in Fig. 2. Due to the open-loop walk engine having no feedback, the robot is unable to adapt to the uneven terrain causing the robot to fall very often. During each fall and non-fall sequence, sensor data listed in Table 1 was captured at a frequency of 100 Hz.

Table 1. Sensor data recorded during fall and non-fall sequences.

Data	Dimension	Unit
Accelerometer	3	m/s^2
Gyroscope	3	rad/s

Given the ubiquity and low cost of IMU sensors (accelerometer and gyroscope sensors), in this work, we will be relying mainly on the IMU data as the input time series sensor observations for our proposed early fall detection model.

2.3 Efficient Early Fall Detection Model

Some of the challenges faced by data-driven approaches for the humanoid robot fall detection/prediction problem include higher false positive rate (FPR) [2,14] and shorter lead time due to their expensive computational requirements - both of them affect their real-time performance [5,8]. To overcome that, we are proposing an efficient neural network model based on the LightTS architecture [15]. LightTS is one of the best-performing architectures for efficient time series modelling. It has achieved superior results on popular time-series benchmarks with less than 5% floating-point operations per second (FLOPS) in comparison to state-of-the-art methods. LightTS was designed based on two main components: 1) two different sampling techniques to capture the temporal dependency in the input sequential data over the short and long term; 2) information exchange blocks to learn the correlations between the extracted sequential features within the input data.

The two different sampling techniques are continuous sampling and interval sampling. Continuous sampling selects consecutive tokens to capture short-term local patterns according to the following equation:

$$Z_t^{\mathrm{con}} \cdot k = \left\{ z_{t-T+(k-1)\cdot W+1}, z_{t-T+(k-1)\cdot W+2}, \ldots, z_{t-T+k\cdot W} \right\} \tag{1}$$

Interval sampling selects tokens with fixed time intervals to capture long-term global patterns according to the following equation:

$$Z_t^{int} \cdot k = \left\{ z_{t-T+k}, x_{t-T+k+\lfloor \frac{T}{W} \rfloor}, x_{t-T+k+2\cdot\lfloor \frac{T}{W} \rfloor}, \ldots, z_{t-T+k+(W-1)\cdot\lfloor \frac{T}{W} \rfloor} \right\} \tag{2}$$

where the sequence $Z_{1:T}$ at the $k-$th column is divided into W chunks.

These sampling methods help the model efficiently capture different temporal patterns. Additionally, LightTS incorporates multi-layer perceptron (MLP) layers, to facilitate information exchange along different dimensions to extract features effectively.

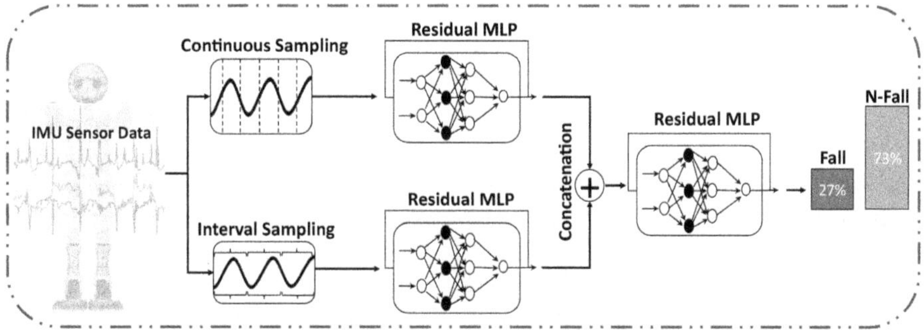

Fig. 3. The proposed framework for efficient early fall detection of humanoid robots.

Similar to LightTS, the main building block of our proposed framework (shown in Fig. 3), Efficient Early Fall Detection (E^2FD), is based on an MLP structure, which was shown recently to be more powerful and efficient (with proper architecture design) in modelling time-series and sequential data [9]. However, unlike the vanilla MLP structure proposed in LightTS, we are proposing a modified version that contains a residual connection (we refer to it as Residual MLP), that allows better modelling of complex relationships that may be difficult to capture with the vanilla MLP structure, especially for noisy sequential sensor observations. As can be seen in Fig. 3, our framework takes as input a short sequence (0.5 s) of IMU sensor data from a humanoid robot, and then this sequence is further down-sampled or chunked using the aforementioned two sampling techniques (continuous and interval) to capture both short and long term temporal dependency among the input IMU sensor observations. The output from each sampling operation is then passed through our proposed residual MLP layers, which generate the feature maps that are concatenated together before being fed to the last residual MLP layer, which in return provides the classification score of whether the humanoid robot will be falling or not in the next 0.5 s.

3 Experiments

In this section, we start by introducing the preparation steps to obtain our fall dataset, and then we describe the different hyperparameters and the procedure utilised for training the proposed E^2FD framework. Finally, we report and discuss the results of the proposed framework when tested on the dataset, in comparison to other baseline techniques from the literature.

3.1 Dataset

Following the procedure described in Sect. 2.2, we obtained a total of 2000 sequences (1000 during applied push forces simulation, and 1000 during uneven terrain simulation) of IMU sensor data involving falling and non-falling sequences, ranging in length between 4 to 20 s. In our first preprocessing step, for each type of fall sequence, we split the 1000 sequences into 70% for training and 30% for testing the E^2FD framework. The split strategy followed ensured that there was no overlap between the training and testing sets using random sampling.

In the second preprocessing step, we localised the humanoid robot's falling window within each generated sequence in the training/testing split. For force-induced falls, we extracted a short sub-sequence of IMU sensor data, starting from the time-step where the force was applied until the robot began the falling action (i.e. before hitting the ground). Given the variable length of these extracted IMU sensor data windows (1–2 s), and to ensure a unified length of the sequences during training and evaluation of the E^2FD framework, we applied a sliding window of length 50 (i.e. 0.5 s since IMU's sampling rate is 100 Hz) with an overlap of 50%. This allowed us to obtain equally-sized short IMU sensor observation sequences. Similarly, for falls triggered by uneven terrain, we first localised the starting/ending time of the robot's unstable movement before hitting the ground. Unlike force-induced falls, which could occur at any starting point, we extracted a sub-sequence of IMU sensor observations 1.5 s before the humanoid robot's falling action and also applied a sliding window of length 50 with an overlap of 50%.

For the non-fall sequences, we randomly sampled fixed-length (of length 50) sub-sequences of IMU sensor observations with starting/ending time-steps outside the starting/ending time-steps of the falling windows described above from all the 2000 sequences. However, we ensured that the total number of extracted sliding windows for the non-falling sequences was equal to the total number of extracted falling sequences, to address the class imbalance problem [3]. After the preprocessing stages, a total of 6862 training samples and 3068 testing samples were collected. Each sample has a size of $(T \times D)$, where T is the sample window length (which is 50, or 0.5 s in our case) and D is the dimension of the IMU sensor data, which is 6.

3.2 Experiments Setup

In the proposed E^{2}FD framework, we empirically used a chunk window size W of 25 in both the continuous and interval sampling operations. In the three residual MLP components, we empirically also used values of 32, 32 and 16 for the hidden units of the three residual MLP layers, respectively. For the objective function of the training, we used the cross-entropy loss function. We trained the E^{2}FD framework using the Adam optimiser, with a learning rate of 0.0001 and weight decay of 0.000001, for 100 epochs using an Nvidia A100 GPU.

In order to quantify the performance of the E^{2}FD framework, we used the following three evaluation metrics: recall, precision and F1 score.

$$\text{Recall} = \text{TP}/(\text{TP} + \text{FN}), \tag{3}$$

$$\text{Precision} = \text{TP}/(\text{TP} + \text{FP}), \tag{4}$$

$$\text{F1} = 2 * (\text{Precision} * \text{Recall})/(\text{Precision} + \text{Recall}) \tag{5}$$

where TP is the true positive count, FN is the false negative count and FP is the false positive count.

Furthermore, we compare the performance of the framework against the following baseline techniques:

- **SVM:** A Support Vector Machine model, similar to the one utilised in [2,14], where the input is the time-series IMU sensor data, similar to our proposed framework. It uses the radial basis function (RBF) as the kernel function.
- **LSTM:** A recurrent neural network model based on LSTM layers, similar to the one presented in [5]. It contains two LSTM layers and one fully connected layer.

- **Conv1D:** A convolutional neural network model based on 1D convolution layers, similar to the one presented in [8]. It contains two 1D convolution layers and one fully connected layer.

Table 2. Performance of the proposed framework (E^2FD) in comparison to other baseline approaches on the test split of the generated fall data.

Model	Precision	Recall	F1
SVM	89.54	88.20	88.10
LSTM	92.66	92.54	92.53
ConvID	93.03	93.02	93.02
E^2FD (ours)	**93.52**	**93.45**	**93.45**

3.3 Results and Discussion

In Table 2, we report the results of the proposed framework E^2FD, in comparison to the baseline techniques from the literature described in Sect. 3.2. As can be seen from the table, E^2FD has achieved superior results according to the three evaluation metrics, outperforming both the SVM and the LSTM models by a relatively large margin. Additionally, our E^2FD has also scored slightly better results than the Conv1D model across the three evaluation metrics. In order to further evaluate the efficiency of our proposed framework, in Fig. 4, we report the number of training parameters required by the two neural networks-based baselines (LSTM and Conv1D) similar to our E^2FD. The number of training parameters influences the computational resource requirements and the overall run-time performance of neural network-based models. As can be seen in the figure, the proposed framework E^2FD only requires about 8K parameters, while LSTM and Conv1D require 30K and 107K parameters, respectively.

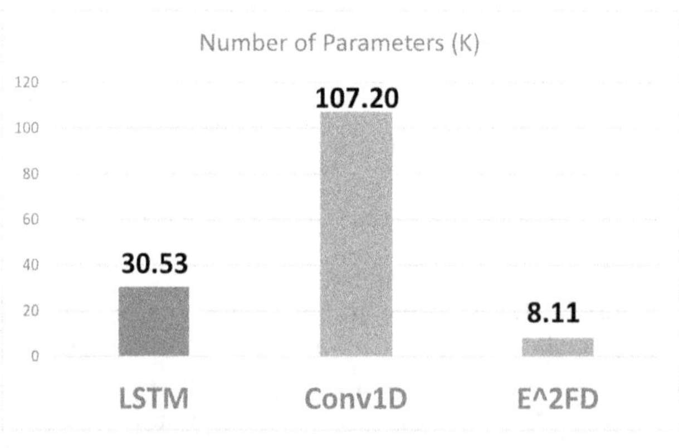

Fig. 4. Comparison between proposed framework and other neural network-based models in terms of number of training parameters.

4 Conclusion

In this work, we introduce an efficient early fall detection framework for humanoid robots, leveraging raw IMU sensor data. The framework relies on a novel lightweight MLP-based architecture capable of delivering accurate and early fall predictions without compromising real-time performance. The proposed framework was evaluated using two distinct fall scenarios, simulated within a realistic environment, and assessed across three different evaluation metrics. Furthermore, the framework was compared against three baseline architectures commonly used for humanoid fall detection and prediction, and it consistently outperformed them.

Acknowledgements. This research is supported by 4Tel Pty Ltd., 4AI Systems Inc. and an Australian Government Research Training Program Scholarship to Ysobel Sims and Thomas O'Brien.

References

1. Allgeuer, P., Farazi, H., Ficht, G., Schreiber, M., Behnke, S.: The igus humanoid open platform: a child-sized 3D printed open-source robot for research. Ger. J. Artif. Intell. (KI) **30**, 315–319 (2016)
2. André, J., Faria, B.M., Santos, C., Reis, L.P.: A data mining approach to predict falls in humanoid robot locomotion. In: Robot 2015: Second Iberian Robotics Conference: Advances in Robotics, vol. 2, pp. 273–285. Springer (2016)
3. Japkowicz, N., Stephen, S.: The class imbalance problem: a systematic study. Intell. Data Anal. **6**(5), 429–449 (2002)
4. Li, Z., et al.: Fall prediction of legged robots based on energy state and its implication of balance augmentation: a study on the humanoid. In: 2015 IEEE International Conference on Robotics and Automation (ICRA), pp. 5094–5100. IEEE (2015)
5. Liu, D., Jeong, H., Wei, A., Kapila, V.: Bidirectional LSTM-based network for fall prediction in a humanoid. In: 2020 IEEE International Symposium on Safety, Security, and Rescue Robotics (SSRR), pp. 129–135. IEEE (2020)
6. Muender, T., Röfer, T.: Model-based fall detection and fall prevention for humanoid robots, pp. 312–324. Springer (2018)
7. Mummolo, C., Mangialardi, L., Kim, J.H.: Numerical estimation of balanced and falling states for constrained legged systems. J. Nonlinear Sci. **27**, 1291–1323 (2017)
8. Mungai, M.E., Prabhakaran, G., Grizzle, J.W.: Fall prediction for bipedal robots: the standing phase. arXiv preprint arXiv:2309.14546 (2023)
9. Oreshkin, B.N., Carpov, D., Chapados, N., Bengio, Y.: N-BEATS: neural basis expansion analysis for interpretable time series forecasting. arXiv preprint arXiv:1905.10437 (2019)
10. Ruiz-del Solar, J., Moya, J., Parra-Tsunekawa, I.: Fall detection and management in biped humanoid robots. In: 2010 IEEE International Conference on Robotics and Automation, pp. 3323–3328. IEEE (2010)
11. Subburaman, R., Kanoulas, D., Muratore, L., Tsagarakis, N.G., Lee, J.: Human inspired fall prediction method for humanoid robots. Robot. Auton. Syst. **121**, 103257 (2019)

12. Tay, J., Chen, I.M., Veloso, M.: Fall prediction for new sequences of motions. In: Experimental Robotics: The 14th International Symposium on Experimental Robotics, pp. 849–864. Springer (2016)
13. Webots. Open-source Mobile Robot Simulation Software. http://www.cyberbotics.com. http://www.cyberbotics.com
14. Wu, T., Yu, Z., Chen, X., Dong, C., Gao, Z., Huang, Q.: Falling prediction based on machine learning for biped robots. J. Intell. Robot. Syst. **103**, 1–14 (2021)
15. Zhang, T., et al.: Less is more: fast multivariate time series forecasting with light sampling-oriented MLP structures. arXiv preprint arXiv:2207.01186 (2022)

Steam Deck: A Handheld ROS 2 Based Rescue Robot Controller

Shubham Pawar(✉), Maximillian Kirsch, Christoph Gollok, and Alexander Ferrein

The Mobile Autonomous Systems & Cognitive Robotics Institute, FH Aachen University of Applied Sciences, Eupener Straße 70, 52056 Aachen, Germany
shubham.pawar@alumni.fh-aachen.de, {m.kirsch,gollok,ferrein}@fh-aachen.de

Abstract. Efficient and rapid deployment of robots by first responders in rescue scenarios is crucial for locating and rescuing more victims faster. Easy to use teleoperating robot interface in urban search and rescue scenario is important to effectively guide the robots through complex environments, alongside having autonomous functions allowing them to operate independently when necessary. In this paper, we propose using the *Steam Deck* as a ROS 2-based Rescue Robot Controller, utilizing its capabilities as a powerful and a portable controller to control robots in the RoboCup Rescue League. We explore the *Steam Deck* for interacting and teleoperating the robot in the context of our Rescue Team *ALeRT*, where we control a quadruped robot Spot which is equipped with a Kinova light-weight manipulator. We show the ROS integration on the *Steam Deck* and discuss the usability of it as a controller.

Keywords: RoboCup Rescue · Teleoperation · ROS 2 · Handheld PC · UI

1 Introduction

Efficient and rapid deployment of robots by first responders in rescue scenarios is crucial for locating and rescuing victims faster. Teleoperation is rather important in Urban Search and Rescue (USAR) robots [8,20,22], along with autonomous robot operations [21]. There have been many advancements in both, USAR robots and their controllers [7]. However, portable controllers for these robots are often overlooked in the literature [14], especially the handheld PC-based controllers. Some of the earlier true portable robot controllers are discussed in [5]. While commercial robots like Boston Dynamics Spot provide a proprietary controller with advanced controls, they cannot be modified to work efficiently in custom scenarios or even allow controlling multiple robots.

In Robocup Rescue League (RRL), many teams make use of the Robot Operating System (ROS) [18,25] as a middleware for their robots. Usually, large computer cases at operator stations are used to launch and control their respective robots [3,13,26]. Each arena of the league has a dedicated operator booth where

E. Barros et al. (Eds.): RoboCup 2024, LNAI 15570, pp. 257–268, 2025.
https://doi.org/10.1007/978-3-031-85859-8_22

the operation system is set up. In a real rescue scenarios, such a comfort is not available, neither in terms of physical space nor time constraints. Especially, the setup time needs to be as minimal as possible [11,19].

Meanwhile, with Valve's introduction of the *Steam Deck* at a competitive price, a new market for gaming handheld PCs has emerged. These handheld devices integrate powerful computational hardware with a touchscreen, display and joystick. These features enable direct access to teleoperation, data visualization, behaviour and mission control [2], from the hands of a mobile operator.

With handheld controllers, the setup times for the operator stations can be minimised and the operator may also switch the operator stations on the go, if needed. First responders may even initiate individual robots in dangerous spaces during on-site missions [7,14], without any restriction on the number of operators and robots.

In this paper, we propose the *Steam Deck* as a ROS 2-based rescue robot controller, utilizing its capabilities as a powerful handheld PC. As a portable controller it is well suited for controlling robots in the Robocup Rescue League.

The rest of the paper is as follows. In Sect. 2, we review related work on portable controllers and user interfaces for USAR robots. Section 3 provides an overview of the Robocup Rescue League and its objectives. Section 4 shows the hardware and control software setup of the ALeRT Rescue Team. In Sect. 5, we introduce the system architecture and the features of the proposed ROS 2-based portable controller for Robocup Rescue Major League and its ROS integration. We briefly compare it with the current setup that comes with Boston Dynamic's Spot robot. Finally, Sect. 6 concludes the paper with a discussion on the significance of the proposed controller.

2 Related Work

Kim et al. [14] propose two different wireless remote controllers offering user friendly operating interface for rescue robots in fire sites. The controller efficiency was analyzed based on a questionnaire survey with a mobile rescue robot system. The use-case of the controller was discussed with firefighters and two applicable portable controllers were suggested: (1) a touch-based Ultra Mobile PC (UMPC), and (2) a joystick based UMPC.

Robotics Task Force (RTF) from the German Rescue Robotics Center (DRZ) used the Robotics Command Vehicle (RobLW), also developed by DRZ, to describe and reflect the missions, in which Unmanned Ground Vehicle (UGV) and Unmanned Aerial Vehicle (UAV) were used. To explore destroyed buildings, the internet independent Robotic Command Vehicle was used as the command centre [27]. For the teleoperation of UAV, both proprietary controller and a gamepad were used.

Idaho National Engineering and Environmental Laboratory (INEEL) developed a user interface to successfully perform teleoperation, safe mode, shared control, and full autonomy, while hierarchically increasing the level of autonomy [4]. Baker, M. et al. further simplified the INEEL system interface [1].

The surge of Augmented Reality (AR) and Virtual Reality (VR) technologies is undeniable. Krückel et al. utilized a VR headset to monitor the teleoperator's head orientation and showcase the present field of view for visually teleoperating UGVs [16]. Further, Luo et al. addressed Distance Perception during teleoperation of UGVs [17]. Walker et al. introduced two AR-based teleoperation interfaces [30]. Gams and Mudry proposed using inexpensive sensors in Wiimote, a gaming controller, for controlling robots instead of using expensive industrial sensors [10].

However, our focus in this paper remains on the *Steam Deck*, equipped with a touch display and joystick, which allows for a more intuitive and user-friendly interface for teleoperation of multiple ROS 2-based robots while being portable and robust in working with minimal operator station setup time.

3 Robocup Rescue League

Robocup Rescue League (RRL) provides an opportunity for international teams to develop and evaluate robot systems to help first responders in rescue scenarios [24]. The objectives of RRL are to create tasks for USAR robots and measure progress in USAR robotic systems. The main tasks in the league for robot evaluation are Mobility and Dexterity challenges [23]. Mobility challenges evaluate the mobility and maneuvering of the robot on different terrains which simulates collapsed buildings and structures, whereas the dexterity challenges evaluate the manipulation performance of the robot which simulates pick-and-place tasks to reach and support the victims. Each of these challenges is located in unique arenas, which try to mimic specific challenges that might occur during a rescue mission. From an enclosed operator booth, an operator controls the robot to perform the different challenges.

Each challenge consists of a 5 min setup phase where the operator station and robot is prepared for the challenge, a 20 min phase where tasks can be performed and a 5 min cleanup phase, where the teams have to leave the arena. Every minute counts as there are continuous rounds with many tasks and the arenas need to be switched in short times.

4 The Alert Spot Rescue Robot System

ALeRT is the RoboCup Rescue League Team affiliated with the MASCOR Institute at FH Aachen University of Applied Sciences. Our challenges encompass a wide spectrum, ranging from mobility, manipulation and exploration, autonomous planning and decision making as well as tasks that necessitate various sensors for perceiving the environment including magnetic sensors and thermal cameras.

For our setup, we utilize an *Intel NUC* mounted on Spot as the onboard PC which is connected via the GXP device by Boston Dynamics, which provides LAN connectivity to the Robot and adds terminals to mount and supply additional hardware with power.

Fig. 1. Full Setup of Team ALeRT Spot in the Rescue League.

An additional 5G and WiFi capable router is mounted on Spot to enable the platform to independently work without the need of a stationary communication system.

The hardware devices are connected either to the switch/router such as the LiDAR system, the Kinova Gen3, cameras, an *ESP32-C3* Micro-controller for the thermal camera and magnetic sensor, or directly to the onboard PC. Figure 1 shows the full setup of our Spot during a challenge of the Rescue League. Ubuntu 22.04 with ROS 2 Humble is installed on the onboard PC, and we have implemented and installed custom services and actions as well as high level agents for behaviour control and decision making. Starting our Software stack we connect the *Steam Deck* to the WiFi network of the router on Spot. Commands are given to the onboard PC over an SSH connection, for e.g., running a tmux session with different programs running in its tabs. Then we start an app as an UI icon, starting Rviz2 and RQT with plugins, setting up multiple buttons to start or stop modules as ROS 2 nodes on the onboard PC.

The Spot ROS 2 driver is always essential to operate Spot. This and other core modules e.g. for mapping, are started together with a button creating a tmux [29] session on the onboard PC. Every module of our stack is then automatically executed in a separate tmux tab which enables the operator to quickly gain an overview of all the running modules and allows them to restart modules in case of an unexpected failure. In addition, multiple users can establish a connection to the tmux session with a tmux capable device which allows the operator to focus on the task at hand by distributing some of the responsibilities to other users.

In the Rescue League, our aim is to adopt a semi-autonomous approach, employing multiple `golog++` agents for various tasks that can be supervised and controlled by an operator using the *Steam Deck*. `golog++` [15] is the action

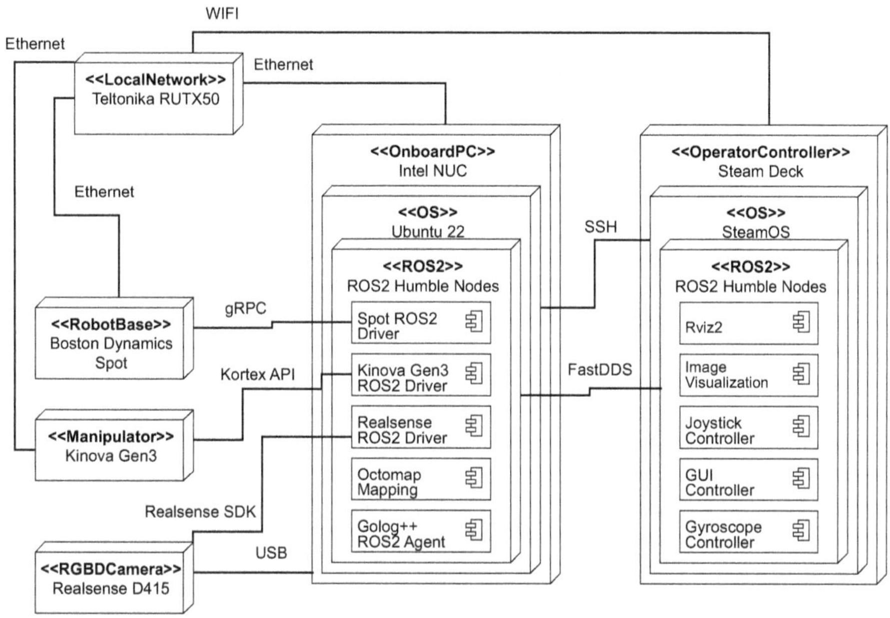

Fig. 2. Deployment Diagram of Team ALeRT's Robotic System with Boston Dynamics Spot and Kinova Gen3 Manipulator.

language which we use for high-level control. A comprehensive overview of the system's hardware components, their interconnections, and the software stack is shown in Fig. 2. The current setup of the operator's workstation is shown in Fig. 3. The workstation is equipped with a laptop, a joystick, and a touchpad. The laptop is used to command the robot, visualize camera streams, and monitor the robot's state. The *Steam Deck* offers greater flexibility compared to a laptop and provides more functionalities than the standard tablet from Boston Dynamics, especially through the ROS 2 interface. On our Github page there are a lot public repositories we are developing for Spot including a stable fork of the *spot_ros2* driver package.[1]

5 Steam Deck

Steam Deck [6] is a handheld gaming PC developed by Valve Corporation. It is a portable device with a 7-in. LCD touchscreen display, a joystick, and a touchpad. It is equipped with a custom AMD CPU, 16 GB of LPDDR5 RAM, and a 40 Wh battery. It runs on a custom version of SteamOS, which is based on Arch Linux. As ROS 2 packages are not precompiled for Arch Linux, we installed ROS 2 packages on the device using RoboStack [9], which consists precompiled ROS 2 packages for different operating systems. System architecture of *Steam*

[1] See https://github.com/RRL-ALeRT.

Fig. 3. Team ALeRT Workstation in RRL2023.

Deck is AMD64, which is same as that of the workstation, and same precompiled packages can be installed or built for both systems. *Steam Deck* is also equipped with a USB-C port, which can be used to connect to external peripherals like a monitor, a keyboard, and a mouse.

5.1 Controls

Figures. 4 and 5 show the button layouts of commands for various modes and actions to control Spot and Kinova Gen3, respectively.

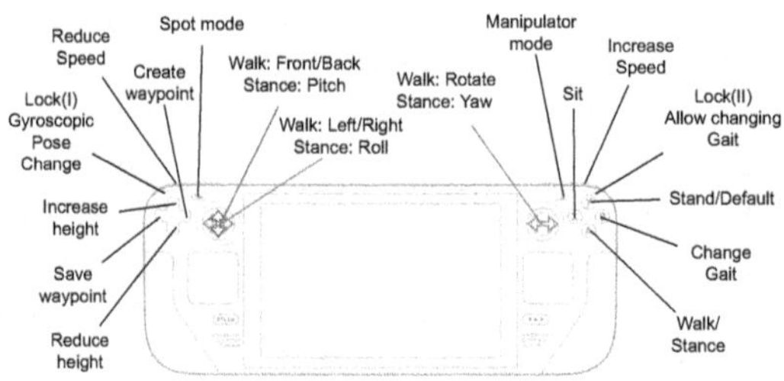

Fig. 4. *Steam Deck* button layout to control Spot.

For Spot, the controls include walking, speed adjustments, waypoint creation, pose changes, and gait changes as show in Fig. 4.

For the Kinova Gen3 manipulator, the controls include changing end effector orientation, Cartesian movements of end effector, gripper operations and calling manipulator home and retract positions. The controls can be extended to include other robots in the overall system. It can also be customised as per the requirements of the operator and the robot.

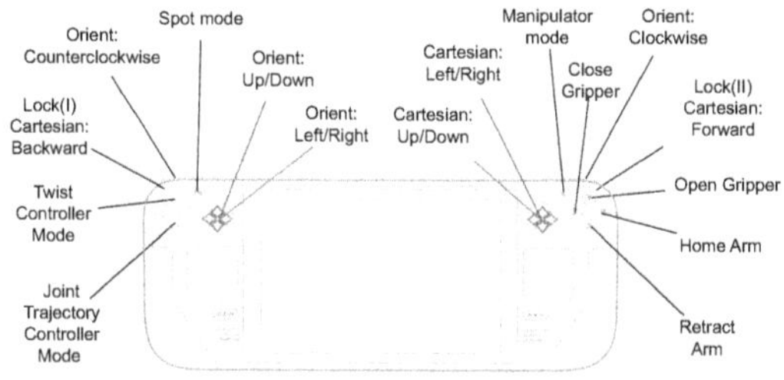

Fig. 5. *Steam Deck* button layout to control Gen3.

5.2 Features

Our robot controller system consists of a GUI along with physical buttons and joysticks of the *Steam Deck* to send commands to Spot or other robots. It runs on two desktop screens, with Rviz2 and RQT plugins on first desktop screen and the ALeRT Dashboard and a terminal on the second desktop screen. This system can be started and stopped with a UI toggle on the *Steam Deck* as shown in Fig. 6a. It was initially developed and tested on a PC and then transferred to the *Steam Deck*. It has the following features:

Visualisation of Camera Streams. The Visualization of camera streams is realized by a modified Image View RQT plugin. This modified plugin, by default, uses FFmpeg image transport plugin to visualise h264 compressed video streams, saving bandwidth and reducing latency. It also subscribes to corresponding bounding boxes, bounding polygons and keypoints to mark them in the same stream as shown in Fig. 6a. Tapping on a camera stream enlarges the camera window as shown in Fig. 6b. The markings are also visible in the enlarged view. Tapping again on the enlarged view makes it smaller again.

Spot RQT. The Spot RQT plugin deals with robot initialisation/stopping, features an emergency stop slider, allows initiating or stopping various RRL related programs and also shows Spot's status, as shown in Fig. 6c. This plugin is also used to initiate `golog++` agents to solve high-level missions, for e.g., the blocksworld problem [15] shown in Fig. 6a and the Frame Runner `golog++` agent, which allows autonomous navigation in the arena. The plugin also allows to start league specific programs like a 2-way audio communication with victims, hazmat detection, mapping, etc. using toggles.

RViz2. In the Rviz2 window, the current state of the robot is displayed using the robot model. An octomap [12], generated using the Realsense cameras, is also visualised in the same Rviz2 window. These are shown in Fig. 6a. An operator can also send navigation goals to the robot using Rviz2's 2D goal pose using a green arrow, as shown in Fig. 7a. The corresponding goal pose's green arrow is also shown in the Rviz2 window in Fig. 6c.

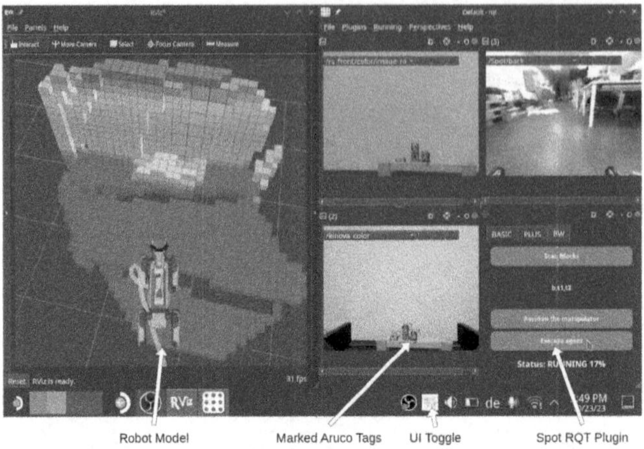

(a) UI toggle to start and stop the controller system.

(b) Enlarged Camera View.

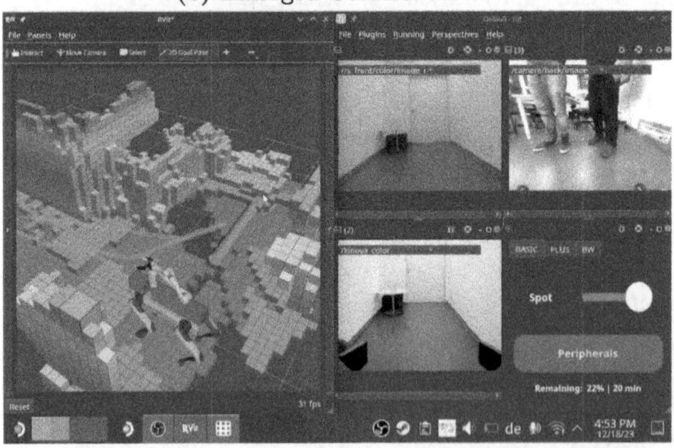

(c) *Steam Deck* Screenshot of Spot RQT Plugin. The green arrow indicates a navigation goal pose is being given to the robot.

Fig. 6. Visualizing Spot's sensors values on the *Steam Deck* (Color figure online)

Utilizing Steam Deck's Internal Sensors. *Steam Deck*'s accelerometer and gyroscope are used to generate a filtered IMU ROS2 message using *imu_complementary_filter* ROS2 package which is based on the work of Valenti et al. [28]. This message allows the operator to instantly control the robot's body pose by holding the left trigger on the *Steam Deck*, as shown in Fig. 7b.

Control Dashboard. On Desktop 2 of the *Steam Deck*, the ALeRT Dashboard RQT plugin along with a terminal runs as shown in Fig. 7c. The Dashboard can run and stop each program of the complete system selectively. If a program is running, its status is shown as *Running* and if it crashes, its status is shown as *Stopped*. Pressing the button beside the program name, corresponding program tab opens up in the terminal, and the operator can see the output of the program. Also, the output of each program is logged in the onboard PC, which can be reviewed.

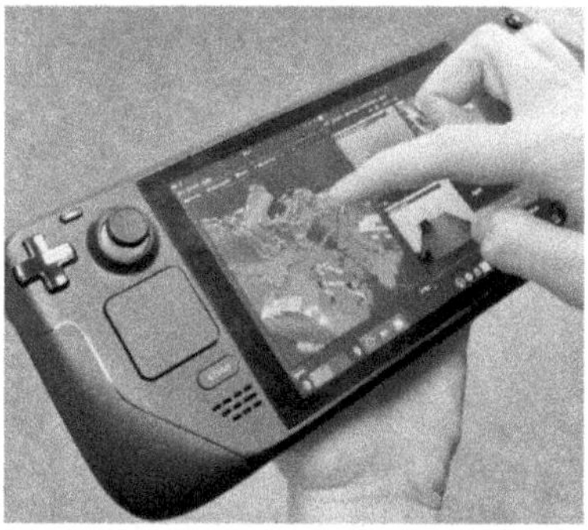

(a) Operator giving a goal pose to Spot using Rviz2's 2D Goal Pose.

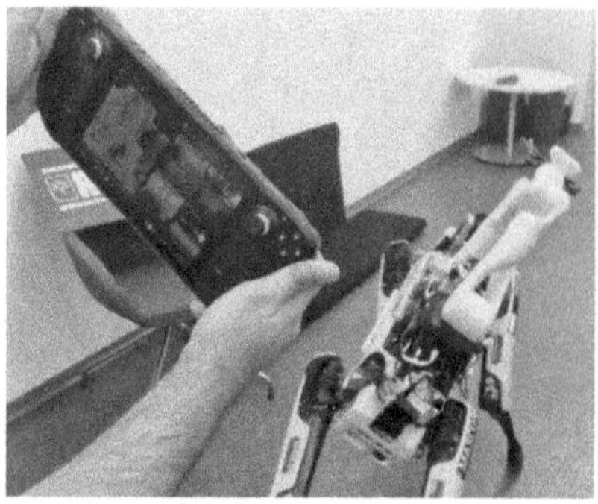

(b) Spot's Body Pose being changed using *Steam Deck*.

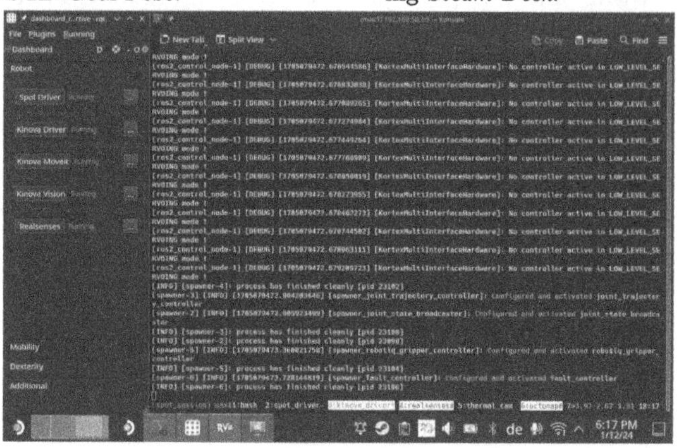

(c) ALeRT Dashboard RQT Plugin with a terminal for debugging.

Fig. 7. Controlling the Spot with the *Steam Deck*

5.3 Comparison Against Current Setup for RoboCup Rescue League

The proposed *Steam Deck* controller system has the following pros and cons compared to the current setup:

Pros:

1. Reduced setup time, facilitating quicker deployment.
2. Enhanced operator flexibility in controlling robots.
3. Simplified switching of operator booths between rounds.

Cons:

1. Increased difficulty in debugging processes.
2. Constraints imposed by limited display size.

However, the cons can be 100% mitigated by connecting the deck to external peripherals like a monitor, keyboard, and mouse, thereby expanding its functionality and overcoming these limitations.

6 Conclusion

In rescue scenarios, the use of a portable controller like *Steam Deck* can be vital for quick robot deployment and efficiently managing increasing number of operators and robots. For RRL, the features of the proposed controller system can make the operator's job easier and more efficient. We have been using *Steam Deck* as a controller for Spot and the Gen3 manipulator in our day-to-day development and testing and the setup times have been reduced drastically.

In the future, we plan to test the proposed system in RRL 2024. We also plan to benchmark the usage with different users having technical and non-technical backgrounds. Further, we would like to extend the controller to include other robots like a UAV in the overall system.

References

1. Baker, M., Casey, R., Keyes, B., Yanco, H.A.: Improved interfaces for human-robot interaction in urban search and rescue. In: 2004 IEEE International Conference on Systems, Man and Cybernetics (IEEE Cat. No. 04CH37583), vol. 3, pp. 2960–2965. IEEE (2004)
2. Birk, A., Schwertfeger, S., Pathak, K.: A networking framework for teleoperation in safety, security, and rescue robotics. IEEE Wirel. Commun. **16**(1), 6–13 (2009)
3. Blattler, A., et al.: 2022 TDP iRAP robot RoboCup rescue robot (2022). https://tdp.robocup.org/tdp/2022-tdp-irap-robot-robocuprescue-robot. Accessed 24 June 2024

4. Bruemmer, D.J., Dudenhoeffer, D.D., Marble, J.L.: Dynamic-autonomy for urban search and rescue. In: Smart, W.D., Balch, T.R., Yanco, H.A. (eds.) AAAI Mobile Robot Competition 2002, Papers from the AAAI Workshop, Edmonton, Alberta, Canada, 28 July–1 August 2002. AAAI Technical report, vol. WS-02-18, pp. 33–37. AAAI Press (2002)
5. Casper, J., Murphy, R.R.: Human-robot interactions during the robot-assisted urban search and rescue response at the world trade center. IEEE Trans. Syst. Man Cybern. Part B (Cybern.) **33**(3), 367–385 (2003)
6. Deck, V.S., Dempsey, P.: The Teardown: the gaming specialist has translated its open-hardware platform into a console. Eng. Technol. **17**(4), 1–5 (2022)
7. Delmerico, J., et al.: The current state and future outlook of rescue robotics. J. Field Robot. **36**(7), 1171–1191 (2019)
8. Doroftei, D., Matos, A., de Cubber, G.: Designing search and rescue robots towards realistic user requirements. Appl. Mech. Mater. **658**, 612–617 (2014)
9. Fischer, T., Vollprecht, W., Traversaro, S., Yen, S., Herrero, C., Milford, M.: A RoboStack tutorial: using the robot operating system alongside the Conda and Jupyter data science ecosystems. IEEE Robot. Autom. Mag. **29**(2), 65–74 (2021)
10. Gams, A., Mudry, P.A.: Gaming controllers for research robots: controlling a humanoid robot using a WIIMOTE. In: Proceedings of the 17th International Electrotechnical and Computer Science Conference (ERK08), pp. 191–194 (2008)
11. Habib, M.K., Bauoptdoitn, Y.: Rescue and hazardous intervention robotics. Industr. Robot: Int. J. **39**(5) (2012)
12. Hornung, A., Wurm, K.M., Bennewitz, M., Stachniss, C., Burgard, W.: OctoMap: an efficient probabilistic 3D mapping framework based on octrees. Auton. Robot. **34**, 189–206 (2013)
13. Khawkhom, A., et al.: 2022 TDP BART lab rescue robotics RoboCupRescue robot (2022). https://tdp.robocup.org/tdp/2022-tdp-bart-lab-rescue-robotics-robocuprescue-robot. Accessed 24 June 2024
14. Kim, Y.D., Kang, J.H., Sun, D.H., Moon, J.I., Ryuh, Y.S., An, J.: Design and implementation of user friendly remote controllers for rescue robots in fire sites. In: Proceedings of SICE Annual Conference 2010, pp. 875–880. IEEE (2010)
15. Kirsch, M., Pawar, S., Ferrein, A., Schiffer, S.: GOLOG++ hits the (right) spot: interfacing GOLOG with a quadruped rescue robot for high-level missions. In: Proceedings of the 16th International Conference on Agents and Artificial Intelligence: ICAART, vol. 3, pp. 1052–1059. INSTICC, SciTePress (2024)
16. Krückel, K., Nolden, F., Ferrein, A., Scholl, I.: Intuitive visual teleoperation for UGVs using free-look augmented reality displays. In: 2015 IEEE International Conference on Robotics and Automation (ICRA), pp. 4412–4417. IEEE (2015)
17. Luo, Y., Wang, J., Shi, R., Liang, H.N., Luo, S.: In-device feedback in immersive head-mounted displays for distance perception during teleoperation of unmanned ground vehicles. IEEE Trans. Haptics **15**(1), 79–84 (2021)
18. Macenski, S., Foote, T., Gerkey, B., Lalancette, C., Woodall, W.: Robot operating system 2: design, architecture, and uses in the wild. Sci. Robot. **7**(66), eabm6074 (2022)
19. Matsuno, F., Tadokoro, S.: Rescue robots and systems in Japan. In: 2004 IEEE International Conference on Robotics and Biomimetics, pp. 12–20. IEEE (2004)
20. Murphy, R.R.: Human-robot interaction in rescue robotics. IEEE Trans. Syst. Man Cybern. Part C (Appl. Rev.) **34**(2), 138–153 (2004)
21. Murphy, R.R.: Trial by fire [rescue robots]. IEEE Robot. Autom. Mag. **11**(3), 50–61 (2004)

22. Ohno, K.: Telerobotics for rescue robots. Nippon Robotto Gakkai-Shi **30**(6), 571–573 (2012)
23. Pellenz, J., Dillenberger, D., Steinbauer, G.: Novel rule set for the RoboCup rescue robot league. In: 2016 IEEE International Symposium on Safety, Security, and Rescue Robotics (SSRR), pp. 282–283. IEEE (2016)
24. Pellenz, J., Jacoff, A., Kimura, T., Mihankhah, E., Sheh, R., Suthakorn, J.: RoboCup rescue robot league. In: RoboCup 2014: Robot World Cup XVIII 18, pp. 673–685. Springer (2015)
25. Quigley, M., et al.: ROS: an open-source robot operating system. In: ICRA Workshop on Open Source Software, Kobe, Japan, vol. 3, p. 5 (2009)
26. Ruffini, A., Schmidt, A., Schnaubelt, M.: 2022 TDP hector darmstadt RoboCupRescue robot (2022). https://tdp.robocup.org/tdp/2022-tdp-hector-darmstadt-robocuprescue-robot. Accessed 24 June 2024
27. Surmann, H., et al.: Lessons from robot-assisted disaster response deployments by the German rescue robotics center task force. J. Field Robot. (2023)
28. Valenti, R.G., Dryanovski, I., Xiao, J.: Keeping a good attitude: a quaternion-based orientation filter for IMUs and MARGs. Sensors **15**(8), 19302–19330 (2015)
29. Victor Quinn, J.: Getting Started with Tmux. Packt Publishing Ltd. (2014)
30. Walker, M.E., Hedayati, H., Szafir, D.: Robot teleoperation with augmented reality virtual surrogates. In: 2019 14th ACM/IEEE International Conference on Human-Robot Interaction (HRI), pp. 202–210. IEEE (2019)

Planning Robot Placement for Object Grasping

Manish Saini[1(✉)], Melvin Paul Jacob[1], Minh Nguyen[2], and Nico Hochgeschwender[2]

[1] Hochschule Bonn-Rhein-Sieg, Sankt Augustin, Germany
{manish.saini,melvin.paul}@smail.inf.h-brs.de
[2] University of Bremen, Bremen, Germany
{minh.nguyen,nico.hochgeschwender}@uni-bremen.de

Abstract. When performing manipulation-based activities such as picking objects, a mobile robot needs to position its base at a location that supports successful execution. To address this problem, prominent approaches typically rely on grasp poses being provided by a planner for a target object, which are then analysed to identify the best robot placements for achieving each grasp pose. In this paper, we propose instead to first find robot placements that would not result in collision with the environment and from where picking up the object is feasible, then evaluate them to find the best placement candidate. Our approach takes into account the robot's reachability, as well as RGB-D images and occupancy grid maps of the environment for identifying suitable robot poses. The proposed algorithm is embedded in a service robot application, in which a person points to select the target object for grasping. We evaluate our approach with a series of grasping experiments, against an existing baseline implementation that commands the robot to a fixed navigation goal. The experimental results demonstrate the validity of our approach, which can serve as a baseline for developing and evaluating more advanced techniques in the future.

Keywords: Robot Placement · Motion Planning

1 Introduction

A common task for mobile robots in domestic and household scenarios is object retrieval, e.g. fetching a cup from a dining table or kitchen counter. Solutions for this task typically involve the robot navigating to a predetermined location and then initiating the picking-up behaviour. Such approaches often do not take into account factors of the environment or physical limitations of the robot, which can result in the robot trying to grasp the object from unfavourable positions, for instance, a far table edge rather than one that is close to the object. Such

This work was supported by the Bonn-Aachen International Center for Information Technology (b-it).

E. Barros et al. (Eds.): RoboCup 2024, LNAI 15570, pp. 269–280, 2025.
https://doi.org/10.1007/978-3-031-85859-8_23

sub-optimal placements can increase the difficulty of the manipulation task, increasing the risk of failure or even making the task infeasible, e.g. when the target object cannot be reached without the robot colliding with the table or with other objects.

To overcome these challenges, we propose in this paper a robot placement planning approach that identifies locations from where a mobile robot can grasp an object more easily. Our approach takes into account occupancy grid maps and RGB-D data to check whether the placement candidates can be navigated to or may be at risk of collision during the manipulation motion. The candidates are then evaluated using a criterion that characterizes the difficulty of the overall navigation and manipulation motion, and the best candidate is selected for carrying out the pickup behaviour. The planning algorithm is embedded in a service robot application, in which a human operator chooses the target object using hand gestures. We evaluate our approach with a series of grasping experiments using the Toyota Human Support Robot (HSR) and compare it against a baseline implementation which grasps from a predefined navigation goal. In summary, our contributions in this paper are two-fold:

- We developed a base placement planning algorithm distinct from prominent approaches addressing the same problem. Our evaluation on a real robot validates the effectiveness of our approach, which can serve as a baseline for developing and evaluating more advanced methods in the future.
- We integrated the proposed planning approach in a Human-Robot Interaction (HRI) scenario for addressing RoboCup tasks which require the robot to retrieve an object from an open environment [5].

The remainder of this article is organized as follows. Related studies will be discussed in the next section. Section 3 describes in detail our robot placement planning algorithm and how we carry out the pickup behaviour using the generated placement candidates. Section 4 describes our experimental setup and evaluates the results of our grasping experiments. Finally, Sect. 5 includes concluding remarks and discusses possible extensions to our approach in the future.

2 Related Work

The traditional approach to improve object grasping performance is grasp planning, which aims to find placement and configuration of end effectors that can best satisfy some criteria relevant to the grasping task [1,10,14]. Grasp planning can be broadly categorized into analytical [14] and data-driven [1,10] methods, with the former typically analysing the target object's shape and/or hand-object contact to evaluate different properties of grasp candidates, such as stability or task compatibility. Empirical or data-driven methods [1,10], on another hand, sample and evaluate grasp candidates based on some existing grasp experience, either characterized by a heuristic or generated in simulation or on a real robot.

Another approach for improving the performance of the robot's grasping behaviour is to consider environmental features during motion planning or control of the robot arm [3]. This can be done in combination with Dynamic Movement Primitives (DMP), in which complex trajectories, e.g. motion of a robot manipulator, are modelled using a system of second-order linear Ordinary Differential Equation (ODE). A learnable forcing term is then introduced to adapt these trajectories to some goal-oriented behaviours using well-defined attractor dynamics [7]. Data from proximity sensors can then be incorporated into the motion plan, e.g. for obstacle avoidance [3], by introducing a coupling term to the DMP formulation. This coupling term can either be derived analytically via computation of the potential field [4,6,16] or learned from sensory data [15].

To address the problem of finding an optimal base placement for grasping an object, several approaches utilize inverse reachability maps (IRM) introduced in [17], which invert a representation of the robot's workspace using its kinematics for a given grasp candidate. The resulting robot placements are then evaluated using some quality metric, typically to minimize the chance of self-collision or singularity. Related research has improved upon various aspects of IRM, including quality metrics for possible robot placements [21] and representations of the robot workspace [9,21]. Burget and Bennewitz [2] extend the approach with constraints specific to humanoid robots to find optimal foot placements for a grasp candidate. Reister et al. [13] apply IRM to the problem of finding time-efficient base placements for picking and placing several objects consecutively, where the placements are evaluated by a combination of manipulation and navigation costs, and reachability inversion is used for the manipulation portion of the cost function. Paus et al. [12] combine IRM with coverage path planning to minimize the number of base repositioning needed to achieve optimal coverage with the manipulator. IRM is also used as priors in machine learning approaches, e.g. for learning approximations of the robot's inverse reachability [18] or training motion models [8]. Aside from IRM-based approaches, Yamazaki et al. [20] evaluate different "motions" for a target end-effector pose by analysing the error distributions associated with carrying out the motion, which consists of moving the base along a trajectory and the arm to a fixed joint configuration. These approaches all rely on the candidate grasp pose being available, e.g. from a grasp planner, which differs from our approach of finding base placements before planning the grasp motion.

3 Approach

Our approach to finding base placements for picking up objects is embedded in a service robot application, illustrated in Fig. 1b). Here, a human operator chooses the target object using a pointing gesture, then our planning algorithm finds a base placement based on the estimated pose of the object, and finally, the according navigation and manipulation motions are planned and executed using existing solutions available on the robot.

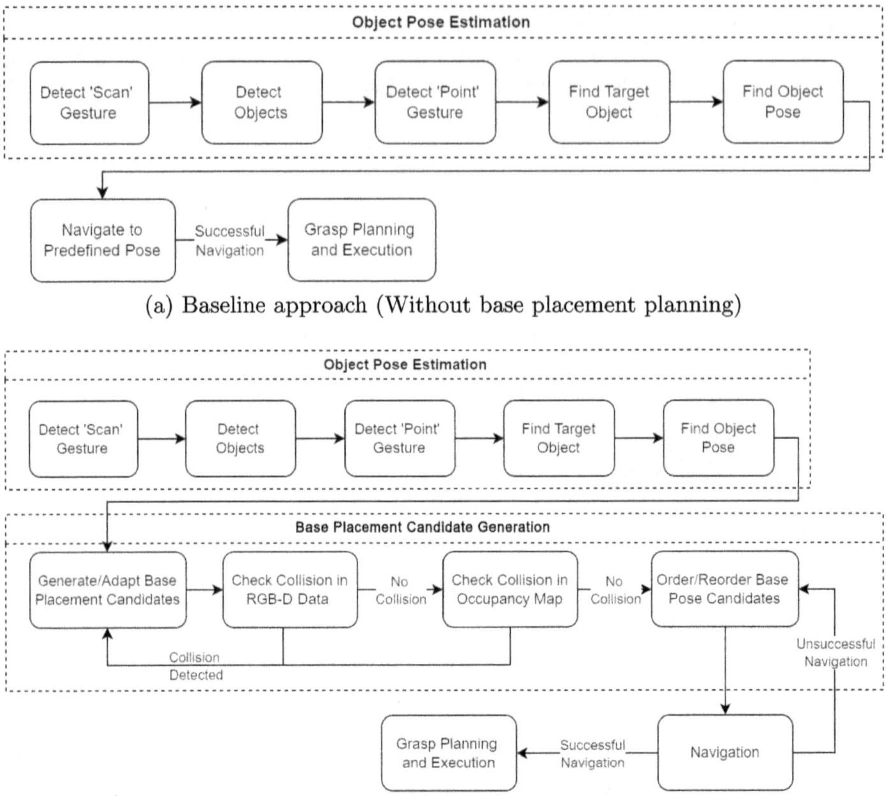

(b) Proposed approach (With base placement planning)

Fig. 1. Execution Flow: The figures describe the flow of the algorithm in the baseline and proposed approaches. The baseline approach lacks base placement planning and instead always goes to a predefined pose defined before initiating pickup. While the proposed approach generates base placement candidates (BPCs) based on the RGB-D data and occupancy grid map before initiating pickup.

3.1 Object Pose Estimation

The object of interest is specified to the robot using gestures. For gesture recognition, we adapt and train an existing MLP architecture[1] to classify pixel values of hand landmarks detected using the MediaPipe library[2] as either *Scan*, *Point*, or *Stop*. Initially, the component waits for a *Scan* gesture from the operator, after which it detects objects in the scene. Next, when the *Point* gesture is recognized, a line is fitted to the detected landmarks of the pointing finger and extends from the fingertip until intersecting either the bounding box of a detected object or the image boundary. The object whose bounding box is intersected is then the target object, and its position in the map frame is estimated from the corresponding depth data in the RGB-D image using the Open3D library [22].

[1] https://github.com/Kazuhito00/hand-gesture-recognition-using-mediapipe.
[2] https://developers.google.com/mediapipe/solutions/vision/hand_landmarker.

3.2 Base Placement Candidate (BPC) Generation

Having obtained the object position in the map frame ${}^{m}\mathbf{p}_{o}$, we generate a set of potential base placements from where the pickup behaviour can be executed and rank them using a metric characterizing the difficulty of carrying out the corresponding navigation and manipulation motions. Algorithm 1 shows the pseudocode for our base placement planning component. For the remainder of this paper, notations of geometric relations will follow the ${}^{originframe}relation_{targetframe}$ convention, where poses are denoted with $\mathbf{q}$, positions $\mathbf{p}$, and orientations $\mathbf{o}$.

Algorithm 1: Robot placement planning algorithm.

Param: Radius of robot footprint r_r, robot height h_r
Param: Minimum and maximum reach of robot d_{min}, d_{max}
Param: Angle increment for generating radial vectors θ
Input: Object position in map frame ${}^{m}\mathbf{p}_{o}$
Input: Detected object width and height w_o, h_o
Input: RGB-D image of the scene $\mathcal{I}$
Input: Occupancy grid map $\mathcal{G}$
Output: Set of base placement candidates $\mathcal{S}$

Set of robot placement candidates: $\mathcal{S} \leftarrow \emptyset$
Generate set of radial unit vectors: ${}^{m}\mathbf{p}_{o}, \theta \mapsto \mathcal{V}$
foreach $\hat{\mathbf{v}}_i \in \mathcal{V}$ **do**
    Initial robot position candidate w.r.t. object: ${}^{o}\mathbf{p}_{ri} \leftarrow d_{min}\hat{\mathbf{v}}_i$
    while $\|{}^{o}\mathbf{p}_{ri}\| < d_{max}$ **do**
        if $\neg$ `HasCollisionRisk`(${}^{o}\mathbf{p}_{ri}$, r_r, h_r, w_o, h_o, $\mathcal{I}$, $\mathcal{G}$) **then**
            Pose candidate: ${}^{o}\mathbf{q}_{ri} \leftarrow \{{}^{o}\mathbf{p}_{ri}, {}^{o}\mathbf{o}_{r}\}$, s.t. robot points in $-\hat{\mathbf{v}}_i$
            `/* Transform to map frame and add to set of candidates */`
            $\mathcal{S} \leftarrow \mathcal{S} + \{{}^{m}\mathbf{q}_{ri}\}$
            `break()`
        end
        `/* Risk of collision detected, try position further away */`
        ${}^{o}\mathbf{p}_{ri} \leftarrow (\|{}^{o}\mathbf{p}_{ri}\| + r_r)\hat{\mathbf{v}}_{\mathrm{i}}$
    end
end
return $\mathcal{S}$

Generating Robot Placement Candidates. We first generate BPCs, one along each of radial unit vectors $\mathcal{V}$ spaced at equal angular intervals θ[3], originating from the projected object's position and pointing outward. Along each $\hat{\mathbf{v}}_i \in \mathcal{V}$, a BPC ${}^{o}\mathbf{q}_{ri}$ (w.r.t. the object) is generated within a predefined distance range $d_{min} \leq \|{}^{o}\mathbf{p}_{ri}\| \leq d_{max}$ and points towards the object, where the distance range corresponds to the robot's reachable workspace. This is done by initializing the position candidate to be at distance d_{min} (minimum safe distance for grasping) from the object and increasing the distance by r_r until d_{max} (max

---

[3] This angle can be calculated based on the robot's reach and footprint radius. For example, the angle to achieve a chord length of $2r_r$ on a circle of radius d_{min} is $\theta = 2\arcsin\frac{r_r}{2d_{min}}$.

reach of the robot) if the risk of collision during pickup behaviour is detected. Repeating this process for each of the radial vectors, we acquire a set of BPCs $\mathcal{S}$.

Checking for Risk of Collision. For each BPC ${}^{o}\mathbf{p}_{ri}$, we process the RGB-D image used for object detection to check if there is a risk of collision when the robot reaches the object (`HasCollisionRisk` in Algorithm 1). This is done by filtering the point cloud to select only points in the space that the robot may occupy during the pickup behaviour, and eliminate the candidate if the number of points found is higher than a fixed threshold k_{obs}. To this end, we perform the check twice, once for the robot body at the base placement pose and once for the manipulator during the reaching motion. The checked regions are visualized as cuboids in Fig. 2, where valid base placement candidates are coloured green, and pruned ones red. The larger cuboids are of size $2r_r \times 2r_r \times h_r$, corresponding to the robot's dimensions. Each smaller cuboid extends from the object position to the position candidate at the object's height, and has dimensions corresponding to the object's detected width and height w_o, h_o.

In addition to RGB-D data, we also process the occupancy grid map provided by the robot to check if placing the robot at ${}^{o}\mathbf{p}_{ri}$ may result in a collision. This is done by transforming a circle of radius r_r centred at ${}^{o}\mathbf{p}_{ri}$ to the grid coordinates of the occupancy map and check if the corresponding cells are occupied. In our experiments, we used only the static occupancy grid map to check for collision, but this step can also be performed on dynamic occupancy maps, if available, to check for dynamic obstacles.

If either of the above checks detects a risk of collision, that BPC is removed from consideration. Otherwise, the corresponding pose candidate at position ${}^{o}\mathbf{p}_{ri}$ and pointing towards the object, ${}^{o}\mathbf{q}_{ri}$, is added to the set of candidates $\mathcal{S}$.

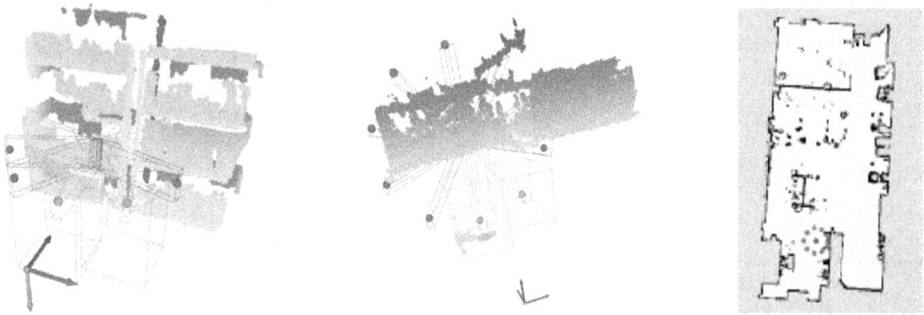

(a) 3D Front View (b) 3D Top View (c) Occupancy Grid Map View

Fig. 2. Checking robot placement candidates for risk of collision during the pickup behaviour using RGB-D data and occupancy grid map. `RGB-D data`: The regions checked for obstacles are visualized by cuboids. Candidates and corresponding cuboids that may result in the collision are coloured red. The larger cuboids correspond to the robot's dimensions. Each smaller cuboid extends from the object position to the position candidate at the object's height, and has dimensions corresponding to the object's detected width and height w_o, h_o. `Occupancy Grid Map`: Red dots represent the candidates checked for collision, while the green dot represents the robot's current position. (Color figure online)

3.3 Navigation and Object Grasping

Algorithm 2 outlines how we carry out the object pickup using the robot placement candidates provided by Algorithm 1. The candidates are evaluated based on the combined distance from the robot's current position to the pose candidate and the distance from the pose candidate to the object, with the assumption that a longer distance would result in a more challenging grasp and closure distance than a limit would result in a collision. The `MotionCost` function in Algorithm 2 performs this evaluation to determine the best candidate. The resulting best candidate will be removed from $\mathcal{S}$ and used as the navigation goal for the robot to carry out the corresponding motions to pick up the object. If navigation fails, the remaining candidates will be reevaluated based on the current robot pose, and a new best candidate will be chosen for executing the pickup behaviour. This process is repeated until either the robot navigates successfully and begins the grasping motion, or if no candidate is left in $\mathcal{S}$. Planning and execution of the navigation motion is done using a modified version of the `move_base` ROS package[4] provided by Toyota. The subsequent manipulation motion is planned and executed using our existing solution previously described in [11].

4 Experimental Results and Evaluation

To evaluate our approach, we carry out a set of grasping experiments using our robot placement planning algorithm and compare the results to a baseline grasp planning approach, in which the robot navigates to a predefined location and initiates the same object pickup behaviour. Our experiments are carried out using a Human Support Robot (HSR) [19] from Toyota, which can be seen in Fig. 3 along with our experimental setup. The remainder of this section will describe this setup and discuss the experimental results in detail.

Algorithm 2: Object pickup based on planned robot placements.

Input: Object position in map frame ${}^{m}\mathbf{p}_o$
Input: Set of base placement candidates $\mathcal{S}$
while $\mathcal{S} \neq \emptyset$ **do**
  Read robot current pose ${}^{m}\mathbf{q}_r^c$
  Best candidate: ${}^{m}\mathbf{q}_r^* \leftarrow \arg\min_{{}^{m}\mathbf{q}_r}$ `MotionCost(`${}^{m}\mathbf{q}_r$, ${}^{m}\mathbf{p}_o$, ${}^{m}\mathbf{q}_r^c$`)` $\forall\, {}^{m}\mathbf{q}_r \in \mathcal{S}$
  $\mathcal{S} \leftarrow \mathcal{S} - \{{}^{m}\mathbf{q}_r^*\}$
  Navigation result: $r_{nav} \leftarrow$ `Navigate(`${}^{m}\mathbf{q}_r^*$`)`
  if $r_{nav} = false$ **then** `continue();`
  Pickup result: $r_{pickup} \leftarrow$ `Pickup(`${}^{m}\mathbf{p}_o$`)`
  return r_{pickup}
end
1. how much distance from robot to propose pose 2. distance between proposed location and object

[4] https://wiki.ros.org/move_base.

4.1 Experimental Setup and Procedure

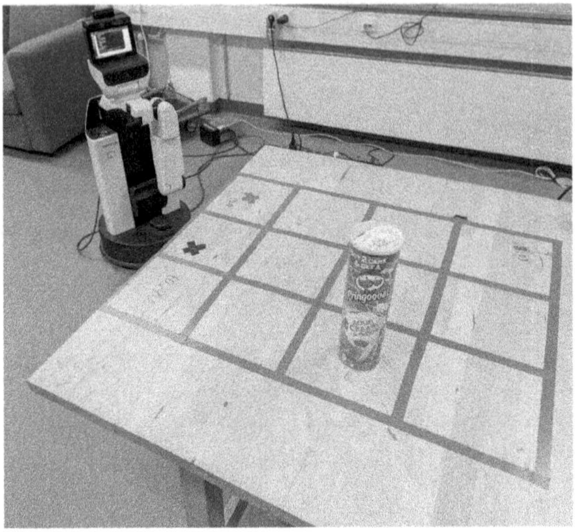

Fig. 3. Experimental Setup

In our experiments, the objects are placed on a standard dining table of dimensions (H × W × L) 74 × 80 × 180 cm. To control for different object placements on the table surface, we tape a 3-by-4 grid on the table, whose cells are squares of dimensions 20 × 20 cm, as shown in Fig. 3. Here, the long sides of the grid are 20 cm away from the long edges of the table, and one short side of the grid aligns with one short edge of the table. We define a 2D discrete coordinate system for referring to specific grid cells, in which a cell can be denoted (x, y) s.t. $x \in [0, 2]$ and $y \in [0, 3]$ are integers. In Fig. 3, cell $(0, 0)$ is marked with a red "x", and the x-axis of the coordinate system aligns with the table's short edge.

For each approach, we perform five grasps of the same object for each grid cell, i.e. 120 grasp attempts in total. A grasp is considered successful if the object remains in the gripper after the pickup behaviour, i.e. after the manipulator returns to its recovery configuration. If the robot is unable to hold on to the object, or if collision with the table occurs, the attempt is considered a failure. For the proposed robot placement planning approach, a human operator presents a "Scan" gesture to the robot to initiate object detection, then points to select the target object. The robot then plans the robot placement poses and carry out the corresponding motions as described in Sect. 3. For the baseline approach, the robot detects and estimates the object's pose, navigates to a predefined location close to the short edge of the table, and initiates the pickup behaviour.

4.2 Results and Discussion

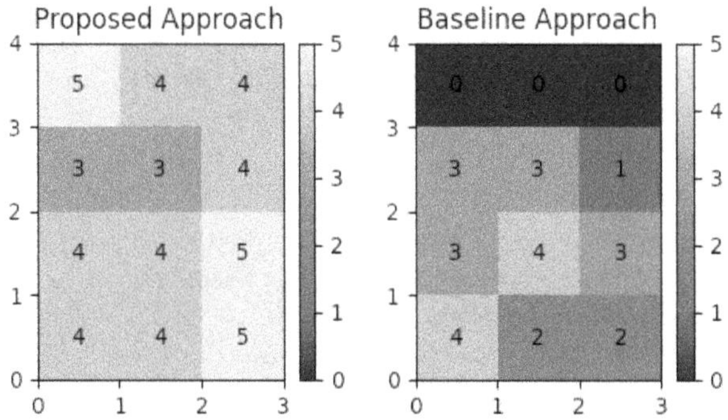

Fig. 4. Heatmap of approach's success out of 5 trials in each grid, corresponding to the experimental setup described in Sect. 4.1. With the baseline approach, the robot can not grasp from the table's longer edges and is unable to grasp when an object is placed far away. The proposed algorithm plans base placements according to the object's pose estimation, resulting in consistent grasp performance for all grid cells.

Table 1. Number of successful and failed attempts during the grasping experiments.

Cell	Proposed Approach		Baseline Approach	
	Success	Failure	Success	Failure
(0, 0)	4	1	4	1
(1, 0)	4	1	2	3
(2, 0)	5	0	2	3
(0, 1)	4	1	2	3
(1, 1)	4	1	4	1
(2, 1)	5	0	3	2
(0, 2)	3	2	3	2
(1, 2)	3	2	3	2
(2, 2)	4	1	1	4
(0, 3)	5	0	0	5
(1, 3)	4	1	0	5
(2, 3)	4	1	0	5

The results of our grasping experiments are shown in Table 1 and the heatmap of same is given in Fig. 4. Overall, the proposed approach had a success rate of 81.7% compared to 40% of the baseline approach. Attempts using the baseline approach are more likely to fail when the object is placed in the grids far from the short edge of the table, i.e. far from the predefined navigation goal. When placed on the last 2 rows (cells $(x, 2)$ and $(x, 3)$), the object is near the limit of the robot's reach, resulting in the robot frequently colliding with the table. In contrast, the proposed approach allows the robot to navigate to other edges of the table before grasping, which makes picking up the object in the last row possible and even at a high success rate.

The experiments described thus far validate the soundness of the proposed robot placement planning algorithm and show how it enables a more flexible means to approach picking up objects, compared to the existing baseline approach. However, they have not clearly shown the benefit of utilizing both RGB-D data and occupancy grid maps in the planning process. This motivates additional experiments, e.g. grasping from a cluster of objects or with obstacles, to show whether the proposed approach can plan robot placements that reduce the risk of collision.

5 Conclusion and Future Work

In this paper, we present an approach to finding a robot placement from where it can pick up an object. Approaches addressing the same problem typically assume an end-effector pose is provided by some grasp planner, then find and evaluate robot placements based on this grasp pose. Instead, we propose to directly find valid robot placement candidates using the estimated object position, RGB-D data and occupancy grid maps, and evaluate them using a simple metric. We evaluate our approach with a series of grasp experiments on the Toyota HSR, in which we compare the approach to an existing baseline implementation that sends the robot to a fixed location before initiating the pickup behaviour. The results validate the effectiveness of our approach in addressing the base placement problem for mobile manipulation and can serve as a baseline for developing and evaluating more advanced methods in the future. Furthermore, the algorithm is embedded in a Human-Robot Interaction (HRI) pipeline, in which a human operator chooses the target object using hand gestures. The pipeline allows an alternative HRI method, complementing standard speech recognition, for Robocup tasks that involve object retrieval in open environments.

As future work, several aspects of the proposed planning algorithm can be extended. First, we used a simple distance range in our approach to represent the robot's reachability, but more elegant methods, such as reachability maps, can be employed that consider the robot's full kinematics. Furthermore, while the cuboid between the object and a pose candidate serves as a simple approximation of the space occupied by the robot's arm while reaching for the object, it does not reflect the actual trajectory that the arm will follow in practice. A more advanced approach may check for obstacles along the planned end-effector trajectory, e.g. to avoid collision in case the trajectory would go under the table surface. Finally, instead of just combining the distance from the pose candidate to the object and the robot's current pose, better metrics can be employed to evaluate the candidates that take into account the potential navigation and manipulation motions that the robot needs to execute, such as one proposed by Yamazaki et al. [20].

References

1. Bohg, J., Morales, A., Asfour, T., Kragic, D.: Data-driven grasp synthesis—a survey. IEEE Trans. Robot. **30**(2), 289–309 (2014)
2. Burget, F., Bennewitz, M.: Stance selection for humanoid grasping tasks by inverse reachability maps. In: 2015 IEEE International Conference on Robotics and Automation (ICRA), pp. 5669–5674 (2015)
3. Frank, F., Paraschos, A., Van Der Smagt, P., Cseke, B.: Constrained probabilistic movement primitives for robot trajectory adaptation. IEEE Trans. Robot. **38**(4), 2276–2294 (2022)
4. Ginesi, M., Meli, D., Calanca, A., Dall'Alba, D., Sansonetto, N., Fiorini, P.: Dynamic movement primitives: volumetric obstacle avoidance. In: 2019 19th International Conference on Advanced Robotics, ICAR, pp. 234–239 (2019)
5. Hart, J., et al.: Robocup@home 2024: rules and regulations (2024)
6. Hoffmann, H., Pastor, P., Park, D.H., Schaal, S.: Biologically-inspired dynamical systems for movement generation: automatic real-time goal adaptation and obstacle avoidance. In: 2009 IEEE International Conference on Robotics and Automation, pp. 2587–2592 (2009)
7. Ijspeert, A.J., Nakanishi, J., Hoffmann, H., Pastor, P., Schaal, S.: Dynamical movement primitives: learning attractor models for motor behaviors. Neural Comput. **25**(2), 328–373 (2013)
8. Jauhri, S., Peters, J., Chalvatzaki, G.: Robot learning of mobile manipulation with reachability behavior priors **7**(3), 8399–8406 (2022)
9. Dong, J., Trinkle, J.C.: Orientation-based reachability map for robot base placement. In: 2015 IEEE/RSJ International Conference on Intelligent Robots and Systems (IROS), pp. 1488–1493 (2015)
10. Kleeberger, K., Bormann, R., Kraus, W., Huber, M.F.: A survey on learning-based robotic grasping. Curr. Robot. Rep. **1**(4), 239–249 (2020)
11. Mitrevski, A., Padalkar, A., Nguyen, M., Plöger, P.G.: "Lucy, take the noodle box!": Domestic object manipulation using movement primitives and whole body motion. In: RoboCup 2019: Robot World Cup XXIII, pp. 189–200 (2019)
12. Paus, F., Kaiser, P., Vahrenkamp, N., Asfour, T.: A combined approach for robot placement and coverage path planning for mobile manipulation. In: 2017 IEEE/RSJ International Conference on Intelligent Robots and Systems (IROS), pp. 6285–6292 (2017)
13. Reister, F., Grotz, M., Asfour, T.: Combining navigation and manipulation costs for time-efficient robot placement in mobile manipulation tasks. IEEE Robot. Autom. Lett. **7**(4), 9913–9920 (2022)
14. Sahbani, A., El-Khoury, S., Bidaud, P.: An overview of 3D object grasp synthesis algorithms. Robot. Auton. Syst. **60**(3), 326–336 (2012)
15. Sutanto, G., Su, Z., Schaal, S., Meier, F.: Learning sensor feedback models from demonstrations via phase-modulated neural networks. In: 2018 IEEE International Conference on Robotics and Automation, ICRA, pp. 1142–1149 (2018)

16. Tan, H., Erdemir, E., Kawamura, K., Du, Q.: A potential field method-based extension of the dynamic movement primitive algorithm for imitation learning with obstacle avoidance. In: 2011 IEEE International Conference on Mechatronics and Automation, pp. 525–530 (2011)
17. Vahrenkamp, N., Asfour, T., Dillmann, R.: Robot placement based on reachability inversion. In: 2013 IEEE International Conference on Robotics and Automation, pp. 1970–1975 (2013)
18. Welschehold, T., Dornhege, C., Paus, F., Asfour, T., Burgard, W.: Coupling mobile base and end-effector motion in task space. In: 2018 IEEE/RSJ International Conference on Intelligent Robots and Systems (IROS), pp. 1–9 (2018)
19. Yamamoto, T., Terada, K., Ochiai, A., Saito, F., Asahara, Y., Murase, K.: Development of human support robot as the research platform of a domestic mobile manipulator. Robomech. J. **6**(1), 4 (2019)
20. Yamazaki, K., Suzuki, S., Kuribayashi, Y.: Approaching motion planning for mobile manipulators considering the uncertainty of self-positioning and object's pose estimation. Robot. Auton. Syst. **158**, 104232 (2022)
21. Yao, H., Laha, R., Figueredo, L.F.C., Haddadin, S.: Enhanced dexterity maps (EDM): a new map for manipulator capability analysis **9**(2), 1628–1635 (2023)
22. Zhou, Q.Y., Park, J., Koltun, V.: Open3D: a modern library for 3D data processing (2018)

Automated Game Statistics for the RoboCup Standard Platform League

Thomas Röfer[1,2](✉), Laurens Müller-Groh[2], Arne Hasselbring[2], and Tim Laue[2]

[1] Deutsches Forschungszentrum für Künstliche Intelligenz, Cyber-Physical Systems, Enrique-Schmidt-Str. 5, 28359 Bremen, Germany
thomas.roefer@dfki.de

[2] Universität Bremen, Fachbereich 3 – Mathematik und Informatik, Postfach 330 440, 28334 Bremen, Germany
{lamu,arha,tlaue}@uni-bremen.de

Abstract. In this paper, we present an application that creates statistics from videos of games in the RoboCup Standard Platform League. The players and the ball are detected in the video using a YOLOv5 network and then projected to the field plane using a camera calibration that is determined automatically. Various statistics are created from the video and the log files of the league's referee application. In a case study, the videos from the 2023 Champion Cup competition were analyzed.

1 Introduction

The RoboCup Standard Platform League (SPL) has made a lot of progress during the past 15 years. It started with soccer games under controlled lighting conditions in which everything was color-coded. Today, games take place under varying lighting conditions, including direct sunlight and hard shadows, all color coding is gone, and teams can even participate remotely by just sending their code that then runs on robots they never touched. During this time, the league also developed a lot of infrastructure that is used to document the progress made. In 2012, our team B-Human developed a new version of the referee application *GameController* that logs all decisions the referee made. Since a project funded by the RoboCup Federation in 2013, these log files are used to create game statistics using the *LogAnalyzer*. They have been published for every RoboCup and some local competitions since then (see Table 1). They count the number of penalties of different types each team received and also contain measures such as *penalties per game*. Thus, each team can compare their statistics with others as well as between different years and identify potential areas for improvement. In addition, the technical committee can monitor the effect of rule changes that were introduced and how well teams cope with them. In another RoboCup-funded project in 2015, the *TeamCommunicationMonitor* (TCM) was developed. It visualizes and logs the messages exchanged between the different robots of each team. These logs have also been collected and published since then.

E. Barros et al. (Eds.): RoboCup 2024, LNAI 15570, pp. 281–293, 2025.
https://doi.org/10.1007/978-3-031-85859-8_24

Table 1. Game statistics of RoboCup 2023 released at spl.robocup.org/downloads (GPM: goals per minute, PPG: penalties per game, ROF: robots on field)

Team	Goal	Timeout	Request for Pick-up	Illegal Position	Motion in Set	Fallen/ Inactive	Local Game Stuck	Ball Holding	Player Stance	Player Pushing	Playing With Arms/ Hands	Leaving the Field	Kick-in Against	Goal Kick Against	Corner Kick Against	Pushing Free Kick Against	Penalty Kick Against	Games	Playing	GPM	PPG	ROF
B-Human	76	0	3	3	0	4	0	1	0	7	0	1	3	7	1	1	0	8	107:50	0,70	2,0	99 %
RoboEireann	67	1	25	16	0	7	0	0	0	6	0	8	5	3	2	4	0	9	115:20	0,58	4,1	71 %
R-ZWEI KICKERS	40	0	18	6	5	9	0	2	0	9	0	15	6	13	0	0	0	9	132:18	0,30	5,1	88 %
BadgerBots	34	0	11	11	2	14	1	0	0	17	0	38	7	6	7	1	0	9	133:47	0,25	9,2	86 %
HTWK Robots	34	1	30	18	0	39	0	0	0	26	0	12	11	3	0	6	0	8	136:29	0,25	11,9	78 %
Dutch Nao Team	27	3	36	16	2	17	0	0	0	8	0	33	14	22	2	0	0	9	137:34	0,20	8,4	83 %
RedBackBots	14	1	30	31	2	7	0	0	0	9	0	52	11	6	2	0	0	7	101:56	0,14	14,4	75 %
HULKs	16	0	49	22	1	31	1	0	0	31	0	46	15	11	0	3	1	8	141:42	0,11	16,5	81 %
Naova	8	2	25	21	20	56	1	0	0	1	0	59	3	0	3	0	0	7	96:54	0,08	22,9	74 %
rUNSWift	10	2	56	15	0	52	0	0	0	21	0	68	32	14	3	7	1	8	138:59	0,07	19,5	78 %
Nao Devils	6	1	22	5	1	50	0	0	0	6	0	10	14	1	4	2	0	6	100:50	0,06	12,0	88 %
NomadZ	5	0	16	15	1	57	2	0	0	16	0	25	5	3	2	0	2	6	92:10	0,05	19,3	79 %
SPQR Team	5	4	38	8	13	45	1	0	0	19	0	67	3	2	0	7	2	7	115:22	0,04	21,9	71 %
Bembelbots	4	2	114	30	6	89	0	0	0	18	0	23	3	1	1	3	1	7	111:22	0,04	23,7	73 %
Berlin United	2	3	9	12	5	13	0	0	0	23	0	32	30	4	0	3	1	6	104:52	0,02	14,2	82 %
UT Austin Villa	0	3	47	0	4	34	0	0	0	0	1	8	0	0	0	0	0	7	74:59	0,00	6,7	17 %
Rinobot-Jaguar	0	0	5	0	0	0	0	0	0	0	0	0	0	0	0	0	0	7	71:47	0,00	0,0	0 %
Average	20,5	1,4	31,4	13,5	3,6	30,9	0,4	0,2	0,0	12,8	0,1	29,2	9,5	5,6	1,6	2,2	0,5	7,5	112:36	0,17	12,5	72 %

Also in a RoboCup-funded project, the team Berlin United developed an automated video recording solution for SPL games. As a result, most games since RoboCup 2018 have been recorded and archived on their website logs.naoth.de, together with the log files of the TCM. Based on some of these recordings, the *Video Analysis Challenge* was conducted at RoboCup 2022. The seven participating teams labeled all robots and balls in 35,000 images from seven of these videos. Then, teams could develop software that would help to automatically analyze aspects of SPL games. We developed the application *B-Human's Video Analysis* and became one of the two winners of this challenge, together with [1]. Its goal is to extend the variety of game statistics available to the teams and the technical committee beyond the ones that can directly be derived from the *GameController*'s log files, e.g. by how many passes are played.

This paper describes the application after it was extended in another RoboCup-funded project in 2023. In Sect. 2, related research is discussed. Section 3 gives an overview of the video analysis application. Our camera calibration approach is described in Sect. 4, followed by the detection and tracking of objects in Sect. 5. Details about the statistics created are given in Sect. 6. The system was applied to real game videos in a case study that is described in Sect. 7, followed by the final conclusion in Sect. 8.

2 Related Work

Nowadays, in professional sports, tracking and analyzing what is happening on the field is a common practice. In general, currently used systems in football competitions rely on optical systems, an overview is given by [6]. TRACAB, a widespread system in football, has been validated as being quite precise [5]. Data generated by such systems is already used for complex football analytics [4,8] as well as for statistics presented to a wider audience, such as running distances, heatmaps, or expected goals [11]. However, in general, the details about the implementations of these tracking systems are not known, as they are proprietary commercial systems. An exception is an early publication about the Hawk-Eye system [9], which is nowadays used for tracking the ball in a variety of sports. All these applications have in common that they require an array of industrial grade cameras at fixed positions. Such a configuration is currently not feasible in the RoboCup context.

However, in some RoboCup leagues, collecting and analyzing game data is a common practice and multiple related works exist. For instance, in both simulation leagues as well as in the Small Size League (SSL), precise information about all players as well as the ball is given at any point of time. These leagues play with 11 players per team, making tactical analysis a relevant issue. An overview of relevant efforts is given by [10]. The simulated data can be considered as perfect, but also the setup of the SSL appears to provide information that allows to apply autonomous refereeing for several years now, starting with [13]. In contrast to other RoboCup robot soccer leagues, the SSL benefits from an external camera setup, which consists of an array of cameras mounted above the field, covering the whole area with almost no occlusion. The camera data is processed by the standard SSL-Vision system [14].

The RoboCup soccer leagues that use fully autonomous robots are not situated in such an environment that would support the straightforward collection of data. To the best of our knowledge, the Humanoid Leagues as well as the Middle Size League do not have any setup that would allow automated game statistics. For several years, the Standard Platform League has a standardized setup for streaming as well as for recording all SPL games at tournaments [7]. A video analysis system for the SPL that has similar features to the one proposed in this paper has been presented in 2022 [1]. However, this approach – in contrast to ours – does not appear to be compatible to the aforementioned standard video setup and has not been validated on recent data recorded by it.

Fig. 1. The user interface of the Video Analysis Application

3 Overview

The application can either run with or without a graphical user interface as shown in Fig. 1. It processes two kinds of inputs: the video recording of a half of a game and a log file that was written by the GameController application. The video can consist of multiple files, as for different technical reasons, the current recording setup might generate multiple files per half. The log file of the GameController contains all the decisions the referee made during the half. Since 2023, it also contains the positions of all players on the field, as they were computed by the self-localization methods running on the robots.

While the video is played back, the video analysis also plays back the events from the GameController log file based on timestamps that are contained in the log. During the games, the recording of the video is triggered by the GameController as well, i.e. when the robots receive the signal about the start of the game, the video recording solution receives this message as well. We estimated a fixed delay between the signal in the log and the actual start of the recording (2.2 s) and a smaller delay when the recording is stopped (0.8 s). The latter is important when chaining together multiple videos of a single half. If the video analysis is run with a graphical user interface, it can be seen how all statistics created develop over time. Eventually, a summary of the statistics is written into a file as comma separated values. The format is designed so that multiple of such files can be concatenated to, for instance, create statistics over all games played at a RoboCup event. An example of such statistics is presented in Sect. 7.

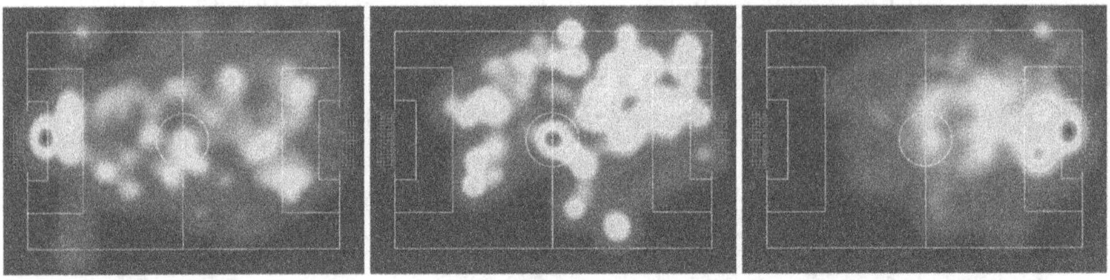

(a) B-Human playing left to right (b) Ball (c) HTWK Robots playing right to left

Fig. 2. Heat maps of the first half of the SPL Champions Cup 2023 final

The application generates three types of quantitative statistics and one type in the form of a visualization:

1. Statistics only based on the GameController logs. They are similar to the ones produced by the *LogAnalyzer* mentioned in Sect. 1. In Fig. 1, these are the statistics shown on both sides of the window down to *Corner Kick*.
2. Statistics based on information extracted from the video. These are based on the detection of the players and the ball in the images. They sometimes also use information from the log file in the form of the game state, as certain

statistics only make sense when the game is in the *playing* phase instead of, for instance, the robots just setting-up for the next kick-off. In Fig. 1, these are all remaining statistics except for the last one.
3. Statistics based on information from both the log and the video. Currently, only the statistics about the average localization error falls in this category.
4. Heat maps (see Fig. 2) about the position of the ball and the position of the robots of each team. These can be viewed in three different tabs, but are also stored as JPEG images at the end of the analysis.

4 Camera Calibration

To transform object detections from image coordinates into field coordinates, an intrinsic and an extrinsic camera calibration are needed. We adapted the code provided by Schlotter [12] that offered the ability to optimize the extrinsic camera calibration using a hard-coded intrinsic calibration. The calibration is performed on a background image that is computed from many images of the video to eliminate moving objects from the field to get a clear view at the field lines. In an iterative optimization process, points on these detected field lines are projected to the field plane and matched to lines in a pre-defined field model, thereby adapting the estimated pose of the camera and minimizing the projection error. We added the optimization of the intrinsic calibration together with the extrinsic one to Schlotter's [12] approach. We also added an inverse transformation from field coordinates back into the image.

The calibration method requires an initial guess for the pose of the camera relative to the field center. Since the camera is moved when the memory card is exchanged, this initial guess is required basically for each half. While the position of the camera cannot change much, the orientation can. Therefore, we simplified the camera calibration by providing an initial guess for tilt and roll based on the gravity vector provided by the metadata stream of the GoPro HERO10 Black cameras that are used for recording. The *telemetry-parser* (https://pypi.org/project/telemetry-parser/0.2.8/) package was used to parse the stream. Since the GoPro cannot know its rotation around the vertical axis relative to the field, the pan angle still has to be manually set.

To extract tilt and roll of the camera, a *rotation vector* (also known as *Euler vector*) $\boldsymbol{r}$ is constructed between the measured gravity vector $\boldsymbol{g}_{\mathrm{m}}$ and a reference gravity vector $\boldsymbol{g}_{\mathrm{r}}$ of a fixed camera pose (Fig. 3a) at the side of the field. An orthogonal unit vector is calculated and scaled by the cosine angle between the gravity vectors:

$$\boldsymbol{r} = \frac{\boldsymbol{g}_{\mathrm{m}} \times \boldsymbol{g}_{\mathrm{r}}}{||\boldsymbol{g}_{\mathrm{m}} \times \boldsymbol{g}_{\mathrm{r}}||} \cdot \arccos \frac{\boldsymbol{g}_{\mathrm{m}} * \boldsymbol{g}_{\mathrm{r}}}{||\boldsymbol{g}_{\mathrm{m}}|| \cdot ||\boldsymbol{g}_{\mathrm{r}}||} \tag{1}$$

The right-handed coordinate system of the GoPro's gravity vector has the z-axis going through the front of the camera. The camera's right-handed coordinate system has the x-axis going through the front of the camera. We therefore rotate vectors in the rotated camera system C' to the reference camera coordinate system F as $T_{C \leftarrow C'} = T_{C \leftarrow G} \cdot T_{G \leftarrow G'} \cdot T_{G' \leftarrow C'}$, where G is the reference gravity vector system, G' is the gravity vector system including the measured rotation and C is the reference camera coordinate system.

$$T_{C \leftarrow G} = \begin{bmatrix} 0 & 0 & 1 \\ -1 & 0 & 0 \\ 0 & -1 & 0 \end{bmatrix} \tag{2}$$

$T_{G \leftarrow G'}$ is derived from $\boldsymbol{r}$ (see Eq. 1) and $T_{G' \leftarrow C'} = T_{C \leftarrow G}^{-1}$. Figure 3b shows the rotated camera. This reduces information entered manually to calibrate the full pose to the translation, which can be easily measured and a fixed rotation of 90° around the z-axis which could also be denoted as $T_{F \leftarrow C}$.

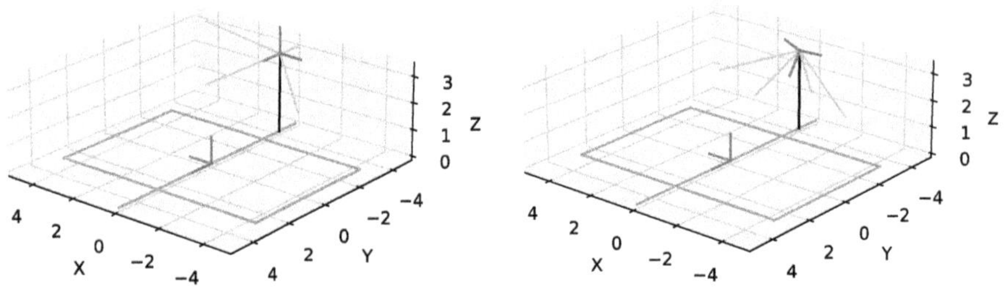

(a) Camera reference rotation (b) Example of a rotated camera

Fig. 3. Field and camera coordinate system highlighted with x-Axes in red, y in green and z in blue. (Color figure online)

Tilt and roll are still considered free variables in the optimization algorithm. Future investigation regarding the accuracy of the gravity vector is needed before one can regard these variables as fixed to decrease complexity and speed up the optimization step. However, the most time is spent with extracting the background image for collecting reference line points, so accelerating the optimization would only have a small impact.

5 Object Detection and Tracking

A YOLOv5 [3] network was trained with an input resolution of 1920 × 1080 with bounding boxes of the ball and the players including their jersey colors. Even at this high resolution, the ball is depicted only slightly bigger than 10 × 10 pixels in the far corners of the field. Only 681 images were used from the original dataset that was created for the technical challenge in 2022. A limitation of that dataset is the absence of a number of jersey colors that are used by the league. The ten colors (see Fig. 4) allowed are defined in the GameController application. 999 additional images were extracted from ten games that were recorded at RoboCup 2023. The focus was to balance the dataset for the official

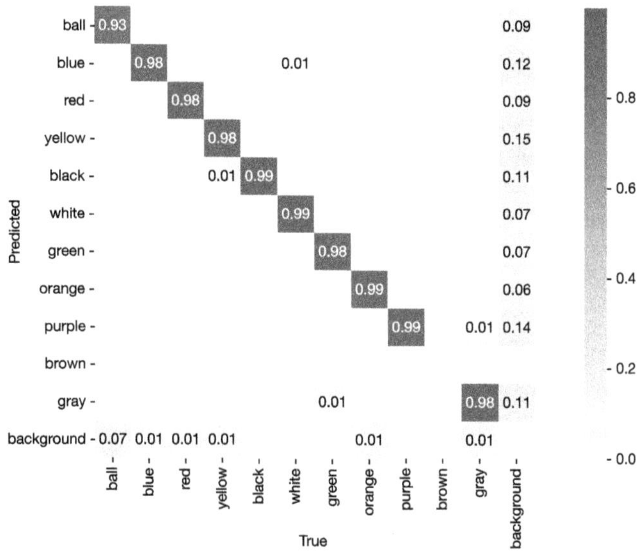

Fig. 4. Confusion Matrix of YOLOv5 trained with the extended dataset

jersey colors. However, the color brown could not be trained, because it was not used in recent years.

For training, we used the YOLOv5-v6.0 nano base model. We maintained a batch size of 8 and trained 400 epochs. We selected the 'best' model as determined by the training process of the YOLOv5 architecture. The resulting confusion matrix, as depicted in Fig. 4, shows some confusion between yellow and black, white and blue, green and gray and gray and purple. The majority of instances is classified correctly. However, the biggest issue is overfitting on the low variety of differing lighting conditions for each color. During empirical testing, we noticed that when confronted with a sufficiently different lighting condition, the model starts to confuse the colors more often. This is not shown in the confusion matrix, as the dataset from which the splits were obtained suffers from said low variety and therefore the test split does not contain samples for this case. The inference takes approximately 39 ms per image on an Apple M1 Max processor. The whole dataset used to train the network is linked from the application's GitHub repository (https://github.com/bhuman/VideoAnalysis).

The bounding boxes of the players are tracked using a centroid multi object tracker [2] ignoring the colors in YOLOv5's non-maximum suppression. For each track, the recent history of colors associated with it is maintained and the most frequent color is assigned as the player's color. False ball detections are filtered out based on an assumed maximum speed of the ball. The centers of the bounding boxes are projected into the world based on an assumed height above ground, i.e. 5 cm for the ball and 26 cm for the players, resulting in the world model (see Fig. 5). If the projection of a player's ground position back into the image is outside its bounding box, the player is assumed to be fallen.

Since the YOLO network does not always detect players with the correct jersey color, we introduced an abstract color class mapping as a post-processing step that is based on the similarity of the detected color to the jersey colors of the two teams that are actually playing, which is provided by GameController log file. The mapping basically distinguishes between saturated colors and unsaturated colors (black, gray, white). For saturated colors, the distance between their prototypical hue values determines the similarity. For unsaturated colors, the brightness is used. Since a number of teams use dark blue as a jersey color, which is often confused with black (they look very similar in the videos even for the human eye), there is also a similarity between these two colors.

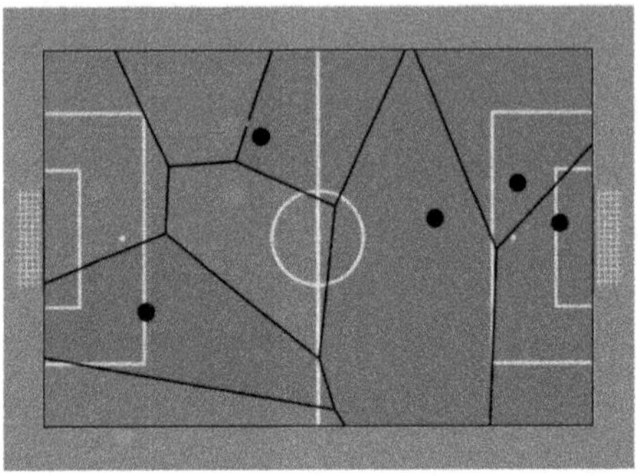

Fig. 5. World model with controlled areas. The black and blue dots mark the robots, the orange dot marks the ball. The controlled areas are shaded in the team colors. (Color figure online)

6 Statistics

6.1 Video-Based Statistics

A number of statistics are computed from the world model. First of all, the number of falls is counted, i.e. the number of transitions from *not fallen* to *fallen* in the world model. To filter out noise, a player has to be in each of these states for at least 1 s before they count.

Other statistics are based on a model of ball possession. A player gets in possession of the ball when it is closer than a distance $p_{\min}$ (currently 40 cm) to the ball, while all players of the opponent team are further away than a distance $p_{\max}$ (60 cm). A player loses the ball, if it distances itself more than $p_{\max}$ from the ball, while the ball is not moving. This means that a player can get in possession of the ball, then enter into a duel with an opponent player while staying in possession until it either loses the ball or continues to keep it. If a player has the ball and kicks it, it stays in possession until the ball stops moving. If this is close to a teammate, the team stays in control of the ball, e.g., during passes.

Based on the model of ball possession, a number of statistics are created: How far a team moved the ball during a half and for how long it was moved. For instance, if a team always performs long distance kicks, it might move the ball quite far, but only for short periods of time. A team that mostly dribbles might move the ball continuously. The time the ball was in motion is currently a value in seconds, but as for most time-based statistics, it should be put in relation to the duration in which the robots could actually play the ball, i.e. the time the half was in the playing state, which is not implemented yet. Also based on the model of ball possession, passes are counted. Passes are detected based on the model for ball possession. A pass is defined as a movement of the ball for at least 75 cm, where the same team is in possession of the ball before and after the movement, but different players are closest to the ball.

For the ball and the players of both teams, the average distance to their own goals is computed. For the ball, this qualitatively corresponds to whether the game took place more in the own or the opponent half. For the players, it should reveal whether teams play more aggressively or defensively, although this positioning obviously is also related to the position of the ball. The statistics about the controlled areas sums up the areas of the field the players of team are closer to than the players of the opponent (see Fig. 5). It reflects how well teams place their players. It is determined as the sum of the areas of the cells in a Voronoi diagram that is computed from all player positions on the field.

6.2 Robot Localization Analysis

The average localization error of the robots is computed using the robot detections in the image and the positions robots sent via the so-called GameController return packets. Starting in 2023, the latter are recorded in the log files of the GameController. As the application does not detect jersey numbers, it has to guess which seen robot belongs to which logged one. This is achieved by solving an assignment problem. For all logged robot positions, the distance $d_{l,s}$ to all seen positions is calculated. Since positions were logged at different points in time (each robot sends its packet individually), these distances are computed per robot when its position is played back from the log file. Then, the assignment is selected that minimizes the overall distance between the logged positions and the seen positions they are assigned to. As not all robots are seen in all images, all distances $d_{l,s}$ where robot s was not detected for at least one logged robot l are removed for all robots before solving the assignment. The assignment ignores the jersey colors of the robots, because their detection is sometimes wrong. Instead, only those assignments are used for computing the average localization error, where the logged robot and the seen one have jersey colors of the same team. Figure 1 shows the detected player positions as solid circles and the logged positions as dashed circles.

There are some additional circumstances in which robots are excluded from the statistics. If a robot is penalized, it is usually removed from the field. Therefore, it is ignored. However, penalized robots are sometimes still detected in the video when standing next to the field. Therefore, the application keeps track of whether a team currently has a penalty and then excludes robots detected in the relevant areas. Fallen robots are also excluded from the localization statistics, as the position that the application computes for the robot is probably not the same as the one teams would use. The application currently assumes that the center of the bounding box that is provided by YOLOv5 corresponds to a point that is 26 cm above the ground for an upright robot and 8 cm above the ground for a fallen one. While the projection to the ground is between the feet for an upright robot, it is not for a fallen one. Therefore, using such positions for the statistics would introduce unfounded errors.

6.3 Heat Maps

Another kind of statistics are heat maps. For each half, three heat maps are created. Two of the heat maps accumulate the positions of the players for each team and the third one accumulates the position of the ball (see Fig. 2). The heat maps are a more visual representation of the statistics *average player distance to own goal* and *average ball distance to own goal.* Positions are accumulated with a resolution of 1 cm^2. For visualization, a Gaussian filter is applied, the result is normalized and then drawn using a pre-defined color map.

7 Case Study

We performed a case study, in which we analyzed the games of the SPL Champions Cup 2023 (see Table 2 and Fig. 6). The result was that out of 32 games, three were not recorded and for one half, the recording started too late. For three games, the application could not distinguish between the jersey colors of the two teams. Dark blue is often confused with black and (dark) red is confused with purple on some fields. The abstract color class mapping of the application can fix such misclassifications, if the wrong color is not actually used in the game. However, in three games it was. In the end, 51 halves could be analyzed, but only for eleven games (22 halves), the automatic camera calibration actually worked. The main problem is that the field lines are not detected correctly in the background image. In 2023, painted lines were used instead of taped lines. They have a much lower contrast relative to the field than the taped ones. In addition, most games of the Champions Cup were played on fields located next to windows, making line detection even harder with the approach the application currently uses. Another problem was that the goals are also detected as field lines. If corners of the field were not shown in the video, i.e. larger parts of the goal lines were missing, the calibration process distorts the projection to match parts of the field model with the goals. In the end, the field lines were manually whitened in the background image using an image editor for the games in which the calibration did not work. After that, the calibration worked fine, i.e. the initial pose of the camera never had to be adapted manually for the calibration to work.

Table 2. The average per half statistics for the SPL Champions Cup 2023. Due to missing game halves, this does not match the values shown in Table 1. Most values are counts. Times are given in seconds, distances in meters, and the controlled area in square meters.

	B-Human	Bembelbots	Berlin United	HTWK Robots	HULKs	Nao Devils	NomadZ	rUNSWift	SPQR Team
Goal for	4.45	0.17	0.00	2.00	1.00	0.64	0.00	0.71	0.50
Goals per Minute	0.66	0.03	0.00	0.24	0.12	0.08	0.00	0.07	0.07
Penalties	1.18	10.50	6.10	5.56	7.82	5.91	12.20	9.57	11.25
Illegal Ball Contact	0.00	0.00	0.00	0.00	0.00	0.00	0.00	0.00	0.00
Player Pushing	0.55	0.83	1.10	1.25	1.71	0.27	1.00	0.86	0.88
Illegal Motion in Set	0.00	0.50	0.50	0.00	0.06	0.18	0.20	0.00	0.13
Inactive Player	0.36	5.75	1.30	2.44	1.76	4.00	6.80	3.43	3.63
Illegal Position	0.27	2.08	1.10	1.13	1.47	0.45	1.60	1.07	0.88
Leaving the Field	0.00	1.33	2.10	0.75	2.82	1.00	2.60	4.21	5.75
Request for PickUp	0.27	7.67	0.60	1.00	3.00	1.27	1.40	3.57	1.63
Pushing Free Kick	0.09	0.25	0.30	0.38	0.18	0.18	0.00	0.50	0.75
Penalty Kick	0.00	0.08	0.10	0.00	0.06	0.00	0.20	0.07	0.13
Goal Kick	0.64	0.00	0.30	0.19	0.59	0.09	0.20	0.71	0.13
Kick In	0.27	0.17	2.60	0.69	0.88	1.09	0.60	1.86	0.13
Corner Kick	0.09	0.08	0.00	0.00	0.00	0.18	0.20	0.21	0.00
Falls	19.00	37.67	30.50	40.44	29.06	44.36	24.60	31.07	39.75
Passes	6.00	1.83	2.00	2.13	1.71	1.18	0.80	1.86	1.25
Ball Isolation Time	46.55	53.08	64.00	43.81	73.06	80.73	66.80	59.57	59.25
Ball Possession	204.00	142.00	220.50	186.38	140.59	193.73	132.40	192.71	118.00
Time Ball Moved	54.27	27.75	40.10	47.88	34.18	36.91	21.00	29.14	24.00
Dist. Ball Moved	51.60	19.15	29.38	35.21	32.22	28.09	18.68	30.38	20.65
Dist. Walked	273.79	266.48	266.19	301.09	347.41	303.34	238.72	375.09	298.91
Dist. to Own Goal	3.69	2.58	3.51	3.18	3.43	2.96	3.63	2.98	2.87
Ball Dist. to Own G.	5.89	3.68	4.48	5.13	5.02	4.28	3.12	4.45	4.55
Controlled Area	35.48	23.48	31.73	23.88	25.13	30.41	27.48	23.63	22.58
Mean Loc. Error	0.12	0.57	0.84	0.23	0.51	0.24	0.34	2.44	0.29

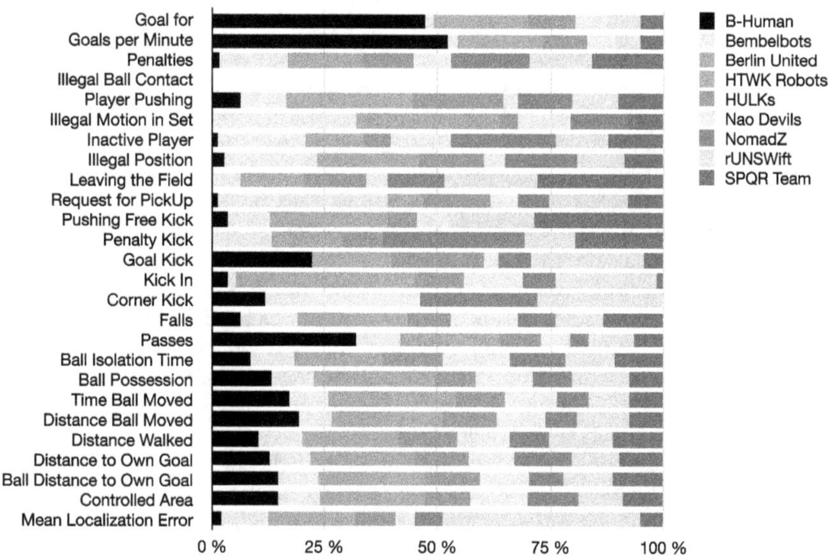

Fig. 6. The statistics shown in Table 2 as ratios for each team (Color figure online)

8 Conclusion and Future Work

In this paper, we presented an application for automated game statistics in the RoboCup Standard Platform League. It is fully integrated into the currently used infrastructure, i.e. the setup for recording and streaming games as well as the league's GameController. The implementation aims to compensate the limits that arise from this setup, such as the single camera that is mounted in an unstable pose. A case study based on a majority of the videos of the 2023 Champions Cup showed that it is possible to provide a number of different game statistics, several of which have never been computed before for the SPL.

In the future, the automatic segmentation of the field lines the camera calibration is based on must be improved. In addition, the detection of jersey colors must be made more independent from the actual lighting condition, e.g. by learning colors while the robots enter the field at the beginning of the game. Furthermore, the setup for recording the games must be optimized to ensure that videos of all game halves are recorded and the videos show the whole field.

References

1. Bloisi, D.D., et al.: MARIO: modular and extensible architecture for computing visual statistics in RoboCup SPL. Technical report (2022). https://doi.org/10.48550/ARXIV.2209.09987. https://arxiv.org/abs/2209.09987
2. Deshpande, A.M.: Multi-object trackers in Python (2020). https://github.com/adipandas/multi-object-tracker
3. Jocher, G., et al.: ultralytics/yolov5: v6.1 – TensorRT, TensorFlow edge TPU and OpenVINO export and inference (2022). https://doi.org/10.5281/zenodo.6222936
4. Link, D., Lang, S., Seidenschwarz, P.: Real time quantification of dangerousity in football using spatiotemporal tracking data. PLoS ONE **11**(12), e0168768 (2016)
5. Linke, D., Link, D., Lames, M.: Football-specific validity of TRACAB's optical video tracking systems. PLoS ONE **15**(3), e0230179 (2020)
6. Manafifard, M., Ebadi, H., Moghaddam, H.A.: A survey on player tracking in soccer videos. Comput. Vis. Image Underst. **159**, 19–46 (2017)
7. Mellmann, H., Schlotter, S.A., Strobel, P.: Toward data driven development in RoboCup. In: RoboCup 2019: Robot Soccer World Cup XXIII (2019)
8. Memmert, D., Raabe, D.: Data Analytics in Football: Positional Data Collection, Modelling and Analysis. Routledge (2018)
9. Owens, N., Harris, C., Stennett, C.: Hawk-eye tennis system. In: International Conference on Visual Information Engineering, pp. 182–185 (2003)
10. Pereira, F.N., et al.: A library and web platform for RoboCup soccer matches data analysis. In: Robot World Cup, pp. 177–189. Springer (2022)
11. Rathke, A.: An examination of expected goals and shot efficiency in soccer. J. Hum. Sport Exerc. **12**(2), 514–529 (2017)
12. Schlotter, B.: Analyse von RoboCup Spielen – Erkennen und Lokalisieren von Nao Robotern. Technical report, Humboldt-Universität zu Berlin (2020). https://www.naoteamhumboldt.de/wp-content/papercite-data/pdf/2020_studienarbeit_schlotter.pdf

13. Zhu, D., Biswas, J., Veloso, M.: AutoRef: towards real-robot soccer complete automated refereeing. In: RoboCup 2014: Robot World Cup XVIII, pp. 419–430. Springer (2015)
14. Zickler, S., Laue, T., Birbach, O., Wongphati, M., Veloso, M.: SSL-vision: the shared vision system for the RoboCup small size league. In: RoboCup 2009: Robot Soccer World Cup XIII. LNAI, vol. 5949, pp. 425–436. Springer (2010)

Development Track

A Light-Weighted Event-Based Simulation for the RoboCup Logistics League

Dominik Lampel[1], Marco De Bortoli[1(✉)], Tarik Viehmann[2], Alain Rohr[3], and Gerald Steinbauer-Wagner[1]

[1] Graz University of Technology, Graz, Austria
mbortoli@ist.tugraz.at
[2] RWTH Aachen, Aachen, Germany
[3] Höhere Fachschule für Technik Mittelland AG, Grenchen, Switzerland

Abstract. In this paper we will introduce an event-based agent simulation for the RoboCup Logistics League (RCLL). RCLL provides a testbed for the automation of flexible production to allow the development and evaluation of novel concepts and algorithms. The development is stimulated by a competition. Competing teams need to develop a team of autonomous robots able to fabricate on-demand product orders embedded into a flexible factory floor. Simulation plays a major role in developing and testing the needed planning and scheduling algorithms. As previously developed full-fledged simulations are too resource-demanding and hard to use we developed a light-weighted abstract simulation. In this paper we will discuss how the abstraction of the real setup to the simulation has been performed. Moreover, to allow a quick adoption of the simulation by teams within the league a standardized perception-action interface was developed. We will present the concepts and implementation of the simulation in detail. In order to evaluate the usability and potential for adoption a user study was performed with members of the RCLL.

1 Introduction

The RoboCup Logistics League (RCLL) [14] is an annual competition established in 2012, wherein teams solve tasks in a mockup production environment. Teams deploy up to three robots to interact with production machines (stations) that are positioned in a configuration which is unknown a priori, fulfilling on-demand production orders provided by a simulated production management system called Referee Box (RefBox). Orders are completed by delivering specific products composed of various pieces to designated delivery stations. To elaborate, each product consists of three types of components: a base, zero to three rings, and a final cap. Each type of piece is mounted on the top of a partial product, provided by a robot, by the corresponding station (base, ring or cap station). Ultimately, the completed product must be transported to a delivery station within a predefined time frame.

E. Barros et al. (Eds.): RoboCup 2024, LNAI 15570, pp. 297–308, 2025.
https://doi.org/10.1007/978-3-031-85859-8_25

Properly testing planning and scheduling algorithms within the RCLL and its Refbox involves real-game scenarios or a Gazebo-based simulation. However, conducting extensive debugging with real setups is challenging due to complex physical arrangements, occasional failures, and time-consuming preparations. Alternatively, the resource-intensive nature of Gazebo-based simulation [15] poses challenges for new teams.

To mitigate these issues and facilitate broad and sound testing and appealing teaching, a lightweight abstracted event-based simulation of RCLL was developed. This simulation abstracts the capabilities and behaviors of real robots, machines, and products while remaining transparent to Refbox and team software by providing a common abstracted interface. This enables teams to evaluate scheduling algorithms without deploying physical robots or delving into the implementation of lower-level software components. This represents the core accomplishment of the simulation and serves as the primary motivation behind its development.

To recap, the simulation offers easier installation compared to Gazebo, consumes fewer resources, it simplifies benchmarking of planning and scheduling approaches, lowers entry barriers for new teams by enabling work on algorithms without complete hardware, and offers various deployment options, from source code to Docker images.

The paper is structured as follow. In the next section, related work is briefly summarized. In Sect. 3, we described how the main components of the league have been abstracted in the simulation. Section 4 delves into the implementations details. Finally, usability and performance of the proposed simulation are evaluated in Sect. 5, before drawing some conclusion in Sect. 6.

2 Related Research

Niemueller et al. [12] proposed the Planning and Execution Competition for Logistics Robots in Sumulation (PEXC). The goal of the PEXC is that it can be used as a test-bed for advancements and testing of the use of planning in real world robotics settings. PEXC is based on the RCLL domain. Similar to the new simulation that will be introduced in this paper an initial task-level planning and execution framework is provided which researcher can extend to address their needs. The paper from Agalianos et al. [3] compares the current literature for discrete-event simulations (DES) and digital twins, concluding that discrete event simulations and digital twins share a lot of characteristics. Much like the comparison between the Gazebo-based simulation and the lightweight approach outlined in this paper, digital twins offer a more precise representation but come with greater computational demands. The GAMA framework introduced by Larsen et al. [9] is an Agent Oriented Programming (AOP) simulation platform based on the belief, desire and intention paradigm (BDI). However, the GAMA platform is not adaptable to work with the RCLL domain, thus it can not be used for the intended simulation. Arguenon et al. [4] proposed a multi-agent system for agriculture robots, featuring an internal representation of the robots which is quite similar to the approach used in the proposed simulation. The paper from Kampa et al. [8] is proposing the usage of discrete-event simulation (DES) for the improvement of manufacturing systems. Their approach with probabilistic models for the human and robot workers is something that is relevant for future extension of the proposed simulation with fault models for actions and tasks. Another related work is the Middleware for Parallel Agent Discrete Event Simulation (MPADES) [13], since it is a simulation framework for language-independent agent simulations.

3 Abstraction

In order to develop an event-based simulation of RCLL the behavior of all involved components such as robots, machines, and products needs to be abstracted. The robot has some capabilities that it can perform and thus need to be represented, in an abstracted way, in the simulation: move from zone to zone, pick up and place products. Regarding the stations, they have a very limited knowledge of their surroundings and only perceive a robot-agent when it interacts with them, or once a production step is required from them. The stations have a few station points that can be interacted with by the robots, which will be elaborated at the end of this section.

The robots used in the RCLL are expected to be able to navigate without collisions on the game field, to identify the machine via visual markers, and to grab and place products from or on the production machines. As each team use their own approach to handle the challenge, a generalized representation was developed. We first introduce how this representation was abstracted.

During the first 3 min of an official game, the robots may try to identify where the machines are placed in order to start production beforehand. This is done via markers, which the robots need to recognize correctly. However, after 3 min the machines' positioning is published. Most teams use cameras on the robot for this purpose. As the simulation should be at a higher abstraction level than the existing Gazebo-based simulation it was decided that the identification of the location of the machine inputs and outputs should be not explicitly modelled, but rather the ground truth on the machine layout is immediately made public by the refbox.

The play field is divided into 14×8 zones of 1 square meter each. For the path planning, many teams use waypoints to represent these zones. Each machine possesses two waypoints (input and output zone, see Fig. 1a). If a robot receives a move task, it usually starts planning his way to the waypoint with the move-base package of ROS [11]. To abstract away the free navigation of the robots in the simulation, the possible positions of a robot were abstracted to the zones of the game field. The zones are mapped onto a graph where all adjacent zones are connected by an edge. For the path planning currently the A* algorithm [7] is used, which calculates a list of zones that the robot needs to traverse to reach its goal. Once the A* algorithm starts with the searching of a path all zones that are occupied by a station are treated as blocked such that the robot can not move through those zones. Other robots are ignored for the path planning. For the execution of the path the robot hops to the next zone on the path with a configurable delay. If there is a zone occupied by a different robot, the avoidance is implemented such that the robot retries up to three times to move to the occupied zone. If after three attempts the zone is still occupied the robot begins with a movement on to the next zone in the list. This jumping over the zone represents an implicitly modeled obstacle avoidance.

Regarding the machines, most of their tasks are initiated by the refbox, leading to rather simple behaviors of the machines. Generally, the positiong of machines are abstracted to a zone that they are placed in and their rotation in this zone (8 discrete orientations). With such information one can already specify the input and output side of the stations (Fig. 1a), which results in a zone where the robot can input a product and a zone where the robot can receive a product from the output. Each machine is equipped with a conveyor belt, which allows a continuous motion of the product on it. The positions on the belt were abstracted to three discrete positions, so called machine points. The three positions that got defined are: (1) the belt input, (2) the belt output, and (3) the middle of the belt, as depicted in Fig. 1. The middle of the belt is used for the manipulation tasks that the machine can execute. Base stations and delivery stations have a total of three machine points. There are also two more machines that need to be equipped with additional machine points: the ring station and cap station. The cap station has an additional shelf where caps on top of colorless bases are stored. These intermediate products can be used to buffer the cap stations and the bases can be used as payment for ring stations.

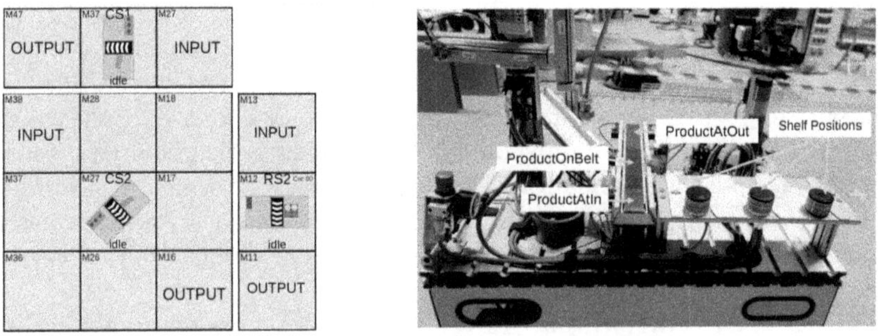

(a) Input and output zones. (b) Machine points.

Fig. 1. Abstraction of the Cap Station.

The cap station shelf is consisting of two rows of three slots each. The robot can be instructed to pickup a product from each of the slots. Thus, the cap station has in sum a total of six machine points, from which the robot can pick and place products (see Fig. 1). Ring stations can be filled with bases to pay for certain rings. This placing of bases can be done at the slide, which has a sensor to get information once a product was placed there. In sum this means the ring stations are consisting of four machine points, three on the belt and an additional one for the slide. These are all the discrete machine points that the robots can interact with. The typical pipeline consists of a robot providing a partial product to the belt input, the station processing the product at the middle of the belt through different steps, depending on specific station, and a robot picking up the resulting product at the belt output. In the real worlds, stations are more complex. They are equipped with different devices, like pneumatic cylinder which are used to mount intermediate pieces on delivered intermediate products. All of these devices and the related steps are abstracted away in the simulation. In our simulation, interactions with a machine is abstracted to a discrete interaction with a machine point. In the real world the robots are equipped with a gripper to pick and place the intermediate products. As this device can be designed and built by every team independently there are several different designs. In the simulation it was defined that the gripper is simply a container where one product can be stored.

The different steps forming the pipeline mentioned earlier are discretized as follow. In order to perform grasping, a robot needs to correctly align to the station, identify and localize the product and, finally, perform the operation. If everything worked out correctly a product is present in the gripping device of the robot. To abstract away several aspects of the real world in the simulation it was defined that a correct alignment is assumed once the correct zone adjacent to the respective station point is reached. For the localizing of the product and to check if a product is present, a method checks if a simulated product is present at machine point. After a product is present a configurable duration will be waited to represent the grasping task of the robot in the real world. The product is then in the gripper and removed from the station. In the real world, the robot must once more align accurately with the station, scan the designated station point, and upon verification, deposit the product onto the conveyor belt or slide. In the simulation, the duration for placement on the station begins upon issuing the placement command, and it can be customized. After this time, the product is removed from the robot and positioned on the designated machine point. If the machine point is blocked by another product the placing will fail. The machine then either needs to process the present product or to be reset which also clears the conveyor belt in the simulation. For the robot, if a picking task has been triggered for a station that is not yet ready, the robot will check for a certain time, which can be configured, the output or input of a station. If the product fails to arrive within the specified time, a timeout occurs, prompting the robot to send a message to the team's scheduler with the 'failed' flag set. This signal informs the scheduler that a task has failed, necessitating replanning or plan repair.

Time is not discretized and remains continuous, and users can adjust the length of tasks to either decelerate or accelerate them. This flexibility allows users to synchronize simulation times closely with real execution or speed them up for debugging or testing purposes. However, adjusting execution time for station tasks requires caution as the Referee Box operates on its own internal timing, potentially conflicting with simulated station timings.

4 Implementation

For the implementation the programming language C# was used. The main components of the implementation can be seen in Fig. 2.[1] The manager components for the machines, the robots and the zones are the key components of the software. They are responsible to create their respective managed resources. The teams's software interact with the simulation by sending ProtoBuf messages to the simulated robots, containing the task to execute, and receiving feedback about the result of tasks' execution. Moreover, it gets information about the game from the RefBox, as it happens in real games or with the Gazebo-based simulation. Given that the Referee Box relies on OPC UA (Open Platform Communications - Unified Architecture, [10]) for station communication, the simulated stations include an OPC UA server.

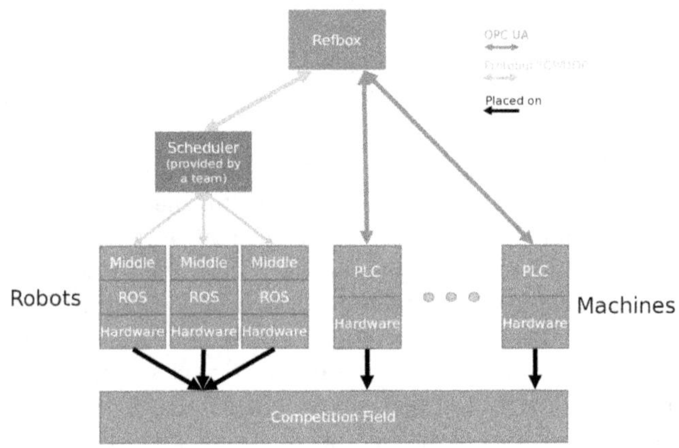

Fig. 2. An overview of the proposed simulation system. All components of the simulation are shown in grey, in orange the refbox provided by the league and in blue the scheduler of a team. The green arrows indicate the OPC UA communication between the refbox and the machines. Communication between simulated robots and the team's scheduler, and between the latter and the RefBox, is implemented with protobuf. (Color figure online)

[1] The simulation is publicly available at https://github.com/robocup-logistics/rcll-simulator.

4.1 User Interface

To keep the simulation light, the representation in the GUI is 2d, picturing the different zones of the field as defined in the rule book [2]. Robots are represented as circles, and machines with rectangles. Information available to the user include the task a robot is executing, the next zone he is moving on, and the status and the resources of a station. The user interface is based on the client/server design pattern [6]. The simulator was extended with a HTTP endpoint that can be connected to, to receive data of the state of the simulation. Data from the simulation is sent in JavaScript Object Notation (JSON) format. As the endpoint can be attached to at any point this also makes the simulation flexible for future uses in parallel deployments. The HTTP endpoint is a listener that waits for requests from clients and answers with the requested data. Currently requests of the type GET and PUT are supported. With the GET requests it depends on the route which data is responded with. The supported routes for GET are /zones, /machines and /robots. The PUT is currently in place to send tasks to the simulation. This is intended for debugging and testing purposes currently.

4.2 Play Field

The zones in the simulation are defined by means of a ZoneId, which is specified by the Refbox throug a ProtoBuf message. Furthermore, they contain their X and Y coordinates as well as a list of all neighboring zones. This list is used for the path planning and to traverse the virtual environment. The `ZonesManager` is the central unit to hold all the zones. It is responsible for the construction of all zones of the game field as well as the placing and removing of objects. It also contains the function `GetPathToZone()` to calculate the paths between the zones, which can be called by the robots to find their way on the virtual map. The currently used algorithm for the path planning is a standard A* algorithm.

4.3 Machines

The machines are designed with a shared base class, which encompasses all the requirements of each of the specialized machines. This includes the OPC UA server and the corresponding node structures. It also includes the lights that are modelled in their own respective class and the belt that is represented by the three variables ProductAtIn, ProductAtOut and ProductOnBelt. The station holds one light of the colors green, red and yellow respectively. Some of the common tasks that all the stations are capable of are also directly implemented in the base class. Those functions are for example `resetMachine`, `handleBelt` which is used to move the products on the belts and the handle lights task where the corresponding light gets changed. Furthermore, the `startTask()` and the `endTask()` functions set the corresponding nodes of the OPC UA server to inform the refbox. Other properties like `SlideCount` and `TaskDescription` are mainly used for the graphical user interface to display the current state of the machines, as the values that are used for the behaviors are the nodes from the

OPC UA server. Derived from base class are specialized classes for each of the machine types in the competition. These classes implement all the functionalities that are not covered by the base class. The base station for example needs the `DispenseBase()` function to place the product on its belt. The following start belt task can be done via the `handleBelt()` function of the base class. For the machines the state design pattern [6] has been used for both the handling of the basic tasks and the machine specific tasks. The state design pattern, also called state machine, is used here. As the behavior of the station has distinct states due to the production tasks, it can be modelled nicely as a state machine. In the case of the machines, the default state is idle and is only changed via a message from the Refbox.

4.4 Robots

The robots have some general properties like the jersey number, team color, name, and the assigned task. The robots methods mirror the capabilities of the real robots. `Move()`, `GripProduct()`, and `PlaceProduct()` are the tasks that are the direct modeling of the respective tasks in the real world. In the `Move()` task the robot calculates a path from the current zone to the goal using the A* algorithm. The goal in this case can be both a machine name with a machine point or directly a zone. The robot model gets back a list of zones it has to traverse to reach its goal. When executing the movement, the robot is waiting at each zone for a preset amount of time before switching to its next zone in the path. Generally, all tasks of the robots are synchronized with their state machine. As with the previous objects the robots also have a manager class, the RobotManager, that holds all the robot instances and creates them initially.

4.5 The Agent_Task ProtoBuf Message

One of the most important contribution of this simulation is the standardization of the interface between teams' schedulers and the simulated robots. This is achieved by the definition of the **agent_task** ProtoBuf message. The message is characterized by three main fields: `Team_color`, `robot_id`, and `task_id`. The first two are used by the robots to identify if the task is assigned to them, while the latter helps the team scheduler to keep track of the tasks internally. Moreover, there is one field for each different type of task a robot can execute. Obviously, only the field corresponding to the task that should be executed by the robot must be set. Depending on the type of task, additional fields on the agent_task message have to be set. This includes waypoints, indicating specific zones or machines that the robot needs to navigate to or align with. Additionally, there are supplementary fields utilized by the RefBox to generate game statistics, such as describing the processing workpiece or the order the robot is advancing with for the current task.

4.6 OPC UA Communication

In OPC UA every entity in the address space is a node. In our case, a server with a node structure that mirrors the real machines had to be realized. To achieve this we used the OPC UA framework from the company Traeger [1]. It has the benefits of already defined import functions for generation of a node structure via XML. There are two main components in the implementation of the OPC UA server of the machines. One can change the behavior of the server, add, and remove listeners for different events. The server itself is a provided class from the OPC UA stack of Traeger [1]. As the server can be updated to the desired behavior, the change of the machine state is handled in the `HandleRequestValidating` function. This function is used to react and validate the write commands to the `Enabled` register. To reduce the CPU load of the machines' threads, the stations are put into sleep mode once a task has finished. The wake up is done once the OPC UA server receives a value update on the enabled node. The second part for the OPC UA connection is the `MPSNodeManager` which is responsible for the creation of the nodes, following the order prescribed by the refbox to mimic a machine. Once the server is up and running we can look at the node structure with tools like the opcuaclient, a python package to read and inspect data of a OPC UA server.

5 Evaluation

Both usability and performance of the proposed simulation was evaluated. Regarding the former, the chosen metric is the standard Usability score (SUS) [5], which assign a value from 0 to 100 % usability. The aim of this work is a simulator that should be easier to setup than the previous Gazebo-based simulator. Thus, we expect the results are better than for Gazebo-based one. The standard usability score consists of 10 standardized questions and was defined by John Brooke in 1996 [5]. According to him its a "quick and dirty" usability scale, first introduced in the mid 1980s. It should be answered rather quickly without too much deliberation about the questions and before some kind of debriefing or discussion about the system. Each question can be answered with a scale from 1 to 5, where 1 represents strongly disagree and 5 represents strongly agree. Questions about the complexity, consistency, usability for both technical and non-technical people, and intuitiveness of the proposed system are asked. The resulting answers can be evaluated with the following formulas: The questions can be separated into two groups. The first group is the positively worded questions and can be transformed with the formula $(x_i - 1)$. The second group, namely the negatively worded questions, are evaluated with formula $(5 - x_i)$. The result of those values is each item's i score contribution. This value can range from 0 to 4. If added up, the score contribution can range from 0 to a maximum of 40 points. This can then be scaled to be in a 0–100% range.

For the evaluation, participants in RCLL, who used Gazebo-based and the new simulation proposed, were needed. For this the team of Carologistics from

Aachen and GRIPS from Graz were asked to participate. This call for participation resulted in 7 participants from Graz and 3 participants from Aachen. The survey has been given to the participants for both the Gazebo simulation and the new proposed simulator. Both teams where asked to give immediate feedback after having played at least one game with both simulators. Their answer should be given quickly upon reading the questions for the specific simulator.

This resulted in the following scores for the simulators: The results of the proposed system (M = 84.75%, SD = 4.931%) is significantly more usable ($t_{(14)} = -15$; $p < 0.0000001$) than Gazebo (M = 30.25%, SD = 4.386%) with the difference of the means being 54.5%. To showcase the results a boxplot for both the RCLL (proposed) and Gazebo simulation is shown in Fig. 3a.

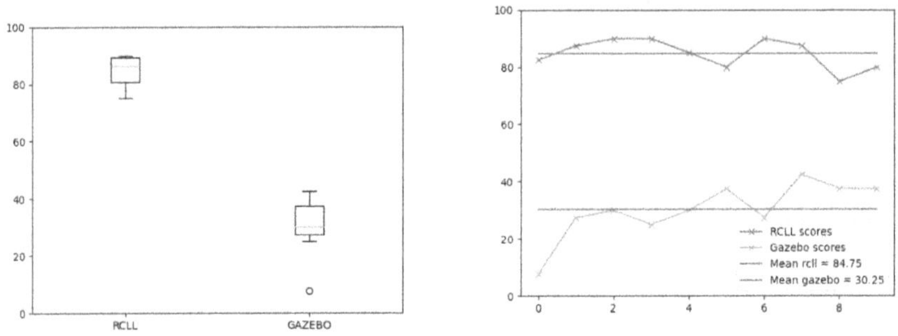

(a) Standard Usability score results

(b) Scores of the different participants and the mean of the according results

Fig. 3. Result figures from the questionnaire. On the left is a boxplot which showcases the point distribution. On the right are the scores in a trend plot, where the red line showcases the mean for the simulator. (Color figure online)

In Fig. 4a and Fig. 4b one can see two boxplots to showcase the different distributions of the simulations. For the boxplot, the score impact of the questions has been taken to show more nicely the distribution of the answers. This means the maximum is 4 and the minimum is 0. What can be seen is the fact that all the answers for the RCLL simulation are relatively close together. The mean of those answers is also close to the maximum value in several of the questions. For Gazebo the opposite can be seen. The questions are quite far apart with a bigger distribution spread. What can be also seen is that the answers in this case are often a lot lower compared to RCLL with some of the mean values close to the minimum of 0.

For the performance evaluation both Gazebo and the RCLL simulation had been used for simulating a full game to show the resource usage. The used computer was equipped with 64 GB of RAM, an Intel Core i9 with 16 logical cores and a Mesa Intel UHD graphics card. The system was running Ubuntu 20.04. The first indicator that will be looked at is the CPU usage. The CPU usage in % can be up to $n * 100\%$ where n is the number of cores, in our case 16. The mean CPU usage of Gazebo is around 775% which means that around

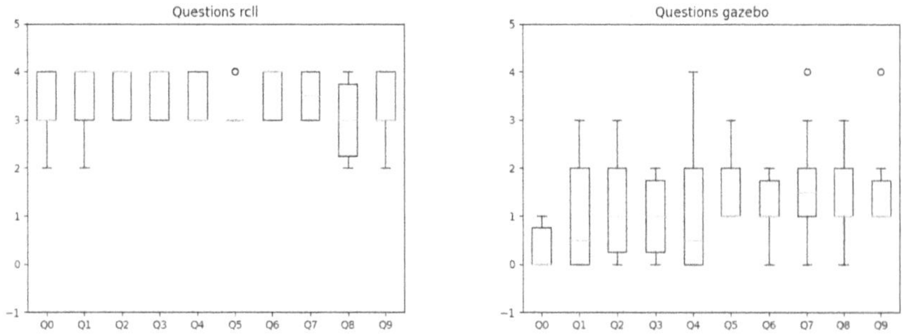

(a) Boxplot of the question results for the RCLL simulation.

(b) Boxplot of the question results for the Gazebo simulation.

Fig. 4. This figures shows the boxplots of the question results for the simulations. The big spread of the Gazebo simulator can be explained by the different experiences of the participants.

8 cores of the CPU were used most of the time. The proposed simulator is at around 2.5% which is a reduction by a factor of 300.

6 Conclusions and Future Work

In this paper we presented the design and implement an event-based agent simulation for the RCLL. An abstraction of the real world capabilities of the robots and stations was proposed and the behavior of the implemented components were described. In order to make the simulation available for all the teams we proposed a definition of a general interface for the agents that each team can follow. The simulation consist of several agents, the machine and robots, which perform tasks and are able to interact with each other. They use different communication protocols, that where already used in the RCLL before, to emulate real machines and robots to both the refbox and team scheduler, replicating the conditions of an actual game. A user interface has been implemented as a web-based solution to give further possibilities in the future with parallel deployments. For example, there is consideration to introduce a simulation subchallenge within the league, enabling new teams to compete with their schedulers making the lack of hardware not a problem. To make future development easier, we have introduced different possibilities to participate in the development, such as continuous integration and a development container. A user study was conducted with several participants to analyze and compare the user experience of both the previous Gazebo-based and the proposed simulation. The study showed that the experience of the participants with the Gazebo-based simulation was on the lower end of the usability score, whereas the proposed system scored highly in comparison. Additionally, a comparison of the resource usage between the Gazebo-based simulation and the proposed system was performed, revealing a significant reduction in CPU usage for the proposed system by 2 orders of magnitude. As part of future work, it is possible to enhance the simulator by incorporating probabilistic models to represent failure and success of activities, enabling more comprehensive testing of team schedulers' robustness. Additionally, Kubernetes could be used to realize parallel deployment, offering the potential for large-scale benchmarks of team schedulers.

References

1. Server Development Guide and Tutorial, Traeger Industry Components GmbH (2022)
2. Technical Committee: RoboCup Logistics League: Rules and regulations. Robocup, 1st edn. (2022). https://github.com/robocup-logistics/rcll-rulebook
3. Agalianos, K., Ponis, S., Aretoulaki, E., Plakas, G., Efthymiou, O.: Discrete event simulation and digital twins: review and challenges for logistics. Procedia Manuf. **51** (2020)
4. Arguenon, V., Bergues-Lagarde, A., Rosenberger, C., Bro, P., Smari, W.: Multi-agent based prototyping of agriculture robots. In: International Symposium on Collaborative Technologies and Systems (CTS 2006) (2006)
5. Brooke, J.: SUS: a quick and dirty usability scale. In: Usability Evaluation In Industry (1996)
6. Gamma, E., Johnson, R., Helm, R., Johnson, R.E., Vlissides, J.: Design Patterns: Elements of Reusable Object-Oriented Software. Pearson Deutschland GmbH (1995)
7. Hart, P.E., Nilsson, N.J., Raphael, B.: A formal basis for the heuristic determination of minimum cost paths. IEEE Trans. Syst. Sci. Cybern. **4**(2), 100–107 (1968). https://doi.org/10.1109/TSSC.1968.300136
8. Kampa, A., Gołda, G., Paprocka, I.: Discrete event simulation method as a tool for improvement of manufacturing systems. Computers **6**(1) (2017)
9. Larsen, J.B.: Going beyond BDI for agent-based simulation. J. Inf. Telecommun. **3**(4), 446–464 (2019)
10. Mahnke, W., Leitner, S., Damm, M.: OPC Unified Architecture. SpringerLink: Springer e-Books. Springer, Heidelberg (2009). https://books.google.at/books?id=de9uLdXKj1IC
11. Marder-Eppstein, E., Berger, E., Foote, T., Gerkey, B., Konolige, K.: The office marathon: robust navigation in an indoor office environment. In: International Conference on Robotics and Automation (2010)
12. Niemueller, T., Karpas, E., Vaquero, T., Timmons, E.: Planning competition for logistics robots in simulation. In: International Conference on Automated Planning and Scheduling (ICAPS) - Workshop on Planning and Robotics (PlanRob) (2016)
13. Riley, P.: Mpades: Middleware for parallel agent discrete event simulation. In: RoboCup 2002: Robot Soccer World Cup VI, pp. 162–178. Springer (2003)
14. Steinbauer, G., Niemueller, T., Karras, U.: The RoboCup logistics league-a testbed for novel concepts in flexible production. In: Worshop on Robotic Assembly – Recent Advancements and Opportunities for Challenging R&D, IEEE International Conference on Automation Science and Engineering (2018)
15. Zwilling, F., Niemueller, T., Lakemeyer, G.: Simulation for the RoboCup logistics league with real-world environment agency and multi-level abstraction. In: RoboCup 2014: Robot World Cup XVIII 18, pp. 220–232. Springer (2015)

Event-Based Vision for Robot Soccer

Seyed Ehsan Marjani Bajestani(✉) and Giovanni Beltrame

Computer and Software Engineering Department, Polytechnique Montreal, Montreal, QC H3T 1J4, Canada
{ehsan.marjani,giovanni.beltrame}@polymtl.ca

Abstract. Object tracking is one of the main challenges in soccer-playing robots. Due to its fast movement, detecting and tracking the soccer ball is challenging for goalkeepers in both humanoid and wheeled robots. To speed up object tracking, we propose the use of Event-based Cameras (ECs). ECs are bio-inspired sensors that asynchronously report changes in brightness for each pixel. Because of their high dynamic range, pixel bandwidth, temporal resolution, low power consumption, and computational simplicity, they are beneficial for vision-based projects in challenging lighting conditions and can detect fast movements with their microsecond response time. We created a dataset using two different event-based cameras from iniVation and Prophesee that recorded events in the lab and during Middle Size League matches at RoboCup 2023. Additionally, we created a Graphical User Interface (GUI) working with the Robot Operating System (ROS) to simplify camera and camera-projector setup calibration for RoboCup participants. The proposed ROS GUI is able to control the camera bias parameters online and publish a stream of events in addition to event "frames" on ROS topics. These advancements will help all RoboCup teams shift from frame-based to event-based technologies, enhancing ball detection regardless of color or lighting. The dataset is available publicly: github.com/MISTLab/event_based_data.

Keywords: Event-based camera · Calibration · Dataset · Soccer robots

1 Introduction

Frame-based standard cameras are widely used on soccer-playing robots in the RoboCup. Typically, robots use these cameras to detect and locate the ball and other robots on the soccer field. Additionally, vision-based sensors provide other important information, such as the field lines and their relative distance to localize the robot. However, frame-based cameras have inherent limitations. They require good illumination, they are susceptible to blurring during fast movements (see Fig. 1), have a relatively low dynamic range (leading to saturation in changing illumination conditions), and may require high bandwidth depending on the output resolution and frame rate.

Executive and Technical committee member of the RoboCup-MSL from 2016 to 2024.

E. Barros et al. (Eds.): RoboCup 2024, LNAI 15570, pp. 309–317, 2025.
https://doi.org/10.1007/978-3-031-85859-8_26

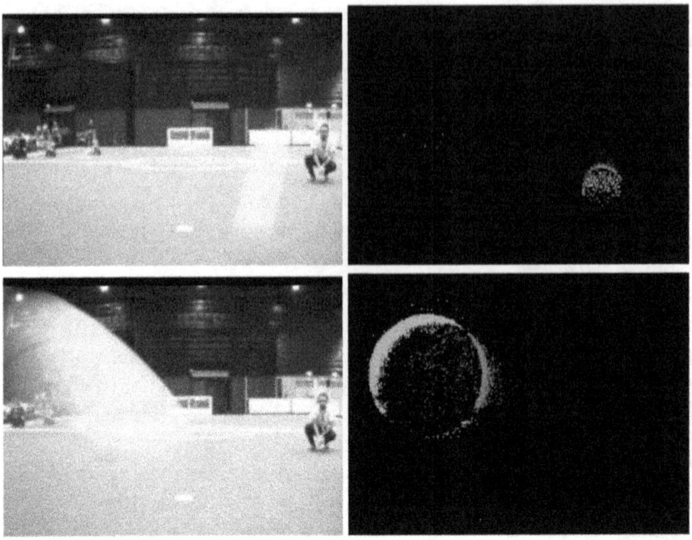

Fig. 1. Comparison between frames captured by the DAVIS346 color event-based camera during RoboCup 2023 on the MSL field. The left column shows RGB frames recorded at 30 fps, while the right column displays gathered events with a temporal resolution of less than 2ms. In this record, the ball approaches the robot and bounces in front of it.

In the RoboCup soccer leagues, real robots mainly fall into two types: humanoid and wheeled robots [1]. Even though robots in the Small Size League (SSL) do not have individual cameras (mounted cameras above the field capture frames, and a central computer reports the locations), detecting and tracking a fast-moving ball individually or cooperatively is challenging for all players in the Middle Size League (MSL) and the Humanoid Leagues (Kid, Teen, and Adult sizes). In recent years, teams have investigated various types of vision-based sensors to achieve the fastest available tracking methods in RoboCup. However, to the authors' knowledge, no research has been conducted on the advantages of the ECs in the RoboCup. ECs (also known as neuromorphic cameras, Dynamic Vision Sensors (DVS), motion contrast sensors, Asynchronous Time-based Image Sensors (ATIS), and asynchronous transient vision sensors) are bio-inspired sensors that produce a "paradigm shift" in the way visual data is obtained [8]. Figure 2, compares standard cameras with ECs.

While these cameras are commercially available, they tend to be relatively more expensive compared to frame-based cameras. Also, due to their neuromorphic nature, employing conventional convolutional algorithms with event-based cameras is not feasible. Overcoming these obstacles is crucial for advancing the adoption and efficacy of event-based technologies in the RoboCup. The main contribution and benefits of this research for the RoboCup participants are as follows:

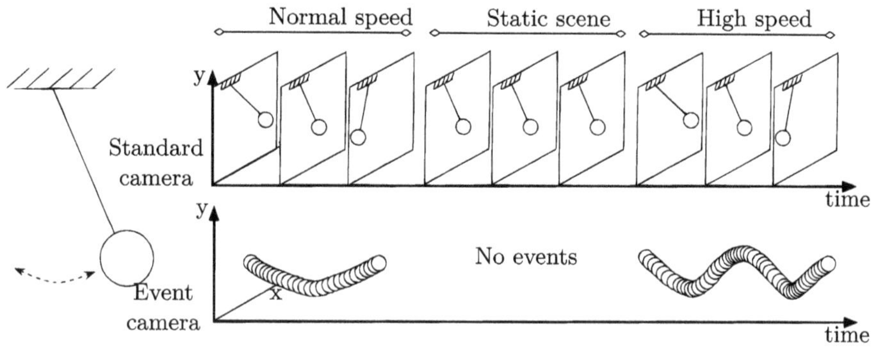

Fig. 2. Comparison of event-based camera output with frame-based camera in different motion modes. Note: The EC shows no activity in static scenes and experiences less blur than frame-based cameras at high speeds.

1. Introduction of Event-based Cameras (ECs) to RoboCup soccer leagues, expanding the technological scope. Which is beneficial in fast object detection and tracking while maintaining computational simplicity, improving overall performance.
2. Providing a dataset containing a recorded stream of events during a RoboCup match, facilitating experimentation and analysis.
3. Development of a Graphical User Interface (GUI) on the Robot Operating System (ROS) [12], enabling the generation of event frames compatible with conventional algorithms.
4. Streamlining camera calibration processes through the ROS GUI, enhancing accuracy and efficiency in camera setup.

Our method provides teams with an open-source code that can be used to feed their current ball detection and tracking algorithm with a faster frame rate. By generating frames gathered from events on ROS topics, our open-source framework seamlessly integrates with existing computational vision-based algorithms, ensuring teams do not need to modify their primary algorithms. Additionally, the provided dataset allows teams to test their code before investing in ECs, aiding in their transition from frame-based cameras to event-based ones.

2 Related Work

ECs do not capture full images; instead, they report a stream of events. However, they can detect movement thousands of times faster than standard RGB frame-based sensors. They are particularly useful in fast-moving detection projects, such as dodging multiple dynamic obstacles with a quadrotor [13]. In [13], the authors used ECs to estimate ego-motion and the motion of moving objects, achieving a 70% success rate, including the detection of objects with unknown shapes in low-light conditions[1].

[1] https://youtu.be/k1uzsiDI4hM.

Researchers have integrated frame-based cameras with ECs to avoid receiving blurred frames during high-speed motions. In [9], they combined these two types of cameras to generate a deblurred high frame rate (HFR) and high dynamic range (HDR) video.

In [11] they presented a perception system for 6-DOF localization during high-speed maneuvers. Their method had robust motion tracking with angular speeds up to 1,200°/*sec*.

In [6], the authors used powerlink $IEEE$61158 industrial network, communicating the FPGA with a controller connected to a self-developed two-axis servo-controlled robot. And they compared frame-based cameras and ECs in terms of the response time and robustness to the variable lighting conditions. By utilizing ECs, they achieved 85% data reduction and 99 ms faster position detection on average compared to the frame-based camera.

The authors of [10], used a DVS to detect and track a fast-moving object. They approximated the 3D geometry of the event stream to motion-compensate for the camera and detect unknown moving objects. They reached over 84% of success rate in detecting multiple unknown moving objects in various lighting conditions[2].

The authors of [7], used an EC on a robotic arm (as a goalkeeper) to block upcoming shots. They achieved an 80% blocking capability even against fast shots, with update rates of 550 Hz and low latencies of 2.2 ± 2 ms. These results were achieved with a peak CPU load of less than 4% and standard USB buses, showcasing practical viability under real-world operating conditions.

3 Event-Based Camera Calibration

To calibrate the camera, we used our Event-based RGBD ROS Wrapper [5]. The provided ROS GUI is able to control the camera setting online and publish a stream of color-stamped events in addition to RGB frames on ROS topics. The GUI is to calibrate the camera with a Symmetric Circles Grid LED Pattern (Fig. 3 top right). Figure 4, shows the provided ROS GUI during the camera-projector calibration.

The ROS GUI distinguishes between events generated by the LEDs on the calibration board and events generated by the projected pattern dots from the projector. As shown in Fig. 4, the GUI has been used first to calibrate the camera by detecting various relative positions of the LED board. Then it has been used to track the calibration board and calculate its relative position to the camera, to calibrate the projector and determine the relative position of the projector to the camera. The camera-projector calibration is integrated into the code, making it convenient for structured light 3D scanning projects. While the projector calibration may not be applicable in RoboCup scenarios, the camera calibration section would be useful alongside the other available software [3].

[2] https://youtu.be/UCAJi0ZFaZ8.

Color-DAVIS346 Khadas VIM3

Fig. 3. Setup for creating the dataset during RoboCup 2023. Top left: Robot number 5 from the French team, Robot Club Toulon, with our standalone setup on the MSL soccer field. Top right: Calibration circle dot-board used for calibrating the event-based camera and camera-projector setup, with white dots from LEDs and red dots projected from a projector. Bottom left: Color-DAVIS346 EC. Bottom right: Khadas VIM3 (Color figure online)

4 Dataset

To create the dataset, we mounted a Color-DAVIS346 [2] EC on top of an MSL robot[3] and gathered data during the RoboCup 2023 (Fig. 3 top left). The camera reports events and frames simultaneously, which can be useful for teams to compare the proposed method with their current camera. It also has a 6-axis (Gyro and Accelerometer) with up to 8 kHz sampling rate. The power consumption of the camera is less than 180 mA at 5 VDC (USB).

To record events we used Khadas VIM3 single-board computer (SBC) [4]. The VIM3 features an Amlogic A311D processor.

The dataset is available publicly: github.com/MISTLab/event_based_data. The provided dataset contains a diverse range of scenarios, including the ball approaching the goalkeeper, leaving the goal area, penalty kicks, dribbling in front of the goalkeeper, and even scenarios involving human dribbling across the soccer field. Figure 5 shows various frames of the dataset captured with the Color-DAVIS346.

[3] Robot Club Toulon.

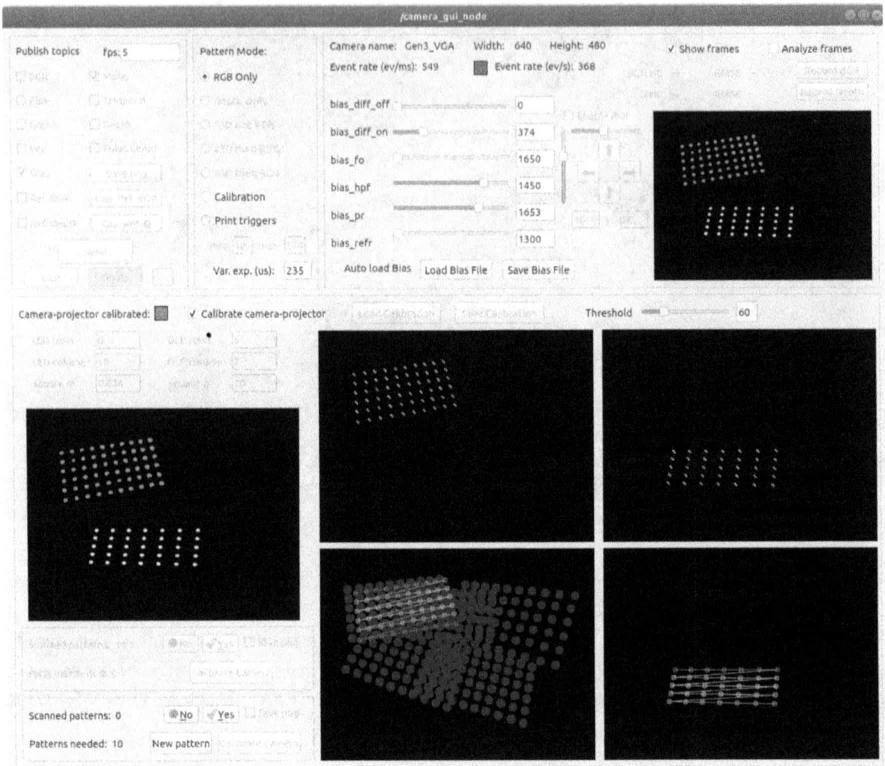

Fig. 4. The ROS GUI to control the bias parameters of the EC and calibrating the camera/projector.

Fig. 5. Various frames of the dataset captured with the Color-DAVIS346

5 Conclusion

In conclusion, our work provides tools for calibrating event-based cameras and offers a dataset for RoboCup participants. Teams can utilize their current convolutional image processing algorithm by generating frames from the event-based camera using our ROS wrapper. This approach simplifies object detection and tracking while maintaining compatibility with existing algorithms.

Acknowledgments. We extend our appreciation to the iniVation company for providing a DAVIS346 color event-based camera in 2023, which facilitated the creation of the dataset and our presentation of this camera to members of the RoboCup community participating in the soccer robot league (Middle Size League) in Bordeaux, France. We also would like to acknowledge the collaboration of the French team Robot Club Toulon for their assistance in affixing the camera onto their robot during intermissions between matches.

References

1. RoboCup Federation. https://www.robocup.org/domains/1
2. The Color-DAVIS346 event-based camera specifications. https://inivation.com/wp-content/uploads/2022/10/2022-09-iniVation-devices-Specifications.pdf
3. The iniVation's documentation page. https://docs.inivation.com/
4. The Khadas VIM3 single-board computer specifications. https://www.khadas.com/vim3
5. Bajestani, S.E.M., Beltrame, G.: Event-based RGB sensing with structured light. In: Proceedings of the IEEE/CVF Winter Conference on Applications of Computer Vision (WACV), pp. 5458–5467. IEEE (2023). https://openaccess.thecvf.com/content/WACV2023/html/Bajestani_Event-Based_RGB_Sensing_With_Structured_Light_WACV_2023_paper.html
6. Barrios-Avilés, J., Iakymchuk, T., Samaniego, J., Medus, L.D., Rosado-Muñoz, A.: Movement detection with event-based cameras: comparison with frame-based cameras in robot object tracking using powerlink communication. Electronics **7**(11), 304 (2018). https://doi.org/10.3390/electronics7110304, https://www.mdpi.com/2079-9292/7/11/304
7. Delbruck, T., Lang, M.: Robotic goalie with 3 ms reaction time at 4% CPU load using event-based dynamic vision sensor. Front. Neurosci. **7**, 223 (2013)
8. Gallego, G., et al.: Event-based vision: a survey. IEEE Trans. Pattern Anal. Mach. Intell. (2020). https://doi.org/10.1109/TPAMI.2020.3008413, https://ieeexplore.ieee.org/document/9138762
9. Messikommer, N., et al.: Multi-bracket high dynamic range imaging with event cameras. arXiv preprint arXiv:2203.06622 (2022)
10. Mitrokhin, A., Fermüller, C., Parameshwara, C., Aloimonos, Y.: Event-based moving object detection and tracking. In: 2018 IEEE/RSJ International Conference on Intelligent Robots and Systems (IROS), pp. 1–9. IEEE (2018). https://doi.org/10.1109/IROS.2018.8593805, https://ieeexplore.ieee.org/document/8593805
11. Mueggler, E., Huber, B., Scaramuzza, D.: Event-based, 6-DOF pose tracking for high-speed maneuvers. In: 2014 IEEE/RSJ International Conference on Intelligent Robots and Systems, pp. 2761–2768. IEEE (2014). https://doi.org/10.1109/IROS.2014.6942940, https://ieeexplore.ieee.org/document/6942940

12. Quigley, M., et al.: ROS: an open-source robot operating system. In: ICRA Workshop on Open Source Software, vol. 3, p. 5 (2009). https://www.ros.org
13. Sanket, N.J., et al.: EVDodgeNet: deep dynamic obstacle dodging with event cameras. In: 2020 IEEE International Conference on Robotics and Automation (ICRA), pp. 10651–10657. IEEE (2020). https://doi.org/10.1109/ICRA40945.2020.9196877, https://ieeexplore.ieee.org/document/9196877

SoS: A Semi-Synthetic RoboCup Soccer Dataset for Visual Segmentation

Ysobel Sims(✉), Trent Houliston, Matthew Amos, Alexander Biddulph, Jonathan Tabac II, Alana Noonan, Angelique Herfel, Joe Bailey, Johanne Montano, and Thomas O'Brien

University of Newcastle, Callaghan 2308, Australia
ysobel.sims@uon.edu.au

Abstract. SoS (Soccer Segmentation) is a computer vision semantic segmentation dataset for RoboCup soccer. It contains raw images with rectilinear and equisolid projections, metadata for each image with lens and positional information, and coloured segmentation masks. The dataset is generated using Blender and uses 360° images from real past RoboCup fields to create a semi-synthetic scene. Our Blender tool used to generate the dataset is available at https://github.com/NUbots/NUpbr. SoS is hosted on HuggingFace and is accessible for download at https://doi.org/10.57967/hf/2099. We provide benchmarks for SoS using the Visual Mesh and U-Net, and conduct real world experiments on the network with fine-tuning on a small amount of real data.

Keywords: Computer Vision · Dataset · Machine Learning

1 Introduction

Computer vision is a vital component of the RoboCup Humanoid Soccer leagues. Robots in these competitions are given no direct information about the position of objects and must use humanoid sensors, such as cameras, to gather this information. Teams use computer vision to interpret the environment and behave accordingly.

Deep learning with convolutional neural networks is a popular object detection method. A survey of computer vision methods in the Humanoid League [1] shows that many teams currently use bounding box methods, such as YOLO [6] architectures. Some teams are using YOEO [9], combining bounding box and segmentation.

Bounding boxes provide a simple and computationally efficient method for detecting objects on the soccer field. However, segmentation provides benefits that bounding box methods lack.

- Segmentation gives more information than bounding boxes. Segmentation can be useful when you need to know not only where objects are in an image, but also what their exact shape is.

E. Barros et al. (Eds.): RoboCup 2024, LNAI 15570, pp. 318–327, 2025.
https://doi.org/10.1007/978-3-031-85859-8_27

- Segmentation can identify overlapping/obstructed objects, such as if a ball is partially behind another robot. While bounding boxes may be able to identify balls in this scenario, it is often more difficult to understand the overlapping situation with bounding boxes.
- Bounding boxes are not suitable for detecting field lines and the field.

The robots used at RoboCup are often low-resource robots and cannot use computationally intensive networks. Segmentation networks are generally more intensive than bounding box networks; however, there are segmentation networks that can run in real-time on low-resource robots, such as the Visual Mesh [5].

The information from bounding box networks may be sufficient in some scenarios, but as the competition progresses and the challenge increases, the importance of finer vision detail will increase. With faster networks and hardware, the disadvantages of segmentation disappear while gaining more information from the vision system than bounding boxes.

A major issue for computer vision in RoboCup is the lack of datasets, and manually labelling and curating datasets is time-intensive and expensive, particularly for segmentation datasets due to the slow nature of segmentation labelling. TORSO-21 [2] provides the Humanoid League with a bounding box vision dataset with segmented field lines. Balls, robots and goals are not segmented in TORSO-21. Participants of the Standard Platform League (SPL) have compiled many datasets, including bounding box and field line segmentation. There exists a segmentation dataset of 10,000 images released on Kaggle [4] and an unsupervised dataset with some issues in accuracy [3].

SPL datasets benefit RoboCup; however, for the Humanoid League, they are not ideal. The field differs between the leagues, and the Humanoid League includes many different kinds of robots and balls, rather than only the NAO robot and standard black and white ball. These differences motivate the creation of datasets for the Humanoid League. While TORSO-21 covers bounding box and field line segmentation, there is no segmentation dataset for the Humanoid League that segments all vision objects relevant for robot soccer, i.e. goalposts, balls and robots. The lack of datasets limits the ability of teams to move to segmentation-based networks.

We introduce the Soccer Segmentation (SoS) dataset to fill this gap. We generate SoS using Blender with physically based rendering, resulting in realistic environments. Full 360-degree high dynamic range (HDR) images from past RoboCup fields provide a further degree of realism.

We obtain a baseline for this dataset using the Visual Mesh and U-Net. Real world tests are conducted using the trained Visual Mesh network, and we further fine tune the network and visualise its performance on a humanoid robot.

2 Data Generation Tool

We compile the dataset using NUpbr[1], our Blender Python tool that automatically generates soccer scenes using physically based rendering. In this section we

[1] https://github.com/NUbots/NUpbr.

introduce NUpbr, with the following section describing how NUpbr is applied to generate SoS. NUpbr is open source on GitHub and publicly available to download and build upon.

NUpbr renders randomised scenes with the following objects.

- **Goals:** The segmentation mask labels all parts of the goalposts, including vertical and horizontal, with the net excluded. We separate back and front goalposts with different colours.
- **Balls:** There could be one or more soccer balls present.
- **Soccer Field:** Includes all of the green parts of the field, excluding the field lines.
- **Field Lines:** The white lines on the soccer field.
- **Robots:** A robot is positioned where the camera mounts in Blender, referred to as the 'self robot'. Additionally, the user specifies the number and types of other robots to render in the scene.
- **Background:** Includes random objects on the field that do not fall into the previous categories.

The Blender tool aims to reduce the gap between synthetic and realistic data. It does this using physically-based rendered (PBR) materials and image-based lighting (IBL) combined with high-dynamic range (HDR) environment maps. For each environment configuration in Blender, we render an image, its corresponding segmentation mask and JSON metadata.

2.1 Field, Goalposts and Background

NUpbr visualises the field, goalposts and background using a HDR environment map of a soccer field. The HDR must have a paired segmentation mask to distinguish the background, goalposts, field and field lines, and any balls or robots in the image. Each HDR environment map has a configuration file with the bounds of the field, and the position and orientation of the camera on the field when the HDR was captured.

2.2 Balls

The Blender tool constructs balls using the Filmbox (FBX) format with colour and normal maps. It can also construct balls from a UV colour map by creating a sphere object and applying the UV map to the object. NUpbr accepts a mean and standard deviation for ball radius, which will randomly determine the scale of each generated ball.

2.3 Robots

Robots are generated by importing FBX models. NUpbr supports colour, normal, texture and material maps for robots. With a JSON file, the robots are assembled according to their kinematic chain and positioned with random joint angles.

The 'self' robot is generated where the camera is located, with the image taken from the robot's perspective. The camera is mounted in Blender to the point where the physical camera would be on this robot. The tool rotates the robot and its neck to look towards an object of interest in the Blender environment, such as the soccer ball, to better balance the presence of a particular object in the environment.

2.4 Clutter and Noise

NUpbr includes the ability to generate random clutter, a form of domain randomisation [8], to bridge the reality gap in synthetic data. This clutter is in the form of random shapes with random textures, including reflective surfaces.

Imperfections are applied over the top of the image to improve realism. These include randomised motion blur, noise and exposure. NUpbr adjusts the red channel by a randomised amount to address an issue with auto white balance in the cameras, which arises from the extensive green presence on the soccer field. This problem occurs because the abundance of green in the field images can lead the cameras to incorrectly compensate, resulting in images with a reddish hue.

3 Dataset Description

The dataset contains 47,575 samples, split into nine sets for easier download and management of the data. We store the dataset on Hugging Face[2]. Ten images in the dataset with their corresponding segmentation masks are shown in Fig. 1.

3.1 Field, Goalposts and Background

We obtain HDRs to generate the field, goalposts and background using a Ricoh THETA S camera. The images contain background, field, field lines and goalposts. Some HDRs also contain robots and balls. The SoS dataset uses HDRs from RoboCup 2017 Nagoya, RoboCup 2018 Montreal, RoboCup 2019 Sydney, RoboCup 2022 Bangkok, RoboCup 2023 Bordeaux, and the NUbots Newcastle Laboratory Soccer Field. We capture multiple HDRs in various locations on each field to get 37 unique HDRs.

3.2 Balls

We collected 122 unique soccer balls to generate the data, including balls previously used at the RoboCup competition, such as Adidas Oceaunz, Adidas Al Rihla, and Adidas Conext 21. Both FIFA and non-FIFA balls are included in the dataset.

[2] https://doi.org/10.57967/hf/2099.

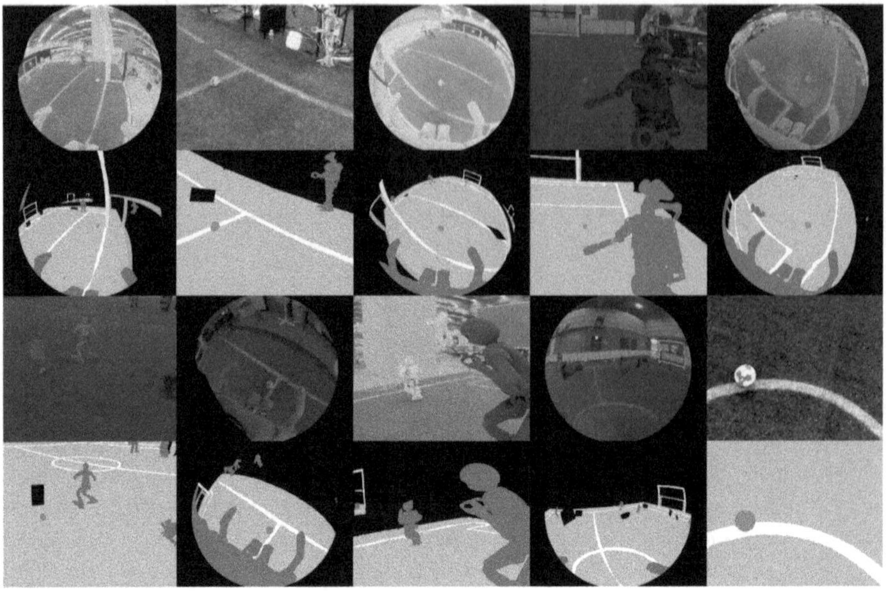

Fig. 1. Images and their segmentation masks from SoS.

3.3 Robots

RoboCup 2021 was conducted virtually, with the Humanoid League using the Webots simulator to run the competition. Each competing team created a Webots PROTO for their robot, defining the model of their robot. After returning to in-person competitions, the Humanoid League continued using Webots in two Virtual Season competitions. This has improved access to models of different robots within the league. We converted these models to FBX files and adjusted them to include the ability to randomise joint angles and materials on each robot. Robots are randomly placed within the field's bounds. SoS includes the NUgus (NUbots), Wolfgang (Hamburg Bit-Bots), Bez (UTRA Robosoccer), Chape (IT-Androids), GankenKun (CIT Brains), Karen (MRL-HSL), SAHRV74 (StarKit), Darwin-OP (Robotis and RoMeLa), and NAO (SoftBank Robotics) robots.

The robot where the camera is mounted is always a NUgus robot, with limits set such that the Blender camera will be within realistic bounds. The head will look towards the ball.

3.4 Metadata

Each image has associated lens metadata in the form of a YAML file. This metadata contains the projection of the image, either equisolid or rectilinear; the focal length, in pixels; the field of view in radians; and the homogeneous transformation matrix from the camera to the field. We use this data to train the Visual Mesh.

3.5 Segmentation

We provide semantic segmentation masks for each image, automatically generated using NUpbr. Each class is represented by a colour, detailed in Table 1. NUpbr automatically generates these masks using the HDR segmentation mask and Blender's knowledge of where objects are in the scene.

Table 1. The colour and RGB value for each class in the segmentation masks.

Class	Colour	RGB
Soccer balls	red	(255, 0, 0)
Soccer field	green	(0, 255, 0)
Field lines	white	(255, 255, 255)
Robots	blue	(0, 0, 255)
Front goalposts	yellow	(255, 255, 0)
Back goalposts	orange	(255, 102, 0)
Background	black	(0, 0, 0)

4 Evaluation

We trained two computer vision networks, the Visual Mesh and U-Net, on the SoS dataset to validate its efficacy and establish benchmark performance. Additionally, we test the Visual Mesh model on a real robot and fine tune it on a small amount of real data.

Table 2. Precision and recall for each class on the test set using Visual Mesh and U-Net trained using SoS.

Class	Visual Mesh		U-Net	
	Precision	Recall	Precision	Recall
Soccer balls	0.80	0.60	0.78	0.50
Soccer field	0.96	0.96	0.98	0.99
Field lines	0.79	0.67	0.89	0.79
Robots	0.81	0.82	0.82	0.79
Goalposts	0.72	0.35	0.72	0.36
Background	0.91	0.94	0.94	0.96

4.1 Visual Mesh

We train the Visual Mesh using SoS and a random 45-10-45 split for the training, validation and test sets respectively. We combine back and front goalposts into one goalpost class. SoS is used directly with no downsampling.

We use the Adam optimiser with a fixed learning rate of 10^{-4} and train the model for 2500 epochs. Our network architecture consists of nine graph convolutional layers, with sizes of 64, 64, 32, 32, 16, 16, 8, and 8, all using the SELU activation function. The output layer employs a softmax activation function. Each epoch comprises 1000 batches, with a batch size of 1. We use a Ring8 mesh.

We record precision and recall on the test set in Table 2. Eight images are shown in Fig. 2 with a mesh overlay with predictions from the trained Visual Mesh model.

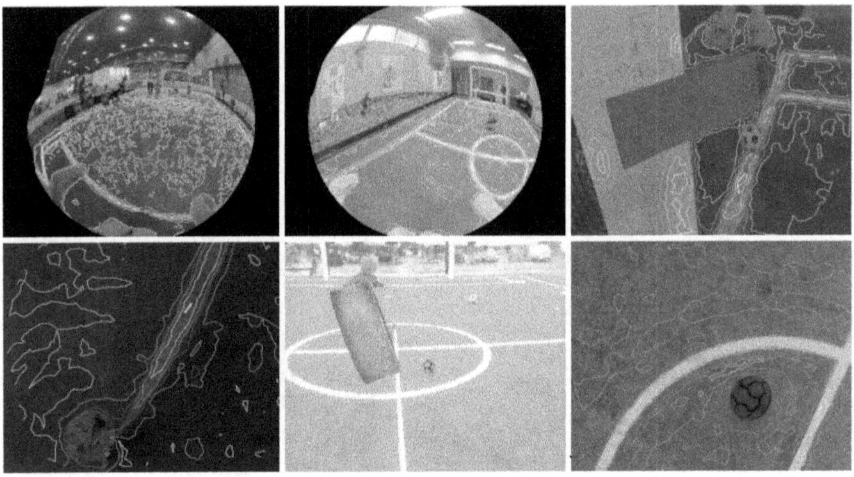

Fig. 2. Images with a mesh overlay of the Visual Mesh predictions from the trained Visual Mesh model.

There is better performance in the background and field pixels due to their over-representation in the dataset. On the other hand, balls and goalposts are under-represented and have a worse performance. The Visual Mesh is sensitive to noise; therefore, the injection of noise in SoS causes a decreased performance overall compared to cleaner datasets. These results show avenues for improvement due to the potential for noise in images from robot cameras.

4.2 U-Net

U-Net is a semantic segmentation network originally designed for biomedical tasks [7]. This architecture was chosen to benchmark SoS due to its simplicity and efficiency. We downsample the images of SoS using nearest neighbour to 256×256 due to the computational load of 1280×1024 images. A batch size of 64 is used and learning rate of 10^{-3} with an Adam optimiser and cross entropy loss. Front and back goalposts were again combined into one class. The network was trained for 44 epochs before early stopping.

Precision and recall for each class is recorded in Table 2. Ten samples with segmentation output from the trained U-Net are visualised in Fig. 3.

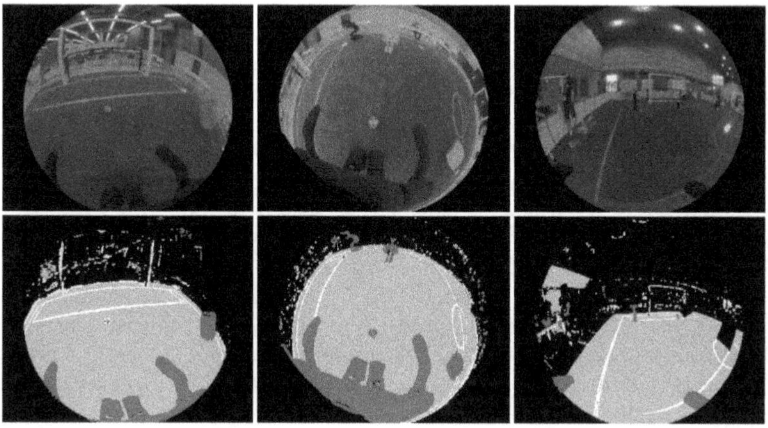

Fig. 3. Pairs of images and their segmentation masks predicted from the trained U-Net model.

Similarly to the Visual Mesh results, we see that under-represented classes under-perform. In both U-Net and the Visual Mesh, the soccer balls have a higher precision and recall to the goalposts. NUpbr rotates the robot so that the camera is looking at the ball. This rotation may result in more balls compared to goalposts in images.

4.3 Real World

We use the Visual Mesh for real world experiments. It is recommended to fine-tune the network on a small amount of real data to bridge the domain gap.

We collect 228 RGB images from a FLIR Blackfly S camera with a Lensation 180° fisheye lens, mounted on a NUgus humanoid robot. Two identical robots are used to collect the data simultaneously in the Newcastle Robotics Laboratory at the University of Newcastle. The images are collected in a stream while the robots autonomously play soccer at a rate of one image every second per robot. Camera pose metadata for each image is collected using an unscented Kalman filter with gyroscope and accelerometer inputs, all running onboard the robot. Segmentation masks are human-annotated using image processing tools such as Photoshop and GIMP. This real data is released alongside SoS on HuggingFace.

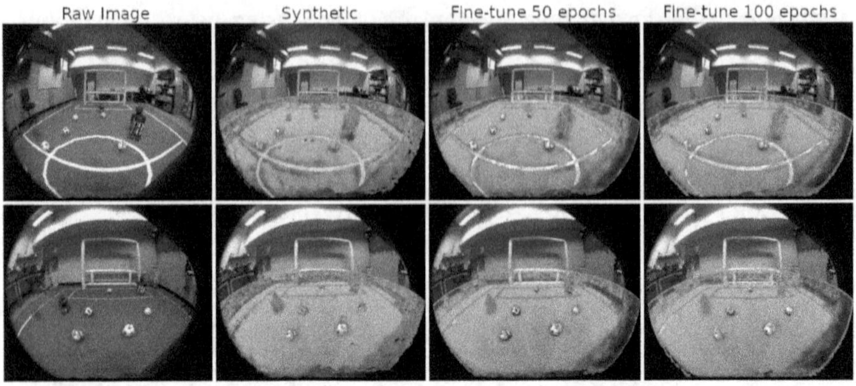

Fig. 4. Real world tests on a NUgus robot, using a visual debugging tool to capture the segmentation in real time. The two scenes are set up with various soccer balls, a NUgus robot and a Darwin-OP robot. The first column shows the raw image from the camera without a Visual Mesh overlay. The second column shows the detections from the Visual Mesh model trained on only the semi-synthetic SoS data. The third and fourth columns show the detections after fine-tuning the SoS model on a small amount of real data for 50 and 100 epochs respectively. Segmentation colours are as defined previously except for field lines which are blue and robots which are magenta, for better visualisation against the raw image. Higher saturation represents a higher confidence for the class. (Color figure online)

The same parameters from the original SoS training are used in fine tuning, with the exception of the number of epochs and number of batches per epoch. The number of batches per epoch is set to 100. We train two fine-tuned models, one for 50 epochs and another for 100 epochs.

We consider the performance of the network in real time using a NUgus robot and a visual debugging tool that displays the robot's images and Visual Mesh segmentation prediction overlay. Figure 4 shows the output of our onboard tests. The first column shows the raw image from the robot's cameras, the second column shows the output of the network only trained on the semi-synthetic data, and the third and forth columns show the output of the fine-tuned networks trained for 50 and 100 epoch respectively.

The semi-synthetic network is able to recognise the balls and robots, and has a high confidence on the field. The background is noisy, but this can be mitigated with post-processing. We cluster field points and create a convex hull around the cluster, representing the bounds of the field, and ignore detections beyond the field. This network is a valuable base for fine-tuning, and with only 50 epochs and a small amount of real data the fine-tuned network has good performance. Notably, the fine-tuned network is able to detect balls and robots (i.e. the Darwin-OP) that are not present in the real dataset.

5 Conclusion

We present SoS, a segmentation soccer dataset with accompanying camera metadata containing 47,575 unique data samples. It is the first computer vision dataset for the Humanoid League with full semantic segmentation annotations. We obtain two benchmarks for SoS using deep learning architectures, one from the Visual Mesh and one from U-Net. While showing room for improvement, these benchmarks demonstrate that the dataset is correct and has use in the computer vision soccer domain.

Acknowledgments. This research is supported by 4Tel Pty Ltd, 4AI Systems Inc and Australian Government Research Training Program Scholarships to Ysobel Sims and Thomas O'Brien.

References

1. Bestmann, M.: Results of humanoid league survey. https://robocup.informatik.uni-hamburg.de/en/2022/07/results-of-humanoid-league-survey-2/
2. Bestmann, M., et al.: TORSO-21 dataset: typical objects in robocup soccer 2021. In: RoboCup 2021 (2021)
3. Blumenkamp, J., Baude, A., Laue, T.: Closing the reality gap with unsupervised sim-to-real image translation. In: Alami, R., Biswas, J., Cakmak, M., Obst, O. (eds.) RoboCup 2021. LNCS (LNAI), vol. 13132, pp. 127–139. Springer, Cham (2022). https://doi.org/10.1007/978-3-030-98682-7_11
4. Broemmel, P.: Robocup spl instance segmentation dataset (2020). https://www.kaggle.com/ds/469203
5. Houliston, T., Chalup, S.K.: Visual mesh: real-time object detection using constant sample density. In: Holz, D., Genter, K., Saad, M., von Stryk, O. (eds.) RoboCup 2018. LNCS (LNAI), vol. 11374, pp. 45–56. Springer, Cham (2019). https://doi.org/10.1007/978-3-030-27544-0_4
6. Redmon, J., Divvala, S., Girshick, R., Farhadi, A.: You only look once: unified, real-time object detection. In: IEEE Conference on Computer Vision and Pattern Recognition, pp. 779–788. IEEE Computer Society, Los Alamitos (2016)
7. Ronneberger, O., Fischer, P., Brox, T.: U-net: convolutional networks for biomedical image segmentation. In: Navab, N., Hornegger, J., Wells, W.M., Frangi, A.F. (eds.) MICCAI 2015. LNCS, vol. 9351, pp. 234–241. Springer, Cham (2015). https://doi.org/10.1007/978-3-319-24574-4_28
8. Tobin, J., Fong, R., Ray, A., Schneider, J., Zaremba, W., Abbeel, P.: Domain randomization for transferring deep neural networks from simulation to the real world. In: 2017 IEEE/RSJ International Conference on Intelligent Robots and Systems (IROS), pp. 23–30. IEEE, Vancouver (2017)
9. Vahl, F., Gutsche, J., Bestmann, M., Zhang, J.: Yoeo -you only encode once: a cnn for embedded object detection and semantic segmentation. In: IEEE International Conference on Robotics and Biomimetics (ROBIO) (2021)

The Director: A Composable Behaviour System with Soft Transitions

Ysobel Sims(✉), Trent Houliston, Thomas O'Brien, Alexandre Mendes, and Stephan Chalup

University of Newcastle, Callaghan 2308, Australia
ysobel.sims@uon.edu.au

Abstract. Software frameworks for behaviour are critical in robotics as they enable the correct and efficient execution of functions. While modern behaviour systems have improved their composability, they do not focus on smooth transitions and often lack functionality. In this work, we present the Director, a novel behaviour framework that addresses these problems. It has functionality for soft transitions between states, multiple implementations of the same action chosen based on conditionals, and strict resource control. The system was successfully used in the 2022/2023 Virtual Season and RoboCup 2023 Bordeaux, in the Humanoid Kid Size League. It is implemented at *github.com/NUbots/DirectorSoccer*, which also contains over thirty automated tests and technical documentation on its implementation in NUClear.

Keywords: Decision Making · Robotics · Software Architecture

1 Introduction

Autonomous robotics is a broad field where robots perform diverse tasks. The actions performed at any given moment depend on state and environment information. Behaviour frameworks allow developers to define rules for behaviour algorithms to manage a robot's actions. A behaviour system should facilitate a smooth transition between actions; account for differences over time in information quality and environment knowledge; be flexible and versatile; impose strict resource control between modules, such as for motors; be composable for quick development; contain state information for debugging; and run in real time.

Looking back at previous research on behaviour systems, the classical subsumption system [5] provided a modular approach but lacked composability and functionality. Behaviour trees are modular, reactive and composable but lack complex functionality and can become cumbersome [4]. They cannot change actions based on the existence of environment knowledge, which research aims to address [1,12,16]. The ABC^2 behaviour system previously used in RoboCup used a queue-based agenda focusing on multi-agent gameplay. It did not facilitate smooth transitions and lacked complexity beyond multi-agent functionality. The Dynamic Stack Decider (DSD) [10] is composable and maintainable but

E. Barros et al. (Eds.): RoboCup 2024, LNAI 15570, pp. 328–338, 2025.
https://doi.org/10.1007/978-3-031-85859-8_28

lacks the desired functionality for soft transitions. The Humanoid Control Module [3] was incorporated with the DSD to abstract lower-level hardware modules from higher-level strategy modules and to avoid conflicts in motor control, as the DSD could not inherently facilitate this.

The literature has developed over time towards composable, functional and transparent systems. However, each system still lacks some desired functionality. Research often focuses on one or a few key components, without considering all aspects needed for a general behaviour system. The Director aims to address these gaps.

In this work, we present The Director, a behaviour framework for autonomous systems that emphasises modularity and transitions. It incorporates functionality for soft transitions to ensure safe robot motions as tasks change. Its modular architecture enables programmers to focus on developing one small and specific functionality for the robot at a time. The framework's versatility facilitates complex behaviours, including defining multiple ways to complete one task chosen based on conditionals. A library of automated tests[1] supports the creation of the Director's backend algorithm. The Director's design integrates many desirable features into a simple, coherent framework. It leverages the popular publisher/subscriber pattern [6] found in many message-passing systems such as Robot Operating System (ROS) [11] and NUClear [7].

The Director exists at a high level of abstraction that oversees all software levels of the system. The Director can work together with algorithms that provide the specific logic for how a robotic agent will achieve its goal, such as large language models (LLMs) [9,13] and knowledge-base systems [2,14], by providing the framework for these systems to work within.

The Director is general-purpose and implementable in reactive message-passing robotic software architectures. We implemented it within NUClear for the RoboCup Humanoid Soccer League, and have used it in the 2022/2023 Virtual Season and RoboCup 2023 Bordeaux, with a game won using the Director in each competition. The Director framework simplified the implementation of new behaviours, provided more flexibility and facilitated published work in using LLMs to power the higher level reasoning of a robot [9].

2 Framework

The Director is a framework for controlling the flow of behaviour in a system. A fundamental aspect of the framework is the concept of Providers and Tasks which build a tree structure, where Tasks are messages requesting functionality, and Providers provide the functionality for those behaviours. Providers can call Tasks themselves, which are considered children of the Provider. The depth and width of the Director tree formed by Providers and Tasks can be of any size. The Director has a wide range of features to solve limitations in existing behaviour systems. Definitions of key terms are in Table 1.

[1] https://github.com/NUbots/DirectorSoccer/tree/main/module/extension/Director/tests.

We use a soccer-playing scenario to describe the concepts in the Director, where a humanoid robot approaches a ball and kicks it. Figure 1 shows the Director graph at the start of this scenario, where the robot has seen the ball and is walking towards it.

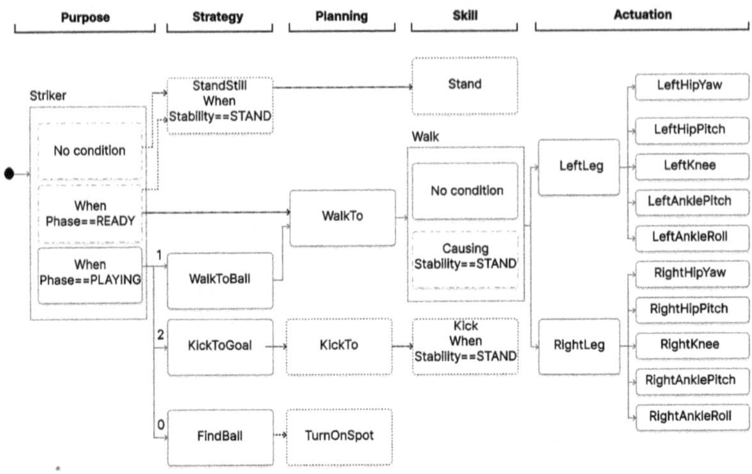

Fig. 1. This figure shows a Director graph for a humanoid robot playing soccer. Arrows represent Tasks and boxes represent Providers. The figure shows active (solid blue), blocked (dashed red), and inactive (dotted black) Providers and Tasks. The values of Tasks indicate their priority. (Color figure online)

Table 1. Definitions for key terms for the Director framework.

Concept	Description
Provider	A function that provides the functionality for a Task
Non-Provider	A function that doesn't provide for a Task
Provider Group	A collection of Providers that service the same Task
Task	A request for a single piece of functionality
Root Task	A Task that is called from a non-Provider
Priority	A value that determines if a Task can take control
Optional	The Task is not required to run and will defer to non-optional Tasks
Done	A Task that indicates that the Provider has completed its Task
Idle	A Task that will keep running the last set of Tasks for a Provider

Table 2. DSL keywords used in the Director.

DSL Keywords	Description
Provide	The normal Provider that provides the functionality for a Task
Start	The Provider that is run when a Provider group gains control
Stop	The Provider that is run when a Provider group loses control
Needs	The Provider needs control of the specified task to run
When	Conditions on when the Provider can be active
Causing	The state that will be achieved by running this Provider
Uses	Retrieves information on a Provider's child task state
RunReason	Gives information on why the Provider ran

The remainder of this section will describe in detail the concepts that form the Director framework. By implementing these together, developers can take advantage of the benefits the Director inherently brings.

2.1 Providers

Providers are functions that perform actions to satisfy the requirements of one particular Task, either directly or by running their own tasks. The function runs when the Task it provides for is requested from anywhere in the system. Providers may have conditions on when they can run, defined in their declaration. Given these conditions are satisfied, the Provider will run when a new task is received.

In our soccer-playing scenario, a Task from the Striker Provider triggers the WalkToBall Provider to execute. It finds the ball position and requests a Task to trigger the WalkTo Provider with this ball position data. The WalkTo Provider will send a Task to trigger the Walk Provider with a determined velocity so that the robot will walk to the ball.

Provider Groups: A group of Providers for one Task type is called a Provider group. Only one Provider in a group can run at a time, chosen based on the conditions of the Providers. If a Provider can no longer run, the Task is reassigned to another Provider in the group.

Striker and Walk are Provider groups in Fig. 1. The Striker is using the 'playing' Provider since that condition is true. If the game phase were to transition to the ready state, the 'ready' Provider would become active. Provider groups allow for a change in behaviour for a specific Task when there is a change in environment or state information. This flexibility is a desired trait explored in the literature [12,15,16].

Provider Types: Provider groups facilitate the inclusion of three unique Provider types. The standard type executes functionality for a Task. The 'start' type sets up the state of the Provider when a Provider group gains control of its Task after not having control previously. It runs once and then the standard Provider will run. The 'stop' type is used to clean up code and only runs once when a Provider group is losing control of its Task. It cannot run without a start or standard type Provider running before it.

In our scenario, the Walk Provider group will have a start Provider that sets up the walk engine. When the Kick Provider takes over, the Walk Provider group will have a stop Provider that cleans up the walk engine.

Needs: The DSL keyword 'Needs' is used to ensure that a Provider can only run if it has priority to take control of its child tasks. In our scenario, both the Walk and Kick Providers specify that they Need the LeftLeg and RightLeg Tasks. This conflict means the Walk and Kick Providers cannot run simultaneously. Because the KickToGoal Task has higher priority than the WalkToBall Task, if both are requested to run then the Kick Provider will take control and the Walk Provider will be blocked from running as it does not have control of its Needs tasks.

When: 'When' is a DSL keyword that only allows a Provider to execute when the system satisfies a specified condition. The condition has three parts - a state type, a comparison operator and a state value. In our scenario, the Kick Provider only runs When the stability state of the robot is equal to standing. This prevents the robot from transitioning from the walk mid-step and falling over.

This functionality, combined with Provider groups, solves the problem described by Veloso et al. [15], where existing systems don't consider the precision of environment knowledge. They proposed a behaviour system that emphasised the accuracy and fidelity of information in determining how to perform a task. A single action, such as localising, could have multiple methods for execution depending on the quality of sensor data. In the Director, each method can have an associated Provider, with the precision level for that method defined in the When conditional.

Causing: The DSL keyword 'Causing' in the Director allows for soft transitions between Providers. It declares that the Provider will cause a condition to be satisfied. Similarly to 'When', it has a state type, a comparison operator and a state value. If a Provider has a 'When' condition, the Director will prioritise lower priority Providers with a matching 'Causing' if the 'When' fails.

In our scenario, the Kick Provider requires the robot to be standing, but the robot is currently walking. A version of the Walk Provider in the Walk Provider group causes the stability state to become equal to standing. Because the Kick Provider has a higher priority, this will run and make the robot stop cleanly and stand still, allowing it to kick safely.

2.2 Tasks

Tasks are jobs that Providers execute and can contain data. They have three pieces of information: Task data, priority level, and an optional flag. Prioritisation of Tasks determines which should run, with non-optional Tasks always taking priority over optional ones. If a Task is optional, other sibling tasks can run if it cannot, but the Director will implement all-or-nothing for non-optional sibling tasks. Both Providers and non-Providers can request Tasks. Tasks from non-Providers are called 'root tasks'.

In our scenario, the Walk Provider requests LeftLeg and RightLeg child tasks. The Provider must have control over both Tasks for them to run. The Walk Provider can also have optional LeftArm and RightArm child tasks, which will run if possible but will not block the other tasks from running.

Root Tasks: Tasks requested from non-Providers are called root tasks and are the starting points of the Director graph. These tasks are siblings at the top of the tree. Root tasks are different from Tasks requested from Providers because they cannot be removed by running a Provider without the Task. Instead, the Task needs to be manually flagged in a way so that the Director will remove it.

Priority: Priority in the Director is determined based on the closest common ancestor of the two competing Tasks. For root tasks, the closest common ancestor is the root element. The priority of each Task's branch from the closest common ancestor will determine which Task has higher priority. The winner takes control and becomes active, while the evicted Task will wait for an opportunity to take back control. Optional Tasks will always lose to non-optional Tasks.

In Fig. 2, the Walk initially has priority over the left and right legs. The Kick is requested and will try to take control of the legs, challenging the Walk Provider. The closest common ancestor of these two Providers is the Striker Provider. Because the KickToGoal Task has a higher priority than the WalkToBall Task, the Kick Provider will take control of the legs from the Walk.

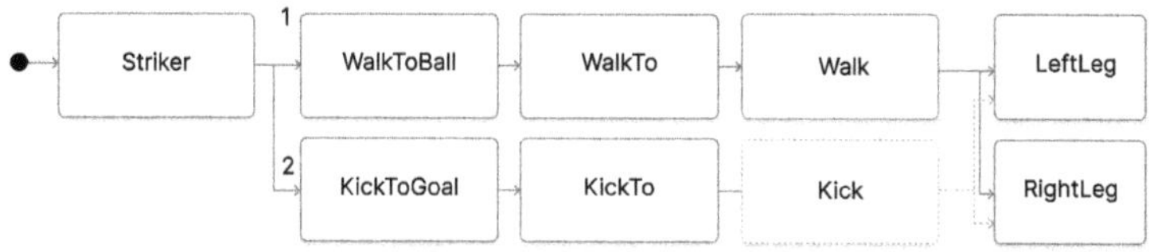

Fig. 2. An example of priority, where the kick challenges the walk for control of the legs and succeeds in taking control due to its higher priority.

Done Tasks: A Done Task is a Task sent by a Provider to notify its parent. The parent is triggered to execute upon receiving this signal from its child. The Done Provider's Task remains in the tree unless it's a root Task.

In Fig. 1, when the LeftHipYaw Provider reaches the desired motor position, it sends a Done Task to its parent. Once all motors in LeftLeg send Done Tasks, LeftLeg itself sends a Done Task, allowing the next sequence of motor positions to run.

Idle Tasks: An Idle Task is a Task a Provider requests to signal to continue running its previous Tasks. For example, in our scenario, the KickTo Provider can send an Idle Task when it is kicking and does not want to re-request the Kick Task. If it is re-requested, the Kick may run from the beginning and not reach the end of its motion. Often, Done Tasks are used to check if a Provider should Idle or run new Tasks.

2.3 Data

Providers can access data about the local state of the Director to assist in making decisions.

Uses: 'Uses' is a DSL keyword used to obtain information about child tasks. It provides information about the run state of the child task and whether it is Done. The run states include whether the child task is currently running, queued to run, or not yet requested by the current Provider. An example of how this information can be used is in Listing 1.

```
def Provide(KickTo):
    # Kick is current running, keep running (idle)
    if kick.run_state is running and kick is not done:
        Task(Idle)
    elif robot is aligned to target and ball in front of robot:
        # Need to kick and waiting to kick, keep waiting (idle)
        if kick.run_state is queued:
            Task(Idle)
        # Need to kick and we aren't trying to kick, send a new kick task
        else:
            Task(Kick)
    # Else no task, Director tree removes any existing Kick task
```

Listing 1: Pseudocode for the KickTo Provider using run state and done information.

Run Reason: The 'RunReason' DSL keyword retrieves information about why a Provider is running. There are five possible run reasons - a new Task was requested, the Provider has become active, the Provider has become inactive, a child task is Done, and the Provider is pushed because a higher priority module wants its Causing state to be true.

3 Evaluation

We consider key traits of the Director that are of benefit to a behaviour system: composability, extensibility, transitions, resource control and versatility. These motivate the adoption of the Director in an autonomous robotic system.

3.1 Composability

It is simple to combine modules in the Director. Requesting relevant Tasks combines desired modules into the program. Calling a 'ChaseBall' Task from a non-Provider function or main loop of the program can easily demonstrate the robot chasing a ball. The Task call will trigger all the necessary modules to chase a ball through subsequent Providers and Tasks. The easy modification and addition of behaviours are critical for debugging and developing in high-pressure scenarios, such as RoboCup. Subsumption-based systems [5] have more difficulty achieving this, as the layers build upon each other and are more tightly coupled.

3.2 Extensibility

In the Director system, adding new components is straightforward and does not require a global reevaluation of priorities. New Providers and Tasks can be created and requested without changes to the rest of the system. Subsections of the system can be easily isolated. This flexibility allows for easy experimentation, modification and debugging.

In our experience, the development of behaviour modules within the Director framework is significantly quicker than in our previous subsumption-like system. After converting our system, the high modularity made it easy to see ways to extend the functionality of the robots. It also allows for quick prototyping of research ideas, motivating the creation of an LLM strategy module with safety systems powered by the Director [9].

3.3 Transitions

In humanoid robotics, transitions are a factor in preventing the robot from causing damage. The Director supports clean and safe transitions through conditionals on Providers to prevent them from running unless the system is in a particular state. Additionally, the Director includes functionality for soft transitions. Rather than immediately transitioning from one action to another, a Provider can handle the transition using the pushing functionality. An example of the pushing functionality involving the kick and walk is provided in the previous section, using the 'When' and 'Causing' DSL words. The smooth transition it creates between walking and kicking is critical for stability and safety. These features facilitate high-priority safety modules critical for practical robotics.

Existing literature rarely addresses transitions, and we are not aware of other systems with soft transitioning functionality.

3.4 Resource Control

The Director has a strict control system where a Provider can only provide for one Task at a time, and only one Provider of a Task type can be active at a time. Other Tasks and Providers are blocked and must wait for an opportunity to take control. This core rule in the algorithm prevents multiple sources from controlling one resource, such as the motors. By grouping motors, the system can ensure that only one module controls a kinematic chain.

In our previous system, all motor commands moved through one module that enforced a similar strict control system. Another solution proposed by Bestmann and Zhang uses the Humanoid Control Module [3] to implement a mutex on the motors. Instead of implementing locking mechanisms directly, the Director handles these tasks on behalf of the user.

3.5 Versatility

The Director is a versatile framework that aims to incorporate all needed functionality for autonomous robotics, including transitions and strict resource control. Another important aspect is the ability to create multiple implementations for one action. Provider groups facilitate this, where one implementation runs based on the system state. Numerous research articles address this concept in the context of the quality and existence of environment information [12,15,16]. Provider groups provide this functionality in a generalised way, where conditions determine the active Provider.

Modern implementations of behaviour trees for autonomous robotics request tasks and act based on the state of the subtask [12,16]. The Uses information and Done Tasks within the Director provide this functionality and could extend to conform to the behaviour tree structure if desired by adding fail and success responses from child tasks.

ABC^2 [8] has a similar Provider-Task relationship with conditionals on nodes. However, they do not address transitions, resource control and multiple implementations for tasks.

4 Conclusion

The Director framework is a unique solution for autonomous robotic behaviour systems. By addressing the limitations of existing frameworks, such as transitions and functionality, the Director offers a comprehensive solution for managing robot actions effectively and efficiently while facilitating safety components and complex behaviours.

The Director's ability to define multiple implementations for the same task based on conditionals adds a layer of flexibility and complexity. This feature enables agents to adapt their actions dynamically to changing environmental conditions, leading to more robust and versatile performance in real-world scenarios. The Director's strict resource control mechanisms, extending to motor control, ensure efficient and non-conflicting usage of resources.

The successful implementation of the Director demonstrates its practical applicability and effectiveness in competitive environments. By simplifying the implementation of new behaviours and providing flexibility for integrating advanced technologies like LLMs, the Director opens up new possibilities for autonomous robotic behaviour.

Acknowledgements. This research is supported by 4Tel Pty Ltd, 4AI Systems Inc and an Australian Government Research Training Program Scholarship to the first author. We acknowledge contributors of the NUbots Robotics Research Group, whose work this publication builds upon. Thank you to Johanne Montano for their review of this work.

References

1. Aisu, H., Unemi, T., Inagaki, Y., Ono, S., Sugie, H.: A robust planning and control system handling fuzziness. In: Proceedings of IEEE International Conference on Fuzzy Systems, vol. 3, pp. 1701–1706 (1995)
2. Beetz, M., Beßler, D., Haidu, A., Pomarlan, M., Bozcuoğlu, A.K., Bartels, G.: Know rob 2.0 - a 2nd generation knowledge processing framework for cognition-enabled robotic agents. In: 2018 IEEE International Conference on Robotics and Automation (ICRA), pp. 512–519 (2018)
3. Bestmann, M., Zhang, J.: Humanoid control module: an abstraction layer for humanoid robots. In: IEEE International Conference on Autonomous Robot Systems and Competitions (ICARSC), pp. 263–268 (2020)
4. Biggar, O., Zamani, M., Shames, I.: A principled analysis of behavior trees and their generalisations (2021). arXiv preprint arXiv:2008.11906
5. Brooks, R.: A robust layered control system for a mobile robot. IEEE J. Rob. Autom. **2**(1), 14–23 (1986)
6. Eugster, P.T., Felber, P.A., Guerraoui, R., Kermarrec, A.M.: The many faces of publish/subscribe. ACM Comput. Surv. **35**(2), 114–131 (2003)
7. Houliston, T., et al.: Nuclear: A loosely coupled software architecture for humanoid robot systems. Front. Rob. AI **3** (2016)
8. Matellán, V., Borrajo, D., Fernndez, C.: Using ABC^2 in the RoboCup domain. In: Kitano, H. (ed.) RoboCup 1997. LNCS, vol. 1395, pp. 475–482. Springer, Heidelberg (1998). https://doi.org/10.1007/3-540-64473-3_85
9. O'Brien, T., Sims, Y.: Exploring gpt-4 for robotic agent strategy with real-time state feedback and a reactive behaviour framework. In: Australasian Conference on Robotics and Automation (ACRA) (2023)
10. Poppinga, M., Bestmann, M.: Dsd - dynamic stack decider. Int. J. Soc. Robot. **14**, 73–83 (2022)

11. Quigley, M., et al.: Ros: an open-source robot operating system. In: ICRA Workshop on Open Source Software, vol. 3 (2009)
12. Safronov, E., Colledanchise, M., Natale, L.: Task planning with belief behavior trees. In: IEEE/RSJ International Conference on Intelligent Robots and Systems (IROS), pp. 6870–6877 (2020)
13. Singh, I., et al.: ProgPrompt: generating situated robot task plans using large language models. In: International Conference on Robotics and Automation (ICRA) (2023)
14. Tenorth, M., Beetz, M.: Knowrob: knowledge processing for autonomous personal robots. In: Proceedings of the 2009 IEEE/RSJ International Conference on Intelligent Robots and Systems, pp. 4261–4266. IEEE Press (2009)
15. Veloso, M., Winner, E.: Multi-fidelity robotic behaviors: acting with variable state information. In: Proceedings of AAAI (2000)
16. Yang, S., Mao, X., Wang, S., Bai, Y.: Extending behavior trees for representing and planning robot adjoint actions in partially observable environments. J. Intell. Rob. Syst. **102**(2), 36 (2021)

A Quantitative Comparison of Vision Performance for the HSR: Gazebo vs. Isaac Simulator

Christopher Duarte(✉), Shengxin Luo, Julio Ojalvo, Katarzyna Pasternak, and Ubbo Visser

Department of Computer Science, University of Miami, 1365 Memorial Dr, Coral Gables, FL 33146, USA
{cduarte,tluo,jojalvo,kwp,visser}@cs.miami.edu

Abstract. Simulators in robotics research are widely used and are the cornerstones of many advances in the field. As time goes on, there are now more and more options available to roboticists than ever before. However, navigating through the choices in search of the right simulator is often non-trivial. There is a lack of quantitative studies to justify the usage of different simulators for different applications, especially regarding the quality of simulated computer vision solutions. A common vision solution with inaccuracies in simulators is object detection. We conduct thorough quantitative experiments and provide in-depth analysis of comparability of object detection performance in the commonly used simulator Gazebo and the newly introduced NVIDIA Isaac Sim to real life solutions using the Toyota Human Support Robot (HSR) as the platform. Our results indicate that Gazebo grossly overestimates in terms of prediction accuracy while NVIDIA Isaac Sim matches much more closely with reality. Additionally, we found that performance in Gazebo can be unstably variant at times. Furthermore, both simulators share highly correlated low-end to high-end performance distribution with reality. We can recommend NVIDIA Isaac Sim for robotic research and developments where computer vision is integral.

Keywords: Simulation · Gazebo · Isaac Sim · Computer Vision · Object Detection · Service Robots · Domestic Robotics · Human Support Robot

1 Introduction

Simulators play a pivotal role in advancing research, development, and testing of robotic systems [1,20,21,28] in the realm of service robotics. They serve as invaluable tools for exploring various aspects of robot perception, navigation, and interaction with the environment and users [3,15,24]. Perception stands out as a cornerstone, with vision playing a critical role, among the various elements crucial for simulating realistic robotic behaviors.

E. Barros et al. (Eds.): RoboCup 2024, LNAI 15570, pp. 339–350, 2025.
https://doi.org/10.1007/978-3-031-85859-8_29

A robotics simulator is defined as an end-user software application that, at a minimum, provides: a physics engine for realistic modeling of physical phenomenon, collision and friction models, a graphical user interface (GUI), import capability for scenes and meshes, API in a programming language used by the robotics community (C++/Python), and readily available models for an array of joints, actuators, and sensors [7].

The effectiveness of a simulator hinges greatly on its ability to accurately replicate the sensory inputs that a robot would encounter in the real world. Vision sensors, in particular, are vital for providing robots with visual information about their surroundings, allowing them to perceive objects, navigate through environments, and interact with external agents.

One issue present when working with robotic simulators is that of the sim-to-real gap [4,12,26,29], evident as missing conditions when modeling scenes from reality to simulator. Several examples of these discrepancies include modeling sensor noise, action latency, and real-world characteristics and dynamics. One simulator common to roboticists which suffers from the sim-to-real gap is Gazebo. Another recently released[1] simulator is NVIDIA Isaac Sim[2] which appears to mitigate this gap through the rendering of more realistic scenes via the application of ray-traced lighting. This led to the following research question: *Is Isaac Sim more performant than Gazebo as a simulator for real-time robotics with regards to vision, on the HSR platform?*

This paper seeks to address this question by providing a comprehensive comparison of the two simulators, Gazebo and NVIDIA Isaac Sim, for the @Home platforms with regards to vision. By examining object detection performances, we seek to analyze the strengths, limitations, and trade-offs associated with each simulator.

Through the provided experimental results and analysis, we hope to provide an educated suggestion to the RoboCup@Home community regarding the most applicable simulator for the needs of the competition and research in the tested areas.

2 Related Work

In recent years, the increase of robotics simulators has allowed for significant advancements in related research, offering researchers diverse tools for modeling and testing autonomous systems in virtual environments [9,16,18,19,30]. Simulators, such as Gazebo, serve as a great platform for testing service robots' capabilities before subsequent verification on physical units. Significant advantages of simulator application include faster development cycles and risk mitigation in both development and testing. Faster development cycles occur by allowing for near-instant, parallel, and continuous access to a virtual emulation of the physical unit for the performance of experiments and testing on a machine meeting

[1] https://forums.developer.nvidia.com/t/isaac-sim-2023-1-0-release-announcement/269863.

[2] https://developer.nvidia.com/isaac/sim.

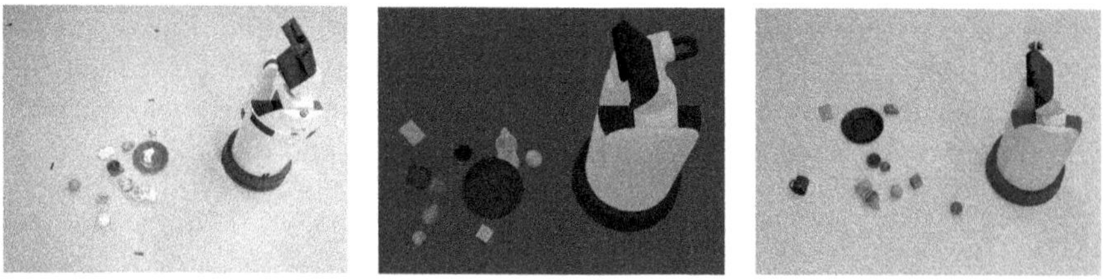

(a) (b) (c)

Fig. 1. Figures from left to right are our default experiment conditions in real life, Gazebo and Isaac Sim.

the specifications of the simulator. By testing in a separate virtual environment from the physical robotic unit, any potential dangers that may be present due to errors are mitigated to both the robotic unit and external agents. Although benefits exist for the experimentation and testing of simulated robotic units, a known significant drawback is that of the sim-to-real gap in the overall performance of simulated and physical robotic units. This is evident in discrepancies present in sensor fidelity, environmental dynamics, and model accuracy among other factors.

Differences between Gazebo and Isaac simulators include physics and vision emulation. By default, Gazebo utilizes the ODE physics engine[3] and Isaac Sim utilizes the PhysX physics engine[4]. These physics engines have been extensively tested in prior works [8,10,11]. In contrast, there exist applications of vision as a necessary dependency for subsequent robotic tasks such as navigation [2], path planning [23], grasping [6], and human-robot interactions [22], but there appears to be a lack of direct analysis of vision with regards to identifying an appropriate simulator that minimizes the sim-to-real gap with regards to the HSR. Previous work(s) in robotic simulator comparisons [17,25,27] have indicated an overall lack of necessary quantitative assessments with regard to the distinct identifiable components of robotic simulators. This study focuses on providing *quantitative* evaluation in robotic perception through vision with measurements on how the rendering quality of each simulator affects object detections, with respect to real-world HSR ground truth.

3 Experiments

Our study focuses on robotic vision with experimental testing of object detection between the real HSR, Gazebo, and Isaac Sim. The experiments were conducted utilizing a YOLOv8s [13] model pre-trained on COCO [14] and fine-tuned on 20 random objects chosen from the YCB dataset [5] from which 10 objects were selected to represent a distribution of easy to difficult to detect objects. The 10

[3] https://classic.gazebosim.org/.

[4] https://developer.nvidia.com/physx-sdk.

selected objects then had their poses randomized 0.5 m around a pivot point at each experiment position. Utilizing the constant object detection model, three distinct experiments were conducted with the following independent variables: HSR relative pivot distance, HSR relative pivot angle, and room lighting conditions.

(a) (b) (c)

Fig. 2. Figure (a) is an example of images used as background of the training image, (b) is a cropped object image from the 3D laser scan of the YCB object dataset [5], and (c) is a composed training image from our data generation pipeline.

In preparation for the experiments, comparable scenes were designed for each experiment scenario as illustrated in Fig. 1. In reality, the robot was moved to the designated poses corresponding to the particular experiment, and object detection results were captured. For simulator testing, a static 3D model of our lab was utilized for consistency amongst simulator environments. For Isaac Sim and Gazebo, separate implementations of the HSR were provided by the Toyota Motor Company (TMC). In the simulator testing procedures, 10 objects were spawned around the pivot position based on a scaled Gaussian distribution with the HSR model generated at the designated experimental poses. This randomization occurs 10 times for each experiment conditions which we will introduce below. Within each randomized scene, 200 detection samples are collected and all 2000 samples are used to computed the statistics for each condition we measured in the results.

(a) (b) (c)

Fig. 3. Figure (a) is the input image to the object detection model, (b) is the prediction with bounding boxes, and (c) is the ground truth.

The object detection algorithm utilized in this work, as illustrated in Fig. 3, functions as part of the data generation framework depicted in Fig. 2. Our custom generation framework composes the training images for the YOLOv8s backbone by taking an isolated object cropping and patching it onto a set of randomly captured background images in an arrangement of 4 rows and 5 columns, all cleanly separated with no overlap.

The generated image is used directly to fine-tune the pre-trained backbone with the default SGD optimizer, a learning rate of 0.001 and a momentum of 0.6. The training lasted for 200 epochs with a batch size of 64 which resulted in a final training IOU loss of 1.64.

(a) (b) (c)

Fig. 4. Figure (a) illustrates the scene for the default configuration of the experiment, (b) is the configuration with the robot 1 m further away from the object scene, and (c) is the configuration with the robot 2 m further away.

The distance experiment (Fig. 4) consists of data captured from setting the HSR at 0.6, 1.6, and 2.6 m away from the pivot position at a fixed pivot rotation at 0°. 0.6-m radius is the optimal camera view from the pivot position for the scene. 2.6 m distance is the maximum distance from which the real robot can still detect the seen object, and 1.6 m is the middle point. This measures the effect of object size scaling due to distance in the image frame for a more robust comparison between simulators.

The angle experiment (Fig. 5) consists of data captured by placing the HSR at a fixed 0.6-m distance and rotating it around the pivot position at 0°, 90°, 180°, and 270° angles. This measures the effect of object reflectance as a result of the HSR's position around the objects.

The lighting experiment (Fig. 6) consists of data captured by varying the test scene's lighting conditions while maintaining the HSR's distance at 0.6 m and 0°. This measures the effect of different lighting conditions through detections in a scene by enabling 1) only rectangular high bay lights, 2) only round low bay, and 3) both lights.

4 Results and Analysis

This section demonstrates the obtained results of the described experiments with subsequent comparative analysis to provide an informed decision when choosing the more comparable simulator to ground truth estimates.

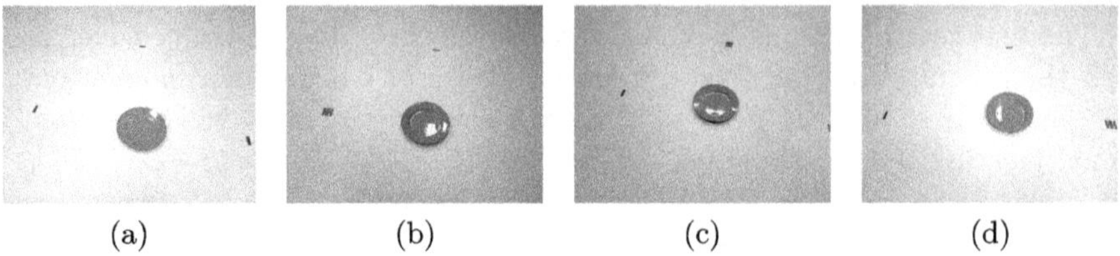

Fig. 5. Figure (a), (b), (c) and (b) are pictures of the same plate object from the YCB dataset from the four different viewing angles permuted in our experiments, demonstrating the effect of reflectivity in real life.

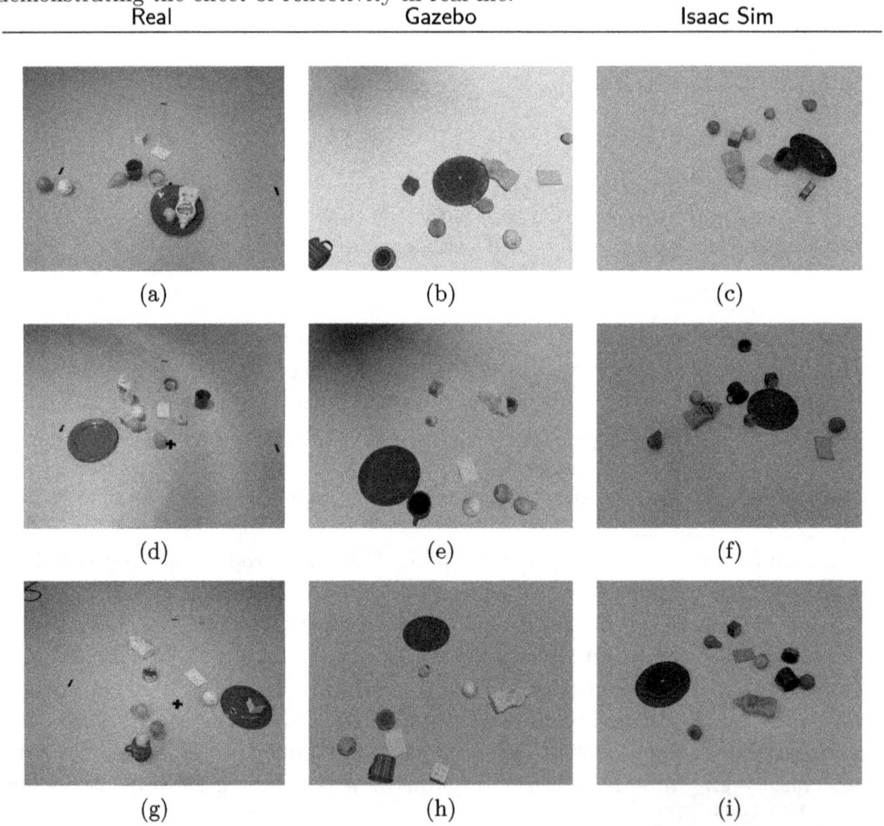

Fig. 6. Figure (a), (b) and (c) are example scenes of both lights on in real life, Gazebo and Isaac Sim respectively. Figure (d), (e) and (f) are example scenes of only the round low bay rights on in the same sequence. Figure (g), (h) and (i) are examples with only the square high bay lights on in the same order.

4.1 Distance

The experiments investigating distance variability aimed to understand how the distance between the robot and objects affects object detection performance in Gazebo and Isaac Sim compared to the real robot. Table 1 reveals interesting insights into the average mAP values obtained for different distances from the scene.

Table 1. Average mAP values for various distances from the scene.

Condition	Real Robot		Gazebo		Isaac Sim	
	mean	SD	mean	SD	mean	SD
0.6 m	38.51	10.63	50.31	9.15	39.94	7.15
1.6 m	21.55	6.62	31.80	4.15	17.41	7.92
2.6 m	2.70	5.70	21.17	7.09	2.53	5.13

For instance, at a distance of 0.6 m, the real robot demonstrated a mean value of 38.51, while Isaac Sim exhibited a slightly higher mAP value of 39.94, resulting in a difference of 1.43. Gazebo exhibited the highest average mAP value of 50.31, resulting in a difference of 11.8 compared to the real robot. At a distance of 1.6 m, the real robot had a mean of 21.55, while Isaac Sim had the mAP of 17.41 resulting in a difference of approximately 4.14. Gazebo had the highest average mAP at 31.80, resulting in a difference of 10.25 compared to the real robot. For the 2.6 distance, we had values 2.70, 21.17, and 2.53 for the real robot, Gazebo, and Isaac Sim respectively yielding a difference of 0.17 between Isaac Sim and real robot and 18.47 between Gazebo and real robot.

Although the mAPs have similar variance across all three simulators and distance conditions, Gazebo consistently yielded higher mean mAP values across all distances, indicating a potential tendency to overestimate. Under conditions of changing robot's position, these results suggest Isaac Sim's ability to more accurately simulate the object detection of the real robot in comparison to Gazebo.

4.2 Angle

The experiments exploring angle variability sought to investigate how object detection performance varied with different viewing angles relative to the objects. Table 2 presents the detailed results of the average mAP values for various viewing angles.

First, when examining object detection performance at a default (0°) angle, Isaac Sim showcased a mean mAP value of 39.94, slightly surpassing the real robot's mean of 38.51 by approximately 1.43. In contrast, Gazebo presented the highest average mAP value of 50.31, indicating a substantial difference of 11.80 compared to the real robot.

Table 2. Average mAP values for various viewing angles.

Condition	Real Robot		Gazebo		Isaac Sim	
	mean	SD	mean	SD	mean	SD
Default	38.51	10.63	50.31	9.15	39.94	7.15
90°	34.13	6.66	67.26	9.34	40.81	7.38
180°	38.31	9.64	55.98	11.18	37.31	5.10
270°	41.47	10.71	50.35	19.69	34.33	7.69

Moving to an angle of 90°, Isaac Sim yielded a mean mAP value of 40.81, while the real robot achieved a slightly higher mean of 34.13, resulting in a difference of approximately 6.68. Again, Gazebo exhibited the highest average mAP at 67.26, showcasing a deviation of 26.45 compared to the real robot. At a 180-degree angle, Isaac Sim yielded a mean mAP value of 37.31, while the real robot achieved a slightly higher mean of 38.31, resulting in a difference of 1.00. Again, Gazebo exhibited the highest average mAP at 55.98, showcasing a notable deviation of 17.67 compared to the real robot. Finally, at an angle of 270°, the comparison between Isaac Sim and the real robot revealed a difference of 7.14, with mean mAP values of 34.33 and 41.47, respectively. Gazebo exhibited a higher average mAP value of 50.35, resulting in a difference of 8.88 compared to the real robot. Furthermore, while in both Isaac Sim and reality, the variance of the mAPs are more consistent, experiments in Gazebo yielded significantly higher variance in one condition suggesting unstable emulation. These findings underscore the varying degrees of simulation fidelity across different angles, with Isaac Sim generally demonstrating closer alignment with real-world object detection performance compared to Gazebo.

4.3 Lighting Conditions

The experiments on lighting conditions aimed to assess how different lighting setups influenced object detection performance in Gazebo and Isaac Sim compared to the real robot. Table 3 provides the average mAP values for various lighting conditions.

Table 3. Average mAP values for various lighting conditions.

Condition	Real Robot		Gazebo		Isaac Sim	
	mean	SD	mean	SD	mean	SD
rectangular high bay lights	38.51	10.63	50.31	9.15	39.94	7.15
round low bay lights	26.28	8.08	48.26	9.34	30.48	10.90
both	34.47	8.90	54.89	7.58	44.95	11.01

When evaluating object detection performance under the condition of using the rectangular high bay lights, the real robot displayed an mAP of 38.51, and Gazebo exhibited the highest average mAP value of 50.31, marking a deviation of 11.80. Isaac Sim got an mAP of 39.94, slightly outperforming the real robot by 1.43.

Switching to round low bay lights, the real robot achieved a mean of 26.28, while Gazebo showcased the highest average mAP at 48.26, representing a substantial difference of 21.98. Isaac Sim yielded a mean mAP value of 30.48, resulting in a gap of around 4.20 compared to the real robot.

Lastly, with both rectangular high and round low bay lights, the real robot produced a mean of 34.47 trailing behind Isaac Sim's mean of 44.95 by 10.48. Similarly, Gazebo demonstrated the highest average mAP at 54.89, exhibiting a notable difference of 20.42 compared to the real robot.

Similar to the experiments of distance conditions, the mAP variance is consistent across all permutations.

These findings suggest that lighting conditions influence object detection performance across simulation environments and the real world, with Gazebo consistently exhibiting higher deviations from real-world performance compared to Isaac Sim.

4.4 Correlation

When examining the correlation between the object detection performance of Gazebo and Isaac Sim with the real robot across different distances, notable correlations were observed as can be seen in Table 4.

The values in the table represent the correlation coefficients, ranging from -1 to 1, where a correlation coefficient to 1 represents a perfect low-end to high-end performance distribution.

For instance, examining the default light condition, both Isaac Sim and Gazebo exhibit high correlation coefficients of 0.92 and 0.95, respectively. In the condition of round lights, both simulators got the same high correlation coefficient of 0.95. Similarly, in the condition of having both lights turned on, both Gazebo and Isaac Sim got the same coefficients of 0.93.

In the context of varying distance setups, at the smaller distance of 1.6 m, Isaac Sim exhibited a correlation coefficient of 0.91, while Gazebo achieved a higher coefficient of 0.96. For the longer distance of 2.6 m, Isaac Sim demonstrated an improved correlation coefficient of 0.96, surpassing Gazebo's coefficient of 0.82.

Regarding the angle setups, Isaac Sim obtained a correlation coefficient of 0.90 for the 90-degree angle, whereas Gazebo achieved a higher coefficient of 0.97. However, for the 180-degree and 270-degree angles, Isaac Sim displayed superior correlation coefficients of 0.98 and 0.94, respectively, compared to Gazebo's coefficients of 0.90 and 0.93, respectively.

Finally, under average conditions involving default rectangular lights, a distance of 0.6 m, and a 0-degree angle, Isaac Sim demonstrated a closer match to real-world conditions than Gazebo, with a correlation coefficient of 0.94 compared to Gazebo's 0.92.

These values suggest a consistent positive correlation between the mAP values obtained in both simulators and those observed in real-world experiments across various experimental conditions.

Table 4. Correlations of sorted mAP values for each experiment conditions between the simulator and the real robot.

	Light conditions			Distance		Angle			
	default	round	both	1.6m	2.6m	90°	180°	270°	Average
Issac Sim	0.92	0.95	0.93	0.91	0.96	0.90	0.98	0.94	0.94
Gazebo	0.95	0.95	0.93	0.93	0.82	0.97	0.90	0.93	0.92

5 Conclusion

We conducted an evaluation of the object detection performance in Gazebo, Isaac Sim, and a real robot across various experimental conditions. Our findings reveal nuanced insights into the strengths and limitations of each simulator in simulating object detection tasks for robotics applications. Both Gazebo and Isaac Sim demonstrate moderate to strong correlations with the real robot under certain conditions, indicating their potential utility as simulation platforms. However, discrepancies are observed, particularly in scenarios involving distance and angle variability, highlighting the need for further refinement to enhance simulation fidelity.

Furthermore, our analysis underscores the importance of considering environmental factors, such as lighting conditions, when evaluating simulator performance. While Gazebo and Isaac Sim exhibit varying degrees of sensitivity to lighting setups, Isaac Sim consistently provides more reliable object detection performance across diverse lighting conditions. This finding suggests that Isaac Sim may offer a more robust simulation environment for tasks requiring accurate perception in different lighting scenarios. Additionally, the correlation analysis highlights the impact of viewing angles on simulator performance, with Isaac Sim demonstrating more consistent correlations with the real robot across a range of viewing angles compared to Gazebo.

Moving forward, several avenues for future research emerge from this study. Firstly, the development of more advanced object detection models tailored specifically for simulation environments could improve the accuracy and robustness of simulated perception tasks. Additionally, exploring techniques for domain adaptation to bridge the gap between simulated and real-world data may further enhance simulation fidelity. Furthermore, investigating the integration of sensor noise models and environmental dynamics into simulators could provide a more realistic simulation environment, better aligning simulated perception with real-world scenarios. Overall, addressing these challenges will contribute to the continued advancement of simulation technologies for robotics applications, ultimately facilitating the development and deployment of autonomous systems in real-world environments.

References

1. Acosta, B., Yang, W., Posa, M.: Validating robotics simulators on real world impacts. IEEE Robot. Autom. Lett. **7**(3), 6471–6478 (2022)
2. Anderson, P., et al.: Sim-to-real transfer for vision-and-language navigation. In: Conference on Robot Learning, pp. 671–681. PMLR (2021)
3. Belo, J.P.R., Romero, R.A.F.: A social human-robot interaction simulator for reinforcement learning systems. In: 2021 20th International Conference on Advanced Robotics (ICAR), pp. 350–355 (2021)
4. Blanco-Mulero, D., Barbany, O., Alcan, G., Colomé, A., Torras, C., Kyrki, V.: Benchmarking the sim-to-real gap in cloth manipulation. IEEE Robot. Autom. Lett. **9**(3), 2981–2988 (2024)
5. Calli, B., et al.: Yale-CMU-Berkeley dataset for robotic manipulation research. Int. J. Robot. Res. **36**(3), 261–268 (2017)
6. Cheng, H., Wang, Y., Meng, M.: A vision-based robot grasping system. IEEE Sens. J. **22**(10), 9610–9620 (2022)
7. Collins, J., Chand, S., Vanderkop, A., Howard, D.: A review of physics simulators for robotic applications. IEEE Access **9**, 51416–51431 (2021)
8. Erez, T., Tassa, Y., Todorov, E.: Simulation tools for model-based robotics: comparison of bullet, Havok, MuJoCo, ODE and PhysX. In: 2015 IEEE International Conference on Robotics and Automation (ICRA), pp. 4397–4404 (2015)
9. Fraichard, T., Levesy, V.: From crowd simulation to robot navigation in crowds. IEEE Robot. Autom. Lett. **5**(2), 729–735 (2020)
10. Giovanni, S., Yin, K.K.: LocoTest: deploying and evaluating physics-based locomotion on multiple simulation platforms. In: Allbeck, J.M., Faloutsos, P. (eds.) Motion in Games, pp. 227–241. Springer, Heidelberg (2011)
11. Hamano, T., Onosato, M., Tanaka, F.: Performance comparison of physics engines to accelerate house-collapsing simulations. In: 2016 IEEE International Symposium on Safety, Security, and Rescue Robotics (SSRR), pp. 358–363 (2016)
12. Huang, P., et al.: What went wrong? Closing the sim-to-real gap via differentiable causal discovery. In: Tan, J., Toussaint, M., Darvish, K. (eds.) Proceedings of The 7th Conference on Robot Learning. Proceedings of Machine Learning Research, vol. 229, pp. 734–760. PMLR (2023)
13. Jocher, G., Chaurasia, A., Qiu, J.: Ultralytics YOLO (2023). https://github.com/ultralytics/ultralytics
14. Lin, T.-Y., et al.: Microsoft COCO: common objects in context. In: Computer Vision–ECCV 2014: 13th European Conference, Zurich, Switzerland, 6–12 September 2014, Proceedings, Part V, pp. 740–755. Springer (2014)
15. Liu, Q., Li, Y., Liu, L.: A 3D simulation environment and navigation approach for robot navigation via deep reinforcement learning in dense pedestrian environment. In: 2020 IEEE 16th International Conference on Automation Science and Engineering (CASE), pp. 1514–1519 (2020)

16. Makoviychuk, V., et al.: Isaac gym: high performance GPU-based physics simulation for robot learning (2021)
17. Santos Pessoa de Melo, M., Gomes da Silva Neto, J., Jorge Lima da Silva, P., Natario Teixeira, J.M.X., Teichrieb, V.: Analysis and comparison of robotics 3D simulators. In: 2019 21st Symposium on Virtual and Augmented Reality (SVR), pp. 242–251 (2019)
18. Moglia, A., Ferrari, V., Morelli, L., Ferrari, M., Mosca, F., Cuschieri, A.: A systematic review of virtual reality simulators for robot-assisted surgery. Eur. Urol. **69**(6), 1065–1080 (2016)
19. Narang, Y., Sundaralingam, B., Macklin, M., Mousavian, A., Fox, D.: Sim-to-real for robotic tactile sensing via physics-based simulation and learned latent projections. In: 2021 IEEE International Conference on Robotics and Automation (ICRA), pp. 6444–6451 (2021)
20. Qin, L., Peng, H., Huang, X., Liu, M., Huang, W.: Modeling and simulation of dynamics in soft robotics: a review of numerical approaches. Curr. Robot. Rep. **5**(1), 1–13 (2024)
21. Reckhaus, M., Hochgeschwender, N., Paulus, J., Shakhimardanov, A., Kraetzschmar, G.K.: An overview about simulation and emulation in robotics. In: Proceedings of SIMPAR, pp. 365–374 (2010)
22. Robinson, N., Tidd, B., Campbell, D., Kulić, D., Corke, P.: Robotic vision for human-robot interaction and collaboration: a survey and systematic review. J. Hum.-Robot Interact. **12**(1) (2023)
23. Sadeghian, R., Zarei, M., Shahin, S., Masouleh, M.T.: Vision based control and simulation of a spherical rolling robot based on ROS and Gazebo. In: 2017 IEEE 4th International Conference on Knowledge-Based Engineering and Innovation (KBEI), pp. 0304–0309 (2017)
24. Skinner, J., Garg, S., Sünderhauf, N., Corke, P., Upcroft, B., Milford, M.: High-fidelity simulation for evaluating robotic vision performance. In: 2016 IEEE/RSJ International Conference on Intelligent Robots and Systems (IROS), pp. 2737–2744 (2016)
25. Staranowicz, A., Mariottini, G.L.: A survey and comparison of commercial and open-source robotic simulator software. In: Proceedings of the 4th International Conference on PErvasive Technologies Related to Assistive Environments, pp. 1–8 (2011)
26. Trentsios, P., Wolf, M., Gerhard, D.: Overcoming the sim-to-real gap in autonomous robots. Procedia CIRP **109**, 287–292 (2022). 32nd CIRP Design Conference (CIRP Design 2022) - Design in a changing world
27. Tselegkaridis, S., Sapounidis, T.: Simulators in educational robotics: a review. Educ. Sci. **11**(1), 11 (2021)
28. Zagal, J.C., Ruiz-del Solar, J.: Combining simulation and reality in evolutionary robotics. J. Intell. Rob. Syst. **50**(1), 19–39 (2007)
29. Zhao, W., Queralta, J.P., Westerlund, T.: Sim-to-real transfer in deep reinforcement learning for robotics: a survey. In: 2020 IEEE Symposium Series on Computational Intelligence (SSCI), pp. 737–744 (2020)
30. Zhu, Y., et al.: robosuite: a modular simulation framework and benchmark for robot learning (2022)

Soccer Gameplay Data Generation: Toward Integrating Computer Simulations and Human Sports Analysis

Hidehisa Akiyama[1(✉)] and Tomoharu Nakashima[2]

[1] Okayama University of Science, Okayama, Japan
hidehisa.akiyama@ous.ac.jp
[2] Osaka Metropolitan University, Osaka, Japan
tomoharu.nakashima@omu.ac.jp

Abstract. This paper presents software that aims to generate extensive soccer gameplay data through computer simulations, addressing the scarcity of human-generated data for analysis. It discusses the challenges of analyzing human gameplay data, the need for computer simulations, and the development of software tools such as rcgamestats and rcg2data. The system uses the RoboCup Soccer Simulator to efficiently generate game data. In addition, it presents a case study on distribution analysis of ball interceptions to demonstrate the potential for various analytical purposes. The provided data includes 78,000 matches, which is equivalent to approximately 8,667 human soccer matches. Future efforts include expanding data collection and improving database system integration.

Keywords: Sports analytics · Sports data · Computer simulation

1 Introduction

RoboCup Soccer represents a form of soccer competition driven by autonomous mobile robots. Its primary objectives include the triumph of robotic teams over human champions and the collaborative engagement of robots alongside humans in the sport. To achieve these objectives, advancements in physical control mechanisms and decision-making frameworks embedded within robots (software agents) are necessary to emulate human-level teamwork.

The mechanisms underlying human decision-making in teamwork must be analyzed and comprehended in order to gain insight into human gameplay. With the advent of sophisticated measurement technologies, the analysis of human gameplay data in team sports like soccer has gained significant attraction. A multitude of data providers in the soccer domain have emerged, not limited to the World Cup but extending to leagues worldwide, attempting data collection. Analytical competitions utilizing such data have been organized, proposing various metrics for evaluating gameplay and engaging in benchmark analyses, such as trajectory prediction employing machine learning methodologies.

E. Barros et al. (Eds.): RoboCup 2024, LNAI 15570, pp. 351–360, 2025.
https://doi.org/10.1007/978-3-031-85859-8_30

While the analysis of human gameplay data is becoming increasingly sophisticated, a notable challenge is the need for more data available for analysis. Although partially open data exists, gameplay data provided by data providers comes at a cost, requiring substantial resources for procurement. Moreover, due to the nature of human gameplay data, there are significant constraints on the number of matches that can be executed for the same match-up, and reproducing matches under identical conditions is unfeasible. Consequently, the collection of gameplay data under specific conditions is a practically challenging endeavor.

One approach to mitigate the data scarcity problem is to generate gameplay data through computer simulation. In this study, we provide software for generating a large amount of gameplay data, aggregating match data, and extracting event data using the RoboCup Soccer Simulator. Furthermore, we use these software tools to generate the gameplay data, resulting in the generated data being sufficiently substantial compared to data obtained from human soccer.

The structure of this paper is as follows: Sect. 2 presents related research and explains the positioning of the software proposed in this paper. Section 3 describes the soccer gameplay data used in the analysis and the software we provide. Section 4 introduces the data we provide. Section 5 describes the case study using the data we provide. Finally, Sect. 6 serves as a conclusion.

2 Related Works

Analysis of human sports primarily revolves around inverse analysis, estimating models from data. Metrics such as shot and pass counts in soccer have long been the subject of data collection and analysis. Recent advancements in measurement and data analysis technologies have facilitated statistical analyses, future predictions, and player evaluations based on such data. Predictive problems in team sports like soccer can be broadly categorized into short-term predictions, spanning a few seconds, and long-term predictions, encompassing events such as shots or decisive moments. However, even short-term predictions in team sports are notoriously challenging, constituting a prominent issue in information science. For instance, numerous studies have focused on the trajectory prediction of players in sports like soccer and basketball [11,12]. Additionally, approaches have been proposed using large-scale datasets to estimate scoring probability and event occurrence probability based on machine learning predictions and evaluate "players' movements that lead to more scores" [4,10]. Algorithms designed for winning games are also employed to conduct long-term predictions. Exploration via such algorithms has been a subject of research, particularly in games such as puzzles and shooters [9]. Such approaches have been attempted even in team sports like soccer. While the RoboCup Soccer Simulator [1,7] serves as a testbed for multiagent systems, algorithm development with a focus on winning strategies is actively pursued within the competition. Conversely, simulators primarily aimed at analyzing group behaviors have also been proposed [5], suggesting a future trend toward not only winning games but also understanding and emulating human players' behaviors. Through such approaches, a deeper analysis of human gameplay necessitates copious amounts of human-generated gameplay data.

Several open datasets are available for analyzing movement data in human-team sports. Analyzing solely positional data of players and the ball, which is challenging in team sports like soccer, is often complemented with event data, including manually recorded events like shots, passes, and fouls. Well-known data providers such as StatsBomb, WyScout, and Opta offer data for matches ranging from WorldCup to European leagues. Soccer gameplay data typically comprises events involving the ball (such as shots and passes) and the corresponding positional coordinates of players [4]. However, not all match data is publicly available, and freely accessible data is often limited.

Gameplay data in team sports is generated through mechanical extraction via image processing from competition footage, supplemented by human experts' labeling adjustments. Despite advancements in automated extraction through image processing, numerous challenges remain, including player and ball tracking, player identification, and estimation of event occurrence time and type, leading to competitions aimed at evaluating performance in data extraction [3]. Various formats have been proposed for representing gameplay data, with existing structured formats like XML, JSON, or commonly used CSV being prevalent. Efforts toward standardizing representations of soccer gameplay data [4], including player attributes, event classification during games, and organization of event-related information, have led to the development of software environments like kloppy[1]. Currently, positional data used in analyzing human soccer gameplay is represented as 2D point coordinates on a plane (the field surface), lacking posture information. Consequently, the RoboCup Soccer 2D Simulation [7] data aligns closely with this format. Being a computational simulation, it enables the execution of numerous matches under identical conditions, potentially addressing the inherent data scarcity issue in human soccer measurements. Constructing a data generation system utilizing the RoboCup Soccer 2D Simulation and aligning team behavior in the simulator with human teamwork tendencies holds promise for collaborative analysis of human soccer data. While attempts have been made to create datasets using the RoboCup Soccer 2D Simulation in the past [6], there is a demand for a more extensive play data generation system tailored to the format of human soccer data.

3 Data Generation System

3.1 Gameplay Data for Soccer

In the analysis of human soccer, information regarding the movements of players and the ball based on their positions is utilized. Positional data, obtained through external observation such as video footage, is the primary source of information. Since directly measuring players' observations or beliefs is challenging, these kinds of information is generally not employed. Currently, the coordinate

[1] https://kloppy.pysport.org/.

system used in analyzing human soccer is two-dimensional rather than three-dimensional. That is, it represents players as single points on the field plane without posture information. Although the ball may be airborne in reality, its positional information is recorded only on the plane in the data. Therefore, these position data are highly compatible with the RoboCup Soccer 2D Simulation.

In the analysis of team sports like soccer, tracking data and event data are often analyzed together. Tracking data records the positional information of players and the ball over time, while event data records specific plays such as shots, passes, and fouls. Advancements in technology have facilitated the automatic extraction of tracking data from video footage, enabling the automated estimation of player and ball positions to some extent. However, cases where the ball's positional coordinates are recorded directly from footage are scarce. When the ball's position is not recorded, it is determined by associating player positions with events involving the ball. Automated extraction of event data from tracking data is challenging, necessitating manual annotation. Manual corrections are also required for tracking data since fully addressing occlusions and accurately identifying players pose challenges in automated extraction. While positional extraction using GPS technology is technically feasible, practical examples are rare due to operational costs.

In tracking data, positional information of players and the ball is quantified for each frame of the video footage. Therefore, it suffices to record the positional coordinates of players and the ball linked to the elapsed time since the start of the match. Event data includes information such as the occurrence time, occurrence position, end time, end position, and involved players. Various data recording formats such as CSV, XML, and JSON are commonly used for both tracking and event data.

3.2 Gameplay Data from the RoboCup Soccer Simulator

In this paper, we employ the RoboCup Soccer Simulator (rcssserver) utilized in the RoboCup Soccer Simulation 2D Competition for data generation. rcssserver is a software that realizes soccer through computer simulation. While it operates in a two-dimensional plane, rcssserver is designed as a distributed multi-agent system for 11 vs. 11 gameplay, effectively realizing competition under rules nearly identical to those of human soccer. As rcssserver employs simplified physics, it is unable to simulate human limb control. However, the tactics that occur when players compete for the ball can be imitated to some extent. Consequently, it is capable of emulating human-like group behavior, including interactions between opponents and teammates.

rcssserver is equipped with the capacity to record game logs, which can be utilized to capture the following information:

- Ball: position, velocity
- Players: Players: state (kick, failed kick, tackle, failed tackle, collision, etc.), position, velocity, body orientation, head orientation, pointing direction, field of view, focus position, stamina, player focused by auditory attention, execution count of each command

The game logs contain error-free numerical information about all objects' positions, velocities, postures, and other attributes. Therefore, there is no need for position extraction through image processing, and issues such as missing information or object identification are avoided. Essentially, it provides more comprehensive information than tracking data in human soccer without incurring the costs associated with extraction processes. Moreover, being a computational simulation, it allows for unlimited repetitions of trials given sufficient computational resources.

However, rcssserver does not support the recording of event data. Consequently, a separate process is required to extract events from game logs. The game logs include flags indicating whether each player has touched the ball. Leveraging this information enables the automated extraction of most event data from game logs with minimal manual labeling efforts, bypassing the need for extensive human intervention.

The game logs recorded by rcssserver are in text format, but Lisp-like format is the default. Starting with rcssserver version 18.0.0, game logs are also available in JSON format. In each case, a separate process is required to extract the necessary information from the game logs.

3.3 Distributed Execution System: Rcgamestats

To address the need for a large number of matches to generate extensive gameplay data, efficient execution of these matches is essential. In response to this challenge, we have developed a system called rcgamestats for facilitating distributed execution of simulations[2]. rcgamestats offers a mechanism for distributing simulator execution, which significantly reduces the time required for match execution, given the availability of computational resources in parallel. rcggamestats makes it possible to efficiently generate gameplay data on a large scale.

Key features of rcgamestats include:

- Distributed execution with any number of hosts: Matches can be distributed across any number of computational hosts within the same LAN.
- Match scheduling: Users can specify arbitrary combinations of teams from the available pool and designate the number of matches to be executed.
- Aggregation and display of match results: Results from each match are aggregated into a database, and the summary of these results is displayed through a web interface(Fig. 1 and 2). The code currently available offers functionality for aggregation and display using Google Spreadsheet as a simplified version(Fig. 3).

3.4 Data Converter and Extractor: Rcg2data

To facilitate the analysis of the game logs recorded by rcssserver and to extract event information in a format suitable for analysis, we have developed a software tool called rcg2data[3]. rcg2data provides two main functionalities:

[2] Available at: https://github.com/hidehisaakiyama/rcgamestats.

[3] Available at: https://github.com/hidehisaakiyama/rcg2data.

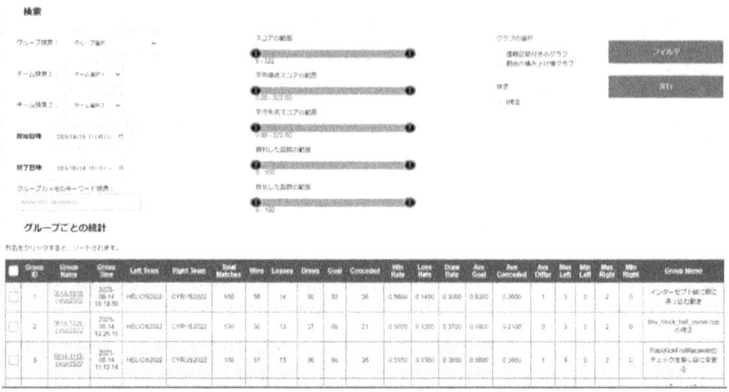

Fig. 1. An example of the aggregated results display. The dedicated web interface allows not only to view the results in table format but also to select the display content using filters and to perform analyses using various indicators.

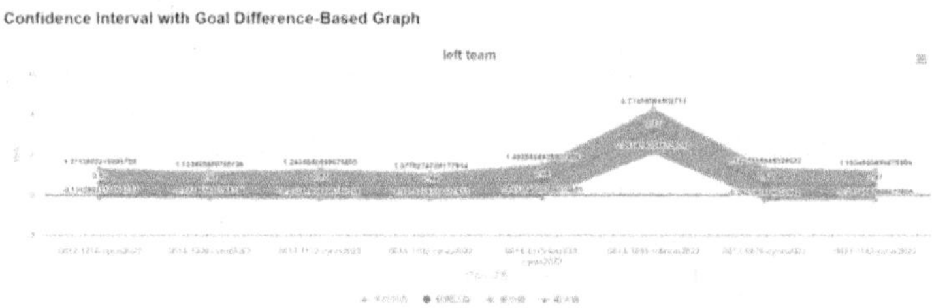

Fig. 2. An example of the visualization. The dedicated web interface provides functions that facilitate graphical visualization and simple statistical analysis.

- Conversion of game logs recorded by rcssserver into CSV format.
- Extracting event information from the game logs recorded by rcssserver. In the current implementation, pass, interception, and shot events can be extracted from the game log and saved in CSV format.

Using rcg2data makes it possible to generate data equivalent to those commonly used in human soccer analysis. Figure 4 shows an example of event data extracted from a game log file. The figure shows a list of plays where the ball was passed, or the opposing team intercepted the ball. The figure shows a list of plays in which the ball was passed to a teammate or intercepted by an opponent player. While it is difficult to analyze team play using tracking data alone, it is possible to analyze it using information from such events.

4 Provided Data

We generated actual gameplay data using the developed system. A total of 1,000 round-robin matches were played by teams participating in the RoboCup

group_name	datetime	target	opponent	tag	# of game	win	draw	lose	goal	conceded	win rate	draw rate	lose rate	ave goal	ave con	max goal	max conc
0706-1202-nc	20210706-120220	alice2021	aras2021	non-anonymous	450	430	14	6	1760	187	95.56%	3.11%	1.33%	3.91	0.42	10	3
0706-1202-nc	20210706-120223	alice2021	cyrus2021	non-anonymous	450	112	139	199	411	545	24.89%	30.89%	44.22%	0.91	1.21	5	4
0706-1202-nc	20210706-120225	alice2021	helios2021	non-anonymous	450	63	135	252	231	580	14.00%	30.00%	56.00%	0.51	1.29	4	6
0706-1202-nc	20210706-120227	alice2021	hfutengine20:	non-anonymous	450	210	105	135	844	699	46.67%	23.33%	30.00%	1.88	1.55	6	5
0706-1202-nc	20210706-120229	alice2021	itandroids202	non-anonymous	450	426	20	4	1913	239	94.67%	4.44%	0.89%	4.25	0.53	9	3
0706-1202-nc	20210706-120232	alice2021	jyo_sen2021	non-anonymous	450	411	35	4	1347	180	91.33%	7.78%	0.89%	2.99	0.40	8	2
0706-1202-nc	20210706-120234	alice2021	mt2021	non-anonymous	450	404	37	9	1180	140	89.78%	8.22%	2.00%	2.62	0.31	7	4
0706-1202-nc	20210706-120236	alice2021	persepolis20:	non-anonymous	450	415	22	13	1831	233	92.22%	4.89%	2.89%	4.07	0.52	10	3
0706-1202-nc	20210706-120238	alice2021	robocin2021	non-anonymous	450	355	70	25	1108	270	78.89%	15.56%	5.56%	2.46	0.60	7	3
0706-1202-nc	20210706-120242	alice2021	thunderleagu	non-anonymous	450	439	8	3	3024	140	97.56%	1.78%	0.67%	6.72	0.31	20	3
0706-1202-nc	20210706-120240	alice2021	yushan2021	non-anonymous	450	42	148	260	106	462	9.33%	32.89%	57.78%	0.24	1.03	2	4
0706-1202-nc	20210706-120244	aras2021	alice2021	non-anonymous	450	7	28	415	222	1682	1.56%	6.22%	92.22%	0.49	3.74	3	9
0706-1202-nc	20210706-120247	aras2021	cyrus2021	non-anonymous	450	9	39	402	155	1232	2.00%	8.67%	89.33%	0.34	2.74	3	8

Fig. 3. An example of displaying the aggregated results using Google Spreadsheet.

Type	Side1	Unum1	Time1	X1	Y1	Side2	Unum2	Time2	X2	Y2	Success
Pass	left	10	105	11.0433	32.3346	left	5	113	-2.7	30.9469	true
Pass	left	5	125	4.4467	29.5977	left	10	128	9.2386	31.489	true
Pass	left	10	143	16.6419	31.1778	left	5	152	0.0918	26.3957	true
Pass	left	5	161	4.2961	25.8656	left	6	169	2.7422	12.9022	true
Interception	left	6	173	4.7946	15.0694	right	7	174	6.834	15.8583	true
Pass	right	7	176	6.5191	16.1724	right	9	182	3.9038	24.3288	true
Pass	right	9	183	3.6503	24.2566	right	7	187	3.1349	19.623	true
Pass	right	7	188	3.1646	19.682	right	9	191	3.0246	25.26	true
Pass	right	9	204	-7.1198	24.3199	right	11	208	-10.6632	17.1693	true
Pass	right	11	209	-10.9034	17.1474	right	9	212	-8.9923	22.7204	true
Pass	right	9	212	-8.9923	22.7204	right	11	216	-12.6582	18.0909	true
Pass	right	11	227	-16.2424	16.4082	right	6	234	-15.0141	2.6168	true
Pass	right	6	234	-15.0141	2.6168	right	8	243	-13.1596	-17.0355	true
Pass	left	7	297	-24.0591	-22.1905	left	6	301	-19.5139	-14.1352	true
Pass	left	6	310	-14.5264	-14.1491	left	7	312	-16.7063	-18.5533	true

Fig. 4. An example of event data extracted from a game log file using rcg2data.

2021 Soccer Simulation 2D Competition. Thirteen teams were involved in the matches: Alice2021, CYRUS, FRA-UNIted, HELIOS2021, HfutEngine2021, ITAndroids, Jyo_sen2021, MT2021, Oxsy, Persepolis, RoboCin, ThunderLeague, and YuShan2021. In 2022, the specifications of the simulator were modified to prohibit players from performing backward dashes. Consequently, some teams were unable to move as intended in RoboCup 2022 and RoboCup 2023. Therefore, we used teams from RoboCup 2021 for this study. This resulted in a total of 78,000 matches.

The data volume for the game log files of 78,000 matches was approximately 500GB after zip-compressed. The match results and team binary information for RoboCup 2021 are available on the simulator's official website[4]. The generated data is available at https://github.com/hidehisaakiyama/RoboCup2D-data/.

[4] https://rcsoccersim.github.io/.

A match played by rcssserver lasts about 10 min, which is one-ninth the length of a human soccer match. Therefore, the generated data is gameplay data equivalent to about 8,667 human soccer matches. It can be said that the gameplay data is sufficiently large compared to that obtained from human soccer data providers.

5 Case Study: Distribution Analysis of Ball Interception

We use the interception information from the event data to estimate the probability distribution of ball interceptions for each matchup combination. While kernel density estimation is a common method for estimating such distributions, we opt for a Gaussian Mixture Model in this study. Since the goal is to analyze the similarity of distributions, we chose a Gaussian Mixture Model, which tends to have clustering characteristics, making it suitable for analyzing the similarity of distributions. Furthermore, to analyze the similarity of the estimated distributions, we perform hierarchical clustering based on distribution distances. We use the Earth Mover's Distance (EMD) [8] as the distance metric between distributions.

Here, we present partial results of the clustering performed for games between HELIOS2021, the runner-up of RoboCup2021, and other teams. Figure 5 shows contour plots of the probability distribution estimation. From these figures, it can be observed that the distribution of ball interception positions exhibits distinctive characteristics for each team, suggesting a relationship between the distribution features and the team's defensive strategies. Figure 6 shows the dendrogram resulting from hierarchical clustering. The results suggest that the team at the bottom (FRA-UNIted) employs a unique defensive strategy, while the top two teams (YuShan2023 and Oxsy), though also distinctive, likely use relatively similar defensive strategies. Although no quantitative evaluation has been made, it is suggested that the characteristics appearing in the distribution and the clustering results may be similar to human observations.

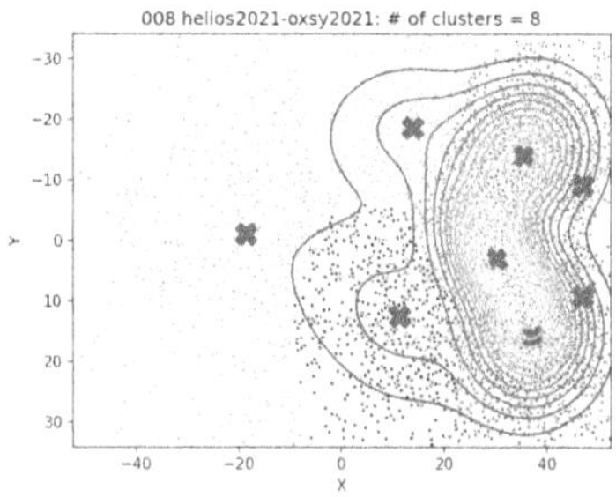

(a) vs. Oxsy

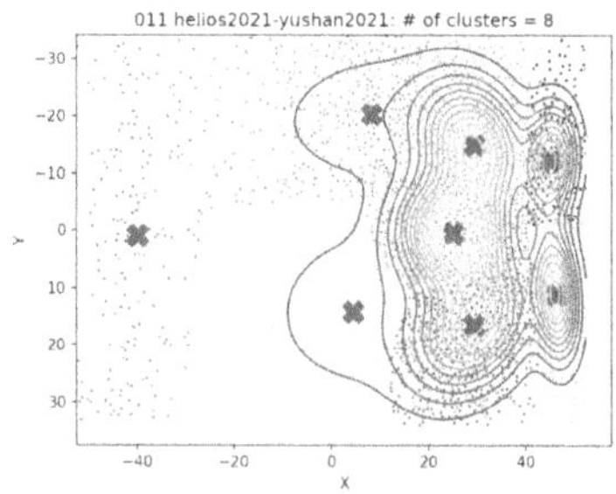

(b) vs. YuShan2023

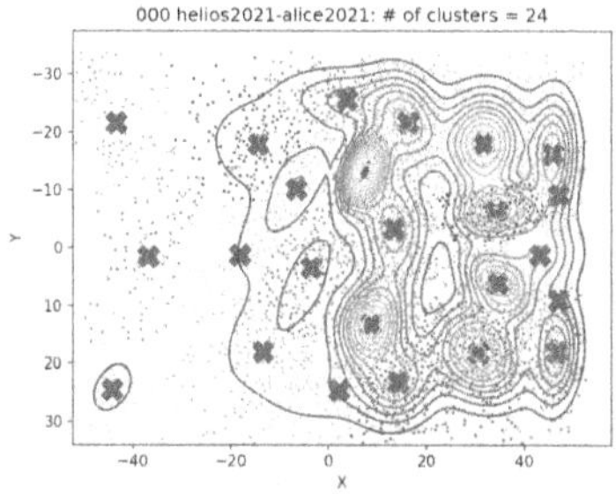

(c) vs. Alice2023

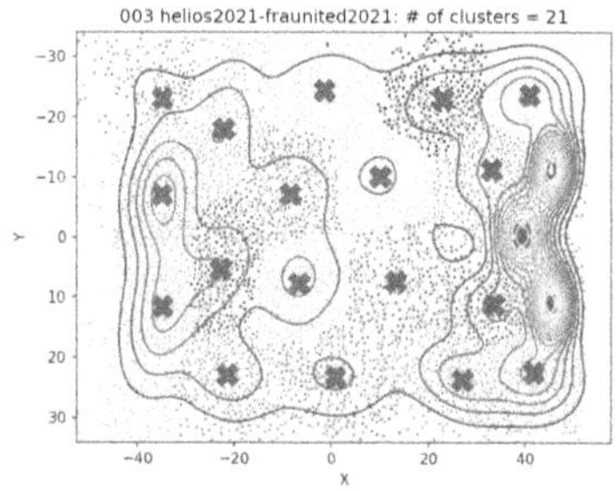

(d) vs. FRA-UNIted

Fig. 5. Results of estimating the probability distribution using interception information obtained from event data between HELIOS2021 and each team. Each uses event information extracted from data for 500 matches in which HELIOS2021 was on the left side.

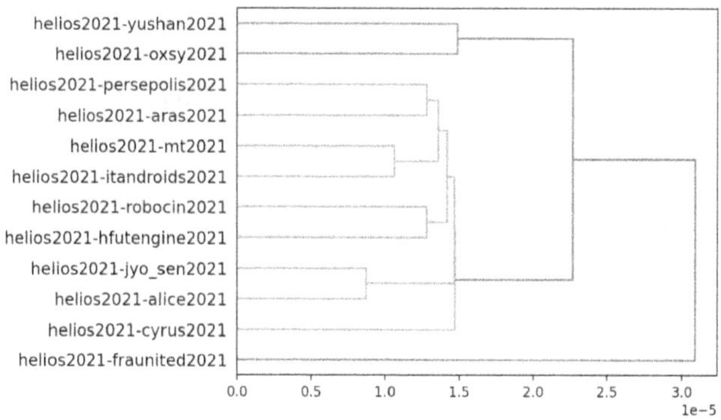

Fig. 6. Dendrogram showing the results of hierarchical clustering using EMD as a distance metric.

6 Conclusion

This paper proposes and implements software for generating a large volume of soccer gameplay data using computer simulation. Furthermore, in the pursuit of merging human soccer with computer simulation, software has been developed to organize data compatible with human soccer. Using the implemented software and team binaries from RoboCup2021, actual data generation was performed and made openly available. Through simple experiments with the generated data, the potential for various analytical purposes was demonstrated.

Future challenges include preparing agents that mimic human play, collecting data from a broader range of match-ups, and improving integration with database systems.

References

1. Akiyama, H., Dorer, K., Lau, N.: On the progress of soccer simulation leagues. In: In: RoboCup 2014: Robot World Cup XVIII. RoboCup 2014. Lecture Notes in Computer Science, vol. 8992, pp. 599–610 (2015)
2. Akiyama, H., Nakashima, T.: HELIOS base: an open source package for the RoboCup soccer 2D simulation. In: RoboCup 2013: Robot World Cup XVII. Lecture Notes in Computer Science, vol. 8371, pp. 528–535 (2014)
3. Cioppa, A., et al.: SoccerNet-tracking: multiple object tracking dataset and benchmark in soccer videos. In: Proceedings of the IEEE/CVF Conference on Computer Vision and Pattern Recognition, pp. 3491–3502 (2022)
4. Decroos, T., Bransen, L., Van Haaren, J., Davis, J.: Actions speak louder than goals: valuing player actions in soccer. In: KDD, pp. 1851–1861 (2019)
5. Kurach, K., et al.: Google research football: a novel reinforcement learning environment. In: Proceedings of the AAAI Conference on Artificial Intelligence, vol. 34, no. 04, pp. 4501–4510 (2020)
6. Michael, O., Obst, O., Schmidsberger, F., Stolzenburg, F.: RoboCupSimData: software and data for machine learning from RoboCup simulation league. In: RoboCup 2018: Robot World Cup XXII. Lecture Notes in Computer Science, vol. 11374 (2019)
7. Noda, I., Matsubara, H., Hiraki, K., Frank, I.: Soccer server: a tool for research on multiagent systems. Appl. Artif. Intell. **12**(2–3), 233–250 (1998)
8. Rubner, Y., Tomasi, C., Guibas, L. J.: A metric for distributions with applications to image databases. In: IEEE International Conference on Computer Vision, pp. 59–66 (1998)
9. Silver, D., et al.: Mastering the game of Go with deep neural networks and tree search. Nature **529**(7587), 484–489 (2016)
10. Spearman, W.: Beyond expected goals. In: Proceedings of the 12th MIT Sloan Sports Analytics Conference, pp. 1–17 (2018)
11. Teranishi, M., Tsutsui, K., Takeda, K., Fujii, K.: Evaluation of creating scoring opportunities for teammates in soccer via trajectory prediction. In: Machine Learning and Data Mining for Sports Analytics. MLSA 2022. Communications in Computer and Information Science, vol. 1783 (2023)
12. Yeh, R.A., Schwing, A.G., Huang, J., Murphy, K.: Diverse generation for multi-agent sports games. In: 2019 IEEE/CVF Conference on Computer Vision and Pattern Recognition (CVPR), pp. 4605–4614 (2019)

The Glee Didn't Last Long: How Continuous Integration Helps Revealing Fundamental Flaws in Team-Play

Thomas Gabel(✉) and Eicke Godehardt

Faculty of Computer Science and Engineering, Frankfurt University of Applied Sciences, 60318 Frankfurt am Main, Germany
{tgabel,godehardt}@fb2.fra-uas.de

Abstract. We present a continuous integration and deployment (CI/CD) framework for Soccer Simulation 2D. On the one hand, we aim to share that system publicly with the community and, therefore, describe its components and their composition. On the other hand, we relate statistics produced by that system to concepts from reliability theory, which facilitates the derivation of reliabilty metrics for assessing a team's defensive performance. In line with that, we present the results of a comprehensive case study in which the CI framework was utilized to find critical game situations, uncover weaknesses in the playing behavior of a soccer simulation team, and implement and evaluate appropriate counter measures.

1 Introduction

The traditional approach to developing and debugging agents in Soccer Simulation 2D – as well as to agent-based programming in general – has often been to program and improve components of their behavior iteratively and episodically: A human developer observes some sub-optimal playing behavior, infers the potential causes in the source code, programs some counter measures or improved versions of existing algorithms, evaluates them by a handful of test situations or matches, and when having approved the changes made, commits them to some code repository. Over the years, a number of approaches, tools, and methodologies were established to improve and support the sketched workflow. Layered disclosure as introduced by Carnegie Mellon's soccer simulation team [13] was one of the successful early approaches frequently adopted by other teams to allow for a goal-directed inspection of an agent's internals boosting the capabilities of developers in debugging agent behavior and in learning from logged data.

Over the years, the official tools maintained by the 2D Soccer Simulation community, most prominently the monitor and log player tools [1], became mature and incorporated more and more facilities that allowed for enhanced match analysis. Likewise, many active soccer simulation 2D teams have developed – and

E. Barros et al. (Eds.): RoboCup 2024, LNAI 15570, pp. 361–372, 2025.
https://doi.org/10.1007/978-3-031-85859-8_31

often released to the public – their own tools to support development, debugging, and agent analysis. Those include the set-play mechanism by FC Portugal [9], the Soccer Reporter and itas2d-window tools by ITAndroids [16], or the AutoTest2D scripts by WrightEagle [2].

While the general procedure discussed above is suitable for prototyping, correcting (obvious) errors, and often implies some (programming) fun, it quickly comes to its limits when questioning the impact of changes to the playing performance of a team. Due to the inherent stochasticity of soccer simulation and the enormous heterogeneity of opponent teams' playing strategies, it is very challenging to foresee the exact influence of specific code changes at large. At this point, evaluations by playing a larger number of games and drawing statistically reliable conclusions from them comes in. While this idea is not new – several robotic soccer simulation teams have published related approaches (cf. Sect. 2.3) –, the system that we outline in the next section and that we share as open source with the community has the property of implementing the continuous integration and deployment (CI/CD) approach. It facilitates the automatic generation of numerous statistics that allow developers to immediately spot and further analyze weaknesses in a team's performance. Moreover, in Sect. 3, we propose casting the problem of defending in robotic soccer as a reliability problem where conceding a goal is considered a failure. Utilizing concepts and approaches from the field of reliability theory and engineering, we then show in Sect. 4 how the outputs created by our CI/CD system can be further processed and deployed to obtain reliability metrics. This enabled us to discover and repair flaws in our (FRA-UNIted) robotic soccer team's tactics.

2 A Continuous Integration Framework for Soccer Simulation 2D

The FRA-UNIted team [4] has an extensive history resulting in a sizable C++ codebase, posing challenges for making confident changes without adequate safeguards. Implementing a continuous integration and deployment strategy can mitigate these risks. However, evaluating the team's performance based on a few games is insufficient. As argued in [6], conducting approximately a thousand games is most often sufficient to obtain a reliable assessment of whether recent changes have had a positive or negative impact.

In order to implement this the flow in Fig. 1 is executed in parallel on 20 computers. This process usually starts at night, when students have left the university. Each one of these computers will first download the current set of instructions, including specific teams for left and right side (dubbed "home" and "away" team, subsequently), or the current team code from git, respectively. In addition, the number of matches and some configuration options can be specified.

Thereafter the envisaged number of games is executed in parallel using the HLM tool —- "Hechi's League Manager", initially developed by team KickOff-TUG's Hechenblaickner [7] and used as official league manager at RoboCup events for years. As all the produced log files would be way to much to keep,

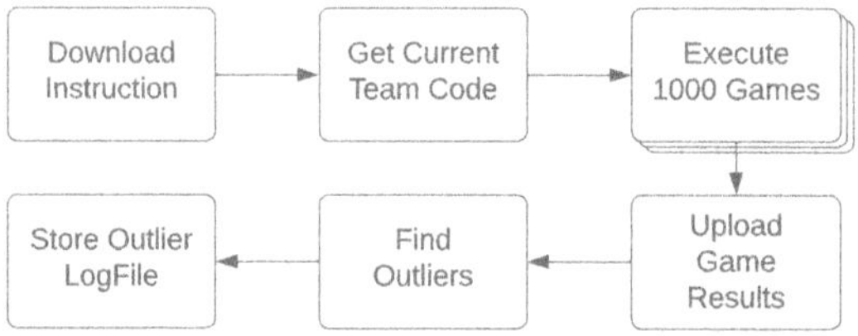

Fig. 1. General Flow of Execution Done Every Night

only a condensed version is upload to the back-end, where finally outliers in this nightly set of games are identified. The main idea is, that outliers are probably either exceptionally good or bad, and might be helpful to replay and beneficial for further analysis in order to improve our team code.

2.1 System Architecture

Besides the general flow of steps, the overall architecture will be explained now. Figure 2 shows both, components involved and the detailed flow of activities that are taking place. The whole process is initiated by all clients by downloading the latest instructions from the back-end at 8 pm. Numbers show the order of activities ending in storing outlier information. In addition, a web front-end is provided to analyze different statistics. Small parts of the front-end are shown in Fig. 3 and will be discussed in Sect. 4. The front-end also enables the user to adjust the instructions to run at night (team setup, number of games etc.).

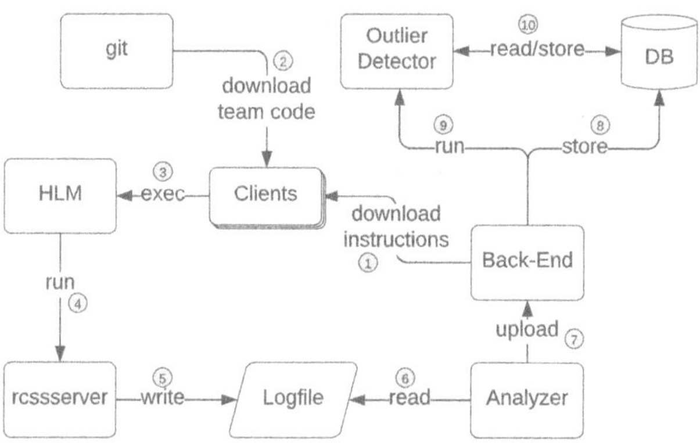

Fig. 2. Mixture of CI/CD Architecture and Activity Diagram

Docker is used on the clients as well as the server side. On the server, a Docker compose is running containing the back-end (together with the compiled front-end), a MongoDB and our outlier detector. The clients also utilize Docker to have a reliable setup and to not interfere with the specific software setup of the client. That sets the stage every night for a clean environment. This is not the same setup, that is run at the world championships, where each and every agent is running in a separate container. Instead all 22 agents and the Soccer Server run jointly within *one* container.

2.2 Open-Source Release

The source code of our CI/CD setup is released as open source in a collection of four GitHub repositories[1]. As described above, these repositories together achieve our night CI/CD setup to run and analyze a thousand games a night.

2.3 Related Work

Approaches similar to the one we have sketched above have already been taken by other Soccer Simulation 2D teams. Team Helios [18] uses a performance assessment system, which leverages SlackBot, Amazon S3, and Google Sheets. Its users are empowered to initiate tasks via SlackBot, specifying branch, opponent details, and the desired number of games. A server orchestrates the allocation of client machines to tasks based on CPU load, abstaining from assigning tasks to heavily burdened computers. Subsequently, client machines execute designated games, process resultant log files into CSV format, and upload them to shared storage platforms such as Dropbox or Amazon S3. These CSV files are then consolidated within a Google Sheet, facilitating user access for performance evaluation purposes. Team Fractals [12] also performed extensive evaluations of its team and variations thereof in the context of a guided self-organization methodology to optimize team performance amidst the fluctuations inherent in the non-deterministic RoboCup simulation environment. The authors developed and analyzed a newly proposed method called Dynamic Constraint Annealing whose execution took approximately three days of computation on a high-performance cluster running 100 parallel games in the RoboCup Soccer Server's synchronization mode, with each game taking approximately 2 min. Team Cyrus has developed the AutoTune2D tool [15] which is an extension of the older AutoTest2D system [2] and which allows researchers to fine-tune parameters that influence a team's playing strategy. Finally, it should be noted that CI/CD approaches are not unique to the simulation league, but have been applied in robot-based RoboCup leagues as well, for example in the Standard Platform League [3].

3 Basics of Reliability Theory

In the subsequent section, we adopt a reliability engineering approach to analyzing the performance of a team (more specifically, the performance of a team's

[1] https://github.com/godehardt/fraunited-backend, https://github.com/godehardt/fraunited-frontend, https://github.com/godehardt/fraunited-outlier-detector and https://github.com/godehardt/fraunited-ci.

defense). For that reason, we need to briefly introduce some basics of reliability theory here, also pointing to [8] and [11] for the interested reader.

Reliability theory is the branch of statistics that focuses on the application of probability theory in an engineering context to the modeling of the occurrence of events such as failures and the prediction of success probabilities. In related research disciplines the same mathematical concepts are applied under the names survival analysis (biostatistics), event history analysis (sociology), or duration analysis (economics). Events of interest may, thus, include the death of a living being, the failure of a mechanical system, or – as in the case of robotic soccer – the conceding of a goal (which somehow represents the failure of a team's defense).

Random Time to Failure. In terms of reliability, the time to failure is modeled as a random variable T where $P(t \leq T < t + \Delta t)$ denotes the probability that the time to failure is in the interval $[t, t + \Delta)$. Accordingly, the failure probability density function f and distribution function F are defined as usually in probability theory as

$$f(t) = \lim_{\Delta t \to 0} \frac{P(t \leq T < t + \Delta t)}{\Delta t} \text{ and } F(t) = \int_0^t f(x)dx \tag{1}$$

where the latter also represents the probability that a failure occurs by time t, which in the soccer domain boils down to the probability that a goal is conceded by t.

Reliability Function. The complement to F is represented by the chance of being successful at least until t, e.g. keeping a clean sheet in soccer. This complement is called the *reliability function* R and denotes the probability that the time to failure is larger than t (i.e. $T > t$):

$$R(t) = P(T > t) = 1 - F(t) = \int_t^\infty f(x)dx. \tag{2}$$

Failure Rate and Hazard Rate. Interestingly, research in reliability theory has shown that the density function f is not very useful in practice which is why the *failure rate* function λ is derived. It represents the ratio of the probability that a failure occurs per unit time within some interval $[t, t + \Delta t)$ *and* the probability that the system has survived faultlessly up to t:

$$\lambda(t) = \frac{P(t \leq T < t + \Delta t)}{\Delta t} \cdot \frac{1}{P(T > t)} = \frac{F(t + \Delta t) - F(t)}{\Delta t \cdot R(t)}.$$

The limit of the failure rate for $t \to 0$ is called the *hazard rate* h, for which we obtain from Eq. 1 that

$$h(t) = \lim_{\Delta t \to 0} \frac{F(t + \Delta t) - F(t)}{\Delta t \cdot R(t)} = \frac{f(t)}{R(t)} = \lim_{\Delta t \to 0} \frac{-(R(t + \Delta t) - R(t))}{\Delta t \cdot R(t)} = -\frac{d}{dt} ln(R(t)). \tag{3}$$

In our notion, the hazard rate is the instantaneous rate of conceding a goal at time t given that the team has not received a goal against up to t.

Goal Rate. Although there is some minor difference in the definitions of hazard and failure rate, they are often used interchangeably in the literature. Therefore, we will subsume them, calling it the (opponent) *goal rate* $g(t)$, subsequently. The goal rate will, in general, change over the course of a match, varying depending on play modes, ball position on the pitch, or playing strategies of the teams. In the next section, we will inspect the goal rate with the help of the presented CI system for a number of specific match situations.

4 Case Study

The case study delineated in the following is meant to showcase the usefulness of the presented CI/CD system and, beyond that, show how ideas from reliability theory can well be applied in the domain of robotic soccer.

4.1 The Changeover Anomaly

When applying the CI system regularly in the course of preparing for the RoboCup 2023 tournament, we soon discovered an anomaly within the visualized results and statistics produced by the React web application that is part of the CI system's back-end. Among the many statistical visualizations [17] is a goal histogram which consistently showed a peak of goals conceded right after the half-time break. Figure 3 (left) provides an impression of that anomaly for a series of 3000 matches of our team, FRA-UNIted, against the 2022 champion team Helios [18]. Using a bin size of 100 time steps, the summed amount of goals seems to be nearly constant on average throughout the 6000 time steps of a game, except for the beginning where both teams score less which can easily be explained by missing knowledge about heterogeneous player types [10] which are typically inferred after a few hundred time steps. Quite remarkably, however, the curve of goals conceded by our team (blue in the left chart of Fig. 3) contains an outlier right after the changeover with almost three times as many goals per bin as during the rest of the match.

We first speculated that this may be caused by defective tactical assignments of players to to-be-marked opponents which are determined by the coach and communicated to players using the Coach Language [14] or by a (partial) reset of those assignments at half-time. Although this calculation and ensuing interaction between agents had proved to be fragile in previous times (as delineated in [5]), we could verify that this is not the root of the anomaly on this occasion.

A second conjecture, which we also soon discarded, was that there might be an issue in the way the side changeover at half-time is realized in our agents' world models. In this context, we once again employed the CI system to generate another series of (9000) matches against the same opponent team, however, with sides flipped, i.e. the fixture was now Helios vs. FRA-UNIted. While the average scores of both series did not show a significant change (0.59 : 1.83 for the first series, and 1.77 : 0.59 for the second one), the distribution of goals along the time looked quite different as shown in the right part of Fig. 3. The peak at

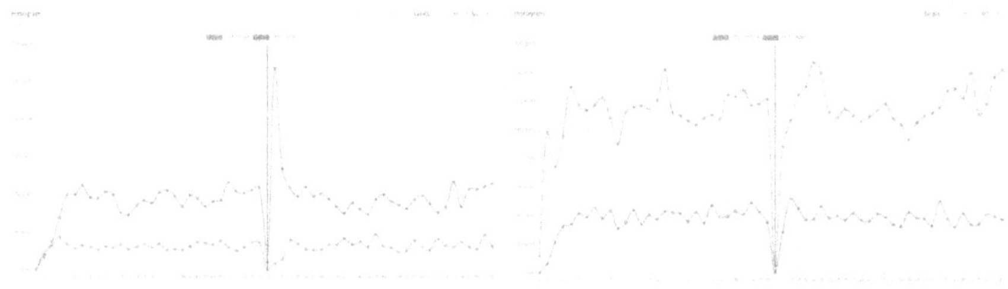

Fig. 3. Original Screenshots from the CI System's React Web Application Visualizing Game Series Statistics Produced by its Python-Based Statistics Tool. Here, the total time of a match is binned using 60 bins, i.e. a window size of 100 time steps. Left: Goal histogram for 3000 matches with FRA-UNIted as the home team, shown in orange, and Helios as the away team, shown in blue. Apparently, something peculiar is going on at half-time breaks. Right: Goal histogram for 9000 matches with sides swapped, i.e. Helios is now the home team (its goals in orange) and FRA-UNIted the away team (blue). Obviously, the goal distribution seems to have changed when swapping sides. Note: Both figures show total number of goals summed over different numbers of matches (3000 vs. 9000). Therefore, the ordinates are scaled differently. For the mid and end of each half-time not much has changed (e.g. about 100 goals for Helios in bin 9 (left) and 300 goals in bin 9 (right) from three times the number of games), but for the beginnings of the halfs the curves differ a lot. (Color figure online)

half-time disappeared, whereas the slope for the team playing from left to right (home team, orange curve, i.e. Helios in the 2nd series) at the very beginning of the match was much steeper.

The Soccer Server lets always start the game with a kick-off for the home team, whereas the away team kicks off to the second half of the match after the half-time break. Given that in the first series the considered opponent Helios was always the away team and, thus, had a kick-off in each game at half-time ($t = 3000$) and in the second series at game start ($t = 0$), we concluded that the initially mentioned peak in goals against FRA-UNIted must be attributed to a poorly-developed and suboptimal behavior of our players during opponent kick-off situations.

4.2 The Glee Didn't Last Long: Conceding Goals After Scoring

According to soccer rules, a single kick-off for the opponent team is unavoidable in any match (either at the beginning or at half-time). Yet, another kick-off is awarded to the opponent after each goal that our team has shot. The conclusion from the previous section, hence, also elicited a profound realization: The joy after having scored a goal may, after all, not last long, if the opponent's probability of scoring a goal right after the immediately following kick-off is high. In order to thoroughly examine this question – and in so doing to confirm that the delineated weakness is really due to kick-offs – we once again utilized the data produced by the CI system discussed above.

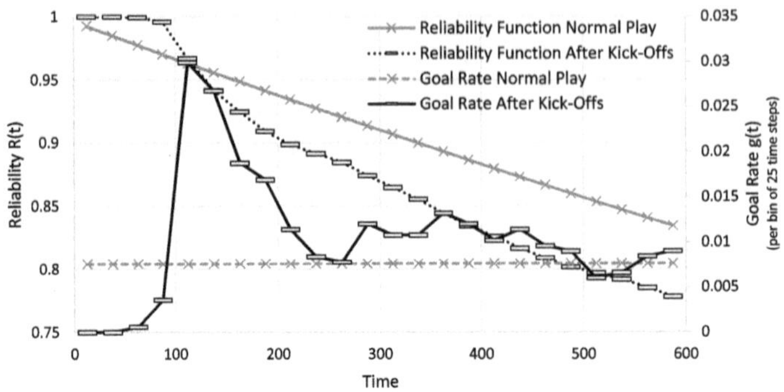

Fig. 4. What Happens After Having Scored: The chart focuses on the 600 time steps after our team has scored a goal and the immediately following opponent kick-off has taken place, aggregating data from 3000 matches. After a little more than 100 time steps, the goal rate of the opponent increases severely while the reliability of our defense drops sharply. This is in stark contrast to the overall "normal play", i.e. the average over all game situations over all 3000 matches, which are drawn in gray color with cross marks, where the goal rate is approximately constant.

The back-end of the CI/CD system we are releasing here also contains a Python-based analyzing tool which is utilized to generate match statistics in JSON format stored in a local database (cf. Sect. 2.1). We used that data and applied various approaches from reliability theory (cf. Sect. 3). Knowing that a kick-off takes place after goals, we selected the subset of match situations unfolding after our team's goals, excluding, however, those that took place near the end of a game or shortly before the half-time break in order to avoid the well-known censoring problem in reliability theory [8].

Figure 4 plots the reliability function $R(t)$ (cf. Eq. 1) for the time after our team has scored a goal (i.e. goal for FRA-UNIted at $t_0 = 0$) where, as discussed in Sect. 3, R refers to the probability of surviving without conceding a goal till time t ($t > t_0$). More interestingly, that chart also contains the hazard rate function $h(t)$, which we refer to as goal rate $g(t)$, that denotes the instantaneous rate of receiving a goal at $t > t_0$. The data is based on 3000 matches with about 1600 goals for FRA-UNIted and immediately following kick-offs for Helios and has been binned with a window size of 25 time steps to produce more readable figures. For comparison, the reliability function and goal rate as they emerge on average during "normal play" are plotted as well. While the goal rate in normal play is constant at $g(t) = 0.0076$ (so many goals are hit within a time window, i.e. within 25 time steps, on average) it peaks with a value almost four times as high (0.03) after circa 100–125 time steps after a kick-off (immediately after a goal by us) has taken place. Note that these numbers exclude kick-offs that took place regularly, i.e. at the start of a half-time. In a separate analysis (not plotted for readability) we confirmed that the reliability function and goal rate for those "regular" kick-offs at half-time or game start are nearly identical.

4.3 Eradicating the Kick-Off Weakness

After acknowledging that our defense's reliability right after having scored a goal, i.e. during opponent kick-offs, is clearly below average, we started working on improvements. The details of the flaws found and belonging corrections are beyond the scope of this paper and can be read in a future team description paper [4]. In brief, we noticed subpar distances between our defenders and their to-be-marked opponent players in conjunction with at times undetected role changes by opponent attackers, often resulting in attackers overrunning our defense line.

Most of all, however, we had to admit that opponent kick-off situations were, in general, far less than perfect tested by our (human) team members. This is because human-based development and testing (even when improved by means of layered disclosure, as described in Sect. 1) focuses very often on *partial* matches with the team under development as home team (i.e. kicking off at game start) and some arbitrary (last year's) opponent binary as away team (thus, not kicking off at game start). Such development test games are often interrupted by the developer as soon as a goal is shot by either team or some other interesting event occurs that seems worth analyzing in the log files. This way, however, often partial matches with a duration of less than a half-time are inspected which do not include any opponent kick-off, which is why those events are extremely underrepresented and flaws are hardly recognized.

Although this delineation is episodical for our team we are, on the one hand, convinced that it holds for other soccer simulation 2D teams as well. On the other hand, the described experience makes a strong case for the introduced CI system which automates much of the testing and assessment work and, in so doing, aims at preventing the mentioned problem of underrepresenting certain match situations.

Results. The effectiveness of the improvements can be read from Fig. 5. Utilizing the CI system once again, we ran another series of 3400 test matches in the same set-up as before, this time, however, employing our mentioned kick-off-related modifications. Again, our focus was on the reliability (top left) of our defense in preventing opponent goals as well as on the goal rate (top right) that emerges after our team's goals and the immediately following opponent kick-off. Apparently, although still worse than during normal play, the defense reliability (top left) after opponent kick-offs could be improved significantly when compared to our team's original (released 2023 binary) version. This is also reflected in the goal rate arising after our goals and the subsequent opponent kick-offs (top right part of Fig. 5), whose peak at $t \in [100, 125]$ could be mitigated clearly.

The top right diagram contains two further curves which refer to the *cumulated* goal rate $G(t)$, for which Eq. 3 yields

$$G(t) = \int_0^t g(x)dx = \int_0^t \frac{f(x)}{R(x)}dx = -ln(R(t)).$$

The curves put this value $G(t)$ in relation to the cumulated goal rate during normal play (plotted on the secondary ordinate, with 100% representing normal

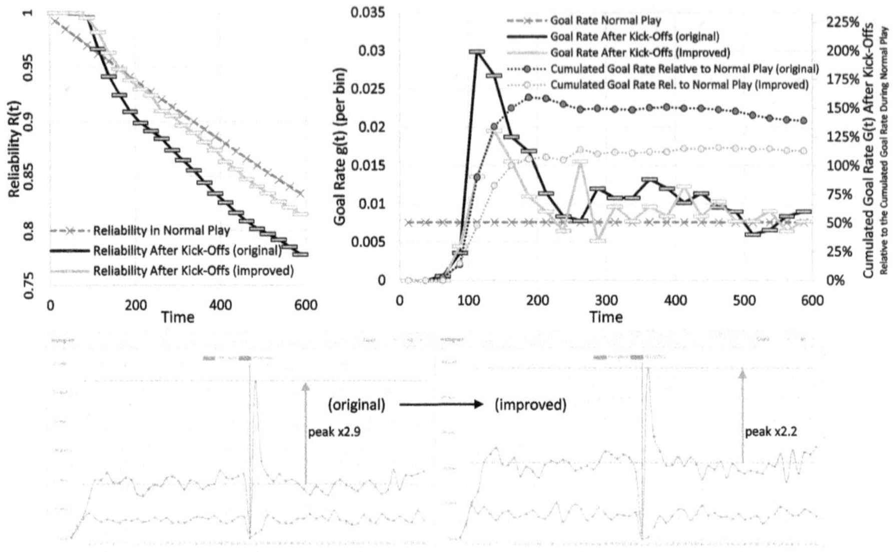

Fig. 5. Efficacy of Counter Measures Against the Detected Kick-Off Weakness: Both charts in the top row contrast reliability and (cumulated) goal rate before ("original") and after ("improved") having implemented counter measures. The goal histogram charts in the bottom row were generated with the presented CI system.

play). Apparently, our team's cumulated risk of receiving a goal (within 600 time steps) after having shot a goal used to be 39.0% higher than during normal play, whereas it is only 12.8% higher after our modifications, hence proving their effectiveness using the CI system.

Returning to the changeover anomaly, the two bottom charts of Fig. 5 which were automatically rendered by the CI system, prove that our modification had the same positive expectable impact on what happens after the opponent's regular kick-offs at half time. The magnitude of the goal peak at half-time relative to the general distribution of goals could be reduced significantly. Note that these histogram charts plot total numbers originating from different amounts of games, therefore being scaled slightly differently.

Discussion. The CI system is composed as a loose coupling of a set of components and, therefore, provides the flexibility to shift the focus to other game events as well. For example, we have done a brief analysis on the vulnerability of our team's playing behavior after opponent free kicks and corner kicks. As can be seen in Fig. 6, we obtain reliability and goal rate progressions that are worth considering. Obviously, opponent free kicks seem to exert only moderate amount of extra danger to our defense (especially between 200 and 300 time steps after the free kick was taken), By contrast, the observed goal rates after corner kicks by the opponent team (with ca. 0.077 per bin at $t \in [100, 125]$ almost three times as high as after kick-offs, cf. Fig. 4) seem to leave room for improvement.

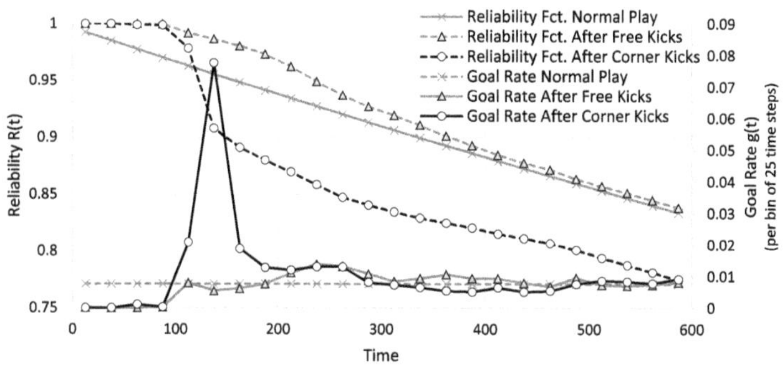

Fig. 6. Reliability and Goal Rate After Further Game Events: This figure contrasts the average "normal play" defense reliability and opponent goal rate with those that are to be observed after opponent *free kicks* and after opponent *corner kicks*. The insight is, that our team's reliability is even higher than average after free kicks indicating well-developed defense behavior. The opposite is true for opponent corners for which our team's behavior seems to be poorly adapted, as indicated by a goal rate that clearly stands out for times in [125, 175] steps after taking the corner kick.

Similarly we might extend the breadth of the analyses by focusing on, for instance, our team's standard situations or on arbitrary game situations, like "ball has left the penalty area" or "an opponent self-pass has been intercepted" to analyze the corresponding subsequent progress of the match. Moreover, so far our focus has been on ultimate outcomes, i.e. goals (received or shot), but, ultimately, other game events and statistics like "share of successful passes" or "ball possession rate" might be considered just as well.

5 Conclusion

We have presented the continuous integration and deployment system that we developed and maintain as part of our activities in the realm of robotic soccer simulation. The system enables the automatic conduction of large series of matches against definable opponents upon any code change conducted, is able to filter out games based on outlier rules, and facilitates the derivation of game statistics that can guide the developers in improving the team. We released the system under MIT licence on Github, making it available to the 2D community. In order to demonstrate the usability of the system, we also presented a case study where that system has been used end-to-end. It helped us uncover some awkward weaknesses in our team's playing strategy that occurred immediately after scoring a goal. Using concepts from reliability theory, it additionally assisted in analyzing the issue in depth and in aiming to ameliorate it.

Acknowledgements. This research has been supported by the German Federal Ministry of Education and Research under grant number 13FH027K11.

References

1. Akiyama, H., Zare, N.: The RoboCup soccer simulator. https://github.com/rcsoccersim. Soccer Server, Soccer Monitor, Logplayer. Accessed March 2024
2. Bai, A., Lu, G., Zhang, H., Chen, X.: WrightEagle 2D soccer simulation team description 2011. Supplement to RoboCup 2011: Robot World Cup XV (2011)
3. Estivill-Castro, V., Hexel, R., Lusty, C.: Continuous integration for testing full robotic behaviours in a GUI-stripped simulation. In: CEUR Workshop Proceedings of MODELS 2018, Copenhagen, Denmark, vol. 2245, pp. 453–464 (2018)
4. Gabel, T., Eren, B., Godehardt, E.: FRA-UNIted – Team Description 2024. Supplement to RoboCup 2024: Robot Soccer World Cup XXVI (to appear)
5. Gabel, T., Riedmiller, M.: On progress in RoboCup: the simulation league showcase. In: Ruiz-del-Solar, J., Chown, E., Plöger, P. (eds.) RoboCup 2010: Robot Soccer World Cup XIV, LNCS, pp. 36–47. Springer, Singapore (2010)
6. Godehardt, E., Allani, M., Vieth, A., Gabel, T.: 1001 games a night – continuous evaluation of an intelligent multi-agent based system. In: Proceedings of the 8th International Congress on Information and Communication Technology (ICICT 2023), London, United Kingdom, pp. 193–208 (2023)
7. Gspandl, S., et al.: KickOffTUG – team description paper 2010. Supplement to RoboCup 2010: Robot Soccer World Cup XXII (2010)
8. Lyu, M.: Handbook of Software Reliability Engineering. McGraw-Hill (1995)
9. Mota, L., Reis, L.: Setplays: achieving coordination by the appropriate use of arbitrary pre-defined flexible plans and inter-robot communication. In: Proceedings of the 1st International Conference on Robot Communication and Coordination (ROBOCOMM), vol. 318, pp. 1–13. ICST/ACM, Athens (2007)
10. Noda, I.: Soccer server: a simulator of RoboCup. In: Proceedings of the AI Symposium 1995, pp. 29–34. Japanese Society for Artificial Intelligence (1995)
11. O'Connor, P.: Practical Reliability Engineering. Wiley (2012)
12. Prokopenko, M., Wang, P.: Fractals2019: combinatorial optimisation with dynamic constraint annealing. In: RoboCup 2019: Robot World Cup XXIII, pp. 616–630. Springer, Sydney (2020)
13. Riley, P., Stone, P., Veloso, M.: Layered disclosure: revealing agents' internals. In: Castelfranchi, C., Lespérance, Y. (eds.) Intelligent Agents VII Agent Theories Architectures and Languages, pp. 61–72. Springer, Heidelberg (2001)
14. Riley, P., Veloso, M., Kaminka, G.: Towards any-team coaching in adversarial domains. In: Proceedings of the 1st International Joint Conference on Autonomous Agents and Multiagent Systems (AAMAS 2002), pp. 1145–1146. Springer, Bologna (2002)
15. Sayareh, A., et al.: Observation denoising in CYRUS soccer simulation 2D team for RoboCup 202. Supplement to RoboCup 2023: Robot World Cup XXV3 (2023)
16. Vasconcelos, D., et al.: ITAndroids 2D soccer simulation team description paper 2022. Supplement to RoboCup 2022: Robot Soccer World Cup XXIV (2022)
17. Vieth, A.: A continuous integration system with diversified opponents and dynamic team configurations for RoboCup 2D. Master's thesis, Frankfurt University of Applied Sciences (2022)
18. Yamaguchi, M., Kuga, R., Omori, H., Fukushima, T., Nakashima, T., Akiyama, H.: HELIOS2021: team description papet. Supplement to RoboCup 2021: Robot Soccer World Cup XXV (2021)

Cleaning Robots in Public Spaces: A Survey and Proposal for Benchmarking Based on Stakeholders Interviews

Raphael Memmesheimer[1(✉)], Martina Overbeck[2], Bjoern Kral[3], Lea Steffen[4], Sven Behnke[1], Martin Gersch[3], and Arne Roennau[4]

[1] Autonomous Intelligent Systems, Computer Science, University of Bonn, Bonn, Germany
memmesheimer@ais.uni-bonn.de
[2] FZI Forschungszentrum Informatik, Karlsruhe, Germany
[3] Business Administration, Free University of Berlin, Berlin, Germany
[4] Intelligent Machines, Karlsruhe Institute of Technology, Karlsruhe, Germany

Abstract. Autonomous cleaning robots for public spaces have potential for addressing current societal challenges, such as labor shortages and cleanliness in public spaces. Other application domains like autonomous driving, bin picking, or search and rescue have shown that benchmarking platforms and approaches in competitive settings can advance their respective research fields, resulting in more applicable systems under real-world conditions. For this paper, we analyzed seven semi-structured, qualitative stakeholder interviews about outdoor cleaning, identified current needs as well as limitations, and considered those results for the development of a benchmarking scenario based on the previous observations.

Keywords: cleaning robots · expert interviews · robotic competitions · benchmarking

1 Introduction

Automation has become an integral part of our daily lives and has transformed various industries and sectors. One such sector that has seen notable advances is the automated cleaning industry. Although considerable research has been dedicated to the development of private autonomous indoor cleaning robots [19,20,28], the exploration of autonomous cleaning robots for public spaces has not yet received the same analysis. Automated public cleaning robots have the potential to address societal challenges, such as maintaining cleanliness and offering a promising solution to labor shortages in the public cleaning sector.

We researched public sector requirements via stakeholder interviews and an analysis of technological requirements for cleaning robots. Based on both and further motivated by the positive impact of robotic competitions, we propose a

E. Barros et al. (Eds.): RoboCup 2024, LNAI 15570, pp. 373–385, 2025.
https://doi.org/10.1007/978-3-031-85859-8_32

benchmarking scenario to foster the development of cleaning robots for public spaces.

The contributions of this paper are as follows:

- *Expert Interviews*: Seven expert interviews were conducted to gain a more profound understanding of the requirements and challenges in communal cleaning of public areas. These interviews provided valuable insights into stakeholders' present requirements and expectations in this domain.
- *Identification of Limitations*: This research identified several limitations of current hardware and software approaches to autonomous cleaning of public spaces.
- *Benchmark Scenario*: Based on our expert interviews and an analysis of current limitations, we developed a benchmarking scenario aimed at fostering advancements in autonomous cleaning in public spaces.

2 Related Work

In the following, we give a brief overview of available cleaning robot solutions and robotic competitions.

2.1 Robotic and Automated Cleaning

Vacuum cleaning robots came onto the market in the early 2000s [20,31] and paved the way for the development and introduction of other cleaning robots for different applications and environments. Husqvarna's robotic lawnmower Solarmower, which appeared in 1996, is considered the role model for the first robotic vacuum cleaners [35]. The first robot vacuum cleaner was the Trilobite from Electrolux, which was commercially available from 2001 [18].

In 2002, iRobot [37] introduced the now well-known Roomba robot vacuum cleaner. In 2012, it had sold more than 8 million units [35]. The robot was able to recognize and avoid obstacles. However, this system was limited in corner cleaning capabilities.

In the 2010s, there were many advancements and, consequently, a rapidly increasing demand for domestic robots – mainly due to advanced sensing and navigation technologies [35]. This led to improved autonomy and flexibility of cleaning robots. Robot-based cleaning systems that were able to move autonomously through complex environments and perform various cleaning tasks became more common [31]. Compared to today's systems, the systems of the time suffered from poor navigability, complexity, frequent failures, and low cleaning performance. In addition, the products were still large and bulky [21].

Since the 2020s, cleaning robots have been increasingly found in commercial scenarios, such as office buildings, shopping malls, airports, hotels, and healthcare facilities. Cleaning tasks they offer include dusting floors, vacuuming, washing windows, and more. Technology is constantly evolving, and the development of artificial intelligence (AI) and sensor technology continues to drive the performance and adaptability of these robots. Current technologies are characterized primarily by achievements in the following two areas [21]:

First, the cleaning performance has increased, e.g. by advanced brush design. This enables cleaning along edges and in tight corners. The battery capacity has also been increased. With a single charge and a service life of over 1,000 charging cycles, several hours of scrubbing or dusting can now be performed.

Second of all, autonomous navigation has been improved with new sensor technology and the combination of distance and collision sensors [34], thus enabling the replacement of inefficient pathfinding using random walks with superior algorithms such as SLAM (Neato Robotics, Samsung Hauzen RE70V, Dyson 360 Eye), fuzzy logic methods (Samsung POWERbot), and the A* algorithm (LG Hom-Bot) [17,33].

The state of the art in commercial, automated cleaning technologies already includes a wide range of proven and established systems. The most commonly required cleaning tasks are classified into six robotic motions: wiping, sweeping, scrubbing, vacuuming, washing and tidying up [20,31]. An excerpt of existing cleaning robots for public spaces are depicted in Fig. 1.

(a) Adlatus CR700 [12] (b) Angsa [13] (c) VIGGO S100-N [15]

Fig. 1. Cleaning robot platforms.

The integration of simple AI methods, robotics, and the Internet of Things (IoT) into cleaning technologies has led to a significant improvement in efficiency, quality, sustainability, and user-friendliness. Systems have already been successfully tested and introduced in the following areas: Firstly, autonomous robots can use sensors and 2D path planning [17] to recognize their surroundings and avoid obstacles. They can be used in various environments, including offices, shopping centers, airports, and warehouses. Such systems are capable of mopping floors, vacuuming carpets, cleaning windows, and other routine tasks. Drones are increasingly being used for outdoor cleaning, especially for hard-to-reach outdoor areas such as high-rise facades or solar panels. These drones are equipped with special cleaning agents and brushes and can work autonomously or remotely. A study specifically on robot-based cleaning of solar installations was presented in [23].

Based on this assessment of the current status, it is possible to identify gaps and weaknesses in existing work on robotic cleaning systems. The combination of different sensors, such as cameras, LiDAR, and infrared sensors for detecting walls, steps, and stairs or encoders for measuring wheel rotation, enables advanced navigation with high precision.

Cleaning systems are currently unable to adapt flexibly to changing environments and only take 2D surfaces into account. For example, future robotic cleaning systems should be able to cope well with changing conditions in a natural environment. This includes darkness, reflections, extreme solar radiation, and heat, as well as heavy rain or wind. On the other hand, an extension to 3D planning would be helpful and would allow the observation of more complex environments.

In addition, cleaning should only take place where it is necessary. This could lead to reduction in water, energy, and chemical consumption as well as a multiple increase in overall efficiency. There are already initial systems that can identify soiling [16,21]. Nevertheless, there is still great potential for innovative developments regarding the identification of contaminated areas to enable the cleaning of selected areas.

Visual perception methods based on recent advances of Convolutional Neural Networks (CNNs) can be applied to identify dirt and therefore focus the cleaning process. The design of many systems also poses a problem for mobility. The smaller the size, the greater the ability to navigate in narrow aisles, corridors, and other confined areas. However, this is in stark contrast to battery life and the associated performance, which tends to require larger designs.

Finally, automated cleaning in public areas requires a positive user experience, as this is the basis for technology acceptance. A distinction is made here between interaction with users and observers who do not operate the device directly (Table 1).

Table 1. Competition overview.

Competition	Focus	Country	Year
RoboCup [8,9,30]	Soccer, Home, Rescue, Logistics, Junior, ...	Int.	since 1996
DARPA Challenges [3,36]	Military	USA	since 2004
European Robotics League	Home, Rescue, Work	Europe	2016–2023
MBZIRC [4]	Military	UAE	2017, 2019, 2023
ANA Avatar XPRIZE [2]	Telepresence	USA	2018–2022
Amazon Robotics Challenge [1]	Industrial/Logistics	Int.	2015–2017
METRICS [5,6]	Domestic, Industrial, Agriculture	Europe	2020–2023
World Robot Summit [10,27,29,38]	Service, Industrial, Rescue, Junior	Japan	2018, 2021

2.2 Robot Competitions

Robotic competitions [1,8,22,32] serve as exciting platforms for researchers, engineers, and students to showcase their designs, push the boundaries of technology, and test the skills of robots against real-world challenges. In this section, we introduce various robotics competitions taking place around the globe.

General Robot Competitions. *RoboCup:* International competition focusing on autonomous robots, with various applications and events, such as soccer [8, 22], service robots [9], and rescue robots [30]. Annual, worldwide, with more than 2000 participants.

DARPA Challenges: US-based competitions focusing on disaster scenarios and advanced humanoid robots and exploration of external environments. Notable events include the DARPA Grand Challenge 2006 [36], the DARPA Robotics Challenge 2015, and the DARPA Subterranean Challenge 2021 [3].

ANA Avatar XPRIZE: US-based competition focused on developing an avatar system allowing human presence to be represented by a remotely controlled robot, with a focus on teleoperation, haptics, and interaction [2,14,24].

Amazon Picking/Robotics Challenge: Challenge to develop robotic systems capable of autonomously picking items in a warehouse environment, with specified objects and warehouse layout [1].

Metrics: EU-funded project focusing on the development of robots in various fields, including healthcare, agile production, inspection, and agricultural robotics [5,6].

Robot Competitions with Cleaning Aspects. The aforementioned competitions focus on various aspects of robotic automation, ranging from autonomous driving, rescue, space, domestic, industrial manufacturing and warehouse scenarios. We now introduce competitions and challenges with a cleaning aspect.

Deutsche Bahn: Automated Cleaning Challenge (2018, Germany). Deutsche Bahn organized a competition in which robots were to be developed that could autonomously clean train stations. The winning team was awarded a two-year contract with Deutsche Bahn to further develop station cleaning. The competition was aimed at innovative companies and start-ups with a focus on automated cleaning. A rule book or a detailed description of the competition are unfortunately no longer available online [7].

World Robot Summit (2018, 2020, Japan). The World Robot Summit (WRS) [10] is an international robotics competition with challenges ranging targeting rescue [27], service [29], industrial [38] and special challenges for juniors. In the Future Convenience Store Challenge (FCSC), robots competed against each other in a supermarket. One task in the FCSC was to clean a customer toilet. The task was semi-automatically scored by calculating a cleaning rate from before and after images under UV light.

UV Robot Design Contest (2021, online) was a design competition for robot designs that to eliminate COVID-19 bacteria using UV radiation.

3 Stakeholders on Cleaning Robots in Public Spaces

To extract meaningful comparison criteria for cleaning robotics in public spaces, stakeholders' opinions were sought through interviews. A semi-structured expert interview approach, according to [11] and [26], was chosen to frame this analysis of requirements for robotic cleaning systems. This allows for adaptability and in-depth exploration of various topics based on the responses and information provided by the experts. An interview guide was created and divided into seven thematic areas addressing economic and technical needs: cleaning tasks and current challenges, the potential for automation through robotic cleaning systems, acceptance and personnel issues, purchasing behavior, potential opportunities and challenges, market development, and trends. The original and English translation of the questionnaire is made available[1]. In total, 82 stakeholders from municipal and urban cleaning service providers, as well as facility management sectors, were contacted, after a conducting stakeholders research. The interviewed persons were mainly managers with a strategic focus but also in contact with executive employees in the city cleaning department. In the end, 8 interviews, each lasting approximately 42 min, were conducted. They revealed a keen interest in future projects within cleaning robotics for both indoor and outdoor cleaning. Only 7 interviews related to public outdoor cleaning are included here.

Table 2. Areas of application (A1-A14) for public space cleaning robots as mentioned from interviews with stakeholders (Mentions in %).

No.	Areas of Application (Tasks)	M. in %
A1	Collecting small, possibly health-hazardous waste of different consistencies	100%
A2	Reaching places that are difficult to access	100%
A3	Vacuuming	100%
A4	Sensory detection/ recognition of objects and people, as well as their quantity	86%
A5	Sweeping of sidewalks, squares, surfaces	86%
A6	Leaf removal	71%
A7	Raking/hooking for weed removal on water-bound paths/areas	71%
A8	Cleaning seams on/in sidewalks or cobblestones	57%
A9	Transporting heavy objects or collected waste	57%
A10	Emptying stationary waste garbage cans	57%
A11	Snow clearing/ gritting	57%
A12	Removing chewing gum or graffiti from surfaces	43%
A13	Mopping of sidewalks, squares, surfaces	43%
A14	Lifting heavy objects such as maintenance hole covers	29%

[1] https://www.roboter-im-alltag.org/aktuelles/publikationen/.

The evaluation of expert interviews regarding stakeholder requirements in the context of robotic cleaning systems revealed relevant insights into application areas and potentials for robotic cleaning. All interviewees highlighted tasks (Table 2) such as collecting or vacuuming small, possibly health-hazardous waste of different consistencies (e.g., crown caps, cigarettes, broken glass, candy wrappers, but also syringes, feces, condoms) as well as reaching places that are difficult to access (e.g., under cars or park benches, near water edges, tree grates and windows, or in corners). Robotic systems were, in the majority of cases, also identified as a potential asset for the sensory detection and recognition of objects and people, as well as their quantity, as well as vacuuming and sweeping sidewalks, squares, and surfaces.

The organizational context and personnel aspects also played a central role in the analysis of the economic needs. The main objective (see Table 3) as to why robots were interesting for outdoor cleaning tasks was the improvement of cleaning quality. That was, nonetheless, closely followed by the mention of the need to clean areas for which the cleaning staff would generally have no capacity, as well as the reduction of downtime caused by both sickness and a shortage of personnel.

Table 3. The most relevant objectives (O1–O7) mentioned by the stakeholders in the semi-structured qualitative interviews (Mentions in %).

No.	Objectives	M. in %
O1	Improvements in cleaning quality	86%
O2	Cleaning of areas for which the cleaning staff would normally have no capacity	71%
O3	Reduction of downtime	71%
O4	Improvement in cleaning speed	57%
O5	Long-term savings and cost benefits	43%
O6	Standardized execution of cleaning with consistent results	43%
O7	Reduction of stress (physical, health) for cleaning staff	43%

The interviews also tackled the question of what boundary conditions robots would have to face (Table 4) to fulfill both their task (e.g., picking up small objects) and the objective (e.g., increasing cleaning quality). Within the most frequently mentioned conditions were having to deal with strongly deviating, heterogeneous substrates, changing weather and lighting conditions, and the varying availability of storage and loading sites, as well as the necessity to be aware of the welfare of nature, animals, and children. Most of all, however, mentioned as a boundary condition for the use of cleaning robots in public outdoor spaces was the role of (non)acceptance of the robots that influences the interaction of both workers and passersby and has the interviewees worried about vandalism.

Table 4. The boundary conditions for task fulfillment (B1–B15) for cleaning robots were identified from interviews with stakeholders.

No.	Boundary Conditions for Task Fulfillment	Mentions in %
B1	Dealing with (non-)acceptance, interactions, vandalism	100%
B2	Dealing with strongly deviating, heterogeneous substrates/surfaces	86%
B3	Dealing with changing weather and lighting conditions	86%
B4	Environmental protection/animal welfare/child protection	86%
B5	Dealing with different storage and loading availability	86%
B6	Dealing with unmapped, unknown areas	57%
B7	Coping with stairs/steps	57%
B8	Sufficient storage capacity of the robot itself	57%
B9	Dealing with grass of different heights	43%
B10	Removing trampled small items of waste	43%
B11	Dealing with noise/volume restrictions	43%
B12	Coping with inclines	29%
B13	Achieving visual improvement through cleaning	29%
B14	Vacuuming without removing or damaging the surface	29%
B15	Dealing with unknown objects	14%

4 Benchmarking

In this section, based on the stakeholder interviews, we derive required basic robotic technologies and hardware requirements. We further propose a benchmarking scenario that combines the technological requirements and the mentioned applications by the stakeholders.

4.1 Technologies and Hardware Requirements for Urban Cleaning

Following the state of the art and the stakeholder interviews, the basic technologies required in the context of urban cleaning can be identified:

Perception is required for environmental perception. Cameras and sensors are used to record the robot's surroundings, recognize obstacles and humans, assess the cleaning requirements, and track the progress of the cleaning. The sensor technology to be used depends on the task. A camera is used to detect contamination, a LiDAR is used to create a map of the environment and detect obstacles, and a camera or LiDAR is used to detect people. It is conceivable that active lighting or cameras in the non-visible range could be used to improve perception. Perception can often be significantly improved by fusing multiple sensors.

Manipulation of objects is task-dependent. For example, dirt can be removed by manipulation using a suction device or a sponge. Picking up garbage can be implemented by manipulation using a gripper. Manipulation is strongly based on the results of perception. If these are deficient, manipulation is usually not possible. Manipulation tasks involving variable objects increase the complexity of the robot and usually require robot arms with several degrees of freedom. There are certain dependencies between the individual basic technologies.

Cognition is necessary for decision-making. The robot must be able to understand the environment and make decisions based on this. There is, therefore, a direct dependency on perception because of which decisions are made. State machines are a simple way of making decisions. However, more complex methods such as behavior trees [25] can also be used here.

Navigation enables the robot to move around in an environment. This includes localization and path planning. Localization can be performed using a LiDAR, movement estimates from odometry (e.g., from wheel rotation), and path planning using a map. The necessary movement commands are transmitted to the robot via a drive and should occur in a closed control loop. There are established localization and path planning methods, which can usually be used on a robot but require initial integration effort.

Interaction is necessary for operating the robot. This includes operation via user interfaces, speech recognition, and gesture recognition. People are recognized by a camera or a LiDAR, speech is recognized by a microphone, and gestures are recognized by a camera or a LiDAR. Interaction with people is, therefore, closely linked to sensor-based perception.

Manipulation, cognition, navigation and interaction are all based on perception. Inadequate perception, therefore, usually has major consequences. Depending on the task, there are also dependencies between the other basic technologies and navigation.

4.2 Benchmarking Scenario: Park Cleaning

Park pathway cleaning is a well benchmarkable task that unifies the criteria stated by the stakeholder interviews and the identified basic technologies, and therefore serves as an interesting benchmarking scenario of cleaning robots for public spaces.

Fig. 2. Exemplary trash from public spaces.

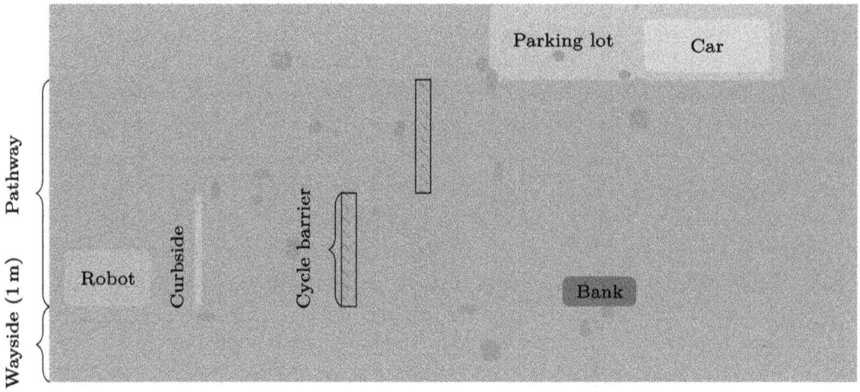

Fig. 3. Scenario layout sketch.

In Fig. 3, we depict a potential setup of a park cleaning benchmark. A pathway containing various types of pollution, and the wayside (up to 1 m distance from the pathway) are subject to being cleaned. The benchmark aims to take place in a real park environment. The contamination is caused by e.g. glass, plastic cups, paper, cigarette butts, etc. (see Fig. 2) and differs e.g. by size, material, moisture, appearance, visibility. Bonus points can be awarded for removing hard-to-reach litter, e.g. under park benches or behind obstacles. Various obstacles (like a curbside, cycle barriers, banks and parking cars) benchmark the handling of obstacles and the cleaning capabilities in hard-to-reach areas (below bank or car). We found this setting to reflect various technical challenges and being highly practical at the same time. The benchmark scoring considers the amount of collected items (in weight or amount) or the time required to achieve the cleaning task.

Technical Requirements. The benchmark is designed to be platform-independent, such that existing platforms can be used. For example, it is possible to take part in the benchmark with unmanned aerial vehicles, unmanned ground vehicles, walking robots or even combinations of several platforms. The technical requirements are checked in the form of a technical acceptance (inspection) at the start of the competition. Participation in the rest of the competition is only possible if all technical requirements are met. The technical requirements are defined as follows:

- Weight $\leq$ 150 kg
- Size $\leq$ 1.2 m $\times$ 0.75 m $\times$ 1 m (L$\times$W$\times$H)
- Well visible and reachable emergency button
- Obstacle avoidance (avoiding people, animals, pathway users and other obstacles)

These requirements are inspired by non-autonomous cleaning machines for public spaces and mobility scooters. Robots being benchmarked should follow size and weight limitations. Further, it is required that benchmarked robots can move on the pathway and potentially the wayside without damaging them. At all time, participating robots should be able to be evacuated from the benchmarking field promptly.

5 Conclusion

In this paper, we discuss the application of cleaning robots for public spaces. Stakeholder interviews were conducted to identify application requirements. Based on that, we derived requirements for basic technologies. The interviews and requirements have been used as the foundation for the design of a practical benchmark for the comparison of cleaning robots for public spaces. These findings underscore the diverse application potential of robotic cleaning systems in public spaces, addressing practical cleaning needs and technical challenges.

Acknowledgments. This work has been funded by the German Ministry of Education and Research (BMBF), grant nos. 16SV8680, 16SV8681, 16SV8683 project: Transferzentrum Roboter im Alltag (RimA).

References

1. Amazon Picking Challenge 2016 rulebook. https://pwurman.org/amazonpickingchallenge/APC_2016_Official_Rules.pdf. Accessed 22 Apr 2024
2. ANA Avatar XPRIZE rulebook v4.2. https://assets-us-01.kc-usercontent.com/5cb25086-82d2-4c89-94f0-8450813a0fd3/bad53d94-c2c6-4c37-bcba-584e56239546/ANA%20Avatar%20XPRIZE%20Rules%20and%20Regulations%20Version%204.2.pdf. Accessed 22 Apr 2024
3. DARPA Subterranean(SubT) Challenge. https://www.darpa.mil/attachments/SubT_Challenge_Finals_Rules.pdf. Accessed 22 Apr 2024

4. MBZIRC robot competition. https://www.mbzirc.com/. Accessed 22 Apr 2024
5. METRICS HEART-MET Challenge rulebook v2.1. https://github.com/HEART-MET/rulebook/blob/master/METRICS_HEART-MET_Rulebook_v2.1.pdf. Accessed 22 Apr 2024
6. METRICS project webpage. https://metricsproject.eu/. Accessed 22 Apr 2024
7. Pressemitteilung DB Cleaning Challenge. https://www.deutschebahn.com/resource/blob/6846088/67db469640f15392e2070fba5d3dda20/PI-reinigungsroboterrennen-data.pdf. Accessed 22 Apr 2024
8. RoboCup Soccer Humanoid League laws of the game. http://humanoid.robocup.org/wp-content/uploads/RC-HL-2022-Rules-3.pdf. Accessed 22 Apr 2024
9. Robocup@home 2023 rulebook. https://github.com/RoboCupAtHome/RuleBook/releases/download/2023.2/rulebook.pdf. Accessed 22 Apr 2024
10. World Robot Summit webpage. https://wrs.nedo.go.jp/en/. Accessed 22 Apr 2024
11. Adams, W.C.: Conducting semi-structured interviews. Handb. Pract. Program Eval. 492–505 (2015)
12. Adlatus Robotics GmbH: Adlatus CR700. https://www.adlatus.eu/en/adlatus/
13. Angsa Robotics GmbH: Ansga. https://angsa-robotics.com/
14. Behnke, S., Adams, J.A., Locke, D.: The $10 million ANA avatar XPRIZE competition: how it advanced immersive telepresence systems. IEEE Robot. Autom. Mag. **30**(4), 98–104 (2023)
15. Beijing Idriverplus Technology Co., Ltd.: Viggo s100-n. https://www.viggorobot.com/autonomous-cleaning-machines/viggo-s100-n.html
16. Bormann, R., Wang, X., Xu, J., Schmidt, J.: DirtNet: visual dirt detection for autonomous cleaning robots. International Conference on Robotics and Automation (ICRA), pp. 1977–1983 (2020). https://doi.org/10.1109/ICRA40945.2020.9196559
17. Edwards, T., Sörme, J.: A comparison of path planning algorithms for robotic vacuum cleaners. DEGREE PROJECT TECHNOLOGY (2018)
18. Electrolux: Trilobite 2.0 (2006)
19. Fink, J., Bauwens, V., Kaplan, F., Dillenbourg, P.: Living with a vacuum cleaning robot - a 6-month ethnographic study. Int. J. Soc. Robot. **5**(3), 389–408 (2013). https://doi.org/10.1007/S12369-013-0190-2
20. Fiorini, P., Prassler, E.: Cleaning and household robots: a technology survey. Auton. Robots **9**(3), 227–235 (2000). https://doi.org/10.1023/A:1008954632763
21. Gausium: What to Expect from a Commercial Cleaning Robot in 2023 (2023)
22. Gerndt, R., Seifert, D., Baltes, J.H., Sadeghnejad, S., Behnke, S.: Humanoid robots in soccer: robots versus humans in RoboCup 2050. IEEE Robot. Autom. Mag. **22**(3), 147–154 (2015)
23. Hashim, N., Mohammed, M.N., Al Selvarajan, R., Al-Zubaidi, S., Mohammed, S.: Study on solar panel cleaning robot. In: International Conference on Automatic Control and Intelligent Systems (CACIS), pp. 56–61 (2019). https://doi.org/10.1109/I2CACIS.2019.8825028
24. Hauser, K., et al.: Analysis and perspectives on the ANA Avatar XPRIZE competition. Int. J. Soc. Robot. 1–32 (2024)
25. Heppner, G., et al.: Risk aware robots - health estimation and capability selection. In: International Conference on Automation Science and Engineering, pp. 1193–1199 (2019). https://doi.org/10.1109/COASE.2019.8843187
26. Kallio, H., Pietilä, A.M., Johnson, M., Kangasniemi, M.: Systematic methodological review: developing a framework for a qualitative semi-structured interview guide. J. Adv. Nurs. **72**(12), 2954–2965 (2016)

27. Kimura, T., et al.: Competition task development for response robot innovation in world robot summit. In: IEEE International Symposium on Safety, Security and Rescue Robotics (SSRR), pp. 129–130 (2017)
28. Mohan, R.E., Rojas, N., Chua, A.: Design principles for robot inclusive spaces: A case study with roomba. In: IEEE International Conference on Robotics and Automation (ICRA), pp. 5593–5599 (2014)
29. Okada, H., Inamura, T., Wada, K.: What competitions were conducted in the service categories of the World robot summit? Adv. Robot. **33**(17), 900–910 (2019)
30. Pellenz, J., Dillenberger, D., Steinbauer, G.: Novel rule set for the RoboCup rescue robot league. In: IEEE International Symposium on Safety, Security, and Rescue Robotics (SSRR), pp. 282–283 (2016)
31. Prassler, E., Ritter, A., Schaeffer, C., Fiorini, P.: A short history of cleaning robots. Auton. Robot. **9**(3), 211–226 (2000). https://doi.org/10.1023/A:1008974515925/METRICS
32. Roa, M.A., et al.: Mobile manipulation hackathon: moving into real world applications. IEEE Robot. Autom. Mag. **28**(2), 112–124 (2021)
33. Raguraman, S.M., Tamilselvi, D., Shivakumar, N.: Mobile robot navigation using Fuzzy logic controller. In: International Conference on Control, Automation, Communication and Energy Conservation (2009)
34. TechHive: How robot vacuums work (2018). https://www.techhive.com/article/583321/how-a-robot-vacuum-navigates-your-home.html
35. Technology, BBC NEWS: Robot cleaner hits the shops (2003)
36. Thrun, S., et al.: Stanley: the robot that won the DARPA grand challenge. J. Field Robot. **23**(9), 661–692 (2006)
37. Wang, Y., Zhang, Z., Yatmono, S., Khairudin, M., Pramono, H.S., Asmara, A.: Development of intelligent floor cleaning robot. J. Phys. **1413**, 12014 (2019). https://doi.org/10.1088/1742-6596/1413/1/012014
38. Yokokohji, Y., et al.: Assembly challenge: a robot competition of the industrial robotics category, world robot summit-summary of the pre-competition in 2018. Adv. Robot. **33**(17), 876–899 (2019)

RoboCup Vision: A Shared Dataset for Object Detection in Robot Soccer

Hoang Anh Pham[1,2(✉)], Marin Dhainaut[3], Tan Minh Cao[1,2], Thierry Soriano[1], and Valentin Gies[2]

[1] Laboratory of COSMER, University of Toulon, La Garde, France
tan-mih-cao@etud.univ-tln.fr, thierry.soriano@univ-tln.fr

[2] Laboratory of IM2NP, University of Toulon, La Garde, France
{hoang-anh.pham,gies}@univ-tln.fr

[3] SeaTech École d'ingénieurs, University of Toulon, La Garde, France
marin-dhainaut@etud.univ-tln.fr

Abstract. RoboCup is an international initiative that promotes research in robotics and artificial intelligence by creating soccer robots capable of competing against humans according to FIFA rules in 2050. One of the main challenges for these robots is to make decisions automatically. This requires them to identify the status of their surrounding robots, such as their teammates, the opponent robots, the ball, and the goal. To improve research and development efforts in the RoboCup community and to help train and evaluate future deep-learning models, a specialized dataset has been developed for the RoboCup Middle Size League (MSL) soccer robot competition. This dataset is recorded and labeled with specific details, and it combines images of the RCT Toulon team and actual RoboCup games. It is available at https://github.com/iutgeiitoulon/MSL_Vision.git and is under an Open Data License, which is expected to significantly speed up the RoboCup community's development process.

Keywords: RoboCup · Image dataset · Deep Learning · Object Detection

1 Introduction and Motivation

Participants in the RoboCup competition [1] aim to develop autonomous robots capable of performing complex tasks under dynamic and uncertain conditions, such as limited communication [2,3] and information sharing when robots compete with humans, the high movement speed of robots and the ball ($5m/s$), and different lighting conditions for competition [4]. These tasks may involve object detection, localization, navigation, and real-time decision-making. Machine learning is one approach to solving the above problems. Deep Learning, which uses Machine Learning to recognize the surrounding environment, is being widely researched and developed. To effectively train and evaluate algorithms for these tasks, it is essential to have a dataset that reflects the specific objectives and challenges of the competition.

E. Barros et al. (Eds.): RoboCup 2024, LNAI 15570, pp. 386–395, 2025.
https://doi.org/10.1007/978-3-031-85859-8_33

The motivation for creating a separate dataset for the RoboCup competition is a need to address the event's unique challenges and objectives, facilitate bench-marking and evaluation, foster community collaboration, and support the training and development of autonomous robotic systems. In particular, the goal is that by 2050, robots can compete with humans in limited communication conditions. Starting from this motivation, we have created a RoboCup MSL dataset with the following objectives:

- By utilizing specialized datasets, participants can push the boundaries of autonomous robotics and accelerate progress toward the ultimate goal of soccer robots capable of competing against humans according to FIFA rules.
- A dedicated dataset for the RoboCup competition provides a standardized benchmark for evaluating the performance of different algorithms and systems developed by participants. Using a shared dataset, researchers and teams can compare their approaches objectively and track progress over time, ultimately driving innovation and advancing the state-of-the-art in robotics and artificial intelligence.
- Creating a separate dataset for the RoboCup competition fosters collaboration within the research community. Researchers, teams, and organizers can contribute their expertise and resources to the dataset-creation process. This collaborative effort ensures that the dataset is comprehensive, representative of the competition's challenges, and beneficial to all participants.
- A dedicated dataset enables participants to train and fine-tune their algorithms using relevant and realistic data, improving the performance and robustness of their autonomous systems. Moreover, the dataset can serve as a valuable resource for education and research beyond the competition, providing researchers and students with real-world data for experimentation and innovation.

This article is organized as follows: Sect. 2, Related Work, presents the advantages and disadvantages of today's popular datasets. Section 3, A Shared Dataset Robocup Vision, introduces how we build the dataset and perform object labeling. Section 4 presents an example of using this dataset to train and test the model. Section 5 is the conclusion and discussion.

2 Related Work

Deep Learning approaches for object detection and classification require diverse, large-scale datasets in order to understand an environment. Here, we briefly introduce existing datasets and compare some of their advantages and limitations in Table 1. However, they also have limitations, highlighting the importance of selecting the most suitable dataset based on the specific requirements of the application or research task. As for the RoboCup soccer robots, to our knowledge, only Sha Luo et al. [5] has published a dataset since 2017 containing 1000 images. Due to the changing robot designs of competing teams each year, as well as the participation of new teams, we have introduced the RoboCup Vision dataset with a total of 8000 images.

Table 1. Some characteristics of current datasets

Dataset	Characteristic advantages	Remarks
COCO[a] [6]	Large number of diverse images with various types of objects labeled, 330k images (>200k labeled), 1.5 million object instances, 80 object categories.	COCO may not have enough samples of certain object classes for specific applications, and contain multiple small objects, which can make it challenging to detect small objects accurately.
ImageNet [7]	The most highly-used subset is the ILSVRC[b] image classification and localization dataset: 1,000 object classes, 1,281,167 training images, 50k validation images and 100k test images.	Images in ImageNet often have different conditions compared to real-world applications and contain only a single object, which may not reflect the complexities of real-world situations.
PASCAL VOC[c] [8]	It contains a diverse set of images labeled for various object classes: 20 objects, 1,464 images for training, 1,449 images for validation, and a private testing set.	The number of images in PASCAL VOC is relatively small compared to other datasets, which may limit the capabilities of deep learning models.
Open Images Dataset [9]	It is a large dataset containing millions of images with thousands of different object classes: 15,851,536 boxes on 600 classes, 2,785,498 instance segmentations on 350 classes, 3,284,280 relationship annotations on 1,466 relationships.	Labeling a large number of images may lead to inaccuracies or incomplete annotations, resulting in noise in the data.

[a] Common Objects in Context
[b] ImageNet Large Scale Visual Recognition Challenge
[c] Visual Object Classes

3 A Shared Dataset Robocup Vision

In this section, we first detail how the data was collected, including data captured from the RCT Toulon team's robot and data from the teams competing at the 2023 competition in Bordeau, France. We then use a tool to perform data labeling.

3.1 Configuring Robots for Data Collection

We have used the RCT robot [10] to collect data. These robots have dimensions of 0.8 m × 0.8 m × 0.8 m (length × width × height). They utilize four omnidirectional wheels, allowing for seamless maneuverability in all directions. Additionally, each robot is equipped with a Lidar 2D sensor and four intelligent JevoisPro[1] cameras, enabling it to accurately ascertain its own position and the positions of other robots and the ball on the field. Moreover, the robots have an onboard computer, the i7 - 10810, to execute a calculation program, and a 32-bit microprocessor control board to execute robot motor control tasks (refer to Fig. 1).

[1] see https://www.jevoisinc.com/products/jevois-pro-deep-learning-smart-camera.

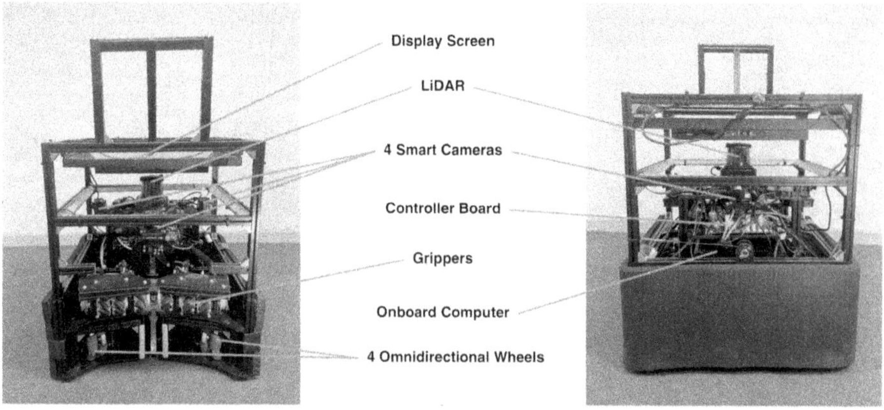

Fig. 1. Visual overview of the robot's hardware components

3.2 Construction of the Database

Step 1: Capture Data Using JevoisPro Camera. The JevoisPro camera boasts high-resolution sensors capable of capturing detailed images that are suitable for machine-learning tasks. It offers adjustable frame rates, allowing flexibility in capturing fast-moving objects or scenes. We used it to collect images of the soccer robot in the stadium at the University of Toulon (see Fig. 2).

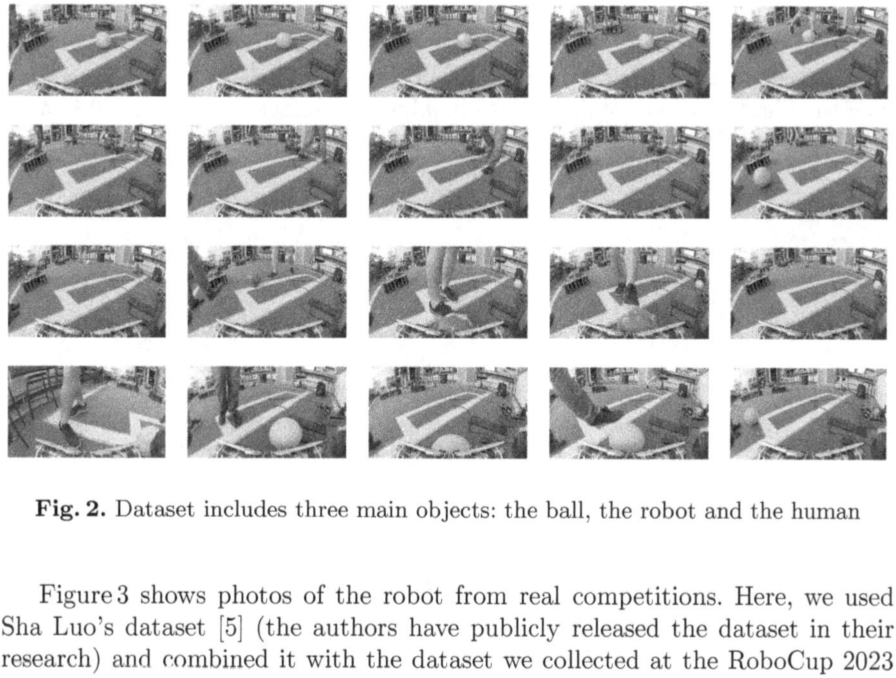

Fig. 2. Dataset includes three main objects: the ball, the robot and the human

Figure 3 shows photos of the robot from real competitions. Here, we used Sha Luo's dataset [5] (the authors have publicly released the dataset in their research) and combined it with the dataset we collected at the RoboCup 2023 competition in Bordeaux, France [11]. This dataset combines many objects in one frame, including balls, robots, and humans.

Fig. 3. Dataset includes two main objects: the ball and the robot

Step 2: Collecting Images from the Other Source. To enrich the images of human and ball detection, we also used data on the internet. The RoboCup Vision Dataset is built based on three data sources. We have used 1,000 images from the Sha Luo et al. [5] datset, the 300 internet images, Coco's 4,000 images from the 2017 dataset, and 2,700 RCT Toulon images. In total, the RoboCup Vision dataset has about 8000 images (see Fig. 4).

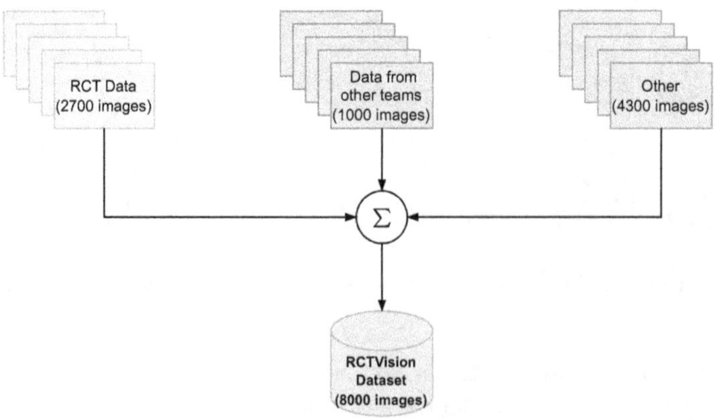

Fig. 4. Combine sources to create a Robocup Vision dataset

Figure 5 represents class instances of the dataset. There, it shows that human subjects and robots account for a large proportion with the purpose of helping robots coordinate with humans in the future.

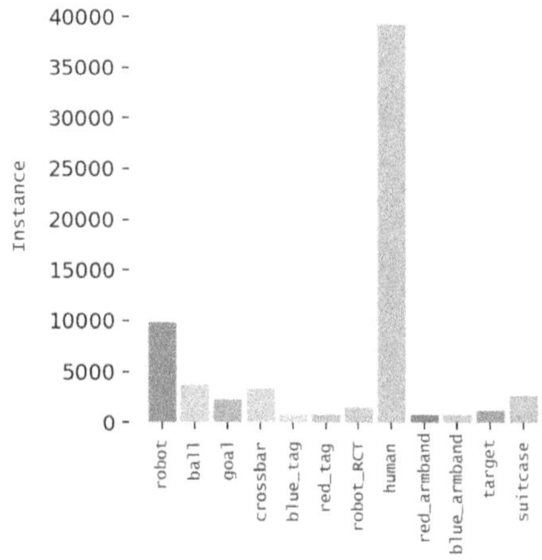

Fig. 5. Distribution of object types in the dataset

Step 3: Labeling Images Using Deeplabel Tool. This step focuses on the process of building the dataset using the images captured with the JevoisPro camera. This involves organizing the images, labeling them with corresponding annotations, and ensuring the dataset's integrity and usability for training machine learning models. (see the list of labels in Table 2).

Table 2. List of assigned labels

Label name	Label description
robot	detect robots of individual teams
ball	detect balls on the field with many different colors
goal and crossbar	detect the goal and crossbar
robot_RCT	robot of the RCT Toulon team
human	detect people on the field
others	it includes: blue_tag, red_tag, red_armband, blue_armband, suitcase, target. The purpose is to test the robot's strategy

In this study, we selected a tool compatible with the JevoisPro camera images, DeepLabel [12]. We manually annotate each image by drawing bounding boxes around objects of interest and assigning corresponding class labels (see Fig. 6). We ensure consistency and accuracy in annotations across all images to maintain the dataset's quality and usability for training machine learning models.

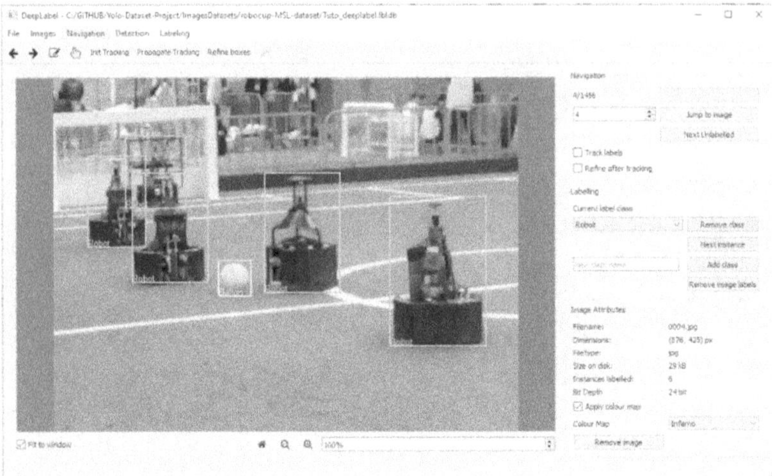

Fig. 6. Manual labeling tool interface

4 An Example of Using a Dataset for Object Detection in the Robocup Competition

In this section, we present the use of the RoboCup Vision dataset to detect and classify objects. The dataset is divided into train, validation, and test splits following the standard proportions of 70%, 10%, and 20%, respectively. This training is performed on a computer with the following parameters: Windows 10, I7 gen10, 16 GB RAM, GTX 3060.

In Fig. 7, the *box, val_box* parameters represent the position and size of the object in the image; *objectness, val_objectness* determine the confidence that a bounding box actually contains an object; *classification, val_classification* represent the probability of classifying the object class in the corresponding bounding box.

Figure 7 also presents the mAP (mean Average Precision) calculated on a test dataset with a mAP@0.5 of 95% by using 200 epochs.

Using the model parameters trained from the RoboCup Vision dataset, we tested the ability to detect and classify objects at the University of Toulon thanks to YOLO v7 tiny [13]. Figure 8 shows an example of simultaneously detecting three objects: a human, a ball, and a goal. The robot can then calculate the relative position between the robot and the objects. A video illustrating this example can be found at the following link https://youtube.com/shorts/83lQt5ryKyk?feature=share.

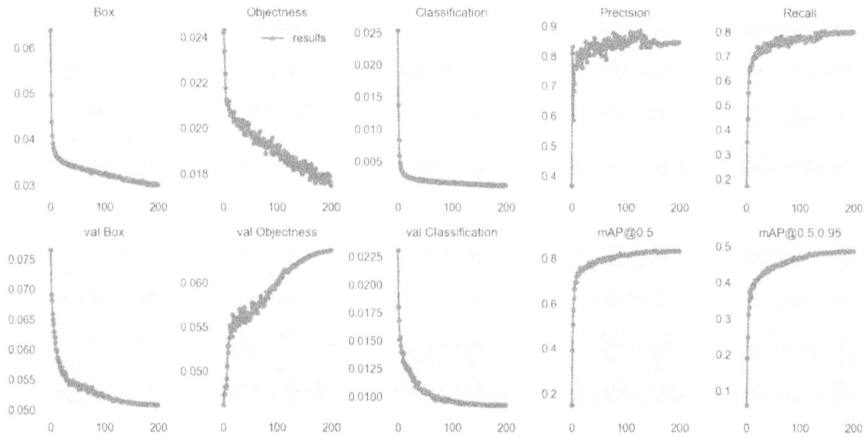

Fig. 7. Parameters of the training model

(a) $t = 0s$ (b) $t = 1s$ (c) $t = 2s$ (d) $t = 3s$ (e) $t = 4s$

(f) $t = 5s$ (g) $t = 6s$ (h) $t = 7s$ (i) $t = 8s$ (j) $t = 9s$

(k) $t = 10s$ (l) $t = 11s$ (m) $t = 12s$ (n) $t = 13s$ (o) $t = 14s$

Fig. 8. Example of using AI Camera to detect and classify objects

5 Conclusion

Creating a separate dataset for the RoboCup competition is a pivotal step toward advancing the field of autonomous robotics and artificial intelligence. Researchers, teams, and organizers can harness the power of machine learning to develop innovative solutions for complex real-world tasks by tailoring datasets to the specific challenges and objectives of the competition. One key benefit of a dedicated dataset is its potential to facilitate collaboration and knowledge sharing within the research community. By providing a standardized benchmark for evaluating algorithms and systems, the dataset encourages participation from diverse teams and promotes exchanging ideas and methodologies. This collaborative effort not only enhances the quality and diversity of solutions but also accelerates progress toward achieving the goals of the RoboCup competition. Moreover, the availability of a comprehensive dataset empowers participating teams to reuse, extend, and develop machine learning algorithms in the future. By leveraging the dataset as a training and validation resource, teams can iterate on their approaches, refine their algorithms, and improve the performance of their autonomous robotic systems.

Acknowledgment. This work was funded by the French ANR/AID agency under the RoboSCo project and the University of Toulon. We would like to thank Kirkland Boyd for his support with text revisions.

References

1. RoboCup. RoboCup-97: Robot Soccer World Cup I. Springer, Heidelberg (1997)
2. Santos, F., Almeida, L., Lopes, L.S., Azevedo, J.L., Cunha, M.B.: Communicating among robots in the RoboCup middle-size league. In: Baltes, J., Lagoudakis, M.G., Naruse, T., Ghidary, S.S. (eds.) RoboCup 2009. LNCS (LNAI), vol. 5949, pp. 320–331. Springer, Heidelberg (2010). https://doi.org/10.1007/978-3-642-11876-0_28
3. Affinita, D., Volpi, F., Spagnoli, V., Suriani, V., Nardi, D., Bloisi, D.D.: Multi-agent coordination for a partially observable and dynamic robot soccer environment with limited communication (2024)
4. Soriano, T., Pham, H.A., Gies, V.: Design of the dynamic behavior of soccer robots based on the Dec-POMDP framework. In: 14th France-Japan Mecatronics (2023)
5. Luo, S., Lu, H., Xiao, J., Yu, Q., Zheng, Z.: Robot detection and localization based on deep learning. In: 2017 Chinese Automation Congress (CAC), pp. 7091–7095 (2017)
6. Lin, T.-Y., et al.: Microsoft coco: common objects in context (2015)
7. Deng, J., Dong, W., Socher, R., Li, L.-J., Li, K., Fei-Fei, L.: Imagenet: a large-scale hierarchical image database. In: 2009 IEEE Conference on Computer Vision and Pattern Recognition, pp. 248–255 (2009)
8. Everingham, M., Van Gool, L., Williams, C., Winn, J., Zisserman, A.: The pascal visual object classes (VOC) challenge. Int. J. Comput. Vis. **88**, 303–338 (2010)
9. Kuznetsova, A., et al.: The open images dataset v4: unified image classification, object detection, and visual relationship detection at scale. Int. J. Comput. Vision **128**, 1956–1981 (2020)

10. Pham, H.A., Gies, V., Soriano, T.: Decision-making strategy for multi-agents using a probabilistic approach: application in soccer robotics. In: 2023 12th International Conference on Control, Automation and Information Sciences (ICCAIS), pp. 298–303 (2023)
11. RoboCup. Robocup middle size league competition. Bordeaux, France (2023)
12. Veitch-Michaelis, J.: Deeplabel Tool (2017)
13. Wang, C.-Y., Bochkovskiy, A., Liao, H.-Y.M.: YOLOv7: trainable bag-of-freebies sets new state-of-the-art for real-time object detectors (2022)

Advancing Humanoid Robotics with Rust: An Open Framework for Runtime Efficiency

Team HULKs(✉), Maximilian Schmidt, Hendrik Sieck, Ole Felber, Konrad Valentin Nölle, Luis Scheuch, and Patrick Göttsch

Hamburg University of Technology, Hamburg, Germany
hulks@tuhh.de
https://hulks.de

Abstract. The development of software frameworks plays a pivotal role in the research on humanoid robotics. This paper introduces a novel robotics framework designed to address challenges in the RoboCup and robotics in general. We present an overview of existing frameworks within the RoboCup Standard Platform League (SPL), highlighting their benefits and limitations. We define a set of requirements that serve as a guiding principle for the development of robotic frameworks. Our novel framework emphasizes modularity and parallelization while optimizing for minimal runtime overhead and complexity. Implemented in Rust, we combine computational efficiency with safety, positioning it as a robust solution for robotic applications. We show that the framework's runtime overhead on a NAO robot has little impact. We conclude with case studies of its application at Team HULKs and other teams, showing its real world use case and impact in the RoboCup SPL.

Keywords: Framework · Middleware · Rust · RoboCup

1 Introduction

Efficient and adaptable software frameworks are crucial for advancing the capabilities of teams participating in RoboCup and robotics in general. In the context of RoboCup Standard Platform League (SPL), the challenge of humanoid robotics extends beyond creating intelligent algorithms for perception, decision-making, or motion planning; it encompasses the efficient implementation and coordination of these algorithms with heavily constrained computational resources.

This paper presents a novel robotics framework designed to overcome challenges and shortcomings of existing solutions. Our framework is engineered to optimize performance, enhance modularity, and establish a seamless interface between robotic hardware and detection as well as control algorithms.

E. Barros et al. (Eds.): RoboCup 2024, LNAI 15570, pp. 396–408, 2025.
https://doi.org/10.1007/978-3-031-85859-8_34

1.1 Robotic Frameworks

Abstraction layers separate concerns into smaller parts, to cope with complexity in the software domain. A common abstraction is a software framework which separates generic code from application-specific code.

In the context of robotics, a multitude of frameworks have been introduced to facilitate the development and execution of robot control software [22]. Notable examples include ROS 1 [18], ROS 2 [15], MIRA [7], YARP [17], LCM [11], Player [8], and Urbi [2], each contributing distinct perspectives and methodologies to the field. The following sections provide an overview of existing frameworks within the RoboCup SPL, highlighting their unique characteristics and design philosophies.

Robot Operating System (ROS) Version 2. Building upon the foundation of Robot Operating System (ROS) 1, ROS 2 [15] addresses several limitations of its predecessor. ROS 2 uses the Data Distribution Service, a publish-subscribe and request-response system. This enhances the robustness and fault tolerance of the middleware compared to ROS 1. ROS 2 maintains an event-driven communication architecture via serialized messages, resulting in similar overheads and complexity as ROS 1. The ROS messaging pattern, while flexible, loses synchronicity, leading to increased complexity in processing nodes that rely on temporally coupled messages.

SPL Frameworks. In the RoboCup SPL league, all teams compete using a standardized robotics hardware platform: the NAO robot by Aldebaran [20]. Teams prefer developing custom robot control systems instead of using established ones like ROS to enable real-time robotic algorithms on the NAO while keeping overheads in the framework as low as possible. This section will take a closer look at the different systems teams have developed for the SPL.

Bembelbots. The team Bembelbots have developed a framework centered around a message passing architecture [6]. Within this framework, each module declares inputs and outputs, which are used to automatically generate a dependency graph. This graph serves as a blueprint for execution, enabling modules to run concurrently while following the specified order of dependencies. Similar to ROS, the message passing actors have the drawback of asynchronicity.

Berlin United. Berlin United uses a sequential blackboard design [16]. Sequential execution per thread ensures that at any given time, at most one module reads from or writes to the thread's blackboard, eliminating the need for explicit synchronization. Each module specifies data it requires and provides, and the framework determines the execution order through topological sorting. Additionally, the framework supports serialization through the use of Protocol Buffers [9].

B-Human. The B-Human framework is based on a 2007 framework of the GermanTeam, written in C++. Since then, the framework has been continuously improved and adapted to the changing requirements of the SPL. The robotics code adopts a modular structure where each module, can both provide and require artifacts from other modules. Communication between modules is handled via memory-sharing, with data being serialized and written in triple buffered channels [19]. While serialization for message passing standardizes the interface between threads, it also leads to additional overheads. Furthermore, a processing task, responsible for merging sensor data from various threads, is activated with each new input, which requires the reprocessing of unchanged data.

NaoDevils. The NaoDevils team employs a framework that originates from the 2009 B-Human framework. The framework defines three distinct domains: cognition, motion, and debug. Within each domain, modules operate in parallel, facilitated by a thread pool managed by Taskflow [12]. A blackboard data structure [10] accompanies each domain. A task graph manages the execution order of modules, ensuring that data is already provided if a module requests to read it. Despite that, the task graph handles thread synchronization, ensuring correct memory access. Between domains, a message queue handles information exchange, copying data to prevent race conditions [14].

rUNSWift. Team rUNSWift uses a framework written in C++, with the robot behavior integrated using Python [1]. Communication among different modules is managed by a blackboard data structure. To prevent conflicting writes to the same blackboard address, only the top-level module of a thread is granted permission to write to a thread-specific sub-blackboard. Furthermore, team rUNSWift will consider the adoption of ROS 2 after RoboCup 2024.

Summary. Despite the popularity of frameworks like ROS in the robotics community, the RoboCup SPL presents unique challenges due to the limited computational resources of NAO robots. As a result, several teams have developed custom frameworks tailored specifically to the demands of the SPL. While each framework has its own design philosophy and implementation details, they all share the common goal of optimizing performance and resource utilization for the NAO platform. These frameworks offer insights into different approaches for addressing the computational constraints of the SPL.

1.2 Requirements

Drawing inspiration from existing frameworks and the design decisions of the NaoDevils team's work [14], we establish a set of requirements that serve as a guiding principle for our framework.

Parallelization: Efficient usage of all available CPU cores is critical to the framework's performance. Performance is directly impacted by the number of cores utilized.

Motion Cycle Priority: The motion cycle has to be prioritized over any other perception tasks. Responsiveness is crucial in dynamic environments where real-time motor control is essential for successful robotic operation.

Low Runtime Overhead: On robotic systems with limited resources, minimizing execution time spent in the framework enables executing more advanced robotic algorithms. Balancing information exchange with computational efficiency is necessary to streamline context switching in a manner that avoids unnecessary computational overheads that may impede overall system performance.

Separation between Robotics Domain and Framework: Separation of concerns in software enhances its flexibility. Establishing a clear boundary between robotic functionalities and the underlying framework decouples the application from its infrastructure. This separation not only ensures adaptability to various robotic platforms and new and evolving functionalities but also guards against overfitting, creating a more versatile and widely applicable framework.

Adaptive Computation: Adopting a computation model based on external triggers ensures that computational resources are allocated in response to environmental changes or incoming data, preventing unnecessary calculations in the absence of new information.

Temporally-Ordered Data: Mechanisms for preserving temporal ordering of incoming data enable robotic algorithms that require temporal order, like filters.

Abstraction over Hardware: Providing abstraction layers over the underlying hardware enables the framework to generalize over the actual hardware it is deployed on. This abstraction enables interoperability and allows using the framework with diverse hardware configurations.

Data Structure Serialization and Reflection: Support for serialization and reflection mechanisms enables efficient data exchange and introspection of the robotics domain. These features allow developers to gain insights into the framework's data structures of robotic algorithms.

Tooling Support: Tools for debugging, profiling, and monitoring enhance the development and maintenance process. Robust tooling support is essential for understanding runtime behavior, diagnosing issues or optimizing performance.

Programming Language: The choice of a programming language is pivotal. The language must be capable of handling the computational demands of robotic applications while providing a high degree of safety and security and supporting modern programming paradigms.

2 Framework

With the foundational requirements established to guide the development of our novel framework, we now introduce the framework itself. Our framework is designed to hide implementation detail from the user, providing a narrow interface for the application of robotic algorithms. To keep the implementation flexible, the architecture strictly separates framework and robotics code. This allows the framework to be used on different robotic platforms and to be adapted to various robotics domains beyond the RoboCup SPL.

This section provides an overview of the architecture, defining core components and concepts. We introduce the modularization of cyclers and nodes, as well as their interaction through hardware interfaces. We conclude with an overview of communication channels, code generation, and our selection of programming language.

2.1 Cyclers

Robots interact in a dynamic environment. To fulfill their tasks, they perceive their environment using sensors and act via actuators. We model this as an event-based system in which sensor measurements trigger computation to produce actuator outputs. Depending on the sensor, the rate of incoming measurement events on robotic platforms varies. For example, the NAO cameras deliver 30 images per second, while the joint position encoders deliver 83 measurements per second. We define a cycler as a unit of computation that encapsulates the data flow from sensor measurements to actuator commands. Cyclers wait for environmental events, process the events, and produce actuator commands. After producing the actuator commands, the cycler waits for the next environmental event. We call this loop a cycle.

The framework allows cyclers to be instantiated multiple times, e.g., for deploying the same detection pipeline to multiple cameras. These instances differ only in their set of configuration parameters. Different cycler instances are executed in individual operating system threads to efficiently use parallel processing resources.

2.2 Nodes

Cyclers modularize their execution by dividing the pipeline into several nodes. Nodes are small units of computation that abstract tasks, e.g., reading an image, detecting robots in the image, or executing a motion. Each node is defined by its inputs, outputs, self-contained state, and its implementation. Figure 1 gives a structural overview of a cycler and its nodes.

Nodes produce strongly typed outputs, each uniquely identified by a distinct name. Inputs to nodes encompass outputs from other nodes, as well as configuration parameters. This allows nodes to form a comprehensive dependency graph. Based on this graph, the framework sorts the execution of nodes topologically, ensuring that each node is executed only after its dependencies have

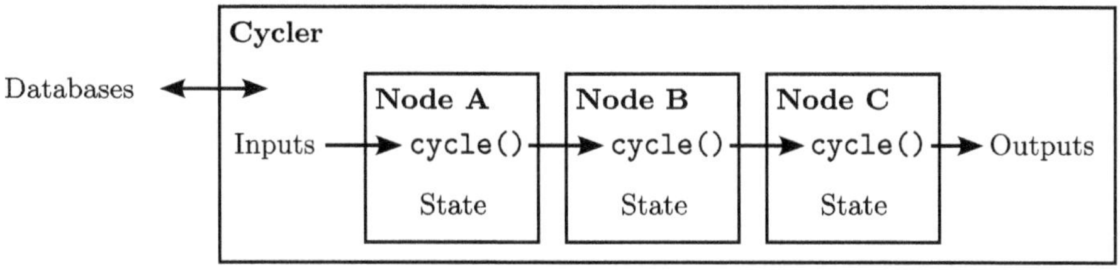

Fig. 1. Overview of a cycler and its execution pipeline of nodes.

been produced. A cyclic dependency between nodes results in a compile-time error. During execution, each cycler traverses its nodes sequentially, ensuring systematic processing of data throughout the framework.

2.3 Starting Cycles

The start of each cycle is triggered by external events, such as new images from the camera. Special nodes, called setup nodes, interact with the environment through a hardware interface and wait for the next external event. After setup nodes are executed, the cycler starts its cycle by executing the remaining nodes.

2.4 Data Exchange Within Cyclers

The framework ensures efficient data exchange within cyclers by storing node outputs in databases local to each cycler. This local storage enables access to other node's outputs through direct memory access. By executing each cycler instance in its own operating system thread, the framework guarantees contention-free access without the need for explicit synchronization. The conclusion of each cycle signifies the readiness of the database for consumption by other entities.

2.5 Data Exchange Across Cyclers

The framework allows nodes to access outputs of other cycler instances. However, these accesses traverse thread boundaries, and therefore demand careful synchronization. The framework provides support for two distinct access semantics: latest non-blocking access using multiple buffering [13] and interleaved temporally-ordered access. The former allows nodes to retrieve the most recent data. The latter ensures a temporal ordering, providing an interleaved sequence based on the timestamps associated with each data entry.

Consider a localization pipeline where the robot's position must synchronize with motion decision-making, while updates need to be processed in order. In this scenario, the localization may depend on outputs of both a long-running cycle, executed every 2 s, and another, every 10 ms. Figure 2 illustrates the timing of four cyclers with interleaved execution.

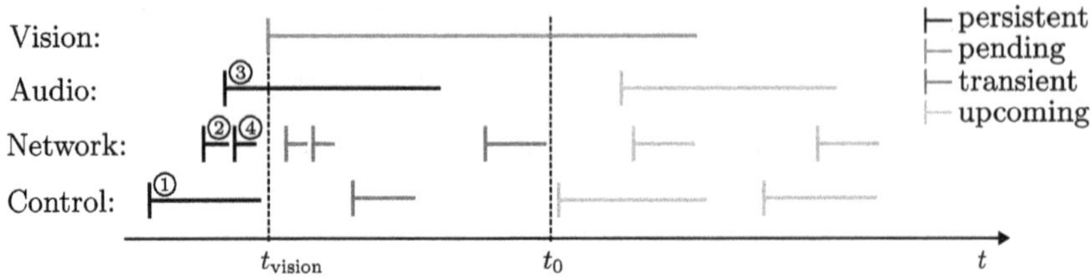

Fig. 2. Timing of four cyclers with interleaved execution.

A straightforward yet inefficient method involves delaying the processing of faster cycle data until the long-running cycle completes its computation, leading to increased latency. Instead, we solve this asynchronous characteristic by queuing futures of pending cycles. A cycler announces the start of a cycle by adding a future to the queue. This future promises the completion of a pending cycle and its associated database. Each entry is associated with a timestamp. Cyclers consuming from the queue are thus able to respect temporal ordering.

Figure 2 illustrates the evaluation of the queue at timestamp t_0. At this point in time, the long-running vision cycle has not yet finished its computation and its results can thus not yet be consumed. Therefore, the queue is split into persistent and transient data. The persistent is all data that is timestamped before t_{vision} and already finished execution until timestamp t_0. All data that is timestamped after t_{vision}, is transient data. Despite their transient nature, nodes may consume this data to produce an estimate on top of the persistent state.

2.6 Configuration Parameters

Execution may not only depend on incoming data, but also on configuration parameters. This allows configuration of algorithm at runtime, e.g., changing the coefficients of a filter. On startup, the initial parameters are read from disk and made available to nodes by the framework. Parameters are organized and stored on disk in a priority-based directory structure. This allows quickly swapping the set of parameters based on the location, e.g., for individual soccer fields. Additionally, parameters may adopt different values for each individual robot.

2.7 Communication

User interaction for debugging and monitoring is tightly integrated into the framework's architecture. A dedicated communication channel allows observing outputs of robotics nodes, altering parameters at runtime, and receiving information about the framework's internal state. Debug client applications can connect via a JSON-oriented WebSocket protocol, which supports many client implementations. The design of communication consists of several asynchronous tasks that manage resources and communicate via message passing.

2.8 Recording and Replay

Real-world interactions with robots may sporadically uncover rare bugs within the robotics domain that are hard to reproduce. To analyze, reproduce, and fix such bugs, the framework incorporates recording and replay functionality. These capabilities are integrated through an adjustment of database storage as the framework manages the execution of nodes and cycler database operations. However, storing all computed outputs from every node across all cyclers proves impractical. Instead, the framework records inputs of each cycle and captures the state of all nodes. Paired with deterministic node implementations, this data is sufficient to replay each recorded iteration without additional dependencies.

2.9 Code Generation and Domain Specific Language (DSL)

The implementation is split into two parts: the framework itself and the robotics code. By analyzing robotics code, the framework automatically generates the infrastructure to start cyclers, spawn operating system threads, create nodes, and share data. The overall structure is specified in a DSL, the framework manifest.

2.10 Programming Language Selection

As highlighted in Sect. 1.2, the choice of programming language is a pivotal aspect of the framework's design. Our selection, Rust, stems from its various advantages. Rust exhibits performance comparable to other leading compiled languages and is specifically crafted for concurrent and secure application development [5]. Notably, a Google survey praises Rust's compiler error messages as "amazing", emphasizing its facilitation of writing correct and review-friendly code [3]. Unique features like ownership and borrowing contribute to more concise and comprehensible code compared to languages like C. Additionally, Rust has an extensive package ecosystem which simplifies the incorporation of external libraries, enhancing flexibility and extensibility.

3 Evaluation

In this section, we present the application of the framework at Team HULKs, quantify its execution time overhead and assess its efficiency in real-world robotic applications. Additionally, we systematically examine the framework against the predefined requirements, offering an insightful analysis of how the framework aligns with each criterion.

3.1 Case Study: HULKs Robotics Domain

Team HULKs employs the presented framework to execute their robotics domain on the NAO robot. Environmental triggers originate from various sources, including new camera images, incoming network messages, microphone samples, and sensor measurements. Each trigger source is processed in dedicated cycler instances: Vision Top, Vision Bottom, Network, Audio, and Control.

The Control cycler executes the motion control algorithm, reading robot sensor measurements and sending actuator commands. The outputs from all other cyclers are treated as perceptions and consumed by the Control cycler in a temporally-ordered fashion. This decoupling allows asynchronous processing without affecting robot motion control. Most other teams run their behavior for every new sensor or camera event. At Team HULKs, we execute the behavior in the real-time cycler based on filtered perception inputs, which allows running behavior on predicted models instead of outdated data.

Team HULKs also develops various debug applications that connect to the communication interface. These applications provide real-time insights into the state of the robot, enabling developers to monitor the execution of individual cyclers and diagnose any potential issues. Over the past two years, the framework has been used in the RoboCup competition, demonstrating its robustness and reliability.

3.2 Quantitative Evaluation of Execution Time Overheads

A critical performance measure is the execution time overhead of the framework, quantifying the duration spent by each cycler executing framework code in contrast to robotics algorithms. While an ideal scenario entails minimal overhead, several features such as database sharing between cyclers necessitate a non-zero amount of additional copying and synchronization.

Experimental Configuration. To conduct our assessment, we evaluate the runtime overhead of the HULKs robotics codebase. Measuring via deterministic profiling accumulates large and difficult to quantify overheads due to node execution times within the microsecond range. Instead, we use a sampling profiler, specifically Intel VTune, to measure the CPU time expended in framework and robotics code. Data collection occurs over a 5-min duration on a NAO robot walking across the SPL field, representing a typical usage scenario for Team HULKs.

Results. The evaluation, summarized in Fig. 3, presents the overhead of our framework in comparison to the time spent in robotics code for each cycler.

The upper bound for the Control cycler is 12 ms, Vision's is 33 ms, while the Audio cycler's is 46 ms. These bounds should not be violated to prevent skipping of input data. As shown in Fig. 3, the robotics code for each cycler operates well below its upper bound. The framework overhead for the Vision cycler is measured at 0.24 ms, while the robotics code averages at 11.26 ms. The framework execution time is approximately 50 times shorter compared to the robotics code. The upper Vision cycler takes approximately 2.5 times more execution time than the lower Vision cycler, attributable to more points of interest in the larger area covered by the upper camera.

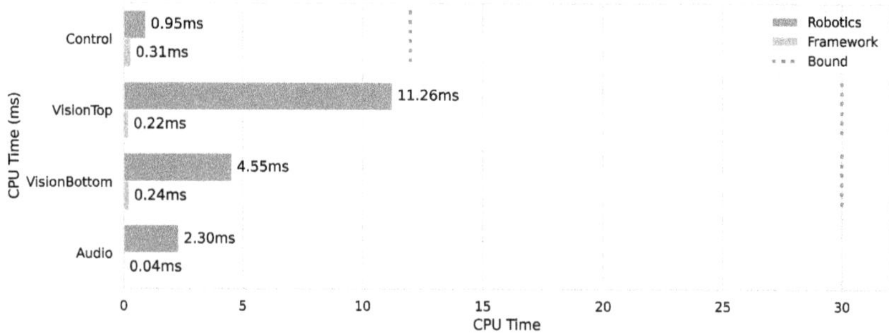

Fig. 3. Profile of the CPU time in the HULKs code base across different cyclers. For each cycler, the runtime is split into the framework overhead and the robotics code execution time, with a red upper bound, if in viewport. (Color figure online)

Notably, the overhead is relatively larger for the Control cycler compared to the Vision cyclers, primarily due to its consumption of futures from all other cyclers. The audio cycler, comprising only two nodes, demonstrates a relatively smaller overhead, measured at blazingly fast 0.04 ms.

Overall, the framework's overhead is significantly lower than both the execution time of robotics code and the bound of the respective cycler, emphasizing its efficiency in real-world robotic applications.

3.3 Qualitative Evaluation of Requirements

This section reviews the predefined requirements (c.f. Sect. 1.2) that serve as benchmarks for our robotics framework.

Each cycler instance operates autonomously via dedicated operating system threads to leverage the *parallelization* from multiple CPU cores. A fundamental aspect is the decoupling of cyclers, ensuring independence in processing. This design enables long-running cyclers to asynchronously conclude their tasks, while giving *precedence to motion cycles.* A substantial amount of resource-intensive computations, including source analysis, node ordering, and execution code generation, is shifted to compile time. This paradigm ensures a *low runtime overhead.* The framework excels in providing a clear *separation* between the robotics code development and the details of node execution. Users can build on enhanced modularity and extensibility as they can extend the robotics domain by incorporating new nodes and cyclers in the framework manifest, dynamically generating fitting execution code. Cycles are initiated by setup nodes, *adapting computation* dynamically to environmental triggers. *Temporally-ordered data* access allows for coherent interaction with filters in real-time cyclers. The framework's *abstraction over hardware* permits seamless execution on diverse hardware configurations without demanding modifications. Intra-process communication between nodes is achieved via direct memory access, minimizing the need for *serialization and reflection.* Only the communication subcomponent that allows external *tooling support* uses *serialization* to encode values for network transfer. The framework and robotics domain are implemented in the Rust *programming language* which provides high computational efficiency. The Rust language's focus on memory safety and concurrency aligns well with the demands of robotic applications, reducing the likelihood of bugs and enhancing overall system reliability. In parallel, ROS, known for its robust middleware in the robotics domain, operates primarily in C++. While ROS offers a wealth of pre-existing modules and community support, the presented Rust-based framework provides a more streamlined and efficient development experience.

3.4 Adoption in RoboCup SPL

Since its open-source release, our framework has been rapidly gaining popularity among teams in the RoboCup SPL. For the 2023 RoboCup competition, the Dutch Nao Team adopted the HULKs framework [4]. Team HULKs helped the Dutch Nao Team getting started both with the framework and robotics code. Using the HULKs framework, they achieved the 4th place in the Challenger Cup at RoboCup 2023 [21]. The Rhinobots team from Brazil considers using the HULKs framework at RoboCup 2024.

4 Conclusion and Outlook

In this paper, Team HULKs present a novel robotics framework designed to overcome challenges and shortcomings of existing solutions. Our framework is engineered to optimize performance, enhance modularity, and establish a seamless interface between robotic hardware and detection as well as control algorithms. The framework has low overhead and fulfills all requirements, e.g., extensibility, temporal ordering, and adaptive computation. The code is developed as open source software at https://github.com/HULKs/hulk. Other teams are already using the framework at RoboCup, and are contributing successfully.

In the future, more features are planned, e.g., profiling, remote procedure calls, and logging. In addition, Team HULKs plans to extract the framework code to increase reuse beside the open development. Due to its separation between robotics and framework domain, this general framework may also be used in many other applications beyond the RoboCup scope.

References

1. Asavkin, M., Gopikrishnan, N., Lizura, M., Sammut, C., Schmidt, P., Vijayan, A.: rUNSWift Team Report 2022. Technical report, UNSW School of Computer Science and Engineering (2022)
2. Baillie, J.C., Demaille, A., Hocquet, Q., Nottale, M., Tardieu, S.: The Urbi universal platform for robotics. In: First International Workshop on Standards and Common Platform for Robotics. Citeseer (2008)
3. Bergstrom, L., Brennan, K.: Rust fact vs. fiction: 5 Insights from Google's Rust journey in 2022 (2022)

4. Bolt, L., Gunnewiek, F.K., Gezegd Deprez, H.L., van Iterson, L., Prinzhorn, D.: Dutch Nao Team - Technical Report. Technical report, University of Amsterdam (2022)
5. Costanzo, M., Rucci, E., Naiouf, M., Giusti, A.D.: Performance vs programming effort between rust and C on multicore architectures: case study in N-body. In: 2021 XLVII Latin American Computing Conference (CLEI), pp. 1–10. IEEE, Cartago (2021). https://doi.org/10.1109/CLEI53233.2021.9640225
6. Ditzel, S., et al.: Bembelbots Team Research Report for RoboCup 2019. Technical Report. Goethe University Frankfurt (2020)
7. Einhorn, E., Langner, T., Stricker, R., Martin, C., Gross, H.M.: MIRA - middleware for robotic applications. In: 2012 IEEE/RSJ International Conference on Intelligent Robots and Systems, pp. 2591–2598. IEEE, Vilamoura-Algarve (2012). https://doi.org/10.1109/IROS.2012.6385959
8. Gerkey, B., Vaughan, R., Stoy, K., Howard, A., Sukhatme, G., Mataric, M.: Most valuable player: a robot device server for distributed control. In: Proceedings 2001 IEEE/RSJ International Conference on Intelligent Robots and Systems. Expanding the Societal Role of Robotics in the the Next Millennium (Cat. No.01CH37180), vol. 3, pp. 1226–1231. IEEE, Maui (2001). https://doi.org/10.1109/IROS.2001.977150
9. Google: Protocol Buffers. https://protobuf.dev/
10. Hayes-Roth, B.: A blackboard architecture for control. Artif. Intell. **26**(3), 251–321 (1985). https://doi.org/10.1016/0004-3702(85)90063-3
11. Huang, A.S., Olson, E., Moore, D.C.: LCM: Lightweight communications and marshalling. In: 2010 IEEE/RSJ International Conference on Intelligent Robots and Systems, pp. 4057–4062. IEEE, Taipei (2010). https://doi.org/10.1109/IROS.2010.5649358
12. Huang, T.W., Lin, D.L., Lin, C.X., Lin, Y.: Taskflow: a lightweight parallel and heterogeneous task graph computing system. IEEE Trans. Parallel Distrib. Syst. **33**(6), 1303–1320 (2022). https://doi.org/10.1109/TPDS.2021.3104255
13. Khan, S., Bailey, D., Gupta, G.S.: Simulation of triple buffer scheme (comparison with double buffering scheme). In: 2009 Second International Conference on Computer and Electrical Engineering, vol. 2, pp. 403–407 (2009). https://doi.org/10.1109/ICCEE.2009.226
14. Larisch, A.: An Efficient Real-Time Capable Multi-Core Module Framework for the Humanoid Robot NAO. Master's thesis, TU Dortmund University (2020)
15. Macenski, S., Foote, T., Gerkey, B., Lalancette, C., Woodall, W.: Robot operating system 2: design, architecture, and uses in the wild. Sci. Rob. **7**(66), eabm6074 (2022).https://doi.org/10.1126/scirobotics.abm6074
16. Mellmann, H., et al.: Berlin United - Nao Team Humboldt Team Report 2019. Technical report, Humboldt-Universität zu Berlin (2019)
17. Metta, G., Fitzpatrick, P., Natale, L.: YARP: yet another robot platform. Int. J. Adv. Rob. Syst. **3**(1), 8 (2006). https://doi.org/10.5772/5761
18. Quigley, M., et al.: ROS: an open-source robot operating system. In: ICRA Workshop on Open Source Software, Kobe, Japan, vol. 3, p. 5 (2009)
19. Röfer, T., Laue, T.: On B-human's code releases in the standard platform league – software architecture and impact. In: Behnke, S., Veloso, M., Visser, A., Xiong, R. (eds.) RoboCup 2013. LNCS (LNAI), vol. 8371, pp. 648–655. Springer, Heidelberg (2014). https://doi.org/10.1007/978-3-662-44468-9_61
20. SoftBank Robotics: NAO - Developer Guide—Aldebaran 2.8.7.4 documentation. http://doc.aldebaran.com/2-8/family/nao_technical/index_naov6.html

21. SPL Technical Committee: Standard Platform League Results 2023 – RoboCup Standard Platform League. https://spl.robocup.org/results-2023/
22. Tsardoulias, E., Mitkas, P.: Robotic frameworks, architectures and middleware comparison (2017). https://doi.org/10.48550/ARXIV.1711.06842

Champion Papers

FC Portugal: RoboCup 2024 3D Simulation League Champions

Miguel Abreu[1(✉)], Pedro Mota[2], Tomás Azevedo[1], Francisco Silva[1], Luís Paulo Reis[1], Nuno Lau[3], and Mário Florido[2]

[1] LIACC/LASI/FEUP, Artificial Intelligence and Computer Science Lab, Faculty of Engineering of the University of Port, University of Porto, Porto, Portugal
{m.abreu,lpreis}@fe.up.pt

[2] LIACC/LASI/FCUP, Artificial Intelligence and Computer Science Lab, Faculty of Sciences of the University of Porto, University of Porto, Porto, Portugal
{pedro.mota,amflorid}@fc.up.pt

[3] IEETA/LASI/DETI Institute of Electronics and Informatics Engineering of Aveiro, Department of Electronics, Telecommunications and Informatics, University of Aveiro, Aveiro, Portugal
nunolau@ua.pt

Abstract. FC Portugal, a simulated humanoid soccer team from the universities of Porto and Aveiro, achieved the third consecutive victory in the main competition of the 2024 RoboCup 3D Simulation League. The team registered 16 wins, 3 ties, and 2 losses, scoring a total of 105 goals while only conceding 17. FC Portugal also ended first in two secondary events: the Scientific Challenge, which evaluates innovative scientific contributions within the league, and the Fat Proxy Challenge, where teams share a common set of low-level skills and compete for the best high-level strategy. The codebase used in this competition was developed in Python after RoboCup 2021. This paper presents a brief overview of its structure along with the new features developed for this year's competition. The key developments include a hierarchical learning framework, presented at the Scientific Challenge, and the release of our codebase to the RoboCup community.

1 Introduction

FC Portugal won the 2024 RoboCup 3D Soccer Simulation League (3DSSL) in Eindhoven, The Netherlands, marking the third consecutive victory after the 2022 and 2023 triumphs [2,4]. The last victory before that was in 2006 when the league was composed of spherical agents. Throughout the competition, the team registered 16 wins, 3 ties, and 2 losses, scoring a total of 105 goals, while only conceding 17.

Over recent years, FC Portugal has contributed to the simulation league through low-level skills for walking, running, kicking and dribbling the ball [1–3,6,7,14,16,21]. Moreover, it contributed with skill development methodologies [15], high-level strategies [5,17,19] and reinforcement learning techniques [8,13].

E. Barros et al. (Eds.): RoboCup 2024, LNAI 15570, pp. 411–423, 2025.
https://doi.org/10.1007/978-3-031-85859-8_35

Following RoboCup 2021, our team rebuilt the codebase from the ground up using Python. Key strategic elements included team coordination, role management, formation, communication, skill management, and path planning. We developed new lower-level skills based on a deterministic analytic model and a shallow neural network that learned residual dynamics through reinforcement learning. This approach, combined with an overlapped learning methodology, improved seamless transitions, reduced learning time, and enhanced the efficiency and stability of behaviors. Notable new skills with seamless transitions included a fast and stable omnidirectional walk, short and long kicking techniques, and an unprecedented close-control dribbling skill. This new formation made its debut at RoboCup 2022, where the team achieved victory in the 3DSSL held in Bangkok, Thailand [2].

In 2023, we implemented updates in response to a new ball-holding rule introduced in the league[1]. These changes included modifications to the dribbling behavior and the removal of the push skill, which had been employed in local RoboCup competitions in Brazil in 2022 and in Portugal in 2023. Additionally, FC Portugal introduced a new programming language called TSAL for defining high-level team strategies in robotic soccer, while exploring the use of deep symbolic reinforcement learning along with human sub-optimal knowledge to optimize team strategies. Other updates in 2023 involved a revised goalkeeper defending strategy and fine-tuning of several modules, leading to a victory in the 2023 RoboCup 3DSSL held in Bordeaux, France [4].

Since RoboCup 2023, we have released a new codebase to the RoboCup community[2]. Our current agent iteration is based on this codebase, which includes adaptations to high-level strategies and formations using TSAL, as well as further fine-tuning. FC Portugal achieved its third consecutive victory in the 2024 RoboCup 3DSSL in Eindhoven, The Netherlands. The main scientific contributions this year were the release of the codebase and the presentation of a new hierarchical learning framework during the Scientific Challenge, where our team secured 1st place.

The remainder of this paper is organized as follows. Section 2 defines the league and the new rules for RoboCup 2024. Section 3 provides an overview of FC Portugal's codebase. Section 4 presents a brief overview of the programming language used to design set plays. Section 5 describes the hierarchical learning framework showcased at the Scientific Challenge. Section 6 outlines the FC Portugal Codebase that was released to the RoboCup community. Section 7 introduces the Ball Throwing Challenge. Section 8 presents the results obtained in the main competition as well as the technical challenge and its constituent events. Lastly, we conclude and outline future research directions in Sect. 9.

[1] Official rules available at https://ssim.robocup.org/3d-simulation/3d-rules/.

[2] Codebase available at https://github.com/m-abr/FCPCodebase.

2 3D Simulation League

The RoboCup 3D simulation league uses SimSpark [12,22] as its physical multi-agent simulator, which is based on the Open Dynamics Engine library. The league's environment is a 30 m by 20 m soccer field containing several landmarks that can be used for self-localization: goalposts, corner flags, and lines. Each team consists of 11 humanoid robots modeled after the NAO robot, created by SoftBank Robotics[3]. Agents get internal data (joints, accelerometer, gyroscope, and foot pressure sensors) with a 1-step delay every 0.02 s and visual data (restricted to a 120° vision cone) every 0.04 s. Agents can send joint commands every 0.02 s and message teammates every 0.04 s. There are 5 humanoid robot types with 22 to 24 controllable joints, and slightly different physical characteristics. Each team must use at least three different robot types during an official game, with a maximum of seven agents of any one robot type and a maximum of nine agents of any two robot types.

2.1 New Rules for RoboCup 2024

For RoboCup 2024, the Technical Committee has approved two new rules. The first rule builds on a 2023 update, which introduced a new *catch* command allowing goalkeepers to grip the ball. The success of this command was inversely related to the ball's distance and speed, but the conditions for success were difficult to meet. To improve its effectiveness, the maximum distance for catching the ball was doubled in 2024. The second rule introduces a new kick pass effector for the NAO robot, which, when activated, simulates a kick by propelling the ball 3 to 5 m as soon as the agent makes contact with it.

3 Team Codebase

This section provides an overview of the code structure used in this year's competition. Please refer to previous work for additional information [2]. Figure 1 illustrates the internal decision flow of the agent and server. The white and orange modules are implemented in Python and C++, respectively. The agent is mainly written in Python, except for the most resource-intensive components such as the 6D pose estimator, role manager, and A* pathfinding algorithm.

The server updates the soccer environment based on agent actions, introducing various types of noise. This includes a constant calibration error affecting the robot's vision sensor, a perception error following a normal distribution that alters object coordinates based on distance, and rounding errors due to a lossy transmitter, rounding all numbers to the nearest hundredth.

[3] https://us.softbankrobotics.com/nao.

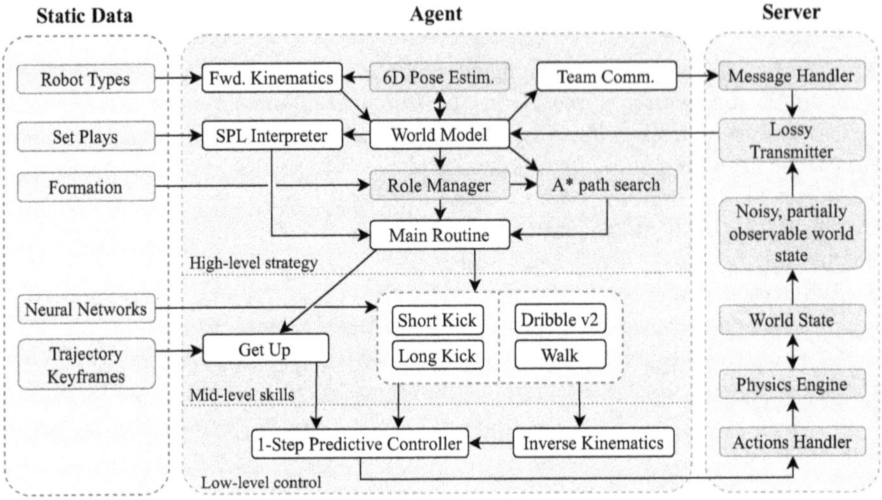

Fig. 1. Overview of the internal decision flow of agent and server, and their external interaction. White modules are implemented in Python while orange modules are implemented in C++. Gray blocks represent static data. (Color figure online)

3.1 High-Level Strategy

As previously stated, agents receive internal data from the server every 20 ms and visual data every 40 ms, consisting of a noisy partial view of the world state. That information is then used to build a world model and devise a common strategy. The main high-level components are briefly described as follows:

- 6D Pose estimator—updates the robot's position and orientation in 3D space. The algorithm uses known noise models to enhance the accuracy of perceived objects, iteratively adjusting the robot's pose [9];
- Forward Kinematics—allows the computation of body part poses for each robot type specification;
- Team communication—ensures all teammates possess a reliable representation of the world state. Messages are limited to 20 characters and are split into three groups, each conveying different game-related information, with specific synchronization and broadcast rules. This protocol ensures efficient communication among agents during a soccer match while adapting to varying visibility conditions;
- TSAL interpreter—manages set plays based on statically specified trigger conditions (see Sect. 4 for a detailed explanation);
- A* path search—divides the soccer field into 70941 nodes (32 m x 22 m, 10 cm grid), mapping the position of goalposts, goal nets, players, and the ball. Role precedence among teammates ensures space allocation for higher-priority roles. The algorithm computes the best path that avoids all obstacles within the time limit of 5 ms;

- Role manager—assigns dynamic roles to players based on the game situation, by considering the position of every player and the ball trajectory. Roles are assigned according to their priority and the agents' distance to the objective, depending on whether the team is attacking or defending;
- Main routine—starts by selecting an intention, such as moving somewhere, dribbling, kicking, or starting a set play. Then, the agent decides the current low-level skill and computes the best way of reaching the chosen target. Shooting is favored if likely to succeed; otherwise, passing is chosen if it aids game progression over dribbling. Information is shared with teammates to synchronize the world model and the execution of set plays.

3.2 Mid-Level Skills

FC Portugal has five major skills, as depicted in Fig. 1:

- Kick—encompasses two distinct kicks: a short kick offering precise control over distance, spanning 3 to 9 m, and a long kick capable of reaching a maximum distance of 21 m. The latter variation is typically used for aiming shots at the goal;
- Walk—omnidirectional walk, able to sustain an average linear speed between 0.70 and 0.90 m/s, depending on robot type and walking direction;
- Dribble v2—second version of the dribble behavior, presented in 2023 [4];
- Get Up—used to get up after falling to the ground. There are three variations of the skill per robot type depending on the falling direction.

4 Set Plays

In 2023, FC Portugal introduced TSAL, a programming language for specifying set plays [17]. Each set play has a name, active roles, and a body that includes an initial trigger condition followed by a series of steps. All agents are initially considered for the set play roles but are gradually eliminated as additional constraints are applied.

The trigger condition defines the initial criteria for starting the set play. During its evaluation, we filter out agents that do not meet the imposed conditions. If no viable candidates remain for a role, the trigger condition evaluates to false, preventing the execution of the set play.

Ultimately, a valid combination of agents is selected, and the set play is started. Every step of the set play includes a set of concurrent actions, each accompanied by a timer for action delay, another timer to establish the set play timeout, and a post-condition that must be satisfied upon completion. Should a timeout or post-condition violation occur, the set play is immediately terminated.

Example in Listing 1.1 implements a triangulation set play where three agents pass the ball between them in order.

```
def setplay 'Triangulation' with agents 'P1', 'P2', 'P3':
    {
        iam(agent='P1') and
        pos(agent='P1', xy = P1Pos, tol = Tol) and
        pos(agent='P2', xy = P2Pos, tol = Tol) and
        pos(agent='P3', xy = P3Pos, tol = Tol)
    }

    pass(agent='P1', to='P2')
        with WaitTime = Time
    {
        has_ball(agent='P2')
    }

    pass(agent='P2', to='P3')
        with WaitTime = Time
    {
        has_ball(agent='P3')
    }

    pass(agent='P3', to='P1')
        with WaitTime = Time
    {
        has_ball(agent='P1')
    }

    where
        P1Pos = (-13, 0);
        P2Pos = (-8, -4);
        P3Pos = (-8, 4);
        Tol = 2.5;
        Time = 1.5
```

Listing 1.1. Triangulation set play

In this set play, three agents, with names P1, P2, and P3, are involved. Once the team has ball possession, the agent holding the ball starts evaluating the triggering condition of the set play, which, in this case, is a conjunction of four predicates. If the triggering condition evaluates to true, then three agents will be assigned the roles of P1, P2, and P3, and the set play may start, which consists of three passes between the agents. After each pass, a post-condition is checked. This post-condition guarantees the execution of the set play. In this case, all post-conditions are similar: if the player receiving the pass doesn't end up holding the ball, then something wrong happen and the set play is aborted.

Currently, there are 8 predicates and 6 actions. Some parameters are optional with default values, and both lists are easily extensible. Each predicate filters candidates for a role; it returns false if no candidates remain after filtering, otherwise true.

In the end, after evaluating all conditions, we will have, for each role, a set of possible agents that can fulfill that role. Note that there is always, at least, one agent for each role since if there was none, the predicate that caused that, would return false, making the trigger condition also immediately false. Then, we simply choose a random candidate player for each role, and start the set play.

The assignment of the players to the roles is not complete, i.e., our approach to filtering candidates may miss some combination that would make the trigger condition true, as the search is done in a greedy way. This design choice was due to time constraints.

The start, progress and completion of the set play is synchronized between the agents with specified messages through the communication channel. If a set play ends due to a timeout or post-condition violation, no announcement is needed, as all participating agents will detect it independently. For further details, please see [4,17].

5 Hierarchical Learning Framework

This work was presented at the 2024 RoboCup 3DSSL Scientific Challenge, where teams showcase research relevant to the league's objectives.

High-level coordination has always been a major research area for FC Portugal. Recent efforts include TSAL [17], a programming language described in Sect. 4, and training two cooperative agents to perform Set-Plays during kick-ins and corners to create goal-scoring opportunities [18].

Building on these approaches, we developed a Hierarchical Learning Framework that leverages existing low-level skills to learn higher-level ones [11]. The learning process stratification follows the Layered Learning principles outlined by Stone [20]. Additionally, a progressive learning method was employed, beginning with a simple two-player corner scenario and gradually unlocking agents' capabilities without altering the environment's state space or reward function.

This work focuses on designing a corner kick set-play, leveraging two existing skills: Kick and Walk, as outlined in Sect. 3.2. The action space includes parameters for the kick's distance and direction, along with target coordinates (x, y, z) for the walking behavior. Additionally, an action switch parameter enables the policy to decide between walking and kicking at any time. The observation space includes the positions of both players, the robots' joint information, and the ball's position.

The first scenario, `Phase1`, features a two-player corner kick. Player R_1 starts at coordinates $(16, y)$, with y randomly selected as either 6 or -6. Player R_2 begins at $(13, 0)$ with a random orientation. R_1 is the passing agent, while R_2 is the receiver and goal scorer. In `Phase2`, the initial conditions remain the same, but R_2 is allowed to walk before the pass and can switch actions. `Phase3` introduces different initial positions for R_2, varying uniformly within $x = [9, 15]$ and $y = [-5, 5]$. Both agents aim to maximize the following global reward function:

$$R(t) = R_g(t) + R_o(t) - \mu(t), \tag{1}$$

$$\text{with} \quad R_g(t) = \begin{cases} 0 & \text{if no goal scored} \\ 10 - 0.5\left(\frac{t}{T}\right)^{0.9} & \text{otherwise,} \end{cases} \tag{2}$$

$$\text{and} \quad R_o(t) = \begin{cases} 0 & \text{if the ball does not go out of play} \\ -\left(\frac{t}{T}\right)^{0.1} & \text{otherwise,} \end{cases} \tag{3}$$

where t is the current time step, T is the maximum number of time steps per episode, and $\mu(t) = 0.001t$ is a time discount applied to favor quick solutions.

R_g and R_o are rewards applied only when a goal is scored or the ball goes out of play, respectively.

A custom single network simulates individual networks, establishing a connection solely through output concatenation. We use the standard Centralized Training Decentralized Execution scheme. Each player has its own actor and critic networks, which differ only in the last layers' activation function for the policy and value heads. The inputs are split at start, fed through linear fully connected feature extractors with *softplus* activation, one for each actor/critic network, then connected to a policy/value head with *softplus* and *tanh* activations respectively. Each hidden layer is composed of 64 neurons.

The model was trained over 14 million steps across various phases. The resulting behaviors include R_1 learning to kick the ball towards a moving R_2, causing the ball to collide with R_2 close to the end line and be redirected into the goal. Subsequently, R_2 learns to position itself while R_1 prepares to kick, ultimately leading to the development of a generalized strategy based on R_2's initial position.

6 Codebase Release

The FC Portugal Codebase is designed to simplify and accelerate development for teams participating in the RoboCup 3D Soccer Simulation League, providing a robust and modern foundation for creating new features or transitioning to Python-based development. It integrates reinforcement learning capabilities via OpenAI Gym, allowing users to train, retrain, and test models within the simulation environment. The codebase automates common tasks from Stable Baselines, displays evaluation graphs directly in the terminal, and allows interactive FPS control during model testing, alongside comprehensive logging of statistics.

The codebase, available on GitHub[4], includes a fully functional team of agents that maintain a basic formation and aim to score by kicking the ball towards the opponent's goal. The main agent is based on the `Base Agent` class, which offers a wide range of functionalities, as shown in Fig. 2. This class incorporates a representation of both the `Robot` and the `World`. The initial state is retrieved from the server and further refined through internal components, such as the `6D Pose Estimator` [9] and the rolling `Ball Predictor`. The agent is equipped with several important tools, including a custom A* pathfinding algorithm, a behavior manager that resets skills as needed, and comprehensive data about the robot and its surroundings. Communication between agents is facilitated by the Radio, which automatically broadcasts information about visible players and the ball.

The codebase release provides essential soccer-related skills, including the latest versions of the Omnidirectional Walk, the underlying Step Baseline skill-set-primitive, and get-up behaviors. It also encompasses the first version of the dribble, introduced in RoboCup 2022, as well as a basic kick and a goalkeeper

[4] FC Portugal Codebase release: https://github.com/m-abr/FCPCodebase.

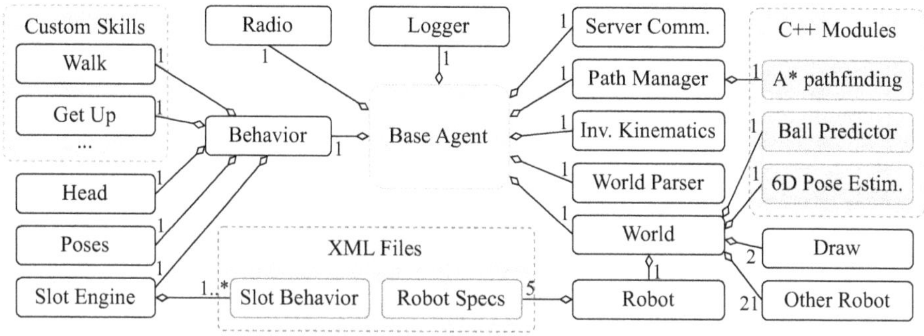

Fig. 2. `Base Agent` structure

dive. Furthermore, the provided agent includes methods for converting low-level actions into magmaFatProxy [10] commands.

The team framework is built for flexibility, allowing multiple agents to be launched either on a single thread or individually across multiple threads. It includes math modules that manage forward and inverse kinematics and reference transformations, allowing for precise tracking of body part positions and orientations, as well as the planning of target poses. A user-friendly interface with menus allows users to access interactive demonstrations, run tests, and utilize various utilities to showcase the key features of the team and agents. Additionally, C++ modules are compiled into shared libraries when changes are detected, ensuring efficiency in development workflows.

Overall, this release offers a robust framework for both new and experienced RoboCup teams, providing tools for simulation, reinforcement learning, and real-time agent behavior control. Alongside FC Portugal, this codebase also served as the foundation for three other teams in RoboCup 2024: BahiaRT, ITAndroids, and Apollo3D.

7 Ball Throwing Challenge

The magmaOffenburg team introduced the Ball Throwing Challenge, included in their magmaChallenge benchmark tool, accessible on GitHub[5]. In this challenge, the ball is placed in front of the goalie within the penalty area. The goalie must walk to the ball, pick it up, and throw it as far as possible. The final score is based on the distance between the ball's initial position and where it stops. The score will be zero if:

- The goalie leaves the 2-meter throwing circle.
- The goalie kicks the ball instead of throwing it (determined by both a tool and a human referee).

An episode ends when at least one of these conditions occur:

[5] magmaChallenge tool https://github.com/magmaOffenburg/magmaChallenge.

- The ball is thrown and its speed drops below 0.01 m/cycle.
- The goalie steps outside a 1-meter circle around the ball.
- 7 s pass and the ball is still within the throwing circle.

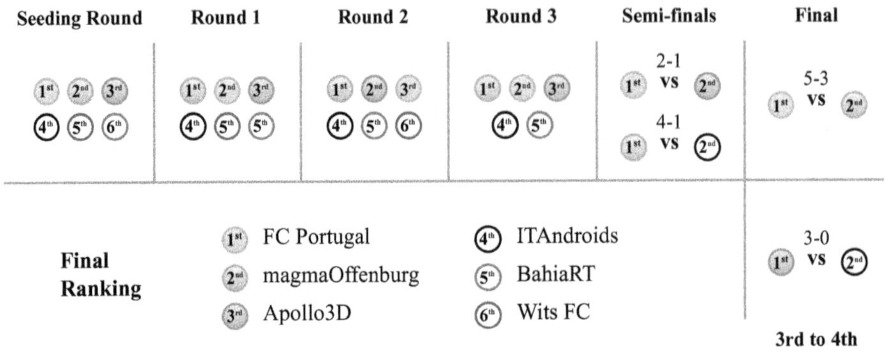

Fig. 3. Main competition results

Table 1. Technical Challenge results based on accumulated points in the Ball Throwing Challenge, the Fat Proxy Challenge, and the Free/Scientific Challenge

Team	Overall		Ball Throw		Fat Proxy		Free/Scientific	
	Rank	Points	Rank	Points	Rank	Points	Rank	Points
magmaOffenburg	1	61.7	1	25	2	18.3	2	18.3
FC Portugal	**2**	**55**	**3**	**5**	**1**	**25**	**1**	**25**
Wits FC	3	23.3	–	–	3	11.7	3	11.7
BahiaRT	4	20	2	15	4	5	–	–
Apollo3D	5	5	–	–	–	–	4	5

8 Results

The results of the main competition are summarized in Fig. 3. FC Portugal finished in first place with 16 wins, 3 ties and 2 losses. During the course of the competition, the team scored 105 goals while conceding only 17. In the final, it defeated the strong magmaOffenburg by 5–3, a team that scored a total of 123 goals while also conceding only 17.

In addition to the main competition, there was a Technical Challenge, which was composed of three events: the Free/Scientific Challenge, where we presented the work outlined in Sect. 5; the Ball Throwing Challenge presented in Sect. 7; and the Fat Proxy Challenge, which was played in a single round-robin tournament using the magmaFatProxy [10]. The purpose of the proxy is to provide the same skills to all teams, preventing the agent from controlling the joints of the robot, thus making the competition exclusively about high-level strategies.

Table 1 shows the scores obtained in each event per participating team. The Technical Challenge ranks teams based on their cumulative points across all challenges. FC Portugal won both the Fat Proxy Challenge and the Free/Scientific Challenge, but magmaOffenburg won the Ball Throwing Challenge and the overall Technical Challenge by accumulating the most points.

9 Conclusion

FC Portugal has developed numerous skills and methodologies concerning the NAO humanoid robot and the simulation league in general. Currently, the team has a very robust code base developed from scratch after RoboCup 2021, which led to the third consecutive victory in the RoboCup 3D Soccer Simulation League. In the main competition, the team registered 16 wins, 3 ties and 2 losses. It scored 105 goals and conceded only 17.

This year, the main scientific contributions included the release of the codebase and the presentation of a new hierarchical learning framework during the Scientific Challenge, where our team secured 1st place. Additionally, the team won the Fat Proxy Challenge and ranked 3rd in the Ball Throwing Challenge, accumulating enough points to finish in second place overall in the Technical Challenge. Despite the good results, there are still many opportunities for improvement. Future research directions include high-level multi-agent coordination strategies, opponent modeling, goalkeeper skills, omnidirectional kicks, optimization algorithms, and more.

Acknowledgments. The first author was supported by the Foundation for Science and Technology (FCT) under grant SFRH/BD/139926/2018. This research was also funded by FCT/MCTES (PIDDAC), under projects UIDB/00027/2020 (LIACC) and UIDB/00127/2020 (IEETA).

Disclosure of Interests. The authors have no competing interests to declare that are relevant to the content of this article.

References

1. Abdolmaleki, A., Simões, D., Lau, N., Reis, L.P., Neumann, G.: Learning a humanoid kick with controlled distance. In: RoboCup 2016: Robot World Cup XX, pp. 45–57. Springer, Cham (2016)
2. Abreu, M., Kasaei, M., Reis, L.P., Lau, N.: FC Portugal: Robocup 2022 3D simulation league and technical challenge champions. In: RoboCup 2022: Robot World Cup XXV, pp. 313–324. Springer, Cham (2022)

3. Abreu, M., Lau, N., Sousa, A., Reis, L.P.: Learning low level skills from scratch for humanoid robot soccer using deep reinforcement learning. In: 2019 IEEE International Conference on Autonomous Robot Systems and Competitions (ICARSC), pp. 256–263. IEEE (2019)
4. Abreu, M., Mota, P., Reis, L.P., Lau, N., Florido, M.: FC Portugal: Robocup 2023 3D simulation league champions. In: RoboCup 2023: Robot World Cup XXVI, pp. 416–427. Springer, Cham (2023)
5. Abreu, M., Reis, L.P., Cardoso, H.L.: Learning high-level robotic soccer strategies from scratch through reinforcement learning. In: 2019 IEEE International Conference on Autonomous Robot Systems and Competitions, pp. 128–134. IEEE (2019)
6. Abreu, M., Reis, L.P., Lau, N.: Learning to run faster in a humanoid robot soccer environment through reinforcement learning. In: Chalup, S., Niemueller, T., Suthakorn, J., Williams, M.-A. (eds.) RoboCup 2019. LNCS (LNAI), vol. 11531, pp. 3–15. Springer, Cham (2019). https://doi.org/10.1007/978-3-030-35699-6_1
7. Abreu, M., Reis, L.P., Lau, N.: Designing a skilled soccer team for robocup: exploring skill-set-primitives through reinforcement learning. arXiv preprint arXiv:2312.14360 (2023)
8. Abreu, M., Reis, L.P., Lau, N.: Addressing imperfect symmetry: a novel symmetry-learning actor-critic extension. Neurocomputing **614**, 128771 (2025)
9. Abreu, M., Silva, T., Teixeira, H., Reis, L.P., Lau, N.: 6D localization and kicking for humanoid robotic soccer. J. Intell. Robot. Syst. **102**(2), 1–25 (2021)
10. Amelia, E., et al.: magmaFatProxy (2023). https://github.com/magmaOffenburg/magmaFatProxy
11. Azevedo, T., Silva, F., Lau, N., Reis, L.P.: Progressive deep reinforcement learning for strategic set-plays in robotic football (2024). https://archive.robocup.info/Soccer/Simulation/3D/FCPs/RoboCup/2024/FCPortugal_SS3D_RC2024_FCP.pdf
12. Boedecker, J., Asada, M.: Simspark–concepts and application in the robocup 3D soccer simulation league. In: Proceedings of the SIMPAR-2008 Workshop on The Universe of RoboCup Simulators. Venice, Italy (2008)
13. Kasaei, M., Abreu, M., Lau, N., Pereira, A., Reis, L.P.: A CPG-based agile and versatile locomotion framework using proximal symmetry loss. arXiv preprint arXiv:2103.00928 (2021)
14. Kasaei, M., Abreu, M., Lau, N., Pereira, A., Reis, L.P.: Robust biped locomotion using deep reinforcement learning on top of an analytical control approach. Robot. Auton. Syst. **146**, 103900 (2021)
15. Kasaei, M., Abreu, M., Lau, N., Pereira, A., Reis, L.P., Li, Z.: Learning hybrid locomotion skills – learn to exploit residual actions and modulate model-based gait control. Front. Robot. AI **10** (2023)
16. Kasaei, S.M., Simões, D., Lau, N., Pereira, A.: A hybrid ZMP-CPG based walk engine for biped robots. In: Iberian Robotics Conference, pp. 743–755. Springer, Cham (2017)
17. Mota, P.: A team strategy programming language applied to robotic soccer. Master's thesis, University of Porto, Porto, Portugal (2023)
18. Santiago, M.: FC Portugal - high-level skills within a multi-agent environment. Master's thesis, University of Porto, Porto, Portugal (2021)
19. Simões, D., Amaro, P., Silva, T., Lau, N., Reis, L.P.: Learning low-level behaviors and high-level strategies in humanoid soccer. In: Iberian Robotics Conference, pp. 537–548. Springer, Cham (2019)
20. Stone, P.: Layered Learning in Multiagent Systems: A Winning Approach to Robotic Soccer. The MIT Press, Cambridge (2000)

21. Teixeira, H., Silva, T., Abreu, M., Reis, L.P.: Humanoid robot kick in motion ability for playing robotic soccer. In: 2020 IEEE International Conference on Autonomous Robot Systems and Competitions (ICARSC), pp. 34–39. IEEE (2020)
22. Xu, Y., Vatankhah, H.: SimSpark: an open source robot simulator developed by the RoboCup community. In: RoboCup 2013: Robot World Cup XVII, pp. 632–639. Springer, Cham (2014)

Team SWOT - Champions of RoboCup@Work 2024

Julian Mueller(✉), Felix Endres, Lucas Reinhart, Martin Loeser, Stanislav Buinitskii, Volker Willert, and Tobias Kaupp

Center for Robotics (CERI), Technical University of Applied Sciences Wuerzburg-Schweinfurt (THWS), Schweinfurt, Germany
{julian.mueller.1,felix.endres,lucas.reinhart,martin.loeser, volker.willert,tobias.kaupp}@thws.de, stanislav.buinitskii@study.thws.de

Abstract. In this paper, we present our approach that earned first place at the RoboCup@Work 2024 competition. We briefly outline the current competition challenges and give an update on our system architecture and methods used for planning, manipulation, perception and navigation. The emphasis is on newly implemented features and relevant changes compared to the design of prior years. Finally, we evaluate the results of the 2024 RoboCup@Work including the additional technical coworker challenge. A performance comparison with other teams is provided and further conclusions are drawn by revisiting the challenges and goals outlined last year.

Keywords: RoboCup@Work · mobile manipulation · factory automation

1 Introduction

The RoboCup@Work league [9] provides a platform for advancing industrial robotics research by challenging participants to solve object-handling problems inspired by real-world applications. Tasks such as transporting drills, metal profiles, and other tools between designated locations are performed across multiple test scenarios. Unlike traditional factory robots, which are designed for static, repetitive tasks, these challenges require intelligent solutions, such as mobile manipulators capable of navigating dynamic environments and interacting with diverse objects. Despite their potential, the adoption of such robots in industrial applications remains limited. Ensuring reliable operation in variable settings and handling different object properties remains challenging and hinders broader deployment.

Previous winning approaches, such as those described in [1,11], have already given some insights into potential solutions, but also highlight the dynamic nature of the league and the need for ongoing development. Our Team, SWOT, has joined the competition in 2021. Comprised of students and employees from

E. Barros et al. (Eds.): RoboCup 2024, LNAI 15570, pp. 424–435, 2025.
https://doi.org/10.1007/978-3-031-85859-8_36

the Center for Robotics (CERI) at the Technische Hochschule Wuerzburg-Schweinfurt (THWS), we have shown consistent performance improvements over the course of six competitions so far. The overall design of our system was previously detailed in [12]. Since then, there have been various changes to the hardware architecture of our robot, shown in Fig. 1, and several of the software components have been updated. These modifications also reflect the evolving competition rules. Therefore, in the following we will provide a brief overview of the 2024 challenge (Sect. 2), present the recent advancements in our system architecture and components (Sect. 3), and discuss the results of the 2024 competition (Sect. 4).

Fig. 1. SWOT mobile manipulator in front of a RoboCup@Work workspace (WS). [1] Mecanum wheel platform, [2] UR3e arm, [3] Robotiq gripper, [4] Azure Kinect, [5] Sick LIDAR, [6] storage trays, [7] e-stops.

2 Current Challenges

The test sets for the RoboCup@Work competition are annually updated based on the latest rule book [6]. Currently they include six stages of increasing difficulty, challenging robots to handle a growing number of targets and workspaces. To evaluate the perception system's robustness, so called "decoy" objects and arbitrary surfaces are included. The inclusion of an advanced object set in the past years has also increased complexity in perception and grasping. Varying workspace height is also a consideration, including floor-level placement tests. Navigational complexity is increased through so called virtual obstacles marked by barrier tape, requiring real-time obstacle recognition and precise path planning. Robots also need to show flexibility in object placements by using different red or blue containers, simulating task sorting and specific placement problems. Additionally, three specialized workstations (depicted in Fig. 2) demand unique pick-and-place skills.

This year, there were no major alterations in the types of tests to complete. Currently the rule book specifies the following tests:

Fig. 2. Different types of workstations encountered in advanced tests, from left to right: rotating table, shelf, precision placement.

(a) BMT: Basic Manipulation Test - moving simple objects from A to B.
(b) BTT1&2: Basic Transportation Tests - increasing the number of tasks and navigational complexity.
(c) ATT1&2: Advanced Transportation Tests - addition of several challenging manipulation tasks and a further increase in the number of tasks.

Each of the tasks within a test is weighed by a score reflecting its difficulty. For example, a successful precision placement is awarded three times the amount of points of a normal placement. Additionally, there are optional technical challenges like the Coworker Assembly Test requiring new robot functionalities to manage a collaborative assembly tasks, further extending the breadth of technical competencies that are evaluated.

3 System Architecture and Components

A full description of the architecture developed over several years has previously been given in [12]. In the following we describe our current hardware and software architecture, with an emphasis on the capabilities developed or improved during the last 12 months.

Hardware. The previous architecture utilized a diverse set of compute platforms. This year, we streamlined our hardware by transitioning to a single AMD Ryzen 7 5700X CPU, suitable for general-purpose compute workloads, paired with an NVIDIA RTX 4060 GPU for parallel processing tasks like object detection.

This shift of course represents a trade off between increased power consumption and increased compute capabilities. However, the change is overall beneficial with regards to solving tasks required for the competition. For example our compute capabilities for neural networks increased by an order of magnitude, whereas the power consumption only increased by a fraction of the overall power draw measured in the prior architecture and does not exhaust our current battery in any of the competition test sets.

Further benefits are a reduction in complexity of the overall system, effectively this eliminates the need for a distributed architecture, alleviating multiple pain points with barley any drawbacks. Deployment of software updates is now faster, freeing up time for more integration testing. Changes to the compute hardware required a restructuring of the components layout to still fit onto the mobile base platform. New mechanical components have been designed and 3D printed. In this process we also made changes to the power supply and added some convenience features and hardware buttons for controlling individual elements of our robot. The remaining components like the, LIDARs (Sick TiM), camera (Azure Kinect), manipulator (Universal Robots UR3e) and gripper (RobotiQ HandE) have not received any updates recently.

Software. Our core software architecture is still based on ROS 1. Even though we do not use multiple compute entities anymore, relying on features like topics and services for separation of software modules remains critical. We previously outlined in our software design the logical grouping of most of our software in either a) task planning, b) manipulation, c) perception, or d) navigation. This has largely remained and we are going to discuss the changes made across all of the individual components.

3.1 Task Planning

Task Planning is responsible for receiving an initial task description from the atwork commander system (the software component used to generate rule book compliant goals) and generating a high level plan of action steps to perform to fulfill the goal. It provides a level of abstraction, interacting with the other components of navigation and manipulation. As mentioned last year, this separation between higher- and lower-level planning can lead to inefficient behavior in some cases. For example, performing multiple placement tasks without leaving a workspace may result in unnecessary repetition of individual image processing steps. We addressed these issues primarily by investing in additional logic within the lower-level behavioral modeling of the manipulation sequences.

3.2 Navigation

Navigation is built on the commonly used Navigation package [10], utilizing sensor readings from 2 LIDARs as well as wheel odometry data. We have further optimized the parameter set for SLAM, local planning and global planning. Significant efforts also went into refactoring the behavior logic between the task planning and the move base system of the navigation package. The new code is easier to maintain and test. Last year we also outlined our separate approach for close proximity navigation when approaching a workspace. There were several changes to the existing code, to get more consistent fine positioning accuracy at the workspace. Another layer has been added, reading sensor data from all LIDARs. The data is constantly evaluated with respect to constant thresholds. Further, we utilize the readings to track directional changes. This also provides safeguards to avoid any potential risk of collision in the case of poor localization estimates.

3.3 Object Detection and Instance Segmentation

One of the main components of the perception subsystem is the neural network based inference for object detection which has received major updates by transitioning to the newer YOLOv8 architecture [7]. Hence we give an outline on our new training process and the performance in our use-case before describing the methods employed for the vision processing of grasping points and depositing areas. An important improvement is the availability of segmentation mask information, which enhances our system's capability of accurate object detection and segmentation. With the recent hardware upgrade, the system's new compute capabilities allow for greater flexibility of running models during the competition. This enhancement, along with the efficient API, enables simultaneous inference across multiple CNNs without risking system overload.

Training Data Generation. To address previously encountered challenges in object detection, particularly with glossy surfaces and under varying lighting conditions, substantial improvements were made to the training dataset. Similar to previous implementations, BlenderProc [3] is utilized to generate realistic images. The synthetic dataset generator script selects a randomized subset of valid objects to position on arbitrary surfaces under diverse lighting conditions. The resulting images are accompanied by automatically generated segmentation masks, as seen in Fig. 3

Fig. 3. Sample of the generated images used for training the YOLO network.

In the latest update, the synthetic dataset was further enhanced with a broader range of lighting conditions, employing an extensive set of HDRI templates that encompass indoor warehouse environments as well as outdoor settings. To reduce the potential impact of false positives, a comprehensive set of decoy elements, provided by [4], has been included in the synthetic scenes.

Additionally, real-world camera data was added in an attempt to increase the overall robustness of the object detection system. To ease the process of data collection for training we use a semi-automated process, by continuously capturing camera data over a workspace scene, moving between different perspectives. In the following, Segment Anything [8] is employed for labeling the

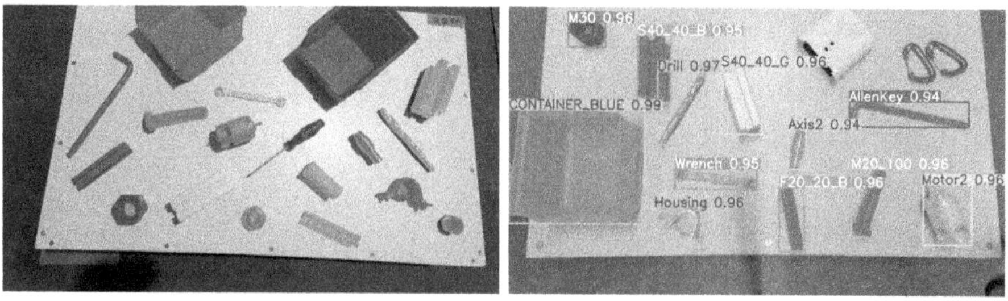

Fig. 4. Left: XMem-based object tracking for automated data labeling. Right: YOLOv8 object detection results.

initial frame. It provides metadata for segmentation, allowing us to automate label generation further for every following frame in the entire video sequence utilizing XMem [2]. This yields approximately 300 labeled images from a single scene. To ensure stable sequences across various lighting and surface conditions, data capture was facilitated by programmed movements of the UR3e manipulator. The automatically generated segmentation for data labeling is shown on the left side of Fig. 4, on the right an example of the detection results during inference.

Model Comparison. We prepared a test dataset which contains 1200 real world images of a competition environment with challenging lighting conditions. To quantify the impact of different training datasets we evaluated multiple versions of our new YOLOv8 model trained either on synthetic data, real data or a mixture of both. The results, as seen in Fig. 5, show that the model trained solely on the synthetic data performs significantly worse than the one with mixed data. For example, the confusion matrix reveals that in this case the detection of the Bearing object failed completely. But even here, adding synthetic data to the training dataset also improved detection compared to models trained purely on real data. Overall we can conclude that improving our training data set has clearly increased our object detection rate. The current ratio of synthetic to real-world data in training dataset is 70:30. However, the optimal balance is yet to be determined.

3.4 Pose Estimation

Grasping. After running the YOLOv8 model inference on the RGB input image, the resulting segmentation masks are processed to estimate the 6D pose of the object, from which the grasping point and the gripper's pose are derived. By filtering for the desired object and its associated inference score, the candidate segmentation mask is identified. Using the depth image and camera intrinsics, the 2D pixel points of the candidate mask are outprojected to generate a 3D segmentation mask of the object. In parallel, a point cloud of the scene is generated from the depth image. This point cloud is transformed into the robot's base

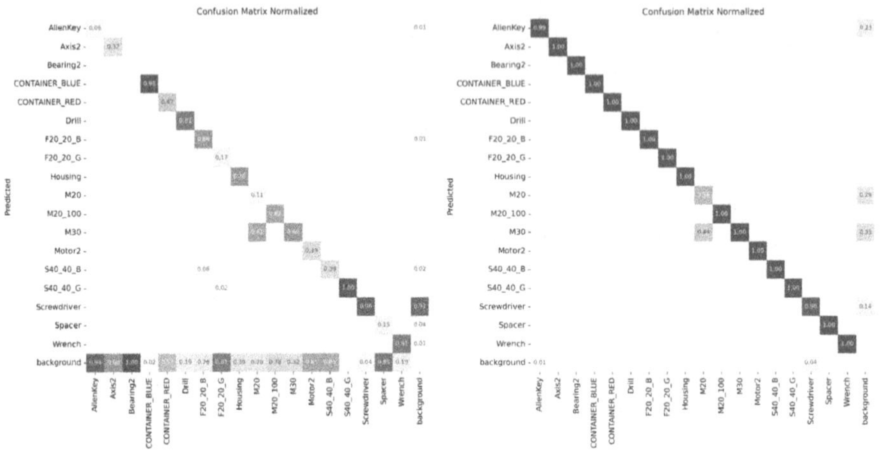

Fig. 5. Confusion matrices: synthetic data(left), real and synthetic data(right).

frame and cropped to match the workspace dimensions. Downsampling is then applied to the point cloud using a voxel grid filter to reduce its size and optimize it for subsequent plane segmentation. To compute the plane equation for the workspace ground, the RANSAC [5] algorithm is employed. This plane equation is subsequently applied to filter out background points from the candidate 3D segmentation mask. For the remaining points, a minimal oriented bounding box is calculated using the algorithm described in [13]. Since the center point of this bounding box closely approximates the actual center point of each competition object, it can be used as the grasping point. The gripper's orientation is aligned with the principal axis of the bounding box corresponding to its longest dimension. The result is visualized in Fig. 7.

Object Placement. The competition tasks include several different modes of placing objects. In the following, we describe our approaches for placing the object on the workspace, precise positioning in cavities and inserting objects into containers.

Workspace Placement. To identify a free area on the workspace for object placement, plane segmentation of the workspace surface is performed using the same process as illustrated in Fig. 6. Subtracting the workspace surface from the cropped scene point cloud isolates clusters corresponding to objects on the workspace. The minimal and maximal extents of these clusters along the width of the workspace are computed to define stripes of the workspace flagged as occupied. The center point of the largest unoccupied stripe is selected as the placement point. A static rotation of 45° relative to the edges defining the workspace is applied to align the placement.

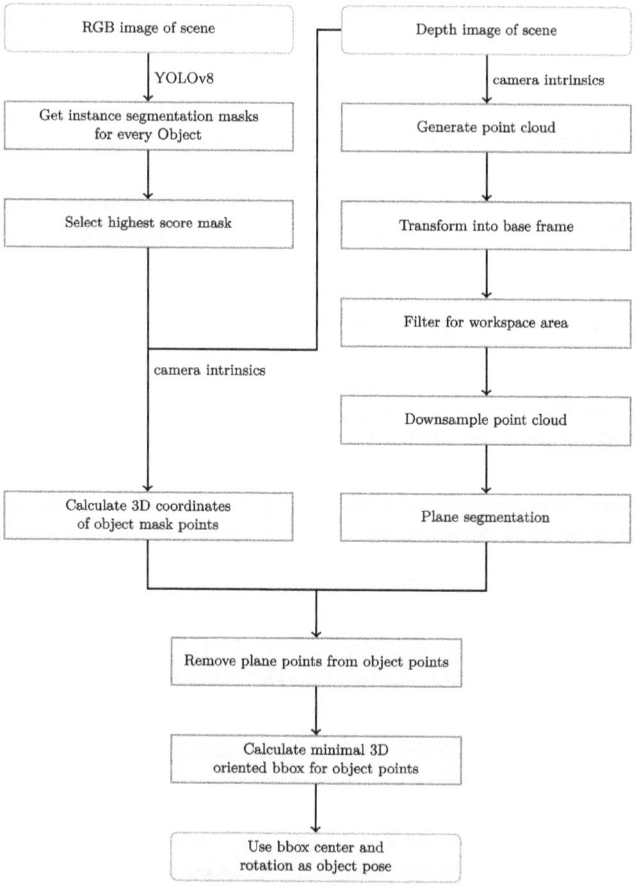

Fig. 6. Flowchart of our 6D pose estimation process. Red boxes represent inputs and outputs. Blue boxes represent intermediate steps. (Color figure online)

Precision Placement. For the precise placement of objects in their cavities, specialized YOLOv8 model weights are used to detect the different cavity types, generating a quadratic segmentation mask around the desired cavity. The camera image is cropped to the square defined by the segmentation mask, and a threshold is applied to generate a binary image. For rectangular cavities, a minimal oriented bounding box is computed using the methods described in [15]. For hexagonal cavities, a contour is first extracted based on [16], and a polygon is subsequently fitted using an algorithm derived from [14], as shown in Fig. 7. In both cases, the 3D coordinates of the polygon's corners are calculated, followed by the computation of the side vectors. For rectangular cavities, the orientation is determined by the vector of the longer side of the bounding box. For hexagonal cavities, differentiation between the two possible orientations is achieved by comparing the angles between the hexagon's sides and those of the square defined by the segmentation mask. By default, the placement point is set to the center of the polygon for both cavity types.

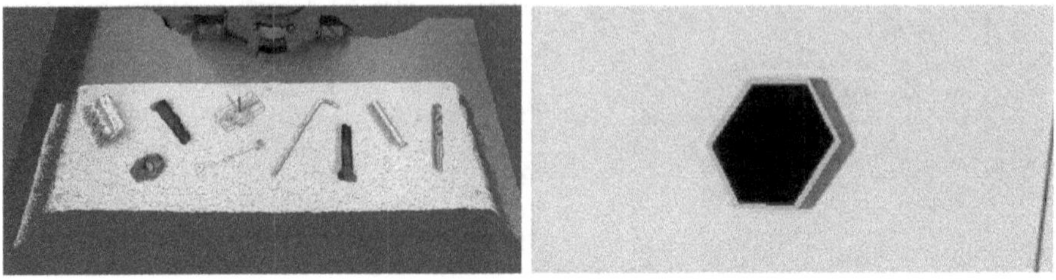

Fig. 7. Left: Oriented bounding box and pose estimation result visualized in the point cloud of the scene. Right: The fitted hexagon overlayed on the detected region for the precision placement task.

Container Placement. To place an object inside a container, the pose of the container on the workspace is estimated using the same algorithm described above. This estimated pose is directly used as the placement pose for the object. This approach achieved a 100% success rate for container placements during the competition, highlighting the accuracy and reliability of our pose estimation method.

3.5 Manipulation

The manipulation logic consists of a set of decisions and behavioral policies. Last year we already moved to an implementation based on a behavior tree framework to manage the complexity. This approach has demonstrated effectiveness to date and the tree structure has been further expanded in its capabilities.

Manipulation path planning for pick and place operations include statically configured positions as well as dynamic path generation according to the 6D pose estimated prior. For pick operations, the gripper is pre-positioned in a x, y plane parallel to the workspace surface. The manipulator is then moved perpendicular to the workspace and picks up the object. This approach results in high accuracy for the vast majority of tasks in the competition but requires the extension of behaviors for specialized tasks. Tree Elements have been added to accommodate the handling of object placements in container boxes and cavities for the precision placement test.

Human Machine Interface. The flexibility of the behavior modeling also allowed us to expand functional behavior by adding a voice based human-machine interface. This enables direct feedback for a human operator, communicating the intended action of the robot. A set of status codes was determined prior to execution, which is used during execution depending on the respective behavior. The system uses a text-to-speech approach for generating the audio commands.

4 Results

4.1 RoboCup@Work

Table 1 shows the results from the competition in 2024. Last year our system showed a strong and consistent performance in the foundational BMT and BTT runs but reached fewer points in tests with higher difficulty. Our focus was mainly on robustness of the core perception, manipulation and navigation capabilities. This year multiple capabilities for advanced tests, like precision and container placement were added, resulting in performance increases across all advanced tests (ATT, final). Unfortunately a hardware malfunction at the start of the competition affected the BMT run.

Table 1. Results of the RoboCup@Work 2024 in Eindhoven. The numbers reflect the achieved scores according to the rule book per test type (rows) and team (columns). Our team reached the 1st place shown in **bold**.

	1st	2nd	3rd	4th	5th	6th	7th	8th
BMT	**0**	650	500	850	300	400	0	0
BTT1	**900**	1000	600	1000	400	150	100	0
BTT2	**1450**	950	1050	100	600	0	0	0
ATT1	**2000**	700	1282.5	1760	0	1126.25	0	0
ATT2	**1440**	975	2075	0	570	0	0	0
FINAL	**1678.75**	2175	743.75	2018.75	187.5	270	0	0
Total	**7468.75**	6450	6251.25	5728.75	2057.5	1946.25	100	0

There are still features which have not been fully implemented so far. Notably, we did not attempt to complete the rotating table task yet. Other lessons learned include the following:

1. Last year highly reflective surfaces caused the object detection to deteriorate. We believed it to be impacted by unrealistic reflective properties of the synthetic image data used for training. The issue was not present in the competition this year, however improvements to the training data set have been made as described in Sect. 3.3.
2. Another issue were inaccuracies in the 6D pose estimation that occasionally lead to pick or place failures. This problem was caused by the initialization of the Iterative Closest Point algorithm used. The changes to the pose estimation pipeline described in Sect. 3.4 significantly increased the overall pose detection rate across the whole object set.

3. The third problem highlighted was related to localization accuracy. We did extensive testing and updated the navigation parameter set as well as refactored parts of the navigation behavior code base leading to a more reliable and accurate localization.

4.2 Technical Challenge - Coworker Assembly

This year, we also participated in the optional Coworker Assembly technical challenge and managed to secure a first place here as well. The challenge simulates the collaboration between a mobile manipulator and a human. The robot is tasked with transporting three objects from the arena to a workspace and placing them there. The human operator assembles the placed objects and the robot waits for a signal from the human to transport the assembled object further. This signal must be recognized by the robot and can be acoustic or visual. The solution approach used to address the challenge utilizes a third-party implementation[1] for visual hand gesture detection. The individual key-points of the hand are localized (refer to Fig. 8) using Google's Mediapipe Hand. After recognizing the correct gesture, the robot finishes its assigned task.

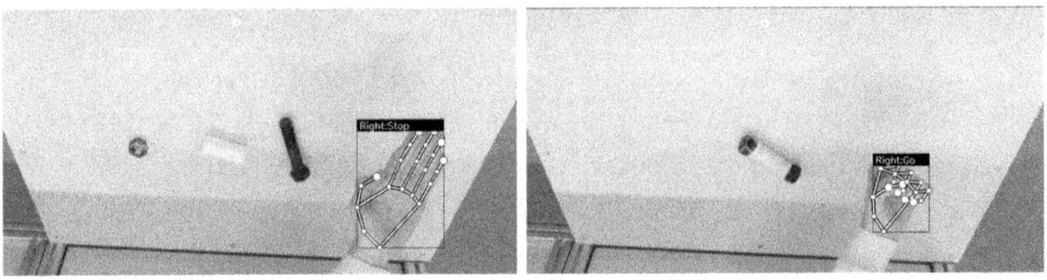

Fig. 8. Gestures for the Coworker Challenge, before and after completion of the task assigned to the human.

4.3 Conclusion

Overall the results indicate that solving the RoboCup@Work tasks consistently in a real world environment remains challenging for all participants. Our recent efforts have demonstrated promising improvements, particularly with the more accurate and feature complete pose detection leveraging the new compute capabilities. Looking ahead, we aim to address remaining gaps, such as the rotating table, and to further incorporate novel approaches improving the robot's capabilities across all aspects of the competition.

Acknowledgments. The authors gratefully acknowledge the contributions made by the GRASS project, funded by the state of Bavaria (Bayrisches StMWi, Grant no. DIE-2010-0009/DIE0128/02).

[1] https://github.com/TrinhNC/ros_hand_gesture_recognition.

References

1. Chenchani, G., et al.: b-it-bots: winners of robocup@ work 2023. In: Robot World Cup, pp. 350–361. Springer, Cham (2023)
2. Cheng, H.K., Schwing, A.G.: Xmem: long-term video object segmentation with an Atkinson-Shiffrin memory model. In: European Conference on Computer Vision, pp. 640–658. Springer, Cham (2022)
3. Denninger, M., et al.: Blenderproc. arXiv preprint arXiv:1911.01911 (2019)
4. Downs, L., et al.: Google scanned objects: a high-quality dataset of 3D scanned household items. In: 2022 International Conference on Robotics and Automation (ICRA), pp. 2553–2560. IEEE (2022)
5. Fischler, M., Bolles, R.: Random sample consensus: a paradigm for model fitting with applications to image analysis and automated cartography. Commun. ACM **24**(6), 381–395 (1981)
6. Fook, C., et al.: Robocup@work 2024 - rulebook (2024). https://atwork.robocup.org/rules/
7. Jocher, G., Chaurasia, A., Qiu, J.: Ultralytics YOLOv8 (2023). https://github.com/ultralytics/ultralytics
8. Kirillov, A., et al.: Segment anything (2023). https://arxiv.org/abs/2304.02643
9. Kraetzschmar, G., et al.: Robocup@ work: competing for the factory of the future. In: RoboCup 2014: Robot World Cup XVIII 18, pp. 171–182. Springer, Cham (2015)
10. Marder-Eppstein, E., Berger, E., Foote, T., Gerkey, B., Konolige, K.: The office marathon: robust navigation in an indoor office environment. In: 2010 IEEE International Conference on robotics and Automation, pp. 300–307. IEEE (2010)
11. Martin, J., Engelhardt, H., Fink, T., Masannek, M., Scholz, T.: Robocup@work winners 2017 team autonohm. In: RoboCup 2017: Robot World Cup XXI 11, pp. 498–508. Springer, Cham (2018)
12. Mueller, J., et al.: Mobile manipulators in industrial environments–robocup@ work and warehouse order picking. In: Australasian Conference on Robotics and Automation. Australasian Conference on Robotics and Automation (2023)
13. O'Rourke, J.: Finding minimal enclosing boxes. Int. J. Comput. Inf. Sci. **14**(3), 183–199 (1985). https://doi.org/10.1007/bf00991005
14. Ramer, U.: An iterative procedure for the polygonal approximation of plane curves. Comput. Graph. Image Process. **1**, 244–256 (1972). https://api.semanticscholar.org/CorpusID:1213794
15. Shamos, M.I.: Computational Geometry. Yale University (1978)
16. Suzuki, S., et al.: Topological structural analysis of digitized binary images by border following. Comput. Vis. Graph. Image Process. **30**(1), 32–46 (1985)

Designing a Rescue Strategy Emphasizing Distributed Control in RoboCupRescue Simulation

AIT-Rescue: RoboCup 2024 Rescue Simulation League Champion

Keisuke Ando[1(✉)], Ryoya Maeda[1], Haruki Uehara[1], Joe Fujisawa[1], Itsuki Matsunaga[1], Ryosuke Suzuki[1], Kota Kato[1], Yuki Shimada[1], Shuntarou Fujii[1], Takeshi Uchitane[1], Kazunori Iwata[2], and Nobuhiro Ito[1]

[1] Department of Information Science, Aichi Institute of Technology, Toyota, Japan
ando@maslab.aitech.ac.jp

[2] Department of Business Administration, Aichi University, Nagoya, Japan
https://www.ait.ac.jp/en/faculty/info-science/,
https://www.aichi-u.ac.jp/english/academics/biz/ba

Abstract. AIT-Rescue is the champion team in the RoboCup 2024 Rescue Simulation League that succeeded in proposing a rescue strategy focused on distributed control. RoboCupRescue Simulation is a competition that aims to develop rescue strategies to save more civilians in disaster rescue simulations. AIT-Rescue employs autonomous distributed decision-making and has a flexible rescue strategy that can be adopted for complex disaster situations. This paper explains the rescue strategy of AIT-Rescue and the implemented module design. The critical features in this system are the methods for determining priority roads and selecting sanctuaries. The processes that these methods consider for civilian rescue in disaster conditions are explained. The research results on multiagent systems are presented in relation to AIT-Rescue's development. This research contributes to developing effective strategies for real-world disaster rescue by exploring multiagent systems and applying them to complex disaster scenarios. In the future, these results will be integrated into agents to obtain better strategies.

Keywords: Multiagent system · Clustering · Queueing theory

1 Introduction

AIT-Rescue is the champion team in the Agent Simulation Competition of RoboCupRescue Simulation League 2024. This team has participated continuously in this competition since its inception. The RoboCupRescue Simulation simulates a city after an earthquake and the operations conducted thereafter by rescue teams to save civilians. Participating teams develop rescue strategies to

E. Barros et al. (Eds.): RoboCup 2024, LNAI 15570, pp. 436–447, 2025.
https://doi.org/10.1007/978-3-031-85859-8_37

compete in saving civilians. Based on the number of civilians saved, the effectiveness of each rescue strategy is evaluated.

The AIT-Rescue strategy emphasizes distributed control, allowing each rescue team to decide autonomously based on the surrounding conditions. Each platoon communicates its actions and coordinates with others to enable more advanced decision-making as a unified rescue team. The functions that comprise the rescue strategy are modular and designed to integrate with the rescue strategies of other teams.

AIT-Rescue is also advancing research on multiagent systems using the RoboCupRescue Simulation. The research areas include developing algorithms for task assignment for each agent (rescue platoon) to efficiently save more civilians [4,7]. The relationship between map complexity and rescue outcomes are analyzed to comprehensively evaluate rescue strategies [3,4]. Based on these results, AIT-Rescue aims to realize more effective rescue strategies.

2 Development of Agents in the Competition

2.1 Agent Simulation Competition

The agent simulation competition is an event in which each participant develops a rescue strategy and competes to demonstrate its effectiveness in rescuing civilians. The strategy is evaluated based on how many civilians it can save under multiple scenarios simulating various disaster situations.

There are three types of rescue platoons: police forces (debris removal teams), fire brigades, and ambulance teams. Each type has a different role and follows a designed rescue strategy to save civilians. The basic flow of rescue operations is as follows:

1. Police forces remove debris and ensure a clear path to civilians and refugees.
2. Fire brigades excavate civilians trapped under the debris.
3. Ambulance teams transport the excavated civilians to a refuge.

Each platoon coordinates with others considering their respective roles and the sequence of activities for rescuing civilians.

2.2 Agent Development Framework

The agents were developed using the Agent Development Framework (ADF) [8]. ADF represents rescue strategies as combinations of modules with different roles, allowing the construction of rescue strategies by developing each module. This framework was adopted as the standard development tool in RoboCupRescue Simulation, and the competition rules require the development of agents using this framework.

The ADF modules address the challenges of group formation, multiagent pathfinding, dynamic resource allocation, information sharing, and information collection, which are problems to be solved in the RoboCupRescue Simulation.

Modules of the same type are interchangeable, allowing the reuse of previously developed or default modules. Therefore, developers can focus on creating modules for the tasks they are interested in. Specifically, they can develop each module based on the interfaces and sample modules provided by ADF. They can also create and add new module types with unique functionalities as required.

2.3 Challenges in Developing a Rescue Strategy

In the RoboCupRescue Simulation, damage varies according to regional characteristics depending on the conditions of disaster occurrence, similar to real earthquake situations. Therefore, the competition involves testing rescue strategies across various scenarios. These strategies require flexibility to adapt to diverse situations; however, agents face physical limitations similar to real rescue teams. Consequently, accurately assessing the problem and constructing effective rescue strategies are challenging.

For example, if the rescue platoons are concentrated in one location at the start of the simulation, they need to disperse and search for civilians. If the platoons are widely scattered, they need to regroup to support areas with a shortage of personnel. Agents can communicate to share position and call for assistance as required. However, their perceptual range is limited, making it challenging to grasp the situation. Communication capacity is also limited, such that careful selection of information becomes essential. Given these constraints, agents must effectively assess the situation and conduct rescue operations.

3 Rescue Strategy and Module Design

3.1 Agent's Rescue Strategy

The AIT-Rescue strategy emphasizes distributed control to respond to various scenarios. Each agent begins operations in an initially assigned area, gathering information about other regions through communication and extending beyond their area as required. Based on the information obtained through perception and communication, agents make autonomous decisions, allowing them to adapt flexibly to different regions and disaster situations.

The agents move by considering the pre-computed priority roads and debris on the streets. Priority roads refer to actively used roads from which debris is removed preferentially. Roads can become impassable due to debris. Therefore, moving along the shortest path to the destination is sometimes impossible. Police forces can clear debris. However, if work proceeds without a plan, it can take a long time. During this period, if a route to the injured civilians cannot be cleared, the civilians may have to wait longer for rescue, gradually becoming weaker, and even risking death. Therefore, establishing and making available a route that connects the rescue platoons and injured civilians, is essential for a designated priority road.

The agents patrol their assigned areas and search for injured civilians. When they hear a voice asking for help, they assess the situation based on the location and content of the voice. They then dynamically plan the order of their search. When there are no civilians to rescue in their assigned area, they move to assist other regions.

The agents share information via communication. This information includes the agent's own and nearby civilians' statuses. The communication process for sharing the agent's status is embedded in ADF's core strategy and is always executed when there is sufficient communication bandwidth. Therefore, other details are not transmitted to avoid overloading the bandwidth and loss of information.

Based on information shared via communication, agent actions should not overlap with those of others, to ensure that useless rescue operations do not occur. For instance, when transporting a civilian, only one ambulance team can transport that individual. If multiple ambulance teams attempt to transport the same civilian, some of the teams will fail to transport. This overlap can waste time and potentially exacerbate the civilian's condition, as the delayed transport process reduces overall efficiency. To avoid this, ambulance teams consider the locations of other teams through communication sharing, assigning the team nearest to the civilian to the transport task.

3.2 Ambulance Team Module Structure

AIT-Rescue naturally extends the ADF module and constructs rescue strategies. Additionally, several functions are developed to implement these strategies as sub-modules. They are also designed to function interchangeably, similar to the main modules. The module structure slightly varies depending on the type of rescue platoon. As an example, this paper explains the ambulance team's module structure shown in Fig. 1.

The ambulance team of AIT-Rescue comprises the following four modules. These are called by the core strategies of ADF and perform processes according to their respective roles.

AITAmbulanceHumanDetector The module determines the transport target for the ambulance team. At each step, the ambulance teams identify civilians eligible for transport based on the information they have perceived and received through communication. These eligible civilians that cannot move due to injuries are those excavated from the debris by the fire brigade. Next, the ambulance team closest to each transportable civilian is identified, and that ambulance team is assigned to transport that particular civilian. If there are multiple candidates, the nearest ambulance team is selected. This method allows numerous ambulance teams to focus on the same target, ensuring efficient transport.

AITExtActionTransport The module determines the commands necessary for transporting targets, calculating the route to the civilian or refuge and issuing commands for movement along those routes. These commands represent the specific actions of agents. For example, commands for ambulance teams include moving, loading, and unloading. Additionally, the model is responsible for selecting the appropriate refuge as the transport destination.

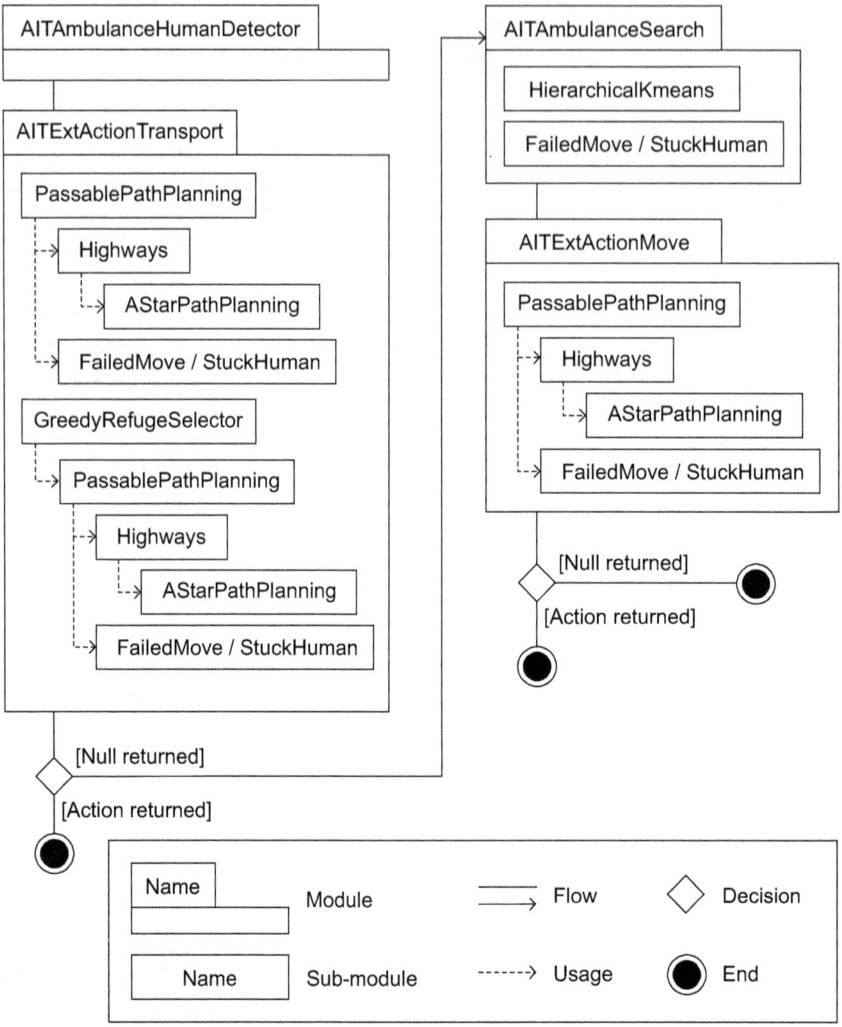

Fig. 1. The AIT-Rescue ambulance team consists of four modules: AITAmbulanceHumanDetector, AITExtActionTransport, AITAmbulanceSearch, and AITExtActionMove. These modules are attached to the basic strategy (DefaultTacticsAmbulanceTeam) provided by ADF for the ambulance team, enabling the realization of the plan through each module's functions. Each module includes several sub-modules used to solve sub-problems derived from complex issues. For example, in the AIT-Rescue ambulance team, the PassablePathPlanning sub-module is employed for pathfinding, considering priority roads and debris.

AITAmbulanceSearch The module determines the destination for locating injured civilians. The ambulance team patrols the unexplored buildings in their assigned area, proceeding in order from the closest. Additionally, they listen to civilian calls for help and move in that direction. There are two types of calls: "Help," which indicates that the civilian is trapped under debris, and "Ouch," which suggests that the civilian is injured and unable to move. Since the ambulance team is responsible for transporting civilians who are wounded and face difficulty in moving, this module searches for buildings in the direction where "Ouch" calls are heard.

AITExtActionMove The module determines commands for moving toward the exploration target, designating a building or road as the destination and executing pathfinding. Based on the result, movement commands are issued.

The ambulance team's sub-modules include the following:

PassablePathPlanning The module performs pathfinding considering priority roads and debris. Based on the A* algorithm [5], it evaluates the routes according to priority and accessibility. In the evaluation formula, penalties are applied to non-priority roads and roads obstructed by debris, enabling the route search to find paths that avoid these difficult-to-pass roads.

Highways This module detects priority roads, providing easy access to buildings across the map.

FailedMove/StuckHuman These two modules detect situations in which an agent in motion cannot move for some reason.

GreedyRefugeSelector This module selects an appropriate refuge for transportation, considering travel time and waiting time for available beds at the sanctuary, thereby selecting the refuge where the transported civilian can be admitted to a bed in the shortest time.

HierarchicalKmeans This module determines and assigns the area of responsibility. Buildings and roads on the map are grouped based on location, with the number of ambulance teams serving as the number of groups, as determined using the K-means++ method. Then, using the Hungarian algorithm, nearby areas are assigned to each ambulance team as the area of responsibility.

3.3 Determination of Priority Roads

The police force removes the debris from the road to allow passage. However, clearing all the debris within the simulation time is difficult. As a result, only a limited number of roads allow passage by the end of the simulation. The police force must prioritize and clear roads that are effective for rescuing civilians within the limited time available.

In the AIT-Rescue strategy, priority roads are determined before the start of the rescue operation, and each rescue platoon acts primarily along these priority roads. The police force aims to ensure passage during the initial phase of the rescue activities by prioritizing the removal of debris along the priority roads. The fire brigades and ambulance teams select the priority road over other routes with uncertain traffic when choosing their paths.

All rescue platoons actively use the priority roads to search for and rescue civilians. Therefore, the priority roads must facilitate locating many civilians.

As civilians wait for rescue inside buildings, the priority roads should ideally provide easy access to as many buildings as possible.

In the Highway module, to satisfy priority roads conditions, a group of roads is selected through the following steps:

1. Cluster all buildings using the K-means++ method.
2. Extract the building closest to the center of each cluster.
3. For all combinations of the extracted centers of clusters, select the road that forms the shortest path using the A* algorithm.

An example of the priority road selection procedure is shown in Fig. 2.

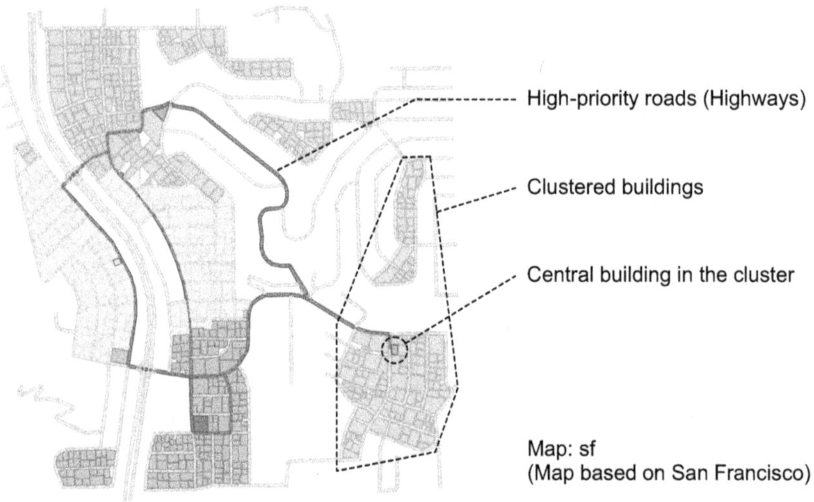

Fig. 2. The blue line indicates the priority road determined by the Highway module. The buildings on the map are divided mainly into two areas on the left and right. The priority road connects each building group, spanning the entire area. In this example, the number of clusters was set to four. Increasing the number of clusters can expand the range of the priority roads. (Color figure online)

3.4 Refuge Selection

Civilians transported by the ambulance team to a refuge are not always guaranteed access to a bed. Each sanctuary has a set number of beds; if all beds are occupied, civilians must wait until a bed becomes available. During this waiting period, a civilian's physical condition may deteriorate depending on the injuries, which could lead to death in some cases. Furthermore, agents cannot assess their current situation if they are far from a refuge. Therefore, the ambulance team must anticipate the status of each shelter and choose a refuge where beds are likely to be available when transporting civilians.

AIT-Rescue designed a new module for selecting refuge. Considering the RoboCupRescue Simulation League 2022, the beds in refuges are a new element. The standard ADF modules do not have a function for determining the destination refuge. Therefore, AIT-Rescue added a new module called RefugeSelector, a submodule of ExtActionMove, to select the sanctuary.

RefugeSelector calculates the travel time to each refuge and the waiting time for available beds at the sanctuary when the ambulance team transports an injured civilian. These calculations determine the refuge where the civilians can be helped in the shortest time for the civilian to be transported. Travel and waiting times are estimated based on the information gathered during the simulation step.

In transporting civilians to a refuge, the time until a civilian is admitted to a bed is determined by the longer of the duration between travel and waiting time. This determination is because the calculated waiting time is based on the time of dispatch, and all or a portion of the waiting time may be spent during transport. If travel time is longer than waiting time, the waiting time has already elapsed by the time of arrival. Consequently, the bed becomes available immediately, allowing the civilian to be accommodated upon arrival. On the other hand, if the waiting time exceeds travel time, the civilian will wait in the refuge for the remaining waiting time after arrival.

The travel time is calculated by dividing the path distance to the refuge by the ambulance team's travel speed. The path distance is computed using the PassablePathPlanning module. AIT-Rescue calculates the length of the road center lines included in the path as path distance. Additionally, values obtained from prior experiments are used to determine the travel speed. This value is calculated by repeatedly moving the ambulance teams between random locations and averaging the observed travel speed.

The waiting time at the refuge is calculated using the queueing model M/M/-m. This model represents a situation where m service counters process a single queue in parallel, applying it to scenarios such as the refuge, where multiple counters (beds) process civilians in parallel.

The average waiting time of W at the refuge is expressed as follows:

$$W = \pi_0 \frac{\rho(c\rho)^c}{\lambda(1-\rho)^2 c!}, \tag{1}$$

where

- c: number of beds,
- λ: number of civilians transported to the refuge per simulation step,
- μ: average number of civilians discharged from beds per simulation step,
- $\rho = \lambda/\mu$: utilization rate of the system, including transportation and treatment at the refuge.

The time required for treatment depends on the civilian's degree of injury, but this module calculates μ based on the average time required. Let the average injury degree of the civilians in the refuge be denoted as $\bar{D}$. Since each bed can restore one injury par simulation step, μ can be defined as $\mu = 1/\bar{D}$. Furthermore, the probability π_0 that no civilians are waiting can be calculated as follows:

$$\pi_0 = \left[\left(\sum_{k=0}^{c-1} \frac{(c\rho)^k}{k!} \right) + \frac{(c\rho)^c}{c!} \frac{1}{1-\rho} \right]^{-1}. \tag{2}$$

4 Competition Results and Discussion

This paper compared the rescue score of AIT-Rescue with that of the standard team (sample agents) using the scenario from the 2024 competition finals. As shown in Table 1, the AIT-Rescue score exceeded that of the standard team in all scenarios, leading to the conclusion that the rescue strategy of AIT-Rescue saves more civilians than the standard team.

Table 1. Comparing the scores of AIT-Rescue for the standard team

Scenario	Standard Team	AIT-Rescue*
sydney1	43.60	44.46
eindhoven2	5.11	5.23
montreal1	31.60	31.83
istanbul1	225.47	225.47
paris1	57.08	58.17
sf1	20.02	24.63
kobe2	183.84	184.59
eindhoven3	19.21	19.48
vc2	37.59	38.05
bordeaux1	13.11	13.11

* : Score is above the standard, : Score is at the standard.

However, in istanbul1 and bordeaux1, the scores of both teams were the same. The results are attributed to the large amount of debris, which interfered with the progress of the rescue operation. In these scenarios, other teams were also unable to rescue any civilians. For reference, Fig. 3 shows the distribution and amount of debris in two scenarios: sf1 and istanbul1. In the simulations, even though AIT-Rescue ensured passage on priority roads, there were cases where the roads ahead offered no passage due to debris. In certain cases, some rescue platoons were isolated by debris, making the rescue of civilians difficult.

Handling the large amounts of debris will necessitate the dynamic planning of priority roads in the future. AIT-Rescue determines the priority roads before the rescue activities; however, this pre-computing cannot use information about

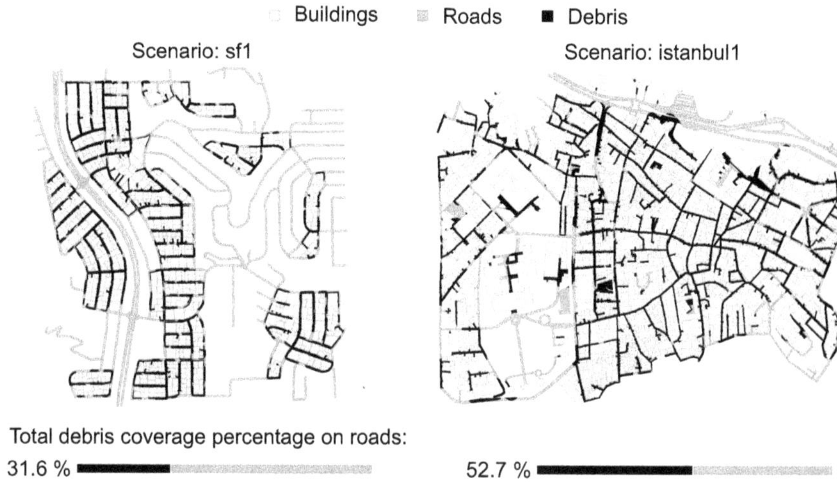

Fig. 3. In istanbul1, debris is present throughout the area, and many roads are impassable. Compared to the 52.7% istanbul1, 31.6% the road area in Sf1 is covered by debris. This difference confirms the extensive impact of the debris.

the civilian positions and debris distribution. The information obtained during the rescue activities, including perceived and shared information from other platoons' details, can make re-determination of priority roads during the operation more effective for rescue efforts.

5 Approach to Research Challenges

In the RoboCupRescue Simulation, AIT-Rescue is working on various research challenges related to multiagent systems to realize effective rescue strategies. Specific research topics include developing task allocation algorithms for the rescue platoon and investigating the relationship between maps and rescue results.

In disaster rescue operations with numerous rescue platoons and injured civilians, assigning the task of which civilian to rescue, significantly impacts the results. To address this challenge, AIT-Rescue formulates this task allocation problem as a distributed constraint optimization problem (DCOP) [2], which has been applied to developing algorithms for solutions [7]. Furthermore, a model called layered-DCOP [6], which incorporates multiple layers, has been proposed to facilitate coordination among heterogeneous rescue platoons. This method seeks solutions that satisfy various constraints, such as having the ambulance team transport civilians dug out from debris by the fire brigade and rescuing civilians within the survival time. In experiments using this model, higher rescue results have been achieved than previous methods [4].

AIT-Rescue analyzes the relationship between map complexity and rescue results, to build rescue strategies that can respond to various situations. In certain environments, rescue strategies excel, and in others, they are less effective.

Therefore, fully evaluating a strategy's effectiveness based on just one environment is impossible. To address this, simulations using a combination of various environments and strategies were conducted to analyze and determine the environments suitable for each strategy. Figure 4 shows the approach of this research [3]. The results of the covariance structure analysis provided three common indicators for evaluating team capabilities, thereby assessing which capabilities are superior among the competing teams using the indicators [1]. One future challenge is to combine the practical functions of each strategy to create a rescue strategy adaptable to various environments.

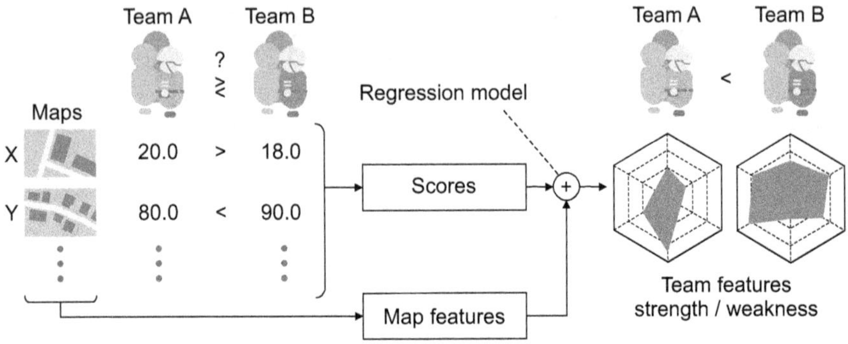

Fig. 4. When comparing two teams, A and B, through simulations on many maps containing X and Y, team A performed better than team B on map X, whereas team A performed worse than team B on map Y. Therefore, determining the superior team is impossible. AIT-Rescue analyzes the relationship between quantified map features and rescue scores in each map using a regression model. Based on the results, each team's strengths and weaknesses regarding the environmental features are evaluated.

In addition to researching technical elements for developing excellent rescue strategies, AIT-Rescue is also engaged in infrastructure building efforts. An ADF compatible with Python, Python-ADF, which is widely used in artificial intelligence technologies, was developed as part of this effort [9]. Python has recently gained in popularity, and its applications extend across many fields, offering a wide range of packages in artificial intelligence. Integrating this module into agent development, enables development of modules and technical expansion of agents.

6 Conclusion

This paper describes the rescue strategy and module design of the AIT-Rescue team, the champion team in the RoboCup 2024 Rescue Simulation League. The AIT-Rescue team designed an autonomous distributed decision-making system that can flexibly respond to complex disaster scenarios, achieving rapid civilian rescue by selecting priority roads and refuges.

Furthermore, AIT-Rescue is advancing research on multiagent systems to realize efficient rescue strategies. The plan is integrate these achievements into competition agents to develop more advanced rescue strategies. Future challenges include strengthening strategies for scenarios with large amounts of debris and further development of Python-ADF.

Acknowledgments. This work was supported by JSPS KAKENHI Grant Number JP17K00317, JP21K12039, and JP23K11225; and the Kayamori Foundation of Information Science Advancement.

References

1. Ando, K., Uchitane, T., Iwata, K., Ito, N., Jiang, Y., Ishii, N.: Social simulations using multi-agent systems. In: Probability and Statistical Models in Operations Research. Computer and Management Sciences: Including Applications to Reliability Models, pp. 117–133. Springer, Cham (2024)
2. Fioretto, F., Pontelli, E., Yeoh, W.: Distributed constraint optimization problems and applications: a survey. J. Artif. Intell. Res. **61**(1), 623–698 (2018)
3. Iwata, K., Ito, N., Koketsu, H., Ishii, N.: Analyzing map features and building information for disaster response using agent-based simulations. In: König, A., Dengel, A., Hinkelmann, K., Kise, K., Howlett, R.J., Jain, L.C. (eds.) KES 2011. LNCS (LNAI), vol. 6883, pp. 616–626. Springer, Heidelberg (2011). https://doi.org/10.1007/978-3-642-23854-3_65
4. Matsunaga, I., et al.: Design of task assignments based on ordering and time window constraints for RoboCupRescue agents. In: 2023 14th IIAI International Congress on Advanced Applied Informatics (IIAI-AAI), pp. 406–411. IEEE, Koriyama, Japan (2023)
5. Russel, S.J., Norvig, P.: Solving problems by searching. In: Artificial Intelligence: A Modern Approach, 4th edn., pp. 81–127. Pearson, Harlow, UK (2022)
6. Suslova, E., Fazli, P.: Multi-robot task allocation with time window and ordering constraints. In: 2020 IEEE/RSJ International Conference on Intelligent Robots and Systems (IROS), pp. 6909–6916. IEEE, Las Vegas, NV, USA (2020)
7. Suzuki, H., et al.: Implementation of pseudo-communication module for DCOP algorithms on RRS and improvement of binary max-sum. In: 2022 Joint 12th International Conference on Soft Computing and Intelligent Systems and 23rd International Symposium on Advanced Intelligent Systems (SCIS&ISIS), pp. 1–7. IEEE, Ise, Japan (2022)
8. Takami, S., Takayanagi, K., Jaishy, S., Ito, N., Iwata, K.: Design of agent development framework for RoboCupRescue simulation. In: Lee, R. (ed.) Computational Science/Intelligence and Applied Informatics, pp. 185–199. Springer, Cham (2017)
9. Uehara, H., Shimada, Y., Ando, K., Uchitane, T., Iwata, K., Ito, N.: RoboCupRescue 2024 TDP Infrastructure AIT-Rescue (Japan). Team Description Paper, RoboCup 2024 (2024)

RoboCup 2024 Humanoid KidSize Winner CIT Brains: The Challenge with the New Robot SUSTAINA-OP2^{TM}

Masato Kubotera(✉)

Department of Advanced Robotics, Chiba Institute of Technology, Narashino, Chiba, Japan
masatokubotera06@yahoo.co.jp

Abstract. The RoboCup Humanoid League has set itself the ambitious objective of developing humanoid robots capable of winning a soccer match against the most recent FIFA World Cup champions by the middle of the 21st century. This paper provides an overview of the development and performance of CIT Brains, the winning team of the RoboCup 2024 Humanoid League KidSize class, within the context of the league's evolving trends and challenges. The SUSTAINA-OP2 robot represents a significant advancement from its predecessor, the SUSTAINA-OP robot, which was first introduced at RoboCup 2022. In response to the ongoing developments of the league, the SUSTAINA-OP2 incorporates newly released actuators and a new computer board. The robot was constructed using components that can be readily procured through online shops in conjunction with custom parts sourced from external manufacturing services. All design data is made available as open hardware on github.com/SUSTAINA-OP2. These developments are based on the league's progress and will facilitate future competition requirements.

Keywords: Open Hardware · Platform Robot · Humanoid Robot · RoboCup

1 Introduction

This paper presents an overview of the CIT Brains team, awarded the world championship in the RoboCup 2024 Humanoid League KidSize class, held in Eindhoven, Netherlands, in July 2024. The team's robot, SUSTAINA-OP2^{TM}, represents a significant evolution from its predecessor, SUSTAINA-OP^{TM}. The latter was developed to address specific challenges faced during previous competitions. The design of SUSTAINA-OP2^{TM} aimed to improve robot durability and reduce preparation time, which proved to be critical factors in the team's success during this competition (Fig. 1).

E. Barros et al. (Eds.): RoboCup 2024, LNAI 15570, pp. 448–460, 2025.
https://doi.org/10.1007/978-3-031-85859-8_38

Fig. 1. The CIT Brains team members are pictured at the awards ceremony (left) and CIT Brains' SUSTAINA-OP2™ vs. KURA's robot in the final match (right)*. (Color figure online)

1.1 Team Overview and Preparation for RoboCup 2024

Since 2007, CIT Brains has been involved in the RoboCup Humanoid League, achieving the World Championship title three times by 2023, in 2014, 2015 and 2022. For RoboCup 2024, the team had four master's students and one advising professor. Despite its small size, the team developed a new robot, SUSTAINA-OP2™, for the competition.

In previous competitions, we encountered several challenges, including the effects of wear on the actuators due to the rigors of competition and the inherent complexities of system development. These issues were particularly evident in the context of the RoboCup 2023 competition, which necessitated a considerable investment of time in preparation for the matches. In light of these experiences, the RoboCup 2024 team concentrated on enhancing the robot's hardware to augment its durability and reduce the preparation time.

1.2 Results at RoboCup 2024

Our team won in the RoboCup 2024 Humanoid League KidSize class, consistently performing well throughout the tournament. In addition to winning the main 4-on-4 soccer competition, the team placed first in the Drop-in Challenge, where mixed teams were formed with robots contributed by various teams. Moreover, CIT Brains earned second place in the Best Humanoid Award, aggregating points from competitions across KidSize and AdultSize classes.

The final match[1] of RoboCup 2024, as shown in Fig. 2, was one of the most intense in recent years. After two 10-minute halves, the score remained tied at 2-2, leading to extra time. The decisive goal was scored during the second half of extra time, extending the match to 40 min. The reliability of the SUSTAINA-OP2™ in performing under such extended conditions significantly contributed to the team's success.

[1] **Final match video:** https://www.twitch.tv/videos/2209867454.

Fig. 2. The 4-on-4 soccer competition, the final match between CIT Brains and KURA in RoboCup 2024*.(Color figure online)

1.3 Participation and Progress in the Humanoid League KidSize Class

At RoboCup 2024, 15 teams from 11 countries participated in the Humanoid League KidSize class, showcasing various robot designs, as summarized in Table 1. Notably, Rhoban Football Club (University of Bordeaux, France), the 2023 champions [1], did not participate in 2024. Their absence created a noticeable gap in the competition, and their presence was notably missed.

Two new teams, KURA (Khalifa University, AE) and Blenders Football Club (Monterrey Institute of Technology, MX), made remarkable debuts. KURA advanced to the final round with a robot based on Rhoban's Sigmaban kinematic design[2], demonstrating the lasting impact of established designs. Meanwhile, Blenders used the ROBOTIS-OP3 platform[3], emphasizing the importance of open hardware platforms for new teams entering the competition.

Compared to previous years, the number of robots participating in the soccer competition increased, and the games became more complex. However, collisions and falls became more common as the robots crowded around the ball. The ability of the robots to recover quickly from falls and to quickly identify and track the ball became essential performance factors.

Only a few teams managed to field all four robots in the 4-on-4 soccer competition, and many struggled with robot preparation. Our team opted to withhold some robots to avoid excessive wear, but localization issues caused frequent exits from the field. Additionally, the intense spotlighting conditions at RoboCup 2024 posed challenges, as the robots needed to adapt to changing lighting. This highlighted the need for more robust systems.

Despite increased participation, performance disparities persisted within the KidSize class. Financial constraints posed challenges for many teams in developing new robots or upgrading their existing systems. Further technological advancement and collaboration are essential to narrow the performance gap and create a more competitive environment in future competitions (Fig. 3).

[2] **RoboCup 2024 KURA Robot Specification:** https://humanoid.robocup.org/wp-content/uploads/2024-kura-specs.pdf.

[3] **RoboCup 2024 Blenders Football Club Robot Specification:**https://humanoid.robocup.org/wp-content/uploads/2024-blenders-fc-specs.pdf.

Fig. 3. The drop-in challenge (left) and the 4-on-4 soccer competition (right)*.

Table 1. Comparison of robots from teams participating in the RoboCup 2024 Humanoid League KidSize class[4].

Team name	Region	Height (mm)	Weight (kg)	Speed (m/s)	Actuator series	Main computer	Camera
Barelang FC	ID	690	6.5	0.34	ROBOTIS MX	NVIDIA Jetson Xavier NX	Logitech C920
Bold Hearts	UK	615	3.1	0.03	ROBOTIS MX	Odroid Xu4	Logitech C920
CIT Brains	JP	750	7.6		KONDO PMX	NVIDIA Jetson Orin Nano	e-con Systems e-CAM50_CUNX
Hamburg Bit-Bots	DE	825	7.1	0.35	ROBOTIS MX/XH	AMD NUC Ryzen 5000U	Basler acA2040-35gc
Ichiro ITS	ID	563	5.0	0.25	ROBOTIS MX	Intel NUC i3-10110U	Logitech C930
ITAndroids	BR	530	3.1	0.30	ROBOTIS MX	Intel NUC i5	Logitech C920
KURA	AE	650	6.8	0.20	ROBOTIS MX	Intel NUC i7	2 × FLIR Blackfly S
NUbots	AU	900	7.65	0.20	ROBOTIS MX/XH	Intel NUC i7-1260P	2 × FLIR BlackFly S
RO:BIT	KR	660	6.2	0.30	ROBOTIS MX	Intel NUC i5-10210U	oCam-1CGN-U
RoboFEI	BR	740	6.8	0.28	ROBOTIS XM	Intel NUC i7-5500U	Logitech C920
Blenders FC	MX	510	3.2	0.07	ROBOTIS XM	Intel NUC i3-7100U	Logitech C920
TH-MOS	CN	597	5.1	0.30	ROBOTIS MX	NVIDIA Jetson TX2	Hongshikang Cmosm
UTRA	CA	500	2.3	0.08	ROBOTIS MX/AX	NVIDIA Jetson TX2	Logitech C920
WF Wolves	DE	860	6.4	0.23	ROBOTIS MX	Intel NUC i7-7567U	Logitech C920
ZJUDancer	CN	673	4.0	0.08	ROBOTIS MX	NVIDIA Jetson Orin NX	Omnivision Ov2710

1.4 The Role of Open Hardware in Accelerating Robot Development

Open hardware platforms such as the Wolfgang-OP [3] and DARwIn-OP [4] have played a critical role in accelerating robot development within the league. By providing access to open-source designs, these platforms allow teams to reduce development time and focus on refining their systems, fostering collaboration and innovation across the league.

The SUSTAINA-OP™ platform, introduced for RoboCup 2022, encourages the development of robots in the league. Its design data is available at github.com/SUSTAINA-OP. As shown in Fig. 4, many teams are adopting elements of its design. This open-source approach enables rapid iteration and improvement by a wider community.

Additionally, the continuous evolution of circuit boards is shown in Fig. 5. The actuator control circuit board based on the FT4232H of the Wolfgang CORE[4], which enabled high-frequency servo communication [2], has been adopted in various robot designs.

[4] **Wolfgang CORE:** https://github.com/bit-bots/wolfgang_core.

This pattern of sharing and evolving hardware components demonstrates how open hardware platforms can drive progress in the RoboCup Humanoid League, leading to the development of increasingly sophisticated and competitive robots.

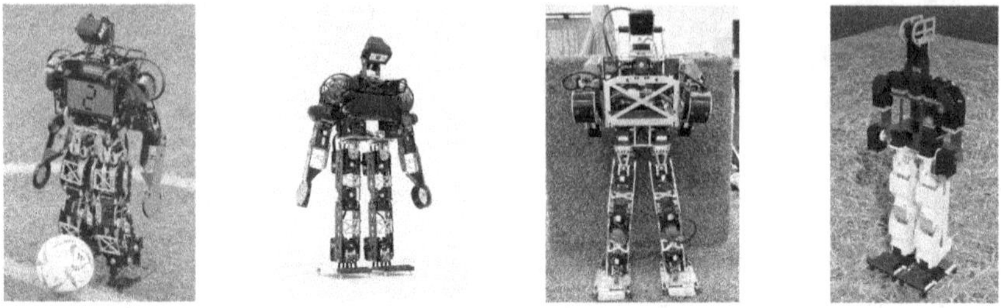

SUSTAINA-OP™ (CIT Brains, JP) | Siber (ICHIRO ITS, ID) | Chul Su OP.4 (RO:BIT, KR) | Susteinaban (RoboFEI, BR)

Fig. 4. SUSTAINA-OP™ and its inspired humanoid robots used by various teams.

1st gen.: Wolfgang-OP | 2nd gen.: SUSTAINA-OP™ | 3rd gen.: Siber

Fig. 5. Inheritance of actuator control circuit boards using FT4232H.

2 Overview of the New Robot SUSTAINA-OP2™

2.1 Development Goals and Approach

The SUSTAINA-OP2™ was developed with two main goals: improving the robots' durability during matches and reducing the time needed for preparation between matches. In addition, to reduce the complexity of system development, we aimed to design it as a platform that is not dependent on computer boards.

Based on SUSTAINA-OP™, SUSTAINA-OP2™ incorporates lessons learned from previous competitions. The hardware design was completed in about two months, and the entire process, from the initial design to the mass production of five units for the competition, was completed within six months. Considering the constraints of being a small team, we adopted a manufacturing approach emphasizing efficiency and flexibility, such as using external manufacturing services to procure almost all mechanical parts and circuit boards.

An overview of the SUSTAINA-OP2™ specifications is provided in Table 2. More detailed technical descriptions can be found in related publications [6].

Table 2. Overview of SUSTAINA-OP2^{TM} specifications.

Category		Specification
Fundamental	Height · Weight	750 mm · 7.55 kg (Battery included)
	DoF	21 DoFs
	Battery	LiPO 11.1V 3S1P 3250mAh MaxAmps MA-3250-3 s-Lipo-Pack Max. 20 min. continuous walking
	Materials	A7075, CFRP, POM, TPU, PLA, etc.
Actuators	Servo motors	8 × KONDO PMX-SCR-9203HV 2 × KONDO PMX-SCR-9204HV 10 × KONDO PMX-SCR-5203HV 1 × KONDO PMX-SCR-5204HV
Sensors	IMU	TDK DK-42668-P
	Camera	e-con Systems e-CAM50_CUNX
	Camera lens	Commonlands CIL926-F2.4-M12A650 168 ∘ (D) · 133 ∘ (H) · 99 ∘ (V)
	Encoders	Contactless magnetic 16bit/round in actuator
	Strain gauge	8 × Sensor and Control SC700-40kg with 2 × 32bit 38ksps ADC
	Audio	1 × DFROBOT SEN0539-EN 1 × DFROBOT DFR0299 with Speaker
	Current & Power	7 × Texas Instruments INA226
Control boards	System-on-Module	NVIDIA Jetson Orin Nano 8GB
	Carrier board	NVIDIA Jetson Orin Nano Developer Kit
	Microcontroller	5 × Arduino Nano ESP32
	Custom boards	12 types 20 boards

2.2 Rapid Development Process

The SUSTAINA-OP2^{TM}'s development relied heavily on external manufacturing services to expedite custom parts production. Components made from materials such as A7075 aluminum, POM, CFRP, and 3D-printed materials were produced by companies such as JLC3DP, MISUMI meviy, and ALLPCB. These manufacturers provided high-precision mechanical components, reducing the time and complexity of in-house fabrication. Printed circuit boards (PCBs) were produced by JLCPCB, which supplied pre-assembled boards based on our design files, significantly reducing manual assembly time and allowing the team to focus on testing and software integration.

Figure 6 shows examples of custom parts essential to accelerating the robot's development.

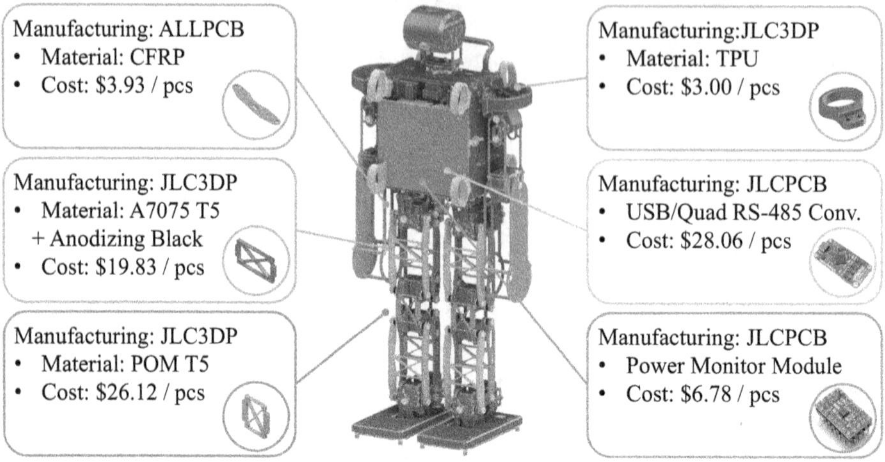

Fig. 6. Examples of outsourced parts used in SUSTAINA-OP2^{TM}, including mechanical components and PCBs manufactured by JLC3DP, MISUMI meviy, ALLPCB, JLCPCB.

The total production cost for a single robot was approximately 12,500 USD (1,800,000 JPY), excluding shipping and customs fees. By outsourcing key components, parts typically arrive within 10 days, and the robot could be fully assembled in about two weeks. This significantly reduced the time and effort compared to traditional in-house production methods, which often require extensive manual machining and soldering. Although outsourcing increased production costs compared to in-house manufacturing, the time savings and reduction in manual labor allowed us to focus on improving the robot's overall performance. Furthermore, the open hardware design of SUSTAINA-OP2^{TM}, available on github.com/SUSTAINA-OP2, supports further customization and adaptation by other teams, fostering collaboration and innovation within the RoboCup community.

3 Mechanical Design Enhancements for SUSTAINA-OP2^{TM}

The SUSTAINA-OP2^{TM} was developed to address specific challenges faced during RoboCup competitions. It improves durability and reduces the time required for robot preparation between matches. By enhancing the robot's ability to withstand impacts and minimizing wear and tear, we aim to streamline maintenance tasks, allowing the robot to perform reliably throughout the games.

3.1 Performance-Oriented Modifications

Several vital modifications were implemented to meet the increasing demands for walking stability and stronger kicks in the RoboCup Humanoid League. The robot's height was increased from 647 mm to 750 mm, allowing for longer strides and improved leg motion. A new pitch axis was also introduced in the foot, improving walking control and increasing kicking power. These changes were essential to maintaining competitiveness within the evolving league. As shown in Fig. 7, adding the pitch axis and the increased height significantly enhanced SUSTAINA-OP2^{TM}'s range of motion compared to its predecessor, SUSTAINA-OP^{TM}.

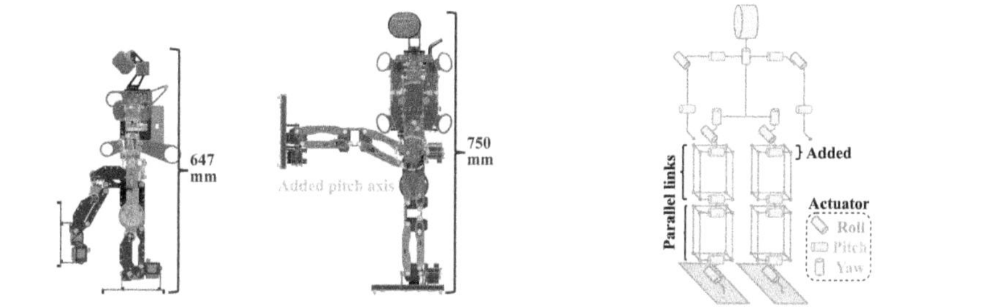

Fig. 7. Range of motion improvements in SUSTAINA-OP2^{TM}. The increased height and the added pitch axis in the foot resulted in more stable walking and stronger kicks.

3.2 Durability Improvements for Collisions and Falls

Durability has always been a critical focus for the SUSTAINA-OP^{TM} series. In the SUSTAINA-OP2^{TM}, this aspect has been further enhanced by adding cross-roller bearings to the hip joint and the joints of the shoulders and neck, which are prone to impact. In addition, the number of 3D-printed bumpers has been increased to 10 to provide optimal protection in the event of a drop. The bumper design was unified for the front and back, as well as the left and right sides, which allowed us to reduce manufacturing costs while expanding the range of protection.

Figure 8 shows the TPU bumper that protects the mechanical structure and precision electronics from damage due to impact. In addition, one-touch resin spacers that prevent distortion and vibration have been added to protect the electronics. These spacers are essential for maintaining stable communication and preventing damage to the circuit board.

Fig. 8. 3D-printed TPU bumpers attached to SUSTAINA-OP2^{TM} (left) and spacers used to prevent damage to the circuit boards (right).

3.3 Actuator Improvements and Reinforcements

The SUSTAINA-OP2^{TM}'s actuator has been upgraded to the KONDO PMX series, which has improved durability by eliminating the spline and adopting an I-cut output shaft. Furthermore, with the exception of joints that require a wide range of movement (shoulder roll, hip yaw, neck yaw, etc.), all joints are equipped with an external reduction mechanism. This mechanism uses maintenance-free plain bearings and an oscillating slider crank mechanism to minimize the direct load on the motor and reduce wear.

Figure 9 shows an example of this mechanism applied to a knee joint. As a result, during RoboCup 2024, the number of fatal failures of actuators was only two in the shoulder roll axis, which did not have this mechanism, and this was the lowest record in the history of the competition.

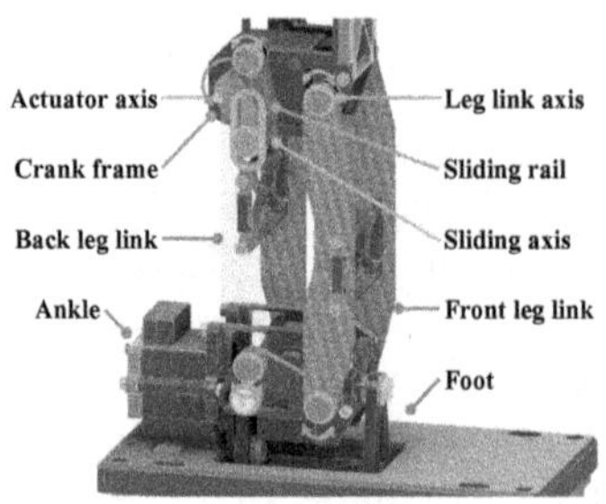

Fig. 9. An example of a knee joint equipped with a deceleration mechanism using a oscillating slider crank mechanism to reduce wear on the actuator.

4 Electronics Design

4.1 Overview of the Electrical System

The SUSTAINA-OP^{TM} series employs the NVIDIA Jetson System-on-Module (SoM) as the primary computing board. The earlier version, SUSTAINA-OP^{TM}, used a Jetson Xavier NX 8GB with a third-party carrier board for I/O expansion. In SUSTAINA-OP2^{TM}, we integrated the Jetson Orin Nano Developer Kit, resolving compatibility issues and simplifying development. This carrier board also supports other modules from the Orin series, offering flexibility for future upgrades.

The sensor system in SUSTAINA-OP2^{TM} was redesigned with all modules standardized to USB interfaces, simplifying hardware integration. Initially, a USB camera was used for its simplicity. However, based on the lessons learned from RoboCup 2022 [5], where we introduced the CSI camera, we reverted to the CSI camera during competition for more stable performance. The USB camera suffered frequent disconnections due to impacts, which the CSI camera avoided under RoboCup's demanding conditions.

In addition to the camera, other components—such as the IMU, system status LEDs, control buttons, voltage/current loggers, audio I/O modules, and foot pressure sensors—are connected via the RS-485 communication bus. This uniform interface minimizes custom connections, simplifying maintenance and ensuring scalability.

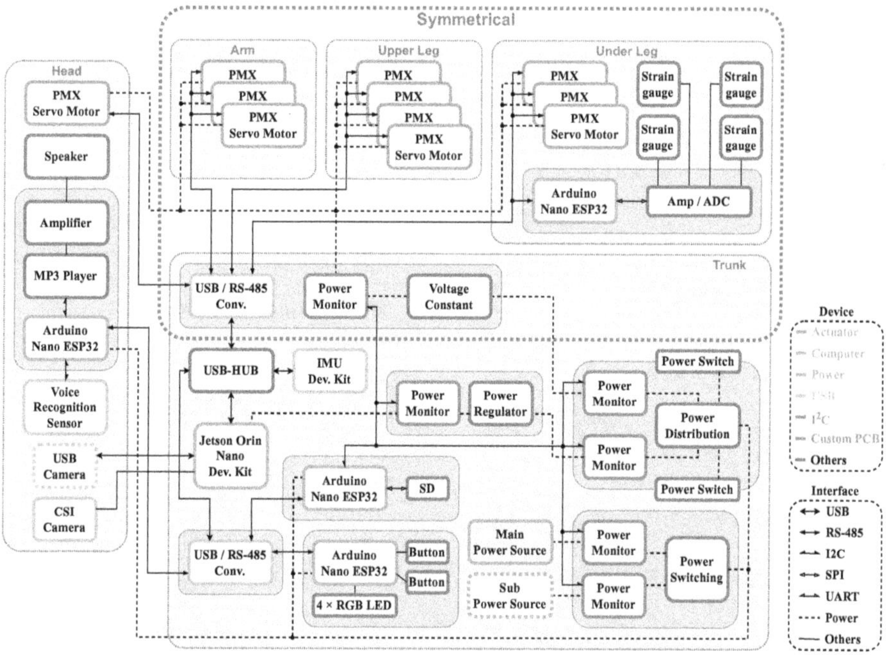

Fig. 10. Electrical schematic of the SUSTAINA-OP2^{TM}.

As shown in Fig. 10, the system architecture integrates these components efficiently, supporting the performance improvements of SUSTAINA-OP2^{TM}.

4.2 Consistent Actuator Performance

The SUSTAINA-OP^{TM}, powered by a 3S1P 2800mAh LiPo battery, enabled the robot to walk continuously for up to 30 min [7]. However, a significant challenge emerged with actuator performance declining over time.

To address this problem, the SUSTAIN-OP2^{TM} incorporates a constant voltage circuit inspired by Wolfgang Constant Voltage[5]. By incorporating this circuit on the left and right sides of the SUSTAIN-OP2^{TM} and supplying a stable power supply to the actuator, it has become possible to maintain a stable voltage regardless of battery fluctuations, as shown in Fig. 11. This has made it possible to eliminate performance variations during gameplay and the performance difference between input from the AC adapter during development and input from the battery during gameplay.

Figure 12 shows a comparison with the original, and the SUSTAINA-OP2^{TM} model has a USB port on the circuit board, so it is possible to control the actuators with maintained performance by connecting the computer board

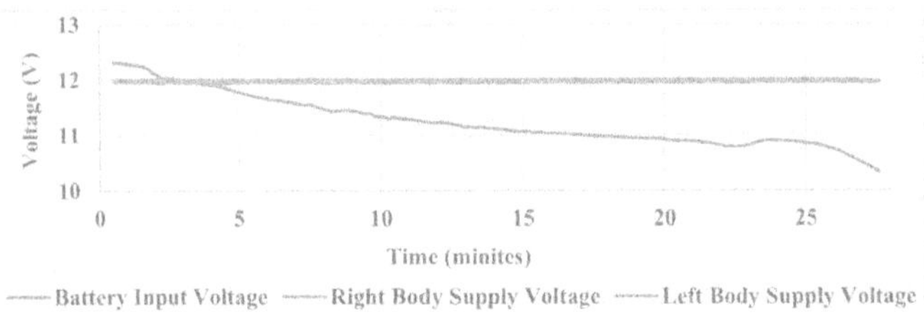

Fig. 11. Voltage of the battery and actuator during continuous walking until battery depletion after introducing the constant voltage circuits.

Fig. 12. Comparison of circuits: Wolfgang-OP (left) and SUSTAINA-OP2^{TM} (right).

[5] **Wolfgang Constant Voltage:** https://github.com/bit-bots/wolfgang_constant_voltage.

and the power supply. Furthermore, it is compatible with a wide range of battery voltages from 9V to 53V to support the low-cell batteries commonly used in the Humanoid League KidSize class.

5 Conclusion

In this paper, we reported on the factors that led to the CIT Brains team's victory in the KidSize class of RoboCup 2024 using SUSTAINA-OP2™ and the technical approaches used. In developing SUSTAINA-OP2™, the primary goals were to improve the robot's durability and reduce the preparation time between matches. These improvements contributed significantly to stable performance during the competition.

Thanks to the addition of an external deceleration mechanism, reinforced bumpers, and circuit protection, the SUSTAINA-OP2™ was able to withstand more shocks during matches than previous models, and there were no withdrawals due to hardware problems. In addition, the reduced wear on the actuators meant that they needed to be replaced less frequently than in previous years, contributing to the reduction in preparation time. Furthermore, adopting a constant voltage power supply has reduced overloads at the end of matches, enabling stable performance to be maintained and wear on the actuators to be reduced.

By utilizing the open platform's characteristics and external manufacturing services, SUSTAINA-OP2™ has a flexible design that allows other teams to customize and improve it quickly. This approach enables cost efficiency and rapid parts procurement, and it is hoped that other teams will use SUSTAINA-OP2™ to improve their technology and contribute to the league's overall improvement.

References

1. Allali, J., et al.: Rhoban Football Club: RoboCup Humanoid Kid-Size 2023 Champion Team Paper. RoboCup 2023: Robot World Cup XXVI, pp. 325–336 (2024)
2. Bestmann, M., Güldenstein, J., Zhang, J.: High-frequency multi bus servo and sensor communication using the Dynamixel protocol. In: Chalup, S., Niemueller, T., Suthakorn, J., Williams, M.-A. (eds.) RoboCup 2019. LNCS (LNAI), vol. 11531, pp. 16–29. Springer, Cham (2019). https://doi.org/10.1007/978-3-030-35699-6_2
3. Bestmann, M., Güldenstein, J., Vahl, F., Zhang, J.: Wolfgang-OP: a robust humanoid robot platform for research and competitions. In: 2020 IEEE-RAS 20th International Conference on Humanoid Robots (Humanoids), pp. 90–97 (2021)
4. Ha, I., Tamura, Y., Asama, H., Han, J., Hong, D.W.: Development of open humanoid platform DARwIn-OP. SICE Ann. Conf. **2011**, 2178–2181 (2011)
5. Hayashibara, Y., et al.: RoboCup2022 KidSize League Winner CIT Brains: Open Platform Hardware SUSTAINA-OP and Software. RoboCup 2022: Robot World Cup XXV, pp. 215–227 (2023)

6. Kubotera, M., Hayashibara, Y.: SUSTAINA-OP2^{TM}: customizable kid-sized open hardware platform humanoid robot for research and competition. In: 2024 IEEE-RAS 23rd International Conference on Humanoid Robots (Humanoids), pp. 706–713 (2024)
7. Kubotera, M., Hayashibara, Y.: SUSTAINA-OP^{TM}: Kid-sized Open Hardware Platform Humanoid Robot with Emphasis on Sustainability. RoboCup 2023: Robot World Cup XXVI, pp. 166–178 (2024)

Hibikino-Musashi@Home RoboCup@Home DSPL Champion 2024

Akinobu Mizutani[1(✉)], Kosei Isomoto[1], Kosei Yamao[1], Ryohei Kobayashi[1], Soma Fumoto[2], Koshun Arimura[1], Naoki Yamaguchi[1], Tomoya Shiba[1], Kouki Kimizuka[1], Yuta Ohno[1], Ryo Terashima[1], Hiromasa Yamaguchi[1], Tomoaki Fujino[1], Ryoga Maruno[1], Wataru Yoshimura[1], Kazuhito Mine[1], Tang Phu Thien Nhan[2], Yuga Yano[1], Yuichiro Tanaka[1], Takeshi Nishida[2], Takashi Morie[1], and Hakaru Tamukoh[1]

[1] Kyushu Institute of Technology, 2-4 Hibikino, Wakamatsu, Kitakyushu, Fukuoka 808-0196, Japan
mizutani.akinobu515@mail.kyutech.jp, hma@brain.kyutech.ac.jp

[2] The University of Kitakyushu, 1-1 Hibikino, Wakamatsu, Kitakyushu, Fukuoka 808-0135, Japan
https://www.brain.kyutech.ac.jp/~hma/

Abstract. This paper provides an overview of the techniques employed by Hibikino-Musashi@Home during their participation in the Domestic Standard Platform League (DSPL). The team developed a robust perception system, navigation system, and task planner, as well as demonstrated their ability to secure first place in the DSPL. In particular, this paper summarizes the technologies employed in the competition.

1 Introduction

Hibikino-Musashi@Home (HMA) is a robot development team comprised of students from Kyushu Institute of Technology and the University of Kitakyushu in Japan. The team was founded in 2010, and has participated in the RoboCup@Home JapanOpen in the Open Platform League (OPL), Domestic Standard Platform League (DSPL), and Simulation-DSPL. Furthermore, the team regularly participates in the RoboCup@Home league since 2017 and secured the first place in the RoboCup 2024 DSPL. In addition, the team participated in the World Robot Challenge (WRC) in 2018 and 2020 as well as in the Service Robotics Category of the Partner Robot Challenge (Real Space). HMA focuses on perception system development, particularly dataset generation systems for training object-recognition systems. The team also develops libraries for primitive tasks, including navigation, human tracking, and object recognition with spatial relationship understanding. HMA is interested in expanding the ability of robots in a real home using a brain-inspired artificial intelligence system. The following Sects. 2–4 are based on our 2024 Team Description Paper [4].

E. Barros et al. (Eds.): RoboCup 2024, LNAI 15570, pp. 461–472, 2025.
https://doi.org/10.1007/978-3-031-85859-8_39

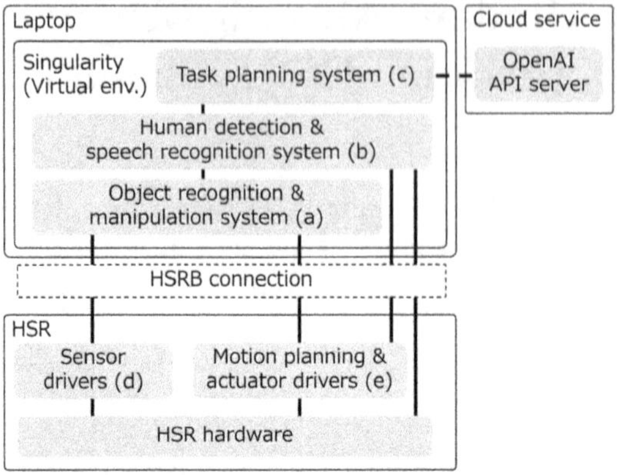

Fig. 1. Block diagram providing an overview of the HSR system. [HSR, Human Support Robot; ROS, robot operating system]

2 System Overview

We used an external laptop (ThinkPad X1 Extreme Gen5) mounted on the back of the TOYOTA Human Support Robot (HSR) to compute systems requiring high computational power. The computer inside the HSR is used to run basic HSR libraries, such as sensor drivers, motion planners, and actuator drivers. The system is mostly complete within the mounted laptop and internal HSR computer, except for the LLM API server.

Figure 1 presents an overview of the software systems used by HMA for HSR [21]. Our system operates on Singularity [19], a virtual environment tool built on a laptop mounted on the HSR. The system comprises an object recognition and manipulation system (a), a human and speech recognition system (b), and a task planning system (c), which are all connected to the sensor and actuator drivers (d) and (e) on the internal computer of HSR, respectively. The task planning system (c) communicates with the OpenAI API server [1] via the Internet.

3 Perception

3.1 Object Recognition

The object recognition system is a crucial component of robot systems. We adopted a strategy leveraging the YOLOv8 [5] and Language Segment-Anything [9]. We selected the ideal system for each task depending on the target objects.

YOLO. YOLOv8 has a low latency with sufficient accuracy to recognize the known objects in the competition. We fine-tuned the YOLO system to recognize the objects used in the competition using a large training dataset generated by the 3D simulation system based on the PyBullet [3] simulator [13]. We first

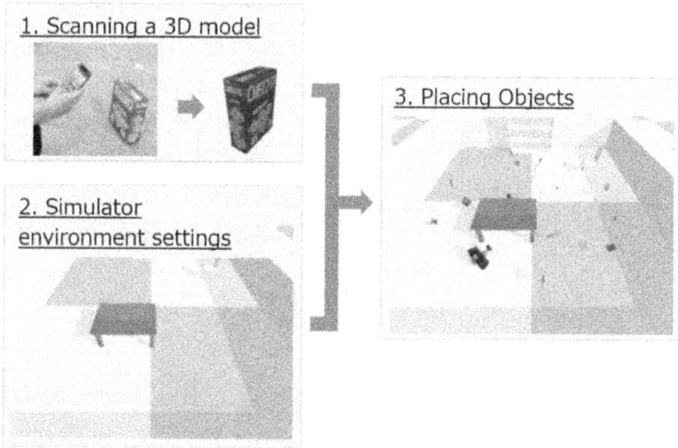

Fig. 2. Placing scanned objects on a 3D simulator.

created a 3D model of each object using a smartphone with LiDAR sensors to generate the training dataset, as shown in Fig. 2. The scanned 3D objects were spawned in the 3D environment. Subsequently, the objects and the environment were simultaneously shot from various angles to create a dataset with 500,000 images in less than 2 h using a six-core CPU. The lighting conditions, furniture placement, and background texture (floor, wall, and ceiling) were changed to randomize a domain at each shot. The annotation data for the training data can be generated automatically by the system; no manual annotation is required.

Language Segment-Anything. Language Segment-Anything [9] is a combination of Grounding DINO [10] and Segment Anything [7]. Grounding DINO is a recognition system that can be tuned by providing text prompts. The segment Anything Model (SAM) can output the segmentation mask of the object without any fine-tuning. In this method, the human has to provide the text prompt, which determines the recognition accuracy. However, the system can be tuned quickly without fine-tuning; thus, the known objects available on the competition site can be recognized without extensive preparation. The target object can be detected by providing different types of prompts, such as color, material, and category, as shown in Fig. 3. Users are required to choose and tune the prompt by checking the recognition results in advance.

3.2 Speech Recognition

We built a real-time speech recognition system. HSR acquires the voice of the speaker in frames and transmits it sequentially to an external laptop computer. Our system uses voice activity detection (VAD) [20] to determine when to start and stop recording. After recording, our system automatically begins speech recognition using only the audio data in the speech section. We employed Whisper [15], a high-accuracy speech recognition method.

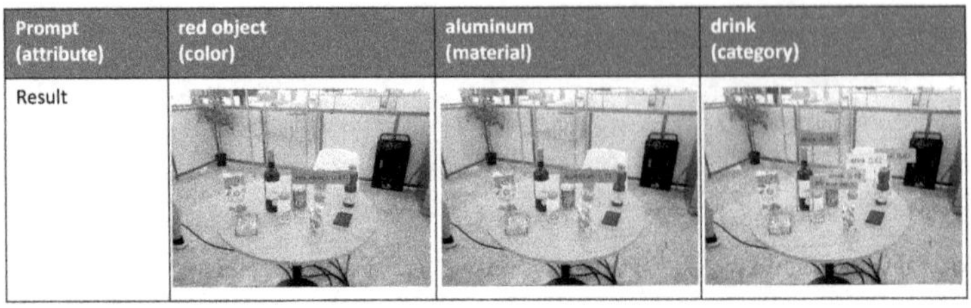

Fig. 3. Example of the prompts for Language Segment-Anything.

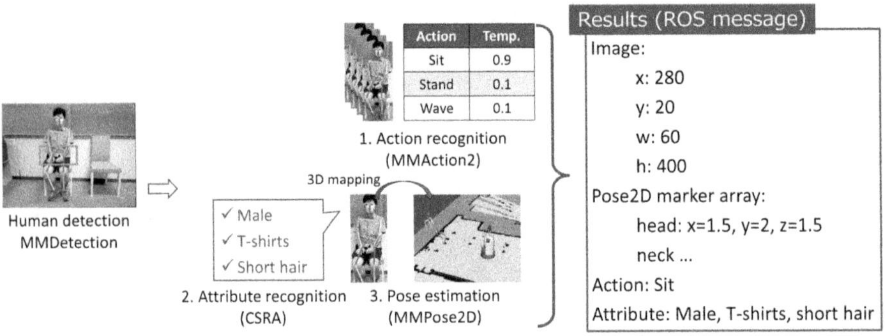

Fig. 4. Placing scanned objects on a 3D simulator.

3.3 Human Detection and Interaction

We employed the MM Libraries provided by OpenMMLab [14] for human recognition. Figure 4 demonstrates our human recognition system. We used MMDetection to detect humans and obtain cropped images. We detected human key points through MMPose and recognized human action using MMAction2. In addition, we used class-specific residual attention (CSRA) [23] to obtain human attributes, such as gender, hairstyle, and clothing.

We developed a human-robot interaction system based on the Restaurant task. However, in a real restaurant situation, customers may request or ask a question beyond the ability of the robot. The robot requests human assistance to complete tasks if beyond its ability. When addressing customer questions, the robot responds based on the situation and pre-existing knowledge. This human-robot interaction task was tested in an environment with customers [22].

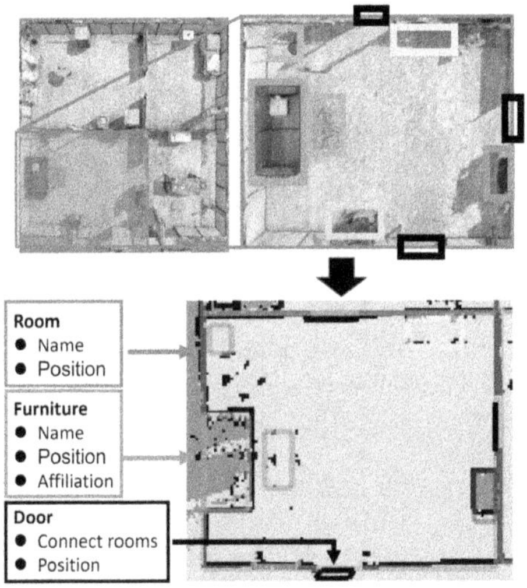

Fig. 5. Example of a semantic map

3.4 Semantic Map

A semantic map is required for the autonomous task execution of service robots. As shown in Fig. 5, we added semantic information about the room, furniture, and door to a pre-acquired environment map created using real-time appearance-based mapping (RTAB-map) [8]. Each room and furniture had a label with the name and location information using an array of two-dimensional (2D) coordinates representing the vertex information of the contours. Moreover, the furniture had information regarding the room in which it was located, and each door had information regarding the room to which it was connected. Before task execution, we defined areas of the room door and furniture positions to input into a configuration file. Subsequently, the robot uses this information to determine the semantic location in an arena to plan the path to the target position.

The path planning algorithm using semantic maps works as follows: First, the robot receives the 2D coordinates of the destination location. Thereafter, it determines the destination room and the current room position of the robot using the inside/outside determination method based on the outer product. Finally, it calculates the shortest path from the current position of the robot to its destination. This calculation includes the Euclidean distance from the position of the robot to the door, between doors that the robot passes through to reach the desired room, and from the door to the specified furniture. The algorithm can change the path of the robot by setting a door as passable or impassable. For example the robot can replan its path by setting a door as impassable after detecting that it is closed.

3.5 Navigation and Human Tracking

Our navigation system, including the path planner, obstacle detector, and human follower, is based on the Pumas navigation system released by the @Home OPL team, Pumas [16]. Notably, we improved obstacle detection functions. We integrated our semantic map system into the navigation system enabling us to influence obstacle information on the map, such as the location of furniture. Furthermore, we optimized the performance of the obstacle detection system to improve the frame rate of the point clouds for quicker obstacle detection. This enhanced navigation system, including obstacle detection and human tracking, enables the robot to navigate safely and follow the person stably.

4 Task Planning

A task planning system is required to accomplish various requests from a user in real-world environments. As shown in Fig. 6, the proposed system plans the task using command recognition results and skill sets based on the SayCan system [2].

The voice requests from the users are converted into text. The provided command may have an ambiguous word; for example, "Bring me the object". In this case, the system asks the user for the proper noun of the ambiguous word/phrase. Then, the system replaces the ambiguous word with the proper noun based on the answer from the user. The skill set is created based on available skills of the robot. The possible skills are selected based on the rule-based constrictions; for example, the same skill is not repeated consecutively, and `grasp` is after `find_obj`. The likelihood of each possible skill is calculated by the LLM, and the skill with the highest likelihood being selected as the next task for the robot until the likelihood of `done` becomes the highest.

The system requires common and environment-specific knowledge to plan the task. For example, to serve a bottle of water to a family, the possible location can be determined by common knowledge and the actual location depends on each home environment. We proposed a brain-inspired memory acquisition model with hippocampus functions to acquire environment-specific information [11, 12]. This model was designed to be implemented on low-power consumption hardware, such as FPGAs and dedicated chips [6,17,18]. We believe this model is necessary for the robot to work in a home environment and the latest research activity will be demonstrated in the *Open Challenge*.

5 Competition Results

Table 1 lists our results and Table 2 summarizes awards we received at the RoboCup 2024 Eindhoven @Home. We obtained the highest scores in Stages I, II, and Final within the DSPL. This demonstrated the effectiveness and stability of our system. However, it remains difficult to fully obtain the score in each task. The current robot system must pause when it plans tasks and recognizes

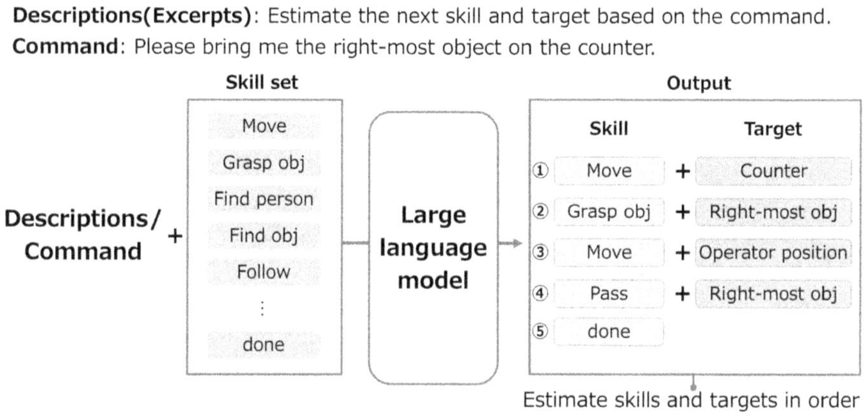

Fig. 6. Overview of the task planning

objects owing to its processing speed. We will enhance our system to continue moving during tasks to obtain the maximum score in the task. The highlights and the technical review are described in the following subsection. The digest video is available on YouTube[1].

5.1 Navigation and Obstacle Detection System

Our navigation systems performed well in all tasks, especially in an unknown environment, in which the robot must operate without a previously acquired map.

The Carry My Luggage task involved following a person to a destination and returning to the origin autonomously in an unknown environment. In the following phase, the robot has to avoid four types of obstacles. Our robot with the Pumas-based navigation system successfully reached the destination and origin in an unknown environment. Although the robot hit small obstacles on the floor, it avoided crowds, a guide pole, and a chair, owing to its fast obstacle detection system.

The Restaurant task involved taking an order from a customer and delivering the item requested by the user in an unknown environment. In the task, the robot must move to and from the start position (kitchen counter) to the customer position twice. Our robot successfully moved while avoiding obstacles, such as chairs and tables in the restaurant.

In both tasks, our robot demonstrated the best performance and received the Smoothest, Safest Navigation Award. However, the obstacle detection frequency is insufficient considering the speed of the robot. We plan to improve it in our future work.

[1] https://youtu.be/ut6FVq6vM-c.

Table 1. HMA result summary in the DSPL

Stage	Task	Score	Summary
I	Carry My Luggage	665/1,015	Reached the goal and re-entered the starting point.
	Receptionist	590/950	Guided two guests.
	Storing Groceries	570/1,140	Picked up three objects and stored two objects.
	Serving Breakfast	145/1,175	Placed two objects.
	GPSR	550/1,500	Executed one task.
II	Clean the Table	15/1,705	Navigated to the kitchen room but did not clean up.
	Restaurant	995/2,050	Detected two customers and served one order.
	Stickler for the Rules	800/2,000	Identified two broken rules by making eye contact.
	EGPSR	950/2,400	Found two persons in need and resolved one task.
	Total[4]	9,033.95	

Table 2. Awards received by HMA

Award Name	Description
Smoothest, Safest Navigation	Best performance of the navigation function
GPSR Overbot	Best in GPSR and EGPSR
Robo-host	Highest score in Receptionist and Carry My Luggage
Robo-butler	Highest score in Restaurant and Stickler for the Rules

5.2 Perception

In the competition, the objects used in each task became available during the setup days. A quick adaptation to such objects is important, especially for manipulation tasks. We only used the head RGB-D camera of the HSR for detection and grasping point estimation.

The Clean the Table task is the manipulation task, in which the robot grasps plates and utensils from the table and then places them into the washing machine. The objects used in the task were standard objects available before the competition. We used our dataset-generating system to train the YOLOv8 system for quick object detection. In Storing Groceries and Serve Breakfast tasks, we used Grounding DINO and SAM for object detection and grasping point estimations. Our system can detect objects by providing prompts to describe the characteristics of each object. The processing speed is lower than that of the YOLO systems; however, the system is considerably easier to adjust. Moreover, in the General Purpose Service Robot task, we applied a language model-powered general object detection system. The robot reported the biggest object on the coffee table, which was a flower base(the item was a decorative object).

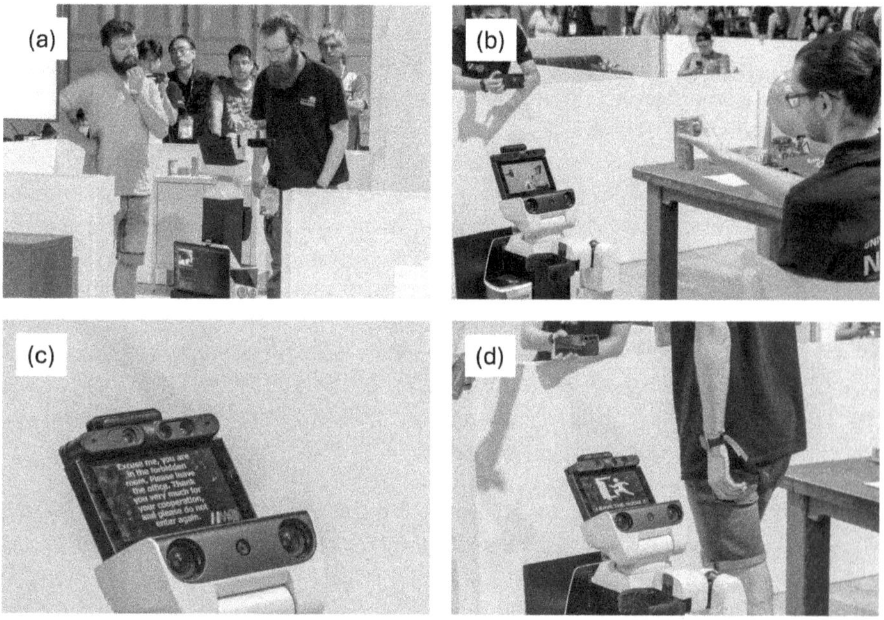

Fig. 7. HRI functions of our HSR. (a) Hight adjustment when listening to the speech. (b) Image displayed to prompt showing a drink. (c) Spoken text displayed. (d) Pictogram displayed.

Thus, we integrated three different object detection systems and switched them according to the task situations to achieve robust and flexible object detection.

5.3 Human-Robot Interaction

The external microphone was admitted to the competition this year owing to the terrible sound conditions on the site. However, our robot could recognize spoken commands using the originally installed microphone. The HSR microphone is attached to the lift part of the robot. We adjusted the height of the lift to ensure that the robot could gather sound close to the mouth of the person. The noise suppression system also contributed to improving the listening ability of the Whisper system. This voice recognition system is fundamental to smoother human-robot interaction. The dictation accuracy of short words, such as human and object names, is insufficient. We hope to improve this aspect in our future work.

In the Stickler for the Rules task, our robot politely told the rule to the person by speaking and showing a pictogram on the head display. This contributed to improving understanding in a noisy environment (Fig. 7).

5.4 Final

The theme of the final of this year is "The robot helps a person in preparing dinner". Our team demonstrated the future vision of @Home robots by expanding the GPSR functions. In the GPSR task, the object locations were predefined and provided in advance. However, in a real home environment, this predefined information is unavailable, instead, the robot must learn about an environment by itself. We introduced a brain-inspired memory model (BiMM) to acquire environment-specific knowledge specific to each home environment. The model was constructed by introducing the brain functions of the hippocampus and related areas to form an episodic memory. BiMM can memorize object locations by observing or experiencing the event, and utilize those memories for future events. Our demonstration scenario was as follows: Robot A returned home with luggage by following family member A. Subsequently, Robot A placed the luggage with snacks near the coffee table. Robot B observed the situation in which Robot A placed the luggage and memorized it. Person B in the kitchen was preparing for dinner and then asked for the help of the robot by waving his/her hand. Robot B detected the person waving his/her hand and then asking for the request. Person B requested mayonnaise and the can next to it. Robot B delivered the mayonnaise on the cabinet and the pea soup can. Here, the specific object name of the pea soup can was not provided; however, Robot B understood the spatial relationship of objects and grasped the target object. Finally, Person A requested the snack from Robot B. Robot B recalled the object location from the memory acquired by observing Robot A and delivered the snack to the coffee table. In this way, our team demonstrated the technological advancement of our robot and future vision for real home environments (Fig. 8).

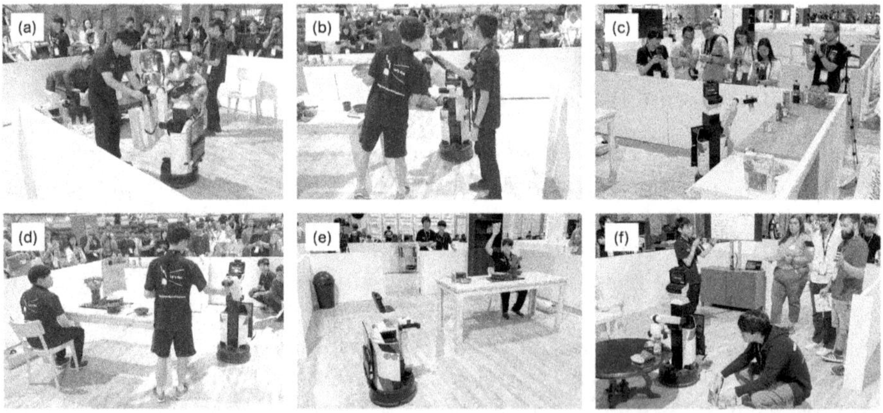

Fig. 8. Summary of the final (a) Handing over the luggage to human A. (b) Understanding the command spoken by human B (c) Grasping the requested object (mayonnaise). (d) Handing over the requested object (mayonnaise). (e) Looking for the person who waving their hand. (f) Picking up the snack.

6 Conclusions

This paper describes the techniques for creating an intelligence system for home-service robots and provides a summary of the competition results. In addition, the team demonstrated the perception, navigation, and task-planning abilities of robot systems in the competition tasks. The team also demonstrated the future vision of the home service robot in the final stage. The effectiveness of the function and the research outcomes were highly rated in the competition and secured the first place in the RoboCup 2024 @Home DSPL.

Acknowledgment. This paper is based on results obtained from a project, JPNP16007 and JPNP20004 commissioned by the New Energy and Industrial Technology Development Organization (NEDO). This paper is also supported by the Joint Graduate School Intelligent Car, Robotics & AI, the Kyushu Institute of Technology Student Project, the YASKAWA Electric Corporation project, JSPS KAKENHI Grant Numbers 23H03468 and 23K18495, JST SPRING Grant Number JPMJSP2154, and JST ALCA-Next Grant Number JPMJAN23F3.

References

1. OpenAI API server. https://platform.openai.com/. Accessed 06 Nov 2024
2. Ahn, M., et al.: Do as I can, not as I say: grounding language in robotic affordances (2022). arXiv:2204.01691
3. Coumans, E., Bai, Y.: Pybullet, a python module for physics simulation for games, robotics and machine learning (2016)
4. Isomoto, K., et al.: Hibikino-Musashi@Home 2024 team description paper (2024). arXiv:2410.06192
5. Jocher, G., Chaurasia, A., Qiu, J.: YOLO by Ultralytics (2023). https://github.com/ultralytics/ultralytics
6. Kawashima, I., Tateno, K., Morie, T., Tamukoh, H.: A memory-based entorhinal-hippocampal model and its FPGA implementation by on-chip rams. In: IEEE International Symposium on Circuit and Systems (ISCAS2022) (2022)
7. Kirillov, A., et al.: Segment anything (2023). arXiv:2304.02643
8. Labbé, M., Michaud, F.: RTAB-Map as an open-source lidar and visual simultaneous localization and mapping library for large-scale and long-term online operation. J. Field Robot. **36**(2), 416–446 (2019)
9. Language Segment-Anything. https://github.com/luca-medeiros/lang-segment-anything. Accessed 06 Sep 2024
10. Liu, S., et al.: Grounding DINO: marrying DINO with grounded pre-training for open-set object detection (2023). arXiv:2303.05499
11. Mizutani, A., Tanaka, Y., Tamukoh, H., Katori, Y., Tateno, K., Morie, T.: Brain-inspired neural network navigation system with hippocampus, prefrontal cortex, and amygdala functions. In: 2021 International Symposium on Intelligent Signal Processing and Communication Systems (ISPACS) (2021)
12. Mizutani, A., Tanaka, Y., Tamukoh, H., Nomura, O., Tateno, K., Morie, T.: A hippocampus-inspired environment-specific knowledge acquisition system utilizing common knowledge with contextual information. In: 2024 International Joint Conference on Neural Networks (IJCNN) (2024)

13. Ono, T., et al.: Solution of world robot challenge 2020 partner robot challenge (real space). Adv. Robot. **36**(17–18), 870–889 (2022)
14. Openmmlab. https://github.com/open-mmlab. Accessed 24 Oct 2023
15. Radford, A., Kim, J.W., Xu, T., Brockman, G., McLeavey, C., Sutskever, I.: Robust speech recognition via large-scale weak supervision (2022). arXiv:2212.04356
16. robot_navigation. https://github.com/ARTenshi/robot_navigation. Accessed 25 Oct 2024
17. Shishido, Y., Nomura, O., Tateno, K., Tamukoh, H., Morie, T.: CMOS digital-analog mixed signal VLSI implementation of a hippocampus-inspired model. In: 2024 International Joint Conference on Neural Networks (IJCNN), pp. 1–8 (2024)
18. Shishido, Y., Nomura, O., Tateno, K., Tamukoh, H., Morie, T.: An efficient spatial representation scheme for memory-based hippocampus-inspired model with vlsi implementation. Nonlinear Theory Appl., IEICE **15**(4), 785–795 (2024)
19. Singularity. https://apptainer.org/docs/. Accessed 06 Nov 2024
20. Wiseman, J.: py-webrtcvad. https://github.com/wiseman/py-webrtcvad. Accessed 24 Oct 2023
21. Yamamoto, T., Terada, K., Ochiai, A., Saito, F., Asahara, Y., Murase, K.: Development of human support robot as the research platform of a domestic mobile manipulator. ROBOMECH J. **6**(1) (2019)
22. Yano, Y., Mizutani, A., Fukuda, Y., Kanaoka, D., Ono, T., Tamukoh, H.: Unified understanding of environment, task, and human for human-robot interaction in real-world environments. In: 2024 33rd IEEE International Conference on Robot and Human Interactive Communication (ROMAN), pp. 224–230 (2024)
23. Zhu, K., Wu, J.: Residual attention: a simple but effective method for multi-label recognition. In: Proceedings of the IEEE/CVF International Conference on Computer Vision (ICCV), pp. 184–193 (2021)

Tech United Eindhoven Middle Size League Winner 2024

Stefan Kempers(✉), Ruben Beumer, Wiktor Bocian, Aneesh Deogan, Adrian Guillot, Danny Hameeteman, Jorrit Olthuis, Wouter Aangenent, Lars Blommers, Ruud van den Bogaert, Patrick van Brakel, Luuk van Bree, Matthias Briegel, Dennis Bruijnen, Hao Chen, Sander Doodeman, Yanick Douven, Dev Joshi, Kayden Knapik, Ivan Kolodko, Abhishek Krishnaswamy, Harrie van de Loo, Ferry Schoenmakers, Peter Teurlings, Luuk Verstegen, and René van de Molengraft

Tech United Eindhoven, De Rondom 70, P.O. Box 513, 5600, MB Eindhoven, Netherlands
{s.t.kempers,techunited}@tue.nl
https://www.techunited.nl/

Abstract. The RoboCup Middle Size League (MSL) is designed to advance robotics research through autonomous soccer played by robots. In this league, two teams of five robots compete on a field measuring 22 by 14 m. Research in the MSL focuses on distributed multi-agent systems with robots that rely solely on on-board sensors. At RoboCup 2024, held in Eindhoven, The Netherlands, the Tech United Eindhoven team from Eindhoven University of Technology claimed victory in the MSL competition, which felt particularly special as the tournament took place in their hometown. This article reflects on the tournament and the key developments that contributed to Tech United's success. We highlight three main areas of progress. Firstly, we showcase a new trajectory planner based on a setpoint generator, which leads to more dynamic and more robust path planning. Secondly, we elaborate on the developments of Tech United towards implementing artificial intelligence for ball and obstacle detection. Finally, we present the progress made in using quadruped robots for the MSL.

Keywords: RoboCup Soccer · Middle Size League · Multi-robot · Setpoint Generator · AI Object Detection · Quadruped

1 Introduction

Tech United Eindhoven is the RoboCup team representing the Eindhoven University of Technology (TU/e) in the Middle Size League (MSL). RoboCup is a global initiative that aims to push the boundaries of intelligent robotics. The MSL contributes to this goal by enhancing distributed multi-agent systems and developing innovative motion control techniques. Since its inception in 2006,

E. Barros et al. (Eds.): RoboCup 2024, LNAI 15570, pp. 473–482, 2025.
https://doi.org/10.1007/978-3-031-85859-8_40

Tech United has reached the finals of the world championship fourteen times, winning eight of those competitions, including a home tournament since this year. The MSL team is made up of six PhD candidates, six master's students, two undergraduate students, seven alumni of TU/e, and five staff members from the university. This paper highlights the important scientific progress achieved by Tech United's soccer robots over the past year and outlines significant developments for future RoboCup events.

Section 2 of this paper provides a comprehensive overview of the fifth generation soccer robot used mainly in the RoboCup 2024 competition. Next, Sect. 3 presents relevant statistics regarding the performance of these robots throughout the tournament. In Sect. 4.1 we show our work on a more dynamic trajectory planner based on a setpoint generator. This is followed by Sect. 4.2, in which the progress of implementing an AI vision module is presented. Section 5.1 then presents the research done on quadruped platforms, which are envisioned to bridge the gap between wheeled robots and humanoid robots. Finally, the paper is concluded in Sect. 6, which presents our outlook for the coming years.

2 Robot Platform

The Tech United soccer robots are called TURTLEs, which stands for Tech United Robocup Team: Limited Edition. Introduced in 2005, they have evolved over the years into the fifth generation TURTLE shown in Fig. 1. Information on the robot design can be found in the publication by Lopez [4]. CAD files of the robots and a detailed list of the hardware are published on the Robotic Open Platform wiki[1].

A high-level overview of the Tech United software is shown in Fig. 2. The software is separated into four modules; Vision, Worldmodel, Strategy, and Motion. Communication between the modules is realized by a real-time database (RtDB) designed by the CAMBADA team [1], depicted in the figure by dashed arrows. Within the four executables, the data flow is governed by Simulink, which is visualized by the solid arrows.

The Vision module processes data from the omni-vision camera to identify the locations of the ball, opponents, and the robot itself. An Xbox Kinect V2 camera, connected to an Nvidia Jetson board, tracks airborne balls that are outside the omni-vision module's field of view.

Position data from both the Vision module and the Jetson board are integrated into the Worldmodel module, where it merges with information from other team members to create a comprehensive representation of the environment. This unified data guides the team's strategic decisions.

Within the Strategy module, high-level decisions are made in the Defcon submodule. This component assesses whether specific actions are needed (such as a free kick mandated by the referee) and determines the team's play style (offensive, defensive, or neutral). The results of this analysis are then relayed

[1] http://roboticopenplatform.org/wiki/TURTLE.

Fig. 1. Fifth generation TURTLE robots, with the goalkeeper on the left-hand side. (Photo by Bart van Overbeeke)

to the STP (Skills, Tactics, and Plays) framework. This framework makes the strategy more easily configurable and reusable by splitting it into separate layers. More information on the STP framework can be found in the work of de Koning et al. [3]. The roles defined by STP are assigned to the available robots, each of which performs tasks associated with its designated role. These tasks detail low-level actions such as passing, intercepting the ball, and shooting.

Lastly, the Motion module receives these actions and applies motion control algorithms for driving, ball handling, and shooting to manage the motors. The driving motion control system is designed to accommodate various driving systems [2]. Since this year, obstacle avoidance in the action handler is performed by a new algorithm, as described in Sect. 4.1.

3 RoboCup 2024 Statistics

Nine teams participated in Robocup 2024 in the MSL: Hibikino-Musashi, Robot Club Toulon, LAR@MSL, VDL Robot Sports, Falcons, BigHeroX, UM CROATIA, IRIS, and Tech United Eindhoven[2]. Two of these teams only participated in the ambition league (matches of up to three vs. three), leaving seven teams to participate in the soccer competition. Tech United played in a total of eight matches, in which we scored 71 goals out of a 101 attempts at target. The robots scored an average of 8.9 goals per match, compared to 9.7 goals in the previous tournament in 2023. The average number of shots during a match also decreased this year, from 15.6 to 12.6. However, the ratio of goals per shot increased from 62% to 70%. According to odometry data, the robots collectively drove 35.1 km during the matches, of which 0.8 km was covered by the goalkeeper.

[2] For detailed results see https://msl.robocup.org/history/2024-detailed-results.

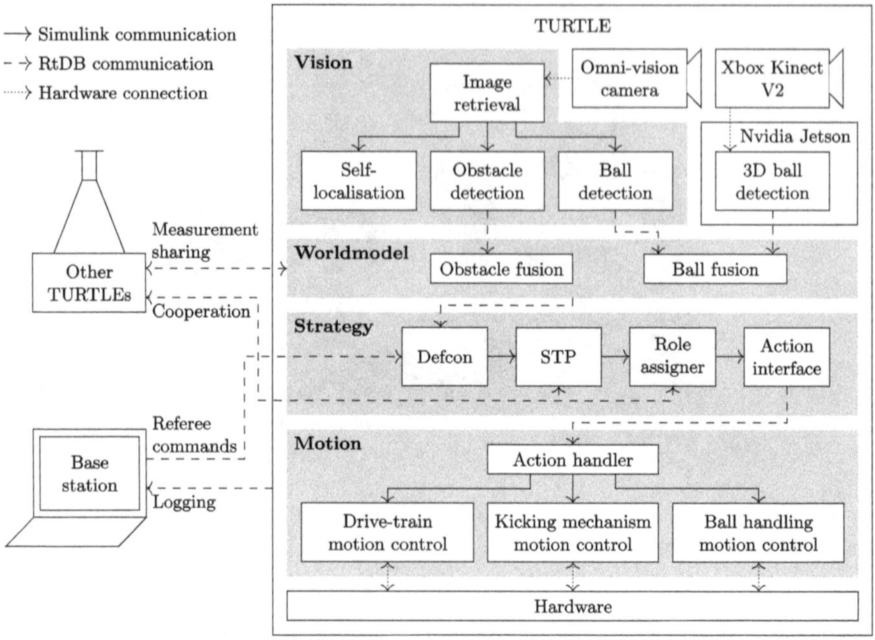

Fig. 2. A simplified, logical overview of the Tech United software architecture.

4 Developments

4.1 Setpoint Generator

The majority of autonomously moving robots have to determine the best path from their current location to their intended target. Whether they are robot vacuum cleaners or robots in a warehouse, they all benefit from a robust and quick trajectory planner. Especially in a dynamic environment, such as a soccer match, the optimal path can vary a lot based on the current positions of the obstacles. We have therefore developed a new method of finding an optimal path between two locations. This setpoint generator (SPG) creates more stable trajectories in much less time than the previous algorithm.

Currently, our robots use a trajectory planner that calculates the optimal path from point A to point B. Whenever an obstacle interrupts this path, the trajectory planner recalculates all possible paths to find the new optimal route to the target. This process is time-consuming and inefficient, as the robot has to slow down and accelerate every time the optimal path is readjusted.

With the new SPG, this problem is solved by integrating the subtarget planning with the trajectory planning and taking the robot constraints into account. The concept of the subtarget is as follows: if the direct path to the desired destination is blocked by an obstacle, another pre-target (so-called subtarget) is calculated, which is always collision-free that the robot will move towards, before heading to the final target. This is shown in Fig. 3, where a moving obstacle of velocity $\vec{v_o}$ is blocking the direct path to the target, so a subtarget is calculated. The small blue dots then represent the motion setpoints towards this collision-free target, with only the first setpoint being used for the low-level motion control. To predict the motion setpoints such that the robots can reach the subtarget quickly, the initial state of the robot is taken into account, namely the position ($\vec{p_r}$), velocity ($\vec{v_r}$) and acceleration ($\vec{a_r}$) of the robot.

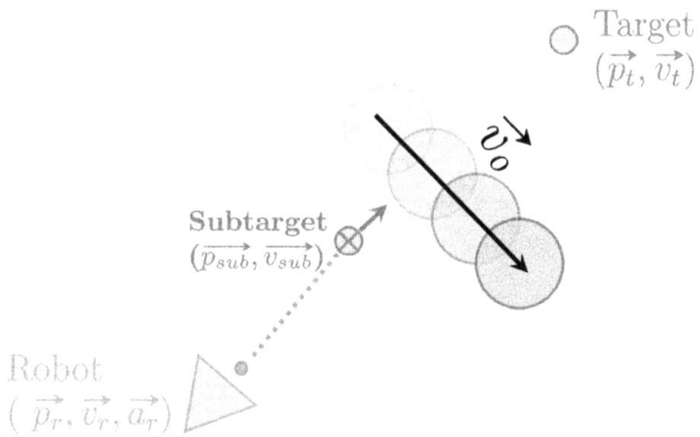

Fig. 3. An example of a scenario where a moving obstacle is blocking the direct path from the robot to the target. The large green dot in front of the robot is the current motion setpoint and the smaller blue dotted line represents the predicted setpoints. (Color figure online)

The framework breaks the trajectory down into smaller sections, each with a subtarget, a setpoint. This saves the robot from recalculating the whole trajectory every time an obstacle obstructs the path, it just has to adjust the next few setpoints. Dividing the problem into smaller manageable chunks makes it much faster computationally.

The SPG is able to find the next subtarget using a heuristic search. This allows it to find the next best setpoint based on previous information and predetermined rules, instead of calculating all possible paths to the target. The overall trajectory consisting of the subtarget is then not necessarily the globally optimal path, but it is a good enough path generated within the given deadline.

Another advantage of the setpoint generator is that it allows the robot to take into account the movement of obstacles. Based on the velocity of the obstacle, it can predict its location up to a certain time in the future. Based on this, it can readjust the subtargets around the future position of the obstacle.

Additionally, Fig. 3 shows that the SPG is able to deal with targets with a velocity and not just a position. Taking into account the constraints of the robot, the new method is able to plan and execute trajectories to fully utilize the robot's capabilities. Altogether, this allows the robot to reach its target as quickly as possible, given the robots' physical constraints, avoiding any collisions with obstacles.

The SPG is a significantly faster solution for finding a good enough trajectory from the robot's location to its target. It is also more adaptable and allows for taking into account the obstacle's future position based on the obstacle's velocity.

The current implementation of the setpoint generator includes some assumptions in the algorithm. Friction and inertia of the robot are not taken into account when determining the subtargets. Including these aspects will increase the accuracy of the framework and is planned to be implemented in the near future. Another future improvement is to include the notion of intent. The subtargets can then be placed based on the intention of the obstacle (a human or another robot). If, for example, a human wants to hand over a tool to a warehouse robot, the future SPG will allow subtargets to be placed accordingly. This is a direct benefit of the adaptability of the framework.

Robot soccer is one example, but it can also be of significant value for warehouse robots or self-driving cars, which have to take into account their constantly varying surroundings, including moving obstacles.

4.2 AI Vision

All mobile robots need a way to perceive and analyze their surroundings. In the case of Tech United football robots each robot is equipped with two cameras: an omnivision camera and a depth camera. The omnivision camera is used to localize the robot and to detect the opponents and the ball. The depth camera is used to detect the ball while it is in the air and helps with decisions on when to shoot on goal. The Xbox Kinect solution used previously required calibration, had a fairly low Field-of-View (requiring 2 Kinects on the keeper), and suffered from stability issues that could not be identified.

To address the stability issue, two stereo cameras that have ongoing support have been tested: OAK D PRO-W and ZED 2. Both of them have proven to be more stable by being capable of running through an entire game without any issues, and have a FOV large enough to replace both Kinects on the keeper, saving roughly 1 kg of weight. During testing, it was observed that the OAK-D camera has a significant drop of depth measurement accuracy when detecting balls further than 3 m away, where the measured distance often had variance of around 0.5 m compared to the actual distance. The ZED 2 camera can reliably detect objects at 9 m with an accuracy of 10 cm. This is sufficient for estimating the ball trajectory at greater distances. Between the two cameras, the ZED 2 showed better depth measurement accuracy, so this camera was chosen to replace the Kinects.

Ball detection on the Kinect camera was previously done using color filtering in the HSV color space, which had to be occasionally recalibrated. This was implemented in a custom C++ implementation, which required significant effort to update and make changes. To avoid needing to calibrate moving forward, a machine learning object detection approach was chosen using a fine-tuned YOLOv8 nano model. At the same time, the software implementation was replaced with a Python version, using pytorch and numpy for performance sensitive code. As a result our implementation is now easier to maintain due to relying on industry standard libraries, as well as providing ball position estimates at a significantly lower latency compared to the previous version.

This transition to using machine learning object detection has improved the TURTLE's depth perception and allows for easy implementation of additional features in the future. As this approach has shown robustness to different lighting conditions, in the future a similar approach will be implemented with the omnivision camera. This change is expected to greatly reduce the amount of calibration effort required during tournaments. Further, machine learning object detection opens the door to using human detection models to enable playing with a human team member.

5 Future Work

5.1 Quadruped Robot Loco-Manipulation

Current MSL robots such as Tech United's wheeled TURTLEs do not align with RoboCup's goal of using humanoid robots to win against humans. To bridge this gap, new research has focused on legged robots, using a quadruped as an intermediate step toward (bipedal) humanoid soccer players. Quadrupeds provide more stability than bipeds when performing loco-manipulation skills, for example when the legs are also used to handle ball manipulation.

This research explores how imitation learning (IL) combined with reinforcement learning (RL) can enable a quadruped robot, the Mini Cheetah, to perform complex ball-handling tasks, such as dribbling and shooting. By leveraging adversarial motion priors (AMP), the study uses limited motion capture data from a German Shepherd [5] to build foundational locomotion and ball manipulation skills, essential for the Mini Cheetah's soccer capabilities. Our approach can be divided into four steps, which are also visualized in Fig. 4. The first step is re-targeting dog motion data to the Mini Cheetah. Then, we train the quadruped to mimic basic walking. In the third step, the agent is reused to manage ball handling. The final step is to deploy and test the model in different environments, including simulations and real-world settings.

The task formulation involves reward functions tailored to each activity: for locomotion, rewards encourage the robot to follow commanded velocities, while for dribbling and shooting, rewards emphasize control over the ball's speed and direction. Specifically, the rewards for dribbling include precise ball orientation and movement, whereas the rewards for shooting prioritize speed and accuracy in directed shots.

AMP allows for simplified task-specific rewards, with training focused on a division between style and task elements to retain a natural movement style. Curriculum learning (CL) facilitated gradual mastery of tasks by increasing task reward complexity in stages, allowing the robot to handle movement directions not present in the original dataset. Domain randomization further ensured transferability across environments by introducing variability in simulation, making the trained model resilient to real-world inconsistencies.

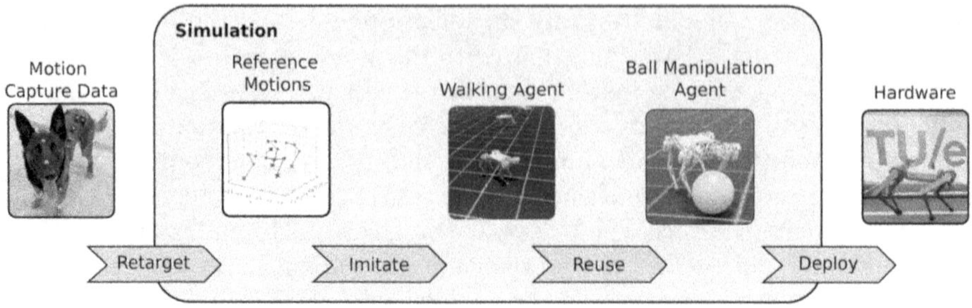

Fig. 4. The approach involves motion capture data to re-target the kinematics of our agent to the Mini Cheetah. Next, a policy is trained to imitate this motion. This policy is used as a basis for the ball manipulation tasks. Finally, the policy is transferred to the real robot.

Using NVIDIA's IsaacSim Orbit, the Mini Cheetah was trained in parallel simulations, leading to an efficient data collection process. To validate before deployment, testing in the MIT simulation and adjustments in controller gain and damping were crucial to managing real-world motor responses, further bridging the sim-to-real gap. Challenges like the lack of a base velocity sensor were noted, with recommendations to develop state estimators for better movement tracking.

The foundational locomotion skills were successfully developed, with CL outperforming constant reward methods by teaching the Mini Cheetah to handle a variety of directed movements smoothly. The dribbling and shooting tasks were built on the locomotion base, demonstrating the AMP architecture's ability to extend the learned skills with minimal tuning. Although the dribbling system was tested only in simulations, the results showed effective ball control within user-commanded directions.

The shooting task highlights the system's adaptability, allowing the robot to independently adjust foot positioning and shot timing for directed kicks. Adjustments to the training data improved this task, showing that the architecture could adapt to new movements while maintaining coherence with the reference dataset.

The project demonstrates that combining IL and RL through AMP is effective in enabling a quadruped robot to perform soccer-related tasks, establishing locomotion as a foundation for more complex manipulation skills. CL allowed safe exploration of new movements without destabilizing the policy, and domain randomization proved essential for real-world application. Future improvements should address sensor limitations, ball dynamics, and control consistency to enhance real-life performance.

6 Conclusion

This paper described the major scientific and technological developments of Tech United in preparation of RoboCup 2024. Part of the work has not actively contributed to the result of winning RoboCup 2024, but already creates a strong foundation to build upon for the coming tournaments.

The first major improvement is the overhaul of the trajectory planner. Instead of using the inefficient approach of finding the optimal path by comparing all possible options, we are now working on using a setpoint generator. This approach splits the total path from robot location to desired target into smaller manageable pieces, each with their own subtarget. These subtargets are based on the robot constraints and on obstacles in the vicinity. Since obstacles velocities are also included, the improved trajectory planner can place subtargets based on these velocities, making it more robust.

We also elaborated on our implementation of an AI vision module for the robots. The ZED 2 stereo camera in combination with the open source YOLO model improves the stability of the system compared to the previous module which utilizes an Xbox Kinect camera. The inclusion of the YOLO model reduces latency and avoids the need to recalibrate ball detection in different lighting conditions. The machine learning obstacle detection also paves the way for human detection, and thus for playing with humans.

Finally, we presented the research done on quadrupeds, which provide more stability than bipedal humanoid robots, especially when also including loco-manipulation skills. The results show that combining imitation learning and reinforcement learning is an effective approach for teaching a quadruped robot to perform soccer-related tasks. Curriculum learning showed to be capable of extending the locomotion skills learned from the original dataset. Showcasing the use of quadrupeds as soccer robots hopefully makes more people enthusiastic about their use in RoboCup.

Overall, the work presented not only pushes the boundaries of the MSL but also contributes to the broader field of intelligent robotics. These advancements aim to make robot soccer more dynamic and engaging for spectators, while preserving its scientific integrity. Continued progress in these areas will help Tech United remain at the forefront of the MSL and contribute to the long-term goal of defeating the human world champion in soccer by 2050.

References

1. Almeida, L., Santos, F., Facchinetti, T., Pedreiras, P., Silva, V., Lopes, L.S.: Coordinating distributed autonomous agents with a real-time database: the CAMBADA project. In: Aykanat, C., Dayar, T., Körpeoğlu, İ (eds.) ISCIS 2004. LNCS, vol. 3280, pp. 876–886. Springer, Heidelberg (2004). https://doi.org/10.1007/978-3-540-30182-0_88
2. Kempers, S. T., et al.: Tech united Eindhoven middle size league winner 2022. In: Eguchi, A., Lau, N., Paetzel-Prüsmann, M., Wanichanon, T. (eds.) RoboCup 2022:. pp. 337–348. Springer International Publishing, Cham (2023).https://doi.org/10.1007/978-3-031-28469-4_28
3. de Koning, L., Mendoza, J.P., Veloso, M., van de Molengraft, R.: Skills, tactics and plays for distributed multi-robot control in adversarial environments. In: Akiyama, H., Obst, O., Sammut, C., Tonidandel, F. (eds.) RoboCup 2017: Robot World Cup

XXI. pp. 277–289. Springer International Publishing, Cham (2018). https://doi.org/10.1007/978-3-030-00308-1_23
4. Lopez Martinez, C., et al.: Tech united Eindhoven team description (2014). https://www.techunited.nl/media/files/TDP2014.pdf
5. Zhang, H., Starke, S., Komura, T., Saito, J.: Mode-adaptive neural networks for quadruped motion control. ACM Trans. Graph. **37**(4) (2018). https://doi.org/10.1145/3197517.3201366

B-Human 2024 – Enhanced Vision and Faster Ball Handling

Thomas Röfer[1,2(✉)], Tim Laue[2], Philip Reichenberg[2], Lukas Gittner[2], and Laurens Schiefelbein[2]

[1] Deutsches Forschungszentrum für Künstliche Intelligenz, Cyber-Physical Systems, Enrique-Schmidt-Str. 5, 28359 Bremen, Germany
thomas.roefer@dfki.de

[2] Universität Bremen, Fachbereich 3 – Mathematik und Informatik, Postfach 330 440, 28334 Bremen, Germany
{tlaue,s_ksfo6n,gittner1,laurens}@uni-bremen.de

Abstract. In 2024, B-Human won the Standard Platform League Champions Cup and the Shared Autonomy Challenge at the RoboCup world championship as well as the RoboCup German Open. This paper provides an overview of some of our new approaches that we believe have contributed most to improving our already very successful code base. This ranges from adaptions to recent rule changes over multiple new vision and motion approaches to the implementation of this year's technical challenge.

1 Introduction

As in previous years, the software used by B-Human during all competitions is an incremental update to last year's software, leaving most of the components untouched. This makes sense as B-Human is undefeated since 2019 and thus the existing code base can be assumed to be very stable and performant. However, updates of parts of the software occur when new approaches that outperform previously existing solutions are found or when new rules require major changes. This paper describes some of these changes that we consider to be most relevant or of scientific interest. An extensive documentation of our system is given online[1].

This year's major rule changes that required to be addressed through appropriate implementations were the visual referee signal that starts a half (Subsect. 2.1) and the new indirect kick rule (Subsect. 2.2). Not implementing these would have been theoretically possible, but would have been accompanied by disadvantages that would have worsened our game performance.

Major improvements to our existing capabilities were made in the areas of vision and ball handling. This includes new CNN-based approaches for goal detection (Subsect. 3.1) and ball and penalty mark detection (Subsect. 3.2) as

[1] https://docs.b-human.de/coderelease2024/.

E. Barros et al. (Eds.): RoboCup 2024, LNAI 15570, pp. 483–494, 2025.
https://doi.org/10.1007/978-3-031-85859-8_41

Fig. 1. The referee signaling the begin of the final at RoboCup 2024. The keypoints MoveNet detected in the three image patches are marked in red. In the middle patch, the signal is not detected, because the network does not place the keypoints on the referee's arms. (Color figure online)

well as step planning approaches that allow a better ball interception (Sect. 4) and a fester kick execution (Sect. 5).

In 2024, the SPL only held one technical challenge, the Shared Autonomy Challenge. A description of our approach is given in Sect. 6.

In addition to the contributions described in this paper, we presented two scientific works at this year's RoboCup Symposium: an approach to quantize neural networks for an optimized implementation [8] as well as our recent work towards automated game statistics for the SPL [7].

2 Major Rule Changes

2.1 Referee Signal Starts Half

One of the significant changes in the rulebook this year is the introduction of a new signal to indicate the start of each half. The referee lifts both arms over his or her head while standing at one end of the halfway line. While standing on the touchlines, the robots have to detect this signal to enter the field early and prepare for the first kick-off. However, if they fail to detect the signal, they receive a delayed signal through the wireless network, leaving them with only 15 s to set up for the kick-off. If they enter the field too early, they face a penalty until 15 s have been played in that half, which can be quite severe.

To detect the referee signal, we employ the same MoveNet-based approach as last year [4, Section 4]. However, we extract a smaller patch from the top of the upper camera image. This is because the referee appears much smaller in the image when viewed from the opposing touchline. The robots assume the referee's position and look for him or her in the upper part of the upper camera image (see Fig. 1). By looking as low as possible, we minimize blooming effects from the ceiling lights.

As misdetections cannot be ruled out, a single robot begins entering the pitch after the signal is detected, giving the referee sufficient time to penalize that robot before the rest of the team walks in, which it would not do if the robot, which we call the "pawn sacrifice", is penalized. This robot enters from the side where the referee stands, ensuring that even if it is removed, the same number of robots can still observe the referee afterwards. There is a maximum of two pawn sacrifices before the robots simply wait for the delayed notification transmitted through the wireless network.

If the team misses the referee's signal and receives the delayed signal, the robots enter the pitch at maximum speed. Most of them manage to reach their kick-off positions within the time limit of 15 s.

2.2 Indirect Kick Rule

The other significant rule change is the introduction of a rule that a team can only score a goal if at least two of its robots have touched the ball after the last set play. To implement this rule, each robot shares the timestamp of the last kick it performed with its teammates. If any of the timestamps received from teammates is more recent than the last set play, a robot is permitted to kick at the goal. The first robot to kick the ball after a set play transmits this information as a priority message [5, Section 3.1] to ensure that its teammates are aware that they can score. To conserve the message budget, which is limited in the Standard Platform League, subsequent kicks are only announced as a consequence of regular team communication.

If a robot is not allowed to kick at the goal, it will either pass the ball to a teammate or dribble instead, just as it would do if the path to the goal is blocked or the goal is too far away [5, Section 2.2].

3 CNN-Based Vision

After having already replaced most of our vision components by solutions based on CNNs in recent years, the field of robot vision remains an important part of our ongoing work. Over the past year, we developed a new goal post detection and replaced our previously used networks for ball, penalty mark and line intersection detection by more sophisticated solutions. While the latter is more or less an incremental update, the others two approaches contain novel contributions and are described in the following subsections. The datasets used for the training are published on the B-Human website[2].

3.1 Goal Post Detection

In 2015, the SPL switched the goal color from yellow to white. For a number of reasons, this made the detection of the goals significantly more difficult. We initially tried to solve this by applying an algorithmic solutions, as described in [6, Section 3.3.1]. However, to avoid any false positive, which would have a severe

[2] https://www.b-human.de/datasets-en.html.

Fig. 2. An illustration of the goalpost detection process. In the first algorithmic step, continuous white line sections are searched. After removing some outliers (not described in this paper), for each line, a surrounding rectangle is computed (depicted in red). In case of multiple overlapping rectangles, the respective rectangles become combined to one (depicted in cyan). This part of the image becomes converted to a 32×32 grayscale image patch, which then becomes classified by a CNN. In case of a positive result, a second CNN is applied to predict the post's base point (marked with a green dot). (Color figure online)

negative impact on self-localization, we had to configure our implementation in a quite conservative way that lead to a very low number of detected goals. Thus, from 2016 on, we decided to play without any goal detection, relying solely on field markings.

For the 2024 competitions, we developed a CNN-based approach that is capable of detecting single goal posts at short and medium distances. The approach aims for the lower parts of the goal posts, as these are – given the perspective of the robot's cameras – surrounded by the field, whereas the upper parts have an undefined background that might contain elements that might lead to false positives, such as light trousers.

The goal post detection consist of multiple stages: multiple algorithmic steps to determine a region within an image that might contain a goal post, a CNN that classifies whether this region contains a goal post or not, and finally a second CNN that predicts the coordinates of the goal post's base point (see Table 1). This process is depicted and explained in detail in Fig. 2. The resulting base points are used as landmarks by the self-localization implementation.

Table 1. Network architecture for goalpost detection. Convolutions reduce the size by two values per image dimension to keep the filter inside the patch bounds.

Layer		Output Shape	
Detector	Classifier	Detector	Classifier
Input	Input	$32 \times 32 \times 1$	$32 \times 32 \times 1$
Conv2D + BatchNorm + ReLU + MaxPooling		$15 \times 15 \times 8$	$15 \times 15 \times 8$
Conv2D + BatchNorm + ReLU + MaxPooling		$6 \times 6 \times 8$	$6 \times 6 \times 8$
Conv2D + BatchNorm + ReLU + MaxPooling		$2 \times 2 \times 16$	$2 \times 2 \times 16$
Conv2D + BatchNorm + ReLU	+ MaxPooling	$2 \times 2 \times 16$	$1 \times 1 \times 16$
Flatten	Flatten	64	16
Dense + ReLU	Dense + ReLU	16	16
Dense + ReLU	Dense + Sigmoid	2	1

Table 2. Network architecture for ball and penalty mark detection. For the two decoders, the predictor is shown on the left and the classifier is shown on the right.

<table>
<tr><th colspan="2">Layer</th><th colspan="2">Output Shape</th></tr>
<tr><td colspan="2">Input</td><td colspan="2">32 × 32 × 1</td></tr>
<tr><td colspan="2">Conv2D + BatchNorm + ReLU + Max Pooling + Dropout (0.1)</td><td colspan="2">16 × 16 × 8</td></tr>
<tr><td colspan="2">Conv2D + BatchNorm + ReLU + Max Pooling + Dropout (0.1)</td><td colspan="2">8 × 8 × 16</td></tr>
<tr><td colspan="2">Conv2D + BatchNorm + ReLU + Max Pooling + Dropout (0.1)</td><td colspan="2">4 × 4 × 16</td></tr>
<tr><td colspan="2">Conv2D + BatchNorm + ReLU + Max Pooling + Dropout (0.1)</td><td colspan="2">2 × 2 × 32</td></tr>
<tr><td colspan="2">Flatten</td><td>128</td><td>128</td></tr>
<tr><td colspan="2">Dense + BatchNorm + ReLU + Dropout (0.25)</td><td>32</td><td>32</td></tr>
<tr><td colspan="2">Dense + BatchNorm + ReLU + Dropout (0.25)</td><td>64</td><td>64</td></tr>
<tr><td>Dense + BatchNorm</td><td>+ ReLU + Dropout (0.25)</td><td>3</td><td>16</td></tr>
<tr><td></td><td>Dense + Softmax</td><td></td><td>3</td></tr>
</table>

3.2 Ball and Penalty Mark Detection

In the past, we used different implementations for detecting balls and penalty marks, which both follow the same structure (which also resembles the one used for the goal post detection): algorithmic detection of possible candidates, patch extraction and CNN-based classification. In addition, the ball detection includes one more step for a CNN-based center point detection (see [3]). Due to these structural similarities as well as due to the fact that both objects are easily confused with each other, we decided to integrate both approaches into a single model, preserving the first steps of candidate detection and patch extraction.

The new network (see Table 2) is based on an encoder-decoder structure and is trained on over 180000 32 × 32 grayscale image patches. Furthermore, to increase the robustness of the model, we manipulate the training dataset with data augmentation.

The encoder is shared and the output is fed into two different decoders. The first decoder classifies the patch as either a ball, a penalty mark, or neither. The second decoder predicts the center coordinates and the radius, which are only used if a ball is classified. Both initially use the same architecture, but the predictor ends earlier.

4 Ball Interception

Intercepting a rolling ball is a vital skill in soccer. It aids in receiving passes from teammates and intercepting kicks from opponents. For an effective interception, three essential components are required: detecting the ball, predicting its trajectory, and executing a motion to intercept it. These components were already present, but the execution of the motion held the greatest potential for improvement. Previously, our approach involved taking side steps towards the

Fig. 3. An illustration of the updated intercepting. In the initial image, the robot initiates a new forward step, which is approximately halfway completed in the third image. At this moment, the behavior detects the necessity of an interception. As evident in the fourth through the sixth images, the robot executes a large side step, all within the same walk step.

assumed interception point. While this approach was straightforward, it encountered several challenges:

- If the ball approached at a sharp angle, the robot would execute numerous side steps, even if a simple combination of a turn and side step could intercept the ball more swiftly.
- If the robot detected a rolling ball immediately after initiating a walking step, it would have to wait until the current step concluded before starting the interception.
- If the interception direction is on the wrong side, e.g., if the robot needed to complete a walking step with its left foot as the swing foot and the ball needed to be intercepted on the left side, the robot would have to wait for up to two walking steps before actually starting the interception. This delay was due to the limitations of the robot's kinematics.
- The ball prediction was not entirely accurate. Errors in the ball's position, roll direction, or estimated velocity made it challenging to precisely stop the ball with the soles.

These issues often resulted in a delay of up to 500 ms until an interception could commence or in an inaccurate step, where the ball could roll between the robot's legs. The delay could even escalate further if the ball was erroneously predicted to stop in front of the robot. To address these challenges, we implemented two significant changes. Firstly, we relocated the step calculation from our behavior to our motion component. Our behavior now solely determines whether an interception is desired, while our motion utilizes this information to calculate an optimized walking step. This walking step adheres to two fundamental rules:

1. Determine the largest side step size feasible to reach the interception point.
2. Determine the extent of forward/backward translation and rotation that can be added while maintaining the stability of the walk. This automatically

Table 3. Competition fall statistics of the teams reaching the RoboCup 2024 quarter-finals. Robots that fell because they were obviously broken are excluded.

Team	Average #Falls per Game					
	German Open 2024			RoboCup 2024		
	Overall	Collision	Walking	Overall	Collision	Walking
B-Human	**15.86**	**13.14**	**2.71**	**16.40**	**12.70**	**3.70**
HTWK Robots	34.00	28.43	5.57	60.40	35.30	25.10
Nao Devils	47.00	17.71	29.29	59.38	17.38	42.00
HULKs	36.17	22.71	9.67	75.60	44.30	31.30
rUNSWift				32.78	22.89	9.89
RoboÉireann				34.40	28.50	5.90
Bembelbots				45.33	34.67	10.67
SPQR Team				46.88	33.50	13.38

results in substantial side steps when the swing foot is closer to the interception point, but it also rotates the robot if necessary otherwise.

Secondly, we introduced a more profound change: the ability to update the currently executing walking step at any time, should an interception be requested from the behavior. This update is relatively straightforward. In each motion frame, we check if an interception is desired. If so, we execute the previously explained walk step generation process to determine a new walk step.

To ensure stability and prevent discontinuities, this new walk step is interpolated from the previously planned step.

For the side step size, the nominal remaining step duration is multiplied by the maximum side walking speed. When the walk direction changes, stability is ensured by reducing the side walking speed for a short period. If the nominal step duration has already been exceeded and no support foot switch has occurred, a remaining time of one frame (12 ms) is used. An extreme case, such as starting the interception in the middle of a forward walk step, is illustrated in Fig. 3.

Every other stability issue that arises from this step update process is handled by our walk, which is already very fast and stable [1,2], as demonstrated in Table 3. This new intercepting technique was introduced at the RoboCup 2024 competition. The average number of falls per game increased by less than one compared to the previous German Open. Therefore, we can conclude that no new significant stability problems were introduced by this new approach.

5 Fast Kick Execution

In 2021, we implemented a change to our so-called "in-walk" kicks. Our primary objective was to enhance the accuracy of the kick direction while simultaneously reducing the time required for a kick to commence. To achieve this, we modified

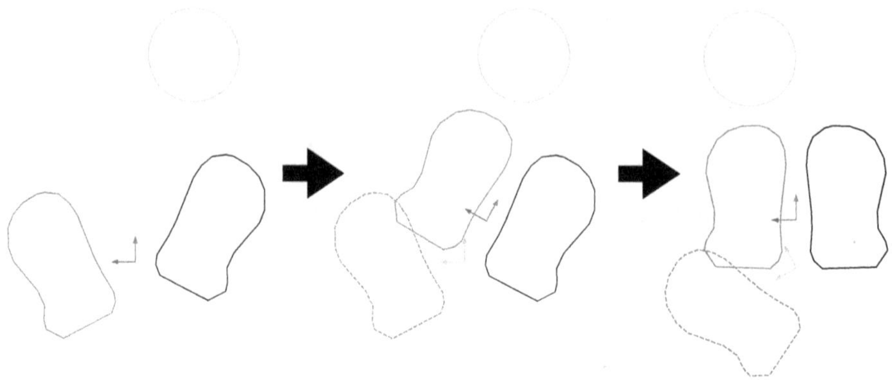

Fig. 4. The coordinate system transformation of relative points from the behavior into the coordinate system of a new walking step. The origin for the behavior is defined as the middle of both soles (left image). When a new walk step starts, a transformation is computed as if the robot would execute a zero walking step (middle image). This places the swing foot (red sole) parallel to the support foot (black sole). This transformation is then used to transform the coordinate system (right image). Here, the ball (yellow circle) is transformed from a position far forward between both soles to a relative one in front of the left sole. (Color figure online)

our infrastructure and relocated the calculation of whether a kick can start and the appropriate path to follow on the field from our behavior component to the motion component. Whenever a new walking step begins, the behavior request is processed once. To facilitate this, we transform all relevant relative points, such as the ball, into a motion-relative start coordinate system. This coordinate system describes how the robot would move if it executed a stopping walk step, with both feet standing parallel to each other. This transformation is illustrated in Fig. 4. For a more comprehensive explanation, please refer to our online documentation[3].

Based on these coordinates, we define our various kicks by specifying the relative ball positions. These 2D coordinates are then converted into walk steps to ensure that the feet are positioned correctly relative to the ball, resulting in foot movements that hit the ball as intended. Additionally, these relative ball positions can be defined as a list of points and utilized as keyframes. This allows us to precisely align the feet with the ball within the same walking step.

After conducting tests over the past year, we identified two issues. Firstly, after executing a significant side step, the robots experienced instability in subsequent walking steps due to residual momentum from the side movement. Consequently, walking steps that did not continue the side movement had significantly shorter durations than intended. To address this problem, we implemented a dynamic side hip shift. We hypothesize that this left-over momentum will always occur after a substantial side step followed by a smaller one. Therefore, we shift

[3] https://docs.b-human.de/coderelease2024/motion/motion-walkkickengine/.

the hip towards the opposite direction whenever the feet move together, with the magnitude of the shift scaled based on the distance covered.

This issue primarily stems from poorly executed kicks and instabilities that occur after side steps. We anticipate that the robots should be able to execute kicks swiftly and accurately after side steps, as if they were simply walking forward to the ball. However, our observations revealed that this was not the case. Either the robots refuse to kick the ball even when perfectly aligned from an outside perspective, or the kick is surprisingly inaccurate, with kick angle errors exceeding 45°.

We discovered that our estimation of the robot's 3D posture is highly inaccurate while side-walking. This error propagates through multiple components including the estimated relative ball position. As a result, even if the robot is standing perfectly behind the ball, the estimated relative ball position differs in the side axis by up to 30 mm. This leads to kicks that no longer hit the ball in the center but instead strike the side, explaining the inaccuracies in the directions.

While a more accurate robot posture estimation would be desirable, given the constraints of the hardware and the difficulty in further improving the current estimation, we opted for a different approach. We had already desired a faster kick execution, including kicking a ball that is not perfectly aligned. Therefore, we decided to adopt a similar approach as in Sect. 4, as the orientation estimation stabilizes itself shortly after the kick is initiated. Consequently, we update the walk kick step while it is already being executed, but only for the first few motion frames of the walk step. We skip the handling of interpolating between the old and new kick variables. Additionally, we increased our thresholds that determine how much the ball is permitted to deviate from the planned position.

6 Shared Autonomy Challenge

In the Shared Autonomy Challenge[4], an autonomous robot and a remote-controlled one play against an opposing team of the same composition. The primary objective is to determine the optimal strategy for incorporating a human into this setup, subject to the constraint that the remote-controlled robot's operator can only perceive the environment through that robot. During each match, one team takes on the attacking role (two field players) and is permitted to score a goal, while the opposing team (a field player and a goalkeeper) cannot score. Each pass is awarded one point, and a goal is worth two points. However, a goal also terminates an attempt, making passing the most effective way to accumulate the highest number of points.

6.1 Interface

The operator of the remote-controlled robot requires sufficient immersion to comprehend the robot's current state but also a comprehensive overview to make tactical decisions. To achieve this, we integrated a 3D view and a 2D view.

[4] Section 2 of https://spl.robocup.org/wp-content/uploads/SPL-Challenges-2024.pdf.

Fig. 5. Interface in the Shared Autonomy Challenge during the game against the team Nao Devils. The remote-controlled robot stands in the opponent's half, facing its teammate (jersey number 3) in the home half.

The 3D view of the robot mimics the motion of the remote-controlled robot. Two rectangles display camera images taken by the robot in its current direction of view. The robot's estimated position on the field is depicted relative to the robot. The robot's ball model is visualized as a transparent orange sphere. Other robots are shown as transparent cylinders in the jersey color of the player (if correctly detected). The robot's feet are surrounded by a ring indicating directions to different objects on the field, such as the ball, teammate, opponent players, and the two goals. The current game state is displayed on the robot's back, including the score, remaining time, game state or set play, and whether the teammate is currently playing the ball, prompting the remote-controlled robot to back off. The 3D view is shown on the right of Fig. 5. Note that the opponent player close to the robot cannot only be seen as a yellow cylinder, but also by the robot taking back its left arm to avoid a collision. However, the operator should be aware that the perspective of the camera images and the 3D drawings is not the same, leading to objects appearing in different locations in one of the images compared to the 3D visualization, such as the halfway line in Fig. 5.

In addition, a 2D overview of the field is displayed, with the opponent's goal always positioned at the top of the screen, as shown on the left of Fig. 5. Two control modes were implemented. Firstly, using a mouse and keyboard, the operator can click within the field to specify a target position for walking, kicking, or dribbling. Additionally, a key can be pressed to pass the ball to a teammate. Secondly, a gamepad can be used to control walking directly, as well as to select a kick target or dribble direction. Passing the ball to a teammate is also an option. The robot's head motion, which determines where it looks, is usually controlled automatically. However, both input devices allow manual control of the robot's neck pan and tilt angles.

6.2 Tactics

Three tactics were defined for the autonomous robot:

Attacking. The autonomous robot positions itself around the halfway line or deeper into the opponent's half, depending on the teammate's position. It attempts to score a goal if the indirect kick rule (refer to Subsect. 2.2) permits it.

Defending. The autonomous robot plays as a goalkeeper, defending its goal.

Passing. The autonomous robot aims to stay at the ball's height along the field, allowing both players to pass the ball back and forth. The remote-controlled robot can decide where this passing occurs by playing the ball to the desired area. As passes are only valid if the ball travels more than 1 m, the autonomous robot maintains a minimum distance of 1.5 m from its teammate.

When playing as the attacking team, the *passing* tactic is the default, but the operator can manually switch to the *attacking* tactic. Conversely, as a defending team, the default is the *defending* tactic, which can be switched to the *passing* tactic.

7 Results

B-Human won the RoboCup German Open 2024 as well as the Champions Cup and the Technical Challenge at the World Cup in Eindhoven (see Table 4). Notably, our performance at the Champions Cup resulted in an impressive goal ratio of 86:1 across ten games, effectively scoring an astonishing 0.64 goals per minute played. This is slightly worse than the 76:0 we achieved in eight games last year (0.70 goals per minute). This primarily stems from the indirect kick rule (refer to Subsect. 2.2), which occasionally hinders the team's progress by requiring additional passes. Our robots demonstrated remarkable stability during their walks, as illustrated in Figure Table 3. Moreover, we significantly improved our ability to intercept rolling balls this year. There were no false positives in the detection of the referee signal (see Subsect. 2.1), but only 14 out of 20 signals were detected successfully, because MoveNet sometimes places the arm keypoints on the cluttered background instead of the referee.

In the Shared Autonomy Challenge, B-Human won all five games we played, each consisting of two attempts. Overall, we amassed a total of 52 points (all achieved through passes), significantly outperforming the other eight participating teams who managed to score only 20 points. During the competition, the mouse and keyboard interface was utilized. In our first game, when playing as the defending team, B-Human's autonomous robot took on the role of a real goalkeeper, i.e. protecting its goal. However, in all subsequent games, the goalkeeper assumed a position at the center circle and adopted the *passing* tactic from the very beginning. So we essentially only played this single tactic, eliminating the need for switching.

Table 4. B-Human's game results in RoboCup competitions in 2024

(a) German Open 2024

Home	Away	Score
Naova	**B-Human**	1:**8**
B-Human	Nao Devils	**9**:0
B-Human	HULKs	**6**:0
B-Human	HTWK Robots	**3**:0
B-Human	R-ZWEI Kickers	**6**:0
B-Human	Nao Devils	**10**:0
B-Human	HTWK Robots	**4**:1

Final →

(b) RoboCup 2024

Home	Away	Score
B-Human	HTWK Robots	**8**:0
B-Human	RoboÉireann	**5**:0
B-Human	SPQR Team	**8**:0
B-Human	HULKs	**8**:0
B-Human	Nao Devils	**10**:0
B-Human	Berlin United	**8**:0
B-Human	Bembelbots	**9**:0
B-Human	Bembelbots	**10**:0
B-Human	RoboÉireann	**10**:1
B-Human	HTWK Robots	**10**:0

References

1. Reichenberg, P., Röfer, T.: Step adjustment for a robust humanoid walk. In: Alami, R., Biswas, J., Cakmak, M., Obst, O. (eds.) RoboCup 2021: Robot World Cup XXIV. Lecture Notes in Artificial Intelligence, vol. 13132, pp. 28–39. Springer (2022)
2. Reichenberg, P., Röfer, T.: Dynamic joint control for a humanoid walk. In: RoboCup 2023: Robot World Cup XXVI. Lecture Notes in Artificial Intelligence, Springer (to appear)
3. Röfer, T., et al.: B-Human 2019 – complex team play under natural lighting conditions. In: Chalup, S., Niemueller, T., Suthakorn, J., Williams, M.A. (eds.) RoboCup 2019: Robot World Cup XXIII. Lecture Notes in Artificial Intelligence, vol. 11531, pp. 646–657. Springer (2019)
4. Röfer, T., Laue, T., Hasselbring, A., Böse, F., Monnerjahn, L.M., van Lessen, K.: B-Human 2023 – object and gesture detection. In: Buche, C., Rossi, A., Simões, M., Visser, U. (eds.) RoboCup 2023: Robot World Cup XXVI. Lecture Notes in Artificial Intelligence, vol. 14140, pp. 395–406. Springer (2024)
5. Röfer, T., Laue, T., Hasselbring, A., Lienhoop, J., Meinken, Y., Reichenberg, P.: B-Human 2022 – more team play with less communication. In: Eguchi, A., Lau, N., Paetzel-Prüsmann, M., Wanichanon, T. (eds.) RoboCup 2022: Robot World Cup XXV. Lecture Notes in Artificial Intelligence, vol. 13561, pp. 287–299. Springer (2023)
6. Röfer, T., et al.: B-Human team report and code release 2015 (2015). http://www.b-human.de/downloads/publications/2015/CodeRelease2015.pdf
7. Röfer, T., Müller-Groh, L., Hasselbring, A., Laue, T.: Automated game statistics for the RoboCup standard platform league. In: In: Barros, E., Hanna, J.P., Okada, H., Torta, E. (eds.) RoboCup 2024: Robot World Cup XXVII. Lecture Notes in Artificial Intelligence, vol. 15570, pp. xx–yy. Springer (2025)
8. Thielke, F.: Quantized neural networks for ball detection on the NAO robot: an optimized implementation. In: Barros, E., Hanna, J.P., Okada, H., Torta, E. (eds.) RoboCup 2024: Robot World Cup XXVII. Lecture Notes in Artificial Intelligence, vol. 15570, pp. xx–yy. Springer (2025)

HELIOS2024: RoboCup Soccer Simulation 2D Competition Champion

Hidehisa Akiyama[1(✉)], Tomoharu Nakashima[2], Takumi Fujikawa[2], Akei Hishiki[2], Shota Yano[2], and Sota Okayama[2]

[1] Okayama University of Science, Okayama, Japan
hidehisa.akiyama@ous.ac.jp
[2] Osaka Metropolitan University, Osaka, Japan
tomoharu.nakashima@omu.ac.jp

Abstract. This paper presents HELIOS2024, the champion team of the RoboCup 2024 Soccer Simulation 2D Competition, which unites researchers from Okayama University of Science and Osaka Metropolitan University. HELIOS2024 has achieved seven consecutive championships since 2022. Our recent advancements focus on refining team tactics by adapting both team strategy and player behaviors based on opponent tactics, utilizing tile coding for improved opponent identification. This enhancement aims to boost computational efficiency, streamlining processes with fewer resources. We also enhanced our performance evaluation system, capable of aggregating data from thousands of distributed simulations to generate reliable statistics, particularly in goals scored and conceded. This system facilitates team development by enabling robust performance analysis and visualization through interval estimates. Although currently focused on goals, ongoing work seeks to incorporate actions like passing and dribbling to provide a more comprehensive assessment of player and team performance. Future directions include collaborating with the machine learning and human soccer analysis communities to explore deeper insights into soccer simulation.

Keywords: Multiagent systems · Opponent Identification · Distributed Computing · Visualization

1 Introduction

This paper presents HELIOS2024, the champion team of the RoboCup 2024 Soccer Simulation 2D Competition, formed by a partnership between Okayama University of Science and Osaka Metropolitan University. This marks the seventh championship win in total for the team, which has achieved three consecutive victories since 2022. The team has released its base code and maintained continuously[1] [1].

[1] https://github.com/helios-base/.

E. Barros et al. (Eds.): RoboCup 2024, LNAI 15570, pp. 495–501, 2025.
https://doi.org/10.1007/978-3-031-85859-8_42

One of our recent research focuses is on the adaptation of team tactics in soccer games. This involves adjusting both the team strategy and players' behaviors based on the opponent's tactics, which is a crucial task for improving the chances of winning. The contribution involves the application of tile coding to enhance the opponent identification method, a technique previously implemented by our team. The primary goal of this extension is to boost computational efficiency and streamline operations with fewer computational resources.

Our contribution includes applying tile coding to improve the opponent identification method, a technique previously developed by our team. The primary goal of this enhancement is to increase computational efficiency and streamline processes, using fewer computational resources.

Additionally, we have improved our evaluation system to enhance team performance. This system enables the collection of game data by running many simulated games across a distributed network of computers. This year, we implemented a feature for statistical analysis of team performance based on the collected game data. Specifically, we successfully facilitated team development by making interval estimates of the average number of goals scored and conceded.

The organization of this paper is as follows. Section 2 introduces the overview of the simulator and the new feature in 2024. Section 3 describes enhancements to make opponent team formation identification more computationally efficient. Section 4 describes enhancements of our performance evaluation system. Finally, Sect. 5 serves as a conclusion.

2 Soccer Simulation 2D Competition

The RoboCup Soccer Simulation 2D Competition, one of the oldest of the RoboCup competitions, is designed as a simulated soccer robot competition on a virtual soccer field [4]. The simulation system[2] enables two teams of 11 autonomous player agents and an autonomous coach agent to play a game of soccer with realistic rules and gameplay.

In 2024, a bipedal dash model was introduced as a new feature. This model closely resembles the differential drive kinematics used in wheeled robots. Previously, players were unable to accelerate and rotate simultaneously, but with this model, they can now do both at the same time. This new feature has added complexity to player movement planning and responses to adversarial situations, resulting in more realistic behaviors. Although participating teams have not yet fully adapted to this change as of 2024, movements that utilize simultaneous acceleration and rotation are often observed among the top teams.

3 Enhancement of Opponent Formation Identification

Opponent modeling stands out as an essential task in soccer [5]. Understanding the tactics employed by the opponent team is crucial for adapting the tactics of

[2] Available at: https://github.com/rcsoccersim.

our own team. As a vital component reflecting a team's cooperative behavior, the tactical arrangement of players, specifically the team formation, is considered the foundational element characterizing a team's behavior. The classification and identification of team formations remain challenging [7]. Presently, we employ a support vector machine for real-time identification of team formations. However, in dynamic games like soccer, where there's no room for prolonged computations, the challenge lies in minimizing the computational resource overhead.

3.1 Basic Data Extraction and Classification Model

If we directly use the coordinate values of players' positions as inputs for the learning model, considering players' uniform numbers becomes necessary, posing a challenge in maintaining the order of players during the learning process. To address this, we express the opponent formation numerically by discretizing the soccer field into a grid (Fig. 1). Each cell's value, representing player count, serves as input for the learning model. These values depict the number of opponent players in a specific cycle, and the results are integrated. The average value is then computed by dividing the accumulated integration by the observed cycles. This set of average values constitutes input data for our classification model. For example, with a 6×4 grid, the opponent formation is represented by a 24-dimensional vector.

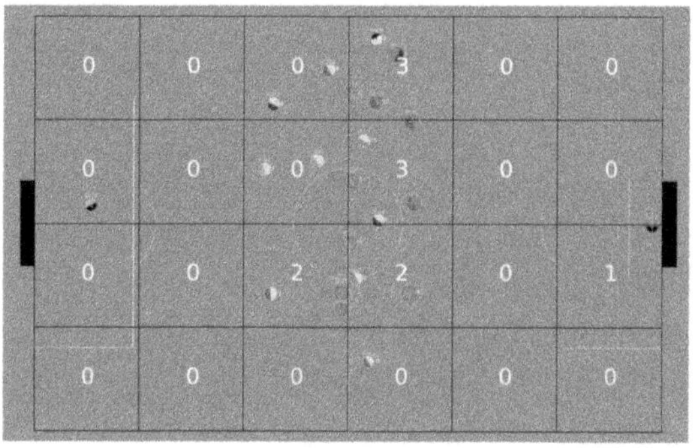

Fig. 1. Example of soccer field discretization using a grid of size 6×4.

We utilized a clustering method to analyze typical formations, employing the Gaussian Mixture Model for this purpose. Subsequently, training data were labeled based on the resulting clusters, and these labeled data were used to train the identification model. At present, our classification model of choice for practical use is a support vector machine with a linear kernel [3].

3.2 Feature Representation Using Tile Coding

The discretization of a soccer field using a grid is effective for handling a group of players without considering their uniform numbers. However, the prediction accuracy depends on the grid's resolution. While higher resolution may yield better predictions, it demands more computational resources and may cause overfitting. To address this problem, we introduce Tile Coding, a well-known state representation method in traditional Reinforcement Learning [6].

Figure 2 illustrates an example of field discretization using tile coding. Lower resolution for each tiling exponentially reduces the demand for computational resources. The linear combination of these tilings is employed as the system output, aiming to maintain prediction accuracy while reducing computational resource requirements for the entire system.

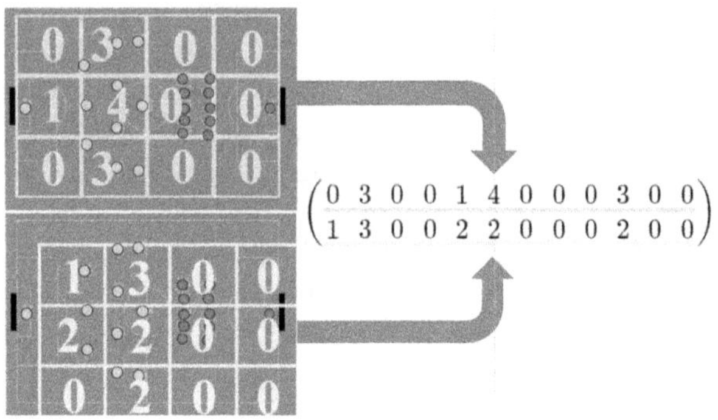

Fig. 2. Example of a soccer field discretization using tile coding. Each tiling in this example is a 4×3 grid.

3.3 Experiment

We conducted a preliminary experiment to assess the accuracy and computational time of the predictions. The primary objective of this experiment is to identify specific team formations. We prepared data for four distinct teams, labeled as A, B, C, and D, generating logs from 200 matches. We focused on cycles where the ball resided in the opponent's two-thirds of the field. As the learning model, we employed a support vector machine with a linear kernel. The feature set included tile counts 5×4 multiplied by the tiling count of 15, in addition to the ball's position represented by (x, y) coordinates, resulting in a total of 302 dimensions. To assess the effectiveness of our approach, we prepared a comparative dataset that uses coordinate values with ordered uniform numbers. Furthermore, we utilized 20% of A+D (merge of A and B) as our test data. The experimental environment was implemented using Python.

Table 1 and 2 show the computational time results for prediction based on two types of inputs. These results indicate the accuracy achieved with tile coding features is comparable to that of direct coordinate values with ordered uniform numbers, while the computational cost remains very similar.

Table 1. Result: coordinate values are used directly as input.

Training Data	Accuracy	Computational Time for Prediction (ms)
A+B	0.5914	0.2403
A+C	0.5732	0.2389
A+D	0.9846	0.2312
A+B+C+D	0.8941	0.3092

Table 2. Result: tile coding is used as input.

Training Data	Accuracy	Computational Time for Prediction (ms)
A+B	0.5914	0.2510
A+C	0.5732	0.2736
A+D	0.9652	0.3311
A+B+C+D	0.9131	0.2936

4 Enhancement of Performance Evaluation System

In team development, efficiently evaluating team performance is essential. We have developed a performance evaluation system to support this process [2]. To make it easier to observe changes in team performance across many games, we are working on visualizing various statistical metrics. Goals scored and conceded are key indicators and currently serve as reliable statistics. This year, we aimed to enhance the visualization of these metrics for improved clarity.

4.1 Overview of the System

To run a large number of games within a reasonable timeframe, an efficient execution system is required. In response to this need, we have been developing a distributed execution system. Our system provides a mechanism for distributing simulator tasks across multiple resources, significantly reducing game execution time when sufficient computational resources are available in parallel.

Our system aggregates the results of numerous games and presents a summary through a web interface. Figure 3 provides an example of the displayed results. For each matchup, thousands of games are run, and the aggregated results are shown in a table.

4.2 Visualizing Game Statistics

Using our distributed system, we can obtain statistical information on how the implemented content changes team performance. Distributed simulation allows us to run a large number of games, making it possible to make statistical estimates that would be difficult to make in the real world. However, it is difficult to

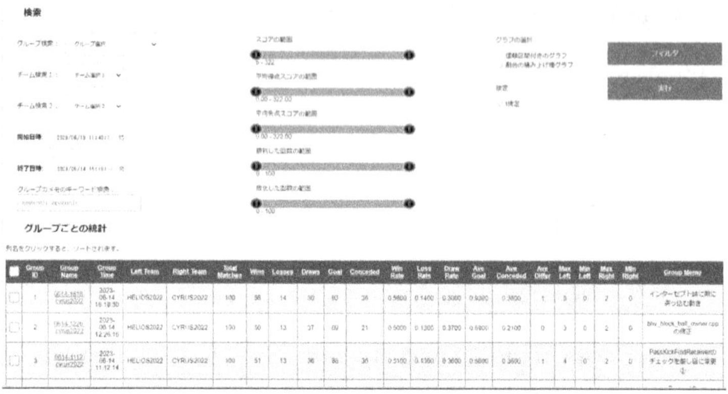

Fig. 3. An example of the aggregated results display. The dedicated web interface allows not only to view the results in table format but also to select the display content using filters and to perform analyses using various indicators.

read differences in results from just a table of numbers, making it hard to grasp changes in team performance over time. Therefore, we are attempting various visualizations using graphs. Figure 4 is an example of a graph showing interval estimates for the average number of goals scored and conceded. By visualizing interval estimations, it becomes easy to see whether a team's performance has changed significantly.

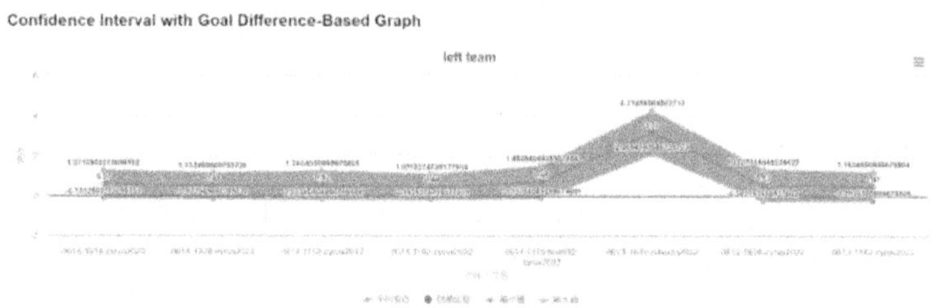

Fig. 4. An example of the visualization showing interval estimates for the average number of goals scored and conceded. The dedicated web interface provides functions that facilitate graphical visualization and simple statistical analysis.

Currently, we use statistics on goals scored and conceded as the most reliable indicators of team performance. However, it is challenging to assess the true performance of a team or individual players based solely on these metrics. To address this limitation, we are also compiling and visualizing actions such as passing and dribbling. Unfortunately, these metrics are not yet effective indicators for directly evaluating team performance. At present, it is particularly difficult to assess the quality of play in the midfield area. A future challenge will be developing methods to evaluate play quality in each specific area of the field.

4.3 By-Product: Soccer Dataset

Our system was originally designed to evaluate team performance. However, it can be applied to not only assess the performance of a single team but also to generate large amounts of gameplay data for any matchup. We already published gameplay data which is 1,000 round-robin games played by teams participating in the RoboCup 2021 and 2024 Soccer Simulation 2D Competition[3].

5 Conclusion

This paper introduced the champion team of the RoboCup 2024 Soccer Simulation 2D Competition. We described our recent efforts to enhance opponent identification and improve the performance evaluation system.

We plan to undertake various initiatives using the generated dataset. In particular, a key future challenge will be to develop more effective methods for analyzing and visualizing team performance. Additionally, we aim to collaborate with the machine learning community and experts in human soccer analysis using our dataset.

References

1. Akiyama, H., Nakashima, T.: HELIOS Base: an open source package for the robocup soccer 2D simulation. In: RoboCup 2013: Robot World Cup XVII, pp. 528–535 (2014)
2. AKiyama, H., Nakashima, T., Hatakeyama, K., Fujikawa, T.: HELIOS2022: robocup 2022 soccer simulation 2D competition champion. In: RoboCup 2022: Robot World Cup XXV, pp. 253–263 (2023)
3. Chang, C.C., Lin, C.J.: LIBSVM: a library for support vector machines. ACM Trans. Intell. Syst. Technol. **2**(3), 1–27 (2011)
4. Noda, I., Matsubara, H.: Soccer server and researches on multi-agent systems. In: Proceedings of IROS-96 Workshop on RoboCup, pp. 1–7 (1996)
5. Pourmehr, S., Dadkhah, C.: An overview on opponent modeling in robocup soccer simulation 2D. In: RoboCup 2011: Robot Soccer World Cup XV, pp. 402–414 (2012)
6. Sutton, R.S., Barto, A.G.: Reinforcement Learning: An Introduction, 2nd edn. MIT Press, Cambridge (2018)
7. Vasconcelos, D.M., Maximo, M.R., Tasinaffo, P.M.: An opponent formation classifier for simulated robot soccer. In: RoboCup 2023: Robot Soccer World Cup XIV (2024). in appear

[3] https://github.com/hidehisaakiyama/RoboCup2D-data/.

RoboCup 2024 Adult-Sized Humanoid Champions Guide for Hardware, Vision, and Strategy

Gabriel I. Fernandez(✉), Yeting Liu, Colin Togashi, Kyle Gillespie, Alvin Zhu, Quanyou Wang, Yicheng Wang, Hyunwoo Nam, Shiqi Wang, Ruochen Hou, Mingzhang Zhu, Aditya Navghare, Alex Xu, Taoyuanmin Zhu, Min Sung Ahn, Arturo Flores Alvarez, Justin Quan, Ethan Hong, and Dennis W. Hong

RoMeLa, Robotics and Mechanisms Laboratory, Department of Mechanical and Aerospace Engineering, Geffen Academy at UCLA, University of California, Los Angeles, CA 90095, USA
gabriel808@ucla.edu

Abstract. Through the course of RoboCup 2024 our team scored 45 goals over 6 seated matches and, ultimately, unseated the longstanding reigning champions in our division with a victory of 6 goals to 1. In this paper we will focus on hardware, vision, and high-level decision making while briefly touching upon others. Our humanoid robot named Artemis is around 1.4 m tall, weighing over 35 kg. Artemis is designed to be lightweight featuring quasi-direct drive actuators with motor housings which serve as drive inputs to the next motor at the hips to save weight. For the tournament the foot was redesigned to allow for increased kicking accuracy, contact rate, and durability when stepped on. For vision we introduce several practical filters and an additional component termed proximity to address potential failure cases when an opponent or obstacle is very near. Finally, we discuss the strategies and overall planning architecture used during the tournament for high level decision making.

Keywords: Perception · Vision · Proximity · Behavior Tree · Strategy · Decision Making · Robot · Humanoid · Autonomous · Soccer · Football

1 Introduction

RoboCup holds a variety of competitions, one of which is humanoid robotic soccer. Soccer presents a variety of unique and complex challenges for autonomous robots, including perception, navigation, and real-time decision making in a dynamic environment. Artemis, our entrant in the RoboCup 2024 adult-sized humanoid league, is designed to meet these challenges through a combination of state-of-the-art hardware, a robust vision algorithm integrating advanced vision techniques with classical methods, and a simple yet effective approach to game

E. Barros et al. (Eds.): RoboCup 2024, LNAI 15570, pp. 502–514, 2025.
https://doi.org/10.1007/978-3-031-85859-8_43

Table 1. Artemis Actuator Specifications [17]

	Hip Roll & Yaw	Hip & Knee Pitch	Ankle Pitch	Arms	Head
Approximate weight (g)	850	3000	350	300	250
Gear reduction	14.5	5.9	50.3	19.2	9
Peak torque (Nm)	85	250	25	32	12
Continuous torque (Nm)	30	80	8	8	3
Velocity (rad/s)	25	23	30	30	50
Reflected inertia (kgm^2)	0.049	0.088	0.020	0.008	0.001

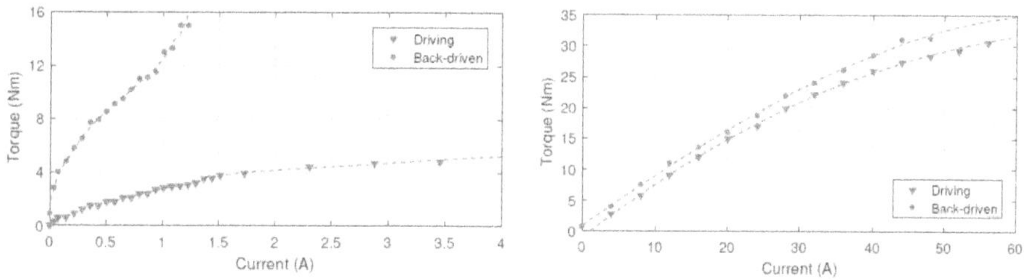

(a) Off-the-shelf Dynamixel MX-106.

(b) Artemis Actuator.

Fig. 1. Drive and Back-Driven Torque Comparison [18].

logic. This paper will primarily focus on these topics and briefly mention several other components of our stack.

Our hardware platform features quasi-direct drive actuators with a high degree of torque transparency [15,16]. Its design provides more than enough torque to potentially sprint like a human. To save weight, the motor shafts at its hip feed directly into the next motor giving us an advantage in speed and stability. Its foot was also redesigned to ensure more consistent kicks.

Our vision system leverages YOLOv8 [13] to detect field features from which we estimate distances to key game features. From these field feature distances Artemis can localize itself on the field. Surprisingly, there were many failure cases in which feature detection would fail. In particular whenever an opponent or obstacle was too close. Due to the fact that Artemis can move up to 2 m/s not detecting a close obstacle could be catastrophic. To address this, we included an additional sub-component, proximity, into vision.

For high-level decision making we use a behavior tree. Though many parameters had to be tuned, it allowed for rapid on-the-fly adjustments depending on the type of opponent we faced. The planner utilized some simple heuristics to determine how to react in the short and long term. Though simple in nature it proved to be much more complex than that of our opponents particularly in cases which required some degree of player coordination.

Our contributions in this paper can be summarized as follows: a description of hardware advances brought about by Artemis, the practical implementations

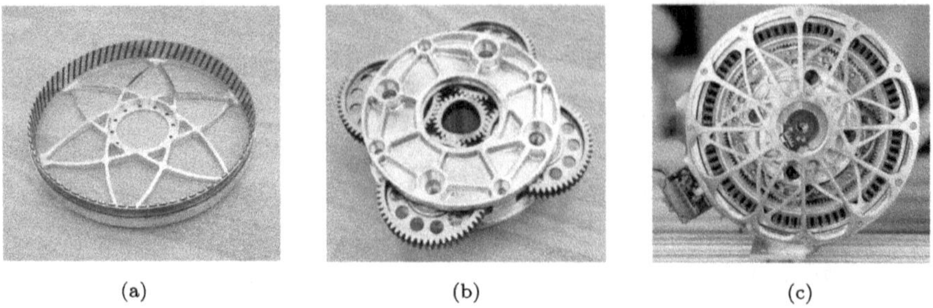

Fig. 2. (a) Rotor, (b) Planetary Gearbox, (c) Assembled Hip Actuator [17].

of vision and introduction of proximity, and high-level strategy control. We hope that readers who are also participants in any of RoboCup's soccer leagues can also utilize many of the approaches laid out in this paper.

2 Hardware Design

Actuator Design. To achieve dynamic locomotion, actuators with low reflected inertia and high transmission transparency are crucial. These enable the robot to effectively employ force control and smoothly respond to impacts.

Most commercially available motors are designed for high efficiency when at higher speeds, which works well for electric vehicles and some robotic arms. However, in legged robots the motors primarily operate at low speeds and require high peak torque. A custom stator and rotor design is necessary to meet this peak torque performance. Our design maximizes the air gap radius to achieve high peak torque, and decreases the gear reduction ratio to improve the torque transparency required for torque control. Table 1 shows the parameters of these actuators on Artemis.

Torque density in actuators is typically increased with a high gear reduction ratio, however this reduces transmission transparency, which affects how external loads are transmitted to the motor. For Artemis' actuators, a gearbox with a low gear ratio is used to enhance transparency and minimize non-linear factors like friction and backlash. This also ensures smoother actuation. Figure 1 compares the Artemis actuators with the Dynamixel MX-106 from ROBOTIS. These Artemis actuators with a single stage planetary gearbox maintain a linear torque response with minimal variance between driving and back-driven torque, apart for some losses to friction at high loads. An extra benefit of this low gear ratio design is that it can absorb external impact forces without destroying the gear train.

Actuator Packaging. As shown in Fig. 2 the motor's large air gap radius provides space at the center of the actuator for integrating the optimized gearbox;

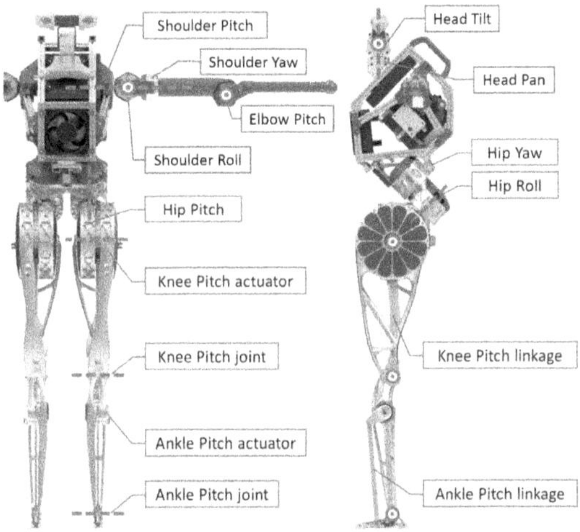

Fig. 3. Artemis upper and lower body joints and actuators locations [17]

Table 2. Artemis Joints Specifications [17]

	Range of Motion (°)	Peak Torque (Nm)	Joint Velocity (rad/s)
Head Tilt	−45–135	10.5	45
Head Pan	−90–90	10.5	45
Shoulder Pitch	−180–90	32	15
Shoulder Roll	−100–75	32	15
Shoulder Yaw	−180–90	32	15
Elbow Pitch	−176–0	32	15
Hip Yaw	−90–45	85	25
Hip Roll	−45–45	85	25
Hip Pitch	−133–78	250	23
Knee Pitch	19–160	250	23
Ankle Pitch	−70–50	25	30

thus creating a compact, space-efficient design with an outer-runner rotor, stator, and gearbox. In addition, the motor driver board and the liquid cooling channel are also integrated in the housing.

Lower Body Design. For Artemis to do highly dynamic behaviors like walking or running, it is necessary to design Artemis with all the essential degrees of freedom (DoF) that humans have. For the lower body, the goal is to achieve a lightweight but robust mechanical design with adequate DoF and minimal moment of inertia to attain highly dynamic motions (Table 2).

Unlike traditional humanoid robots which utilize 6 DoF legs, Artemis' leg is designed with only 5 DoFs, omitting the ankle roll to decrease the leg's distal mass Fig. 3. This design enables faster leg acceleration during the swing phase, which is advantageous for fast walking, running, and dealing with disturbances. The trade-off is that, without the ankle roll, the robot cannot balance on one leg. Since ARTEMIS is dynamically stable, we do not encounter single leg balancing.

Another design novelty in the lower body is the coupled hip roll and yaw joints. For humanoid robots with hip joints configured like humans, the hip roll requires much more torque than the hip yaw. Typically this demands for differently sized actuators. However, by tilting the hip yaw and roll axes forward 45°, the torque is more evenly distributed, allowing the same actuator size for both joints and therefore simplifying the system. This configuration also positions actuators toward the back, increasing clearance for hip pitch, enabling a human-like squatting motion.

The lower body design aims to reduce distal mass to enable more dynamic motion. This goal was commonly achieved by placing actuators closer to the torso and using mechanisms like belts or chains for torque transmission. However, chains can create inconsistent transmission ratios, and belts can lack stiffness, leading to unwanted deflection [14]. To address this, Artemis utilizes parallel four-bar linkages to bring actuators near the torso. As shown in Fig. 3, the knee actuator is placed co-axially with the hip pitch actuator, and the ankle pitch actuator is placed right below the knee joint. This design concentrates over 60% of the leg's mass around the hip, enhancing leg acceleration and overall stability.

In high DoF robots, modular actuators are often reused across joints to simplify design and maintenance; though this can lead to material waste and lower

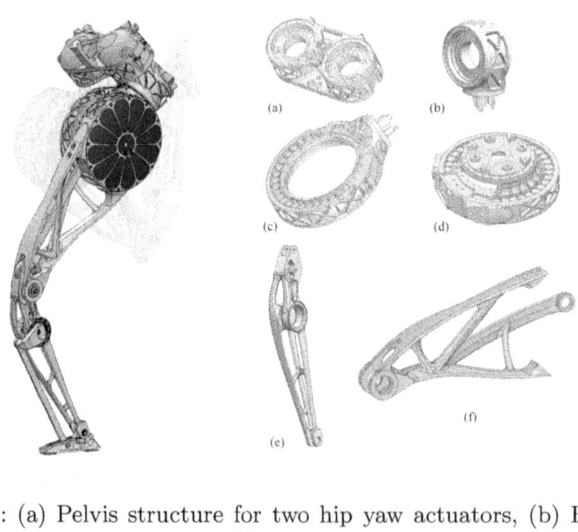

Fig. 4. Depicts: (a) Pelvis structure for two hip yaw actuators, (b) Hip yaw output and housing for the hip roll actuator, (c) Hip roll output and housing for the hip pitch actuator, (d) Hip pitch output and housing for the knee actuator, (e) Tibia structure with integrated ankle actuator housing, and (f) Femur structure connecting the hip actuators to the knee [17].

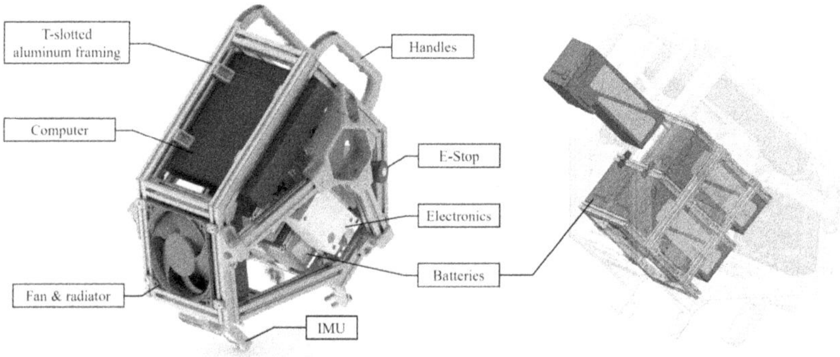

Fig. 5. Artemis torso structure and components [17].

torque density. Artemis avoids this issue by integrating its actuator housings directly into the robot's structure, thus reducing bolted connections and eliminating extra parts, as shown in Fig. 4. In addition, topology optimization is used in the part design process to achieve the balance between lightweight and rigidity, especially for structural components like the femur and tibia.

Torso Design. The torso of Artemis is shown in Fig. 5, which is constructed from a T-slotted aluminum frame which securely houses the electronics and batteries. This roll-cage-like structure protects components in falls, and has handles on the upper back aid to in transport. The HP Elite Mini 800 G9 computer mounted near the top, runs control algorithms and vision tasks with an Intel Core i7 and NVIDIA RTX 3050 Ti GPU. The independent battery cage, designed to prevent failures during impact, holds four RB56100 batteries and various electronic modules. Additionally, a MicroStrain 3DM-CV7 IMU is mounted in the torso's belly area, which is crucial for maintaining balance and stable walking.

Foot Design. As seen in Fig. 6(b), the foot is made up of: a *snap cover* which is attached to the foot's *main body*, a *front bill* which directly impacts the ball during kicks, and a *side bill* which helps side kicking and prevents the ball from

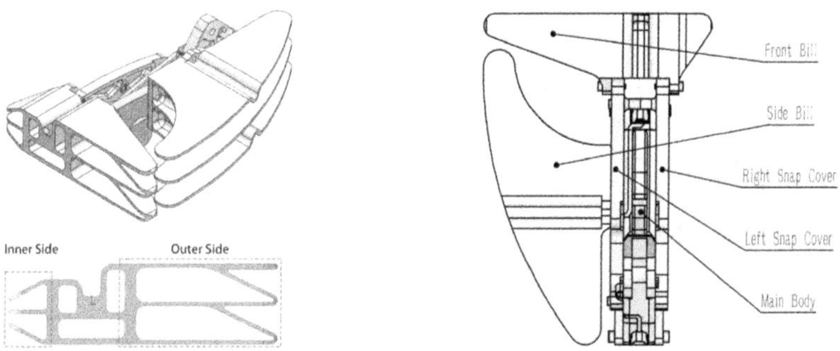

(a) (b)

Fig. 6. Shows: (a) Foot design and front bill and (b) Components.

rolling backward during foot retraction. Rather than using a symmetrical design, the inner width of the front bill is reduced to prevent self-interference during in-place turning, while the outer width is expanded to increase the kicking contact area. The contact surface of the front bill is designed as a flat plane to ensure the force exerted is along the foot's axis.

Foot Compliance. The front bill design maintains stiffness in the horizontal direction while maximizing flexibility in the vertical direction, allowing the foot to deform under pressure when stepped on by other robots. This configuration reduces the risk of damage and helps prevent the robot from toppling, without compromising its kicking performance. To achieve this, the large holes in the foot are oriented horizontally, forming a structure that can be conceptualized as three vertically stacked planes, as shown in Fig. 6(a).

On the inner side, the ends of the upper and lower planes taper toward the center, forming a triangular structure. This configuration enables the planes to guide the feet outward upon contact, thus, preventing the robot from overlapping if it steps on itself. On the outer side, angled supports are incorporated between each plane, enabling load sharing across the three planes. When the top plane is compressed by an external force (such as by a step), it transfers the load, promoting coordinated deformation rather than bearing the force independently. This design reduces the risk of fracture and improves the overall structural strength of the outer side.

Foot Durability. In nearly every match, at least one of the front bill or side bill components on the robot incurred damage. Damage to the front bill predominantly occurred on the upper side, suggesting that it was primarily due to being stepped on by other robots. Conversely, damage to the side bill was mostly observed on the lower side, indicating that it likely was from stepping on other robots. Simulation results indicate that this damage may be caused by insufficient material strength. Future development will aim to address this.

3 Vision

Stereo Camera. The ZED 2i camera provides both RGB images and estimates depth information. The high frame rate (60 FPS) and wide field of view (110°) ensures that the system can capture dynamic scenes reliably. The camera's intrinsic calibration parameters, such as focal length and optical center, are dynamically adjusted based on the robot's orientation, ensuring accurate 3D perception. The calibration parameters for both the left and right cameras are automatically selected based on the robot's head orientation.

Object Detection. During competition we deployed a custom-built version of the YOLOv8 model, which has been tailored for detecting specific objects in the Robocup environment. The speed of the medium-sized model was too slow for our application. Thus, we deployed a custom-built one that is roughly 80% of the size of the medium variant to increase speed at the cost of some performance.

However, given our relatively small class size, the smaller model's accuracy only slightly dropped. To further accelerate inference, the model is optimized using the NVIDIA TensorRT SDK, which compiles the network into a highly optimized runtime suitable for NVIDIA GPUs. This setup allows the system to perform real-time inference at high frame rates with minimal latency, a critical requirement for a robot as fast as Artemis. Multiple optimizations resulted in a 70% decreased inference time compared to the standard YOLOv8 model.

Our detection model is trained to recognize: soccer balls, robots with red or blue uniforms, and landmarks such as goalposts and intersections (T, X, or L-shaped). Bounding boxes are computed for each detected object, along with confidence scores. The pixels from ZED's 2D images are converted into 3D world coordinates using stereo matching. A cost function using the model confidence of a detection and its distance from the robot is used to provide the best 6 landmarks for localization. This conversion and calculation is essential for calculating the positions of the ball, robots, and best field landmarks.

Estimation. For each detected object, the centroid of its bounding box is computed, and its 3D position is estimated by averaging the depth values within the bounding box. In the specific case of ball detection, if depth data is unreliable or unavailable, the system employs a geometric depth estimation technique. This method uses the pixel diameter of the detected ball and the camera's intrinsic parameters to estimate the ball's real-world distance from the robot. This approach serves as a backup to ensure continuous tracking of the ball, even in the absence of depth information.

Ball Detection. As the ball is the focal point of the game, we take several steps to ensure that the ball is detected if it is in frame while weeding out false positives. *Green*: Since the soccer ball is typically surrounded by green turf, the system verifies that a significant portion of the region around the detected ball contains green pixels. *Dimension*: The system checks that the dimensions of the detected ball are within expected ranges for the actual soccer ball. Objects that do not meet these criteria are filtered out. *Height*: An additional filter checks the height of the center of the ball relative to the field.

4 Proximity

Proximity is a newly envisioned component developed out of necessity from our prior RoboCup matches. As our robot moved so fast when a close object was suddenly detected our momentum would be too great causing us to frequently run into opponents. From our understanding this component is unique from all our competitors. Compared to other works in obstacle avoidance like Vector Field Histogram (VFH) [3] or dynamic window approach [6], this module functions at a much lower level in the navigation pipeline.

Preprocessing. From ZED's depth map we filter out pixels further than a threshold as well as special values (Inf, NaN). Connected Component Analysis (CCA) [10] is used on the depth map to find the two closest components by which a bounding box is drawn to flag a detected object. If the box's size or aspect ratio don't meet a certain threshold, it is filtered out.

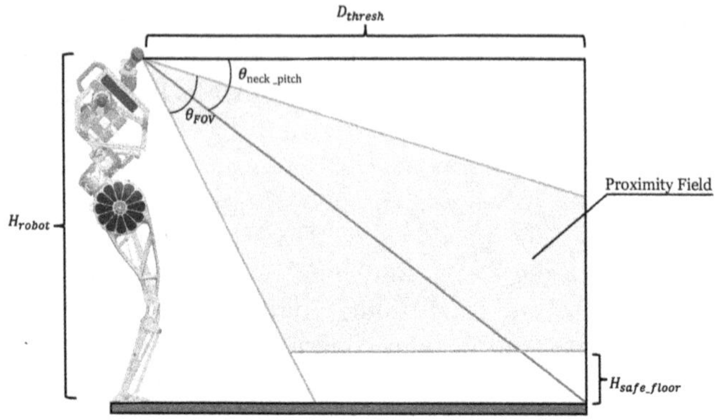

Fig. 7. Visualization of the Field-of-View approach, filtering out depth map readings and appending alien depth map values within the proximity field.

Detection. A Field-of-View (FoV) technique utilizing simple trigonometric calculations, Fig. 7. The FoV parameters from the camera specifications and the robots height are used to generate an array of angles by which the distance from the camera to the ground floor can be calculated with simple geometry. These distances can be compared with the depth map generated from the stereo camera, the inconsistencies can be checked to see if they meet the criteria of an obstacle. This simple yet robust algorithm provides an accurate and efficient way of detecting objects within a certain proximity. The observed field is calculated in under 2 ms. This method was paired with CCA to get appropriate bounding boxes.

5 Localization

We developed a new localization method called CLAP [5]. CLAP uses geometry to match relative camera observations with the previously known global map of the field features. A minimum of two features is required for localization, but additional correctly-identified features naturally form a cluster to improve the reliability of the state estimate. We also tested an optimization-based localization method [11].

6 Locomotion

The locomotion stack used to walk and kick during the Robocup 2024 competition improves upon previous work on Artemis [1]. The stack starts off with a gait scheduler [2] that propagates cyclic phases for each leg based on specified swing and stance times. During the competition, a symmetric walk was used in which both the swing and stance times were the same values, with no double support phase. On a touchdown event, the opposing leg is triggered to liftoff immediately to ensure the gait is always in single stance.

To move the foot during the swing phase from one contact point to the next, a ninth order polynomial is fit using a boundary problem optimization for each x, y, z position [1]. The optimization seeks to minimize the acceleration over the trajectory while prioritizing hitting a midpoint during the swing. In the case of foot z position, the step height was chosen as the midpoint for each trajectory. Meanwhile, the x,y optimizations either used a linear interpolation of the contact points or a kinematically limited ball location in the robot frame for the midpoint.

A footstep planner aimed at controlling the angular momentum about the contact point was used [8] to choose the next touchdown location of the swing foot. Simple center of mass (CoM) planner was constructed to track the swing of the linear inverted pendulum based on the gait phase progression. The desired transformations and velocities for both feet as well as the CoM position and velocity are then tracked by a lower level whole body controller [1].

7 Path Planning

In order to navigate a dynamic, obstacle-rich environment, with four robots, two referees, and four handlers constantly moving on a crowded 14 m by 9 m field, we implemented a real-time path planning and tracking system. Our dynamic augmented visibility graph approach calculates optimal paths efficiently with turning angle considered. Linear interpolation is then applied to maintain a smooth trajectory. For trajectory tracking, we developed collision-free MPC, which balances obstacle avoidance with robot dynamics without the need for switching modes. Detailed process can be found in our paper [12].

8 Behavior Tree

There are a multitude of key decisions that need to be made during a soccer game. Behavior trees have become widely used decision models in tackling these sorts of problems [7]. Compared to traditional finite state machines (FSM), behavior trees generate significantly fewer nodes [4]. The design of behavior trees focuses on composing action nodes instead of states in a hierarchical structure [9] (Fig. 9).

Approach. Our structure was designed such that the high level strategic decision making (i.e. to kick the ball) was separated from the more nuanced calculated decisions (i.e. where to kick or how hard to kick). This required a multi-segmented behavior tree in which three components, which we will refer to as

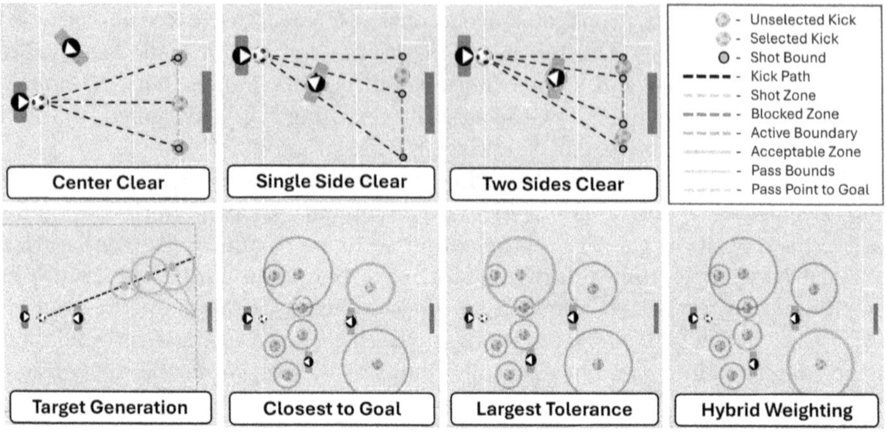

Fig. 8. The top row displays three generalized shot placement configurations. When an opponent obstructs the shot the shooting algorithm finds the best possible shooting location with enough tolerance. Otherwise, it will pass or move the ball to a more advantageous position using the pass algorithm depicted in the lower half. The lower left image shows roughly how the field is broken apart to generate placement of potential kicks shown by blue circles, which are calculated from the triangles in the field division based on obstacle and important points on the field shown in different colored dotted lines. This is then filtered based on desired heuristics until there is a single option depending on the style of play the robot is in. (Color figure online)

Fig. 9. This figure displays an oversimplified version of the behavior tree.

decisions, calculations, and communications, are linked via a common shared memory.

Behaviors. Calculations are composed of a series of parallel behaviors. One such behavior decides the optimal location for the player and generates kick commands. The resulting position goals are then filtered to avoid rapid jumps. There are two categories for choosing the ball's goal position, which are shooting and passing. Passing is chosen when there is no direct path from the ball to the goal or the accuracy of the required kick would be unreasonable. In this case, the ball needs to be passed or moved to an open space chosen via a pass finding algorithm, depicted in the bottom figures of Fig. 8. When shooting on goal, there's a separate algorithm governed by how much of the goal line is unobstructed with reference to the ball as seen in the top figures of Fig. 8.

Another type of behavior handles the system's memory of the field and object permanence. There are 4 primary ball conditions: lost, in view, remembered, and predicted. When the ball is no longer identified by the camera the state of the ball will transition from in view to remembered. In the remembered state the position of the ball is locked in its last known location until the ball is detected, remains unseen for too long, or the memory position is within the calculated field of view. To account for other players and obstacles obscuring the ball, shadows projected by the obstacles are also considered. The predicted state is employed when the ball has a significant estimated velocity. Here we use an estimated final position of the ball.

9 Conclusion

Our success at RoboCup 2024 can be attributed to the integration between all the components discussed throughout this paper. State-of-the-art hardware allows for better tracking for low-level control. This allows trajectory generation and tracking to move and adjust quickly relative to play. This then opens the way for more complex planning and interactions which relies on vision providing accurate landmark estimates to localization. Our on-going goal is to get Artemis to play soccer like an actual human. We had to develop the new methods and technologies laid out in this paper to reach just a fraction of what is needed. We hope to continue to push boundaries with our fellow competitors in the league going forward.

Acknowledgments. We would like to acknowledge other significant previous team members: Junjie Shen, Jingwen Zhang, Ji Sung Ahn, and Luke Mariak.

References

1. Ahn, M.S.: Development and real-time optimization-based control of a full-sized humanoid for dynamic walking and running. In: PhD Thesis. University of California, Los Angeles (2023)
2. Bledt, G., Wensing, P.M., Ingersoll, S., Kim, S.: Contact model fusion for event-based locomotion in unstructured terrains. In: 2018 IEEE International Conference on Robotics and Automation (ICRA), pp. 4399–4406. IEEE (2018)
3. Borenstein, J., Koren, Y.: The vector field histogram-fast obstacle avoidance for mobile robots. IEEE Trans. Robot. Autom. **7**(3), 278–288 (1991). https://doi.org/10.1109/70.88137
4. Colledanchise, M., Parasuraman, R., Ögren, P.: Learning of behavior trees for autonomous agents. IEEE Trans. Games **11**(2), 183–189 (2019). https://doi.org/10.1109/TG.2018.2816806

5. Fernandez, G., Hou, R., Togashi, C., Xu, A., Hong, D.: Clap: clustering to localize across n possibilities, a simple, robust geometric approach in the presence of symmetries. In: 2025 IEEE International Conference on Robotics and Automation. (Under Review)
6. Fox, D., Burgard, W., Thrun, S.: The dynamic window approach to collision avoidance. IEEE Robot. Autom. Mag. **4**(1), 23–33 (1997). https://doi.org/10.1109/100.580977
7. Ghzouli, R., Berger, T., Johnsen, E.B., Dragule, S., Wąsowski, A.: Behavior trees in action: a study of robotics applications. In: Proceedings of the 13th ACM SIGPLAN International Conference on Software Language Engineering, pp. 196–209. SLE 2020. Association for Computing Machinery, New York, NY, USA (2020). https://doi.org/10.1145/3426425.3426942,
8. Gong, Y., Grizzle, J.: One-step ahead prediction of angular momentum about the contact point for control of bipedal locomotion: validation in a lip-inspired controller. In: 2021 IEEE International Conference on Robotics and Automation (ICRA), pp. 2832–2838. IEEE (2021)
9. Gugliermo, S., Cáceres Domínguez, D., Iannotta, M., Stoyanov, T., Schaffernicht, E.: Evaluating behavior trees. Robot. Auton. Syst. **178**, 104714 (2024). https://doi.org/10.1016/j.robot.2024.104714. https://www.sciencedirect.com/science/article/pii/S0921889024000976
10. He, L., Ren, X., Gao, Q., Zhao, X., Yao, B., Chao, Y.: The connected-component labeling problem: a review of state-of-the-art algorithms. Pattern Recogn. **70**, 25–43 (2017). https://doi.org/10.1016/j.patcog.2017.04.018. https://www.sciencedirect.com/science/article/pii/S0031320317301693
11. Hou, R., Zhu, M., Nam, H., Fernandez, G.I., Hong, D.W.: Fast and robust localization for humanoid soccer robot via iterative landmark matching. arXiv preprint arXiv:2503.11020 (2025). https://arxiv.org/abs/2503.11020
12. Hou, R., Fernandez, G., Zhu, M., Hong, D.: Model predictive control with visibility graphs for humanoid path planning and tracking against adversarial opponents. In: 2025 IEEE International Conference on Robotics and Automation. (accepted)
13. Jocher, G., Chaurasia, A., Qiu, J.: Ultralytics YOLO. In: Github (2023). https://github.com/ultralytics/ultralytics
14. Liu, Y., Shen, J., Zhang, J., Zhang, X., Zhu, T., Hong, D.: Design and control of a miniature bipedal robot with proprioceptive actuation for dynamic behaviors. In: 2022 International Conference on Robotics and Automation (ICRA), pp. 8547–8553 (2022). https://doi.org/10.1109/ICRA46639.2022.9811790
15. Wensing, P.M., Wang, A., Seok, S., Otten, D., Lang, J., Kim, S.: Proprioceptive actuator design in the mit cheetah: impact mitigation and high-bandwidth physical interaction for dynamic legged robots. IEEE Trans. Rob. **33**(3), 509–522 (2017). https://doi.org/10.1109/TRO.2016.2640183
16. Zhu, A., Tanaka, Y., Rafeedi, F., Hong, D.: Cycloidal quasi-direct drive actuator designs with learning-based torque estimation for legged robotics (2024). https://arxiv.org/abs/2410.16591
17. Zhu, T.: Design of a Highly Dynamic Humanoid Robot. Ph.D. thesis, UCLA (2023)
18. Zhu, T., Hooks, J., Hong, D.: Design, modeling, and analysis of a liquid cooled proprioceptive actuator for legged robots. In: 2019 IEEE/ASME International Conference on Advanced Intelligent Mechatronics (AIM), pp. 36–43 (2019). https://doi.org/10.1109/AIM.2019.8868596

RoboCup@Home 2024 OPL Winner NimbRo: Anthropomorphic Service Robots Using Foundation Models for Perception and Planning

Raphael Memmesheimer(✉), Jan Nogga, Bastian Pätzold, Evgenii Kruzhkov, Simon Bultmann, Michael Schreiber, Jonas Bode, Bertan Karacora, Juhui Park, Alena Savinykh, and Sven Behnke

Autonomous Intelligent Systems, Computer Science Institute VI, Lamarr Institute for Machine Learning and Artificial Intelligence, and Center for Robotics, University of Bonn, Bonn, Germany
memmesheimer@ais.uni-bonn.de
https://www.ais.uni-bonn.de/nimbro/@Home/

Abstract. We present the approaches and contributions of the winning team NimbRo@Home at the RoboCup@Home 2024 competition in the Open Platform League held in Eindhoven, NL. Further, we describe our hardware setup and give an overview of the results for the task stages and the final demonstration. For this year's competition, we put a special emphasis on open-vocabulary object segmentation and grasping approaches that overcome the labeling overhead of supervised vision approaches, commonly used in RoboCup@Home. We successfully demonstrated that we can segment and grasp non-labeled objects by text descriptions. Further, we extensively employed Large Language Model (LLMs) for natural language understanding and task planning. Throughout the competition, our approaches showed robustness and generalization capabilities. A video of our performance can be found online (https://www.ais.uni-bonn.de/videos/RoboCup_2024).

1 Introduction

NimbRo has a well-established track record of successful participation in robotic competitions ranging from humanoid soccer in the RoboCup AdultSize class [21], mobile manipulation in unstructured environments at the DLR SpaceBot Cup [23] and the DARPA Robotics Challenge [27], cluttered bin picking at the Amazon Picking / Robotics Challenges [25,26], multiple UGV and UAV tasks at MBZIRC 2017 [1,24] and 2020 [2,12], and immersive telepresence at the ANA Avatar XPRIZE competition [13]. After winning RoboCup@Home three times in a row 2011–2013 [29], we participated again at RoboCup@Home 2023 in Bordeaux [17] and now won the RoboCup@Home 2024 competition in the Open Platform League. Figure 1 shows our team at RoboCup 2024 in Eindhoven, NL.

E. Barros et al. (Eds.): RoboCup 2024, LNAI 15570, pp. 515–527, 2025.
https://doi.org/10.1007/978-3-031-85859-8_44

Fig. 1. The NimbRo@Home team at RoboCup 2024 in Eindhoven, NL.

In this paper, we give an overview of the hardware setup, describe the approaches and methods used in the competition and present the results of the RoboCup 2024 world championship in the @Home Open Platform League. Our team won the competition with a final score of 8,852, followed by team Tidyboy-OPL (South Korea) with a score of 7,495 and SocRob@Home (Portugal) with a score of 6,901. Novelties of this year's participation include a modified robot platform, improvements in our grasping and vision approaches and the integration of LLMs for task planning. We focused on the integration of open-vocabulary approaches for object segmentation.

2 Hardware

For RoboCup@Home 2024 participation we used a modified TIAGo++ robot [20] (see Fig. 2) which is equipped with an omnidirectional mobile base, a linear liftable torso with two 7-Degrees of Freedom (DoF) arms and a pan-tilt-unit with an RGB-D camera. A ZBOX QTG7A4500 with an NVIDIA RTX A4500 is used for model inference and is mounted on the robot's back. An Ouster OSDOME-128 with a 180° FOV is used to gather a frontal hemispherical view of the robot for small obstacle avoidance and precise estimates for distant 3D perception. The Light Detection and Ranging (LiDAR) is calibrated against a wide FoV IDS uEye+ Camera to colorize the point cloud and to project detections from the camera to the LiDAR frame. For 2D mapping and localization, two Sick TiM 571 LiDAR sensors are used to cover the robot's surroundings. A 10-inch IPS touch screen is mounted at the front of the robot to improve human-robot interaction. For speech recognition, a Zoom Am7 microphone is used. A Teltonika RUTX50 Wi-Fi + 5G router served as a hybrid Wi-Fi and 5G connection for the

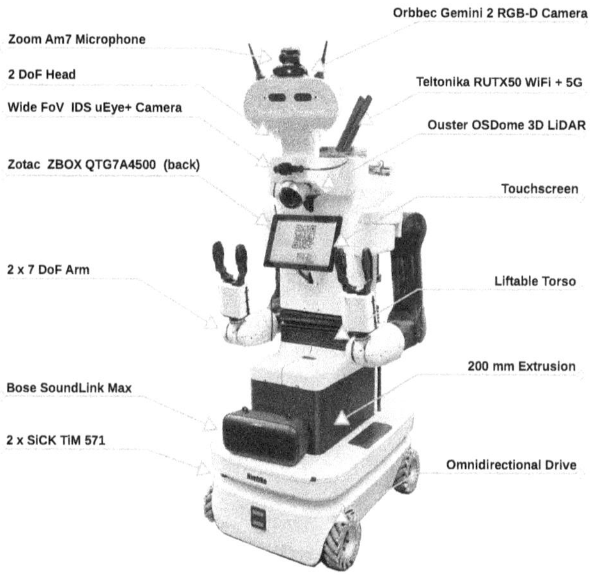

Fig. 2. Enhanced TIAGo++ omnidirectional robot platform.

robot, using the 5G connection when it couldn't connect to the Wi-Fi network to ensure connectivity to online API services we utilize. We increased the height of the robot by 200 mm to improve the grasping workspace and limit the extent of the elbow joints when grasping objects from table and shelf heights. The speaker of the robot was upgraded to Bose SoundLink Max to enhance its audibility in noisy environments. We use ROS 2 Foxy [16] on the robot's back computer and bridge ROS 1 topics from the robot's onboard computer. A second robot with a similar configuration was used for redundancy and to allow for parallel testing.

3 Software for Perception and Planning

The developed software modules address mapping and navigation, person and object perception, human-robot interaction, and task planning using LLMs.

3.1 Mapping and Navigation

We employ the SLAM Toolbox [15] to perform the mapping and utilize AMCL for localization. SLAM toolbox is a graph-based approach with high mapping accuracy due to loop closure support. When the operation area is unknown in advance (Carry My Luggage task), we use the SLAM Toolbox localization mode that updates the graph to new regions. In known environments, we utilize pose location markers to encode poses of interest. In addition, we can use those markers to define regions that can be used to distinguish between different areas

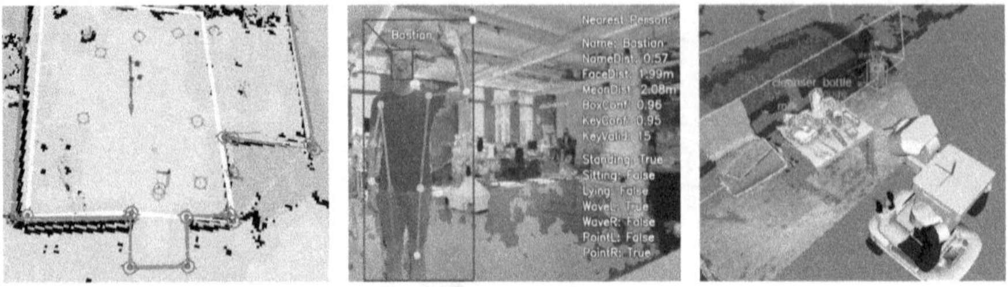

(a) Mapping and navigation (b) Person perception (c) Promptable object segmentation

Fig. 3. Software modules used in the competition. (a) Map including location markers and annotated regions. (b) Person detection using YOLO V8, body pose estimation, action and face recognition. (c) Projected object segments using mmGrounding-DINO.

(rooms), to constrain person and object search areas, or to restrict specified areas for the robot. An example of the underlying map is shown in Fig. 3a. We edit the map in a web interface created with Viser Studio.

3.2 Person Perception

The exemplary person detection shown in Fig. 3b uses YOLO V8 [9] models for both pose and face detection. Both methods are combined by computing the Mean Intersection over Union (MIoU) of the bounding boxes of the face detection and the estimated face from the pose. For face recognition, we employ a VGG-Face [5] embedding model from DeepFace [28]. Compatible with both the Gemini and IDS cameras, the system can access depth for each detection, allowing it to naively recognize gestures such as hand waving, and discard detections of persons outside a specified area, such as the competition arena.

For tracking, we employed a combination of 2D person detector from an RGB-D camera and a re-identification approach [32] that continuously collects features of the tracked person to distinguish the operator from the remaining crowd. In case the operator is lost, the re-identification approach is used to re-identify the operator. If that fails, the robot asks the operator to wave to the robot to reinitiate the tracking. During the tracking phase, we adjust the robot's head to continuously look at the operator. This improves the interaction and should minimize that the operator's track is lost when the robot's navigation is not optimally facing the operator.

3.3 Object Perception

In this year's RoboCup participation we utilized both, supervised and open-vocabulary object segmentation approaches and could flexibly switch between the two approaches. The closed vocabulary training and detection pipeline is supported by a dataset of household objects spanning 63,516 object instances

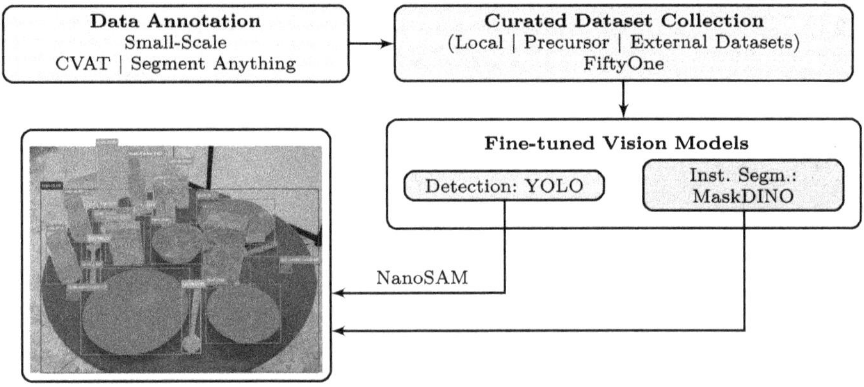

Fig. 4. Object perception pipeline including annotation, curation, and backbone models. We annotate data semi-automatically using CVAT and Segment Anything. This data is then curated using FiftyOne and combined with external datasets. The curated data is used to fine-tune YOLO and MaskDINO models. Additionally, we employ NanoSAM to recover segments from YOLO detections.

from 104 classes in 5,088 frames. It was captured in our lab in Bonn as well as at previous competitions and annotated using SAM [11] interactively. At RoboCup, the dataset was extended to include the local objects in cluttered arrangements. Over the setup days, more data was collected for objects which were not performing well in the detection metrics and for difficult scenarios such as faraway objects on the floor. These local datasets can be mixed with the base dataset by remapping labels to visually similar local object classes to improve recall or mixing in unrelated objects as negative examples to improve precision. Our object perception pipeline is depicted in Fig. 4. Fine-tuning of detection (YOLO [9]) or instance segmentation (MaskDINO [14]) models is done on a task per task basis, targeting only the object classes required in that task. Our base models are pretrained on large image datasets (COCO, OpenImages), to assure that the feature extraction layers are performant from the start. In this setup, fine-tuning a task-specific model on a single RTX 4090 takes between 10 and 30 min. In Eindhoven, we used MaskDINO models rather than YOLO because they proved more robust to the changes in lighting given our training data.

While open-vocabulary detectors are not yet as performant in terms of inference speed and detection metrics as their closed vocabulary counterparts, we find mmGrounding-DINO [33] to suffice for many household tasks. In this year's RoboCup vision strategy, we used this model when there were few relevant object classes (Serving Breakfast, Clean the Table). The prompts were manually designed using our locally captured dataset for evaluation and could be changed on the fly during the task depending on its state, such as when checking for chairs, searching for cutlery and tableware or looking for the dishwasher tab in the Clean the Table task, respectively. Since Grounding-DINO models output bounding boxes, we use these as prompts in NanoSAM to obtain the instance segmentations we require for grasping.

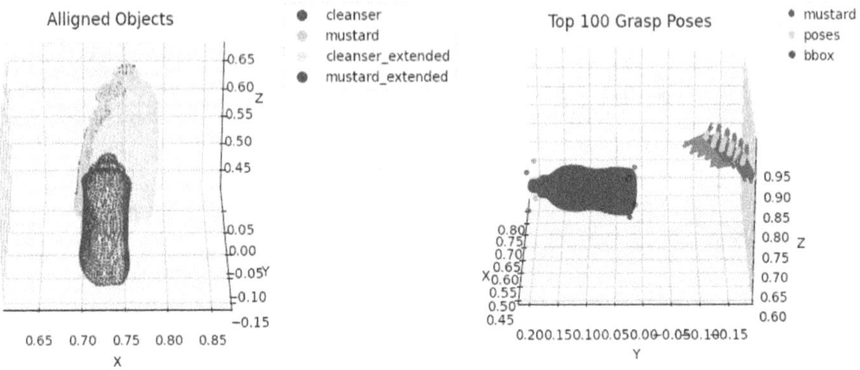

(a) Object registration (b) Grasp proposals

Fig. 5. 3D object perception and grasping. (a) If available, 3D models can be registered to partial point clouds of all detected objects. (b) The grasp proposals minimizing the grasping cost function for approaching a bottle of mustard lying on a surface.

3.4 Grasping

For manipulation, the robot is aligned based on the orientation of the object and a reachability map precomputed using cuRobo [30]. Masking the object in the depth image yields a partial point cloud, which is completed by registration to a 3D model if one is available for the corresponding class label. The final point cloud is then approximated by a 3D oriented bounding box.

Next, potential grasp poses are sampled on a quadrant sphere covering the side of the object that is facing the robot, their base orientations placing the gripper opening towards the object CoM with the fingers oriented vertically. These base poses are augmented by twist angles around the forward axis in the end effector frame.

In a subsequent filtering step, grasp poses which are in collision with the environment are identified using a KD-Tree lookup in a composite point cloud from the RGB-D camera and 3D LiDAR. This check is repeated for the approach trajectories of the remaining candidate poses. Then, the object 3D oriented bounding box is transformed into the frame of each grasp pose. Poses in which the object width exceeds the gripper width are removed. From the remaining poses, the most affordable one is selected for execution using a heuristic which considers the availability of similar precomputed pre-grasp poses which are not in collision with the environment, the distance from obstacles and the margin between grasp pose and the borders of the robots' workspace. Figure 5 b shows example grasp proposals.

3.5 Speech Synthesis and Recognition

The foundation of our audio processing pipeline is the JACK Audio Connection Kit [6], which provides capabilities for real-time audio processing and interfacing to connected audio hardware. To cope with challenging acoustic conditions in downstream tasks, the microphone signal is pre-processed using the NVIDIA Maxine toolkit [18], which applies denoising and dereverberation to isolate clean foreground speech from background noise. To retrieve speech commands at specific times during task execution, we use a voice activity detection model [4] to determine beginning and end-of-speech boundaries. Speech segments are then passed directly to a local instance of Faster Whisper [31] for speech recognition, implementing Radford et al. [22], which is capable of transcribing 99 different languages and translating them into English. Thus, our speech recognition pipeline can be characterized as robust, grammar-free, and multilingual.

For text-to-speech synthesis, we utilize the Coqui.ai library [7], which implements the end-to-end approach of Jaehyeon et al. [10]. We embed this model between custom pre- and post-processing modules for text normalization of numerals and punctuation, as well as loudness normalization between passes and loudness maximization to cut through loud environmental noises.

3.6 Task Planning Using Large Language Models

To allow the robot to understand and act on complex natural language instructions where naive keyword searching is not sufficient, we use LLMs, i.e. *GPT-4o* [19], which is accessed via our 5G router. We aimed for a general solution that includes both the *General Purpose Service Robot (GPSR)* and *Enhanced General Purpose Service Robot (EGPSR)* tasks provided by non-expert operators.

Our approach is based on encapsulating the robot's capabilities, such as *communicating with a person*, *driving to a location*, or *grasping an object*, in a general way, so that a successful execution of a typical command can be achieved by calling about 3 to 15 functions. In order for the LLM to keep track of progress and possibly react to unexpected situations, it is important that these functions are not only general and robust, but also provide appropriate textual feedback. The LLM is then used to execute one function after another until the command is accomplished, using the *function calling* feature provided by many SOTA models. The LLM can determine that the command has been accomplished by calling an appropriate function that advances the state machine of the underlying task. We have also worked on analyzing the performance of different prompting methods in a similar context [3]. In addition, we use LLMs to reject commands that require capabilities that the robot either does not have or that take a long time to execute, so that moving on to the next task increases the overall score.

4 Competition Results

We briefly present the results of the predefined tasks and the final demonstration of the RoboCup@Home 2024 competition. For complete task descriptions, we refer to the rule book [8]. In this year's competition, the tests were executed twice in different arenas.

4.1 Stage 1

Stage 1 consists of the tasks *Carry My Luggage*, *Receptionist*, *Serve Breakfast*, *Storing Groceries* and *GPSR*. The task duration is limited to 5 min for all tasks.

(a) Carry My Luggage (b) Receptionist (c) GPSR

Fig. 6. Impressions from Stage 1 tests.

- In *Carry My Luggage* (Fig. 6a), our robot successfully detected the correct bag to carry, picked it up successfully, memorized the operator and followed the operator while passing a crowd, a tiny object and a hard-to-see object (chair). Our robot lost track of the operator when it was avoiding the hard-to-see object.
- In *Receptionist* (Fig. 6b), our robot welcomed two guests, identified their names and favorite drinks via speech, estimated distinguishable attributes by face- and pose analysis to describe the guests to the other guests and offered free seats. It was limited in time for offering the second seat.
- A low score in *Storing Groceries* was caused by a hardware defect which prevented the robot from utilizing the arms properly.
- For the *Serve Breakfast*, task our robot successfully grasped a spoon and a bowl, placed the bowl, and placed the spoon next to it. Finally, it perceived the cereals.
- In *GPSR* (Fig. 6c), our robot received two commands by a naive operator: "Tell me what the smallest object on the kitchen counter is." and "Navigate to the office and hand me a pear." The robot successfully executed the first command and was limited in time for the second command. This performance yielded the highest score among all sub-leagues in the *GPSR* task.

After Stage 1, our team was ranked second with a score of 2,128—behind Tidyboy-OPL (2,717).

4.2 Stage 2

Stage 2 consists of the tasks *Clean the Table*, *EGPSR*, *Restaurant* and *Stickler for the Rules*. The duration for the tasks is 10 min, while the *Restaurant* task is limited to 15 min.

- In *Clean the Table* (Fig. 7a), our robot successfully grasped and placed a cutlery item conveniently in the dishwasher and pushed in the rack.
- In *Restaurant* (Fig. 7b), our robot detected waving guests and navigated through the unknown environment towards them. When reaching customers, the robot took their orders using speech recognition. If environmental noise proved too challenging, the robot fell back on a touchscreen interface. Following this pattern, our robot took orders from two different customers. Communicating with the barman, the robot then picked up the ordered items and delivered them to the recipients. In addition, the robot was also able to interact with detected waving guests who did not want to order anything, returning to the loop of searching for new customers and handling their orders. We received the *Waitress Captain (Best in Restaurant Test)* award as our team scored highest in the Restaurant task among all sub-leagues.
- In *EGPSR* (Fig. 7c), our robot followed a pre-designed path, scanning for trash with a closed-vocabulary detector and instructing the judge to dispose detected objects. Using the wide-angle IDS camera, it identified all waving persons, collected tasks, and executed them sequentially, starting with the closest non-rejected task, following our Stage 1 *GPSR* approach. In the first run, we hit the time limit during the initial task. In the second run, our robot faced issues receiving a task from a quiet-voiced operator due to nearby robot band noise.
- For the *Stickler for the Rules* task, we employed open-vocabulary detection models together with a pre-trained one. The pre-trained model detected known floor objects. To minimize false positives, training data was collected in all arena rooms with varying backgrounds. Open-vocabulary models detected shoes, socks, and drinks—allowing for unknown item detection. Using the same model saved GPU resources. The robot patrolled the arena, stopping to detect rule offenders, managed by a custom state machine. In unexpected situations, it returned to the main patrol cycle.

After Stage 2, we led the competition with a score of 4,918, followed by SocRob@Home (4,247) and Tidyboy-OPL (4,213).

4.3 Final Demonstration

This year's theme for the final demonstration was "The robot helps a person in preparing dinner". We aimed to showcase approaches and tasks that had not been shown in the predefined stages of the competition. Due to the limited time of 10 minutes available in the final demonstrations, we employed two robots in a time-splitting manner. The first robot was used to scan the environment to find

(a) Clean the Table (b) Restaurant (c) EGPSR

Fig. 7. Impressions from Stage 2 tests.

out which objects are present in the kitchen. Next to a 2D map and marked locations, no further input was provided. This part of our final demonstration should showcase how open-vocabulary vision approaches can be practically employed in domestic service robots to gather information about the environment and utilize this information for task planning based on user input. The second robot was used to pour an egg into a pan. This part should story-wise be after the scan of the environment to showcase that open-vocabulary approaches can be utilized to grasp non-labeled objects and allow achieving complex tasks like pouring an egg into a pan. Impressions of our final demonstration are shown in Fig. 8. For the final, our team received the highest scores from both the internal and the external jury members (1,783 + 2,152), followed by Tidyboy-OPL (1,545 + 1,738) and SocRob@Home (1,185 + 1,469).

(a) Egg pouring (b) Apartment scanning (c) Human interaction

Fig. 8. Impressions from the final demonstration.

5 Lessons Learned

Closed-set object detection approaches lack generalization in domestic service robotics. Open-vocabulary instance segmentation proved valuable in this competition. In the final demo, we used multimodal foundation models with open-vocabulary segmentation, enabling the robot to gather semantic scene information and grasp unseen objects. Capturing object relevance and attributes surpasses generic class label limitations. We successfully used a hybrid approach, combining closed-set detectors with open-vocabulary models for challenging categories like drinks, shoes, and garbage. For future tasks, we aim to reduce reliance on custom closed-set models and enhance open-vocabulary segmentation integration with LLM agents for arbitrary task planning in unseen environments.

Robustness and generalization are key for successful RoboCup@Home participation. We used hybrid Wi-Fi and 5G for connectivity, sensor watchdogs for reliability, and promptable object perception models for quick adaptation. Non-successful grasps were detected by reading the gripper's encoder states to reattempt the grasp. After too many failures, we triggered a handover procedure.

From last year's participation, we learned to prioritize natural interaction, emphasizing speech support and visual feedback on a touch screen interface. If speech commands are unclear, a graphical user interface allows users to select options or cancel phases. We also displayed object perception results for transparency and debugging.

6 Conclusion

In this paper, we summarized our hardware, approaches, and performance of the NimbRo@Home team at the RoboCup@Home 2024 competition in the Open Platform League. For this year's participation, we successfully employed open-vocabulary approaches for object segmentation and LLMs for task planning and execution. We successfully demonstrated that open-vocabulary approaches can be utilized to grasp non-labeled objects. During the competition, we scored in all tasks of Stage 1 and Stage 2. In the final demonstration, we showcased how open-vocabulary object perception approaches can be practically employed in domestic service robots to gather information about the environment and utilize this information for task planning based on user input and finally execute complex tasks like pouring an egg into a pan. Our team NimbRo@Home won the overall competition in the Open Platform League, followed by team Tidyboy-OPL (South Korea) and SocRob (Portugal). Further, we received a *Waitress Captain (Best in Restaurant Test)* award. We believe that robustness and generalization are key for successful RoboCup@Home participation.

Acknowledgments. This work has been funded by the German Ministry of Education and Research, grant 16SV8683: Transferzentrum Roboter im Alltag (RimA).

References

1. Beul, M., Nieuwenhuisen, M., Quenzel, J., Rosu, R.A., et al.: Team NimbRo at MBZIRC 2017: fast landing on a moving target and treasure hunting with a team of micro aerial vehicles. J. Field Robot. (JFR) **36**(1), 204–229 (2019)
2. Beul, M., et al.: Target chase, wall building, and fire fighting: autonomous UAVs of team NimbRo at MBZIRC 2020. Field Robot. **2**(1), 807–842 (2022)
3. Bode, J., Pätzold, B., Memmesheimer, R., Behnke, S.: A comparison of prompt engineering techniques for task planning and execution in service robotics. In: IEEE-RAS 23rd International Conference on Humanoid Robots (Humanoids) (2024)

4. Bredin, H., Laurent, A.: End-to-end speaker segmentation for overlap-aware resegmentation. In: Interspeech Conference, pp. 3111–3115 (2021)
5. Cao, Q., Shen, L., Xie, W., Parkhi, O.M., Zisserman, A.: VGGFace2: a dataset for recognising faces across pose and age. In: 13th IEEE International Conference on Automatic Face & Gesture Recognition (FG), pp. 67–74 (2018)
6. Davis, P., Letz, S.: (2023). https://jackaudio.org
7. Eren, G., Coqui T.T.S.: Coqui TTS (2021). https://github.com/coqui-ai/TTS
8. Hart, J., et al.: RoboCup@Home 2024: Rules and regulations (2024)
9. Jocher, G., Chaurasia, A., Qiu, J.: Ultralytics YOLOv8 (2023). https://github.com/ultralytics/ultralytics
10. Kim, J., Kong, J., Son, J.: Conditional variational autoencoder with adversarial learning for end-to-end text-to-speech. In: 38th International Conference on Machine Learning (ICML), pp. 5530–5540 (2021)
11. Kirillov, A., et al.: Segment anything. In: IEEE/CVF International Conference on Computer Vision (ICCV), pp. 4015–4026 (2023)
12. Lenz, C., et al.: Autonomous wall-building and firefighting: team NimbRo's UGV solution for MBZIRC 2020. Field Robot. **2**(1), 55–74 (2022)
13. Lenz, C., Schwarz, M., Rochow, A., Pätzold, B., et al.: NimbRo wins ANA avatar XPRIZE immersive telepresence competition: human-centric evaluation and lessons learned. Int. J. Soc. Robot. (SORO) (2023)
14. Li, F., et al.: Mask DINO: towards a unified transformer-based framework for object detection and segmentation. In: IEEE/CVF Conference on Computer Vision and Pattern Recognition (CVPR) (2023)
15. Macenski, S., Jambrecic, I.: SLAM toolbox: SLAM for the dynamic world. J. Open Source Softw. **6**(61), 2783 (2021)
16. Macenski, S., Foote, T., Gerkey, B., et al.: Robot operating system 2: design, architecture, and uses in the wild. Sci. Robot. **7**(66), eabm6074 (2022)
17. Memmesheimer, R., Bode, J., Splietker, M., Bultmann, S., Imbusch, B.T., Behnke, S.: NimbRo@Home 2023 Open Platform League team description. RoboCup@Home Team Description Papers (2023)
18. NVIDIA: NVIDIA Maxine Audio Effects (2023). https://github.com/NVIDIA/MAXINE-AFX-SDK
19. OpenAI: GPT-4 Technical report (2023)
20. Pages, J., Marchionni, L., Ferro, F.: TIAGo: the modular robot that adapts to different research needs. In: International WS on Robot Modularity, IROS, vol. 290 (2016)
21. Pavlichenko, D., Ficht, G., et al.: RoboCup 2023 humanoid AdultSize winner NimbRo: NimbRoNet3 visual perception and responsive gait with waveform in-walk kicks. In: RoboCup 2023: Robot World Cup XXVI. Springer (2024)
22. Radford, A., Kim, J.W., Xu, T., Brockman, G., McLeavey, C., Sutskever, I.: Robust speech recognition via large-scale weak supervision. In: International Conference on Machine Learning (ICML), pp. 28492–28518. PMLR (2023)
23. Schwarz, M., et al.: Supervised autonomy for exploration and mobile manipulation in rough terrain with a centaur-like robot. Front. Robot. AI **3**, 57 (2016)
24. Schwarz, M., Droeschel, D., et al.: Team NimbRo at MBZIRC 2017: autonomous valve stem turning using a wrench. J. Field Robot. **36**(1), 170–182 (2019)
25. Schwarz, M., et al.: Fast object learning and dual-arm coordination for cluttered stowing, picking, and packing. In: International Conference on Robotics and Automation (ICRA) (2018)

26. Schwarz, M., et al.: NimbRo picking: versatile part handling for warehouse automation. In: IEEE International Conference on Robotics and Automation (ICRA) (2017)
27. Schwarz, M., Rodehutskors, T., Droeschel, D., Beul, M., Schreiber, M., Araslanov, N., et al.: NimbRo rescue: solving disaster-response tasks with the mobile manipulation robot Momaro. J. Field Robot. (JFR) **34**(2), 400–425 (2017)
28. Serengil, S., Ozpinar, A.: A benchmark of facial recognition pipelines and co-usability performances of modules. J. Inf. Techn. **17**(2), 95–107 (2024)
29. Stückler, J., Schwarz, M., Behnke, S.: Mobile manipulation, tool use, and intuitive interaction for cognitive service robot Cosero. Front. Robot. AI **3**, 58 (2016)
30. Sundaralingam, B., Hari, S.K.S., Fishman, A., Garrett, C., Van Wyk, K., et al.: cuRobo: parallelized collision-free robot motion generation. In: IEEE International Conference on Robotics and Automation (ICRA), pp. 8112–8119 (2023)
31. Systran: Faster Whisper (2024). https://github.com/SYSTRAN/faster-whisper
32. Wojke, N., Memmesheimer, R., Paulus, D.: Joint operator detection and tracking for person following from mobile platforms. In: 20th International Conference on Information Fusion (FUSION). IEEE (2017)
33. Zhao, X., et al.: An open and comprehensive pipeline for unified object grounding and detection. arXiv preprint arXiv:2401.02361 (2024)

RoboCup 2024 SSL Champion TIGERs Mannheim—State-of-the-Art Dribbling and Path Planning Methods

Nicolai Ommer(✉), André Ryll, Michael Ratzel, and Mark Geiger

Department of Information Technology,
Baden-Württemberg Cooperative State University,
Coblitzallee 1-9, 68163 Mannheim, Germany
info@tigers-mannheim.de
https://tigers-mannheim.de

Abstract. In 2024, TIGERs Mannheim won the RoboCup Small Size League competition in Division A for the fourth time in a row.

This paper presents our latest improvements of ball control and path planning algorithms. First, the paper will focus on state-of-the-art methods for dribbling a ball and the employed control architecture. Furthermore, many implementation details and improvements to our trajectory-sampling-based path planning are depicted. This includes generating and executing trajectories, handling dynamic obstacles, and dealing with corner cases.

1 Dribbling Methods and Control

SSL robots are allowed to control the ball by actively exerting a backspin on it. They must not remove all degrees of freedom of the ball and an area of at least 80% when viewed from above needs to be outside the robot's convex hull[1]. The part of the robot which is exerting backspin is commonly referred to as a dribbling device. These devices appeared first around 2002[2], which is only 5 years after the league was founded in 1997. Dribbling devices were mainly used with straight forward or backward movement only, as they had little lateral control of the ball. Nevertheless, this allows to pull back the ball from opponents and it is essential during ball placement procedures (introduced 2017 and mandatory in Division A since 2018).

Dribbling got more advanced in 2015 when team CMDragons introduced dribbling while turning [1]. A circular path is followed to pass around a single opponent. Because of this skill, among other things, CMDragons won the world championship in 2015. The next step of dribbling device and ball control evolution happened in 2018 when team ZJUNlict demonstrated outstanding movement abilities with the ball. Their so called *break skill* was able to move

[1] cf. SSL rules Sect. 3.2.3.

[2] Archive images of CMDragons team with dribbling device: https://www.cs.cmu.edu/~robosoccer/image-gallery/small/.

E. Barros et al. (Eds.): RoboCup 2024, LNAI 15570, pp. 528–539, 2025.
https://doi.org/10.1007/978-3-031-85859-8_45

with the ball on arbitrary paths, not limited to circular movement [3]. This led to two consecutive world champion titles in 2018 and 2019 for them.

Especially the achievements in recent history show the importance of a good dribbling devices and ball control to become a top team of the SSL. Section 1.1 describes our current dribbler design and two common methods to control the ball. Section 1.2 gives a detailed description of the motor controller used for successful ball handling.

1.1 Dribbler Design

Figure 1 shows the dribbler design of our current v2020 robot generation at two different states. The forward dribbler position is the default position when the robot is not in contact with the ball or when it just made contact. In this state, the ball only has two contact points: with the dribbling bar and with ground. The rearward dribbler position is limited by the chip shovel position. In this state there is an additional contact point between ball and chip shovel. Over the full range of movement the robot does not violate the coverage rule as indicated by the dashed vertical line.

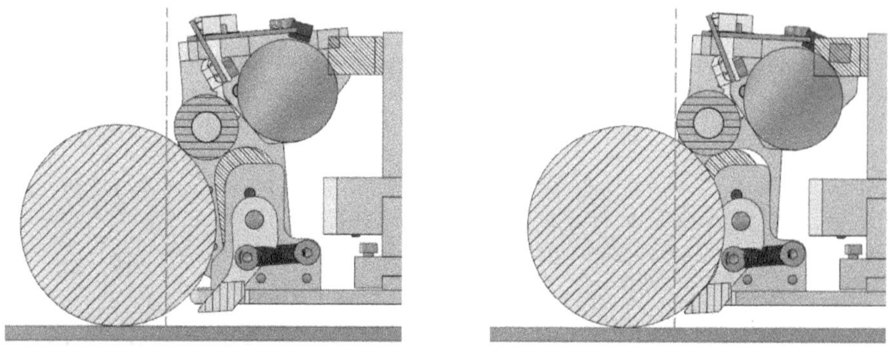

(a) Forward dribbler position, inclination 5° (2-point contact).

(b) Rearward dribbler position, inclination −3° (3-point contact).

Fig. 1. Half section view of two different dribbler positions with highlighted elements being: ball (diagonal section lining), dribbling bar (horizontal section lining), chip shovel (vertical section lining), damping elements (fine diagonal section lining). The vertical dashed line indicates the ball coverage limit according to SSL rules.

High Speed and Low Speed Dribbling. After the success of ZJUNlicts dribbling in 2018, we first tried to recreate their design. We observed that they are using high dribbling speeds and they employ a 3-point contact mode as seen in Fig. 1b. In this mode, the ball is constantly pulled onto the chip shovel and drops back to ground, leading to a periodic dynamic steady state [2].

Ultimately, we failed at recreating the exact same method of dribbling. We could either have a good dribbling or a good ball reception, but not both. To achieve a 3-point contact, the dribbling bar must be at a more rearward position. In this position, we were not able to receive balls well as it hit the chip shovel during the process and bounced back from the dribbler. Then, we tried a more forward position. The problem then was to get into a 3-point contact state with high dribbling speed. If there is sufficient traction between the ball and ground and between the ball and dribbling bar we noticed a strong force pushing onto the ball. This also pushed the dribbling bar back to a 3-point contact but the required motor torque was high and reduced the ball speed. Hence, 3-point contact and high speed was not achievable.

After multiple tests with the dribbler it turned out that a low speed 2-point contact dribbling can also work very well to control the ball. A key factor is to use a torque controller for the dribbling motor (see Sect. 1.2). By controlling the torque, we can effectively control how far the dribbler moves back and how far the ball enters into the robot. The chip shovel only acts as a final end stop and ensures the coverage rule is not violated. As torque is limited, the dribbling speed reduces as soon as the balls' friction forces exceed the torque limit. In some situations, the ball comes to a full stop. In this case we have a firm *grip* on the ball with a well controlled force.

Properties of Different Dribbling Methods. The methods of dribbling described above have notable differences and have various benefits and drawbacks.

Ball Centering. Achieving ball centering requires a specific spiral shape and a rotating dribbling bar. Unfortunately, our approach lacks a consistent rotating dribbling bar and lacks the required spiral shape, rendering ball centering unattainable in our case.

Dribbling Bar Wear. High speeds contribute to increased wear on bearings, particularly on the dribbling bar material due to abrasion. Our deliberate use of low-speed dribbling proves advantageous in mitigating wear. Notably, we did not need to replace any dribbling bar during the 2023 World Championship.

Kicks with Backspin. Kicking a ball with a backspin is a good way to improve chip kick ball control. A lobbed ball with backspin rolls less far or even rolls back. The same applies for flat kicks but in this case the behaviour is usually not desired. Fast kicks will be slowed down by a large backspin. Kicks with backspin are in general not possible with our dribbler approach.

Danger of Lost Balls. In scenarios where the ball is lost during high-speed dribbling (e.g., skirmish situations), it retains considerable rotational energy, leading to unpredictable acceleration. This makes it challenging to regain ball control. Opting for low-speed dribbling proves advantageous as the ball remains closer, reducing the risk and facilitating easier ball control recovery.

Ball Control. Both dribbling methods can offer good ball control after successful tuning to a given carpet. There is no common metric for dribbling performance yet which makes a scientific comparison difficult. Observations show that ZJUNlicts performance is slightly better at the moment but this may also be due to better higher-level systems (e.g., better path planning with the ball) which are not covered in this paper.

In summary, our design decisions prioritize robust dribbling and effective ball reception, accepting trade-offs in ball centering and backspin kicks.

1.2 Dribbler Motor Control

Figure 2 details the control architecture of our dribbler motor. The motor itself is a brushless DC (BLDC) motor with three hall sensors. The three motor windings are energized according to the common 6-step commutation scheme. This is the simplest mode of control for a BLDC motor and results in characteristics and mathematical model equivalent to that of a brushed DC motor. Its main drawback is a small torque ripple as the rotating magnetic field is only adjusted six time per electrical revolution.

In addition to the hall sensors there is one low-side shunt sensor for current measurements. The shunt circuit has a voltage offset to allow bidirectional measurements (accelerating and braking motor). Our dribbling motor is not equipped with an encoder.

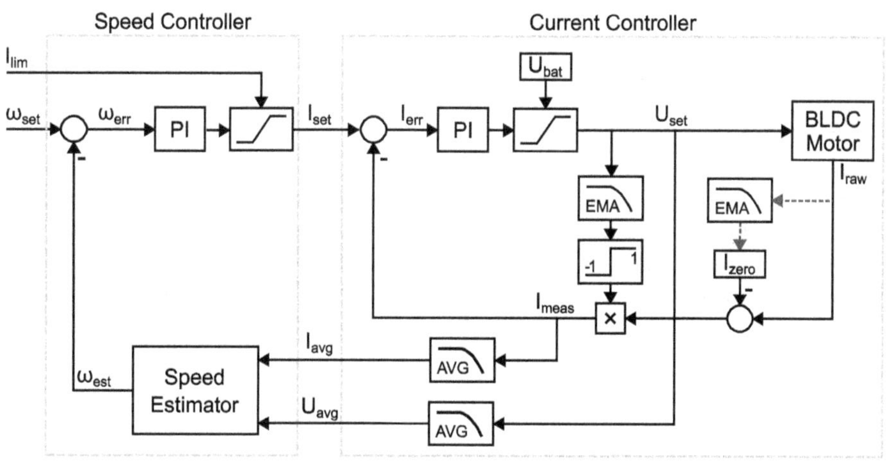

Fig. 2. Outer speed control loop (1 kHz) with estimator and inner current control loop (40 kHz) with filtering.

Architecture. The motor is controlled by a cascaded architecture of an outer speed control loop and an inner current control loop. The speed loop runs at 1 kHz, the current loop at 40 kHz. The loops are implemented on a single STSPIN32F0A microcontroller which also includes gate control logic for the inverter MOSFETs. To achieve the control frequency all computations are done with fixed-point arithmetic and without any division operations. They would be very slow, because this microcontroller does not have a floating-point unit or hardware divide instructions.

The electrical system of the motor can be modeled as

$$L \cdot \dot{I} + R \cdot I = U - K \cdot \omega \tag{1}$$

with motor inductance L, motor resistance R, back-EMF constant K, current I, speed ω, and applied voltage U.

Current Control Loop. Section 1.1 emphasizes on the importance of controlling the motor torque τ for good ball handling. The motor torque is not directly measurable but it is related to the motor current I by $\tau = K \cdot I$, where K is the motor torque constant. Hence, the controller uses current as controlled unit.

The input to the current controller is a desired current I_{set} and its output is the voltage U_{set} applied to the windings via pulse-width modulation (PWM). During each PWM cycle, the current of the motor windings I_{raw} is measured. Due to the bidirectional measurement there is an offset current I_{zero} which is subtracted to get the real current reading. I_{zero} is adjusted via an exponential moving average (EMA) filter when the motor is off to account for manufacturing tolerances, aging, and temperature changes.

The motor current is measured by a single common shunt resistor to ground. This setup cannot measure the direction of current flowing within the motor windings but only its magnitude. Hence, I_{raw} will mostly be positive values, except for very short periods where current within a motor winding changes direction. For proper current control it essential to have actual positive and negative current measurements as it represents positive and negative torque.

To solve this problem, we multiply the measured current by the signum of a filtered U_{set} value. U_{set} is passed through an EMA filter to simulate the effect of the inductance. Without this filter I_{meas} would change signs immediately whenever U_{set} changes signs. This is not realistic and the reason given as follows: The step response (voltage change) of a LR circuit like the motor winding is a first-order response with a time constant of $t_c = L/R$. The step response reaches 99.3% of the target value within $5t_c$. Our motor has $L = 35\,\mu\text{H}$ and $R = 0.48\,\Omega$ resulting in $5t_c \approx 365\,\mu\text{s}$ which is larger than our control period $T_{\text{ctrl,cur}} = f_{\text{ctrl,cur}}^{-1} = 25\,\mu\text{s}$. Hence, the inductance cannot be ignored in the state estimation for this control loop.

I_{meas} and I_{set} now form the current error I_{err} for the PI controller. The PI values have been tuned to the motor to have minimum overshoot. The controller output is limited by the battery voltage U_{bat}. Although shown separately in Fig. 2 limiting is implemented in the controller to use anti-windup techniques for the integral part.

Speed Control Loop. The input to the speed control loop is a desired speed ω_{set} and a maximum output current I_{lim} for saturation. The output is the desired current I_{set} for the inner control loop. The controller is of PI type with integrated saturation as well. The gains are tuned manually. Currently, we use a high-gain P-only setting.

A challenge for this control loop is a frequent measurement of motor speed ω. An apparent choice is the use of the hall sensors. Our motor has only one pole-pair which results in 6 pulses per revolution. An update frequency of 1 kHz requires at least 10000 rpm. This is impractical, especially since we operate at low speeds or even standstill (see Sect. 1.1). To overcome this problem, we are using a speed estimator based on average setpoint voltage U_{avg} and average current I_{avg}. The average values are computed from block filters with 40 samples each (all samples from the current control loop within one speed control period). The motor model from Eq. (1) can be rearranged to

$$\omega = \left(U - R \cdot I - L \cdot \dot{I}\right) \cdot K^{-1}. \tag{2}$$

For the speed control loop we can omit the inductance because its time constant t_c is much smaller than $T_{\text{ctrl,speed}} = 1\text{ms}$. This results in

$$\omega_{est} = (U_{avg} - R \cdot I_{avg}) \cdot K^{-1}. \tag{3}$$

The speed estimator has a fixed update frequency of 1 kHz independent of the motor speed. ω_{est} and ω_{set} form ω_{err} for the speed PI controller.

It is worth noting that the speed controller output is usually saturated at I_{lim} and the actual speed does not equal the desired speed. This is intentional, as we prioritize current control over speed control to have a well defined force on the ball.

This architecture has proven to work well for controlling the ball, even at low speeds. Furthermore, it does not need an additional encoder for speed measurements. Nevertheless, a possible improvement is to use an encoder to enable field-oriented control instead of 6-step control. This will reduce torque ripple and eventually result in less vibrations during dribbling. An open task for future work is a precise controller performance analysis (e.g. bandwidth/margin, overshoot, and robustness to parameter deviations).

2 Path Planning

Path planning is a common problem not only in the SSL, but also in general robotics. A lot of work has been published about this already. In 2019, we described our novel trajectory-sampling-based path planning approach in detail [5], which we started to develop and use in 2015 already. Many teams were using an RRT-based approach back then. In 2020, team ER-Force changed their path planning from an RRT to a similar trajectory-sampling-based approach [6]. In 2023, team RobôCIn compared our solution and that of ER-Force and based their own implementation on that work [4].

Since the last publication in 2019, we have tuned the path planning implementation further. While the basic idea is still the same, much of the original implementation has changed. This chapter describes our current implementation and points out some differences that we applied since our last publication.

With our approach, we committed about 3 fouls due to collisions where our robot was significantly faster than the opponent (henceforth called crash) on average per match during RoboCup 2023[3] and only 1.8 fouls during RoboCup 2024.

2.1 Overview

The following sections describe our current implementation in detail. The code can be found in our open-source release.

Path planning is initiated by a specific skill, the *MoveToSkill*. It is performed individually and independently for each robot with the following steps:

1. Generate a list of obstacles: Each robot may have individual requirements for path planning. A supporter wants to keep a larger distance to the ball, while an attacker needs to touch it. A defender wants to respect opponents in a more defensive/aggressive way than other robots. Details on how obstacles are modeled can be found in Sect. 2.5.
2. Create and adapt the path finder input: The input to the path finder consists of the robot's current 2D position and velocity, the robot's movement constraints, like maximum velocity and acceleration, the list of obstacles from the previous step and the target position.
3. Find a path: The path finder will return a path finder result, consisting of the trajectory to be executed and a list of collisions along its path. Collisions consist of the obstacle and the first collision time. Sections 2.2 and 2.3 describe the process of generating trajectories and finding collisions along the path and Sect. 2.4 describes how resulting path finder results are accepted or rejected.
4. Execute the trajectory: Based on the returned path finder result, the *MoveToSkill* will either execute the trajectory, or perform a fast brake, if a collision is imminent. This is outlined in Sect. 2.6.

2.2 Generate Trajectories

The basic approach is straightforward: First, create a trajectory from the current state to the target position. If its path is acceptable, return it. Else, iterate through a finite list of intermediate targets. For each intermediate target, create a trajectory from the current state to the intermediate target. Next, step over the resulting trajectory in discrete time steps $t_{\text{intermediate}} = 200\,ms$ and create a new trajectory consisting of two parts. The first part is the intermediate trajectory with an upper time limit of $t_{\text{intermediate}}$, the second part is a new trajectory with the initial state of the intermediate trajectory at $t_{\text{intermediate}}$ and the final

[3] https://ssl.robocup.org/match-statistics/.

target position. So far, we never created more than one intermediate target for our trajectories. This was sufficient for our use cases. However, it would be an option if more fine-grained paths are needed.

The way of generating the intermediate targets has not changed much in recent years. We still have two different implementations. One that generates a finite list of random targets and one that generates a systematic list. Currently, we use the random-based implementation with five targets. Having such a small number of intermediate targets is acceptable, because we run path planning continuously every frame (about every 10 ms) and can thus eventually find a good path. Additionally, the target from the previous iteration is also added to the intermediate targets. This caches good results and stabilizes the resulting path over time.

Initially, we always calculated paths for all intermediate targets and selected the best one. Now, we choose the first acceptable path and stop. This reduces the overall runtime at the cost of not finding a potentially faster path. With this lazy approach, the order of the intermediate targets has become relevant, so for the random-based implementation, we sort the targets by the angle between current position to target and current position to intermediate target, smallest first. This favors paths pointing towards the target.

2.3 Finding Collisions Along a Trajectory

We apply a simple iterative approach, but also added several optimizations. Basically, we step over a given trajectory and for each time step t, we iterate over all obstacles to check if there is a collision.

In the initial implementation, we used fixed time steps and a binary collision result (colliding or not colliding). In the current implementation, the time steps are dynamic and the obstacles return the distance to the currently checked point. This enabled two improvements. First, the next time step can now be calculated based on how close the closest obstacle is. This can reduce the total number of collision checks significantly. Second, we can apply an extra margin between obstacle and robot. We chose a dynamic margin depending on the robot velocity v_t at the given time step, defined by

$$m = \left(\frac{\min\left(v_{\max}, v_t\right)}{v_{\max}}\right)^2 \cdot m_{\text{base}} \tag{4}$$

with $v_{\max} = 3\,\text{m/s}$ and margin $m_{\text{base}} = 0.2\,\text{m}$. With this dynamic margin a robot can drive very close to an opponent robot, when slow, but considers an appropriate safety distance when driving fast.

In Fig. 3, the collision check procedure is depicted. Every dot on the paths is one collision check for one obstacle. Path P_1 is checked first and at time t_3, the collision check determines that the point is inside obstacle B and will stop. The second path P_2 is tried and this time, there are no collisions. One can also see, that the time steps t_4 to t_6 are closer to each other. The step size is smaller here, because they are near the penalty area, a close obstacle.

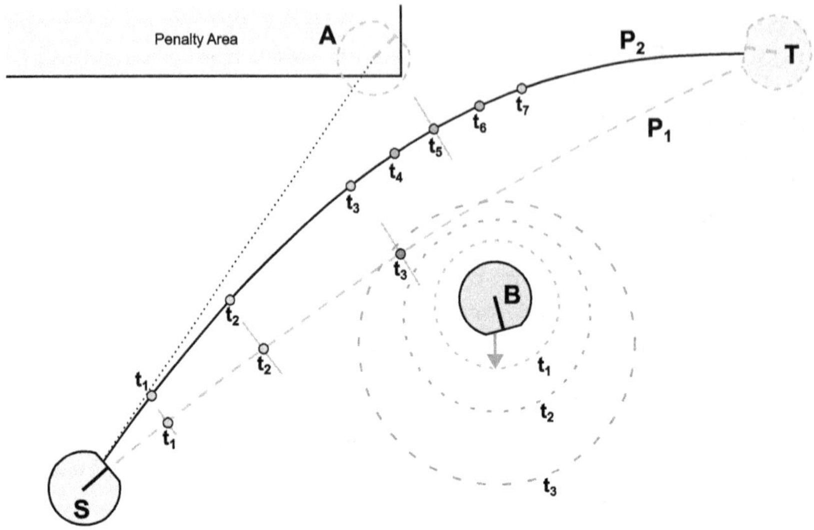

Fig. 3. The path planning situation visualizes how a collision check is performed. The path is planned from start S to target T with an intermediate target A, avoiding Obstacle B, which is moving slightly down. Path P_1 has a collision at time t_3 and path P_2 is free of collisions. The dynamic obstacle size is illustrated through the dashed circles at times t_1 to t_3, which correspond to the collision check points along the paths. The dynamic margin of the robot is depicted as an orthogonal line for some of the collision points.

Another optimization that was introduced recently is the separation of moving obstacles from motionless obstacles, as they have some distinct differences. A motionless obstacle, like the penalty area, is much simpler than an opponent robot that moves in an unpredictable way. There are two main reasons to separate those two kinds of obstacles. First, motionless obstacles are always checked before moving obstacles. If there is a collision with a motionless obstacle, the path is not accepted and the moving obstacles are not checked. Second, we have different implementations for accepting a path with a collision. They are explained in the next section.

2.4 Accepting or Rejecting Path Finder Results

Matches in the Small Size League are very fast and competitive. The best path is not necessarily the fastest one without a collision. We cannot be too careful, because then the opponent may catch the ball before us. Most obstacles are moving robots that can change their direction any time, so the situation has to be reevaluated every frame. Caring about collisions which happen one second in the future are just not worth to consider. However, this is not true in general. There are some static, motionless obstacles like the field boundary and the penalty area. On the other hand, moving obstacles can also be categorized into different behaviors. For our own robots, we know very well, where they will move along. Movement of opponent robots has to be estimated, while avoiding to be pushed or otherwise influenced by the opponents.

Our solution to those specifics are two acceptors, one for moving obstacles and one for motionless obstacles. They are applied to a path finder result and their output is binary: accepted or rejected.

Since last RoboCup (2023), we tuned the moving obstacle acceptor to more reliably intercept a ball before the opponent. Previously, our own robots got too nervous about a crash with the opponent ball interceptor and thus lost the ball against it. The optimization has been successfully evaluated during RoboCup 2024.

2.5 Modeling Obstacles

In practice, an obstacle is not just a simple geometric shape. That's why we have several different implementations for different kinds of obstacles. Some consider the current time on the trajectory to account for moving objects. For the field border and penalty area, we have specific obstacles for their geometric shape. Our own robots are modeled by their current trajectory. If they have no trajectory (because they perform some special skill, or because they are broken/off), they are instead modeled by a simple tube shape, which is constructed by position and velocity of the robot. Opponent robots have two different obstacle types that depends on the desired aggressiveness. If we want to be more aggressive, we only assume constant velocity over a short time window, otherwise we expect that robots will accelerate up to a certain maximum velocity.

For that, we calculate a circle r_{dyn} depending on time t that defines the area in which the robot could potentially move within this time based on its movement limits. Figure 3 visualizes such an opponent obstacle for multiple time steps. The radius $r_{\text{obstacle}}$and circle center $\boldsymbol{p}_{\text{obstacle}}$is calculated with Eqs. (5)–(8).

$$t_c = \begin{cases} 0 & \text{for } t < 0 \\ t_{\max} & \text{for } t > t_{\max} \\ t & \text{otherwise} \end{cases} \tag{5}$$

$$r_{\text{dyn}} = \frac{|f_+(t_c) - f_-(t_c)|}{2} \tag{6}$$

$$\boldsymbol{p}_{\text{obstacle}} = \boldsymbol{p}_{op} + [\boldsymbol{n}_{\text{op}} \cdot (f_-(t_c) + r_{\text{dyn}})] \tag{7}$$

$$r_{\text{obstacle}} = r_{\text{op}} + r_{\text{dyn}} \tag{8}$$

f_+ and f_- are the 1D bang-bang trajectories from position zero to positive and negative infinity with the current opponent speed and its velocity and acceleration limits, $\boldsymbol{p}_{\text{op}}$ is the current opponent position, $\boldsymbol{n}_{\text{op}}$ is the current opponent normalized move direction and $r_{\text{op}} = 0.09\,\text{m}$ is the robot radius. The limits can be adapted to individual opponents, but are usually around $3\,\text{m/s}$ and $3\,\text{m/s}^2$. The maximum time $t_{\max}$ is set to about $0.5\,\text{s}$, which allows for enough lookahead to react to direction changes of opponents. A higher maximum time results in larger obstacles and thus longer paths. A small tweak is applied to this obstacle to make it less pessimistic. Instead of a circle, only a tube is created. The width of the tube is the robot width and the length is the circle radius. Additionally, for non-moving robots, the dynamic radius is set to zero, effectively reducing the obstacle to a small circle. Without this tweak, our robots would circumvent opponents widely, as they expect them to accelerate in any direction soon.

The ball is modeled by its ball trajectory. If it would simply be modeled with a tube from start to the point where it will stop, this would create a wall across the field that robots could not cross easily, so modeling the ball by time is quite important.

For ball placement, a virtual ball is modeled, as if it would be kicked to the placement position now. This also avoids the wall issue.

2.6 Executing a Trajectory

Executing the trajectory is generally straightforward. Our robots require a target position as input. We take the next (intermediate or final) target position from the trajectory and send it to the robot every frame.

However, before the trajectory is applied, the *MoveToSkill* will check if it is safe to do so. The trajectory may have a collision and reports the time until the first collision will happen. The skill will calculate if it can reduce the robot velocity to a safe amount before hitting the obstacle. If it is still safe, the path is applied. Otherwise, the skill brakes until it is safe again. The skill will use a larger acceleration for braking, than the path planning considers. This makes it more likely to actually brake in time.

Incorporating the emergency brake feature into the skill offers several advantages. Our current bang-bang trajectories lack the ability to differentiate between acceleration and braking, yet the robots demonstrate a significantly faster braking capability compared to acceleration. Consequently, addressing this within path planning proves challenging. Additionally, planning a path with a reduced brake acceleration enables us to account for inaccuracies and devise a more risky trajectory.

2.7 Summary

Since we switched from an RRT-based approach to our novel trajectory-sampling-based approach in 2015, we improved our path planning performance continuously. Recently, other teams, like ER-Force and RobôCIn, adopted our approach as well and reported good results. While the basic idea is simple, there are a lot of options in detail. We showed how to handle different kinds of obstacles accordingly and how to assess and accept collisions in order to not being pushed too much by opponent robots.

We are still using the same bang-bang trajectories that we introduced back in 2015, mainly because they are really simple and fast and can also easily be implemented and reproduced on the robots. This held us back from switching to another version that also supports non-zero end-velocities, like other teams did.

There is at least one major disadvantage of our current approach. We have tuned it to return an acceptable path fast and optimize it over time (over multiple frames). Also, we only use one intermediate target, so longer paths might be rather rough at the beginning. For path planning itself this is usually not an issue, as the path will adapt throughout the journey. However, the exact path and thus the estimated total time can change a lot, which makes it less useful for the AI, for example to estimate which robot can intercept a ball the fastest. For that reason, we generate simple trajectories without path planning in all estimations, like for checking which robot can intercept the ball best.

References

1. Biswas, J., et al.: CMDragons 2015 Extended Team Description (2015)
2. Huang, Z., et al.: ZJUNlict Extended Team Description Paper for RoboCup 2019 (2019)
3. Huang, Z., et al.: ZJUNlict Extended Team Description Paper for Robocup 2020 (2020)
4. Oliveira, A., Gomes, C., Silva, C., Alves, C., Souza, D., Xavier, D.: RoboCIn—Extended Team Description for RoboCup 2023 (2023)
5. Ommer, N., Ryll, A., Geiger, M.: TIGERs Mannheim—Extended Team Description for RoboCup 2019 (2019)
6. Wendler, A., Heineken, T.: ER-Force—Extended Team Description for RoboCup 2020 (2020)

SinfonIA Uniandes: Winning Team of the RoboCup@Home Social Standard Platform League 2024

David Cuevas[1,2](✉) and Luccas Rojas[1,2]

[1] IMAGINE: Computación Visual, I+D+i, SinfonIA Uniandes, Bogotá, Colombia
{d.cuevas,sinfonia}@uniandes.edu.co

[2] Universidad de los Andes, 111711 Bogotá, Colombia
https://sinfoniauniandes.github.io/SinfonIA-web/home,
https://www.uniandes.edu.co/es

Abstract. This work explores the improvements and methods that led to SinfonIA Uniandes' success in winning the RoboCup@Home Social Standard Platform League (SSPL) 2024, using the Pepper robot from SoftBank Robotics. Considering the challenges due to human-robot interaction (HRI) and the hardware constraints, our focus was on improving Pepper's ability to offer practical assistance in home tasks. Key improvements include a robust person-following system that combined YOLO-based visual detection with a PID controller, achieving 80% accuracy in tracking individuals during short walks (under one minute). To improve General Purpose Service Robot (GPSR) tasks and perception capabilities we integrated OpenAI's GPT-4o, significantly enhancing Pepper's interaction and functionality.

This enabled Pepper to do more complex operations like determining whether a person is wearing shoes or interpreting gestures with an 89% success rate in executing autogenerated GPSR tasks. The integration of GPT-4o with OpenAI's locally deployed Whisper system provided robust speech recognition, facilitating smoother and more natural conversations, crucial for complex human-robot interactions. Additionally, GPT-4o's multimodal capabilities enabled advanced image processing, enhancing the robot's understanding of its surroundings. Our work with Pepper underscores the potential of AI to address key hardware and perception challenges, empowering social robots to effectively assist humans in dynamic environments.

Keywords: RoboCup@Home · RoboCup · Social Standard Platform League · Pepper · SinfonIA Uniandes · YOLO · ChatGPT · Whisper · Human-Robot Interaction

1 Introduction

In the year 2024, SinfonIA Uniandes participated in the RoboCup@Home Social Standard Platform League that was held in Eindhoven and won. The team consisted of four undergraduate engineering students and one undergraduate law

E. Barros et al. (Eds.): RoboCup 2024, LNAI 15570, pp. 540–551, 2025.
https://doi.org/10.1007/978-3-031-85859-8_46

student working together with a single objective: facing challenges posed during the competition.

This paper is organized as follows: Sect. 2 introduces the RoboCup@Home Social Standard Platform League competition and its challenges. Section 3 describes the Pepper robot and its hardware. Section 4 details the software architecture and key innovations. Section 5 discusses the current research. Lastly, Sect. 6 concludes the paper with a summary and outlook.

2 RoboCup@Home Social Standard Platform League

SinfonIA Uniandes has been an active participant in the **RoboCup@Home** Social Standard Platform League since 2019, always using the Pepper robot manufactured by SoftBank Robotics. This league evaluates robots in domestic and social environments, forcing teams to create software applications to facilitate everyday tasks. In 2024, our team participated in RoboCup in Eindhoven with a focus on advancing the development of social robotics that prioritize generalization over task-specific capabilities.

The Social Standard Platform League competition is designed in three stages. The first stage benchmarks core functionalities, including person tracking and following, speech understanding, recognition of objects, and navigation. Tasks included Carry My Luggage, where a robot helps a person transport their belongings, and Receptionist, where a robot greets and guides visitors. The rest of the tasks included grocery storage, breakfast setup preparations, and implementation of General Purpose Service Robot (GPSR) commands ranging from determining if a person had their shoes on to recognizing specific gestures.

During the second stage, all the core functionalities were combined in more involved tasks. The robots performed tasks like Clean the Table, which involved clearing objects from a table, and Restaurant, where they retrieved and served orders to customers in a simulated restaurant, detecting and reaching tables without prior guidance. The Enhanced General Purpose Service Robot (EGPSR) task required the robot to locate individuals in the arena and respond to auto-generated commands.

The final round featured the top-performing teams, with a focus on innovative applications of social robotics. SinfonIA Uniandes stood out for its advanced human-robot interaction capabilities and very efficient help solutions. Our participation in RoboCup demonstrates the potential of social robots to address practical problems while advancing both the research and applications of the robotics domain.

3 Hardware Setup

In alignment with the regulations established by the RoboCup@Home Social Standard Platform League, our hardware configuration adhered to the league's stipulations that disallow any alterations to the standardized robot platform. For this year's competition, SinfonIA Uniandes utilized a Pepper robot supplied in the competition, necessitating a comprehensive reinstallation of our software on this device.

The Pepper model has fixed hardware, including a 3D camera, microphones, tactile sensors, and a tablet interface. The robot is functional but has serious limitations. The mechanical design is limited by a reduced range of motion, featuring weak arms with very restricted mobility. The fingers close all together, not one by one, which makes grasping tasks difficult. In addition, the maximum speed of Pepper is just 0.5 m/s, which is very slow compared to other robots.

The robot's sensors also have significant shortcomings. The depth camera only operates effectively from 40 cm in front of the robot and is both imprecise and low quality, making precise grasping tasks nearly impossible. Similarly, Pepper's regular cameras struggle with performance; higher resolutions cause significant slowdowns, forcing us to use very low resolutions. The laser sensors are insufficient for robust localization, adding to the difficulty of reliable navigation.

To overcome most of these challenges, the majority of computations were offloaded to an external computer using the ROS distributed node system. This setup handled resource-intensive tasks such as Whisper speech recognition, YOLO object detection, and face recognition. By leveraging external processing, we were able to extend the capabilities of the robot despite its hardware limitations (Fig. 1).

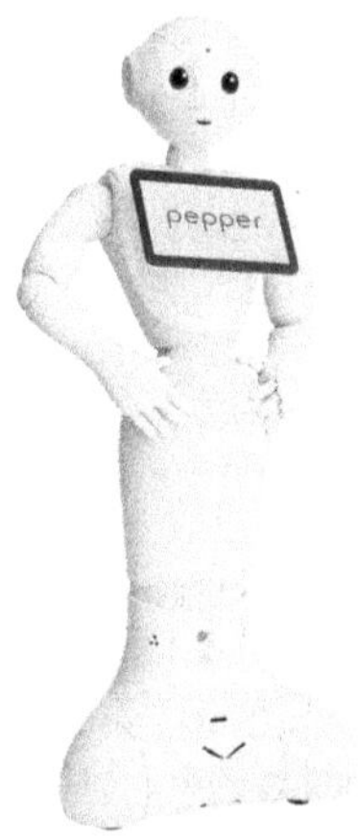

Fig. 1. Pepper Robot. Source: SoftBank Robotics (https://corporate-internal-prod.aldebaran.com)

4 Methodology

Architecture. Since we did not have root access on the Pepper robot, we could not install the required software (ROS) directly on its onboard computer. To overcome this limitation, we used Gentoo Prefix, which is a minimal user-space portage system. In addition, we have included the ros-overlay (based on ROS Kinetic), with additional changes to make Pepper's capabilities more complete by integrating the latest available software. The foundation of our system consists of the raw Pepper hard disk image version 2.5.5.5, which acts as a cross-compilation environment.

To integrate ROS into the Pepper robot, a proprietary driver was developed to replace the current naoqi driver. This new driver has two separate parts: a driver for basic functionalities written in C++ and an extended functionality driver built in Python. The C++ part is in charge of the basic functionalities such as navigation, perception, or speech processing, while the Python part is in charge of less intensive operations like displaying images on the robot's tablet. This separation brings better performance and modularity.

Together, both drivers provide low-level instructions for control, and modules like navigation, perception, speech, and manipulation handle higher-level tasks. At the highest level, the task module connects all of these elements to perform complex tasks, ensuring seamless interaction between the robot's capabilities and enabling advanced operations. The software architecture is visually represented in Fig. 2, which illustrates how these modules interact and are organized within the system.

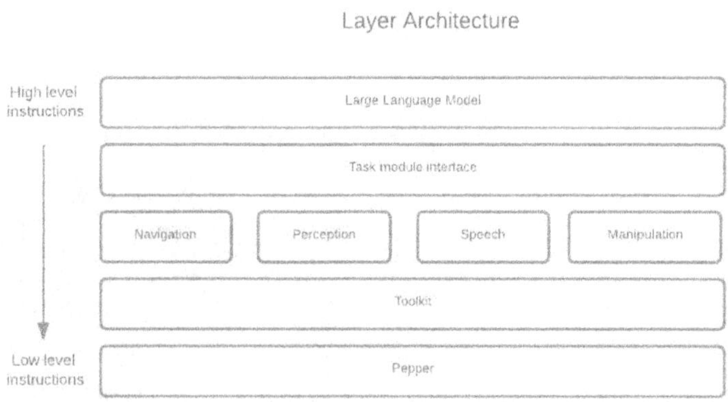

Fig. 2. Software Architecture

Environmental Awareness. Environmental Awareness is an integral part of robotics, especially in dynamic environments such as those found in the

RoboCup. It encompasses a robot's ability to perceive and understand its environment, which is necessary for making good decisions and navigating complex environments. In our framework, we include object perception, detection, and mapping to enable the robot to operate autonomously and intelligently within its environment.

On the object perception and detection side, we use YOLO (You Only Look Once) together with CVBridge. YOLO is one of the state-of-the-art deep learning-based methods, which prevails in speed and accuracy in real-time object detection. CVBridge serves as an interface between ROS and OpenCV; it converts images taken by the cameras of the robot into a format easily readable by tools compatible with ROS. Such a setup enables the robot to perceive many objects in its environment, such as obstacles, people, and other robots, thus increasing the number of possible decisions.

Regarding the processes of mapping and localization, the ROS Kinetic Navigation Stack serves as a reliable framework that facilitates path planning and autonomous navigation. The robot builds and maintains an environmental representation using the Navigation Stack, keeps track of its location, and navigates dynamic environments. This integrated approach enables the robot to automatically adapt to changes in the environment, avoid obstacles, and optimize routes in real-time. The combination of YOLO, CVBridge, and the Navigation Stack allows the robot to remain continuously aware of its surroundings, making it a strong contender in RoboCup competitions that require real-time perception and navigation to succeed (Fig. 3).

Fig. 3. Person detection and distance calculation

Human-Robot Interaction. Human-Robot Interaction lies at the heart of any autonomous robot, and in this case, social robotics, where the robot is required to understand and be aligned with human instructions. Our HRI approach incorporates speech recognition, object perception, and memory through face recognition in a single framework where the robot can interact with the environment seamlessly. For this, we implemented a system based on Whisper for speech-to-text conversion, complemented with Silero Voice Activity Detection (VAD) for real-time audio evaluation. This backend calls the robot's listening mode at critical moments in time, recording and processing just the speech of interest. Silero VAD makes sure that background noise is excluded, allowing Whisper to recognize the words said by the user and transcribe them into text. This approach improves the robot's capability to hold meaningful conversations while minimizing errors due to background noises. In the case of speech understanding, we followed a hybrid approach that relies on the complexity of the tasks. For simple commands, the robot exploits a set of pre-defined functions that match a limited set of instructions.

On face recognition, the robot employs a technique in which several images of the individual are taken; the system generally takes three distinct photos for identification. The photos are then averaged by computing the median of the 128 dimensional encoding vectors for a proper representation of the individual's face. This is advantageous over averaging the vectors as the median has less sensitivity to outliers. It achieves this by using five images to save a face, and only three are used in the recognition. Stored encodings are then compared against new face images for accurate identification of individuals, such that the robot can recognize and remember its users over time.

When more complex tasks are considered, such as those required in the General Purpose Service Robot Task (GPSR), the robot makes use of Large Language Models (LLMs) to understand a wider class of instructions. In line with the contribution of Becerra et al. (2024), which focuses on optimizing task execution in social robots using large language models (LLMs), our system includes advanced natural language processing mechanisms to improve the performance of tasks executed in dynamic and unpredictable environments. The GPSR tasks often involve human-level complex instructions that can noticeably differ depending on contextual dependencies, and our approach addresses the widespread gap between provided instructions and the robot's ability to execute them adequately. With LLMs, we can provide the robot with a better understanding of open-ended commands, improving its autonomy and the quality of responses it can generate. In particular, the study showed that 55% of tasks generated passed the automatic runtime execution assessment, highlighting the significant progress made in improving task execution in robots. The best success rate was achieved by GPT-4, which underlines the effectiveness of using an LLM in complex and context-sensitive tasks. This double-focal approach allows the robot to handle both structured, systematic tasks and more flexible, conversational interactions, significantly enhancing its practical applicability in real-world settings (Fig. 4).

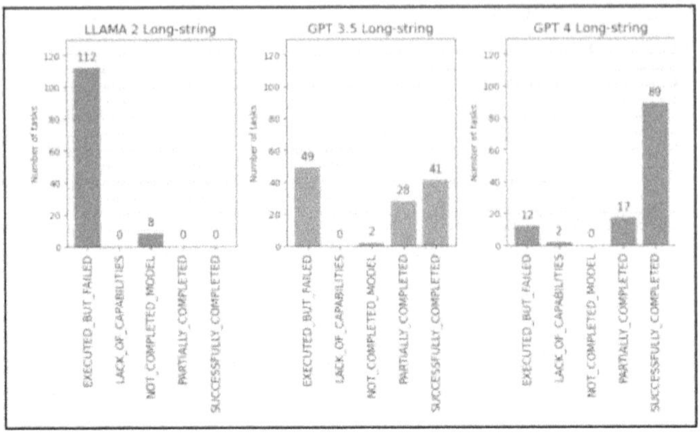

Fig. 4. Task results [4]. Reproduced from [4], with permission.

In our system for operator following, the robot detects, tracks, and follows a single operator through a combination of visual detection and motion control. The algorithm relies on data from Pepper's camera to locate the closest person in its visible range. By estimating the position and size of the person's bounding box, the robot calculates the distance and angle to the operator. The robot then adjusts its movement—both linear and angular—ensuring it maintains a safe following distance while reacting to changes in proximity.

The robot's motion is controlled based on these calculations:

Inputs:

- max_width: Maximum width of the detected person (typically 140 pixels)
- $person\_width$: Current width of the detected person
- $speed$: Predefined speed factor
- $followed\_person[1]$: X-coordinate of the left edge of the person
- $current\_head\_angle$: The current yaw angle of the robot's head

Outputs:

- $calculated\_vel$: Robot's linear velocity
- $angular\_vel$: Robot's angular velocity

Algorithm:

1. **Linear Velocity Calculation:**
   Calculates the robot's movement speed based on the width of the detected person, ensuring a minimum speed even when the person is close.

$$calculated\_vel = \begin{cases} speed \times (max\_width - person\_width) + 0.05 & \text{if } person\_width < max\_width \\ 0.01 & \text{otherwise} \end{cases}$$

2. **Person's Center Calculation:**
   Computes the center of the detected person based on their left edge and width to determine their position in the camera frame.

$$person\_center = followed\_person[1] + \frac{person\_width}{2}$$

3. **Yaw Angle Calculation:**
   Converts the person's position (in pixels) into an angular value (in degrees) relative to the robot's field of view, considering the robot's head angle.

$$person\_degree\_yolo = (person\_center \times 0.16875) - 27$$

4. **Angle Difference:**
   Determines the difference between the detected person's angle and the robot's current head angle to align the robot's orientation.

$$person\_degree = person\_degree\_yolo - current\_head\_angle$$

5. **Angular Velocity Calculation:**
   Determines the rotational speed needed to align the robot with the detected person's yaw angle, taking into account a scaling factor to limit the robot's turning speed.

$$angular\_vel = -\min\left(0.5, \frac{person\_degree}{|person\_degree|} \times 0.5\right)$$

Explanation of Constants:

- $max\_width = 140$ pixels: Chosen based on expected person size at average distance.
- 0.05 m/s: Ensures a minimum speed even when the person is very close.
- 0.16875: Scaling factor to convert pixels to degrees based on camera field of view.
- $-27°$: Offset in degrees to align the detected person's position with the robot's frame.
- 0.5 m/s: Controls the robot's rotation speedin meters per second.

The system also includes obstacle avoidance algorithms and recalibration methods, enabling the robot to reroute or reverse in response to obstacles, while speech functionalities keep the operator informed about the robot's status or requests for help.

Combining speech recognition, natural language processing, and perceptual awareness, these integrated systems give the robot the ability to understand and respond to human interaction in a more appropriate manner, thereby creating a more natural and intuitive human-robot interaction experience.

World Interaction. World interaction is a critical aspect of social robotics, especially in dynamic environments where the robot must navigate and manipulate objects.

The quality of the camera and the manipulation capabilities of Pepper's arms are quite poor and limited, which seriously impairs the capabilities when performing manipulation tasks. The limited range of the depth camera, together with the ineffective grasping capabilities of the robot, makes the implementation of conventional manipulation strategies—such as trajectory planning based on accurate targeting of the end-effector—difficult. As a result, we changed our plan to rely on human operators' assistance using the "Deus Ex Machina" clause allowed by RoboCup rules. This allowed us to request an operator to place an object directly directly onto the robot's open hands. In addition, we developed specific poses that allowed Pepper to securely grasp objects once they had been placed accurately on its hands thus saving the need for complex manipulation planning. While this was not ideal, it proved to be the most effective way of working within the restrictions of the robot in the competition.

Finally, the ROS Navigation Stack was run directly on Pepper's processor to minimize latency. Our navigation setup uses AMCL, move base, global planner, and many other essential elements from the ROS Navigation Stack to enable reliable navigation in dynamic environments (Fig. 5).

Fig. 5. Succesful grasp

5 Current Research

Enhancing Autonomous Task Execution Through Large Language Models. Our work follows that of Becerra, Colmenares, and Manrique (2024) in improving autonomous tasks of social robots using Large Language Models. In the present research, deep integration of LLMs is performed to advance autonomy and task execution by social robots, like Pepper in complex dynamic scenarios. The key research focus is towards developing the robot's understanding, planning, and execution of tasks carried out autonomously. That builds up to expand the abilities beyond rigid, predefined task structures to more flexible, context-aware task management.

We believe that, by integrating LLMs, we can enhance the instruction-interpreting capability of the robot, making it capable of performing tasks with greater flexibility in response to changing environmental clues.

The robot achieves this by developing a strong context-awareness system that enables it to understand situational context, predict what should come next in a task, and adapt its behavior accordingly. This is made possible through a systematic methodology that involves three core steps. First, verbal instructions are transcribed into text, enabling the robot to analyze and process them. Second, the transcribed text is processed by a large language model, which generates precise code instructions tailored for the robot's execution. Finally, the robot carries out the task by executing these instructions.

This approach therefore leverages the power of computation that LLMs bring about to enhance the decision-making processes of the robot so that at its maximum capacity, the robot can do not only instruction following but also real-time adaptation on new tasks. Additionally, the research establishes how LLMs can be trained to identify and understand ambiguous or incomplete instruction for enhanced handling of dynamic and unpredictable situations by a robot.

Future Research: Towards Continuous Autonomy with AutoGPT. Following our victory in the RoboCup@Home Social Standard Platform League this year, a new generation of work will center on combining AutoGPT, an open-source AI agent that autonomously breaks down goals into sub-tasks and executes them in a continuous loop, in an effort to harness the most significant level of autonomy. This approach allows the robot to set its own agenda and keep learning to respond to new and evolving environments, rather than relying on a user to provide a defined task. AutoGPT presents a possibility: give the robot the ability of self-improvement of its abilities over time, learning from past interactions and adapting to new challenges on its own, without human intervention.

The present research will attempt to give the robot the capability to become an independent agent that can recognize new problems and solve them on its own in real time. With AutoGPT, it will be possible for the robot to judge which tasks have to be done independently, manage its priorities, and find novel solutions in complex and uncertain environments. When the reasoning and decision-making abilities of LLMs are combined with the generative powers of AutoGPT, the robot will be capable of working independently with minimal supervision in a variety of settings. This may redefine the role that social robots are going to play and will be more capable of withstanding long-term engagements in dynamic environments where they can take responsibilities autonomously, adapt to shifting contexts, and provide consistent service to users. The role of robots has evolved from being merely task executors to intelligent, autonomous agents that understand, learn, and respond to their environment in real time, calibrating their behavior to better serve needs and changes in the environment.

6 Summary and Outlook

SinfonIA Uniandes is pioneering work in social robotics, focused on improving the interaction capabilities of robots like Pepper. Our current research combines state-of-the-art technologies in perception, speech recognition, and autonomy to enable robots capable of engaging in flexible, open-ended interactions with human users. The objective of this research is to enhance the capacity of robots to comprehend and react to their surroundings, identify individuals, retain memories of prior interactions, and adjust to various social contexts. Such improvements are crucial for rendering robots more human-like, relatable, and proficient within social settings.

By using cloud-based multimodal models and distributed systems like ROS, we enable efficient robot operation, even with limited on-board computing resources. The method is crucial in bringing up the accessibility and performance of social robots in highly variable global settings, particularly in developing nations, where the existing infrastructure may not be able to support the advanced robotics computational requirements.

Looking ahead, SinfonIA Uniandes will be devoted to taking the functionalities of social robots further in terms of autonomy and personalized interaction. We envision a future where robots can make decisions independently while being adapted through continuous interaction, engaged in meaningful and contextually relevant conversations. While we work on expanding the frontiers of social robots, our aim is to contribute to the global conversation on the future of interaction among humans and robots, while ensuring that such technologies become usable and beneficial to people everywhere.

Acknowledgments. We would like to express our deepest gratitude to the Universidad de los Andes for their unrelenting support, to all members of RoboCup for giving us this great opportunity, and to Luccas Rojas and Juan Jose Garcia for their invaluable guidance throughout the process.

References

1. SoftBank Robotics: Pepper Robot. https://corporate-internal-prod.aldebaran.com/themes/custom/softbank/images/full-pepper.png.webp. Accessed 17 Nov 2024

2. OpenAI: Whisper: A general-purpose speech recognition model. GitHub repository (2024). https://github.com/openai/whisper
3. Silero Team: Silero VAD: pre-trained enterprise-grade Voice Activity Detector (VAD), Number Detector, and Language Classifier. GitHub repository (2024). https://github.com/snakers4/silero-vad,email:hello@silero.ai
4. Becerra, L.R., Colmenares, J.R., Manrique, R.: Enhancing autonomous task execution in social robots with large language models. In: 2024 10th International Conference on Automation, Robotics and Applications (ICARA), Athens, Greece, pp. 40–44 (2024). https://doi.org/10.1109/ICARA60736.2024.10552978
5. United Robotics Group: Pepper Technical Specifications. United Robotics Group Support. https://support.unitedrobotics.group/en/support/solutions/articles/80000958735-pepper-technical-specifications. Accessed 6 Dec 2024
6. Redmon, J., Divvala, S., Girshick, R., Farhadi, A.: You Only Look Once: Unified, Real-Time Object Detection. arXiv preprint arXiv:1506.02640 (2015). https://arxiv.org/abs/1506.02640. Accessed 6 Dec 2024
7. Memmesheimer, R., Seib, V., Paulus, D.: Homer@UniKoblenz: winning team of the RoboCup@Home open platform league 2017. In: Akiyama, H., Obst, O., Sammut, C., Tonidandel, F. (eds.) RoboCup 2017. LNCS (LNAI), vol. 11175, pp. 509–520. Springer, Cham (2018). https://doi.org/10.1007/978-3-030-00308-1_42
8. Holz, D., Ruiz del Solar, J., Sugiura, K., Wachsmuth, S.: On RoboCup@Home – Past, Present and Future of a Scientific Competition for Service Robots. Academia.edu. https://www.academia.edu/93013980/On_RoboCup_at_Home_Past_Present_and_Future_of_a_Scientific_Competition_for_Service_Robots. Accessed 6 Dec 2024
9. Hart, J., et al: RoboCup@Home 2024: Rules and Regulations. GitHub. https://github.com/RoboCupAtHome/RuleBook/releases/tag/2024.1. Accessed 6 Dec 2024
10. Quigley, M., et al: ROS: an open-source robot operating system. In: ICRA Workshop on Open Source Software (2009)
11. Holz, D., del-Solar, J.R., Sugiura, K., Wachsmuth, S.: On RoboCup@Home – past, present and future of a scientific competition for service robots. In: Bianchi, R., Akin, H.L., Ramamoorthy, S., Sugiura, K. (eds.) RoboCup 2014. LNCS (LNAI), vol. 8992, pp. 686–697. Springer, Cham (2015). https://doi.org/10.1007/978-3-319-18615-3_56
12. Matamoros, M., Seib, V., Paulus, D.: Trends, Challenges and Adopted Strategies in RoboCup@Home. CoRR, vol. abs/1903.02516 (2019). http://arxiv.org/abs/1903.02516. Accessed 6 Dec 2024
13. Significant Gravitas, AutoGPT: A collection of tools and experimental open-source attempts to make GPT-4 fully autonomous. https://github.com/Significant-Gravitas/AutoGPT. Accessed 6 Dec 2024

Author Index

E. Barros et al. (Eds.): RoboCup 2024, LNAI 15570, pp. 553–556, 2025.
https://doi.org/10.1007/978-3-031-85859-8

GPSR Compliance
The European Union's (EU) General Product Safety Regulation (GPSR) is a set of rules that requires consumer products to be safe and our obligations to ensure this.

If you have any concerns about our products, you can contact us on

ProductSafety@springernature.com

In case Publisher is established outside the EU, the EU authorized representative is:

Springer Nature Customer Service Center GmbH
Europaplatz 3
69115 Heidelberg, Germany

www.ingramcontent.com/pod-product-compliance
Lightning Source LLC
Chambersburg PA
CBHW072204270425
25801CB00004B/62
* 9 7 8 3 0 3 1 8 5 8 5 8 1 *